# RELIGIOUS THOUGHT IN THE REFORMATION
## Second edition

Bernard M. G. Reardon

Longman
London and New York

*1981*
*1995.*

**LONGMAN GROUP LIMITED,**
Longman House, Burnt Mill,
Harlow, Essex CM20 2JE, England
*and Associated Companies throughout the world.*

*Published in the United States of America*
*by Longman Publishing, New York*

First published 1981
Second edition 1995

ISBN 0 582 25960 6 CSD
ISBN 0 582 25959 2 PPR

**British Library Cataloguing-in-Publication Data**

A catalogue record for this book is
available from the British Library

**Library of Congress Cataloging-in-Publication Data**

Reardon, Bernard M. G.
    Religious thought in the Reformation/Bernard M. G. Reardon. – 2nd ed.
        p.    cm.
    Includes bibliographical references and index.
    ISBN 0-582-25960-6 (hard). – ISBN 0-582-25959-2 (pbk.)
    1.| Theology. Doctrinal – History – 16th century.  2. Reformation.  I. Title.
    BT27.R36  1995                                                        94-36908
    230′.09′031–dc20                                                      CIP
                                                                         AC

Set 14A in Monotype 9½ on 12 Times
Produced by Longman Singapore Publishers (Pte) Ltd
Printed in Singapore

# CONTENTS

# Contents

It is the function of learning to assert what is known,
and to leave perverse ingenuity steadily alone.

Mandell Creighton

# PREFACE

Of the making of books on the Reformation there would seem to be no end. An author therefore who presents the reading public with yet another should be prepared to state his reasons for so doing. My own may be given readily. Most historians, in treating of this subject, are concerned, very properly, with the course of events and the persons who figured in them: how those events cohere and what were their causes, and the parts played in them by human agents, whether or not such roles were acted out either in full consciousness of motive or with much inkling of the possible outcome. The task thus envisaged is a highly complex one and the scholar who embarks on it, if he encompasses the period as a whole, must follow multiple lines of research and not just confine himself to arbitrarily selected data. There is little reason for wonder, then, that in dealing with a movement like the Reformation simplistic views, content merely to highlight the corruptions of the medieval church or the evangelical vision and single-minded courage of a Martin Luther, should appear inadequate. Nowadays especially the economic and social conditions, as well as the pressures and strains of political ambition, must be taken fully into account. On the face of it of course the Protestant Reformation was a religious revolution, but men's religious beliefs and aspirations are certainly not undetermined by historical circumstances, and changes that affect the life of an epoch have to be seen in a wide context. Nevertheless, in the events which the history of western Europe in the sixteenth century recalls, religion was a powerful if not a dominating factor. Why else should we continue to speak of the 'Reformation' at all if the reform and renewal of religious faith and practice which then occurred be parenthesized or accorded only passing notice? My purpose here, rather, is to concentrate on the very things such parenthesis would be likely to contain and to examine them in their own right and for their own sake. In short, my concern is with the religious, not to say more strictly theological, aspect of the movement, on the grounds that, all too often, this receives less attention from historians than might fairly be expected, even when allowing for their other legitimate interests or necessary preoccupations.

Thus the question I have sought to answer is: What in fact were the religious convictions which the reformers upheld, taught, struggled for and sometimes died for? To a Luther or a Calvin, to a Zwingli, a Melanchthon or a Cranmer, these matters were of absolutely primary significance, since the whole meaning of life, as they saw it, turned on them. To suppose that because in a secularist age, in which religious principles are likely to be equated at best with a few simple ethical precepts, the notions of justification by faith alone, or predestination to eternal bliss or perdition, or the living presence of Christ in the eucharist may have little intelligibility, is no excuse for neglecting or minimizing their historical importance, even apart from the theologian's concern with their truth.

Thus what I have set out to do is to examine the teachings of the principal reformers in turn, but also in more detail than is commonly found in histories either of the Reformation itself or of Christian doctrine generally. Many full-length studies of the individual leaders and their beliefs are indeed available, but these do not as a rule supply the reader, and more especially the younger student (with much already on his academic plate), with the kind of synoptic view which is probably what he feels himself to be most in need of. The only work known to me which attempts anything of the sort is Henry Strohl's *La pensée de la Réforme* (Neuchâtel and Paris, 1951). Even so, the method he adopts – that of treating theological doctrines or themes in systematic sequence – is one which I have not seen fit to use. But although I have aimed to do more than offer a mere sketch of my subject, that subject is a very large one and I have still been obliged to compress severely. The bibliographical references, both in the notes and in the chapter bibliographies at the end of the book, are sufficiently ample for the reader who wishes to pursue his study into greater depth to find adequate guidance from them.

The world-historical significance of the Reformation has not lessened with the passing of time. Not only does it mark a new epoch – the Protestant era – in the history of Christianity, but modern civilization itself may look back to it for its beginnings. With the break-up of the western church European culture was to be freed, willy-nilly, from the control of a unitary religious tradition subject to a single ecclesiastical authority. Not that it was the intention of any of the reformers that temporal affairs should be secularized, as the word is used nowadays. Protestant society was still Christian society and Calvin's 'holy commonwealth' of Geneva can be cited as a prime example of what a community deemed to have been ordered in accordance with the word of God ought, in Protestant eyes, to aspire to be. But the breach with the past which the sixteenth-century religious upheaval caused was such as to render it possible for new intellectual and social forces, to which the blanket-term Renaissance is conveniently affixed, gradually to secure the emancipation of the secular life from ecclesiastical tutelage. Christendom remained a reality, but its definition became ever less precise as a growing movement of autonomy revealed itself over large areas of human interest and endeavour. In fact, the Reformation and Renaissance are difficult to correlate in any positive way. In important respects the former was a reaction, medieval in ethos, against certain evident tendencies of the contemporary world. If Erasmus was a typical Renaissance figure then the attitude towards him of both the reformers and the Catholic authorities is instructive in this way, in that both realized that he stood for the freedom of the questing human intelligence in a manner that each sensed as a threat to supernatural authority, however mediated.

Yet although neither Luther nor Calvin saw religious renewal in terms of the claims of a subjective individualism – and where such claims were asserted, as by some of the more innovative spirits of the time, their own disapprobation was emphatic – nevertheless their invocation of the rights of conscience in repudiating a traditionary system of belief and piety which appeared to them false and oppressive, was a move fully consonant with the humanistic bias of the Renaissance and in after generations was to bear fruit which the original reformers would have found little to their taste.

Further, the disposition of Protestantism, manifest from the start, to break up into mutually discordant groupings, each with its own confession and polity, meant in practice, despite the exclusivism that none of them was willing to forego, that a degree at least of liberty and tolerance came to be admitted. To all of them the arch-enemy was Rome; and in any case rejection of the whole principle of hierarchical-sacerdotalist mediation rested on the assurance that the gospel demanded the unconstrained response of the individual heart and mind. But this again was tacitly to concede that the human understanding has its proper needs and requirements, and whatever, by the criteria of a supposedly biblical theology, the defects of the 'natural' reason may be it cannot be entirely prohibited from trenching on the preserves even of divine revelation itself, in so far as that revelation employs human means. I do not say that Protestantism, by its declared tenets, made entry for reason and freedom and tolerance, for the open, critical intelligence hailing truth wherever it might be discovered, but that such were the conditions in which it began – as such, also, were certain assumptions fundamental to its own enterprise – that post-Reformation developments in western European culture were inevitably facilitated and hastened by the sweeping changes which it brought about.

But once autonomous reason is allowed its head who can foretell its course or the speed of its progress? The modern outlook has been transformed by immense advances in scientific and historical knowledge and by the technological industrialism which the application of new knowledge has effected. And in no area of life has this transformation had such far-reaching consequences as in the religious. In the light of the historical critical examination of the authority on which they were based, namely the Bible, the reformers' theological assumptions have faded away. No longer can one scripture text, taken in its literal meaning, be correlated with another to provide the premises of an inferred doctrine, which then, in its turn, is aligned with others, similarly arrived at, to produce a scheme of ideas the very self-consistency of which is regarded as testimony of its truth. Rather has the whole morphology of religious belief come to be seen in respect of the intellectual and social settings accompanying its successive stages, with the result that almost nothing of the theological systems of earlier centuries appears to have escaped the desuetude into which, with time, all human ideas to some extent fall.

Roman Catholicism, supported by the unified organization of an international authoritarianism, has been able to defy modernity with a bolder face than has Protestantism, the very nature of which, in its diversity, its individualism and its openness to the manifold extraneous influences at work in the intellectually progressive societies with which its own history is intertwined, has left it in a more vulnerable situation. The outcome has been that Protestant religious teaching, apart from certain more or less restricted enclaves within the main Protestant communions, or in the obscurer sects on their fringes, has moved away from the positions held by the great reformers themselves and so uncompromisingly defined in its classic confessions of faith. In fact it is no exaggeration to assert that the central doctrines of historic Protestantism – original sin, atonement, justification *sola fide*, predestination, the verbal inspiration of scripture – not to mention those which the reformers received from antiquity through their Catholic inheritance and themselves fully endorsed – the dogmas of the Trinity and the person of Christ – all of them stressing the sovereignty and prevenience of God and the incapacity and depen- dence of man, are now almost unintelligible without the aid of an extended historical commentary.

I do not presume, in this book, to offer the prospective reader anything so comprehensive as that. But what I have written should serve, I think, as an informative guide to the religious beliefs actually current in the century wherein the main Protestant churches had their origin. Thus my purpose has been to expound and clarify, not, except very incidentally here or there, to criticize. If at the end the persevering student should feel himself nearer to an understanding of what his forbears of four to five hundred years since could, as Christians, in all sincerity believe, he will not have spent his time in vain. For the history of human ideas, of what men have thought and taught, often with deeply passionate convic- tion, can surely never be without interest and indeed importance, if only because it is by his beliefs and the ideals which they are framed to enshrine that man seeks to establish his self-identity. Even when he changes them he does so as part of a continuous process in which nothing is wholly pointless or is ever entirely lost.

It is altogether beyond the scope of my engagement here even to attempt to suggest how, in the heritage of Reformation Christianity, what is still living and valuable might be separated from what is otiose or dead; that, more suitably, is the job of the systematic theologian. Varying types of theological 'liberalism' or 'modernism' have, needless to say, already ventured to accomplish as much, and their success has by no means been unqualified. The problem lies in the totally different orientation of the modern mind, the discrepancy between its own funda- mental assumptions and those which prevailed in the ages of faith. What the reformers stressed, more insistently even than their Catholic opponents, was man's utter inadequacy. 'We have no power of ourselves', states the Anglican liturgy, 'to help ourselves.' Yet despite the efforts of a Karl Barth to restore the emphasis of classical Protestantism in this all-significant regard, modern man, including the modern Christian, is now unshakeably persuaded that his salvation (whatever this to the modern mind can be explained to mean) rests with him. That he can contrive nothing for his own ultimate destiny except by aid of divine grace communicated to him by supernatural media is an assertion which leaves him at most in a state of pious incomprehension, even though he may still repeat the time-honoured phrases which state it. Herein lies the great difference between the presuppositions of the Reformation era and of our own. Any refurbished orthodoxy which ignores it will be flawed. Yet any 'new' or 'radical' theology which accepts it and adopts the modern standpoint will have abandoned the historic creed, not in merely peripheral matters, but in its focal affirmation.

Catholic and Protestant Christianity alike were unambiguously supernaturalist. Neither could possibly have interpreted the gospel in terms of an activist humanism, since for both it was the revelation of divine power and purpose. Without God man could indeed know nothing and do nothing for his own salvation, here and hereafter. And the agents and instruments of that salvation were providentially given and unique. Where the two great systems of belief diverged was on the nature of those means and agencies, or how, in certain regards, they were to be correlated and appropriated. Catholic and Protestant together acknowledged scripture, the church and the sacraments; but they parted company on the priorities. Further, their differences on this were so far-reaching that each in the end presented widely discrepant conceptions of what the Christian religion essentially is. In other words, their disparity arose not simply because one accepted whereas the other rejected this or that specific doctrine; rather was it that the very teachings they held as a common legacy were approached in different ways, seen in different lights and given diverse orientations.

Thus for the Catholic, broadly speaking, the Christian religion furnishes the means whereby the believer is confronted with an objective order, represented on earth by the institutional church with its sacramental system and a hierarchy divinely appointed to be that system's custodian and administrator. The sacraments themselves, each of them ordained by Christ as a direct channel of his grace, are therefore effective *ex opere operato*, by virtue of what they themselves are, not *ex opere operantis* – in dependence, that is, on subjective qualities of ministrant or recipient. Nonetheless the divine grace, made in all certainty available to those who seek it, depends for its efficacy not simply on its own inherent power but on the use which is made of it. To this extent the will of man must be free to cooperate with God's saving purpose. Not even the sinful inheritance of Adam is sufficient to render him incapable of this. Thus the way of salvation is an ever-present, objectively manifest and unchanging divine reality offered for the needs of men. Their appropriation of its benefits is a responsibility with which they are morally charged. As they accept it and turn it to account in good works so, at the last, will they be judged.

For the Protestant this divine reality is no less 'given' and no less objective, but it is primarily to be apprehended not in the sacerdotal-sacramental institution, but in the word of revelation, which for practical ends is to be found in the divinely inspired testimony of scripture. Further, this testimony has to be communicated, the word expounded. Hence the importance which Protestantism attaches to the ministry of the word – again, for practical purposes, the sermon, the biblical preachment. But Protestantism does not hold that the divine reality is in any way identified with this communication, or even confined to it. To put it otherwise, there is no *opus operatum* of the word. The Bible and biblical preaching are means, vehicles, but what they purport to convey altogether transcends them. In a similar way the 'word' which imparts their significance to the sacraments also transcends them. Hence for Protestantism the divine reality has a living, free, not to say elusive quality that contrasts strikingly with the formalism of the Catholic concept. Formalism renders what it signifies or communicates much more readily apprehensible by the ordinary man, but the dangers to which it is exposed – legalism, mechanism, materialism – are never far away. Protestantism, on the other hand, while appealing to a reality and a truth much more personal and dynamic, to something therefore that demands an inwardness of conviction which in the nature of things is not easily attained, likewise involves risks of one kind or another – literalist biblicism, subjectivism and an inability to resist the dissolvents of a secularized environment. For whereas Catholicism has, at the price of dogmatic fixity and institutional rigidity, maintained over the post-Protestant era a self-identity which is still quite unmistakable, Protestantism now shows, apart from some scattered areas of self-conscious and self-isolating conservatism, a wide divergence from the type of belief and piety enshrined in its historic documents. This may in part be explained by the extended influence of the more radical elements within the Reformation movement itself, but mainly by the exposure, especially within the past century, to cultural forces which increasingly have weakened the sense of any authoritative revelation of suprahuman truth.

The plan of the present book indicates no novelty of approach to its subject, and I have been content to deal with the thought of the reformers as the historian, taking the chronological route, is almost bound to see it. I have not, that is, followed a procedure which would appear to wrest ideas and doctrines from their historical matrix. If one is to appreciate an idea or doctrine aright one must first encounter it, like the archaeologist's finds, *in situ*.

My opening chapter is concerned much less with the causes of the Reformation than with the many and various anticipations of it which occurred during the preceding two centuries. For the reformers' teachings were in themselves by no means the novelty which has often been claimed. Indeed the latter ought properly to be seen as a continuation of the former in changed circumstances favourable not only to their further efflorescence but to their institutionalization in formal systems and confessions. To Erasmus I have assigned a separate chapter; the significance of the great humanist, both as one of the most eminent men of his era and as indicative of what might have been a *tertium quid*, a reformed and 'liberal' Catholicism, justifies it. In any case he stands out as a paragon of rational amenity in a violent and vociferous age. The leading reformers themselves – Luther, Zwingli and Calvin – I have endeavoured to treat in as much detail as my space allowed; but I have also not neglected the secondary figures – a Melanchthon, an Oecolampadius, a Bucer – who all too often in general surveys of the Reformation movement are simply passed over. Rather fuller notice too is taken than usual of the classic confessions of Protestant doctrine. The so-called radical thinkers and activists – anabaptists and others – present a problem to the historian who does not wish to entangle himself inextricably in the complexity of the subject. But their diversity, their intrinsic interest and the long-term effects of their views and attitudes demand, again, as full an account as a single chapter can hope to encompass. Recent scholarship has disclosed much more about these worthies (so greatly misunderstood and, alas, ill-used in their own day) with the result that they can now be seen in a clearer and more sympathetic light. The reader who desires to explore the byways of the subject had best turn to G. H. Williams's formidably bulky *The Radical Reformation*, to which my own debt is obvious.

To the Reformation in Britain, commonly supposed to be of relatively slight interest doctrinally, I have given what some may feel as over-generous attention. But the emergence of Anglicanism in the sixteenth century, alongside Lutheranism and Calvinism, is a phenomenon of sufficient import in itself to warrant some extended notice, quite apart from the fact that my personal interest in the subject may be held to excuse at least a modicum of bias in its favour. The 'judicious' Hooker, it will be observed, has received more than a passing nod of respect. The book concludes with a look at the Roman Catholic reply to Protestantism at the Council of Trent, one of the most momentous synodical gatherings in the history of the Christian church. The admirable work of the Görres Society in making known the detailed course of its deliberations has earned the gratitude of more than simply professed students of sixteenth-century events.

Bernard M. G. Reardon

# PREFACE TO THE SECOND EDITION

In preparing a new edition of this book my aim has been not only to correct errors and bring the documentation reasonably up to date, but also to supplement text or notes at those points at which it seemed necessary or desirable to do so. The whole has been carefully reviewed in the hope that it will prove more acceptable for the purpose I originally had in mind when bringing it before the public. That purpose, as must be evident at a glance, is to present the student of the Reformation period, perhaps coming to it for the first time, with the complex theological issues involved, issues which in my judgement were absolutely central to it; and to do this in an *ouvrage d'ensemble*, which will at the same time offer, not just an outline sketch, but a considerable amount of the detailed information requisite to their proper understanding. To this end the page footnotes, replacing the original endnotes to each chapter, are of importance, especially for their bibliographical references. To the Protestant Reformers, as to their Catholic opponents, theology was a science in the sense of a precisely statable scheme of knowledge, and their writings accordingly assumed a technical character of the sort we nowadays far more readily expect to encounter in other and more mundane areas of knowledge and research. Indeed, the difficulty for the modern reader in approaching this subject is to enter into the condition of mind that admitted such exactitude with regard to matters which to his way of thinking belong only to the realms of remote or fanciful speculation. The ethos of Reformation religion is certainly not easy for us to imbibe and to attempt it demands no small effort of intellectual empathy. I can but hope that my book, on this its second début, will do something to facilitate this for the type of individual – not simply the professed student, but also that more elusive personage, the general reader – who may make it his interest to do so.

Bearing in mind the shift in the perspective from which historical studies are sometimes now viewed – a move away from the more familiar angle of narrative history towards a sociological or 'contextual' or synchronic one – it may not be irrelevant to stress again that this book was conceived as an essay in historical *theology*. Its concern is with beliefs and ideas: how they arose, were stated and were developed; and of course with the ideological disputes, usually vigorous and often bitter, which they occasioned. The ultimate reason for advancing these beliefs may not have been wholly present to the minds of those who held them, but in their conscious and deliberated form they were operative forces with an observable effect on the process of events. I trust the book will serve to show this.

A good deal of attention has in recent years been given to what may broadly be called the intellectual background of the Reformation, and in particular later medieval philosophy, as providing the methodological and conceptual framework within which the Reformers' thinking has to be set. This is an important subject, now receiving the appraisal which was its due. But it is a study in itself and should not be seen merely as prolegomena to what was to come. Accordingly I have not felt the need, in view of the work done by others, to extend my opening chapter beyond its present limits by attempting a summary which would have the alternative disadvantages of being either too short or too long; too short, in all likelihood, to serve any really informative use, yet too long, in actually serving such a use, to avoid the impression of assuming disproportionate space. In any case, what possessed the minds of the Reformers was their sense of entering new spiritual territory, and if progress was to be made much of the baggage of the past had to be discarded. A parallel may be suggested: Descartes, as modern scholarship has taught us, owed not a little to his medieval forbears; but what really matters about him is his having earned, in historical retrospect, the designation of 'Father of Modern Philosophy'.

In re-reading what one wrote several years previously the feeling inevitably occurs that the emphasis here or there might well have been different from what it was. Thus in the treatment of Luther, the most difficult because the most complex of the religious teachers under review, more perhaps might have been done to indicate the nuanced character of his thought and the fluctuations to which, over the years, it was subject. But this would have meant a closer investigation of his writings, which always were occasional rather than systematic, than the limits of my task would have practically allowed. What I have attempted in the two chapters allotted to him is no more than an overall account, or a distillation, of what his religious thinking produced. What is offered, therefore, is not 'Luther complete' but the identifying features made clear even at the cost of simplifying abstraction. This is all that an introduction can reasonably supply. For further and more searching inquiry there are treatises in abundance, especially if the reader's linguistic capabilities stretch to a knowledge of German. I believe, however, that the titles listed in the select bibliography should meet the needs of the type of student for whom I have written. If more is wanted the footnotes provide some amplification.

The chapter on Melanchthon and the earlier development of Lutheranism in its theological reach retains, I believe, its usefulness. Luther's favourite disciple has not, it would seem, in the English-speaking world won the recognition, or even commanded the interest, which his place in the history of Protestantism deserves. At any rate, quite apart from his role in the formulation of the *Augsburg Confession*, he points the way which Lutheranism was to take in its subsequent scholastic phase. With Zwingli, however, and the emergence of the Reformed (and initially Swiss) variety of Protestantism, one leaves the academic atmosphere, in which Lutheranism arose and took shape, for a more open scene and an enterprise less dominated by purely doctrinal considerations, and where the social and ethical dimensions of religious concern became more insistent. Zwingli was, in the old sense of the word, a humanist; the impress of Erasmus upon his mind was never lost. In certain regards one may find him the most interesting of all the Reformers. I have not thought fit to extend my account of Calvin's teachings beyond the bounds set by Calvin's own work: what came to be known as 'Calvinism' were developments, not always upon uniform lines. Such transformations, subtle or radical, of an original teacher's ideas are to be expected and are not simply to be identified with them: later Calvinism is better referred to as the 'Reformed' doctrine. Calvin's own theology as set out in the *Institutes* was presented as a hermeneutical prolegomenon to the study of the Bible – or as he himself put it, 'a key and an entrance to give access to Holy Scripture' – and his supreme achievement, as is nowadays generally agreed, is in his biblical commentaries. It was unfortunate – and witnesses to the manner in which Calvin's teachings were sometimes 'adapted' by his followers – that he should have been saddled with a theory of the verbal inerrancy of scripture which depicts it as literally of divine authorship. The great Genevan theologian himself distinguished between the words written and 'the Word of God'.

The Radical Reformation, as it is now frequently called, is still probably the side of the sixteenth-century religious revolution that has been least studied theologically, although modern research has done much to rectify this imbalance. Moreover the affinity of certain present-century expressions of an idiosyncratic evangelical religiosity with earlier forms having a certain similarity has given these latter a notable topicality of appeal, as they also appear to anticipate some contemporary social and political attitudes. Indeed evangelical Protestantism today, at all events as popularly manifested, would seem to have drawn its inspiration more from the 'radicals' than from the dogmatic systems now usually referred to as classical or 'magisterial'. The freedom of the Spirit has evidently more to offer than any assurance of being among the Elect.

No excuse, I fancy, need be made for continuing to assign two chapters of this book, published initially in England, to the Reformation in Britain, and of which the major part covers the emergence of what has come to be known as Anglicanism. The English, or British, Reformation was not theologically original: for instruction in doctrine it looked to the European continent. North of the Scottish border medieval Catholicism was replaced by Calvinism, with the consequence that the Scottish religious tradition has always displayed a degree of homogeneity that England did not achieve, whatever the thinking behind the Elizabethan Settlement might have envisaged. The doctrine of the Church of England, as indicated in its Articles of Religion and its successive Prayer Books, is not all of a piece, and for a proper commentary upon it one must repair to history for the actual ways in which the Anglican form of post-sixteenth century Christianity has as a living entity taken shape. Some however will think that the recent history of the Church of England, as of Anglicanism at large world-wide, has been such that a recollection of its sixteenth-century beginnings would be salutary – a worthwhile look at the rock whence it was hewn, especially in the considered utterances of that most judicious of Anglican teachers, Richard Hooker, who would seem, I suspect, to have slipped somewhat out of mind among those who could yet learn from him. To what I have already written – all too briefly, I fear – on this admirable divine I have added a short section on his doctrine of civil governance. But it is time, I venture to suggest, for a new full-length appraisal of the author of the *Laws of Ecclesiastical Polity*.

As for the final chapter there is little that calls for explanation or enlargement. Again I have made no attempt to treat of those aspects of the Counter-Reformation which are not my concern in a volume of this scope. That movement was not, as has long been understood, a mere papal backlash for the loss of the lands formerly of the Roman obedience. On the contrary it was a movement in its own right, with its own sources of inspiration and spirituality. The Roman Catholic church of the seventeenth century and after owed much of its distinctive character to the course which Catholicism took not only in the aftermath of the Protestant upheaval but contemporaneously with it. However, although 'Catholic Reformation' is now the preferred designation the word 'Counter' is by no means inapposite. The Papacy could not have ignored the doctrinal challenge of what it denounced as heresy any more than it could have disregarded the internal pressure for searching reform at a number of levels. Notice of the latter has not, as I have said, been to my purpose. But the Catholic doctrinal response, as formulated at Trent, is altogether relevant. The renewal of the Catholic tradition in Europe which then came to pass did not fail to learn from those whose beliefs it resisted, just as in after times the legatees of the Protestant heritage were in their turn to profit from the immemorial Catholic experience. If the present century has still not succeeded in uniting the two great spiritual inheritances within some kind of institutional framework it at least has witnessed a welcome growth in their mutual understanding and appreciation. Perhaps, too, the mere historian of Christian conviction and belief, modest though his work may be, can contribute something of value towards the dissemination of spiritual wisdom.

Bernard M. G. Reardon

# ACKNOWLEDGEMENTS

We are grateful to the following for permission to reproduce copyright material:

SCM Press Ltd. and The Westminster Press for extracts from *Calvin: Institutes of the Christian Religion* Vols. XX and XXI, The Library of Christian Classics, edited by John T. McNeill and L. E. Battles, translated by The Westminster Press, Copyright 1960 by W. L. Jenkins. Used by permission.

Chapter 1

# THE EVE OF THE REFORMATION: ANTICIPATIONS OF REFORM

## Antipapalism

The succession of events which identifies the Reformation as a religious movement begins, by common consent, with the protest of Martin Luther, on the eve
of All Saints' Day, 1517, against what he regarded as a flagrant ecclesiastical evil.
Yet the historian is confronted with abounding evidence of the church's decline
in prestige and spiritual influence long before this, a decline attributable not to
any marked lessening of popular religious sentiment (the facts, rather, show the
contrary to have been the case)[1] but to the worldliness, corruption and venality
rife among its official representatives, including, most signally, the papacy itself[2].
Demands for reform were voiced as early as the fourteenth century, and in the
fifteenth the necessity was everywhere recognized by men of conscience. The
difficulty was that so many persons judged their professional interest or material
advantage to depend on the continuance of the existing system that agreement
seemed impossible, not simply as to the means of reform but even on its real
aims. Moreover, although widespread abuses in the ecclesiastical administration,
financial exactions by the authorities of all ranks – 'The Lord desireth not the
death of a sinner,' remarked a papal official, 'but rather that he should pay and
live' – and the ignorance and immorality all too common among the clergy at
large were the usual reasons for complaint, the basic principles on which the
medieval church order rested were, on the whole, not the object of critical
questioning. With the exception of a few exponents of ideas clearly heretical
according to Roman standards, the traditional dogmas and the beliefs underlying
familiar religious practices were taken for granted. What was lacking was forceful
leadership at once conscious of an overriding religious mission and capable of
harnessing religious discontent to the innovative tendencies of the age. In the
sixteenth century such leadership did emerge, but by that time the need for change
had become so insistent that reform swelled into revolution, the result of which
was that the unity of western Christendom was shattered and startlingly new

---

1. See B. Moeller, 'Piety in Germany around 1500', in *The Reformation in Mediaeval
   Perspective*, ed. S. E. Ozment (Chicago, 1971), 50–75. For the not dissimilar situation
   in England see P. Janelle, *L'Angleterre catholique à la veille du schisme* (Paris, 1935).
2. For anti-clericalism in Germany see H.-J. Goetz, *Pfaffenhass und gross Geschrei: die
   reformatorischen Bewegungen in Deutschland 1517–1529 (Munich, 1987)*. But anticlerical
   feeling was not always soundly based and rumour-mongering was rife. See P. Heath, *The
   English Parish Clergy on the Eve of the Reformation* (London, 1969).

forms of faith and piety all but effaced the old Catholic tradition over large areas of Europe.

Responsibility for the church's secularization must to a very considerable extent be laid at the door of the papacy, with its increasingly inflated claims to the *plenitudo potestatis*, explicitly asserting an absolute authority over the affairs of men, as well temporal as spiritual. For although the Roman pope was held to be supreme in the religious sphere – a supremacy which few in Catholic Europe contested – the medieval doctrine of the 'two swords' had envisaged a shared authority: the spiritual order and the civil possessed each its own realm by divine right. This division was one which the secular ambitions of the papacy, abetted by its canon lawyers, consistently tried to remove. The emperors for their part opposed the claim vigorously, and if for a time the popes triumphed their success was of short duration. Boniface VIII (1294–1303), in the bull *Unam Sanctam* of 1302 occasioned by his quarrel with Philip IV of France, declared that outside the 'One, Holy, Catholic and Apostolic Church' there is 'neither salvation nor remission of sins', reasserted the papal supremacy in uncompromising terms and urged the principle that to reject the pope's authority was tantamount to ceasing to be a Catholic or even a Christian. He also contended, virtually as a matter of dogma, that the temporal and spiritual 'swords' were alike committed to the church, the latter to be wielded by the clergy directly, the former, though delegated to the secular authorities, to be used on behalf of the church and under its direction. To resist the spiritual power divinely conferred on St Peter and his successors was to contravene the law of God himself. This pronouncement marked the zenith of the papal pretensions in the medieval period. But in uttering it Boniface overreached himself. Arrested and imprisoned by the French, he died shortly afterwards, a broken and humiliated man. The so-called 'Babylonish Captivity' at Avignon followed (1309–77), and with it an inevitable fall in the papacy's universal standing, accelerated moreover by John XXII's ill-judged intervention in the quarrel over Louis IV of Bavaria's election as emperor. Exiled from Rome and subject to pressure from the French king, the Avignon popes were not only bereft of political power but suffered a loss of ecclesiastical prestige as well, especially from the scandal of the Great Schism (1378–1417), with its absurd and humiliating spectacle of anti-popes. Thus the way was prepared for the promotion of 'conciliarist' ideas in the next century.

The papacy's exorbitant jurisdictional claims, resisted in practice by temporal rulers like Philip IV and Edward I of England, were impugned on theoretical grounds by civil lawyers who appealed to ancient Roman law in support of the royal authority in both temporal and ecclesiastical concerns, and by such philosophical thinkers as William of Ockham (*c.*1285–1347) and Marsiglio of Padua (*c.*1275–1342). The former, a Franciscan friar teaching at Oxford, became involved in a dispute with John XXII at Avignon, whence he sought refuge with the Bavarian prince, under whose protection he remained for the rest of his life. It was during these latter years that he inveighed against the pope in favour of the imperial authority and its policies, arguing not only that the pope had no right to determine the validity of an imperial election but that the emperor, on the contrary, had a positive duty to depose a heretical pope, as he himself deemed John XXII in fact to be.[3] Marsiglio, who also became a protégé of Louis's, is best known as the author (in collaboration with John of Jandun) of the famous treatise 'Defender of the Peace' (*Defensor Pacis*) (1324). In this work, in which the influence of Aristotle's *Politics* is evident, he maintains that the state, which derives its authority from the people themselves – who retain the right to censure and even overthrow the ruler – is the great unifying power in society, and to it as such the church, which has no intrinsic jurisdiction temporal or spiritual, must be wholly subordinate. Its legal rights no less than its property are conferred upon it by the civil power. Marsiglio further held that the ecclesiastical hierarchy is of human not divine institution, that St Peter was never accorded the primacy among the apostles, and that the popes cannot be proved to be his successors. In his own opinion a general council, comprising laymen as well as clerics, is the true authority in ecclesiastical matters. That so audacious a book should have been condemned by the papal censors at Avignon and Marsiglio himself excommunicated can have surprised no one, least of all its author. Translated first into French and then into Italian and English, it was known to Wycliffe and Luther, and could scarcely have failed to influence Reformation thinking. Certainly in England Thomas Cromwell made it the subject of assiduous study.[4]

Nothing abashed, the papacy in no way moderated its ambitions, as was demonstrated by the bull *Execrabilis et Pristinis* of Pius II (1460), and that of Leo X, *Pastor Aeternus* (1516), published on the eve of the Reformation itself. The difficulty lay not simply in the popes' temporal pretensions but in their spiritual absolutism, amounting to the doctrine that all religious and ecclesiastical authority so far lies with the pope as universal bishop that members of the episcopate have no other role than that of delegated functionaries. Indeed in this context the very word 'spiritual' carries a more material significance than authority in faith and morals; all church property was covered by it, in the aggregate a vast territorial domain in the governance whereof the pope ultimately had sovereign rights the exercise of which, since the clergy everywhere were in a quite literal sense the pope's subjects, could and did involve perpetual incursions on those of temporal princes all over Europe. So closely intertwined were the spiritual and the temporal that to separate them might at times be impossible. In the nature of the case therefore the vexation which resulted from a repeated clash of interests did nothing to enhance respect for an establishment whose boast was in possessing the sole power under God to dispense the means necessary for man's salvation.

Conflict, had the ecclesiastical administration been a thoroughly enlightened one, would in the prevailing circumstances have been unavoidable; but when, as so commonly in the fifteenth and early sixteenth centuries, it revealed itself as

3. *Dialogus super dignitate papali et regia (c.1334), Breviloquium de principali tyrannico (c.1340–2)*, and *Tractatus de imperatorum et pontificum potestate (c.1437)*. Modern editions of the *Breviloquium* by L. Baudry (Paris, 1937) and R. Scholtz (Leipzig, 1944), and of the *Tractatus* by C. K. Brampton (Oxford, 1927). Cf. G. de Lagarde, *La Naissance de l'esprit laïque au déclin du moyen âge (1942–6; rev. edn., Louvain, 1970)*.
4. There are critical editions of the *Defensor Pacis by C. W. Previté-Orton (Cambridge, 1928) and R. Scholtz (Hanover, 1933). On Marsilius see C. K. Brampton, 'Marsiglio of Padua: Life', in English Historical Review*, xxxvii (1922), 501–15, and A. Gerwith, *Marsilius of Padua: The Defender of the Peace* (2 vols, New York, 1951, 1956).

avaricious and corrupt, when in fact the very fount of spiritual authority on earth, as the mere iteration of the names of Alexander VI (Borgia), Julius II (della Rovere) and Leo X (Medici) serves to remind us, had become a by-word for a worldliness that even secular princes did not surpass, there can be little wonder that to some at least any effective reform of the ecclesiastical institution was not compatible with the papacy's continuance.

## The growth of heresy

It was this conviction that gave impetus to certain of the heretical movements of the later Middle Ages. Heresies had appeared at intervals during the medieval period (for example, the Albigensians in southern France in the twelfth and early thirteenth centuries) but had not hitherto posed any serious threat to the unity of Christendom. However, the increasing authoritarianism of the papacy now furnished for such movements more urgent grounds for dissent. Thus a radical reformist programme was advanced during the Avignon years by the English scholar-statesman John Wycliffe (*c*.1330–84).[5] His career was spent mainly at Oxford, except for the final decade of his life when he held the benefice of Lutterworth in Leicestershire. From 1371 he was employed in the service of the government, and more particularly of the Black Prince and John of Gaunt, on whose behalf he entered into negotiations with the Roman Curia in 1374; indeed it was Gaunt and the prince's widow who later protected him against ecclesiastical censure. He first gained a reputation for himself as a philosopher, attacking nominalism and upholding a Platonist-Augustinian realism not unmixed with Thomas Bradwardine's determinism; but as a theologian his inspiration came from the Bible – 'God's law', as he was wont to call it – and the early church Fathers rather than from the philosophical schools.

His biblical and patristic interests also led him to rethink the doctrine of the church as such, and although his distinction between the ideal or 'invisible' society, which, like Augustine, he identified with the totality of the elect, and the visible, historic institution, to which he ascribed no authority that did not derive from the former, was by no means novel, it was one which, in the conditions of the age, could only detract further from the spiritual standing of the ecclesiastical order. At first his views took a less critical course, expressing no open opposition to tradition or to the hierarchy, but as time passed he became increasingly dissatisfied with the religion of his day, and in his treatise 'On Civil Dominion' (*De civili dominio*) (1375–6) he argued that all authority, whether ecclesiastical or secular, depended on the grace of God, and that bishops or priests who manifestly ceased to be in a state of grace could be lawfully deprived by the civil power. These opinions were quickly condemned by Pope Gregory XI and thereafter Wycliffe's hostility towards the papacy sharpened. In three more writings – 'On the Church'

5. H. B. Workman's *John Wycliffe* (2 vols, Oxford, 1926) remains authoritative, although K. B. McFarlane, *John Wycliffe and the Beginnings of English Nonconformity (London, 1952) is the best biography. See also* M. Aston, *Lollards and Reformers: Images and Literacy in Late Medieval Religion (London, 1984).*

(*De Ecclesia*), 'On the truth of sacred scripture' (*De veritate sacrae scripturae*) and 'On the power of the pope' (*De potestate papae*) (1377–8) – he insisted that the Bible is the only valid criterion of doctrine, to which ecclesiastical tradition may add nothing, and that papalism has no real basis in scripture. His ecclesiology, moreover, took on a more rigid Augustinianism: it was improper to describe the church as 'the whole body of faithful travellers', or to say that 'Christ is the head of all men, both of the faithful and the unfaithful', inasmuch as the Lord is the head of the elect only, even though 'as each man shall hope that he is safe in bliss, so he should suppose that he is a limb of the Church'.

In a later work, 'On apostasy' (*De apostasia*) (*c*.1382) Wycliffe launched a scathing attack on monasticism, for which again he found no scriptural warrant, and he appealed now to the government to reform the whole English church system. The pope, he declared, so far from being the church's *jure divino* head, might not, on predestinarian doctrine, even be a member of it, any more than was Judas, although he had been numbered among the apostles. For the same reason much of the traditional sacramentalist piety – absolution, confirmation, extreme unction, even the priesthood itself – was of dubious authority or value. Assuredly on matters of faith papal decisions were worthless unless based on scripture. Wycliffe further held that the theory as well as the practice of indulgences was to be rejected, along with clerical celibacy, useless church dignities and the not very edifying custom of begging as adopted by the mendicant orders.

But it was his teaching on the eucharist which finally led to his breach with the university of Oxford and retirement to Lutterworth. Transubstantiation he denied outright, as unsound philosophically, an encouragement to popular superstition and the main prop of sacerdotal power. Christ, he believed, was indeed present in the eucharist, but 'sacramentally, spiritually and virtually' (*sacramentaliter, spiritualiter et virtualiter*), not corporeally – phraseology which sometimes suggests receptionism, or the view that the presence is dependent on the state of mind of the recipient himself.

Wycliffe's ideas, reaffirmed in his *Trialogus*, dating from about 1382, are easy enough to grasp. A clear-minded, not to say doctrinaire, academic, he expressed his opinions with lucidity and forcefulness, if sometimes also at inordinate length and with no very exact appreciation of what was or was not practicable. Save for government patronage he would undoubtedly have suffered the fate of a convicted heretic. On 18 May 1381 he published a defence of his views in the form of a *Confession*, which resulted in a condemnation both of his doctrines and of his followers' by Archbishop Courtenay at a council held at Blackfriars, London, in 1382.[6] It is significant that the condemnation did not include Wycliffe himself, despite the widespread if erroneous impression that his writings had in large measure been the cause of the Peasants' Revolt, rather as Luther in his day was

6. For the text of the *Confessio* see *Fasciculi Zizaniorum, a collection of anti-Wycliffite documents attributed to Thomas Netter (c.1377–1430)* and edited in part by W. W. Shirley (1858). Most of Wycliffe's works were published by the Wycliffite Society, London, 1883–1914 in 35 vols. The *Trialogus* was edited by G. V. Lechner at Leipzig in 1863. A. Hudson, *The Premature Reformation: Wycliffite Texts and Lollard History (Oxford, 1988)* provides a useful compendium.

to be blamed for a similar uprising in Germany. As a man indeed Wycliffe is not readily assessable, since we know little about his inner disposition. Always very much the theorist, ideas interested him more than people, and he seems to have been deficient in religious feeling: anything resembling the doctrine of justification by faith appears not to have occurred to him. A rebel by temperament, his dislike of ecclesiasticism may have been deepened by his failure to gain preferment. The upshot was that his conception of church – state relations developed into a thoroughgoing erastianism, while his detestation of clerical wealth became almost obsessive, with his blistering denunciations of 'the religion of fat cows'. (His attacks on the pope – 'a poisoned weed', 'the head vicar of the fiend', and so on – were as embittered as those of Luther himself.) Undoubtedly he had courage, even if he did enjoy the royal protection, but it can hardly be said that his character attracts; with all his evangelical zeal, charity and forbearance were somehow lacking.

What then of his influence? Of greater consequence probably than any of his original writings, at least in England, was his sponsorship of a vernacular translation of the Bible. This to begin with was crudely literal, but it was replaced by an improved version for which his secretary at Lutterworth, John Purvey, was mainly responsible.[7] The fact that some two hundred manuscripts of it survive, most of them produced subsequently to the council at Oxford in 1407 which forbade the making of any fresh translations (or the use of any translation done 'in the times of John Wycliffe or since') except with diocesan or synodical approval, suggests that the popular demand for the scriptures in English was considerable.

Towards the end of his life Wycliffe's views began to carry less weight even with his sympathizers, proving too extreme for those who genuinely wanted reform; in any case the impact of his teaching was localized rather than nationwide. Nevertheless the so-called Lollard movement sprang from it and maintained a more or less underground existence until well into the sixteenth century, when it gave way to continental influences.[8] The real extent to which Lollardy spread is not easy to estimate, especially as in its later phases it became somewhat amorphous, being confined, apart from a few priests, merchants and professional men, mainly to the uneducated. During the fifteenth century Lollards were to be found in London and Essex, in the Chiltern country, in Coventry and in parts of northern England. Their religious outlook reduced itself to a simplified Wycliffism: Wycliffe, that is, without the academic sophistication and polemical edge. They believed firmly in the sufficiency of holy scripture as against either church tradition or scholastic reasoning, rejected transubstantiation, were anti-papal in sentiment and scorned most of the current religious practices – confession, indulgences, pilgrimages, veneration of images and even the ringing of church bells. On the other hand they had no very clear body of positive tenets, and their naive scripturalism was sustained by the

7. Although the preface repeats St Jerome's assertion that the Hebrew canon alone is of divine authority this Wycliffite version comprises the Apocrypha as well. See M. Deanesly, *The Lollard Bible and Other Medieval Biblical Versions (Cambridge, 1920)* and S. L. Fristedt, *The Wycliffite Bible*, pt I (Stockholm studies in English, IV, 1953); and more generally F. F. Bruce, *The English Bible (London, 1961)*.

8. J. Gairdner, *Lollardy and the Reformation in England (4 vols, London, 1908–13) provides a detailed study of the movement, but underestimates the extent of the Tudor revival of Lollardy.*

underhand circulation, in much-thumbed manuscripts, of their vernacular Bible.[9]

The effect of Wycliffe's teachings, however, was not limited to his fellow-countrymen; it was potent, if indirectly, as far away as Bohemia. The marriage of Anne, sister of King Wenzel (Wenceslaus) IV to Richard II of England in 1382 greatly stimulated intercourse between the two countries. Thus scholarships were founded at Oxford expressly for Czech students, who brought home with them copies of Wycliffe's writings, which were eagerly read in Prague. That the Czech leader Jan Hus drew many of his own opinions straight from the English divine is obvious; his treatise 'On the Church' (*De Ecclesia*), for instance, reveals a dependence nothing short of plagiarism.[10]

Born *c.* 1372 of a peasant family at Husinec, from which he took his name, Hus studied at Prague university, graduating as master in 1396. In 1401, soon after his ordination to the priesthood, he was elected dean of the philosophical faculty and was also licensed to preach at the Bethlehem chapel, where it was the custom to address the congregation in the Czech language. Not himself an original thinker, his first encounter with Wycliffe's writings marked the turning-point of his life. The Englishman's vehement denunciation of clerical worldliness and greed especially moved him, and it was to the task of practical reform that he henceforth devoted himself. Theologically cautious, there was much in Wycliffe's provocative teaching, on the eucharist in particular, which he did not himself endorse. The authority of scripture he ranked supreme, however, and Wycliffe's views on the church he fully shared, predestinarian though they were. Encouraged at first by the archbishop of Prague, Zbinck von Hasenburg, who welcomed his attack on popular superstitions, his sermons on clerical shortcomings met with strong opposition from the Prague clergy, and in 1407, on the instructions of Pope Innocent XII, he was inhibited from preaching. But he still retained the favour of the king, who relied on the help of the university in holding a neutral stance between the claims of the rival popes Alexander V and Gregory XII at the forthcoming Council of Pisa, whereas the archbishop supported Gregory.

Hus's national standing was further enhanced when in 1409 a royal decree transferred control of the university to the Czech 'nation' in place of the Germans who had exercised it hitherto. Unfortunately, on the archbishop's suddenly changing his allegiance to Alexander, a papal bull was issued condemning Wycliffite doctrines and ordering the destruction of Wycliffite books. Finally, on the accession of the Antipope John XXIII, Hus was excommunicated and his followers placed under an interdict. But his person was safe as long as he enjoyed the king's protection, and on his retirement from Prague he seized the opportunity to compose his treatise 'On the Church', in which, as we have said, he borrowed liberally from Wycliffe. Having announced his readiness to appeal to a general council,

9. A vernacular Bible seems to have been a rare thing in later fifteenth-century England, at least as compared with Germany, where twenty complete translations of the scriptures are said to have been produced between 1466 and 1522, or even France, where a thirteenth-century translation was reprinted seven times between 1487 and 1521. See P. Janelle, *op. cit.* pp. 15ff.

10. On Hus's concept of the Church see M. Spinka's volume of that title (Princeton, 1966). There is an English translation of the *De ecclesia* by D. S. Schaff (New York, 1915; repr. Westport, Conn., 1974).

excommunicate though he was, were such to be convened, he left Bohemia in 1414 for Constance, with a safe-conduct from the Emperor Sigismund. Here, however, he found himself arraigned on a vaguely formulated charge of heresy, and on his refusal to recant the opinions attributed to him he was burned at the stake on 6 July 1515. No doubt in attending the council at all he was fully aware of the risk he ran.

Hus's very moderation demonstrates the inability of the ecclesiastical authorities to meet the demand for reform at any level. In his preaching he felt bound to appeal to the freedom of the gospel against the dead weight of legalist institutionalism and the corruptions which it sheltered; but he refused to confess to errors he did not share, even if he stood by his belief that the church's sole head was Christ and not the supposed successor and representative of St. Peter. His death, followed a year later by that of his friend Jerome of Prague, made him a national hero no less than a martyr of faith. His attempted reform, unlike Wycliffe's, had at least stirred up a wave of popular feeling such as those who in any age seek profound changes in society must sooner or later enlist.[11]

Oddly perhaps, his adherents, in their revolt against persecution in 1419, adopted a principle which he himself did not insist on or even consider until near the end of his life, namely that of 'utraquism', or the doctrine that the laity as well as the clergy should receive the holy sacrament in the forms of both bread and wine (*sub utraque specie*). But the Utraquists or 'Calixtines', as they were sometimes called (from the Latin *calix*, meaning a chalice), constituted a moderate element in the Hussite movement; the more extreme, known as Taborites after Mount Tabor, their fortified stronghold south of Prague, were fanatical zealots who under their leader Zizka sought to promote the Kingdom of God by force of arms, scorning reasoned theological debate in favour of revolutionary social ends. One Utraquist group later (1467) separated from the main body and acquired the name 'Bohemian Brethren'. Embracing the teachings of a certain Peter Chelĉický, whose death had occurred a few years earlier, they became known for their strict moral discipline, dislike of urban life and disapproval of private property, as well as their pacifism. In course of time this rigorism was modified, and they eventually joined the Lutherans, though still retaining some features of their old practice. A generation or so later they established their centre in Moravia, whence the name 'Moravians', by which they are now remembered. What was left of the sect united with Zinzendorf's Herrnhuter in 1722. John Wesley, it may be recalled, was himself markedly influenced by Moravian teaching and piety.

A third group of medieval dissidents to call for mention here are the Waldensians of southern France and Piedmont, who in the fifteenth century had definite links with the Hussites. Their founder had been a twelfth-century *lyonnais*, Pierre Waldo, who on conversion turned to a life of poverty and gospel preaching, from which his subsequent excommunication in no way deterred him. But although strongly biblicist his followers were chargeable with no heresy apart from their dislike of the doctrine of purgatory and the practices associated with it, a fact which,

11.  On the Hussite movement as a whole see H. Kaminsky, *A History of the Hussite Revolution* (Berkeley, Los Angeles, 1967).

unhappily, did not spare them from persecution. Later their hostility to Rome grew, as too did their opposition to the cult of Mary and the saints, auricular confession and the prevalent teaching on the mass, on which last their own views anticipated Zwingli's. With the coming of the Reformation they sought relations with both Lutherans and Zwinglians, though their natural affinities were with the latter. At a meeting at Cianforan in September 1532 attended by Guillaume Farel and other Protestants a declaration was drawn up stating their main convictions. But it cannot be said that they themselves provided any real stimulus to Protestantism; rather was it the rise of the latter that gave them a new lease of life. Indeed the sect survives to this day.

### The conciliar movement

The perpetuation of the papal schism after 1378 was a manifest scandal to Christendom, although the initial efforts to terminate it were if anything productive of even more dismay and confusion than the schism itself, since the attempt on the part of the cardinals at the Pisan council in 1409 to bring it to an end resulted only in the emergence of Alexander V as a third pontiff, with a successor a year later in John XXIII, a man whose personal conduct was such as to bring the papal office into yet further disrepute. This situation was intolerable and had to be resolved. Thus at the behest of the Emperor Sigismund John summoned the council of Constance – reckoned afterwards to be the sixteenth general council of the church – in 1414. The attendant circumstances of intrigue and plot, counter-plot and counter-intrigue need not detain us. It is sufficient to observe that the only satisfactory solution lay, as it seemed, in the limitation of the papal power itself, a limitation to be based partly on the theories of Ockham and Marsiglio and partly on what were deemed to be the principles of the natural law, though also on the precedents of the early church. The leading apologists of the conciliar movement were the French theologians Pierre d'Ailly (1350–1420) and Jean Gerson (1363–1429), the former's tractate 'On the Reformation of the Church' constituting the third part of an elaborate work on the nature and function of a general council (*De materia concilii generalis*) to which Gerson too made an important contribution. The argument was that in the Catholic Church supreme authority must rest with such a body and not in the pope, d'Ailly going so far as to maintain that bishops and priests receive their jurisdiction directly from Christ and not mediately through the Roman pontiff. In any case he considered neither pope nor council to be infallible. One of the assembly's most significant acts was the decree *Sacrosancta* (15 April 1415), which declared that as a general council it had plenary authority and that 'all men, of every rank and condition, including the pope himself, are bound to obey it in matters concerning the faith, the abolition of the schism, and the reformation of the Church of God in its head and members'; while another, *Frequens* (9 October 1417), enacted that a general council was in future to be held at intervals of not more than ten years, each such assembly having already been announced by its predecessor.

Unfortunately the 'nations' represented at Constance could not agree on a common programme of reforms, their individual interests proving too diverse. The schism was at last brought to an end with the election in November 1417 of a new pontiff, Martin V, who displaced the other three, and the council dealt also with the heresies of Wycliffe and Hus, condemning no fewer than two hundred propositions attributed to the former, besides burning the latter in person. A further council, held this time at Basel and meeting at intervals between 1431 and 1439, endeavoured like its predecessor to tackle the twin problems of heresy and reform; yet it too failed, largely because the rulers of western Europe found it more expedient to settle their differences with the papacy independently, by means of concordats. The result was that the pope, sensing the threat of wholesale reform to have passed, could now turn his attention to the more congenial matters of his own political ambitions and the cultivation of the arts. The high noon of the Renaissance papacy was shortly to be reached, and when the pressure for reform again became heavy Rome was to show itself even less willing to deal with it constructively than before. The French clergy, however, recognizing the extreme improbability of any general ecclesiastical reform with the pope's support or acquiescence, persuaded Charles VIII to convoke a national synod to carry out specific reforms in France itself. By the Pragmatic Sanction of Bourges in July 1438 the principle of the supremacy of general councils was reaffirmed, together with an assertion of the rights of the French church to administer its temporalities without interference from Rome, to disallow papal nominations to vacant benefices and to limit the number of appeals from the French courts to the Roman Curia. Although superseded by the Concordat of Bologna in 1516 these articles provided the basis of the Gallicanism of a later age. Thus although the conciliar movement, regrettably, brought no solution to the problems troubling the western church, the demand for reform was in no way silenced; conditions, rather, were developing which were to make it even more urgent. On the other hand what is noteworthy is that no clear plea was voiced for changes in doctrine, and heresy was still looked on as the gravest of evils.[12]

## Late medieval piety

The later fifteenth century was not at all an age of religious indifference; on the contrary, religious sentiment ran high and easily spilled over into superstition, for which the popular saint cult gave ample scope. Religious confraternities, especially in Germany, were numerous; devotional books, for which in England there was a keen market, were particularly favoured; sermons (where they could be heard) were gladly listened to, above all when fervent; and hymns and pilgrim songs were well loved. Preaching, in fact, which was reasonably supposed to demand a good deal more of a priest than a mere ability to mumble his way through the missal, enjoyed

12. On the conciliar movement of the fifteenth century see B. Tierney, *Foundations of the Conciliar Theory* (Cambridge, 1955); P. de Vooght, 'Le conciliarisme aux Conciles de Constance et de Bâle', in *Le Concile et les conciles* (Paris, 1960), E. F. Jacob, *Essays in the Conciliar Epoch* (rev. edn., Notre Dame, Ind., 1963), A. J. Black, *Council and Commune: the Conciliar Movement and the Council of Basel* (London, 1979).

a measure of esteem never previously known in the Middle Ages. There were even manuals available to help the sermonizer in his task; for example, the *Biblia Pauperum* – the Bible for the Pauperes Christi, 'the poor in Christ', or the preaching monks – containing pictures illustrating Bible stories along with short explanatory comments, or, for the more learned, a work like the *Postilla* of the Franciscan Nicholas de Lyra, a commentary that passed through at least six editions between 1471 and 1509 and was praised by Luther himself. Sermons were also sometimes published, such as those of Jean Herlot, which were often reprinted and widely circulated. One of the most highly regarded of contemporary preachers was Johann Geiler of Keyserberg in Alsace, a member of the Strassburg circle of humanists renowned for his fierce denunciations of the vices and superstitions of the age, including relic worship, indulgences and the corruption in the religious orders. Nor, we may add, did he spare the logic-chopping of the scholastic theologians.

But of all the preachers of righteousness at that time the Dominican friar Girolamo Savonarola (1452–98) has left by far the most vivid impression upon history. Believing himself to be divinely inspired, he harangued the Florentine populace like an Old Testament prophet, calling on them in language of apocalyptic menace to burn or otherwise destroy their 'vanities', by which he meant their profane books and 'pagan' ornaments, and to turn again to God. But his sermons were not simply pulpit rant; he urged a drastic moral reform within the church itself and in his *Rule and Government of the City of Florence* set out the principles of a democratic theocracy; in fact, in December 1495 the citizens of Florence were induced to accept a new constitution devised along the lines of that of the Venetian republic. But although he moved the people deeply by his fervour, as well as by the uncanny accuracy of at least one of his prophecies (relating to the death of Pope Innocent VIII), he made enemies for himself no less surely. Summoned to Rome by Alexander VI to render account of his activities, he refused to budge from Florence, with the consequence that the pope inhibited him from further preaching. Undismayed, he continued to attack the Roman Curia and Alexander personally, and in 1497 he was excommunicated. Disregarding even this, he demanded the summoning of a general council to bring about the pope's own deposition. But when his supporters turned against him the end came quickly and he was burnt in the Piazza della Signoria in May 1498 as a schismatic and a heretic, even though his treatise *The Triumph of the Cross*, for all its apocalyptic and mystical tone, was an open apology for traditional Catholicism in face of the sceptical and pagan tendencies of the age.[13]

During this late medieval period the reading of the vernacular Bible should not be overlooked, as it often tends to be. We have referred to the Lollard Bible in England, but the English in this respect were much less well provided for than the Germans. These German versions, made of course from the Vulgate, usually had no official sanction, and for that reason were suspect in the eyes of the ecclesiastical authorities. The reading of the scriptures, in spite of their authority in all matters of faith and morals, was judged to be dangerous for the uninstructed and likely to

---

13. The best recent study of Savonarola is R. Ridolfi, *Vita di Girolamo Savonarola* (2 vols, Rome, 1952), although J. Schnitzer's *Savonarola* (2 vols, Munich, 1924) is still indispensable.

foster heresy, as in the case of the Albigenses. Nevertheless no general prohibition was laid on bible reading and in the hands of persons considered to be reliable – and laymen were not necessarily excluded – it was at least tolerated. After the invention of printing vernacular Bibles, like other forms of religious literature, were of frequent appearance; besides *Plenaria* (little books containing translations of scripture passages used in the church services), copies of the psalter and of the gospels and epistles multiplied; for example, of the gospels twenty-two were made before 1509 and twenty-five before 1518, while as many versions of the whole Bible in both High and Low German were printed during the late fourteenth and early fifteenth centuries, from that of Johann Metzel of Strassburg in 1466 to the Augsburg edition of 1518. For the most part these were displaced by the subsequent publication of Luther's translation, but they did not entirely vanish and were often to be found in German households down to the eighteenth century.

At this point it is appropriate to say something of the influence of the medieval mystics, for whom religion meant basically the practice of the presence of God and a life of dedicated piety. The attraction of mysticism for those who were not themselves by temperament mystical lay in its evident simplicity and directness: theological intricacies were not so much repudiated as ignored, while the import- ance of rites and ceremonies (apart from the sacraments) was minimized. In short, mysticism signified religion of an inward and personal kind rather than external and institutional. It was not by implication hostile to the church, but it could become so; at all events it encouraged a certain detachment from the traditional ecclesiasticism. The end of the mystical experience was held to be a union with God to which all else is subordinate if not an actual obstacle. To quote from an anonymous late fourteenth-century writing known as the *Theologia Germanica*, the first printed edition of which was supervised by Luther himself:

> [*The meaning of this union*] is that we should be of a truth purely, simply, and wholly at one with the One Eternal Will of God, or altogether without will, so that the created will should flow out into the Eternal Will, and be swallowed up and lost therein, so that the Eternal Will alone should do and leave undone in us. Now mark what may help or further us towards this end. Behold, neither exercises, nor words, nor works, nor any creature, nor creature's work, can do this. In this wise, therefore, must we renounce and forsake all things, that we must not imagine or suppose any words, works, or exercises, any skill, or cunning, or any created thing can help us or serve us thereto. Therefore we must suffer these things to be what they are, and enter into union Gods.[14]

The most famous of the German mystics was the Dominican Meister Eckhart (*c*.1260–1327), at one time regarded as more or less of a pantheist but whose work is nowadays better understood and appreciated.[15] For instance, although in his

14. S. Winkworth's translation, chap. xxvii. *The Theologia Germanica* is believed to have been written at Sachsenhausen, near Frankfurt, by a priest of the Teutonic Order. The English version by Miss Winkworth was first published in 1854 (rev. edn., with an introduction, by J. Bernhart, New York, 1949).

15. See e.g. V. Lossky, *Théologie négative et connaissance de Dieu chez Maître Eckhart* (Paris, 1960). The 'mystical' movement in medieval theology, especially in Germany, has to be seen as a counter-weight to scholasticism, particularly in its nominalist form (see p. 48 below, n.13). It signified a reversion to the practical type of religion for which

*Opus Tripartitum* he can say *Deus est esse*, or that God and existence are the same, his meaning is fundamentally Augustinian; in any event his practical religious convictions were definitely theistic. His young disciple Johann Tauler (*c.*1300–61), likewise a Dominican, stood firmly in the Thomistic tradition. His sermons, which stressed the divine indwelling in the soul and taught that the mystical way consists chiefly in the pursuit of virtue through humility and resignation to the will of God, were highly esteemed by Luther.[16] Yet another Dominican friar who came directly under Eckhart's influence was Henry Suso (Heinrich Seuse, *c.*1295–1366), whose 'Little Book of Eternal Wisdom' (*Das Büchlein der ewigen Weisheit*) dating from about 1328, became one of the German classics in this field. Devised as a practical aid to meditation it was much used during the fourteenth and fifteenth centuries, not least by Thomas à Kempis.[17] Finally there is the Flemish mystic Jan van Ruysbroeck (1293–1381), founder in 1349 at Groenendael, near Brussels, of a community of canons regular whose prior he was until his death. Groenendael later became associated with the religious movement known as the *devotio moderna* and thus had associations with the Brethren of the Common Life.[18]

This orthodox mystical tendency had its heretical counterpart in a group of sectarians known as the Brethren of the Free Spirit, whose teachings appear to have been both pantheistic and antinomian.[19] But there were also other types of 'Brethren' (the name was loosely applied) to be found chiefly at first in Germany and more akin in their beliefs and ways to the English Lollards, adhering to a simple evangelical creed, studying the Bible in the vernacular and adopting a

15. *continued* knowledge of divine things was to be acquired less by the speculative intellect than by penitence of heart. Whereas scholastic theology aimed to clarify and demonstrate by rational processes, mystical theology sought understanding by 'vision', by intuitive feeling, resulting in an ineffable sense of union with God. The circumstances and conditions in which such mystical religion developed and the literary expression it assumed set it quite apart from the academic teaching of the universities. It pertained essentially to the monastic life and to the kind of spiritual training given there, as also to the popular style of preaching intended to evoke an immediate emotional response. Its concern was markedly eschatological and gave rise during the fourteenth century to phenomena of prophecy announcing the approaching end of time and the appearance of Antichrist. John Eckhart was teaching at the University of Paris in 1300, but the rest of his life was spent in Germany, where as vicar-general of his order he gained a high reputation by his preaching and doctrine and by his reforms of the Dominicans in Bohemia. But he had his opponents among the Franciscans, who eventually (1329) secured the condemnation at Rome of some twenty-eight of his theses.

16. See *Johannes Tauler. Ein deutsche Mystiker*, ed. E. M. Filthaut (Essen, 1961), a volume issued to commemorate the six hundredth anniversary of Tauler's death.

17. There is an English translation of the *Little Book of Eternal Wisdom, as also of Suso's earlier and more speculative Little Book of Truth*, by J. M. Clark (London, 1953). On Suso generally see E. M. Filthaut, ed., *Heinrich Seuse* (Cologne, 1966), which like the volume on Tauler referred to above was published to commemorate the six hundredth anniversary of Suso's death.

18. Much of Ruysbroeck's work was written in Flemish, although several Latin versions appeared in his own time. There is a *Life of Ruysbroeck* by Evelyn Underhill (London, 1915).

19. Cf. G. Leff, *Heresy in the Later Middle Ages* (Manchester, 1967), I, 308–407, and N. Cohn, *The Pursuit of the Millenium* (London, 1957), 149–94.

moralistic pattern of life. Recruited mainly from the urban artisan class, they suffered, like the Lollards, intermittent persecution. They seem to have been especially active, again like the Lollards, during the last decades of the fifteenth century and the first quarter of the sixteenth.

The so-called 'modern devotion' (*devotio moderna*), probably in its day the most influential religious movement in northern Europe, originated towards the end of the fourteenth century in the Low Countries and in the circle of Gerhard (or Geert) de Groote (1340–84), a layman of mystical bent and founder of the Brethren of the Common Life. A native of Deventer, he was educated at Paris, where as a youth he showed promise of a brilliant intellectual career. But in 1374 he underwent a conversion experience and entered a monastery in Holland. Later, under the influence of Ruysbroeck, he took up mission preaching in the diocese of Utrecht and was forward in denouncing the abuses of his time, an activity which eventually cost him his licence. The semi-monastic life he passed in company with a few priests at Deventer became the nucleus of a type of community which stood, so it has been said, 'halfway between a medieval friary and a devout Puritan or Quaker household of the sixteenth or seventeenth century',[20] and received its most revered literary expression in *The Imitation of Christ*.[21] It consisted for the most part of free associations of secular priests and laymen, although among the religious the Windersheim canons were its principal representatives, and their members were drawn from various classes of society and noted, in contrast to the begging habits of the friars, for their industriousness. Yet to speak of them as 'reformers before the Reformation', as has sometimes been done, is erroneous. They had no distinctive doctrines, while de Groote himself was an orthodox Catholic with no leanings towards heresy and suspicious even of the mystical ideas of his admired Ruysbroeck. What the Brethren aimed at was the cultivation of the personal religious life under the guidance of the Spirit. It was the revivification of belief, not its revision, that they sought. They valued the study of the scriptures and encouraged the laity to read them in the vulgar tongue: private meetings of an informal character for the exposition of the Bible were quite common among them. But their main influence lay in the sphere of education and the school at Deventer so closely linked with them became famous throughout Europe. Religion of course received strong emphasis but they made no effort to induce their pupils to enter the religious life; they set much store by the humanities and certainly did not forbid the reading of the pagan classics. By modern standards no doubt the routine was harsh and narrow, often petty and sometimes even brutal: Erasmus, who had

20. D. Knowles, *The Middle Ages* (vol. II of *The Christian Centuries*, London, 1969). On the Brethren see A. Hyma. *The Brethren of the Common Life* (Grand Rapids, Mich., 1950) and *The Christian Renaissance* (rev. edn., Hamden, Conn., 1965).
21. Thomas à Kempis (Thomas Hemerker, *c.*1380–1471) was in all probability the author, or at least part-author, of this famous work. Educated at the Brethren's school at Deventer, he joined the canons of the Agnietenberg, near Zwolle, a daughter-house of the Windersheim community, of which his elder brother Jan was co-founder and prior. Thomas spent virtually all his life there. The *Imitation* is only one of his numerous writings, all of them imbued with the 'modern' devotional spirit. Many editions of it have been printed. S. Kettlewell, *Thomas à Kempis and the Brothers of the Common Life* (2 vols, London, 1882) is still a useful source of information.

himself been a schoolboy at Deventer, later accused the Brethren of trying to break the spirit of their charges. Nevertheless many such schools were established, in Germany as well as in the Netherlands, and in general the quality of education which they offered was in their day unsurpassed elsewhere.

But there was a group of fifteenth-century teachers, Netherlanders or Rhinelanders, who could in a sense not too strained be described as 'pre-reformers' on account of their marked Augustinianism as well as their exaltation of scripture and opposition to ecclesiastical abuses.[22] The best known of them are Johann Rucherat (*c*.1400–81), usually called John of Wesel, Johann Wessel of Groeningen (*c*.1420–89) and Johann Pupper of Goch (d.1475). Wesel, a canon of Worms, was accused of preaching Hussite doctrines on the church and sacraments and was brought to trial in 1479 by the Inquisition, and although he publicly recanted was kept in confinement until his death two years later. Maintaining that the Bible alone is the final authority in matters of faith, he rejected the dogma of transubstantiation, indulgences, compulsory fasting and extreme unction. Wessel, a nominalist in philosophy and, like Ockham, a critic of the papacy, taught for many years in Paris, though later he came under the influence of Italian humanism. He too attacked indulgences and indeed so far anticipated Luther that when the latter came across his writings in 1522 he expressed gratification to find him 'in accord with me in all things'. 'If', he even declared, 'I had read this earlier on it could well have given my enemies the impression that I copied everything from Wessel, so much are our two minds at one.'[23] Pupper also was acclaimed by Luther, who contributed a preface to an edition of his *Fragmenta*.[24] For these writers at least therefore the designation 'reformers before the Reformation' could be said to have some justification.

## Humanism

But a major factor behind the demand for reform is to be seen in the changes in intellectual outlook which occurred during the fifteenth century, changes marking a point at which Renaissance and Reformation clearly interlink. Here the rediscovery of the literature of classical antiquity – *literae humaniores* – was the most potent influence, introducing as it did a standard of human cultural achievement by which Christian civilization itself might be judged. In any case humanistic studies aroused a new critical spirit contrasting sharply with the narrowness and formalism of the theological tradition. No doubt the enthusiasm engendered by this 'new learning' was itself at times rather naïve and uncritical, resulting, especially in Italy, in a posturing 'classicism' that merited only ridicule.[25] But the outcome of the

22. See C. H. Ullmann, *Reformatoren vor der Reformation* (2 vols, Hamburg, 1841–2; English trans. by R. Menzies, *Reformers before the Reformation, London, 1885*).

23. On Wessel see E. W. Miller and J. W. Scudder, *Wessel Gansfort: his life and writings* (2 vols, New York and London, 1917).

24. On Pupper see O. C. Clemen, *Johann Pupper von Goch (Leipzig, 1896)*.

25. The view, as stated by P. O. Kristeller, *Renaissance Thought and its Sources* (New York, 1979), that humanism was for the most part a cultural and educational movement and that its concern with philosophy and other matters of intellectual substance was secondary, is hardly to be challenged. Renaissance philosophising was, in general, eclectic and rather shallow.

movement was a great increase in the knowledge not only of classical literature but also of the early church Fathers, the biblical texts and the age-old heritage of Judaism. Its effect was enlarged by the rapid dissemination of the new knowledge by the lately invented printing-press. No longer was learning confined to the universities or the cloister but was placed within reach of an increasingly literate and cultivated public. Inevitably the outlook and methods of the schoolmen began to lose credit.

Moreover scholasticism was itself divided by internecine disputes. It had in its heyday made possible, through its endeavour to systematize the faith by means of the resources of speculative philosophy, an impressive synthesis of human learning as a whole, the finest expression of which was in the work of Thomas Aquinas. But Thomist realism had largely given way to the nominalism of Ockham and Gabriel Biel, the latter a member of the Brethren of the Common Life and a teacher not without influence on Luther himself. This came to be known as the *via moderna* in distinction from the older *via antiqua*, and was dominant at a number of centres of learning, including the university of Erfurt, where Luther graduated. The 'modern way' drastically limited the role of reason in man's knowledge of things divine; a realm where truth, so its exponents held, is not rationally demonstrable, but must rest on authority alone, which in the end means simply the biblical revelation. Thus dogmatic positivism or fideism had its basis in a thoroughgoing scepticism. Towards the close of the century, however, a reaction set in, chiefly at Paris and Cologne, against the *via moderna* in favour of the 'old way' of Aquinas (and also Duns Scotus), so that once again reason could be invoked in support of faith. In Luther's time its most able exponent was the Dominican Cardinal Cajetan – Tommaso de Vio, called Cajetan or Gaetano from the name of his birthplace, Gaeta – with whom in person the reformer was to be confronted at Augsburg in 1518.

But from scholasticism of whatever brand the humanists dissociated themselves utterly, even if none overtly denied the doctrinal tradition which the scholastics purported to explain and codify. It was scholarship, the knowledge of men and of letters, which absorbed their interest, not the logomachies of philosophical argument, for which they felt only aversion and contempt. This attitude was typified by Erasmus even in his early years when, as the protégé of the bishop of Cambrai, he was obliged to attend theological lectures at the Sorbonne, where the 'wrinkled brows, bulging eyes and purple faces' of supposedly learned doctors disgusted him.

The beginnings of the humanist movement can be traced to Italy in the fourteenth century, where its earliest representative was the poet Petrarch, who already in his schooldays had developed a love of Cicero and who, when in later life he received a gift of manuscripts of Homer and Plato, kissed them with awe and reverence, unable though he was to decipher the language in which they were written, the mere sight of the Greek script being an inspiration to him. His successors set about applying themselves to a close study of such texts and thus for the first time devised a critical literary technique. Lorenzo Valla (1405–57), for example, in his 'On the Donation of Constantine' (*De falso credita et ementita Constantini donatione declamatio*, 1440) was able to demonstrate that the document on which the pope's temporal sovereignty purported to rest, instead of dating from the days of the

Emperor Constantine, was a forgery of the eighth century.[26] The same author's 'Collation of the New Testament' (*Collatio Novi Testamenti*, 1444) signified a fresh departure in New Testament studies by attempting a critical comparison between the Vulgate and the Greek original. But Valla did not confine himself to literary scholarship; in his disputations 'against the Aristotelians' (*Dialecticae disputationes contra Aristotelicos*, printed posthumously in 1499) he poured ridicule on the whole scholastic method in philosophy, while in his book 'On the Religious Profession' (*De professione religiosorum*) he attacked monasticism not only in its current practice but in its very ideals. Naturally enough Valla was suspected of heresy, but he escaped persecution and his influence on subsequent Renaissance thinking was profound.[27]

In some ways the most interesting aspect of the humanist movement in Italy was its revival of the study of Plato, exemplified in the activities of the Platonic Academy of Florence under the patronage of Cosimo and Lorenzo de' Medici, whose enthusiasm had been kindled by the arrival in the city of the Greek savant Gemisthos Pletho. The luminaries of the Academy were Marsiglio Ficino (1433–99) and Giovanni Pico della Mirandola (1463–94). Ficino worked for years on a Latin translation of all Plato's dialogues (printed 1483–4) and thereafter on the writings of Plotinus, Porphyry and Dionysius the Areopagite. Ordained to the priesthood in 1473, he preached Plato no less than Christ from the cathedral pulpit, but his ideas, an often fanciful amalgam of Christian theology and neo-Platonist mysticism, were rather more systematically expounded in a treatise *De religione christiana*, published in 1477, in which he presents Christ, the divine Logos, as the true 'artist' behind the manifest beauty and harmony of the world and asserts that all religious truth, however and wherever disclosed, is essentially one. Unfortunately his lively imagination outstripped his critical judgement, and of any sense of historical perspective he was devoid. His musings thus lose themselves in daydreams.[28]

Ficino's quest of the ultimate unity of all truth and reality was indeed intensified by his noble compatriot Pico, for whom all religions were in their differing ways but an utterance of the soul's yearning for God. A perpetual student moving from one centre of learning to another, he yet amassed a substantial library and by the age of twenty-five he knew, so it was said, 'everything which a man can know'. Besides being a good classic he also studied Hebrew and was familiar with the Kabbala, in which he discovered, as he thought, a clue to the Christian mysteries. But his speculations led him beyond the bounds of orthodoxy and at one time he had to seek refuge from the church authorities in France. The range of his interests is indicated by the nine hundred theses on various topics the truth of which he

26. Modern edn. by C. B. Coleman (New Haven, Conn., 1922). On Valla see F. Gaeta, *Lorenzo Valla: filologia e storia nell' umanismo (Naples, 1955)*.

27. See G. Radetti, 'La religione di Lorenzo Valla', in *Medioevo e Rinascimento. Studi in onore di Bruno Nardi*, II (Florence, 1955), 595–620.

28. His principal philosophical work was his *Theologia platonica de immortalitate animorum, composed in 1474 and obviously inspired by Plato's Phaedo* (modern edn. in the Guillaume Bud series, 2 vols, 1964). On Ficino's thought as a whole see P. O. Kristeller, *The Philosophy of Marsilio Ficino* (New York, 1943) and R. Marcel, *Marsile Ficin* (Paris, 1958).

declared himself ready to defend. As some at least of them appeared heretical at Rome, however, Pico abandoned this ambitious project and passed the rest of his days in the retirement of a simple and even ascetic life. In his book 'On Human Dignity' (*De hominis dignitate*), which summarizes his philosophy, he discussed the centrality of man in the universe and stoutly defended the freedom of the will. As he put it, 'the only condition to which man is subject on earth is that there are no conditions for him'. In short, man is, as a modern existentialist might say, his own means and end; by his rational understanding he can resolve all antitheses, since propositions that at first sight look irreconcilable may in fact be complementary, their meeting-point and focus being the human mind itself – an interesting pre-echo of Hegel. But as the friend and disciple of Savonarola religion for Pico was a deeply personal matter, founded on prayer and the study of the Bible. When he died his body was dressed, as he himself had requested, in a Dominican cowl.

Outside Italy the humanist movement assumed a somewhat different character, less secular in outlook and more concerned with the implications of the new learning for Christian thought and life. The love of classical antiquity remained strong, but the text of the Bible and the writings of the early Christian Fathers claimed more attention.[29] In fact many humanists saw in antiquarian scholarship not only a source whence Christendom might draw renewed intellectual vitality but a standard by which both church and society could be reformed. Thus an enthusiasm which otherwise might have ended in a sterile dilettantism was geared to a practical need. On the other hand the Christian humanists of Spain, France, England and Germany had none of them any programme for sweeping change; they exposed corruptions in the institutions of their time, especially in monasticism, the ideals of which had been widely lost sight of, but they had no wish to question the accepted principles of belief or to see the universal church replaced by a congeries of newfangled sects. They were far more interested in conduct than the abstractions of theology, although they were confident that moral improvement would be brought about by advancing knowledge.

In Spain the humanist tradition combined with the native seriousness of temper in religious matters to produce a group of Catholic intellectuals for whom scholarship and faith were certainly interrelated. Thus Cardinal Ximenes (Jiménez) de Cisneros (1436–1517), archbishop of Toledo, a Franciscan of ascetic life and great personal dedication who from his own purse established the university of Alcalá, was responsible for the production there of the first printed edition of the text of the New Testament, an enterprise which antedated that of Erasmus by some two years, even though actual publication was delayed until 1520; as also that of the Complutensian Polyglot Bible (so called from *Complutum*, the Latin name for Alcalá) of 1522, a vast work in six volumes, including vocabularies and a Hebrew grammar, in which the Old Testament was set out in parallel columns containing the Hebrew text and the Vulgate and Septuagint versions.[30] Other Spanish

29. See J. H. Bentley, *Humanists and Holy Writ: New Testament Scholarship in the Renaissance* (Princeton, N.J., 1983).
30. On Ximenes and his circle see L. Fernandez de Retana, *Cisneros y su sigla* (2 vols, Madrid, 1928–30) and W. F. Starkie, *Grand Inquisitor, being an account of Cardinal Ximenez de Cisneros and his times* (London, 1940).

humanists comprised Elio Antonio de Nebrija (c. 1442–1522), whose attempt to correct the Vulgate aroused the suspicions of the Inquisition; Juan de Valdès (*c.* 1500–41), biblical translator and commentator and author of a book (*Alfabeto cristiano*, 1536) on Christian perfection which stressed the importance of personal faith; his twin brother Alfonso (*c.* 1500–32), who became a notable figure in the entourage of Charles V; and perhaps most influential of all, Juan Luis Vivés (1492–1540), the greater part of whose career was spent in the Low Countries and in England. Vivés, a *littérateur* and a master of Castilian prose, was deeply concerned with contemporary social problems (witness his *On the Help of the Poor* printed in 1526) and education (*De tradendis disciplinis*, 1531), both of which interests were underpinned by a strong religious conviction: education especially, he thought, should be made to serve the ends of Christian living; indeed he was more interested in the moral and spiritual development of individuals than in ecclesiastical reform. All these men were admirers of Erasmus, who in the early decades of the century was highly esteemed in the Iberian peninsula, the statesmen and courtiers surrounding the young King Charles being proud to call themselves Erasmians. But by 1530 the humanist vogue, which the Dominicans certainly never favoured, had declined, thanks at least partly to a common mind on the subject between Charles and the pope.[31]

In France, on the other hand, the humanist movement had King Francis I's warm support. Its most famous scholar was Guillaume Budé (1467–1540), a friend and mentor of the young Calvin.[32] Budé, who had studied in Italy, had an unsurpassed command of the classical languages, – in Greek, unquestionably, he had no rival in western Europe – and was well versed in Roman law and Greek philosophy. He was also personally influential with the king, who not only entrusted him with the charge of the royal library but at his suggestion founded and endowed the seat of learning now known as the Collège de France. More directly involved with religious issues was Jacques Lefèvre d'Etaples (Faber Stapulensis; 1455–1536). He too was a keen classicist, especially drawn to Aristotle, but he later turned his attention to the Bible, producing in 1512 a Latin commentary on St Paul's epistles which Luther used in preparing his Wittenberg courses. In 1518 his critical studies caused difficulties with the church authorities and in 1521 he was condemned for heresy by those staunch upholders of scholastic orthodoxy, the doctors of the Sorbonne. Finally his sympathy with the religious changes afoot in Germany embroiled him with the French government and in 1525 he fled the country, seeking refuge at Strassburg, though fortunately for him the king's sister, Marguerite d'Angoulême, queen of Navarre, who was herself both a patron of humanism and drawn to the reform, accorded him her protection. (As the author of a well-known book on spirituality, *Le Miroir de l'âme pécheresse*, even she had elicited the disapproving notice of the Sorbonne professors.) But Lefèvre, although he questioned the doctrine of transubstantiation, never accepted the characteristic teachings of the Reformation

31. See M. Bataillon, *Erasme et l'Espagne* (Paris, 1937).
32. See J. Bohatec, *Budé und Calvin: Studien zur Gedankenwelt der französischen Frühumanismus* (Graz, 1950).

and the sort of reform he hoped for was on the Erasmian not the Lutheran model.[33]

The most understanding of Lefèvre's pupils was Guillaume Briçonnet (1470–1533), a member of an illustrious family, who in 1516 became bishop of Meaux. A man of great personal piety, Briçonnet conceded the need for church reform and gathered round him a number of like-minded scholars, but again the sort of renovation he envisaged coincided with the aims of conciliarists like Gerson and was not otherwise revolutionary, while he was confident that sound learning could only strengthen traditional Christian faith and devotion. It was Christian humanism of this type which in his younger days attracted John Calvin, who himself had links with the Meaux group, particularly through Nicolas Cop, the future rector of the university of Paris. Its objectives were never more vigorously stated than by François Rabelais who in his letter of Gargantua to Pantagruel urges the necessity of a knowledge not only of Greek, 'without which a man may be ashamed to account himself a scholar', but Hebrew, Arabic, Chaldean and Latin as well, to which were to be added (besides of course a good literary style) civil law, philosophy and above all the Old and New Testaments in their original tongues. All very utopian, no doubt, but it is astonishing how close some of these eager spirits came to achieving their goal.[34]

Although in England the beginnings of humanism might be traced back to Chaucer, it is with two Oxford teachers and personal friends, both of whom had studied in Italy, William Grocyn (*c.*1446–1519) and Thomas Linacre (*c.*1460–1524), that the movement really becomes identifiable. However, it acquired its distinctive character and tendency from John Colet (*c.* 1467–1519), the son of Sir Henry Colet, a rich London merchant and sometime lord mayor. He too had lived in Italy, where he picked up a good knowledge of Greek, and in all probability had been in Florence at the time of Savonarola's mission. At least his Italian sojourn was such as not only to imbue him with a keen taste for the New Learning but also with a seriousness of outlook that was to condition his whole subsequent career. On his return to England in 1497 it was as a determined student of the Bible and of those ancient church Fathers who were especially congenial to latterday Platonists: Origen, Jerome and Pseudo-Dionysius. Erasmus, then on his first English visit, met Colet in 1499, and was greatly impressed alike by his learning and by

33. Other scholarly works by Lefèvre include the first printed edition (in Latin) of the epistles of St Ignatius (1498) and a French translation of the New Testament from Vulgate (1523), a similar rendering of the Old Testament being completed in 1528. On Lefèvre's religious standpoint see A. Renaudet, 'Un problème historique: la pensée religieuse de J. Lefèvre d'Etaples', in *Medioevo e Rinascimento,* II, 621-50; as also, more largely, the same writer's *Préréforme et humanisme à Paris pendant les premières guerres d'Italie (1494-1517)* (2nd ed., Paris, 1953) and E. Doumergue, *Jean Calvin, les hommes et les choses de son temps,* I (Luasanne, 1899), 79-112.

34. Rabelais's real intention here is ironic. He himself had no sympathy with religious zeal, Catholic or other. Though himself a Franciscan and a student of theology both scholastic and biblical, his religious opinions were idiosyncratic and quirky. His writings were eventually placed on the Index Librorum Prohibitorum. See M. A. Screech, *The Rabelaisian Marriage: aspects of Rabelaisian religion, ethics and comic philosophy* (London, 1958).

his high principles, which were evidently borne out in practice. The two men became close friends.

Colet's spirit was not only pious and ascetic, it was critical as well, as was apparent from his Oxford lecture courses on the Pauline epistles, which for the first time approached these writings as personal utterances having their proper historical context. He was concerned, that is, to show what manner of man the apostle himself was and what were the circumstances in which he wrote: it would no longer suffice to use the epistles merely as a source for theological 'texts' or to interpret biblical statements by a free-ranging allegorism; nor was he content simply to quote patristic comments. In short, he dismissed the scholastic exegesis for something more recognizably modern. Doctrine, though, he left aside, not seeing himself as a theologian.

But Colet was a conscientious churchman (in 1505 he was appointed dean of St Paul's) and like all serious-minded men was scandalized by the corruption he witnessed everywhere about him. Reform, he believed, would have to begin with the bishops, on whom responsibility primarily fell and who even under the existing canon law had the means at their disposal. His interest in education received a lasting memorial when in 1509 he refounded St Paul's school with money he had inherited from his father, his aim being to instil into the one hundred and fifty-three young scholars who constituted the initial intake sound Christian instruction and a good knowledge of the classical languages.[35]

One whose home at Chelsea was frequented by Colet was the lawyer Thomas More (1478–1535), afterwards Speaker of the House of Commons, High Steward of the universities of Oxford and Cambridge, and eventually, on the fall of Wolsey in 1529, Lord Chancellor of England. Erasmus too was on close terms with him, having first met him in 1499 and then again in 1506, and whose 'Praise of More' (the title *Encomium Moriae*, or 'The Praise of Folly', carries an obvious play on More's name) was at once a tribute to a much admired personality and a joke to be enjoyed, its satirical purpose being quite undisguised, by both men. More's own most famous work, *Utopia*, was published at Louvain in 1516 and was clearly intended for readers with a humanist bent, although its author also had an eye on the more discerning type of public official. It describes an ideal commonwealth devised in accordance with natural law, all its citizens living in a state of political, social and economic equality, reflected in democratic institutions, and practising, rather curiously, a kind of deistic natural religion, although this last feature is certainly not to be taken as an indication of More's personal views, since he remained a devout Catholic until he died – in the event tragically.[36] But between the years 1515 and 1520 More warmly supported Erasmus's humanistic ideals in religion as in scholarship. On the other hand he had no sympathy with Luther's

35. On Colet's teaching see E. W. Hunt, *Dean Colet and his Theology* (London, 1956); also L. Miles, *John Colet and the Platonic Tradition* (La Salle, Ind., 1961).

36. *Utopia*, written in Latin, was not translated into English until after More's death. The Yale edition of the *Complete Works* (New Haven, Conn. and London, 18 vols) began publication in 1963, but is still far from finished. The standard modern life has been that of R. W. Chambers (London, 1935), but in some respects has been superseded by E. E. Reynolds, *The Field is Won: the life and death of Saint Thomas More* (London, 1968).

opinions, and for Henry VIII's *Defence of the Seven Sacraments* in 1522 he himself acted as 'a sorter out and placer of the principal matters'. Indeed when Luther answered Henry, More, under the pseudonym of Gugliemus Rossaeus, sought to vindicate his theologically-minded monarch in a learned if also somewhat scurrilous *Responsio ad Lutherum* (1523). Later, in an *Epistola ad Pomeranum* (first printed in 1568), he attacked all the Saxon reformer's main positions.

In Germany the humanist movement had its closest contacts with the Italians, German students regularly making their way southwards to Italian centres of learning. Among them the linguistic interest was particularly strong, some of them, Reuchlin pre-eminently, mastering Hebrew as well as the classical languages. But religion was usually their prime concern, with the Bible and the Fathers as the ultimate focus of their studies, from which reformist ideas inevitably germinated. The earliest of the German humanists, unless we except Gregor von Heimberg (1410–72), was Rudolf Agricola (1442–85), who was educated by the Brethren of the Common Life at Deventer and who subsequently became leader of the humanist fraternity at the university of Heidelberg. Indeed, according to Erasmus, he was the first 'to bring out of Italy the breath of higher culture'. Others included Jakob Wimpfeling (1450–1528), a product of the Brethren's school at Schlettstadt and an alumnus of Heidelberg, whose interests were principally those of a historian and educationist (he came to be known, even before Melanchthon, as *Praeceptor Germaniae*, the 'teacher of Germany'); Sebastian Brand (1457–1521), satirist and author of the widely read *Narrenschiff*, 'The Ship of Fools'; Konrad Celtes (1459–1508), a notable propagandist both of the New Learning and of German nationalism; Konrad Peutinger (1465–1547), the city archivist at Augsburg and an antiquarian; and Willibald Pirkheimer (1470–1528), a rich young Nuremberger in love with the arts and all scholarship, and the translator of a number of classical authors – in fact, a typical Renaissance figure in whom the Latin and Teutonic aspects of humanism were strikingly combined.

The university of Erfurt, where Luther studied, vied with Heidelberg in its humanist enthusiasm. The leader here was Konrad Mut (1472–1526), commonly known as Mutianus Rufus, the designation referring to his red hair. Another Deventer schoolboy and a pupil of Hegius's, he afterwards studied at Erfurt and Bologna, where he took a doctorate in law, finally to settle down as a church dignitary at Gotha. Yet at one time, under the influence of Pico della Mirandola, he all but abandoned orthodox Christianity in pursuit of an eclectic Platonist mysticism, looking on traditional religion as fit only for the untutored masses, not men of higher enlightenment:

> Thus the true Christ [*he protested*] is not a man, but spirit and soul, which do not manifest themselves in outward appearance, and are not to be touched or seized by the hands.

And again, more darkly:

> There is only one god and one goddess; but there are many forms and many names – Jupiter, Sol, Apollo, Moses, Christ, Luna, Ceres, Proserpina, Tellus, Mary. . . . In religious matters we must employ fables and enigmas as a veil. Thou [*he is addressing his friend Heinrich Urban*] who hast the grace of Jupiter, the best and greatest God,

shouldst in secret despise the little gods. When I say Jupiter, I mean Christ and the true God. But enough of these things, which are too high for us.[37]

Mutianus wrote no book of importance, but his correspondence is illuminating on certain facets of Renaissance thought. His paganizing fancy he later curbed, but his contempt both for scholasticism and for ecclesiastical officialdom persisted.

However, on the eve of the Reformation the two outstanding representatives of German humanism were the great Hebraist, Johann Reuchlin (1455–1522), and Ulrich von Hutten (1488–1523), an impoverished Franconian nobleman. The former, who after schooling from the Brethren of the Common Life at Schlettstadt studied the classical tongues at Freiburg, Paris and Basel in turn, became so excellent a Hellenist that the Italians spoke of him as the 'transalpine Greek', though he also compiled a Latin dictionary which for many years was highly regarded. But it was on his knowledge of the Hebrew language and literature that his fame later rested.[38] He began to learn Hebrew in 1485, receiving instruction from scholarly Jews. Thereafter his neo-Platonist interests, stimulated by contact with the Platonic Academy during a visit to Italy, led him to the doctrines of the Kabbala, the supposedly Christian implications of which he expounded, first in a book called 'On the Wonderful Word' (*De verbo mirifico*) (1494) – a farrago of theosophical speculations – and then, many years later, in *De arte cabalistica* (1517). His most important work was a Hebrew lexicon and grammar (*De rudimentis hebraicis*) published in 1506. This gave a new and scientific impulse to the study not only of the Hebrew language but of the Old Testament generally, which could now be approached through the original tongue. Unfortunately his researches into Judaism kindled the suspicions of the Dominican friars of Cologne, who, scenting heresy or worse, backed the efforts of a converted Jew, one Johann Pfefferkorn, to secure the seizure and destruction of all Jewish books that could be found. Any idea of such a holocaust Reuchlin strongly opposed and advised the Emperor Maximilian I accordingly. Indicted at Cologne, he was twice acquitted (in 1514 and again in 1516), but on an appeal by his adversaries to Rome in 1520 the decision went against him and he was even made to bear the costs of the hearing. This prolonged controversy aroused bitter feelings on both sides, Reuchlin's case being supported by the celebrated satirical broadside 'Letters of Obscure Men' (*Epistolae obscurorum virorum*, 1515–17), in which the Cologne theologians, and especially the inquisitor, Jakob von Hochstraten, were boisterously ridiculed. Who exactly the authors were – for there were two series – was not at the time known, but it is fairly certain that the first was from the pen of the humanist Crotus Rubeanus (Johann Jaeger of Dornheim), whilst the second was the work of that literary knight-errant, Hutten.

Hutten, poet, controversialist and one-time soldier (he had taken part as a *Landsknecht* in Maximilian's Italian campaign of 1512), a man whose faults of

---

37. C. Krause, *Briefwechsel des Mutianus Rufus* (Kassel, 1855), 94, 28.
38. The biography of Reuchlin by L. Geiger (Leipzig, 1871) has still not been rendered obsolete, but on the Hebraist's religious views see L. W. Spitz, 'Reuchlin's philosophy: Pythagoras and Cabala for Christ', in *The Religious Renaissance of German Humanism* (Cambridge, Mass., 1963).

character – impulsiveness, ill-temper and a loose mode of life – may in part be attributable to chronically poor health, was a scathing critic of the old order whether as embodied in the papacy, the monks or the scholastic theologians. In his younger days a wandering scholar – Bologna, Cologne, Wittenberg and Vienna were among the universities he had attended – he brought out in 1519 an edition of Valla's *Donation of Constantine*, at the same time proclaiming his adherence to the cause of Luther, whose ardent admirer he had become. But whether he had much understanding of or even sympathy with the deeper aspects of the reformer's teachings is open to doubt. His real passion was German nationalism, and he saw in Luther's protest a likely means of delivering Germany from the Roman yoke, as is evident from his writings, in German and in Latin, of 1520–21. On his dismissal from the service of the archbishop of Mainz, whose counsellor he had been, and the issue from Rome of an order for his arrest, he took refuge for a time with his friend and fellow-knight Franz von Sickingen. He even sought the protection of Erasmus, but the ever-cautious scholar was not the man to compromise himself by embarrassing associations, and it was Zwingli at Zurich who in the end gave him shelter. Disappointed, disillusioned and riddled with syphilis, he died soon afterwards, in abject circumstances.[39]

It would be misleading to claim that the humanist movement represents an initial phase of the Reformation, or even in any direct sense an anticipation of it: rather is it yet another face of late medieval Catholicism. But it did prepare the way for the Reformation intellectually, above all in the field of biblical study, where it fastened attention on the literal or historical meaning of the original instead of the more arcane interpretations – allegorical, moral, tropological – elaborated by the schoolmen. Its essential nature, and not least its somewhat ambiguous relation to the cause of the Reform, is best seen in the personality and work of Erasmus, of all humanists the prince, in the eyes of his contemporaries. Such indeed are the Dutchman's intrinsic interest and historical significance that he merits a chapter to himself.

39. D. F. Strauss wrote a 'Life' of Hutten (Leipzig, 1958; new edn., 1927), an English version of which by G. Sturge was published in 1874. A more recent study is that by H. Holborn, *Ulrich von Hutten and the German Reformation* (trans. R. H. Bainton, New Haven, Conn., 1937).

Chapter 2

# DESIDERIUS ERASMUS

## The humanist and biblical scholar

The well-known saying that Erasmus laid the egg which Luther hatched was an embarrassment to the celebrated humanist from the day he first encountered it. 'I laid a hen's egg,' he retorted, 'but what Luther hatched was a bird of a quite different sort.' Nonetheless at the time it was commonly believed, on one ground or another, to be true. Aleander, Leo X's envoy at the imperial court, declared that both men disseminated much the same doctrine, save that Erasmus's poison was the more deadly. At any rate a speculatively-minded humanist like Mutianus could gladly acclaim the Dutchman as the 'restorer of theology' and looked on the Reformers generally as his spiritual progeny. Luther himself, in his earlier days, respected him profoundly not only as a great scholar but as a fellow-fighter in the same cause. Erasmus's ever-popular *Adages*, his *Enchiridion Militis Christianae*, with its simple gospel piety, and the Lucianic satire of the *Encomium Moriae* ('In Praise of Folly') were plainly, it could be said, the work of a man in whose eyes the old order stood condemned. Yet the humanist's attitude to the Reform movement was ambiguous and fluctuating, and throughout his voluminous correspondence it is virtually impossible to discover a consistent standpoint. Much depended on whom he was addressing; in any case he was a pastmaster in the art of nuanced and qualified statement, especially when he felt that he had the best of reasons for not showing his hand. For this he has been accused of dissimulation, and by the time of his death he had succeeded in alienating both sides in the great quarrel, the Catholics distrusting him as subversive, the Protestants as pusillanimous and shifty. But although he did not himself become an active partisan in the reformers' cause there can be no question but that his influence went far to promote it.[1]

1. The *editio princeps* of Erasmus's collected works was issued by his friend Beatus Rhenanus and published at Basel in nine volumes, 1540–1. The standard edition of the *Opera omnia* is still that of the Arminian theologian and biblical scholar, Jean Leclerc, published at Leyden between 1703 and 1706 (repr. 1963), but a new and critical edition under the patronage of the Union Académique Internationale and the Royal Netherlands Academy of Sciences and Letters is now in course of publication. For Erasmus's letters see P. S. and H. M. Allen, *Opus epistolarum Des. Erasmi Roterodami*, in twelve volumes, with index (Oxford, 1906–58). An English translation of the *Collected Works*, from the University of Toronto Press, is to be completed in about forty-five volumes. Modern translations have been published of the *Adages* by M. M. Phillips (Cambridge, 1964), the *Colloquies* by C. Thompson (Chicago, 1965), the *Enchiridion* by R. Himeleck (Bloomington, Ind., 1965) and the *Encomium Moriae* by H. Hudson (Princeton, 1941). A selection in English of Erasmus's epistles, in three volumes, was made by F. M. Nichols (London, 1901–08). For a general selection from Erasmus's writings, also in translation, see J. C. Olin, *Christian Humanism and the Reformation* (New York, 1965).

Desiderius Erasmus, although he called himself Roterodamus, was in all probability born not at Rotterdam but at Gouda, where his father lived. There is uncertainty about the date of his birth, as well as the place; 1469 would seem to have been the year, but he himself chose for personal reasons to give the impression that it was earlier, as early even as 1466. That his birth was illegitimate – a fact about which he was acutely sensitive – is not in doubt, his father being a priest. He received his schooling first at Gouda and then with the Brethren of the Common Life at Deventer, where he was taught by the humanist Alexander Hegius. It was only with reluctance, presumably because he lacked any real sense of vocation, that he became an Augustinian canon at Steyn before reaching his twentieth year, but already his scholarly interests were fast developing. In 1492 he was ordained to the priesthood, and shortly after acquired a patron in Henry of Bergen, bishop of Cambrai, whose Latin secretary he became, an appointment that at least relieved him of his servitude to the cloister. Some three years later he began a course of studies at Paris, entering the same Collège de Montaigu at which Rabelais had been a student and which Calvin and Ignatius Loyola were also to attend.

In 1499 he accompanied a pupil of his own, William Blount, Lord Mountjoy, who also materially befriended him, on a visit to England, where he met both Thomas More and John Colet, whose company and friendship he found entirely congenial and by whom he was markedly influenced. Colet's lectures at Oxford on the epistles of St Paul in particular captivated his imagination, not least perhaps because the apostle's doctrine was freely spiced with a neo-Platonism culled from Origen, Pseudo-Dionysius and Marsiglio Ficino. Returning to the continent in the following year he for a while resumed his interrupted Paris studies, after which he moved to Louvain, although, fearing the restrictions of a routine occupation, he declined the offer of an academic post there. It was then that he commenced the serious if laborious study of Greek.

A second visit to England took place in 1505, but by July 1506 he had arrived in Italy, to remain there until the summer of 1509, when he once more set out for England. His Italian sojourn, rather surprisingly, afforded him less intellectual stimulus than he had expected, but in England, and notably during his stay at Cambridge, where for a time he assumed the newly created Lady Margaret's professorship in divinity, he was happily occupied in lecturing, writing on education, translating the classics and preparing his edition of the Greek New Testament. In the autumn of 1514 he was back again on the continent, reaching Basel in August and wintering there. From 1515 until 1521 he was mainly in the Low Countries, with Louvain as his centre, though he met the Elector Frederick of Saxony at Cologne in November 1520, when the latter sought his advice on the problem of Martin Luther. The years 1521 to 1529 were spent at Basel, with accommodation at the home of his friend the well-known printer Johann Froben.

Erasmus had by this time become one of the most famous men in Europe, with an unrivalled reputation as a scholar, prelates, princes and even kings being proud to hold correspondence with him. Official appointments were offered him that would have been irresistible to a man of more worldly ambitions, and all were declined. If one of his ruling passions in life was his love of learning, the other was his personal freedom. In 1529, when Basel espoused Zwingli's reform movement, he left the city for Freiburg-im-Breisgau, his home for the rest of his life. But it was at Basel that he died, in June 1536. His splendid public funeral testified to the honour in which he was held, despite the detraction of his enemies.

It was his edition of the Greek New Testament, prudently dedicated to Pope Leo X, which of all his works had probably the widest theological repercussions. But although Latin could almost be said to have been his mother-tongue, he did not find that proficiency in Greek came at all easily. 'It is nearly killing me', he wrote in March 1500 – he was then back again in Paris, after his visit to England – 'but I have no time, no money and no teacher.' However, he persevered: Greek was a necessity if the classics were to be understood and enjoyed. Moreover, he longed to study not only the Greek Fathers but the original text of the New Testament itself so as to reach down to the very sources of Christianity; away from the stuffy atmosphere of the Vulgate, redolent as it was of generations of scholastic interpretation, the simple, rational *philosophia Christi* might be freely breathed in. Valla and Colet had been pioneers in New Testament study, but both had used the Latin version only; what Reuchlin was doing for the Hebrew Old Testament should now be done for the writings of the apostles.[2] A fresh Latin translation of the New Testament had been made by Erasmus himself in 1506, but his work on the Greek text was very probably hastened by a rumour of the forthcoming appearance of Ximenes's Complutensian edition. The fruit of his efforts came out at Basel in March 1516 from the publishing house of Froben under the title *Novum instrumentum omne, diligenter ab Erasmo, Rot., recognitum et emendatum*. For it Erasmus had used ten manuscripts, four of which he found in England, and five more at Basel; the tenth and best of all had been lent him by Reuchlin. His undertaking was modest enough in comparison with the achievements of more modern scholars, but it was sound so far as it went, being critical in temper and resting on a genuine collation of manuscripts, besides drawing on Erasmus's extensive patristic knowledge.[3] It became with but a few emendations the *textus receptus* of modern times until the whole problem of the New Testament text was tackled afresh and much more scientifically by Tischendorf in Germany and Westcott and Hort in England during the nineteenth century.

Hardly less influential than Erasmus's Greek Testament was the new Latin version which accompanied it.[4] A number of changes were made from the Vulgate, such as the substitution of *sermo* in the opening verse of St John's Gospel for the Vulgate's *verbum*, as being closer to the meaning of *logos*, or the rendering of the Greek *metanoeite* in St Matthew 3:2 by *resipiscite* ('be mindful') or *ad mentem redite* ('come to yourselves') instead of *paenitentiam agite*, with its strong suggestion of

2. Valla's 'Notes' on the New Testament, in which he had exposed the deficiencies of the received Vulgate text, had not been printed, but Erasmus found a manuscript copy in the Praemonstratensian Abbey of Parc, near Louvain.

3. Unfortunately the last six verses were missing, which Erasmus made good by producing a none too brilliant translation of his own from the Latin. The second edition (1519), for which he had recourse to several other manuscripts, contained a large number of alterations. It was from this second edition that Luther made his German version of the New Testament. See A. Bludau, 'Die beiden ersten Erasmus-Ausgaben des Neuen Testaments und ihre Gegner' (*Biblische Studien, vii*, 5, Freiburg-im-Breisgau, 1902).

4. First published in 1519.

doing penance. It was in fact this latter alteration which so much affected Luther's own thinking, causing him to stress the inwardness of repentance far beyond any outward act of 'satisfaction'. Indeed when Erasmus's work first appeared the Wittenberg teacher had no doubt that it would provide the indispensable foundation for his courses in New Testament exegesis, and even though the accompanying *annotationes* became as time went by less and less to his liking he never repudiated the debt which the new theology owed to the humanist's labours. As he himself observed: 'There never has been a great revelation of the Word of God unless he has first prepared the way by the rise and prosperity of languages and letters, as though they were John the Baptists.'[5] Both the Greek and Latin editions were adopted in universities all over Europe and became the basis for numerous vernacular translations.

The truth is that Erasmus was much more than a sequestered scholar and man of letters, even if in after years he did shun publicity in any other capacity. What was ever uppermost in his thoughts was the cause of religious reform, and the drift of his theological views was evident long before Luther wrote.[6] Thus in the *Paraclesis* or Introduction to his Greek Testament he makes it abundantly clear that he thinks scripture the prime authority in religion and believes that it should be open for all to read.

> I strongly disagree [*he writes*] with those who would not have the Holy Scriptures read by layfolk and translated into the vulgar tongues, as though Christ had imparted a teaching so obscure that it could be understood only by a handful of theologians, or as though the safety of the Christian religion lay in ignorance of it. It is right perhaps for the secrets of kings to stay hidden, but Christ wishes his own to be as widely proclaimed as possible. I should like all women to read the Gospel and the Epistles of Paul. Would that they were translated into all languages so that not only the Scots and the Irish but Turks and Saracens might be able to read and know them.

His favourite New Testament books were the four gospels, but he also prized the First Epistle of Peter, the First Epistle of John and the whole of the Pauline *corpus* apart from Hebrews, which nevertheless was then held to be Pauline.[7]

Erasmus was wary however of venturing, in his actual comments, into the realm of dogmatic theology, not merely from a sense of incompetence in matters so abstruse but from a conviction that Christian doctrine, so far from being abstract

5. In a letter to Eoban of Hesse, leader of the humanist circle at Erfurt. See *Luther's Correspondence* and *Other Contemporary Letters*, ed. P. Smith and G. M. Jacobs, (2 vols, Philadelphia 1913–18), ep. 180.
6. See E. W. Kohls, *Die Theologie des Erasmus* (2 vols, Basel, 1966).
7. Among Erasmus's critical opinions regarding the New Testament was the view that Mark's gospel is an abridgement of Matthew's (itself, he thought, in all probability originally written in Hebrew), and that Luke was not an eyewitness. The authorship of Hebrews, 'written in a rhetorical rather than an apostolic style', could well, he suggested, be attributed to Clement of Rome. The Epistle to the Ephesians he considered Pauline in thought but not in language. The Apocalypse he did not care for. It has fairly been said that 'malgré sa vaste erudition, il fondait l'enseignement du dogme sur un petit nombre de textes: les paroles du Christ dans l'Evangile, d'abord, puis les Epîtres apostoliques: le reste, pour Erasme, comptait peu à ses yeux' (A. Renaudet, *Erasme, sa pensée religieuse et son action d' après sa correspondance (1518–1521)* [Paris, 1926; repr. Geneva, 1970], 27).

and complicated, is essentially simple and practical, as befits the needs of the ordinary man.

> To my mind he alone is a theologian who teaches, not with the aid of learned syllogisms, but with an internal fire, with expression of his feeling – in a word, with his life itself – that the riches of this world are to be despised and that a Christian ought not to trust in earthly defences but rather to put his whole confidence in Heaven and refrain from all injustice, praying for those who condemn us.

It is just such 'popular' theology as this, he contends, which is to be found in the Bible.

> Why then do we not occupy ourselves exclusively with the great writers of Scripture? Why do we not carry their words around with us, having them always in our hands, imbibing them, examining them, probing into them ceaselessly? Why do we give so much time to Averroës instead of the Gospels? Why do we spend our lives almost entirely with the Commentaries and their mutually contradictory opinions?

It was not the speculative intellect to which theology should address itself but the moral conscience enlightened by the teachings of Christ. There was no profit to the soul in the rationalism of the schoolmen, and between the religion of the gospels and the standpoint of such a book as the *Sentences* of Peter Lombard (let alone of his innumerable commentators) there was a complete gulf.

In saying this Erasmus was well aware that he could count on many sympathizers, some of them, a Guillaume Budé or a John Colet, for example, among the most clear-sighted and thoughtful men of his day;[8] men who realized that any genuine renewal of either faith or morals would in no small degree depend on education and knowledge. Moreover, there can be little doubt that for some years after the publication of his Greek Testament Erasmus's views had the support of Luther and his followers. Luther himself indeed may all along have had misgivings on certain points, but at the time of the Heidelberg meeting of the chapter of his order (April 1518) Martin Bucer, a Dominican friar who also happened to be present, could readily affirm that the Wittenberg professor, with whom he had already corresponded, was in open agreement with the humanist on all the main issues. A year later Luther wrote to Erasmus in almost fulsome terms, expressing gratification that his own ideas were known to and approved by the scholar, and saluting in turn the latter's 'noble spirit, which has enriched me and all men'. In fact, until 1521 Erasmus was virtually Luther's guide and mentor.

Such, then was the opinion held of the celebrated humanist wherever the reformed doctrines were taking root, and the influence of his biblical theology was invariably at work. At Strassburg, for instance, Matthäeus Zell, the pioneer of the Reformation in that city, undertook a continuous exposition of the Epistle to the Romans in a side chapel of the cathedral, and a couple of years later Bucer was doing the same for the Pastorals. At Basel Oecolampadius was preaching on the biblical text to large congregations, as likewise was Andreas Osiander at Nuremberg. At Zurich as early as 1519 Zwingli had begun his lecture-sermons in the

---

8. See, e.g., a letter of Budé's, 1 May 1516 (Allen, ep. 403) and of Colet's, 20 June 1516 (ep. 423).

minster with a series on St Matthew, afterwards extending them to cover other books of the New Testament as well, always using the actual Greek text. But the appeal of Erasmus was nowhere more explicit than in the case of a layman, Joachim de Watt, usually known as Vadianus (b.1484), a scholar and theologian and a practising physician, who eventually became burgomaster of St Gall. As with Zwingli, his change of mind on religion found immediate expression in humanism, but it soon took a more radical turn leading to a complete break with tradition, although never to the extent of abandoning Erasmus's moralism. Thus while his writings betray a definite Lutheran influence his idealizing of primitive Christianity is no less Erasmian, as too are his notions of *fiducia*, or 'fiducial faith', the *lex evangelii* and his pacifism.[9]

## Erasmus and the reformers

Among the leading reformers none was more deeply in the humanist's debt than Huldrych Zwingli, despite some attempt in recent years to play it down.[10] In the first place due weight should be given to the effect on the Swiss divine of a poem of Erasmus's first published in 1514, his 'Expostulation of Jesus with Man' (*Expostulatio Jesu cum homine*). In its praise of Christ the one Mediator as the heart and soul of all real Christian piety it may be said to have contributed in no small measure to Zwingli's conversion in 1514–15.[11] As he himself put it:

> Eight or nine years ago [*he wrote in 1523*] I read a deeply consoling poem of the learned Erasmus of Rotterdam, in which he addresses our Saviour Christ, and in which, in the most beautiful words, Jesus laments that men do not seek their good in him; for he is the foundation of all satisfactions, a redeemer, a consolation and a treasure of the soul.[12]

Again, when he read Erasmus's *Plan or Compendium of True Theology* he declared that he could not remember having discovered elsewhere 'so much fruit in so small a space', and as soon as his Greek Testament came out he bought a copy and studied it carefully, seeing in it a deliverance from the empty theologizing of the schools. This 'Christ-centredness' of Zwingli's faith had developed, that is to say, before he encountered Luther's teaching, overmastering though this proved to be. In 1516, when still a parish priest at Glarus, he travelled to Basel especially to meet the man he so greatly esteemed, following up his visit with a letter expressing his gratitude for all that he had done for him;[13] although it is evident from Erasmus's reply that the young man's admiration was rather for the scholar's literary achievements than his religious doctrine.

9. Erasmus's *Querela Pacis* ('The Complaint of Peace') was published in 1517.
10. On Zwingli's early enthusiasm for Erasmus's writings, virtually all of which we know that he possessed, see J. Rogge, *Zwingli und Erasmus. Die Friedensgedanken des jüngen Zwingli* (Stuttgart, 1962).
11. See W. E. Köhler, *Huldrych Zwingli* (Leipzig, 1943), I, 92ff.
12. E. Egli *et al.* eds., *Zwinglis Sämtliche Werke* (Zurich, 1905ff.), II, 217.
13. Allen, ep. 401.

I am very glad [*the latter wrote*] that my works commend themselves to one so generally approved as are you; and for this reason they displease me the less. I congratulate Switzerland, of which I am very fond, that you and men like you polish and ennoble her with learning and character – particularly Glarean [*Heinrich Loriti of Glarus, the most distinguished of the Swiss humanists, and a friend of both Erasmus and Zwingli*], a man singularly respected by me on account of his varied learning and uprightness, and one wholly devoted to yourself. . . . Ulrich, exercise your pen, that best teacher of style: I see that natural talent is there, if only practice be added.[14]

That Zwingli's attitude to scripture was basically Erasmus's own is hardly to be questioned.[15] The humanist, as we have seen, had always maintained that there can be no sound theology which is not biblical, because only in the New Testament will a man discover the living Christ:

Here [*he urges in his New Testament introduction*] Christ lives, breathes and speaks to us today; almost, I might say, with greater effectiveness than when he himself was here on earth. The Jews saw him and heard him less than you do now in the Gospel writings. You have only to open your eyes and ears.

Others took up and popularized such teachings, they did not originate them. But whereas Luther rested his interpretation of Christianity mainly on St Paul, Erasmus looked to the central figure of the gospels, and especially to the words of the Sermon on the Mount, which for him contained the very essence of the 'philosophy of Christ'. Yet to infer from this that Erasmus neglected the Pauline epistles would be quite wrong. He had commented on them as early as 1500, long before he compiled his notes for the Greek Testament or wrote the paraphrase of Romans published in 1519.

Nor was his understanding of the apostle any less 'vital' or 'evangelical' than that of the Swiss reformer.[16] Another Zuricher, the bell-founder Hans Füssli, could write (in 1521) of 'the splendid, famous and learned man, Erasmus of Rotterdam, who opened up the right way in which we may safely go to the true Holy Scripture, which surpasses all things', adding, 'Where have you seen that anyone brings forward Paul as fairly as Erasmus has done?'[17] One could indeed as reasonably argue that Zwingli's own view of the New Testament is 'humanistic' and determined primarily by the respect due to a classical text. It may also be said, at this point, that too much should not be made of the distinction often drawn between Erasmus's purely humanistic interests before the turn of the century and the more definitely religious concern which is supposed to have developed subsequently.[18] The Dutchman, as we have said, was never merely the detached scholar, uncommitted in any personal way to the challenge of religion; although why such non-commitment, to use no more forceful a word, was

14. Allen, ep. 404 (8 May 1516).
15. Cf. Kohler, *op. cit.*, 126ff.
16. Contrary, that is, to the opinion of A. Rich, *Die Anfänge der Theologie Huldrych Zwinglis* (Zurich, 1945), 44ff.
17. O. Schade, *Satiren und Pasquille* (1859), I, 119; cited P. Smith, *Erasmus* (New York, 1923), 375.
18. R. H. Bainton in *Newsletter of the American Council of Learned Societies*, no. 19 (1968), 1–7.

eventually such an offence to the Protestant reformers we shall shortly have to consider. From the standpoint of the Catholic conservatives of Louvain, of whom Latomus was typical, Erasmus's dubious religious opinions were only too much in evidence. The truth is that in the case of Zwingli the Erasmian influence was of fundamental importance; or to put it a little differently, Zwingli was the most distinctively *humanist* of all the reformers, not even excepting Melanchthon or Bucer, and in this Erasmus was his inspiration. Indeed, as we shall see later, he stands in this respect apart from all the others, in Switzerland or elsewhere.[19] The affinity of the two men's thinking on such subjects as the *regnum Christi* or the *militia Christi* is obvious.

How far does this hold good of Erasmus's ideas on the eucharist, that crucial issue in contemporary debate? It has been claimed that both Zwingli and Oecolampadius, the Basel reformer, generally echo his beliefs, and this decidedly was Melanchthon's opinion. But Erasmus's statements are ambiguous, although there are indications that he was already in sympathy with the position which Zwingli adopted. Thus in October 1525 he wrote to the bishop of Langres, Michel Buda, that 'a new dogma has arisen, that the Eucharist is nothing but bread and wine. Not only is it naturally difficult to refute, but Oecolampadius has supported it with such copious arguments and reasons that it appears that even the elect may be seduced.' Erasmus had been asked by the town council of Basel to give them his opinion of Oecolampadius's tract 'On the True Understanding of the Word of the Lord, "This is My Body" ', and in reply did not conceal his appreciation of the author's argument, as well as commending his learning and eloquence. What he could not do was to approve it as a doctrine, since it plainly differed from that of the church, 'something which it is always perilous to reject'. But what precisely he himself believed, as distinct from his professed adherence to the accepted dogma, is less than clear.

> Oecolampadius's idea of the Eucharist would not [*he confessed*] displease me were it not opposed to the consensus of the Church. For I do not see what is the function of a body which cannot be apprehended by the senses, provided that the spiritual grace be present in the symbols. But the authority of the Church binds me.[20]

Rationally speaking the Swiss view was, he thought, a plausible one, but a man should not play fast and loose with the dogmas of the church when claiming to be a loyal member of it. Even so, not a few of Zwingli's followers understood Erasmus to be, on this issue, definitely of their persuasion. The Swiss reformer, Leo Jud, for instance, author of a pseudonymous pamphlet *The Opinion of the Learned Erasmus of Rotterdam and Dr Martin Luther on the Lord's Supper* (1526), made it appear, by an adroit selection of passages from the humanist's writings, that in the latter's eyes the eucharistic elements were only 'signs or symbols of the Lord's Body and Blood'. Not surprisingly Erasmus himself took vigorous exception to this interpretation of his statements and repudiated Jud's tract as the product

19. See J. Rugge, 'Zwingli und Erasmus', in *Arbeiten zur Theologie*, II (Stuttgart, 1962), 11, 22ff, 40ff.
20. From a letter to the German humanist Willibald Pirkheimer, 6 June 1526 (Allen, ep. 1717).

of both ignorance and malice.[21] But by this time his break with Luther also was complete and in his own judgement the Reform movement had shown itself to be negative and divisive. Henceforward he saw himself as a conservative for conscience's sake, however much he might detest the obscurantists who automatically identified new knowledge with heresy.

Before we leave the subject of Erasmus's reformist influence something needs to be said on the position of Martin Bucer. The Strassburg divine was early attracted to humanism, admitting a dual allegiance to Erasmus and to Luther as men between whose teachings he found no essential divergence. Even as late as 1530 he published an anonymous 'Apology' for the Reform in which he not only defended the Protestant cause and celebrated its advance, but, in reply to Erasmus's then recently published *Epistle against those who falsely boast that they are Evangelical* (November 1529), sought to demonstrate that the reformers' principles were still essentially the humanist's own, even if the latter now received such compliments with distaste and embarrassment. Bucer's chosen role, however, was that of a conciliator, and the traditionalist element in his thinking is further evidenced by his advocacy of a rite of confirmation such as that adopted, on his advice, by the church of Kassel in 1539. Yet the idea of a ceremony of this kind, focusing on the renewal of baptismal vows, had been proposed by Erasmus likewise many years previously, not indeed as a sacramental act but as a means of instructing the young in the full meaning of their baptismal commitment, a point on which he conceived himself to be following the usage of the primitive church. Actually it was Zwingli who drew Bucer's attention to this suggestion, but it certainly was from his reading of Erasmus that the Strassburg reformer deepened his own understanding of baptism as at once a divine gift and an observance of human obligation. Already in the *Enchiridion* Erasmus had exhorted 'the Christian soldier' to remember that he twice owed his life to the Lord – by natural birth and by the supernatural regeneration of baptism – and that through solemn vows he was now wholly dedicated to 'this generous Prince'. 'What does the cross on your forehead signify, if not that you are to fight all your life long under his banner? And what the holy oil of anointing, if not that you embark on an unending struggle against evil?'

In Erasmus's mind the two aspects of the sacrament, the objective and the subjective, that is the spiritual grace given and the moral effort demanded, are reciprocal.[22] Yet it is the pedagogical side of baptism that especially interests him, an interest which was also Bucer's. In the latter's catechisms of 1534, 1537 and 1543 (Erasmus, we may note, had published one of his own in 1533) the starting-point is not, as with Luther, the Ten Commandments, but holy baptism, an approach entirely consonant with the Erasmian ideal of a *communio sanctorum*, a 'communion of saints', as outlined in Bucer's last treatise *De regno Christi*,

21.  It has even been argued that Erasmian ideas underlay the thinking of the more radical reformers on baptism. Balthasar Hubmaier visited Erasmus at Basel in 1522, and undoubtedly the humanist saw much to admire in the purity of the anabaptists' way of life and their fortitude under persecution. But their baptismal doctrine and practice he could not accept, and regarded the general tendency of their beliefs as dangerously anarchistic. See Allen, epp. 1313 and 1369.

22.  Cf. Kohls, *op. cit.*, 73ff and 122ff.

composed in England with an eye on the religious situation in that country during the reign of the young king Edward VI.[23]

## 'Christ's philosophy'

Why, then, if Erasmus so far anticipated the teachings of the Protestant reformers that they could hail him as a colleague, did they later turn against him as he too turned against them? To answer this question we have first to consider what really it was that he meant by the *philosophia Christi*. It was plainly set forth, at least for all Latinate readers, in the *Enchiridion militis christiani*, the 'Handbook [or, better, Dagger] of a Christian Warrior', where the subject is the *imitatio Christi* and the emphasis is on the inwardness of true religion.[24] It was written at the request of a pious woman whose knightly husband led a boorish and dissolute life (his identity has never been firmly established) in the hope that since, virtually illiterate though he was, as a friend and admirer of Erasmus the latter might succeed in persuading him to heed the teachings of religion and to amend his ways. But in it the humanist offers far more than a conventionally elevating tract; for what it contains is an expression of personal belief that altogether minimizes the importance of external observances, which in his opinion only pander to superstition. Not that he condemns them in themselves – they have their place – but what matters is the state of a man's heart..

> To observe these things is salutary, but to lean upon them is pernicious. Paul does not forbid you to use rites and ceremonies, but it is not his wish that he who is free in Christ should be bound by them. He does not condemn the law of works if only one uses them lawfully. Without these things perhaps you will not be pious, but they do not make you pious.

The true way of piety is in following Christ. He is 'the sole archetype, from which if anyone swerve by even a nail's breadth he goes astray and deviates from the way'. Christ's 'philosophy' is for Christians nothing other than the meaning of Christ himself, 'no empty voice' but, on the contrary, simplicity, patience, purity; in short, whatever he himself taught. Christ's ethical precepts are not to be explained away or glossed over but taken literally, although in the spirit no less than the letter. The heart of Christian doctrine is charity: 'For this cause chiefly was Christ born and did die, that he might teach us not to do as the Jews do, but to love.' Thus the Apostle Paul, in writing to the Corinthians, rightly puts charity foremost, before miracles, prophecy, or even the tongues of angels. By charity he means 'edifying your neighbour, counting all men members of the same body, thinking of them all as one in Christ, rejoicing in the Lord over your brother's good fortune as over your own, relieving his misfortunes, correcting with gentleness such as err, instructing the ignorant, lifting up the fallen, consoling the dejected,

23. See below, p. 245.
24. Translations appeared subsequently in several languages: English in 1518 (made probably by William Tyndale), Czech in 1521, Dutch in 1524, Spanish in 1527 and French in 1529.

helping those who toil, succouring those in need'. Above all let a man strive to keep himself from pride, the most odious and the most insidious of vices. For in the end what is he? 'Filthy at birth, a bubble throughout life, the food of worms at death.' Even so, God for his sake became man too.

The *Enchiridion* was inspired not only by its author's reading of the gospels but by Plato's *Phaedrus* and Pico della Mirandola's *On the Dignity of Man*.[25] The spirit of the work is that of the *Imitation* – a simple, practical and undogmatic piety, wholly suited to its pastoral aim of delineating the ideal of the good man who tries his best to walk in Christ's footsteps. Dogma is not denied, nor is it dismissed, but it is not primary: indeed for Erasmus Christ was always more of a model than a mediator. As for worship, the truest sacrifice is a broken and a contrite heart. It is also obvious that despite the influence of German mysticism and the *devotio moderna* the author himself was nothing of a mystic, but a moralist through and through, looking to the example and precepts of such ancient worthies as Socrates and Cicero as well as the New Testament. Finally, all we know of Erasmus himself leaves no doubt that the externals of the religious life had little interest for him, with the consequence that he was in no sense a radical if by radicalism is meant an insistence on a literalist return to New Testament patterns. Custom, modified where necessary by reason, was his accepted standard.

The *Encomium Moriae* (completed in the summer of 1509, though not published until two years later) had an entirely different aim, namely to mock, although the mockery was by no means without a serious and a reformatory purpose. As Erasmus himself puts it in his dedicatory epistle to Thomas More, if 'nothing is more trifling than to treat serious questions frivolously, so nothing is more amusing than to treat trifles in such a way as to show yourself anything but a trifler'. Thus many persons and things receive the whiplash of the writer's satire, not least the conventional pietism of his day, and especially the professional religiosity of the monks and friars, for whose whole mode of life Erasmus seems to have had a rooted dislike. But notably pointed are his facetious observations on contemporary theologians and their futile speculations:

> They will explain the precise manner in which original sin is derived from our first parents; they will satisfy you in what manner, by what degrees and in how long a time our Saviour was conceived in the Virgin's womb, and demonstrate how in the consecrated wafer the accidents can exist without the substance. Nay, these are accounted trivial, easy questions; they have greater difficulties behind, which, nevertheless, they solve with as much expedition as the former – namely, whether supernatural generation requires any instant of time? whether Christ, as a son, bears a double, specially distinct relation to God the Father and his Virgin Mother? whether it would be possible for the first Person of the Trinity to hate the second? whether God, who took our nature upon him in the form of a man, could as well have become a woman, a devil, an ass, a gourd or a stone?

The point of *In Praise of Folly* is to reduce everything to a jest, but the constant raillery is ironical as well, the mockery serving only as a disguise for a serious

25. Erasmus's initial acquaintance with Pico may have been through Rudolf Agricola, though later, quite certainly, by way of More and Colet. Eventually however he came to read the Florentine for himself. See *Opera omnia*, I, 1009.

criticism of life. 'Christ himself', says the author, 'became a fool when he was found in fashion as a man that he may bring healing by the foolishness of the cross. "For God has chosen the foolish things of the world to confound the wise, and the weak things of the world to confound the mighty." '

The New Testament *Paraphrases* were Erasmus's response to a request by Colet that his critical edition of the text be supplemented by an explanatory commentary.[26] He takes the scriptural material in order, elucidating and expounding it freely but simply, so that 'the farmer, the tailor, the mason, prostitutes, pimps, and Turks' might read it to their profit. His guiding method, particularly in the case of the Pauline epistles, with which he began, was, he said, 'to close up gaps, to soften abrupt transitions, to reduce the confused to order, to smooth out involved sentences, to explain knotty points, to illuminate dark places, to grant Hebraisms the Roman franchise, in short to modernize the language of St Paul, heavenly orator as he is'.[27] Perhaps the overall effect is a shade too literary, as several contemporaries did not fail to note. ('How ridiculous', exclaimed Luther, 'are those who, for the sake of style, put the Bible into paraphrases!') But Erasmus's intention was not to substitute his own graceful erudition for the inspired word itself, but rather to induce his readers to return to it. The first of the *Paraphrases* to be finished was dedicated to Cardinal Domenico Grimani in November 1517, the four gospels, which came later, being inscribed in turn to the Emperor Charles V, King Francis I of France, King Henry VIII of England, and the Archduke Ferdinand of Austria, king of Hungary and Bohemia. Composed in Latin, they soon appeared in vernacular versions, French, German, Czech and English.[28]

Erasmus's method of interpretation follows tradition in distinguishing the differing senses that attach to the words of scripture. Thus in addition to the literal or historical meaning an allegorical also is to be sought for, that is, a deeper, spiritual significance relating to Christ and the church; often too a tropological meaning, conveying moral instruction, as well as an anagogical, giving assurance to the faithful reader of the heavenly realities to come. But Erasmus is insistent that the historical sense, determined by the actual situation described, must first be grasped. Apart from a few of the psalms, Old Testament exegesis, doubtless because so much in the ancient Jewish scriptures seemed to him alien to the spirit of Christianity, is avoided. His allegorical interpretation, in which Platonist influence is present, aims to discover the spiritual beneath the material.[29] For example, in commenting on the miracle of the loaves and the fishes Erasmus sees the bread not even as Christ's sacramental body, but rather as the bread of heaven, the gospel itself, readily available to all who desire it. 'First consider what you have at home', he adds characteristically, 'and bring that to the Lord. He will bless it and give it

26. They are contained in the fifth volume of the *Opera omnia*. Cf. Allen, epp. 710, 196, 956.
27. Allen, ep. 710.
28. By Edward VI's Injunctions of 31 July 1547, copies of the gospel paraphrases were ordered to be displayed in all churches. See H. Gee and W. J. Hardy, *Documents Illustrative of English Church History* (London, 1896), 421 and 425.
29. On Erasmus's biblical exegesis see H. de Lubac, *Exégèse médiévale* (Paris, 1964), 472–87 and H. Schlingensiepen, 'Erasmus als Exeget', in *Zeitschrift für Kirchengeschichte*, xlviii, 1 (1929), 16–57.

back to you to distribute. The people will then receive more benefit than if some superstitious Pharisee, some arrogant philosopher, some eloquent orator should come with a carefully prepared discourse.' Above all, the parable of the Prodigal Son appealed to him for its simple and straightforward teaching about the love and the forgiveness of the heavenly Father.

It is of interest to note that it was on a point of biblical exegesis that the earliest intimation reached Erasmus of the existence of Martin Luther. Spalatin (Georg Burkhardt of Spalt), chaplain and librarian to the Elector Frederick the Wise of Saxony, wrote to Erasmus in December 1516 informing him that a certain Augustinian friar (unnamed but asserted to be 'no less famous for his life than for his theological learning') disputed his interpretation of the Epistle to the Romans, but the two men did not enter into correspondence until, some two and a half years later, Luther himself wrote to Erasmus in the letter already referred to. But by that time the latter had become acquainted with the *Ninety-Five Theses* and had actually sent copies of them to his English friends More and Colet.[30] His own view of the indulgences question is apparent from what he said to Colet: 'In all royal courts counterfeit theologians rule. The Roman Curia has simply cast aside all shame. What is more impudent than these incessant indulgences?'[31] The impression he had formed of Luther's *Theses* can be inferred from a letter of his to Johann Lang of Erfurt: 'I hear [*he says*] that Eleutherius [*Luther*] is approved by all good men, but it is said that his writings are unequal. I think his Theses will please all, except a few about Purgatory, which they who make their living from it do not want taken from them.'[32] He had also seen the refutation of them by the Roman theologian Pierias which he considered 'bungling'.

To begin with, then, Erasmus was sympathetic towards Luther and observed that his detractors were condemning passages in his works which were judged entirely orthodox when paralleled in those of St Augustine and St Bernard. Yet as the Wittenberg professor became increasingly violent in his language, not only about the papacy but about the Catholic church generally, he modified his attitude. Reform, not least at Rome itself, was now urgently necessary and drastic measures would certainly have to be taken, but he was loath to contemplate the 'tumult' which would almost inevitably accompany it. Would that Luther himself were 'more civil and less mordant'! 'I see sedition under way', he wrote to Melanchthon. 'I hope it will turn out to be to the glory of Christ. Scandals it may be have to come, but I have no wish to be their author.'[33] Yet to some it seemed that the hour had arrived for him to throw the full weight of his personal prestige into Luther's movement. Obviously there was need for caution. When Hutten came to see him at Basel at the end of November 1522 he avoided him. A few months later Erasmus took stock of his own position in a letter to a correspondent at Bruges.[34] He confessed that he was temperamentally opposed to dissension as well as finding it contrary to the principles of Christ. He saw himself to be between two fires:

30. See Allen, epp. 785 and 786.
31. Allen, ep. 786.
32. Allen, ep. 872.
33. Allen, ep. 1113.
34. Allen, ep. 1342. The letter is dated 1 February 1523.

Each side pushes me and each reproaches me. My silence against Luther is interpreted as consent, while the Lutherans accuse me of having deserted the gospel out of timidity. Luther's abusiveness can be condoned only on the ground that perhaps our sins deserve to be scourged with scorpions. . . . I cannot be other than what I am, and cannot but execrate dissension. I cannot but love peace and concord. I see how much easier it is to start than to assuage a tumult.

His words however drew bitter reproaches from the fiery Hutten, who commented on them in a harshly phrased *Expostulation*:

You render us invidious [*the latter wrote*] by saying that we [*i.e. his own and Luther's supporters*] are responsible for stirring up tumult and dissension. Did not Christ say that there would be hate and dissension, wars and bloodshed, because of his teaching? . . . You say that Luther casts the apple of discord. Anyone who proclaims the gospel does so. Have you not declared that if Luther is destroyed evangelical truth and liberty will suffer a great loss? How can you then oppose? . . . I grieve over your defection.[35]

This attack forced from Erasmus an answer, and his words are so typical of the man that their sincerity is beyond doubt:

I do not [*he states*] deny that I seek peace wherever possible. I believe in listening to both sides with open ears. I love liberty. I will not, I cannot serve any faction. I have said that all of Luther's teaching cannot be suppressed without suppressing the gospel; but because I favoured Luther at first I do not see that I am called upon to approve everything he has said since.

He had never called Luther a heretic, he says, and goes on to affirm that he has always deplored tyranny and vice in the church, but if the corruptions at Rome were sufficient to destroy the church then indeed there would be no church. It might be that the papal primacy was not instituted by Christ; nevertheless the church still needed a head. Again, taking up Hutten's statement that one should be ready to die for the gospel he declares that he would not refuse even this if the need arose, 'but I am in no mind to die for the paradoxes of Luther'. The sort of questions currently at issue were essentially theological problems; they were subjects for discussion in the schools, not principles of faith demanding martyrdom.

Erasmus's rejoinder not unnaturally encouraged the Romanists to think that, when it came to the point, he would support them against heretical innovations. The pope himself (Adrian VI from Utrecht, and an old friend of Erasmus's) urged him as a man renowned for his learning to rise up in defence of the church and refute Luther's doctrines. But the humanist's reply was evasive: 'Who am I to write? What understanding have I? I am said to be a Lutheran because I do not attack Luther, yet I am resisted by the Lutherans.'[36] Duke George of Saxony pressed him similarly, and once more Erasmus retorted that the matters in dispute were not such as he himself – no dogmatic theologian, for sure – was competent to handle, and in any case they were not fundamental. Besides, he protested, he could not read Luther in German; the best thing was to treat the whole controversy with silence. To which the prince answered that the real reason why Erasmus would not

35. On the whole document see E. Böcking, *Ulrichi Hutteni opera*, I (Leipzig, 1859), 180–248.
36. Allen, ep. 1352.

write against Luther was that he agreed with him! Little wonder, perhaps, when the humanist in a letter to Zwingli remarked that 'I seem myself to have taught what Luther teaches, only not so savagely, and without paradoxes and enigmas.'[37]

Indeed it would appear that basically Erasmus's reformism differed from that of Luther, Zwingli and the rest less in specific content, although the key-doctrine of predestination he deemed monstrous, than in the temper of mind by which it was imbued. And this was something that Luther had detected from the outset. What the latter owed to the celebrated scholar he never dissembled, but when he came to study his annotations to the New Testament he discovered that he had missed the vital truth of justification by faith alone, enshrined (as Luther himself believed) in the golden words of Romans 1:17, even though Erasmus's actual determination of the text coincided with his own against St Jerome's. As early as March 1517 he had to confess that his respect for Erasmus 'daily decreases': 'I fear he does not sufficiently reveal Christ and the grace of God; . . . for with him human considerations prevail more than divine.' By September 1521 he had come to see him as one 'far from the knowledge of grace' and looking for peace and quiet rather than at the cross of Christ. The humanist's tactic of 'civility and benevolence' would, he judged, accomplish nothing.

The consequence was that neither side in the great conflict really trusted him and in the end he was to be repudiated by both. As a powerful ally against Rome the reformers at first welcomed him, but when he declined to throw in his lot with theirs they repudiated him as a timeserver and a coward. It is clear that on many counts Erasmus continued to think well of Luther, but he disliked his loud-mouthed aggressiveness. 'I have never ventured [*he wrote*] to judge Luther's spirit, but I have often feared that the appearance of arrogance and vituperation would injure the cause of the Gospel, now happily reviving. . . . Would to God that he were gentler.'[38] Luther for his part deplored the scholar's 'guile' even while admitting that 'he has done what he was called to do'. Perhaps like Moses he would die 'in the land of Moab', but 'to come to the promised land of better pursuits was not for him'.[39]

### *'Vox clamantis in deserto'*

Erasmus's *Diatribe on the Freedom of the Will*, a work on which he embarked, under Catholic pressure and only with reluctance, brought matters to a head, resulting in a total breach with the German leader.[40] The theme was one that could well be considered academic, at any rate in the sense of having no direct bearing on Luther's practical reforms. That the human will is not free in all that relates to man's salvation Luther had long been known to deny. Back in April 1518, at Heidelberg, he had maintained that 'free will, after the fall, was only a name, and

---

37. Allen, ep. 1384.
38. Smith, *Luther's Correspondence*, ep. 580. Cf. epp. 1186 and 1188.
39. Smith, ep. 591. The letter was to Oecolampadius, 20 December 1523.
40. The *Diatribe* was first published at Basel in September 1574. There is a critical edition of it by J. von Walter in *Quellenschriften zur Geschichte des Protestantismus* (1910; repr. 1935).

that when a man acted according to his own being he sinned mortally'. Erasmus presents his argument succinctly and in moderate terms, although he suffuses it with a good deal of ironical wit. He points out the difficulty of deducing anything conclusive on such an issue from the letter of scripture, the interpretation of which is all too often only an expression of the exegete's personal assumptions. In any case the subject is an abstruse one with no immediate significance for faith. Nevertheless the will's freedom has to be maintained, since without it repentance would have no meaning and punishment of sin would be unjust – a view sustained by numerous biblical texts which clearly imply that men do have the responsibility which freedom alone can confer. Erasmus agrees that divine grace is necessary but concludes that the opinion of those who attribute a positive role to the will please him most. How little, on the contrary, his arguments pleased Luther, and why, we shall have to discuss later. But it may be said here that the *Diatribe* does not show Erasmus at his best and that his treatment of a difficult and for Luther himself a deeply emotive topic is superficial, whereas the reformer's answer, *On the Bondage of the Will*, is one of his most carefully composed works, albeit that courtesy and urbanity are entirely lacking. In excuse of Erasmus it should be remembered that he had no personal desire to tackle it. Luther sent him a copy of his own treatise with a covering letter that has not survived. But Erasmus's answer is extant.

> The whole world [*he told the reformer*] knows your nature, according to which you have guided your pen against no one more bitterly and, what is more odious, more maliciously, than against me. . . . How do your scurrilous charges that I am an atheist, an Epicurean and a sceptic help the argument? . . . Wish me any curse you will except your temper, unless the Lord change it for you.[41]

It is true that Luther's academic colleague and theological mentor, Philipp Melanchthon, always held Erasmus in high esteem and continued to profit from his writings; but he himself did not escape branding as a traitor to the evangelical cause, suffering so much indeed from the 'rage of the theologians' that he even longed, he said, for death. Calvin too, for all his own humanist training, could scarcely bring himself to utter a word of praise for Europe's greatest scholar, although he quotes him repeatedly and makes free use of his ideas; while Theodore Beza, who on Calvin's death became the leader of Swiss Protestantism, dubbed him an Arian. Even so he was more restrained in his abuse than the swashbuckling Guillaume Farel, to whom Erasmus's very name was anathema.

On the other hand Catholic suspicions were not allayed by Protestant hatred. More and more readily was it believed, especially after 1530, that the humanist had fathered the new heresy, and dissemination of his works was prohibited in one Catholic country after another. At the Council of Trent he was openly denounced as a heretic, and official condemnation soon followed, Pope Paul IV in 1559 consigning his entire literary production to the newly instituted Index. Yet he was not without his defenders, notable among whom was the leading Jesuit in Germany, the Dutch-born Peter Canisius, who lauded his educational treatises while at the same time regretting the imprudence which had led him to dabble in theological matters. In the main, however, he was no more beloved of Catholic theologians

41. Allen, ep. 1688.

than of Protestant, who thus could agree at least in reviling a man who appeared false to whichever set of principles one side could condemn the other for teaching.

Theological dogmatism of any kind was repugnant to Erasmus: too many things had been defined, or acrimoniously debated, on which it would have been more becoming to confess ignorance. Fellowship with Father, Son and Holy Spirit, for instance, was possible without a grasp of all the niceties of trinitarian doctrine. If religion was to bring peace and reconciliation then theological definition would have to be minimal and personal opinion given its freedom. Faith, certainly, would never be created by coercion. The great affirmations of the creed – God, Father and creator, the incarnation, redemption, the church as Christ's body into which we are implanted by baptism – are sufficient. For the rest let a man die to the lusts of the flesh and the world and live according to Christ's precepts and example, bearing adversity with patience and looking for the recompense of the reward undoubtedly in store for all the godly at the Lord's second coming. Thus will he progress from virtue to virtue, ascribing nothing to himself, but whatever is good in him to God alone.

Erasmus insisted, then, on drawing a necessary distinction between the essentials and the non-essentials of belief, between *fundamenta* and *adiaphora*, permitting with regard to the latter a proper openness of mind. In this a consensus could be achieved among men of faith and good will, and therefore that spiritual *concordia* which he valued so much. He himself held that history in fact witnessed to the existence of such a *consensus omnium* and that it was a Christian's duty to adhere to it. Hence his dislike of the acrid partisanship and contentiousness that led only to disruption and schism. To leave the church, the Roman church even as it was, he had no desire, and so would take no action which might have the effect of separating himself from it, for the church was his spiritual home. Of infallibility, however, whether of popes or councils, what evidence was there? Neither indeed is reason infallible, and he declined to judge matters as though he thought it were. Traditional beliefs and institutions, for all their faults, embody a wisdom gained from long corporate experience, and as Protestantism won ground he feared increasingly that the price of the church's reform would be its division or even abolition.

As one who in so many respects was ahead of his time Erasmus advocated what may fairly be described as a liberal or 'humanist' Catholicism, bearing fruit in a learned piety.[42] He assuredly left behind him no church or sect carrying his name or perpetuating his doctrine. Bigotry and factiousness were as antipathetic to his nature as a man as they were to his ideals as a scholar. Circumspect and clear-sighted, and ever aware of the obscurity pervading so many things on which men feel deeply, he could always appreciate the strength of opposing arguments, knowing that truth and justice are rarely an exclusive possession. Extremism he saw as, only too often, prejudice, blindness to facts, and the temper which, when its own judgements are involved, admits no possibility of error. To acquire knowledge, he realized, demands application and patience, and sound opinions are reached only after due reflection and self-critical candour, qualities he himself exemplified to a

---

42. See B. Bradshaw, 'The Christian Humanism of Erasmus' (*Journal of Theological Studies*, 33, 1982, 411–47).

singular degree. He understood well enough the need for change, perhaps far-reaching change in societies long established, but also for preserving what the past had so slowly and painfully built up.

No doubt he had his weaknesses. A natural solitary and an individualist to the core, he was averse from committing himself wholeheartedly to any public cause, and he found the discipline of institutions, whether ecclesiastical or academic, irksome. He was by no means always frank about his own views and altered his tone markedly to suit the opinions or the status of his correspondents. He was wary, and even afraid, of personal confrontations and avoided them whenever possible, and he could be irritatingly evasive or equivocal when a situation threatened to become embarrassing: the Elector Frederick once said that 'you never know where you are with him'. His indeed, as he readily admitted, was not the spirit that imbues martyrs, and he was apt to hide the audacity of his thinking behind a screen of diplomatic phraseology.

Again, although cherishing his intellectual independence he was, as a man under religious vows, notoriously solicitous for his creature comforts and not above toadyism where he hoped for personal, not to say pecuniary, advantage. At the same time he was not petty-minded, nor, as his hostile critics have persistently maintained, was he ultimately lacking in the courage of his convictions. His difficulty lay in his being a reasonable and peaceable man in a violent and unreasonable age, and if he took care for his own safety it was because the perils that surrounded him were real. Of the sincerity of his religion, however, there surely can be no question: religious belief was for him the underlying concern of his life. But he could not persuade himself that the salvation of men's souls depended on abstruse theologizing, just as he was convinced that truth is attained only under conditions of responsible liberty. That the Catholic church of his day was in urgent need of spiritual and moral renewal he recognized as plainly as did anyone; but he refused to contemplate a revolution such as would have altered its fundamental character or destroyed its unity. As we look back on him from the vantage-point of an era certainly no less tumultuous than his own, we cannot but applaud in him, in Huizinga's words, 'the profoundly serious advocate of that gentle state of spirit which the world needs so badly'.

Chapter 3

# MARTIN LUTHER:
# I. THE RELIGIOUS REVOLUTIONARY

## The age and the man

It has been said that 'they who do not rightly estimate the Reformation cannot rightly understand Luther, since Luther apart from the Reformation would cease to be Luther'.[1] This certainly is true, but no less true is it that apart from Luther the Reformation itself cannot be understood. He is its key figure, protagonist and spokesman alike, upon whom all others zealous for change were more or less dependent. Indeed, whether but for Luther the Reform movement of the sixteenth century would have swept over Europe in the way it did is highly questionable. What he achieved was rendered possible because the time and the milieu were matched in him by the man also, so that all the necessary elements were present to issue in events such as, in the most authentic sense, were epoch-making. That achievement was not therefore something external to him, but the utterance of the man himself and of his profound personal experience. Over the preceding century voices had repeatedly called for the reform of abuses and corruptions, but there had emerged no guiding principle on which Reformation could successfully be carried through, nor a dominant personality to give it impetus.

As opinions varied so counsels differed, whereas what was needed – the outcome proved it – was the dynamism of a spiritual conviction that struck at the very heart of the evils which men of conscience yearned to see cast out. Luther it was who reached such a conviction and proclaimed it forthrightly and fearlessly. Yet to begin with it was one the full implications of which he himself did not comprehend. Only as opposition mounted did he sense the extent either of the changes that would perforce be necessary or the risks and temptations to which he, a monk and an academic, was to be exposed when thrust upon the stage of world politics. But as he was wont afterwards to declare: 'I simply taught, preached, wrote . . . otherwise I did nothing. . . . The Word did it all.' That, politically speaking, he could have set Europe alight, he realized, but he knew too that this was no game for him to play. For the remarkable thing is that he did not feel himself to be an autonomous agent, deploying his own resources against however powerful odds – in short, a hero challenging fate – but the instrument rather of an overriding providence and purpose. Quite apart from his talents as a man, which in any case were outstanding, Luther's sense of mission, of doing the work to which he firmly believed, despite every doubt and difficulty that might confront him, God had called him, made him in truth a prophet; for even the soberest historian can scarcely withhold the word. Moreover, his ability to communicate verbally his overwhelming

1. The words are Charles Julius Hare's (*Vindication of Luther*, London, 1855, 3).

intimations of the reality of God has rarely been equalled in Christian history. In this not even St Augustine surpassed him.[2]

Yet the presentation of Luther's thought, and it is with this aspect alone of his work as a religious leader that we are here concerned, is not altogether easy for an Englishman writing for English readers. As he contemplates his task he will perceive more and more how beset he is with problems. For the great reformer, as his modern compatriots always tell us, is *echt deutsch*, a German to the core, expressing himself (when of course not using the scholar's medium of Latin) very much in the German idiom of his time, an idiom that repeatedly taxes the skill of the translator. Further, Luther's ideas have to be culled from a vast number of diverse writings – polemical treatises, pamphlets, tracts, exegetical commentaries, lectures and sermons in multitudes, not to mention the letters and the famous *Table Talk*: a treatise a fortnight, it has been estimated, sustained over a period of twenty-five years.[3] And the difficulty is enlarged by the fact that although as an author he was so prolific Luther was not, as was Melanchthon or, still more signally, Calvin, a systematic expositor of his own teachings. He wrote as occasion demanded, often impulsively, sometimes violently, never without prejudice, with the result that he does not always appear self-consistent, and views and opinions can readily be cited in support of even sharp differences of interpretation. But this, as he would have said himself, 'is what happens when things were moving. . . . Now this work has to be done, and now that.'[4]

Again, the leader of the German Reformation has always been a highly controversial figure: to some, as to Adolf Harnack for example, he is a spiritual hero whose authority is only a little below that of the New Testament itself, a Mr Valiant-for-Truth contending manfully against the embattled powers of error embodied in the Roman Anti-Christ; whereas for others he is, not indeed the grotesque caricature drawn by Cochlaeus (or even, in modern times, by Heinrich Denifle),[5] yet still the unhappy disruptor of Christendom and harbinger of the secularizing individualism of the Enlightenment.[6] But perhaps the chief obstacle to a sympathetic understanding of Luther from our standpoint in time is the sheer medievalism of his outlook; for of all the reformers he is apt to strike us today as

2. 'Only Augustine is his equal in the capacity to express in words the depth and paradoxical complexity of religious emotions', see W. Pauck, *The Heritage of the Reformation* (rev. edn., Oxford, 1961), 169.
3. Cf. E. G. Rupp, *The Righteousness of God: Luther Studies* (London, 1952), 5. The critical Weimar edition, ed. J. C. F. Knaacke *et al.* (begun in 1883; referred to here as *W.A.*), comprises over 80 volumes, superseding the Erlangen edition (1826–57) in 67 volumes. An English translation of Luther's collected works, edited by J. Pelikan and H. T. Lehmann (referred to here as *W.M.L.*), begun in 1958, has now been completed in 55 volumes (Concordia Publishing House, St Louis, Missouri). There is also the six-volume edition of *The Works of Martin Luther* in a translation edited by H. E. Jacobs (Philadelphia, 1915–43) (referred to here as *P.E.*). Other selections include those of H. Wace and C. A. Buchheim (*Primary Works*, London, 1876), B. L. Woolf, *The Reformation Writings of Martin Luther* (2 vols. London, 1952ff.), and the volumes (XV–XVIII) in the Library of Christian Classics, Philadelphia and London, 1955–69.
4. See *P.E.*, V, 373.
5. *Luther und Luthertum in der ersten Entwicklung* (Mainz, 1914).
6. As portrayed, for example, by J. Maritain, *Trois Réformateurs* (Paris, 1925).

the most medieval, the most unmodern, so little touched was he, in any essential respect, by the spirit of contemporary humanism. Between him and us, that is, there stands an intellectual barrier such as makes him appear remote in comparison with an Erasmus or a Montaigne, or even, in some ways, a Zwingli, and it is only with a real effort of the imagination that one can hope to surmount it. In fact, Luther's medievalism so conditions his thinking that in the opinion of a modern Catholic historian, Josef Lortz, it was not he but the great Dutch scholar who posed the true threat of 'dogmatic dissolution within the church'. For although Luther challenged the church it was on its own, not on alien, principles.[7] Both sides in the momentous controversy could comprehend one another's meaning because fundamentally their presuppositions were the same. Now, however, it is only with some difficulty that even Christians, be they Protestant or Catholic, can grasp what exactly either the reformers or their opponents meant by what they said. Both Protestantism and – if only more recently – Catholicism have themselves changed greatly since the sixteenth century and much that was vital to the Reformation debate today seems distant and archaic.

Nevertheless, if we are to attempt to appreciate what moved a Luther as well as a Loyola we must make every endeavour to elucidate their ideas. Certainly in the case of the German reformer it is with the religious teacher and theological thinker that the modern student must come to grips if his historical significance is to be properly assessed. Other 'Luthers' – Marxist, Freudian – can be and have been trotted out and need not be summarily dismissed; but whatever the factors that combined to bring about revolutionary changes in sixteenth-century Europe, the dynamic of the Reform movement which Luther himself undoubtedly precipitated must be sought above all in his personal experience as a Christian believer. Indeed, but for the religious convictions that dominated his mind from early manhood until his death in 1546 at the age of sixty-three he would have no identity. Neither in theory or practice was he a political or social reformer, just as he was not in any modern sense a humanitarian or even a moralist. To understand what he accomplished, designedly or not, we must therefore see the man for what he preeminently was, a religious genius. As for unconscious psychological pressures, all men are affected by them, and what we loosely call temperament played no small part in shaping Luther's attitudes in particular.[8] Those however who took up his cause were inspired by what he consciously believed and deliberately taught. Thus for all its strangeness to the mind of a secular age Luther's faith has proved itself of sufficient historical importance to claim our attention still. Moreover, what men in any age have thought about the profoundest issues of human life must, as such, always command respect.

Martin Luther was brought up in accordance with the ordinary Catholic teaching and piety of his day. At Magdeburg he attended a school run by the Brethren of the Common Life; then after three years at Eisenach he entered the university of Erfurt in 1501 with the purpose, encouraged by his father, of studying law. Erfurt at that time was the main centre of humanistic culture in Germany, but there is

7. J. Lortz, *Die Reformation in Deutschland* (2 vols, Freiburg-im-Breisgau, 3rd edn., 1948).
8. See E. H. Erikson, *Young Man Luther: a study in psychoanalysis and history* (New York, 1958).

no evidence that he was in any way deeply influenced by it. He seems to have shown little intellectual curiosity and no aptitude for philosophy, even if some years later he was sent by his order, the Augustinian Eremites, which he had joined in 1505, to lecture on the subject at the newly founded university of Wittenberg. The truth is that, well-endowed though he was with humane good sense, he had no feeling for the spirit of the new age that was dawning. His choice of the religious life, whatever the circumstances that immediately prompted it, was natural to him and appropriate. The monastic house at Erfurt, strict in its observance of the order's rule, afforded him exactly the type of vocational environment for which he was suited by disposition and conviction alike. His life there was uneventful and in itself entirely satisfying. His ordination to the priesthood, which took place on 2 May 1507, he regarded with profound seriousness. Looking back on it many years afterwards he recorded the powerful emotions which then seized him; while on the occasion of his first mass he was all but tongued-tied at the thought of the sudden realization, at the moment of consecration, of the very presence of God. By the words *Hic est Corpus meum* he was, he confessed, 'stupefied and terror-stricken. I thought to myself, "With what tongue shall I address such Majesty, seeing that all men ought to tremble at the presence of even an earthly prince?".' He felt himself to be but dust and ashes, and full of sin.

None of the doctrines or practices of his religion did he at this time question; he was to all showing wholly without intellectual difficulties. He accepted the current supernaturalism with the simplicity of a peasant and had no doubt that the Catholic system was entirely adequate to meet the needs of the spiritual life. At least this was so until he became by degrees aware that in its actual operation it was indeed *not* adequate, at all events for himself. But he discovered this inadequacy only by putting the system to practical test. To those who took it with something less than the absolute seriousness of his own attitude, or by recognizing that between the precept and its fulfilment there is always, men being what they are, some shortfall, that system was serviceable and effective. The vicar-general of Luther's order in Saxony, Johann Staupitz, a thoughtful and conscientious man, understood this and advised the over-scrupulous young monk accordingly. The latter, nevertheless, was not satisfied – far from it. But his theological revisionism – and theologically he was not especially well read – was the consequence of his practical dissatisfaction; there was no speculative aim behind it whatever.

It thus is no occasion for surprise that Luther never systematized his theological thinking. His interest was essentially in the needs and conditions of the religious life itself. He was not even interested in the reform of ecclesiastical institutions simply as such. Changes, he realized, there would have to be, consonant with the principles of his own teaching, of the truth of which he had the firmest possible inner assurance. But in themselves they were largely peripheral, and to give them detailed effect, like the proper schematization of his own theology, was something he was content to leave to others.

## Luther's experience

For Luther the monk 'natural' man was a sinner in need of redemption. Furthermore, this sinfulness was deeply seated, the result of a condition described only too aptly as fallen. Even in the beginning man, in the person of Adam, had lapsed from his original state of righteousness and was now totally unable to deliver himself from the moral depravity and spiritual corruption, which were the consequences of his fall, without supernatural aid. Divine 'grace' was a necessity therefore, and was dispensed by the church through a variety of means, chief among which were the sacraments, seven in number, though the most important were baptism, the eucharist and penance. Habitual or sanctifying grace, according to the current teaching, was a supernatural quality which, when added to, or infused into, the soul united it with Christ and rendered it acceptable to God by producing in it a new 'habit' (*habitus*) or disposition by which the recipient was enabled to perform virtuous acts. Such grace was *sufficient* in that it conveyed the power to obey God, but it was not automatically *efficacious* since its efficacy depended on its appropriation by the human will. A perpetual effort therefore was demanded for a man to acquire merit in the sight of God and so, in a true sense, earn the heavenly reward promised to the righteous. Further, entry into a religious order was held to be a kind of second baptism – St Thomas Aquinas himself had thus characterized it – offering an assured way of salvation to all who conscientiously pursued it. ('Keep this rule,' Luther was told at his profession, 'and I will promise you eternal life.') Detachment from a world essentially evil was deemed to be a most laudable thing, an anticipation of the bliss to come hereafter. This present life being merely probationary, self-denial, self-discipline and self-sacrifice, which the monastic vows of obedience, poverty and chastity served to achieve, were a challenge to all who sought to take religion seriously. One who in this way responded to the divine call with his whole heart could not fail to attain justification *coram Deo*.

The question, then, was whether a man could in fact lead a life of sufficient spiritual merit really to be certain of acceptability in the eyes of God. Luther (and his own testimony is not to be refuted) observed his monastic rule with unusual scrupulosity.

> I was a good monk [*he afterwards recalled*] and kept my order so strictly that I could claim that if ever a monk were able to reach heaven by monkish discipline I should have found my way there. All my fellows in the house, who knew me, would bear me out in this. For if it had continued much longer I would, what with vigils, prayers, readings and other such works, have done myself to death.[9]

At first he was too much occupied to be unduly troubled, but with time came doubts. In spite of his diligence and conscientiousness, his repeated confessions and penances, he could not feel sure of success. 'The more I tried to remedy an uncertain, weak and afflicted conscience with the traditions of men, the more each day found it uncertain, weaker, the more troubled.'[10] Those well-tried austerities,

9. *W.A.*, *Tischreden*, IV, 303, 16.
10. *W.A.*, XL (ii), 15, 15.

fasts and vigils, were unavailing. Peace and tranquillity of mind eluded him, self-effort only increasing self-distrust.[11] 'Who knows,' he would ask himself, 'whether such consolations are to be believed?'[12] Too much, it seemed, was demanded of the mere human will, a condition which his nominalist training, with its emphasis on volition (*fac quod in se est*), did nothing to alleviate. The virtue of perseverence thus was undermined by scepticism.[13] And behind all this was that fear of God's wrath and damnation by which he had been haunted since childhood

---

11.  *W.A.*, XXVI, 12, 12.
12.  *W.A.*, XL (ii), 411, 14.
13.  Nominalism, which in opposition to Thomist realism denied the reality of universal concepts and maintained that in human discourse only 'names' (*nomina*) have universality, was the favoured philosophy in German universities during the fifteenth century. Its most eminent exponent had been the English Franciscan William of Occam (c.1300–c.1349). His arguments against the existence of universals were not new, having been already employed in the eleventh and twelfth centuries, and went back indeed to Boethius's discussion of Aristotle's criticism of Plato. See E. Gilson, *History of Christian Philosophy in the Middle Ages* (London, 1955), 489–520. At Erfurt Luther received his theological training under two nominalist teachers, Joducus Truttveter and Bartholomäus Arnoldi of Usingen, and when he entered the Augustinian convent he continued his studies under Johann Nathin, who had himself been a pupil of the leading German Occamist Gabriel Biel (c.1420–1495), one of the founders of the university of Tübingen. Indeed the scholastic teaching was known to Luther mainly in its nominalist form (the *via moderna*), his knowledge of Thomism (the *via antiqua*) being relatively slight. He was wont to speak of William of Occam as his 'master', or even as his 'dear master', if sometimes not without irony. In the shape of the *via moderna* nominalist influence on Luther is discernible, but it is not pronounced, although it was from his scholastic training that he doubtless acquired the logical rigour evidenced in the more carefully considered of his theological treatises, namely those against Latomus, Erasmus and Zwingli. See P. Vignaux, in *Wilhelm Ockham, 1349–1949* (Münster, 1950), and H. Junghans, *Ockham in Lichte der neueren Forschung* (*Arbeiten zur Geschichte und Theologie des Luthertums*, XXI, 1968). But Occamism had more specifically theological implications as well as exerting a largely unchallenged influence in philosophy. A feature of its teaching was a stress on the arbitrariness of the divine will, thus diminishing the possibility of a rational understanding of the being and ways of God. The result in certain instances was a pessimism concerning man's ability to rehabilitate himself in the sight of God. Here the tendency was markedly Augustinian; hence its designation as the *schola Augustiniana moderna*. It was sharply opposed to what it saw as the 'Pelagianizing' drift of the 'modern school'. Archbishop Thomas Bradwardine's *De causa Dei adversus Pelagium* was highly polemical in this respect (the printed edition [London] dates from 1618). See S. Hahn, *Thomas Bradwardinus und seine Lehre von des menschlichen Willensfreiheit* (Münster, 1905). Also H. A. Oberman, *Archbishop Thomas Bradwardine, a Fourteenth Century Augustinian: a Study of his Theology in its Historical Context (Utrecht, 1957)*. Luther belonged to an Augustinian order, in which this theological stance was presumably congenial. See H. A. Oberman, 'Headwaters of the Reformation: Initia Lutheri – Initia Reformationis', reprinted in *The Dawn of the Reformation: Essays in Late Mediaeval and Early Reformation Thought* (Edinburgh, 1986), 39–83. That at Wittenberg Luther came under the influence of the *schola Augustiniana moderna* there can surely be little question. By 1517 his disillusionment with scholastic methods was complete, as is demonstrated by his university *Disputatio contra scholasticam theologiam*, aimed at Gabriel Biel. See L. Grane, *Contra Gabrielem: Luthers Auseinandersetzung mit Gabriel Biel in der Disputatio contra scholasticam theologiam 1517* (Gyldendal, 1962).

and of which even 'the rustling of a dead leaf' was enough to remind him.[14] For such assaults of conscience Luther used the word *Anfechtung*, 'temptation'.[15] Later he wrote movingly of these awful experiences, in which it would come upon him that he was past redemption, with nowhere to turn for help. It was like a momentary glimpse of eternal punishment; momentary because, mercifully, the mood would not last. It is not of course difficult to see in this a state of mental anxiety verging on the pathological, but any attempt at a psychological analysis of Luther's condition at the time is likely in the nature of the case to be too speculative to be of serious use to the historian.

The doctrine which troubled him was that of the *justitia Dei*, God's 'justice' or righteousness. He took it in its formal or 'active' connotation to mean the divine righteousness as manifested in judgement and retribution; and faced by that what conceivable hope could there be for a sinner like himself? Long afterwards, in a biographical fragment prefacing the Wittenberg edition (1545) of his Latin works, he confessed that he had even come to hate the expression, 'the righteousness of God' because 'in accordance with the usage and custom of the doctors' he had been taught to understand it only thus. It seemed to him therefore that he had been driven to utter in his heart an appalling blasphemy. For divine judgement appeared to be pronounced not only by 'the law of the Ten Commandments' but by the gospel itself, if the words of St Paul in the first chapter of Romans were true: 'The righteousness of God is revealed in it.' The divine command, that is, covered not only the outward act but the inward motive. However, pondering day and night the meaning of these words, along with the added phrase, 'The righteous shall live by faith', illumination came at last.[16] At that point, he relates, he began to perceive that God's 'justice' is the gift by which a righteous man in fact lives, namely *faith*.

> Now I felt as though I had been immediately born anew and had entered Paradise itself. From that moment the face of Scripture as a whole became clear to me. My mind ran through the sacred books, as far as I was able to recollect them, seeking analogies in other phrases, such as *opus Dei*, that which God works in us; *virtus Dei*, that by which God makes us strong; *sapientia Dei*, that by which he makes us wise; *fortitudo Dei, salus Dei, gloria Dei* – the strength, the salvation, the glory of God.[17]

The offending expression, *justitia Dei*, ceased henceforth to cause offence.[18] On the contrary, he now 'longingly praised this sweetest of words'. A subsequent reading of St Augustine's *On the Spirit and the Letter* gave him further assurance: the

14. *W.A.*, XIX, 226, 16.
15. A good discussion of this is in P. Bühler, *Die Anfechtung bei Martin Luther* (Zurich, 1942).
16. For a full documentation see O. Scheel, *Dokumente zu Luthers Entwicklung (bis 1519)* (2nd edn., Tübingen, 1929), and for a translation of the more important passages see E. G. Rupp and B. Drewery, *Martin Luther* (*Documents of Modern History*, London, 1970).
17. *W.A.*, LIV, 179–87.
18. Years later, in 1526, Luther could still write: 'I myself have more than once been offended [by the doctrine of the *justitia Dei*] almost to the very depth and abyss of despair, so that I wished I had never been created a man until I realized how salutary was this despair and how near to grace' (*W.A.*, LVIII, 719, 7ff.).

righteousness of God was indeed 'the righteousness with which God clothes us and by which we are justified'. And he goes on to record that, armed with these considerations, he began a second course of exposition of the Psalms, a task interrupted, alas, by the imperial summons to attend the Diet of Worms in the spring of 1521.

This much-quoted passage, with others in Luther's *Table Talk* that appear to refer to the same discovery, has given rise to prolonged discussion by Luther scholars in the present century. According to the *Table Talk* allusions (which are far from precise) insight came to him in the tower *hypocaustum*, or heated dayroom, of his Wittenberg friary. He also remarks that it was at this time that he learned to understand the true distinction between the law and the gospel. Even so, these references pose certain problems, both chronological and theological. Here we can do no more than summarize the issue.

In the first place, very diverse datings have been given for this illumination. (Incidentally too much should not be read into the so-called 'tower-experience' [*Turmerlebnis*]: that it was some kind of mystical enlightenment or emotional conversion experience may be discounted.) At one extreme it has been assigned to a time as early in Luther's career as 1508 or 1509, soon after he had moved from Erfurt to Wittenberg and when he was still a philosophy lecturer expounding Aristotle's *Nichomachean Ethics* and the *Sentences* of Peter Lombard.[19] At the other it has been postponed until 1518, when the dispute arising from his protest against Tetzel's indulgence sale was rapidly gaining momentum.[20] Otherwise it has been dated between 1513 and the outbreak of the church struggle in 1517.[21] The question of date is inseparable from that of understanding what Luther's new perception really amounted to. Here valuable primary evidence is afforded by his early Wittenberg lectures on scripture, the texts of which have survived partly in his own hand, partly in those of his students. Four complete courses are extant, those on

19. Such is the view of Reinhold Seeberg, as stated in the fourth volume of his *Lehrbuch der Dogmengeschichte* (Leipzig, 1917). The Danish scholar, Regin Prenter, has more recently argued that the discovery antedated the lectures on the Psalms and assigns it to 1512. See his *Der barmherzige Richter* (Copenhagen, 1961).

20. So H. Grisar, *Martin Luther, his life and work* (St Louis, 1935, based on the 2nd German edn [Freiburg-im-Breisgau, 3 vols, 1911–12] by F. J. Eble, ed. A. Preuss); U. Saarni-vaara, *Luther's Discovery of the Gospel* (St Louis, 1951); and E. Bizer, *Fides ex auditu* (Neukirchen, 1958).

21. Erich Vogelsang (*Die Anfange von Luthers Christologie nach der ersten Psalmenvorlesung*, Berlin, 1929) thinks it took place 1513–14, i.e. before the time of his lectures on the psalter. E. G. Rupp is disposed to date it before the delivery of the course on the Epistle to the Romans (*Luther's Progress to the Diet of Worms*, Harper Torchbook edn, New York, 1964, 5). 'I cannot believe', writes Rupp, 'that this fine and powerful commentary could have been the work of one prevented from entering the Pauline world by theological (and emotional) difficulties about the concept which is the very heart of the epistle.' Others might prefer to say that what the lectures on Romans make clear is that the Augustinian theology had by then become 'alive' and spiritually fruitful for Luther; it was no longer a matter simply of repeating a 'received' doctrine. Luther owed his knowledge of Augustine's writings to humanist scholarship, and he most likely used the Amerbach edition, a humanist enterprise. Erasmus did not begin his own work on Augustine until 1510. Luther's knowledge of Hebrew, moreover, and the Hebrew text used for his lecture-course, were thanks to the Hebraist Reuchlin.

the Psalter (1513–14), Romans (1515–16), Galatians (1516–17) and Hebrews (1517–18). Other material to be taken into account is to be found in certain sermons of his delivered during this period, and in an uncompleted second course on the Psalms, dating from 1518 to 1519. Agreement is general that these were the years which saw the formation of Luther's cardinal doctrine of justification by faith alone (*sola fide*). But did he arrive at it complete in a single moment of penetrative insight, as the statements referred to suggest, or was it the outcome only of a process of reflective thought, even if hastened at the end by the pressure of external events?

Of critical importance is the extent to which Luther's thinking continued to be controlled in this matter by Augustinian doctrine. It is hard to believe that he could at any time have hit on the latter, well known as it was, as a new and decisive discovery. What Luther came to realize, in the light of Romans 1:17, was that *justitia Dei* did not mean God's retributive justice but rather that merciful endowment of unmerited grace in the power of which alone the sinner could even begin to meet the 'law's demands'. Yet according to the Augustinian teaching justification was a gradual inward renewal, involving spiritual cleansing, healing and restoration, in which man's reactivated will plays a positive and necessary role. In what respect, then, could this be described as a break through? It was already familiar ground in the schools: as Denifle was at pains to show, some sixty medieval authors had interpreted *justitia* in terms of God's unmerited grace. Thus Luther's experience as explained, for example, by a scholar like Karl Holl would have meant no more than a reaffirmation of the traditional Augustinianism, which maintained that the sinner was unquestionably justified by grace, but not without personal effort as well.[22] This idea was, we repeat, no novelty to Luther, and his lectures on Romans reveal that it still dominated his mind at the time of their delivery: to be 'justified' a man had to *become* righteous – the criterion was an ethical one. We may note indeed that Luther's exposition of the epistle shows not only that he was acquainted with the newly published Greek Testament of Erasmus but also with the writings of the German mystics, especially Tauler, whose sermons he had read on the advice of Staupitz, and the *Theologia Germanica*, a devotional book then supposed to have come from Tauler's hand and an edition of which Luther himself brought out. These studies certainly deepened his feeling for the inwardness of religion, but there is no clear evidence in the lecture courses of these years to show that his thought had moved in any significant way beyond the Augustinian orbit.

Towards the end of 1518, however, he published his *Sermon on the Threefold Righteousness*, followed early in 1519 by another on *The Twofold Righteousness*, in which at last his own view of the meaning of justification is made plain.[23] In the former Luther distinguishes three kinds of sin, and therewith three kinds of righteousness corresponding to them. The first, both the sin and the righteousness, are such as are recognized by the laws of states. No misunderstanding arises here. Again, the third kind of sin, sin in the properly religious meaning of the word, is what is usually classified as actual, sin for which the individual is himself responsible; and the righteousness which corresponds thereto is also his, being the fruit

22. See Holl's 'Die Rechtfertigungslehre in Luthers Vorlesung über den Römerbrief' (1910), in *Gesammelte Aufsätze*, I (Tübingen, 1938), 111ff.
23. *W.A.*, II, 41ff., and 143ff.

of that faith by which, through God's grace, the sinner now walks. But the second type of sin, and the righteousness which contrasts with it, is less easy to comprehend. This sin is inherent, innate, 'original'; it is not constituted, that is to say, by the individual's own acts, but, on the contrary, it is 'alien' to him because really it is Adam's sin, the consequences and indeed the guilt of which descend on him also: he himself has to bear the imputation of it. But this 'alien' sin is counter-balanced by a no less alien righteousness, namely the righteousness of Christ, which, through the work of redemption, is likewise counted as the sinner's own, provided he embraces it by *faith*. In the second sermon, on *The Twofold Righteousness*, this teaching is repeated and re-emphasized. Here again Christ's righteousness is set against Adam's sin, both alike being foreign to the sinner himself. Yet as a man's actual sins are the outcome of his 'alien' but nonetheless intrinsic sinfulness, so his actual or empirical righteousness can flow only from the 'alien' righteousness of Christ, who alone is meritorious. The gospel is nothing other or less than the good news of what the sinner owes to his Redeemer and Lord.

This doctrine, which certainly may be seen as a fresh insight into the meaning of the Epistle to the Romans, could very understandably have seized Luther with revelatory force, taking him far beyond anything he had hitherto believed, since it taught a 'righteousness of God' which covered the sinner as he is, even in his sinfulness. Thus it is we arrive at the great teaching – the very *articulus aut stantis aut cadentis ecclesiae* – with which Luther's name is always associated, and which in the technical language of theology is often referred to as the 'material' principle of Reformation doctrine, the 'formal' principle, also vital to Luther's thinking, being that of the sufficiency and perspicuity of scripture. This 'material' principle, justification *sola fide* 'by faith alone', we now must look at in more detail.

## Justification by faith alone

The term 'justification' (Latin, *justificatio*, from *justificare*, the word by which the Vulgate translates the Greek *dikaioō*) means literally, 'to make righteous' (*justum facere*) before or in the sight of God. This interpretation of it goes back to St Augustine, who regarded salvation as the free work of God, while conceiving of the grace (that which is bestowed *gratis*) whereby this is achieved as an infusion of supernatural life into fallen human nature by divinely appointed means, although his emphasis was on the divine impartation rather than on the human attainment. Thus sinful man is justified by being transformed into the image of Christ, justification and sanctification (*sanctum facere*, 'to make holy') being to all intents one and the same process. This Augustinian doctrine became the accepted pattern of medieval teaching, which acquired a standardized form in the *Summa Theologica* of St Thomas Aquinas, where justifying grace (*gratia justificans*) is described as 'something real and positive' (*quiddam reale et positivum*) within the soul, an infused supernatural quality by which alone the 'theological' virtues of faith, hope and love, as constitutive of the Christian life, can be produced. Moreover, in the nominalist teaching especially, particular stress was laid on the cooperative response of the will.

Behind the Augustinian – Thomist doctrine lay the Pauline, from whence of course it was derived. In Romans the word rendered by the Latin *justificare* means not 'to make righteous' but simply 'to declare (or account) righteous', to treat as righteous, and in the apostle's use signifies remission of sins. So to one 'to whom God reckons righteousness apart from works' St Paul applies the words of the Psalmist: 'Blessed are those whose iniquities are forgiven, and whose sins are covered.'[24] That is, God no longer counts his sins against him, 'acquitting' him by an act of sheer grace. But the response on man's part, in accepting a gift made available to him through Christ alone, whose death and resurrection are the fullest and most vivid manifestation of the divine mercy, is described as faith: 'For we hold that a man is justified by faith apart from works of the law'; and again: 'Since we are justified by faith, we have peace with God through our Lord Jesus Christ.'[25]

In St Paul the expression translated by 'justify' (*dikaioō*) is largely confined to Romans and Galatians. Of the twenty-nine occurrences of the word and its derivatives in the entire Pauline *corpus* twenty-five are in these two writings; its meaning therefore cannot properly be understood apart from the context of the Judaistic controversy. But within this context Paul's claim emphatically is that because of what God has done in Christ man's justification no longer depends on his own moral achievements – for God actually justifies the ungodly – but on his faith in Christ, meaning thereby not simply assent to a fact, but complete trust in and obedience to God, a putting of one's whole life at his disposal. But because sin is forgiven and the sinner acquitted the latter's status *coram Deo* is also changed,[26] bondage giving place to freedom. The consequence of this new relationship, whether one calls it reconciliation, redemption, adoption or salvation, is a hitherto unknown 'peace'.

It was this aspect supremely of the apostle's teaching which took possession of Luther's mind, borne out as it had been by his personal experience – an exceptional experience, no doubt, but one by no means unique.[27] What was new, radically new,

24. Rom. 4:6f.
25. Rom. 3:28, 5:1. In the Old Testament to 'justify' is equivalent to 'acquit', as in Isaiah 5: 23: 'who acquit the wicked for a bribe'; or Exodus 23:7: 'I will not acquit the wicked'; although elsewhere it can mean to 'deliver from oppression', to 'vindicate'. In the gospels it occasionally has the sense of 'showing oneself in the right' (Luke 10:29, 16:5), as also to 'receive the divine approval' (Mark 12:37). The word *dikaios* means, not holy, but 'free from guilt'.
26. Rom 5:22, 3:24f.
27. It was not of course the apostle's sole teaching; no less important for Paul was the soul's mystical union with Christ. Thus in Romans itself (6:5) he says: 'For if we have been united [or grafted together] with him [Christ] in a death like his, we shall certainly be united with him in a resurrection like his'; and he constantly speaks of the believer as being 'in Christ' (e.g. 'Alive to God in Christ Jesus' [Rom. 6:11], or 'If anyone is in Christ he is a new creation' [2 Corinthians 5:16]). Cp. Colossians 1:27: 'Christ in you the hope of glory'. The same idea is vividly expressed, again, in Romans (7:1–4) by the metaphor of marriage (particularly 7:4): 'Likewise my brethren, you have died to the law through the body of Christ, so that you may belong to one another, to him who has been raised from the dead in order that you may bear fruit for God.' Another way of putting it is to say that Christians live in the Spirit, or that the Spirit of Christ dwells in them (Rom. 8:11).

was what he deduced from it. Thus he saw himself as a man *already saved* and not merely plodding along the road to salvation. In other words, the Christian life with its required 'good works' was not the condition of salvation but its consequence. 'Merit', however hard it was striven for, had nothing to do with it. Assuredly the traditional teaching declared that meritorious works could not be done without grace, but it was necessary to use grace rightly, to prove oneself worthy of it by producing its fruits. For Luther, on the other hand, merit as such was an irrelevance. In God's sight, no man could *deserve* to be saved, or even helped on the way to salvation, no matter how assiduously and conscientiously he tried. For no work of man could appease the wrath of God, which for Luther signified not the divine judgement only, terrible though this would be, but rather that *aversio Dei*, that turning away of God from the sinner, abandoning him to his own hopeless condition: 'God is most angry when he shows no anger at all. He then sends the godless to go their own way, to increase and further their own interests'. Thus the most dire of all punishments is to continue in sin and reap the inherent reward of so doing. The only way of deliverance is to throw oneself upon God's merciful grace, the great counterweight to his wrath. Indeed, it was the horror of that wrath which moved Luther more even than the repugnance of sin itself. He states as much in his treatise against the Louvain theologian Latomus, a work in which he chose his words with unusual care:

> As wrath is a greater evil than the corruption of sin, so grace is a greater good than the health of righteousness, which we have said comes from faith. For there is no one who would not prefer (were such a thing possible) to be without the health of righteousness than without the grace of God.[28]

Plainly this conviction is religious rather than ethical: a man's standing with God is far more important than any moral end which he himself can achieve even with God's help.

What precisely Luther means by faith he never quite defines, though he emphatically denies that it is mere intellectual assent. What he does do is to delineate its effects.[29] Faith, that is, is primarily an experience and not a formal theological concept. It embraces at once God's act and man's response. Through faith alone, by divine grace, are we enabled to do God's will. It is, says Luther, 'a divine work in us. It changes us and causes us to be born anew of God; it kills the old Adam and makes altogether different men, in heart and spirit and mind and powers, and it brings with it the Holy Ghost. Oh, it is a living, busy, active, mighty thing, this faith.'[30] Subjectively, it engages man's being not at one level only but in his 'wholeness', committing him in all his faculties. Hence

> The reason why some do not understand how faith alone justifies is that they do not know what faith is . . . imagining that it is a quality latent in the soul. But when the Word of God sounds forth, which is truth, and the heart cleaves to it through faith, then is the heart imbued with the same truth of the Word, and . . . soon all the powers

---

28. See *Luther: Early Theological Works*, ed. and trans. by J. Atkinson (Library of Christian Classics, London, 1962), 349.
29. Cf. H. Strohl, *La pensée de la Réforme* (Paris, 1951), 30.
30. Preface to the commentary on Romans (1522), *P.E.*, VI, 451.

and members act in accordance with the inclination of the heart, whether that be good or bad.[31]

Faith, then, is a life-transforming force, not a mere 'notional' belief. The objection that the devil himself has faith, inasmuch as he too believes that God became man in Christ, is promptly answered: 'Does the devil believe that God is God and Lord unto him? . . . He has no faith whatever of this kind.'[32] For faith is no mere idle thought, 'but just as water heated by fire certainly remains water, yet is no longer cold, but hot and quite a different water, so faith, the work of the Holy Spirit, creates a different spirit and a different mind, and makes a quite new man.'[33]

To regard faith in this way is to perceive why Luther insisted on describing justification as by faith *alone*. The inclusion of the words *sola fide* in his rendering of Romans 3:28 had aroused strong criticism among his opponents, who objected that any such addition to the sacred text was intolerable. To this Luther replied that he was doing no more than what many of the early Fathers, notably Origen, had already done, and in any case he was only exercising the translator's right and responsibility to make clear the meaning of the original; here the sense of the passage itself demanded *sola* and forced it on him. The essential point was, as St Paul's words indicate, that justification is by faith in Christ *without the works of the law*. Were Christ's death and resurrection 'works' of ours? Obviously not. 'Faith alone, nay utterly alone, without any works, lays hold on this death and resurrection when it is preached by the Gospel.' The sinner himself is passive, unable of his own strength to take a single deliberate step to secure his justification. As Luther in a later composition, the Preface to his 1531 commentary on Galatians, categorically states: 'We work nothing, we render nothing to God, but only receive and suffer the action of another, namely God. Therefore one is pleased to call this righteousness of faith, or Christian righteousness, a passive righteousness.'[34] But the same idea is present in his much earlier course on Romans, for there too he insists that man can do nothing of himself, inwardly or outwardly, to deserve God's forgiveness or win his favour. Indeed any 'good' that man accomplishes by his own effort is better described as sinful.[35]

Yet it is of the very nature of faith, in the active sense of *fiducia*, that the good works which the law requires are its necessary outcome. The law of itself cannot bring peace of conscience, any more than it can ensure righteousness of life; it is the grace of the gospel alone that renders either possible. The law, we may say, exacts, but it is the gospel which gives. The former, by revealing our sinfulness, serves only as a baleful warning of the judgement to come. Yet thus it is that we are prepared for grace. When justified, however, a man performs good works as naturally as a good tree brings forth good fruit. In his pamphlet on *The Freedom*

31. *W.A.*, VI, 94, 7.
32. *W.A.*, XI, 472, 12.
33. *W.A.*, XLII, 482, 17.
34. *W.A.*, XL (i), XLI, 15–21.
35. As Luther succinctly puts it in his *De servo arbitrio*: 'Quod vero gratia Dei non facit, bonum non est. Quare sequitur liberum arbitrium sine gratia Dei prorsus non liberum, sed immutabiliter captivum et servum esse mali, cum non possit vertere se solo ad bonum' (*W.A.*, XVIII, 636, 4–6).

*of a Christian Man*, written towards the end of 1520 – a little work to be reckoned among his very best – Luther speaks in terms that are eloquent in their simplicity of the relation between saving faith and a good life.[36]

> Good works [*he says*] do not make a man a good man, but a good man performs good works. Evil deeds do not render a man evil, but an evil man commits evil deeds. Hence, as always, it is necessary that the substance be previous to good works [*ante opera bona*], and that good works follow and proceed from the person who is good.[37]

Again:

> Since works justify no one and it is necessary for a man to be just before he does a good deed, it is most clear that it is faith alone which, by the pure mercy of God through Christ in his Word, and with nothing wanting, justifies and saves the person; so also that the Christian man needs no work and no law to be saved [*et nullos opere nulla lege christiano homini opus esse ad salutem*]; for through faith he is delivered from all law, and by an act of sheer liberty he does all things gratuitously, seeking in no way either his own interest or salvation; for already, by the grace of God and through his faith, he has enough and is saved. But he does what he does solely to please God.[38]

To the modern mind such statements are utterly paradoxical, but what Luther himself again and again says is a firm rebuttal of the charge that his teaching is antinomian, or that it sees good works as indifferent in comparison with faith. Any such suggestion would have horrified him, as his sermons and his two great catechisms surely demonstrate. He repeatedly urges that the justified sinner must apply himself to understand God's Word in order to make it the practical rule of his life; that self-discipline is at all times a necessity; that the forces of evil have constantly to be repelled; that spiritual perfection is ceaselessly to be aimed at. No doubt through faith a man will come 'to take pleasure in God's commandments', but it is faith only that justifies him; good works cannot. Aware though the Christian will always be of the inevitability of moral struggle in the advance towards personal holiness, he will also know that such efforts do nothing, of themselves, to affect his standing in the sight of God.

For the justified sinner is nevertheless a sinner still, *simul justus et peccator*, at once spiritual and carnal: spiritual inasmuch as Christ acts in and for him, carnal inasmuch as his being is still contaminated by sin, so that what he himself does is not free from sin, a condition persisting through life. But although no man can rid himself of his sinful nature, and therefore of its effects likewise, justification does not admit of degree. His sins are either wholly forgiven or they are not; either he is under God's favour or he is under his wrath. Upon this Luther's statements in answer to Latomus are explicit and unhesitating:

> Wrath and grace are so constituted (since they both act from outside us) that they are poured out upon the person in his entirety. Consequently he who is under wrath has the whole of him under the dispensation of wrath, and he who is under grace has the whole of him under the whole dispensation of grace, because grace and wrath

36. See *W.A.*, VII, 49–73 (*W.M.L.*, XXXI, 327–77).
37. *W.A.*, VII, 61, 26–31.
38. *W.A.*, VII, 62, 7–14.

have to do with persons. It is man in his entirety God receives when he receives a man in grace; it is to man in his entirety God shows his favour when he shows favour to a man. And in the same way it is with the whole man God is angry when he shows his anger to a man. For he does not portion out this grace as he portions out gifts; he does not love the head and hate the feet, nor favour the soul and hate the body. . . . Grace must be sharply dissociated from a man's other gifts, since it is grace alone that is life eternal, and wrath alone that is death eternal.[39]

Again there is paradox here. For if on the one hand Luther stresses the power of faith as life-transforming, while on the other he recognizes that man remains a sinner, how can the latter be thought of as righteous at all? Because, Luther insists, the righteousness by which a man is justified is not his but Christ's alone. 'Thou and I are holy, church, city and people are holy, not by our own but by an alien holiness, not by active but by passive holiness.'[40] Nevertheless, when a man through faith 'puts on Christ' the presence of Christ thus realized in his soul has the inevitable effect of changing him from within, so that not only is he accounted other than he is but actually becomes so. Yet, once more, it is not the alteration as such which justifies but faith, or rather the grace which faith impetrates.

## Christian freedom

However, it is only because the justified sinner is as a person fully received into grace that he can feel himself at last to be a free man. The Christian life is essentially one of liberty. He who trusts in God as a loving and merciful Father will have no need to fear, because his salvation, so far from depending on his own persevering efforts, is already complete; here and now he is a child of God by adoption, and as such free of the bondage of the law. The latter will indeed have served its purpose of making known God's righteous will and hence of revealing sin, but it will no longer impose its negative control. Thus in *The Freedom of a Christian Man* Luther can assert that the believer is 'the most free lord of all things and subject to no one'. Every Christian is by faith 'so exalted above all things that in spiritual power he is completely lord of all. . . . A Christian man needs no work, no law for salvation, for by faith he is free from all law and in perfect freedom does whatever he does gratuitously, seeking neither profit nor salvation, but only what is well-pleasing to God, since by the grace of God he is already saved and rich in all things through faith'.

The principle here stated was, in its implications, of epoch-making significance. The works righteousness of traditional religion was wholly discounted: salvation is God's gift, not man's laboured achievement. For although the sinner was, in one sense, no more than a passive recipient of divine grace, in another he was truly free and capable. And where he most obviously was free was in his relation to the institutional church, in that his eternal destiny no longer depended on the rules and prescriptions of a legalistic system. Church, sacrament and ministry continued, for Luther, to have an appropriate place in the Christian life and to serve a

39. Atkinson, *op. cit.*, 350.
40. *W.A.*, XL (i), 70, 19f.

necessary end; but the kind of dominion which they hitherto had exercised must now be broken, as he himself makes abundantly clear in his explosive tract *On the Babylonian Captivity of the Church (De captivitate Babylonica)*, which, published in the October of 1520, immediately preceded that on *The Freedom of a Christian Man*.[41] Hierarchical power Luther now saw as nothing less than a spiritual bondage from which Christendom had to be freed if the needed reform – in head and members – was to come. The familiar antitheses of the church and the world, the clerical state and the lay, the 'religious' vocation and the 'secular', were either false or misconceived. Indeed any honest earthly calling provides the conditions for a vocation (*Beruf*) by means of which a man can fulfil God's will for him, so that his daily task in the world is no less sacred, and a good deal more useful, than the cloistered security offered by monasticism. It might, says Luther, *look* a fine thing when a monk renounces the 'world' and devotes himself to prayer and ascetic practices, in comparison with the humble chores of home and hearth, but where God commands true service can always be rendered. Nay, it is his express command that a man should honour his father and mother by all the means in his power, not that he should become a monk as an easier way to greater holiness. Religion, in other words, pertains to the people in their ordinary affairs, and not, whether exclusively or even primarily, to the clergy: a cobbler belongs to the spiritual estate as truly as a bishop. The clerical order represents the people but only by ministry. Furthermore, every baptized Christian is a priest in God's sight and therefore is not dependent on another for the reception of divine grace. In this fundamental respect there is no difference between the 'spiritual' estate and the 'temporal'. To assert the contrary is 'an artful lie and hypocritical invention'. For the spiritual estate is constituted by the whole body of Christians together. Certainly an ordered ministry is requisite, but only as a delegated function.

This doctrine of the priesthood of all believers was never to receive more forthright and vigorous statement than in the first of Luther's great 1520 tracts, his *Address to the Christian Nobility of the German Nation*.[42] A truly revolutionary document which deeply affected public opinion and gave an immense boost to nationalist sentiment, it was in form an impassioned appeal to the emperor, the princes and the nobles of Germany. The papacy, it declares, has entrenched itself behind a triple wall of spurious ('straw and paper') claims, namely, that the spiritual power is in all things superior to the temporal, that the pope alone has the authority to interpret scripture, and that he alone may summon a general council of the church. The papacy is in fact the embodiment of a tyrannous clericalism, the ubiquitous control of which in Germany can be overthrown only by the magistrates. The responsibility for so doing, now manifest as a duty, is theirs by divine right, inasmuch as 'the temporal power has been ordained by God for the punishment of the wicked and the protection of the good' without respect of persons, whatever their status or however 'holy' their office; hence Luther launches a virulent attack on the Roman pontiff personally for his grossly unapostolic display of wealth and pomp, and on the cardinals and the curial court for their avarice and chicanery. He concludes by outlining a wide range of ecclesiastical reforms, including the

41.  *W.A.*, VI, 497–573 (*W.M.L.*, XXXVI, 3–126).
42.  *W.A.*, VI, 404–69 (*W.M.L.*, XLIV, 115–217).

complete abolition of the papal authority over the state, the creation of a German national church with its own synod, parallel to the German imperial diet, as a final court of appeal, reform of the religious orders and the permission of a married priesthood to end the scandal of clerical concubinage.

By the beginning of 1521 Luther's prophetic message to the German people had thus been made clear, especially in its more radical and destructive implications, providing as it did a plain directive to practical action in church and state alike. Six months earlier Pope Leo X had already issued his bull *Exsurge Domine*, relatively mild in its wording but lamenting the revival in Germany, hitherto so loyal, of the errors of the Greeks and the Bohemians, and listing forty-one propositions, allegedly taught by Luther, which are forthwith condemned as 'heretical, or scandalous, or false, or offensive to pious ears, or seducing to simple minds, and standing in the way of the Catholic faith'. Exactly which propositions were heretical in the strict sense the bull does not specify. Curiously, Luther's views on the sacraments are largely passed over and his teaching on the priesthood of all believers is ignored, but his assault on the doctrine of purgatory, the penitential system, indulgences, and of course the papal authority are given prominent place. Luther himself was also inhibited from preaching – he had already refused to come to Rome to submit himself to 'instruction' – his books were ordered to be burned and he and his followers were bidden to make public recantation within sixty days, failing which they were to be treated as heretics subject to the usual penalties.

Luther's eventual clash with the papacy was inevitable, and had been so from the moment he raised the issue of indulgences in the autumn of 1517. Leo X had at first indeed regarded the whole affair as of little consequence, dismissing it, as did the Curia generally, as a mere quarrel among monks. It was even reported that he had spoken of the *Ninety-five Theses* as only the scribble of a drunken German who when sober would think differently. Luther himself had been sanguine enough to suppose that the pope might approve his denunciation of Tetzel's practices. But instead of a benediction from Rome he got, as he said, only 'thunder and lightning'. 'I was treated like a sheep which had fouled the wolf's water. Tetzel went scot-free, and I must submit to be devoured.' Gradually he came to realize that religious renovation with papal support and protection was an idle dream. Yet he admitted the conviction only with reluctance; he still wished to distinguish Rome from the pope personally, whose loyal spiritual subject he considered himself to be. But everything he said, whether in discussion or debate with Prierias, Cajetan or Eck, that touched upon the papal supremacy made it clear that his views struck at the whole ecclesiastical system in and over which the pope exercised authority. Thus his own account of the Leipzig disputation reveals him as having maintained that the bishop of Rome's unqualified jurisdiction was scarcely four hundred years old, and that the Eastern church had never recognized it any more than had the general councils or the Fathers of the early church. To Eck's taunts he replied that he was unable to admit that all of Christ's sheep were committed to Peter, for in that case what had been assigned to Paul? 'When Christ said to Peter, "Feed my sheep", he surely did not mean that no one else could feed them without Peter's permission?' Nor would Luther agree that the Roman pontiff could not err or that he alone was competent to interpret the scriptures. The papal theory was no more than a man-made doctrine which turned the words of Christ, 'Thou art Peter', into 'Thou art the primate'.[43] His encounter with Eck served in fact to clarify Luther's mind remarkably and he now saw himself to be at the parting of the ways. From Rome he could henceforth expect nothing but hostility and obstruction, compromise being impossible.

At last, on 10 October 1520, the papal bull reached him, and he had sixty days grace in which to recant. His immediate impulse was to act on the assumption that a document which 'condemned Christ himself' must be spurious. But he could not forbear from answering it, and in violent language, declaring that whoever was its author – Eck possibly? – was assuredly Antichrist. 'I protest,' he retorted, 'before God, our Lord Jesus Christ, his saints and angels, and the entire world, that with my whole heart I dissent from the damnation of this bull, that I curse and execrate it as sacrilege and blasphemy.'[44] So much for his recantation! Nor did his antagonism towards Rome lessen with the years; it became obsessive, rather. The actual pronouncement of his excommunication, in the bull *Decet Romanum Pontificem*, was not communicated to him until after the publication of the imperial edict against him at the Diet of Worms towards the end of May 1521, but his own breach with Rome had already been dramatically sealed by the public combustion of the bull *Exsurge Domine*, along with copies of the canon law and works of scholastic theology, outside the Elster gate of Wittenberg on the morning of 10 December 1520. Luther's own stabbing comment on this act was: 'Since they have burned my books I burn theirs. Their canon law was included because it makes the pope a god on earth.'[45] For he was certain, as he wrote at the time to a friend, that unless a man 'fight with all his might, and if need be unto death, against the statutes and laws of the pope and the bishops, he cannot be saved'.

## Note on the indulgence controversy

Although the change in Luther's religious convictions which set him on the road to far-reaching reform can in origin be traced back to his earliest Wittenberg lecture courses on biblical theology, the crisis which was to end in his breach with Rome did not begin until the late autumn of 1517, with the publication of the famous *Ninety-five Theses against Indulgences*, prompted by the indulgence-selling mission of the Dominican Johann Tetzel, which came close to but not actually within the territory of Luther's prince, the Elector of Saxony. In principle an indulgence was a remission by the church of the temporal penalty due on account of forgiven sin. The practice of dispensing indulgences presupposed, first, a retributive theory of divine justice according to which sin must be punished, either on earth or in purgatory, unless satisfaction be made even after confession and absolution; and secondly, the doctrine of the 'treasury of merits' (*thesaurus meritorum*), according to which not only the infinite merits of Christ but those also of the Blessed Virgin Mary and the saints were available to the church through the *communio sanctorum*,

43. *W.A.*, II, 180–239.
44. *W.A.*, VI, 597–612 ('Against the Execrable Bull of Antichrist').
45. *W.A.*, VII, 161–82 (*W.M.L.*, XXXI, 379–95).

in which all Christians are united with Christ and with one another as members of his Mystical Body. For the church possessed both the power and the right to administer the benefit of these merits in consideration of the prayers or the good works offered or rendered by the faithful. This advantage was extended even to souls in purgatory, and by the end of the fifteenth century a 'pardon' for such could actually be purchased for a money payment regardless of any contrition on the part of the purchaser, a practice which readily lent itself to flagrant abuse quite apart from the dubiousness of the principle itself. Luther's concern indeed was provoked less by its squalid commercialism than by its theological and moral defects: of the agreement reached among themselves by Pope Leo X, the archbishop of Mainz and the Augsburg banking house of Fuggers he probably at the time knew nothing. It has to be said however that Luther's objections are somewhat repetitive and not always clearly expressed (see *Documents Illustrative of the Continental Reformation* ed. B. J. Kidd, (Oxford, 1911), no. 11, for Latin text; English trans. in B. L. Woolf, *Reformation Writings of Martin Luther*, I, 32–42). The gist of them is: (1) that the church can remit only what she herself has imposed, God being by no means bound by her action; (2) that an indulgence cannot remit guilt, a condition over which the pope has no authority; (3) that the church cannot remit the divine punishment of sin, which remains exclusively in the hands of God; (4) that the penalties remitted by her apply to this life only: the pope has no authority over souls in purgatory, although they can be helped by prayer; (5) that true repentance alone brings divine forgiveness and so renders indulgences unnecessary; and (6) that the treasury of merits is an ill-defined concept, and that in any case the merits of Christ and his saints are not at the disposal of the pope, the church's true treasure being 'the sacrosanct Gospel of the glory and grace of God'. Early in 1518 Luther published a *Sermon on Indulgences and Grace* which is rather more explicit than the *Theses* and was circulated even more widely. Thus the theory of indulgences and, in fact, the entire penitential system of the late medieval church were seen by him only as blunting the conscience and encouraging a false sense of security (*tentatio cogitationum de securitate*) which was 'the mother of hypocrites and the cause of hypocrisy' (*W.A.*, LVI, 281, 5ff.). He insisted that the word *poenitentia*, used in the Vulgate to translate *metanoia*, means 'penitence', not the mere doing of penance, and that there is no penance apart from the love and righteousness of God, a truth which he himself, as he confessed, had learned from his monastic superior and spiritual guide Staupitz (*W.A.*, I, 525).

# Chapter 4

# MARTIN LUTHER:
# II. THE FOUNDER OF PROTESTANTISM

## The authority of scripture

It is said that when Luther joined the Augustinian convent at Erfurt he was warned by one of his instructors there: 'Brother Martin, let the Bible alone; read the old teachers. . . . Reading the Bible simply breeds unrest.' In Luther's own case the unrest it bred was rather with the 'old teachers' themselves; and when at Wittenberg in 1513, a year after he had graduated as doctor of holy scripture, he came to lecture on the Bible his whole theological outlook, after much painful soul-searching, was by degrees transformed. For it was his study of the scriptures which, as we have seen, led him to that belief in justification by faith *alone* through which he at last found spiritual liberation. Scripture, in contrast to the overblown tradition of the church, testified directly to the original gospel. Therein lay its signal and unique authority, since what it contained was the very Word of God by which faith is ever and again rekindled in men's hearts. That it could do so was, in its way, a sheer miracle, far surpassing, as evidence of divine truth, any merely physical wonder.

Yet Luther did not understand by the Word simply the letter of the scriptures, for the Word had been preached by the apostles before ever it came to be written down. Merely as a document it has no power to create faith; it needs to be used – read or preached with penetration and a real grasp of its meaning.[1] Hence, it is what the Bible *conveys* that has saving power. This truly is 'gospel' – something which, when received with an open heart, is self-authenticating. Luther's own mind was steeped in biblical material. All other authorities were for him utterly outdistanced by it.

> I believe [*he declared*] I owe this duty to the Lord, of crying out against philosophy and turning men to Holy Scripture. For perhaps were anyone else to do it . . . he would be afraid, or would not be believed. But I who have already wasted many years on such things, and have encountered and hear of many like myself, see that it is a vain pursuit, doomed to perdition. . . . It is high time now to be carried away from other studies and to learn Christ and him crucified.[2]

What could not be proved out of scripture or supported by its clear indications was, as regards faith and salvation, irrelevant or false. Thus it was from the testimony of the Bible that Luther rejected indulgences, in theory as in practice, denied the authority of the pope and felt bound to assert, as at the Leipzig disputation, that general councils could err. It was by it alone that he himself, when

1. *W.A.*, XXI, 466, 36.
2. *W.A.*, LVI, 371, 17 and 26.

questioned at the Diet of Worms concerning his own teachings, would submit to be judged. 'Unless [*he then answered*] I am convicted of error by the evidence of Scripture, or . . . by manifest reasoning I stand convicted by the Scriptures to which I have appealed, and my conscience is taken captive by God's word, I cannot and will not recant anything.' Once scripture and conscience were in accord, that is, the authority of the church could no longer interpose between them. The power of the word to create faith had already been sufficiently demonstrated in his own experience to prevent him from questioning it.

Luther's method of biblical exegesis, as he makes clear at the beginning of his earlier lectures on the Psalms,[3] rested on a distinction between the spirit and the letter. But to draw this distinction effectually the guidance of the Holy Spirit himself was necessary, 'for nobody understands these precepts unless it is given him from above. . . . Therefore they most sadly err who presume to interpret the Holy Scriptures and the law of God by taking hold of them by their own understanding and study.'[4] The mere phrases of scripture will not of themselves bring enlightenment and inward comprehension, for what is uttered *vocaliter* needs to be understood *vitaliter*, in the heart and conscience. The Spirit, it could be said, is hidden within the letter, since the letter itself may proclaim only the law or the wrath of God, whereas the Spirit conveys the word of grace, the gospel. Moreover it follows from this that the interpretation of scripture is not something that can be settled once for all as a fixed tradition of belief; on the contrary, it is a task that each and every man must assume for himself if the knowledge of the Word is not to sink once again to the level of a dogmatic literalism. The true reading of the Bible is a continuous process of, as it were, bringing faith to birth, a constant renewal and recreation of the spiritual understanding.

Nevertheless, in this stressing of the role of the Spirit, Luther was well aware of the dangers of the kind of 'illuminism' preached by some of the more radical and individualistic reformers of his own day. Spiritual 'experiences' could easily mislead and required to be guided or corrected by the objective witness of the written revelation. Hence the importance he attached to the historical sense, even while not denying the usefulness of the secondary senses recognized in the medieval hermeneutics.[5] At first indeed he considered that each of these – allegorical, tropological, anagogical – had its appropriate place, so long as the all-important distinction between the letter and the spirit was not forgotten;[6] but two of them at least soon ceased to have any practical significance for him. What really mattered was the *prima facie* or literal-historical meaning, which he took, however, to cover an implicit Christology. 'All prophecies and all the prophets ought', he claimed, 'to be understood of Christ our Lord, unless it appears by plain words that they

---

3. *W.A.*, III, 12, 2ff.
4. *W.A.*, LVII, 185, 21, Cf. LIX, 19, 4,
5. See above, pp. 36. The traditional scheme was not rigidly applied and medieval exegesis varied, in fact, quite considerably in its procedure. Luther was of course thoroughly familiar with the scholastic exegesis according to the *quadrige*, 'the fourfold sense of scripture'. Ironically, he uses it as an instrument against scholasticism. See G. Ebeling, *Die Anfänge von Luthers Hermeneutik* in *Lutherstudien* (Tübingen, 1971), 1–68.
6. See e.g. *W.A.*., III, 11, 33.

treat of something else.'[7] For in Christ 'all words form but a single Word'.[8] Once this primary sense was established it was, of the other three, only the tropological that retained for him any point, namely as applying the work of Christ to the individual, a truth which can be summed up in one word: the Cross. Christian theology, Luther believed, is through and through a *theologia crucis*, an expression coined by him in 1518, in the course of the dispute over the indulgences issue. It is this type of interpretation which creates faith in the heart of the individual, bearing always in mind that it is the Spirit alone who can bring this necessary insight.[9]

Yet Luther was, as we have said, very far from equating God's saving Word with the word as written; not all the biblical books had the same revelatory value or the same power to elicit faith. The touchstone of their spiritual authority lay in the extent, greater or less, to which they witness to Christ – *soweit sie Christum treiben*. And first the traditional division must be recognized between the Old Testament and the New. Basically it is the law which the Old Testament promulgates, its core being the Mosaic legislation which exacts, warns, accuses and condemns. The New Testament, on the other hand, proclaims the gospel, the good news of the benefits of God in Christ for mankind. But while accepting the division Luther declines to press it too far, since the Old Testament itself contains gospel, even as the gospel itself contains law. Law and gospel, command and promise, are in fact two different aspects of God's one Word, and as such can be found throughout the Bible.

Yet if all scripture thus testifies in some measure to Christ there are parts of it which do so with unique force and authority, as Luther explains in the preface to his translation of the New Testament. Of supreme value, he judges, are St John's gospel and the same writer's first epistle, the epistles of St Paul, especially Romans, Galatians and Ephesians, and the First Epistle of St Peter. These, he tells his readers, 'are the books that show you Christ and teach you all that it is necessary and good for you to know for your salvation, even though you were never to see or hear any other book or teaching'.[10] By contrast the Epistle of St James, which stresses the importance of works in comparison with mere 'faith', is dismissed as 'straw', having nothing of the nature of the gospel about it.[11] But of Romans in particular he says that it is 'really the chief part of the New Testament and the very purest Gospel'. As for the Old Testament, the heart of it is contained in the

7. *W.A.*, III, 137; as also III, 225, 37 and IV, 379, 35.

8. *W.A.*, IV, 439, 20f.

9. 'For who would realize that one who is visibly humbled, tempted, rejected and slain, is at the same time and to the utmost degree inwardly exalted, consoled, accepted and brought to life, unless this were taught by the Spirit through faith?' (*W.A.*, IV, 82, 19–24).

10. For translation of this preface see J. Dillenberger, *Martin Luther, Selections* (New York, 1961), 14–19.

11. But Luther by no means looked on the Epistle of James as worthless. 'I think highly', he says, 'of the Epistle of James, and regard it as valuable although it was rejected in the early days. It does not expound human doctrines, but lays much emphasis on God's law.' Nevertheless he did not consider it an authentic writing of any apostle. See Dillenberger, *op. cit.*, 35f. The New Testament book least to Luther's taste was the Revelation of St John – a favourite with many of the sectaries of his day.

psalter, 'a little Bible' in itself, so that whoever could not read the whole Bible would here have almost an entire summary of it, 'comprised in a single small book'.[12]

It is evident therefore that Luther was by no means a biblical literalist of the kind which Protestant sectarianism has so often fostered. Any given passage must be interpreted in relation to scripture as a whole, the subject matter of which is always in itself perspicuous – intelligible, that is, and coherent; and because of this perspicuity of scripture as a whole its several parts are their own mutual interpreters. Moreover, once the Bible's fundamental clarity is recognized its occasional obscurities and difficulties of detail may be readily admitted.[13] As to the nature of biblical inspiration Luther had no particular doctrine, and he certainly propounded no theory of its literal inerrancy.

But how does the Bible stand in relation to the tradition of the church? More especially, if scripture is superior to and therefore corrective of ecclesiastical tradition, how is the fact to be explained that it was the latter which actually determined the canon? To this Luther's answer is that the question of canonicity was settled in the early and relatively uncorrupt days of the church's existence; and with the 'external' or historic guarantee must also be reckoned another and an 'internal' one, that of the content of the books themselves, of their own firm consistency of witness; the extent, in short, to which they proclaim (albeit in differing ways) the gospel of God in Christ. Finally, there is the reliability of their authors, whether as eye-witnesses of the events they describe, particularly in respect of the life, death and resurrection of Christ, as in the instance of the apostles themselves; or else, when not bearing such personal testimony, as inspired by the Holy Spirit, a consideration which has special applicability to the writers of the Old Testament.[14] Thus the written word has for Luther an authority that cannot be attached either to the 'traditions of men' – doctrines and practices which have appeared only in the course of the church's historic life – or to the 'inner word' of the more radical and innovative reformers of his time. It certainly is true that Luther emphasizes the function of the *spoken* word: 'Christ', he remarks, 'did not command the Apostles to write, but only to preach' (or more aphoristically, 'the Church is a mouth-house, not a pen-house');[15] yet the written word is necessary both to sustain and to authenticate the church's oral proclamation, so that the word continuously preached remains consistent with the primal witness of revelation. In other words, its function is at once to inspire and to correct. Not even the best of the early Christian Fathers, weighty though their teaching is, could dispense with the Word as originally, under divine guidance, committed to writing.

But Luther's most signal contribution to the resuscitation of scriptural authority was his own translation of the Bible, beginning with the publication of the New Testament in September 1522, the latter task having been completed with remarkable speed during his 'protective custody' at the Wartburg. Illustrated by Lucas

---

12. For the 1528 Preface to the Psalms see Dillenberger, *op. cit.*, 37–41.
13. See K. Holl, *Gesammelte Aufsätze*, I, 544ff.
14. See H. Bornkamm, *Luther und das Alte Testament* (Tübingen, 1948).
15. The Bible, Luther held, is the Word of God 'put into letters' (*gebuch stabet*) (*W.A.*, XLVIII, 31, 4). But simply as written (or printed) it is unable to create faith *extra usum*.

Cranach, the first edition of three thousand copies was sold out within three months. The Old Testament took much longer, appearing in four successive parts, the last as late as 1534. Made not from the Vulgate but from the original tongues (although Luther needed help with the Hebrew), it is in many respects an achievement of genius, a landmark, it has been well said, in the linguistic and cultural history of the German nation.[16] Unlike the English Authorized Version of 1611 it was deliberately 'modern', cast in a racy idiom. 'My teachers', Luther averred, 'were the housewife in her home, the children at their games, the merchants in the city squares; I tried to learn from them how to express and explain myself'; though to this should be added also another and indispensable personal qualification, 'his own inrooted simplicity and his capacity to think within the biblical worlds'.[17]

## The church

But if it is scripture which, as embodying the Word of God, provides the rule and standard of saving faith, what then for Luther is the role of the church? In response to this question it must be said at the outset, and with emphasis, that he did not teach the sufficiency of mere 'private judgement' or seek to inculcate individualist pietism. On the contrary, the idea of the church was central to his whole theological outlook. In his early lectures on Genesis he claimed that the first 'theological' word in the Bible refers to the church, for when God planted the Tree of Life in the midst of the Garden he erected, so to speak, a temple wherein Adam might worship him. From this it follows that the church is the primary institution, antecedent to the state and even the home. Likewise it will prove to be the ultimate one; all others will have an end, whereas the Kingdom of Christ is everlasting;[18] for the church is the Kingdom in its present, earthly manifestation, inasmuch as it is a specific 'people', 'God's people', the community of believers, or, in the language of the creed, the *communio sanctorum*.

> I believe [*Luther wrote in 1520*] that there is on earth, through the whole wide world, no more than one holy, common Christian Church, which is nothing else than the congregation or assembly of the saints, i.e., the good, believing men on earth, which is gathered, preserved, ruled by the Holy Spirit, and is daily increased by means of the Sacraments and the Word of God.[19]

And again, many years later: 'The Creed indicates clearly what the Church is, namely, a Communion of Saints; that is, a group or assembly of such people as are Christians and holy.'[20] The word 'church' (*Kirche*) itself Luther disliked; he thought it lacking in definite meaning and even 'un-German', preferring to translate the Greek *ekklesia* by expressions like *Gemeine* (congregation), *Gemeinde* (community) or *Versammlung* (assembly). Another term he favoured was *Christenheit*, or

16. A. G. Dickens, *Martin Luther and the Reformation* (London, 1967), 64.
17. E. G. Rupp, 'Luther and the German Reformation to 1529', in *The New Cambridge Modern History* (1958), 83.
18. *W.A.*, LII, 522.
19. *P.E.*, II, 372.
20. *P.E.*, VI, 264.

Christendom, the unity of all Christian people. But although these designations seemed to him to convey the spirit of the New Testament much more readily – and it was this which above all he sought to recreate in place of the legalistic institutionalism of his own day – he did not regard the New Testament forms as in any prescriptive manner normative of the changes he wished to see brought about. His concern rather was with discovering the true nature of the church as a fellowship of believers the source of whose spiritual life was Christ; such a fellowship, in fact, as could truly be identified with the *corpus Christi mysticum*. The church, for Luther, was the *locus* in which personal faith in Christ, the faith which justifies, is naturally and necessarily exercised.

Far, then, from opposing scripture and the church, Luther saw them as alike constituted by the Word.[21] Christ is 'preached' in both, and is the substance and vivifying power of each, *tota vita et substantia ecclesiae in verbo Dei*. He is directly witnessed to in the one and constantly reproclaimed in the other. The Word's presence within it is thus the church's pre-eminent mark or 'note'. The Word of God and the People of God cannot be separated. But this clearly implies that whatever in the church's tradition of faith is not capable of being justified by the testimony of the Bible must be without divine authority. Hence Luther's scorching criticism of the Rome-dominated church of his day. Everywhere he saw declension from the original gospel purity: in the whole elaborate structure of hierarchical government, in sacerdotalism, legalism and monasticism, in 'merit', above all in the papacy itself. None of these things – and, in their sum, Catholicism was equated with them – had any place according to the witness of scripture, and virtually all were antagonistic to its spirit if not to its letter. The Christian religion would therefore have to be reconstituted on an evangelical basis, cleared not simply of the gross abuses few would wish to hide, but of doctrines and institutions which were generally thought to compose its actual fabric.

Yet although Luther presents the church as a visible organization, identifiable by the preaching of the Word and the due administration of the gospel sacraments (though not in respect of specific ecclesiastical forms) it is, as the 'communion of saints', in a necessary sense invisible: *abscondita est ecclesia, latent sancti* – 'the Church is concealed, the saints hidden'.[22] For God alone can read into the hearts of men and know whether they have been really touched by grace. To unbelievers the idea of an invisible church is meaningless, but where faith exists its truth is evidenced from personal experience. 'As this rock [*Christ*] is invisible and only to be grasped by faith, so too the Church [*apart from sin*] must be spiritual and invisible, to be grasped only by faith.'[23] The invisible church is the company of all who possess the gift of faith and the true 'apostolical succession' is that of those who, age upon age, respond to grace with faith. Thus the visible and the invisible

---

21. 'The Church does not make the Word of God, but she is made by the Word of God' (*W.A.*, VIII, 491, 31; see also III, 259, 18; III, 139, 19; III, 425, 25; IV, 173, 34; IV, 179, 14).
22. 'For Christ is concealed in the Church, which is hidden from men but manifest to God' (*W.A.*, III, 124, 36). And again: 'The Church is invisible and recognizable by faith alone' (*W.A.*, IV, 189, 17).
23. *W.A.*, VII, 710, 1.

churches are not and cannot be coterminous. For Luther, unlike the so-called radicals of the Reformation, did not suppose that the 'true' church of faith, 'without spot or wrinkle', could also receive a visible and tangible embodiment.

This, let us repeat, is not to say that the visible church is of merely secondary importance and that its fellowship can in the end be ignored. On the contrary, the visible church is indispensable, inasmuch as it is where Word and sacrament are to be found and where the Holy Spirit is certainly operative, enlightening and sanctifying. Hence Luther can say, with no more hesitation than Cyprian in the third century: *Extra ecclesiam nulla salus* – outside the church there is no forgiveness and no holiness. Indeed he affirms quite explicitly that the church is the 'gathering of all Christians upon earth'.[24] That it should have an outward shape and character is natural and to be expected; more, it is an 'ordinance of divine wisdom' that God should reveal himself to men under a sure and visible form, 'which can be seen with the eyes, grasped by the hands, and apprehended by the five senses'.[25] Only it has to be remembered that as the things of creation are, as it were, *larvae Dei*, 'masks of God', so too the church at once reveals and conceals God. However, there can be no question that the outward manifestations of his purpose are instruments by means of which he works upon men and speaks to them, so that, as Luther wisely remarks, 'a child of seven years old knows what the Church is'.

That is why, at any stage of his career, Luther had no notion of placing himself outside the institutional church, or of disowning the historic tradition of Christendom, and still less of founding some new body. Rome herself possessed the scriptures and the sacraments of baptism, the eucharist and absolution, while saintly lives had been and continued to be lived under the old system. But if the church, humanly speaking, was to survive and further its witness to the gospel it would have to be purged of its errors.[26] Thus in the actual course of the reform which, willy-nilly perhaps, Luther had set in motion, drastic changes were brought about involving the repudiation of the papacy, and with it the entire system of hierarchical government: the closure of the monastic houses, the reduction of the traditional seven sacraments to two, the total rejection of the scholastic philosophy in any of its forms, the radical simplification and purification of the liturgy and the abolition of most of the old rites and ceremonies. On the other hand the fundamental dogmas of the faith, the legacy of the patristic age, were retained, with the result that Lutheran orthodoxy never for one moment saw itself as departing from the historic credal positions: the word 'heresy' was held to be altogether inapplicable to the teachings of Luther and his followers, but rather to the innovations for which Rome had culpable responsibility, such as false doctrines of the eucharist and purgatory. In fact, the very suggestion that he was propounding a theology of his own to be designated by his name was something which the Wittenberg leader indignantly rejected. 'I am not,' he insisted, 'and do not want to be, anybody's master. Along with the Church I have the one universal teaching of Christ, who alone is the Master of us all.'[27]

24. *W.A.*, VI, 293–6.
25. *W.A.*, XLII, 625, 30.
26. *W.A.*, XXXIX (ii), 167, 20.
27. *W.A.*, VIII, 685, 6ff.

At the heart of Luther's concept of the church was however his strongly held conviction of the priesthood of all believers, to which we referred in the last chapter. Its practical application would, he realized, transform the character and ethos of the existing church. Within the latter the role of the laity was subordinate and passive, the word 'church', as commonly used, denoting virtually the clergy only. In all matters relating to ecclesiastical doctrine and governance laymen as such had no part. But in a church ordered by the Word, now freely preached, the laity would assume a new responsibility, or rather the responsibility which already was theirs in principle as members of the Body of Christ. Authority in the church rested, that is, not with a select and privileged few, a sacerdotal caste, but with all its members, as between one and another of whom there is in this regard no essential difference. As Luther put it in his lectures on Galatians, 'there is neither cleric nor layman, nor status of this or that order, not he who prays nor he who reads, but to all these things a man is indifferent, doing or not doing them as shall help or take away from charity'.[28] Hence when the need for thorough reform became evident it might prove necessary for laymen – in practice those most powerful and influential – to take the required measures in hand. It was for this reason that Luther issued his *Address to the Christian Nobility*, those so addressed including the knights and the authorities of the imperial cities as well as the ruling princes. The clerical element, controlled by Rome, had refused to summon a free reforming council. The task of inaugurating change therefore fell to lay leaders who had both the will and the means to discharge it.

Did Luther seek to erase all differences or distinctions between the clerical state and the lay? To this the answer is a definite negative. On the contrary, he held that the church's ministry was divinely instituted, but as a ministry of *function* rather than of status. For ministry *per se* is the property of the whole congregation, as the idea of the priesthood of all believers clearly implies. The capacity and responsibility for ministering resides, that is, in the Christian community as such, and there only: *Nos omnes aequaliter sacerdotes, quotquot baptisati sumus.*[29] Nevertheless, were the principle that all believers are priests taken to mean that any one may at will personally exercise ministerial functions, the result would be anarchy, resembling, as Luther puts it, only the chatter of women in the market-place, all of them talking and none listening.[30] Order would be gone. But his objections are not purely practical: his stress on the necessary implications of the doctrine of the universal priesthood belongs rather to his earlier years than to his maturity; later he is more concerned to urge the church's responsibility under God to appoint recognized and accredited ministers, properly called, qualified and ordained.[31] His position is indeed quite unambiguous: 'We are all priests in so far as we are Christians, but those whom we call priests are ministers (*Diener*) selected from our midst to act in our name, and this priesthood is our ministry.' What he means is that the minister is ordained not to a hierarchical *sacerdotium* conferring an indelible 'character', but to a *ministerium* in the sense of a function or office

28. *W.A.*, LVII, 64, 2.
29. *W.A.*, VI, 564, 6.
30. *W.A.*, X (iii), 397, 17.
31. *W.A.*, XVI, 33ff; XVII (ii), 493, 14; XVII (iii), 570ff. *Tischreden* IV, 113, 483.

(*Amt*) recognized only so long as such service is discharged by the authority of the congregation which had called him. In particular, the power of the keys, the absolution of sins, belongs to every Christian by right of the universal priesthood, but its exercise is permitted only to those who have received public authorization. Regarding the rite of ordination itself, although Luther concedes that in extreme circumstances it is possible for laymen to administer it,[32] the rule is that it is ministers only who ordain to the ministry: *Sed nos qui iam habemus ministeria, commendabimus in nostrum ministerium.*[33]

Yet the whole concept of different degrees of ministry *jure divino*, a concept ancient as well as medieval, was superseded. For Luther the New Testament, where the words *episcopos* and *presbyteros* appear as interchangeable terms, provided no evidence for it. No doubt he might have retained something resembling the traditional structure had the conditions of the time allowed it, but they did not. It proved impossible in Germany (unlike England) to impose a reformed doctrine on the episcopal system, and when a choice had to be made between the two there could be no doubt where it would fall: in comparison with the unimpaired truth of the Word forms of ministry were altogether secondary.[34] Moreover, the episcopate as Luther knew it was not simply an ecclesiastical order; it had become secularized, bishops appearing to the world rather as temporal princes or nobles than representatives and ministers of the gospel. In short, the entire structure of Catholic clericalism could be left with no place in a church effectively reformed and renewed. In the latter clerics would enjoy no sacral privileges as compared with laymen, although they would, on the other hand, be invested with the full responsibilities of ministry, inasmuch as no ministerial capacity belongs to bishops which is not, in principle, that likewise of priests or pastors.

But because all members of the *communio sanctorum* have their appropriate responsibilities there can be no discrimination of spiritual standing in terms of vocation or office. Instead the Christian life must itself be understood as vocational in an absolute sense. Thus the notion of a 'higher' way of asceticism, the 'religious' life *par excellence*, with its supposed distinction between gospel 'precepts' and 'counsels', is disallowed. Rather, Luther points to the ethic of the 'calling', *Beruf*, whereby the roles of all Christian believers in the ordered scheme of divine creation are duly consecrated. Normally, that is, a man's 'calling' will provide the particular sphere, wherever and whatever it might be, within which he finds himself charged to fulfil the will of God. Here he can learn to do his part in the realization of the Kingdom of Christ on earth and so render a willing service to God and to his neighbour. Normally, be it said; for Luther was of course by no means unaware of the moral problems posed by certain forms of 'vocation'. Plainly, criminal or immoral ways of life can never be blessed. The difficulty arises with respect to those callings, necessary to civil society, through which the authority of the state is

---

32. *W.A.*, VI, 407f.
33. *W.A.*, XV, 721, 1ff. Luther did not, however, hold that an episcopally-ordained ministry is necessary to the church's existence. The preaching of the true gospel was the essential requirement. Where the word is, he would say, there is faith, and where faith is there is the church.
34. *W.A.*, XXX (ii), 340ff; see also XXXVIII, 236, 23 and XLI, 241, 1.

enforced. Luther's own view is that if the state and the sword it wields are actually themselves a divine service, given the conditions of a sinful world, there is no moral or spiritual danger in them. 'For as was said: Love of neighbour seeks not its own, how great or small, but considers how profitable and needful for neighbour and community such works are.'[35] But to this issue, which involves Luther's idea of the Two Kingdoms, we shall return later.

Although the church on earth is in its essence a 'communion of saints', full expression of its nature is never a completed achievement. Its members, albeit forgiven and declared righteous, are sinners still, even when on the road to sanctity. In this aspect the ideal Christian community is always in process of becoming, of being built up. Externally realized, it is recognizable as the *corpus Christianum*, reaching out to embrace the whole social life of the community; and it is because society can be thus Christianized that it is possible for the communion of true believers to live and grow. But nature and history have brought into being certain orders or hierarchies (*Ordnungen*), as Luther called them, namely the family (*oeconomia*), which is the basic natural 'order', the state or magistracy (*politia*), the protective order, and the church (*ecclesia*), the spiritual order. All these orders have their rights and proper authority, through whose interaction the *communio sanctorum* can exist and manifest itself among men.

Luther's faith in the Word, then, obliged him, in the actual historical situation in which he found himself, to work out a doctrine of the church in many regards strikingly different from that on which contemporary Catholic practice rested. He did so, however, in no spirit of iconoclasm – he agonized over the question whether he alone could be right and all the Catholic teachers before him wrong[36] – but in the conviction that he was cleansing not destroying, correcting not abolishing, and that the reformed church he envisaged and sought to bring about would be not simply a return, *per saltum* as it were, to the church of the New Testament, but a continuation of that whose life and fundamental witness to the truth in Christ Jesus had persisted through the centuries. At first it was his hope and even expectation that the Roman papacy itself would awaken to the true light of the gospel. These were dashed when he and his followers were denounced and excommunicated. The upshot was the establishment of new institutions devised in accordance with the principles which his reading of the scriptures had led him to embrace. Thus 'Lutheran' churches came into being, embodying a reformed order of their own. Luther himself, though, looked on these not as new creations but as reforged links in a chain uniting the present with the more distant past. The Word had remained steadfast; it was the papacy that had strayed into ways of corruption. Luther's own work, accordingly, was essentially one of restoration: he would destroy nothing which his knowledge of the gospel would enable him to preserve. It was for this reason that he so bitterly opposed not only the radical sects, mere *Schwärmer* to him, but even more moderate reformers whose sacramental doctrine struck him as so defective as to be impious.

35. *P.E.*, III, 249.
36. *W.A.*, XXIII, 421, 26ff.

## The sacraments

For as the church is, basically, constituted by the Word of divine grace so too are the sacraments, which similarly draw their whole meaning from it. The outward sign, the 'element', becomes significant when the Word is added to it. Thus to the believer the sacraments, by God's express ordinance, are channels or instruments of his grace, even though not, as Catholic teaching avers, effective of themselves as visible things, *ex opere operato*. Indeed, Christ himself, the incarnate Logos, can with all propriety be described as the original *sacramentum Dei*, or 'sign of God'.[37] The specific sacraments of the church are of his foundation, being rendered efficacious through the agency of the Holy Spirit. According to the *Confession of Augsburg*, drafted in 1530 by Luther's disciple Melanchthon, their purpose generally is to serve 'not only as marks of profession amongst men, but still more as signs and testimonies of the will of God towards us, set forth for the purpose of arousing faith in such as use them'.

Luther dealt polemically with the prevailing Catholic doctrine and use of the sacraments in his tract, *The Babylonian Captivity of the Church*, addressed to the clergy. The traditional seven, as fixed dogmatically by the Council of Florence in 1439 – namely baptism, the eucharist, penance, confirmation, holy order, marriage and extreme unction – are reduced to two, or at most three: i.e. baptism, the eucharist and perhaps penance. Baptism is the primary sacrament. 'Every Christian', says Luther in his *Larger Catechism* (1528), 'has enough in Baptism to hear and to practise all his life. For he has always enough to do to believe firmly what Baptism promises and brings, namely, victory over death and the devil, forgiveness of sin, the grace of God, the entire Christ, and the Holy Ghost with his gifts.' From the very day of his baptism a man has to die unto sin for the remainder of his life if he is to reap the benefits bestowed on him by it. He must, so to say, return to it again and again. In itself therefore it is the work of God alone, not of the minister, and signifies the completeness of our justification, although in this regard its efficacy is inseparable from faith. When rightly administered and received it is spiritually regenerative, and by it one becomes a member of the church. In the moving phrases of the *Short Catechism* (1529): 'It signifies that the old Adam in us is to be drowned by daily repentance and penance, and is to die, with all sins and evil desires, and that daily is to arise and emerge a new man, who is to live before God in righteousness and purity for ever.'[38]

Despite Luther's unwavering emphasis on the necessity of faith, he stoutly supported the practice of infant baptism. And he did so by simply denying that infants are without faith, trying in this way to avoid the errors, as he saw them, both of the Roman *opus operatum* doctrine and of anabaptism. Faith, he maintained, is *unconsciously* present in the child brought to baptism by virtue of the proclamation of the Word there made, along with the conscious faith of the sponsors, although naturally an *infans* is incapable of faith in the sense of an understanding trust and obedience. The essence of Luther's view presumably is that

37.  *W.A.*, X (i), 2, 15 and 21.
38.  Kidd, *Documents*, 215. A translation of the *Short Catechism* is printed as no. 97 in this collection.

the baptized child is set in a new relationship to God, receiving thereby forgiveness of sin and the promise of salvation, while a full personal comprehension of what his baptism involved must develop as he matures. The stress, one should notice, falls characteristically on the objectivity and prevenience of the divine promise and grace.[39]

As is well known this same stress marks Luther's doctrine of the eucharist. For here again the act is emphatically that of God in Christ, in bestowing his saving grace. But for the grace to be received, the promise to be fulfilled, faith must be present, elicited by the Word. This implies that the traditional idea of the mass as a meritorious work whereby God is propitiated by the church's daily repetition of Christ's sacrifice is rejected. To Luther – and here he broke decisively with Catholic belief and piety – the mass is no sacrifice. We cannot, he said, offer Christ sacrificially, it is Christ who offers us.[40] The one and only sacrifice pleasing to God was made once and for all on Calvary. However, the gift of grace is denoted by a sign (*Zeichen*) instituted by Christ himself, namely the consecrated bread and wine. By means of it he offers the merits of his death to all who partake of them: hence the demand, which all the reformers reiterated, that the cup should be restored to the laity. But on one thing Luther was insistent, that the bread and wine are, through consecration, no longer simply bread and wine: Christ himself is really and substantially present therein. The Roman doctrine of transubstantiation, as defined by the Fourth Lateran Council of 1215, he indeed utterly repudiated as, to quote the words of the *Babylonian Captivity*, 'an invention of human reason, based neither on scripture nor on sound reasoning', and thus preposterous when advanced as an article of faith. But he did hold that the words 'This is my body' etc. mean what they say, so that one is bound to accept that the substances both of the body and blood of Christ and of the bread and wine co-exist in union one with another, a theory of Christ's eucharistic presence usually known as consubstantiation, although the term is one which Luther did not himself use.[41] The presence did not, however, depend on a priestly miracle wrought at the moment of consecration, but on the truth, as Luther conceived it to be, of the natural ubiquity of the Lord's glorified body, this natural presence becoming sacramentally significant by virtue of the divine promise attaching to the eucharistic rite, the purpose of which is communion with the living Christ and appropriation of the merits of his atoning death. It was on this issue that Luther disagreed so sharply

39. On Luther's baptismal teaching generally see his treatise *Concerning Rebaptism* (*W.A.*, XXVI, 144–74; *W.M.L.*, XL, 225–62).

40. In the *Babylonish Captivity* Luther denounces the doctrine of the sacrifice of the mass as 'the most wicked abuse of all' and one that 'has brought an endless host of others in its train'. He resumed his attack in two later pamphlets, *The Misuse of the Mass* (1521) and *The Abomination of the Secret Mass* (1525) (English translations of both in *W.M.L.*, XXXVI, 127ff. and 307ff.). In the *Schmalkald Articles* of 1537 he still rejects the mass as 'the most precious papal idolatry' and as 'the dragon's tail' that has brought forth 'a brood of vermin and the poison of manifold idolatries' (Part II, article 2). See T. G. Tappert, ed., *The Book of Concord* (Philadelphia, 1959), 293ff.

41. Luther insisted that his doctrine of the real presence was truly scriptural, quoting Mt. 26:26, 1 Cor. 10:16–33, 11:26–34. See D. C. Steinmetz, 'Scripture and the Lord's Supper in Luther's Theology', in *Luther in Context* (Bloomington, Ind., 1986), 72–84.

at the Marburg Colloquy of 1529, thus preventing any coordination of the German and Swiss reform movements.

But the proper context of Luther's teaching on the sacraments is his still more fundamental convictions about the atonement, which theologically is the root of his whole belief, the doctrine of justification *sola fide* itself deriving directly from it. Here again the objectivity of God's truth and grace are seen as all-important, the certainty on which the uncertainties of mere human feeling can come finally to rest. Luther's theology is, as we have stressed, *theologia crucis*, a theology of the cross. Scripture itself, he insists, is pervaded by the cross: *Crux enim Christi ubique in scripturis occurrit.*[42] Christ, Luther would have us never forget, 'was made a curse for us, and truly died on account of sin', having taken all our sins upon himself.[43] The result was an actual change in God's attitude towards us, a transforming of his wrath into grace, so conquering death and sin. In fact, it is by what Christ did, the work he alone accomplished and could have accomplished, that we recognize his divinity, see that he 'must needs be truly and naturally God'.

## The work and person of Christ

A common misapprehension of Luther's teaching on justification is that he seeks to explain it purely in terms of *imputation*, as though Christ's work on behalf of men brings him, the sinless one, no nearer to the sinner whom he had redeemed. Any such notion misrepresents what he did teach, although such a doctrine certainly made its appearance in later Lutheranism. That it is Christ's righteousness, not man's, which saves is of course a cardinal principle for him, but all that he says concerning justification must be understood in the light of his belief in Christ's *uniting* himself with us by his incarnate life and atoning death, even as we are united with him through faith. (Indeed when a man is separated from Christ he is again under the law.) For Christ not only acted *for* us, he identified himself completely *with* us, taking the very guilt of our sin upon himself, even to the extent of feeling at the moment of his death upon the cross that he himself was forsaken of God. The measure of this substitution, of him who knew no sin being made, as St Paul says, sin for us sinners,[44] is also therefore the measure of the respect God has for the individual human personality, sin-stained though it is, whose response in trust and love he desires. Thus the forgiven sinner learns his own true worth as a child of God, a child in whom, reconciled to and made holy by God, God's own righteousness achieves a personal realization. For what the believer sees in Christ is the eternal love and goodness of God, ever seeking to draw men to him. Again and again in his sermons Luther dwells on the truth of the believer's union with Christ, his incorporation into Christ, so that all Christ has is his, the sinner himself assuming Christ, so to speak, as his own body. Given this union, nothing, neither the world, nor the devil, nor calamities of any sort, can hurt him or overwhelm him. By faith he is bound to Christ, so that there arises, as it were, one person,

42. *W.A.*, IV, 87, 35.
43. *W.A.*, III, 426, 28; cp. III, 548, 23.
44. 2 Cor. 5:21.

enabling the believer to declare, 'I am Christ, not indeed in my very person, but by sharing in his righteousness, his victory, his life'.

It has to be said, though, that Luther offers no detailed theory of the atonement, important as his principles were for the influence they exerted on Reformation theology generally. His fullest statement occurs in his comment on Galatians 3:13: 'Christ redeemed us from the curse of the Law, having become a curse for us', in his commentary on that epistle published in 1535.[45] Here he depicts the death of Christ as a legal penalty rendered for the sin of mankind. Sin and its penalty being laid upon and accepted by this one man – who also was God – we sinners are henceforth set free.

> If the sins of the whole world are upon that one man, Jesus Christ, then they are not upon the world. . . . Further, if Christ himself was made guilty [*ipse factus reus*] of all the sins which we all have committed, then we are absolved from all sins, yet not through ourselves, our own works or merits, but through him.

Luther does not consider whether the wrong involved in human sin can be righted by another wrong inflicted on the innocent, or whether outraged justice can ever in such a case be morally satisfied. The atonement is regarded as a purely objective event in which man himself has no part, the salvation which Christ brought to pass being adequately proportioned to man's sin. Yet it would scarcely be fair to Luther not to view his doctrine in a broader perspective, for what his whole teaching emphasizes is that it is in Christ that we see God, and in his death, to which he was willingly submissive, that supreme manifestation of God's love for us by means of which saving faith is kindled in us. Yet this does not alter the fact that, in his eyes, the atonement is essentially the reconciliation of God to man. Such is made unmistakably plain in the third article of the *Augsburg Confession*, which states plainly that Christ having 'truly suffered, been crucified, dead and buried, that he might reconcile the Father to us, and might be a victim [*ut reconciliaret nobis Patrem, et hostia esset*] not only for original guilt but also for all actual sins of men'.[46]

We have already remarked that Luther's conception of Christ's person depends on that of his work. The christological dogma as defined in the fourth and fifth centuries he accepts wholeheartedly, not merely from a respect for its antiquity but as embodying the conditions which made Christ's work possible. Christ himself was not and could not have been a sinner, or a mere man however good, or even a demi-god. He is one with man in his humanity, certainly, but as touching his divinity he is raised infinitely above him. So whatever our own state of sin we have 'a brother in heaven who is at the same time Son of God'. Moreover, it is God's will that he himself should be known only through Christ, who is 'the mirror, the means, the way' to this end.[47] He therefore who does not know God in Christ will never and nowhere find him outside Christ: nay, 'to seek God outside Jesus is the Devil'.[48] God, that is, is known to us (and the fact is for Luther of decisive

45.  For the Galatians commentary (1535) see *W.A.*, XL (ii), 1–184. Part of it (chaps. 5 and 6) is translated in *W.M.L.*, XXVII, 1–149.
46.  Kidd, *Documents*, 263.
47.  *W.A.*, XL (i), 602.
48.  *W.A.*, XL (iii), 337, 11.

importance) solely through the medium of Christ's humanity, especially in its humility, its weakness and its suffering. And this is possible only because of the complete unity of the two natures in Christ, the divine and the human, so allowing, Luther thinks, the full significance of the doctrine of the *communicatio idiomatum*, 'the interchange of the properties', the view, in other words, that both natures, while separate, are yet so intimately related that the attributes of the one may be expressly predicated of the other.[49] In this regard Luther stands firmly with Cyril of Alexandria, as against the possibly Nestorianizing tendency of Zwingli and even of Calvin. It is a christology which is clearly consonant also with his doctrine of Christ's eucharistic presence.

### God, providence and predestination

In saying that we can know God only in Christ Luther does not of course exclude what may be called a 'theology of the natural', but by this should not be understood the scholastic natural theology. The latter, based on Aristotle, Luther wholly disclaimed, as was manifest from his academic *Disputatio contra scholasticam theologiam* of September 1517. 'It is an error', he there declares, 'to say that without Aristotle no one becomes a theologian. On the contrary, one only becomes a theologian when one does so without Aristotle. . . . The whole of Aristotle is related to theology as darkness is to light.'[50] 'Natural theology,' as the product of the supposedly 'natural' reason of fallen man, could better be described as 'unnatural'. It is misleading to assume that man can arrive at a sound but incomplete 'rational' knowledge of God, to which revelation adds only the necessary supplement and completion. The truth is rather that all man's knowledge of God is and must be *revealed*, in that revelation is not a mere appendix to reason but something the acceptance of which requires a transformation of reason itself – a critique of reason, one might say, carried out on the ground of faith and grace. This means that the Christian doctrine of God is contained in the *whole* of Christian doctrine, from which no purely rational 'idea' of God can be abstracted, the centre and focus of the entire Christian creed being Christ himself. Thus to speculate on the attributes of God apart from what Christ disclosed concerning him in his historical mission is a futile exercise.[51] Further, it introduces a dichotomy into the distinction between natural and supernatural, the human and the divine, nature and grace which amounts – and here Luther again points his finger accusingly at scholasticism – to

---

49. Cf. A. Harnack, *A History of Dogma* (English trans., London, 1894–99), VII, 198f.: 'God's grace is only manifest in the historical work of the historical Christ. On the one hand we see in Christ that "God has entirely emptied himself and kept nothing which he could have given to us" – so there is the firmest assurance of the full deity of Christ, – on the other hand we see him in the manger and on the cross. The two, however, are not side by side with each other, but in the abasement faith sees the glory.' The thought of the *infant* Jesus, we may note, always had an intense appeal for Luther.
50. *W.A.*, I, 226, 14ff, 26ff.
51. God as he is in himself, in his absoluteness, says Luther, sinful man can neither understand nor commune with. Only as he is revealed (*revelatus*), dressed and clothed (*vestitus, indutus*), in his word and promises can we approach him.

a gross misconception. For the notion that revelation is no more than a 'supplementing' of reason is paralleled by that which sees in grace only a 'perfecting' of nature. In this way the worldly and the heavenly are contrasted in a manner which is doubly false, since the former is both worse and better than scholasticism pretends.

A theology of the natural, on the other hand, approaches nature in the light of divine revelation, and in so doing can still have ample use for 'reason', except that it does not try to render God an object of speculative philosophizing – 'playing blind man's buff with God and making vain error and always missing the mark, calling God what is not God and not calling God what is God'.[52] Nevertheless he is certainly known to us to exist, since all creatures serve as 'masks' by means of which his own being is at once concealed and revealed (*absconditus et revelatus*).[53] And this implies not only that all natural orders are instinct with the divine presence but that human history too is the sphere of God's operation. For the omnipotence of God does not entail his capacity to do what in fact he does not will to do – and a vast deal of scholastic disputation had been devoted to such absurdities – but rather the power whereby he actually controls, governs and effects all things. 'All things which we do, though they may appear to be done by change and chance, are yet done necessarily and immutably if you have regard to the will of God.' And again: 'God foreknows nothing by contingency, but he foreknows, purposes and does all things according to his immutable, eternal and infallible will.'[54] So we reach that most profound of Luther's doctrines which sees God's presence and action in the very least of things no less than in the greatest, allowing us to say that, in truth, he is nearer to all creatures than they are to themselves. Thus his absolute transcendence is balanced by his omnipresent immanence.

The reformer's trust in divine providence was a characteristic of his personal piety throughout his life. That there were hostile demonic powers he did not for a moment doubt – did he not, during his stay at the Wartburg, throw his inkpot at the devil when the evil one visited him there? – but neither did he doubt that God had them in leash. Before setting out for Worms in 1521 he declared to his friend Spalatin that he would thither go even if there were as many devils in the place as tiles on the roofs to prevent him. God would protect his own!

This thought brings us to Luther's beliefs on predestination. The doctrine had, following St Augustine, been taught in one way or another by all the leading medieval theologians. Peter Lombard, for instance, had maintained that in God all passivity or dependence on men's decisions is absent, while St Bonaventura upheld the principle that the divine predilection is the cause and not the effect of such goodness as is shown by his creatures; and although St Thomas Aquinas employed the same idea in seeking to reconcile the mystery of predestination with God's purpose that all men should be saved, the nominalists urged the absolute, not to say arbitrary, freedom of the divine choice, whether for salvation or damnation. Luther's conviction is that God's purposes are not and cannot be thwarted by the human will, just as all notion of merit on man's part must be ruled

---

52.  *W.A.*, XIV, 206, 31ff., and 207, 3–13.
53.  *Ideo universa creatura eius est larva*; see *W.A.*, XL (i), 174, 3.
54.  *W.A.*, XVIII, 615, 31 and 12.

out.[55] Human aspiration after righteousness could never be the cause of election.[56] But what really interests Luther is the positive aspect of the doctrine, which so far from being intimidating is to him infinitely comforting. To the elect, he says, and to those who have the Spirit, predestination is 'the very sweetest of all doctrines', although to the worldly, as is scarcely to be wondered at, 'the bitterest and hardest of all'.

> Thus [*God*] proves through all these things, not our will, but his inflexible and sure will of predestination. For how would it be possible for a man to break through all these in which a thousand times over he would despair, unless the eternal and fixed love of God led him through them, and the Spirit himself by his presence led us and made intercession for us with groanings that cannot be uttered?[57]

Unfortunately in his exchanges with Erasmus in 1525 Luther seems to have been driven, all too like Augustine in the latter's prolonged dispute with the Pelagians, to more extreme and negative conclusions under the pressure of his own arguments. The humanist's *Diatribe on Free Will (De libero arbitrio)* was published by Froben in the autumn of 1524, and is to this day eminently readable, shot through as it is with the author's ironic wit. He was not, for example, quite taken in by the reformers' insistence in referring everything to the test of Holy Writ: 'Whatever men read in the Bible they distort into an assertion of their own opinion, just as lovers incessantly imagine that they see the object of their love wherever they turn.' But the subject raised, basically that of the omnipotence of God, was of profound importance theologically, and when Luther answered Erasmus with a treatise *On the Bondage of the Will (De servo arbitrio)* he treated the matter with the highest seriousness, voicing his own impatience with what he considered 'so unlearned a book from so learned a man'.[58] His reply does not, it must be admitted, show the reformer in the most engaging light, with his frequent abusiveness and repeated insinuations as to the humanist's personal levity and scepticism. Nevertheless it is one of Luther's most carefully contrived essays in systematic theology, and he himself was proud of it. Certainly Erasmus was no professional theologian, for all his doctor's degree, and while he tends to view the whole issue as perhaps hardly more than an interesting topic for debate, Luther felt that it was one that touched his religious convictions at their heart.

In any case Erasmus had not really understood Luther's position in accusing him of denying human volition. Luther did not regard man as an automaton; psychologically he is free in respect of 'things beneath him'. Where for the reformer he is not free is in his inability, through the corruption of his nature, to fulfil God's commands, which are not relative but absolute. Thus there can be no admission of 'congruent' (or approximate) merit as distinct from 'condign' (which could be

---

55. *W.A.*, LVI, 83, 27.
56. *W.A.*, LVI, 89, 15.
57. *W.A.*, LVI, 382, 4.
58. See Smith, *Luther's Correspondence*, ep. 645. *De servo arbitrio* is printed in volume XVIII of the Weimar edition (600–787). There is an English translation of both Erasmus's *Diatribe* and Luther's answer in E. G. Rupp and P. S. Watson, eds., *Luther and Erasmus: free-will and salvation* (Library of Christian Classics) (Philadelphia and London, 1969); see also *W.M.L.*, XXXIII.

seen as placing God under an obligation), something which Erasmus himself conceded to be beyond man's reach. Luther fell back on a striking simile to describe the human condition:

> The human will is like a beast of burden. If God rides it, it wills and goes as God wills; if Satan rides it, it wills and goes as Satan wills. Nor can it choose its rider, nor betake itself to him it would prefer, but it is the riders who contend for the possession.[59]

But if this is so then surely man's will is constrained, and in a fashion that seemed to Erasmus Manichaean? Luther's rejoinder is to insist that human reason cannot comprehend God's ways and that it is the summit of faith to believe that God, 'who saves so few and condemns so many', is nonetheless merciful, and that 'he who has made us necessarily doomed to damnation' is at the same time just, even though, in the eyes of such as Erasmus, 'he would seem to delight in the tortures of the wretched, and to be more deserving of hatred than of love'. If reason, that is, cannot accompany faith, then faith must venture on alone. Virtue for a Christian, however, lies in faith, not in reason. Granted that God is both omniscient and omnipotent only one conclusion is possible: 'God foreknows nothing subject to contingencies, but he foresees, foreordains, and accomplishes all things by an unchanging and efficacious will. By this thunderbolt free will sinks shattered in the dust.' In short, the divine will is absolutely sovereign and is not to be questioned, a truth which to the man of faith is no terror but an infinite consolation. Luther, who on this point is as emphatic as Calvin, is writing not to satisfy the curiosity of the worldly but to reassure the faithful. Let a man direct his mind to what God most mercifully has revealed of himself in Christ, for by the light of grace we can perceive much that is only a riddle to us by that of nature, although to that most baffling of all questions, why God should damn men who by their own strength cannot but sin, only the light of glory in the life to come will disclose the answer.

## Sin

The fact of our sinfulness is revealed to us by the Law. 'Before the Law came we were living at ease, secure, imagining nothing was wrong; but afterwards the Law entered in, and showed us what kind of people we were, and commanded those things which, even had we so wished, we could not have performed.'[60] The sins we actually commit stem from, to quote Luther's words in his Romans lectures, 'an inclination to evil, a distaste [*nausea*] for what is good, an aversion from truth and wisdom, a delight in error and darkness, a hatred and avoidance of good works, and a headlong course towards the bad';[61] in a word, from *original sin*, the effect of which is a dislike of all that is sound and a fatal attraction to all that is harmful.

---

59. Rupp and Watson, *op. cit.*, 140. The analogy goes back to St Augustine (*Libri III Hypomnesticum contra Pelagium*, a work however of uncertain attribution). 'Hence it follows', says Luther, 'that free choice without the grace of God is not free at all, but immutably the captive and slave of evil, since it cannot itself turn to good' (141).
60. *W.A.*, XXXIX (i), 558, 2.
61. *W.A.*, XVI, 312, 10.

Here Luther is doing more than simply to reiterate the accepted doctrine; he goes beyond Aquinas, who regarded original sin as consisting formally in *privatio justitiae originalis*, loss of original righteousness – or even indeed Augustine.[62] Rather is it a condition which affects man's entire nature, spreading disharmony and corruption throughout his whole being. In this sense man is *totus depravatus*, 'totally depraved'. But his resulting concupiscence (*concupiscentia carnis* is Luther's most frequent expression) is not to be confused, as was usual in the scholastic theology, with a psychological 'fleshliness'. When he says *totum hominem esse carnem*, that 'the whole man is flesh',[63] he is deliberately falling back on Pauline ways of thought and implying not simply 'sins of the flesh' but all moral evil, the greed, envy, strife, hatred and so forth which the apostle himself lists, as in Galatians 5:19ff. For the essence of sin lies in man's disposition always to seek his own ends, even in his morality, even indeed in his religion. Not only is he, as Augustine held, *curvatus*, 'bent' (towards the things of the world) but *curvatus in se*, 'bent in upon himself', enclosed in a vicious circle of egocentricity.[64] It is for this reason that his will is not really 'free will' at all, but only 'self will', the medium of an unremitting self-concern and self-interest issuing in self-righteous virtue as well as self-regarding vice. All the same, it would be wrong to suppose that Luther teaches man's incapacity for any good, especially in regard to the ordinary affairs of life. Between the recognizably good man and the evil liver there obviously remains a vast difference.

The origin of human sinfulness Luther attributes of course to the fall of Adam.[65] Adam, for him as for all other Christians at that date, was, it need hardly be said, a historical figure and his lapse a historical event. However, he was not looked on merely as an individual at the beginning of human history, but the 'head' of corporate humanity, our 'first parent', so that what affected him affects his entire posterity also. Man today therefore stands in complete contrast with what he was before the fall, when the 'image of God' (*imago Dei*) in which he was first created was destroyed or at least defaced. For as Luther understands it the 'image of God' signifies not simply man's soul, his rational nature as such, but more properly the relationship in which he stands to God. When this state of original righteousness, in which man clearly reflected his Maker, was lost by sin, the 'image' likewise could be said to be obliterated, since if a man ceases to reflect God he is bound to reflect the devil instead. But Luther, we should note, is more concerned with the effect of original sin than with explanations of its cause, although he does not attribute this

62. St Thomas (esp. *Summa Theol.*, II, i, 99, 81–84), like certain of his predecessors, distinguishes the formal element – loss of original righteousness – in original sin from the material element, *concupiscentia*, concupiscence. But he further distinguishes from these a prelapsarian state of *prima naturalia*, pure nature, whereby man was able to direct himself to a supernatural end. Thus for Aquinas the fall left man in a state of nature in itself unimpaired, a view very much less pessimistic than Augustine's, let alone Luther's.
63. *W.A.*, XVIII, 742.
64. 'For Scripture describes man as bent inwards upon himself, and seeks himself in all things' (*W.A.*, LVI, 356, 4). Cf. LVI, 359, 9 and 361, 15.
65. Luther's teaching on the fall is fully presented in his *Sermons on Genesis* (*W.A.*, XXIV) and *Lectures on Genesis* (*W.A.*, XLII–XLIV).

to God himself. To such questions as why God permitted the fall in the first place, or allowed its consequences to descend to the human race as a whole, there is no answer. One can say only that the divine will has neither cause nor reason. God is ultimately hidden in his own majesty (*absconditus in majestate*), and for us to try to penetrate this divine obscurity is both impious and futile.

## Man and society: the two kingdoms

The presence of sin in the world inevitably affects the structures of human society itself, and it is to the problem which this raises for Christian belief that Luther devotes some of his most fruitful thinking.[66] Here on earth he distinguishes, following St Augustine, two 'kingdoms' or 'realms': that of God or Christ, and that of the world. The citizens of the first kingdom are the true believers in Christ, Christ's own subjects. The citizens of the second are those, the vast majority, who are not subject to him, and who thus, as Luther was wont to put it, are under the law. This distinction is registered in the difference between the church, where the gospel is operative, and the state, the organized society of men. But over each realm, the temporal as well as the spiritual, God exercises a final sovereignty. Were the whole world indeed, so Luther supposes, to consist of true and faithful Christians no civil government, 'no prince, king, lord, sword or law', would be needed. What would be the use of earthly rulers exerting coercive authority in a world made up of Christians having 'the Holy Spirit within their hearts, who instructs them to wrong no one, to love everyone, and willingly and cheerfully to suffer injustice and even death from everyone'?[67] But as, on the contrary, the world consists very largely of unbelievers and sinners – for Luther is not persuaded that true believers are other than few – the civil power is necessary, enacting laws and wielding the sword in order to preserve the society of men from anarchy and satanic destruction. 'The law is given for the sake of the unrighteous that those who are not Christian may through the law be externally restrained from evil deeds.'[68] In this respect the state is the servant of God, performing what Luther characterizes as God's *opus alienum*, his 'strange work' of forcible restraint and punishment; strange because at once needful yet alien to his nature and purposes. Thus the state may be called, thanks to the presence therein of sin, the 'Kingdom of God's left hand', whereas God's *opus proprium*, his 'proper work' declared in the gospel, has for its instrument the church, the 'Kingdom of his right hand'.[69]

God's purposes in the world are, as we have already said, realized through the

---

66. See in particular his treatise *Von weltlichen Obrigkeit* ('Of Worldly Authority') written in 1523 (*W.A.*, XI, 229–80; (*W.M.L.*, XLV 75–129). But his views are also given free utterance in his *Address to the Christian Nobility*, in his writings against the 'fanatics', and, notoriously, in his pamphlet attacking the peasants in the uprising of 1524–5.

67. *P.E.*, III, 234. Luther's use of the terms 'kingdom' and 'government' is not without ambiguity. See W. D. J. Cargill Thompson, 'The "Two Kingdoms" and the "Two Regiments": Some Problems of Luther's *Zwei-Reiche-Lehre*,' in *Studies in the Reformation: Luther to Hooker* (London, 1980), 42–59.

68. *P.E.*, III, 235; cf. 249.

69. *W.A.*, LII, 26f.

natural 'orders': the family, men's differing vocations, the state itself. All these have their requisite function in human life and so their appropriate place in God's design, either to secure the continuance of his creation, as with the first two, or, as with the third, to prevent the devil from having his full way with it. Accordingly all three demand men's honour and respect. The idea of the 'natural law' (*lex naturae, lex naturalis*) Luther accepts as expressive of the will of God and therefore as a vehicle of his self-revelation; but he does not concede that it is so plainly written in the human heart that any one at all is in a position to act in obedience to it. 'Natural law and reason are a rare thing among the children of men', whereas 'natural idiots' are many.[70] Luther, we may add, was no democrat, at any rate in the modern, egalitarian sense; of peasant stock himself, he had a shrewd understanding of, as well as a natural sympathy with, the common people, and he was not sentimental about their weaknesses and limitations. He feared what Erasmus called the 'tumult' no less than did that fastidious scholar himself, stressing non-resistance as a Christian duty. He was in no way therefore an apologist for rebellion, whatever the supposed justice of the cause. Only duly constituted authority had the right to use the sword, which was why, in principle, he denounced the Peasants' Revolt. But he insisted that princes had their obligations also, and needed to be reminded of them, especially as, more often than not, they were either fools or knaves.[71]

But whatever the quality of secular rule, whether good or bad, the spheres of the two kingdoms should never be confused. In other words, the church must never become political, as had the papacy, just as the state should in no wise endeavour to impose the gospel by force of law. By overstepping its proper limits both alike could frustrate the will of God.[72] Hence any attempt to bring about the Kingdom of Heaven by coercive means will only result in disaster. Nevertheless Luther's deep-rooted differences with radicals like Thomas Müntzer, for example, induced him more and more to press on external authority the obligation to maintain the teaching of sound doctrine as well as the liberty of true worship. Heresy accordingly was not to be tolerated: to propagate, for instance, the notion that Christ was not divine but a mere man, as certain anabaptists, so Luther believed, did do, he considered to be not simply heresy but sheer profanity and blasphemy, and to be punished accordingly. Moreover it would appear that, in the last resort, the actual determination of what constitutes heresy falls to the civil authority – an effective subjection of the church to the state, even in spiritual matters, such as Calvin could not for one moment have contemplated.

The influence of Luther's beliefs and ideas on the whole Protestant movement

70. *W.A.*, LI, 212, 14.
71. *P.E.*, III, 258.
72. *P.E.*, III, 237. 'The devil is always trying to cook and brew the two Kingdoms into one another. The temporal ruler tries to teach and rule Christ in the devil's name and tell him how he ought to manage the Church as well as the civil power. The false Papists and the fanatics are always trying to teach and manage the temporal order. So the devil busies himself on both sides and has much on his hands. But God will teach him!' (*W.A.*, LI, 239, 24). On Luther's view of the difference between divine and worldly standards of justice see F. E. Cranz, *An Essay on the Development of Luther's Thought on Justice, Law and Society* (Cambridge, Mass., 1959).

can hardly be overestimated. There were elements in it, no doubt, both doctrinal and ecclesiological, which did not stem from him and which, on certain matters, he vigorously opposed. The divergences in outlook between himself and the Swiss leaders were sometimes, as we shall see, sharply edged. Yet all but the most radical, perhaps, owed him much, and often far more than they were disposed to admit. Spiritually he was a true creator, the Reformation's most powerful personality and most fertile mind. When he died, prematurely aged, early in 1546, his disciple Melanchthon, the always-faithful 'Master Philipp', could only lament, 'Alas, gone is the horseman and the chariots of Israel!' For the Protestant cause had lost one who, as history already had shown, did more for it than any other human agent. But although Luther proved so great a force for change, giving rise to what was virtually a new religion in Christendom, his thought still stayed within the orbit of Catholic orthodoxy. Essentially, his viewpoint was medieval and he was little drawn to the insights and attitudes of the Renaissance. Thus his break with Erasmus resulted not simply from a theological difference, however significant: the two men were remote from one another, in outlook as in temperament, Luther's resting on the theocentricity of traditional belief, the humanist's on his sense of the inherent capacity of men to fashion their own destiny. The former's medievalism is apparent in his insistence on the objectivity, the sheer 'giveness', of revelation and grace, which is the real reason why the charge, so often brought against him by his critics, of individualism and subjectivism is misdirected. That Protestantism in some of its aspects was soon to manifest both is not in question. But Luther himself cannot rightly be accused of them, for what he strove to do was to make religion at once prophetic and personal, to teach men to see it as a relationship between God and humanity which the Almighty in his sovereign freedom himself determines but which is also to be gladly acknowledged and gratefully accepted by each and every man who recognizes himself to be a sinner. Hence Luther's consistent message was that the gospel of redemption which the scriptures so unambiguously proclaim must be met with the response of a living faith. But to say that he was interested only in individual salvation and the state of the believer's mind is refuted by his entire doctrine of the church, of the sacraments, and not least of the Christian life itself.[73] For there is, again, no substantial truth in the further charge that Luther failed to draw out the ethical, and more particularly the social-ethical, implications of faith by inculcating a pietism that would effectually abandon the social order to secular authoritarianism. A distinction, in other words, has to be pressed between Luther's own teachings and the 'Lutheranism' subsequently moulded by historical circumstances, notably in Germany. Such later Lutheranism departed in important respects from Luther's spirit and characteristic positions. This is not to deny that the great reformer's work did lead to the establishment of new, 'Lutheran' churches and wrought large changes not only in theology but in the whole

73. Luther saw human morality as having a wider basis than Christian ethics, which is grounded in his cardinal doctrine of justification by faith. The performance of civic and social duties is thus a Christian obligation. Public office must be counted among such responsibilities. The state exists for certain purposes which the church itself cannot achieve. See Steinmetz, 'Luther and the Two Kingdoms', *op. cit.*, 112–25.

conception of the nature of the ecclesiastical institution and its role in society. Much of this, however, was more or less accidental, neither directly prompted by him nor of special concern to him.

Chapter 5

# HULDRYCH ZWINGLI

### Reform at Zurich

Although the Reformation had its beginnings in Germany they were quickly followed by a parallel movement in Switzerland. But the parallelism should in no way obscure the differences, for in its Swiss centres the reforming movement from the start took on a distinctive character, determined by the peculiar circumstances of the country, geographical, political and cultural. No less important, however, was the constraining personal influence of its two great leaders, men of a very different temper and cast of mind from Luther's and whose convictions, aims and attitudes were to give to the Swiss Reformation and the churches which were its heirs a propagandist edge and thrust such as its German counterpart never came to possess. The scene of Huldrych (or Ulrich) Zwingli's activities was Zurich, in German-speaking Switzerland, and of Calvin's (though Jean Chauvin was himself a Frenchman from Picardy) Geneva, where French was the native tongue. The Zurich-based reform, which spread from the lakeside city to Bern and then Basel, preceded that of Geneva and was complete some years before Calvin's extraordinary enterprise began. But with the death of Zwingli on the battlefield of Cappel on 11 October 1531 – as also that, no less premature though from natural causes, of his follower Oecolampadius of Basel – its momentum slackened, yielding the leadership to the sister city to the south-west. By an agreement, the *Consensus Tigurinus*, arrived at in 1549 the two wings of the Swiss movement became one at a time when the cause of Protestantism in Germany had suffered a severe reverse.

Zwingli himself is an arresting figure, of considerable originality as a thinker, independent and consistent in his judgements and of an ambition in his political schemes which, had the extent of them been known to him, would have alienated the sympathies of Luther still further. Moreover, as Zwingli differed from Luther, so too did Calvin from Zwingli; indeed the contrasts between all three open up an intriguing study. Calvin, writing in 1540 to Guillaume Farel, declared of the two older men that 'if they are compared with each other you yourself know how greatly Luther exceeds'.[1] It is an opinion with which, in the light of history, none would quarrel. Luther is of so commanding a stature as to overtop any of his contemporaries on the European stage. But comparison is not really to the point; it is better to understand wherein the two diverge and to appreciate what Zwingli had especially to contribute. The Zuricher was always somewhat concerned to stress his independence of Luther's views, while at the same time acknowledging the power of the latter's teaching. Modern research has shown fairly conclusively that

---

1. 'Si inter se comparantur, scis ipse quanto intervallo Lutherus excellat.' See A. L. Herminjard, *Correspondance des Réformateurs dans les pays de langue française* (Geneva, 1866–97), VI, 191.

from 1518 onwards the impact of the Wittenberg leader on Zwingli's theological thinking was strong,[2] but the Swiss cleric had already become imbued with reformist ideas, arising mainly from his humanist approach to the Bible. Disillusioned as he was with the Catholic penitential system, he had been deeply impressed by Hus's treatise on the church, but what he needed was an organizing principle for a consistent body of evangelical doctrine, and it was this which he found in Luther's writings.[3] Nevertheless he admitted no particular debt to Luther for what was, and was to remain, basic to his own religious outlook, namely that assurance of the overriding authority of scripture on which his whole subsequent programme of ecclesiastical reform was constructed. This he had discovered for himself.[4]

A month or so younger than Luther, he was born on New Year's Day, 1584, at the little town of Wildhaus, high in the Toggenburg about forty miles from Zurich. His father was a peasant proprietor in easy circumstances and chief magistrate of the district. His uncle, Bartholomäus Zwingli, dean of Weesen a few miles to the south-west, was a man of intellectual interests who saw to it that the boy was properly schooled, first at Basel and then at Bern, until at the age of sixteen he was old enough to attend the university of Vienna. From the first he showed an aptitude for Latin, as too for dialectic and music, which last indeed was to be a lifelong joy to him, so long as it played no part in church worship. At Bern he was taught by a humanist of repute, Heinrich Wölflin (Lupulus), who did much to imbue him with the spirit of Renaissance scholarship, although it was while there that he nearly joined that most scholastically-minded of religious orders, the Dominicans – not, perhaps, surprisingly, since he was well-grounded in the *via antiqua* of Thomism. His stay at Vienna lasted until 1502, when he entered the university of Basel, taking his bachelor's degree in arts two years later and his master's in 1506. It was in his final year here that he came under the influence of Thomas Wyttenbach (1472–1526), another keen humanist who himself afterwards went over to the Reform and whom Zwingli was wont to praise as 'the most learned and holiest of men', and one who had already taught him 'at a time when none of us had ever heard of Luther, except that he had published something on indulgences . . . what a cheat and delusion indulgences were'. It was from Wyttenbach also, as he tells us, that he learned to look to scripture as the supreme authority in matters of faith.[5] Among Wyttenbach's other pupils subsequently to take a lead in the reform movement were Wolfgang Capito (1478–1541), who for a time was a councillor of the archbishopric of Mainz, Leo Jud (1482–1542), afterwards pastor of St Peter's, Zurich, and Konrad Kürschner (1487–1550), who became professor of Hebrew at Zurich. In 1506 Zwingli was himself ordained priest and appointed to a charge at Glarus which he held until 1516.

2. See. W. Köhler, *Ulrich Zwingli und die Reformation in der Schweiz* (Tübingen, 1919); also A. Rich, *Die Anfänge der Theologie Huldrych Zwinglis* (Zurich, 1949).
3. Cf. R. Seeberg, *Lehrbuch der Dogmengeschichte*, 2nd ed. (Leipzig, 1908), IV, 356f.
4. 'I am not ready to bear the name of Luther, for I have received little from him. What I have read of his writings is generally found in God's Word', *Zwinglis Sämtliche Werke* (ed. E. Egli, G. Finsler *et al.*) (*Corpus Reformatorum*), II, 145f. This edition, which began publication in 1905, is referred to here as *S.W.*
5. See O. Farner, *Huldrych Zwingli, seine Jugend, Schulzeit und Studentjahre 1484–1506* (Zurich, 1943), Cf. *S.W.*, VIII, 84n and V, 718–20.

It was during these Glarus years that he first began a serious study of Greek, managing to teach himself, despite the paucity of adequate textbooks, in order, he says, 'that I might learn the doctrine of Christ from the original sources'. But he also read many classical authors and early church Fathers, among them Origen, Gregory of Nazianzus and Gregory of Nyssa, as well as Augustine and Jerome, although he did not neglect moderns like Pico della Mirandola and Erasmus, the latter's works probably being supplied to him by his friend Beatus Rhenanus, who was employed by several printers at Basel. Zwingli's admiration for the Dutch scholar grew, and from 1514 onwards his own beliefs were more and more a reflection of Erasmus's moralist 'philosophy of Christ'; for this was the time when his humanist enthusiasm was at its height. Later, when Luther's ideas began to affect him, differences arose between them. Erasmus was becoming uneasy at the course of events in Switzerland as well as in Germany. He did not approve of Zwingli's association with Hutten, whom he heartily disliked, and feared the direction which his erstwhile disciple might now be taking. On 9 December 1522 he wrote to Zwingli regarding an attack on the then pope, Adrian VI, a fellow-Netherlander and personal friend of Erasmus's, which, although anonymous, was generally, and correctly, considered to be from Zwingli's pen: 'I could', he averred, 'easily bear with the rashness of others did it not compromise good learning and good men and the evangelical cause, which they promote so stupidly that if anyone wished Christianity extinct he could not devise a better method of bringing this about than theirs.'[6] To this sharp rebuke Zwingli did not take kindly, and thereafter it was only a matter of time before the breach between the two men was complete, though the humanist's feelings seem to have remained more bitter than the Reformer's.[7]

From Glarus Zwingli moved to nearby Einsiedeln, the site of a popular shrine dedicated to the Blessed Virgin. Here he acquired a reputation as a biblical preacher, while greater leisure as well as the availability of a good library gave him further opportunity to pursue his patristic and New Testament studies. But the post was not one to retain him long and in December 1518 he accepted that of *Leutpriester* or 'people's priest', which carried the responsibilities of general ministry but offered also occasions for preaching of which from the first he made the most.[8] He at once started a continuous exposition of the New Testament on Sundays, a task which occupied him for several years, while on market days he preached on the psalter to country folk in the town square – for them a quite unfamiliar experience. No manuscripts of these sermons survive and it would appear that they were for the most part delivered extemporarily. Zwingli's pulpit style was fluent but subdued – it was a frequent complaint that he could not be clearly heard – but he was always forthright, simple and free, with homely

6. *S.W.*, VII, 631f. See C. Christ, 'Das Schriftsverständis von Zwingli und Erasmus im Jahre 1522', *Zwingliana*, 16 (1983), 111–25. Also G. W. Locher, 'Zwingli und Erasmus', *Zwingliana*, 13 (1969) 37–61.
7. Erasmus's last letter to Zwingli dates from the end of August 1523; see Allen, *Erasmi epistolae*, no. 1384.
8. See Farner, *Huldrych Zwingli, seine Entwicklung zum Reformator 1506–1520* (Zurich, 1946), 298–301.

illustrations.[9] Rhetoric, gestures and learned allusions were avoided. His denunciation of abuses, however, was not muted, and included an attack on the indulgence-vending of one Bernardin Sanson, although in this he had the approbation of his diocesan, the bishop of Constance, and even of Pope Leo X himself. More importantly perhaps, Zwingli's preaching was warmly endorsed by the city council, which as early as 1520 ordered that all preachers should keep to the New Testament and prove their doctrine from the Bible alone. The following year he became a canon of the minster and a citizen of Zurich, having renounced the papal pension he had hitherto drawn on account of his former service with Swiss mercenary troops. (He was by then a vigorous opponent of the mercenary system on grounds both patriotic and moral.)

Convinced as he was that the sole standard of truth in religion is provided by the *Schriftprinzip*, the letter of scripture, Zwingli was also won over to the Lutheran doctrine of justification by faith, seeing redemption only in the free grace of God through Jesus Christ as the one mediator.[10] Yet his private life was still by no means above reproach; certainly he lived in a state of concubinage, though this was so common in the Swiss dioceses as almost to have received official recognition.[11] In 1522 he contracted a secret marriage with a widow, Anna Reinhart, a woman of higher social rank than himself; but it was an act which could not long be concealed and so caused him, along with a number of other priests, to petition the bishop of Constance, asking for formal countenance of clerical marriage, even if he could not have been in any doubt about what the answer would be.

The Reformation at Zurich, the miniature prototype of reformed Christianity, was effected more or less completely between the years 1522 and 1525, under Zwingli's leadership and by the inspiration of his evangelist preaching. Like Luther he believed that theological principle was primary, although, in this respect very unlike Luther, he was himself actively concerned to give it a radically practical application. Opportunity came in 1521 when, as a newly instituted member of the minster chapter, he also acquired a seat on the city council. On the other hand, he never attempted to force legislative changes upon laymen unprepared by instruction to receive them. The upshot was a religious revolution carried through with minimal opposition and a remarkable degree of smoothness. Scripture was recognized as its platform and its requirements, as interpreted by sound opinion, were to be enforced by public authority. Immediate issues were the practice of fasting, clerical celibacy and the cult of the saints, all of them hitherto sanctioned by immemorial usage but without, as it was now contended, biblical warrant. The approved method of settling matters was by public disputation organized by the council, such as that

9. Zwingli's preaching was until recently known only from some formal discourses published during his lifetime or from reports of his hearers. In 1957 however the indefatigable Oskar Farner published a translation of a manuscript attributed to Zwingli containing expositions of the gospels of Matthew, Mark and John (*Aus Zwinglis Predigten zu der Evangelien Matthäus, Markus und Johannes*). In the same year sermons on Isaiah and Jeremiah were also brought to light (*Aus Zwinglis Predigten zu Jesaia und Jeremia*). Both were published at Zurich.

10. See A. Rich, *op. cit.*

11. See G. R. Potter, *Zwingli* (Cambridge, 1976), 78f.

held towards the end of October 1523 on images and the mass.[12] The decision on this occasion was critical; the council ruled the elimination of both and unequivocally placed themselves outside the jurisdiction of the bishop of Constance and thus of Rome itself, their action being explained a few days later by Zwingli in his *Short Christian Introduction*. On Christmas Day communion was administered in both kinds in the minster and biblical preachments took the place of the daily celebration. The break with the old order was finally sealed when in reply to the bishop's attempt to justify the impugned practices both were explicitly rejected by the council on 15 June 1524, which set up a new church on the basis of the commune or congregation (*Gemeinde*). The dismantling of the church buildings (even organs were cast out) and the closure of the religious houses quickly followed.

Zwingli, still not satisfied, demanded the complete abolition of the mass and its replacement by a 'love feast', with, instead of an altar, a table covered with a white cloth and with unleavened bread on wooden platters and wine in wooden beakers passed round among the communicants. The sermon of course was given the central position. On 25 June Bible-readings or 'prophesyings' ousted the observance of the canonical hours, while by 1527 the number of holy days had been drastically reduced. Church government was assumed by the town council, which set up a court of discipline and regulated marriages. Zwingli himself attached high importance to an educated ministry, founding in 1525, with the aid of Jud and Myconius, a seminary for the training of pastors.

Thus the work of religious reform at Zurich was carried through, thanks to Zwingli's energy and single-minded pursuit of principle, with a consistency and thoroughness which Luther, who had no thought-out scheme of practical change and whose arrangements therefore were generally piecemeal, failed to accomplish. All in all it was a remarkable achievement.

### Zwingli's biblical theology

As a writer Zwingli is always clear and forthright, but often hasty; usually he took up his pen only to meet the demands of a pressing occasion.[13] The result was a certain partiality and superficiality; the searching profundity of Luther and the balance and system of Calvin were alike lacking. His most carefully considered work was his *Commentarius de vera et falsa religione* ('On the True and the False Religion'), published in the spring of 1525.[14] He had laboured at it for over three

---

12. M. Schuler and J. Schulthess, *Zwinglis Werke* (Zurich, 1828–42), VII, 311f. (referred to here as *S.S.*).
13. In addition to the collected editions of Zwingli's works already cited there is a selected edition, *Zwinglis Hauptschriften*, ed. F. Blanke, O. Farner and R. Pfister (Zurich, 1940–63; referred to here as *H.*) For English translations of a number of Zwingli's writings see *Ulrich Zwingli (1484–1531): Selected works*, ed. S. M. Jackson (New York, 1901), G. W. Bromiley, *Zwingli and Bullinger* (Library of Christian Classics, XXIV) (Philadelphia/London, 1953), and G. R. Potter, ed., *Huldrych Zwingli* (*Documents of Church History*) (London, 1978). On recent Zwingli study see V. Gäbler, *Huldrych Zwingli im 20 Jahrhundert. Forschungsbericht und annotierte Bibliographie (1897–1972)*.
14. *S.W.*, III, 590–911. There is a detailed discussion of it in P. Wernle, *Der evangelische Glaube nach der Hauptschriften der Reformation, ii: Ulrich Zwingli* (Tübingen, 1919), 246–306.

months and intended it to be read as a comprehensive account of his personal theological position. But it was not without a pragmatic aim also, being meant for the eyes of Francis I of France as himself a possible reformer, and it included a preface addressed to the king as dedicatee. Its influence in France however was slight (its Latin was never rendered into French) except in so far as its ideas found embodiment in Calvin's *Institutes*. Its leading theme is the contrast between the false religion of Rome and the truth as taught in scripture, through which alone God's saving word is uttered. But not the least important aspect of the book's message was the assurance it sought to convey that the state has nothing to fear from reformed religion, whatever might have to be said of the eccentric radicalism then being voiced in certain quarters, including Zurich; on the contrary, good Christian men would always make good magistrates, since church and state are of necessary mutual support. A subsequent and more pithy statement of Zwingli's teachings, likewise drawn up for the benefit of the French king, was his *Fidei expositio* (1531), the last theological work he ever wrote.[15] In this he informs the humanist monarch that on attaining Paradise – which who could doubt? – he would share the company of such heroes of pagan antiquity as Cato, Scipio, Socrates, Aristides and even Theseus and Hercules.[16]

In Zwingli as in Luther the restatement of Christian doctrine rests on two fundamental principles, a formal and a material. The formal principle, again as in Luther, is that of the supremacy of scripture, but the material principle differs; here it is not justification by faith alone but the sovereignty of God. First, however, let us consider Zwingli's attitude to the Bible, since it too is quite distinct from Luther's. The Swiss reformer approaches the sacred book from the angle of humanism; he sees it initially as an ancient text – indeed much of its authority derives directly from its primitiveness – to be studied as such, with scholarly care as well as reverence. The paramount importance of the scriptures for Christian belief was of course a doctrine in no way new: it was held alike by the early Fathers and by the scholastics. But Zwingli further holds that it must become a matter of individual conviction grounded in deep personal study: he himself had committed whole passages of St Paul's epistles to memory in their original language. The consequence was that the actual written words of scripture seemed to him sacred and to have an authority of their own.[17] Hence the canons of both the Old Testament and the New he accepted *in toto* and without question, although at first he appears to have had reservations about the Apocrypha, and in the New

---

15. *S.S.*, IV, 44–78. G. W. Bromiley, *Zwingli and Bullinger*, provides an English version (239–79).

16. Zwingli's first major statement of his beliefs was his *Apologeticus Architeles* (*S.W.*, I, 249–384), which, as its name implies, is an 'apology' or defence, 'once for all', of the reforming point of view. It was addressed to the bishop of Constance. 'Unremittingly', the author declares, 'I shall endeavour to restore the unity of the primitive Church. . . . The nearer ancient customs are to the Gospel, the more we should honour them.' Zwingli's programme of reform as a whole is set out in the Sixty-seven Articles (*Schlussreden*) published in January 1523 in preparation for the great public disputation arranged to take place at the end of that month. See *S.W.*, I, 458–65; and Potter, *Zwingli (Documents)*, 21–5, for an English translation.

17. See C. Nagel, *Zwinglis Stellung zur Schrift* (Freiburg-im-/Breisgau/Leipzig, 1896).

Testament some particular doubts as to the Apocalypse, probably because of its too materialist imagery. But it was plain to him that if scripture is directly inspired by the Holy Spirit, as he firmly believed it to be, then its study is a prime Christian duty and one must learn to submit oneself to its teaching in all things. No other authority had any right to impose doctrines or obligations of which this book knows nothing. But for the task of interpreting the Bible Zwingli was well equipped by his other studies, classical and patristic, and his treatment of the scriptures always remained humanist in spirit. In this he differed markedly from Luther, to whose own reading of the Bible, for all his indebtedness to Erasmus's Greek Testament, humanist disciplines contributed virtually nothing. Moreover the Swiss divine's attitude was stamped by his more rationalist cast of mind. At any rate it seems clear that for Zwingli the Bible was not directly related to a personal religious experience, as the Epistle to the Romans had been revelatory to Luther. Although his outlook as a reformer, that is to say, was determined through and through by scripture, it was so objectively, by the divine Word as a compendium of laws or principles more than as an inward light and inspiration. Here again he contrasts with Luther significantly.[18]

Zwingli's ideas on the role of scripture were first expounded in a sermon he delivered in the summer of 1522, at the behest of the city council, to a community of Dominican nuns at the Oetenbach convent, across the river from Zurich, a discourse printed later in the same year under the title *Von Klarheit und Gewissheit des Wortes Gottes* ('Of the Clarity and Certainty of the Word of God').[19] His aim was to explain to the pious ladies of this house, disturbed and confused as they were by the novel opinions then being voiced, the reasons for accepting the sole authority of the Bible, and to extol both its spiritual power and intrinsic lucidity, speaking out of his own experience and with copious illustrations from the sacred text itself. Thanks, he declares, to the image of God in all men, despite their sin, there is within them a deep though often hidden longing for God's saving Word, which the regenerative work of the Holy Spirit will both elicit and satisfy; for it is only from the Word that man's nature will draw the light and sustenance it needs. This power is inherent in it and does not require to be endorsed or reinforced by the church. Although Zwingli can assure his audience on the testimony of scripture itself that the divine promises will be fulfilled, he does not shirk the difficulty that the meaning of scripture is often on the face of it obscure and uncertain. 'If God', it will be asked, 'wants his Word to be understood, why does he speak in parables and riddles?'[20] But the impression is no more than superficial. By careful study the truth will emerge, partly because the saving message is essentially plain and intelligible to those who earnestly seek to profit from it, but also and principally because when the divine Word shines on the human understanding it enlightens it in such a way that it 'comprehends and confesses the Word and knows the certainty of it'. This again is the work of the Spirit, for what the Word states may be perfectly clear without its being heeded and taken to heart, as many passages in the Old Testament can be cited to prove. 'Even if you hear the Gospel of Jesus Christ from

18. Cf. F. Loofs, *Leitfaden zum Studien der Dogmengeschichte* (Halle, 1890), 799.
19. *S.W.*, I, 238–384. English translation in Bromiley, *op. cit.*, 59–95.
20. Bromiley, 72.

an apostle you will not follow it unless the heavenly Father teaches and draws you by his Spirit. . . . You must be *theodidact*, that is, taught of God, not of men.'[21] Accordingly it is not for us to judge scripture, we must ourselves be judged by it.

What precisely it is that constitutes the Word Zwingli does not lay down.[22] It is not necessarily the written word, since the spoken precedes this and may be independent of it. Indeed in many of the instances which Zwingli gives it is the latter which is shown to be really effective. Often he passes from one to the other without any attempt to explain their relationship. Nor however does he propound any theory of inspiration, and he is not apparently committed to the sort of literalism that became such a feature of later Protestantism. The written revelation, that is, is not exactly equivalent to the Word itself, but it is the form in which the divine utterance reaches us and thus has an authority of its own which must at all points be respected. Yet we do not find in Zwingli, as we do in Luther, an internal evaluation of the Bible, involving a comparison of part with part. For him it is in all its parts a disclosure of God's will for man, and he increasingly used it as such in dispute with adversaries. It was this view of scripture which was adopted by the earliest reformed confessions of faith, namely the *Basel Confession* of 1534 and the *First Helvetic Confession* of 1536.[23]

## The sovereignty of God and the mediation of Christ

We turn now to the material principle of Zwingli's theology, the doctrine of the divine sovereignty. All things, he holds, were foreseen, because foreordained, by God; indeed 'we call God Father because he can do what he pleases with us'. To have been the object of an incomprehensible divine choice is the most manifest proof of grace. But what lay behind this belief? Did it spring from a personal sense of election on Zwingli's part, or was it conceived as a controlling dogmatic principle independent, in the final resort, even of the scriptures?[24] The Zurich leader seems never to have undergone a religious experience comparable with Luther's, and this fact combined with his humanism may well account for his more detached and objective approach to doctrinal reform. It would be an error to minimize the emotional element in Zwingli's personal conviction: that the whole world is in God's hands like the clay in the hands of a potter was for him a deeply religious

21. *Ibid.*, 89.
22. 'By the Gospel we mean not only the writings of Matthew, Mark, Luke and John, but . . . all that God has revealed to man in order that he may instruct him and give him a knowledge of his will' (*Zwinglis Hauptschriften*, I, 106).
23. The *Basel Confession* was the work of Oswald Myconius and is based on a shorter formulary drawn up by Oecolampadius. The *First Helvetic Confession*, sometimes known as the 'Second Confession of Basel', was compiled by Heinrich Bullinger. Essentially it is Zwinglian, but Lutheran influence is also detectable. An English translation of the text of both Confessions is given in A. C. Cochrane, ed., *Reformed Confessions of the Sixteenth Century* (London, 1966), 89–111. The original text is in H. A. Niemeyer, *Collectio Confessionum* (Leipzig, 1840), 78–122. The *First Helvetic Confession* is also included in P. Schaff, *Creeds of Christendom*, III (London, 1877), 211–31.
24. The former was the view of E. Zeller (*Das theologische System Zwinglis*, 1853), the latter of C. Sigwart (*Ulrich Zwingli: der Charackter seiner Theologie*, 1855).

sentiment. At the same time his logical bent enabled him to deduce the theological consequences unflinchingly: if a principle were sound its implications also had to be accepted; his teaching has thus the merit of consistency. Yet he was no mere dogmatician but always a practical reformer, a man of action, and his doctrinal statements were usually framed, at times over-hastily, to meet a pressing need. The suggestion that, for example, his concept of God had its source in the speculations of Pico della Mirandola is quite unnecessary, for his theology was rooted firmly in the Bible.[25] That he was led to the doctrine of predestination, central to his whole idea of the divine providence and purpose, only by his reading of the scriptures he himself expressly states. He could allow no knowledge of God which was not a revealed knowledge.

Nevertheless there is in Zwingli's teaching a rationalist tone that is foreign to Luther. In his classical studies he had been impressed by the Stoicism of Seneca, while of the moderns the influence of Pico he would have admitted. The truth is that he had a religious philosophy of his own in which a determinist note is certainly present. Hence although the positive content of Zwingli's theology is biblical in origin, the style of its presentation indicates an attitude of mind which is less scriptural than humanist. This is especially evident in his main theological work, the short treatise *De providentia Dei*, 'On the providence of God'.[26] But a certain stiffness in the exposition of his beliefs disguises only partially the intensity of the feeling underlying them. Zwingli never undertook a fully systematic formulation of doctrine – his immersion in affairs and his premature death gave him no chance to do so – but the concise summaries of his teaching which he did draw up are enough to show the general coherence of his position. Whether had he lived he would have given the Swiss Reformation anything similar to what Calvin achieved in the *Institutes* it is idle to surmise.

Zwingli's stress on the unity of God arose from his insistence that the divine sovereignty cannot possibly be divided or shared, which in turn may have been a reaction against the popular piety, familiar enough at Einsiedeln, which assumed a variety of intermediaries between God and his worshippers. Although he in no way denies the doctrine of the Trinity his acceptance of it appears as no more than conventional. Certainly his view of it is monistic. Also he seems to conceive of God less as a heavenly Father than as the creator and ruler of the universe, always emphasizing his omnipotence and omniscience. Thus he thinks of God as eternally active and all-controlling, to the extent indeed of being the immediate cause of every event: *Providentia est perpetuum et immutabile rerum universarum regnum et administratio.*[27] That this in turn implicates God as the cause of evil as well as good

25. On Zwingli's indebtedness to Pico see J. M. Usteri, *Theologische Studien und Kritiken*, IV (1885), 625ff.
26. It was originally delivered unscripted as a sermon in the presence of Philip of Hesse at Marburg on 29 September 1529. For the text see *S.S.*, IV, 79–144 and *H.*, II, 81–250. Wernle (*op. cit.*, 246–306) provides a detailed commentary.
27. *S.S.*, IV, 84. On Zwingli's doctrine of providence see Wernle, 249, 251f. and G. W. Locher, 'Die prädestinationslehre der Theologie Huldreich Zwinglis in Vergleich mit der jeniger Martin Luthers und Johannes Calvins', in *Zwingliana: Beiträge der Geschichte Zwinglis, der Reformation und der Protestantismus in der Schweiz*, XII (1967), 470–509, 545–95.

he does not blink. 'If in man there is absolutely no free counsel, then are we compelled to confess that thefts, murders, and all manner of crimes are the work of divine Providence. For thus I say, we acknowledge Providence as carrying out and accomplishing all things.'[28] Or rather, if what men call crimes have God as their author, mover and instigator, then they are not crimes; whereas man, as their actual perpetrator, does act criminally. For although God is not bound by his revealed law man is, and is condemned by it. 'What God does he does without constraint; the other does it by a wholly evil disposition.' Hence God must logically be conceived as absolute power, above all law; were it not so he would be limited and his sovereignty impaired. Man is a sinner because he infringes a law to which he, as God's creature, is subject. On the other hand his dignity lies in the very fact that this same divine law is inscribed in his heart.

It is in full accord with this view that Zwingli underlines the doctrine of election much more firmly than Luther does. God's eternal choice of those whom he purposes to redeem is for the Swiss teacher the sole ground of our hope. 'The elect are the children of God even before they believe.' Election, in other words, precedes faith, which of itself not only is without merit but is not the means of our salvation. For although faith normally is the sign or mark of election it is not necessarily so; those who are of the number of the elect do not always come to a knowledge of the truth. Not only is this the case with children dying in infancy, it applies even to the heathen who can never have heard of Christ. Zwingli sees no reason, that is, why the saving purpose of the omnipotent God should not altogether transcend the means of grace which he has himself provided. So in his *Exposition* of 1531 he states that not only Old Testament worthies – Abel, Enoch, Noah, Abraham and the rest – but those also of classical history and even mythology are likewise considered to be saved: 'In short, there has not lived a single good man, there has not been a single pious heart or believing soul from the beginning of the world to the end, which you will not see there [*in Paradise*] in the presence of God.'[29] Nor will Zwingli concede that salvation so understood in any way renders otiose the work of Christ: he alone gives men access to the Father, inasmuch as it is in him only that the redeemed are elected. But Zwingli is content to maintain that where faith is not possible virtue will suffice, so long of course as it is not regarded as meritorious. For the law, as St Paul teaches, is written in the hearts of all men and the knowledge of God which this entails must obviously in certain circumstances be independent of the conscious knowledge of Christ.[30]

Zwingli's doctrine of predestination is, to use the technical term, *supralapsarian*, which means that he does not see the predestinating decree of God as consequent on the fall of Adam. His reason for holding it is, clearly, its intrinsic logic, and when in this matter he does seek guidance from antiquity – for he seems to have owed little or nothing to St Augustine – it is from Seneca, 'that noble and divine soul', in whom he admits to discovering a far higher spirituality than in the tortuous

28. *S.W.*, IV, 113. Zwingli's predestinarianism, resting as it does on a philosophical theory of divine omnipotence, amounts virtually to determinism. God is not only the ultimate cause, he is effectively the *only* cause, secondary causation having no real place in the system.
29. Bromiley, op. cit., 273f.
30. *S.W.*, III, 180.

argumentation of the scholastics.[31] Nor, again, does he hesitate to say that the fall was itself ordained by God, since the occurrence of sin in the world afforded the Almighty opportunity to manifest both his justice and his mercy, for if providence contrived the fall it also planned the redemption. In any event falsehood and injustice are the shadows which highlight justice and truth.[32]

The actual origin of sin Zwingli ascribes to the contrariety of soul and body, the tension between spiritual aspiration and the downdrag of carnal appetite.[33] Thus by the 'flesh' he means the 'fleshliness' of the actual physical body, so narrowing the sense in which St Paul uses the word. Indeed it was characteristic of Zwingli always to distinguish sharply between man's spiritual capacity and the animality of his physical nature, and he even thinks of God as actively assisting the former against the latter in the interest of man's true being. That the argument is more rationalist than biblical Zwingli himself is frank enough to admit at the close of his discourse. Nevertheless the assurance that all things are of God's determining induces, he believes, not fatalism but rather a joyful confidence, since the elect know that evil cannot finally overwhelm them. To be aware that one is the instrument of God and therefore entirely at his behest is the highest privilege.

The body-soul dualism in Zwingli's thought is not simply a moral but an ontological antithesis. The soul, which comes directly from God, has the principle of life within itself: *entelechy*, as the Greeks called it, 'an inexhaustible power, operation, activity and purpose'. Death accordingly does not affect the soul except to liberate it from its physical constraints, existence in this world being captivity rather than freedom. The body itself, after death, Zwingli regards as 'sleeping' until the final resurrection, when it will be reunited once more with the soul. But the latter, like God himself, cannot sleep, any more than air can fail 'to be clear and transparent when the sun arises on the earth'.[34]

Zwingli of course follows tradition in holding that sin began with Adam, who by his disobedience to divine law lost his primal innocence, and that from his transgression all mankind suffers, being unable now by nature to fulfil God's will. On the other hand Zwingli does not see the divine image as having been obliterated, although it has been obscured and in individual instances virtually effaced. Original sin itself he regards as more a state of disease (*morbus est et condicio*) or radical defect than of guilt.[35] However, albeit that man's actual condition is one which he inherits from birth without his own fault, he is, like a marred vessel, worthy only of destruction. Yet God in his mercy has elected some to eternal life, a redemption achieved through the mediation of his Son Jesus Christ.

> When supreme Goodness willed to give the supreme gift, it gave the most costly of all its treasures, namely itself. . . . Thus the Son of God is given to us as a confirmation of mercy, a pledge of grace, a requital of justice and an example of life, to assure us of the grace of God and to give us the law of true conduct.[36]

31. *H.*, II, 117–22.
32. *H.*, II, 156ff., 163f., 199–223.
33. *H.*, II, 135–40, 150–3.
34. Bromiley, 273f.
35. *S.W.*, IV, 307.
36. Bromiley, 250.

So, for all his emphasis on God's sovereignty, it is unquestionably Christ who is the vital centre of Zwingli's faith, as the one in whom God's justice is reconciled with his love by a sacrificial act of atonement for human sin, the second Adam making good the havoc wrought by the first. On this subject Zwingli writes with a devotional fervour approaching Luther's and far removed from the frigid dogmatism which is sometimes attributed to him in contrast to the warmth of the German reformer. At the same time his christology is in line with the distinctions he consistently draws between God and humanity, spirit and letter, substance and form. Thus he seems to juxtapose the two natures in the incarnate Son in a manner verging on Nestorianism:[37] 'The attitudes and properties of both natures are reflected in all Christ's words and works, so that the pious mind is able to see without difficulty which is to be accredited to each'; although he insists that 'the difference of nature does not involve a division of the person' and that 'the unity of the person continues in spite of the diversity of the natures', since Christ assumed manhood into the hypostasis or person of the divine Son.[38] According to his humanity, says Zwingli, he was born of a virgin ('without any violation of her virginity'), and after his ascension his omnipresence obtained only of his divinity, the humanity being localized in heaven after a manner consistent with the intrinsic nature of bodies. Here again that sense of the absolute unity of the one Christ which to Luther meant so much is attenuated, and its implications for his sacramental doctrine became only too apparent in the eucharistic controversy of Zwingli's last years.[39]

Although the gospel of Christ proclaims man's redemption it in no way permits us, according to the Swiss reformer, to infer that law as such is abrogated. Christ's work, in its essence, is a revelation of God's will and is therefore not to be set in contrast with that general revelation of truth and righteousness which attaches to the divine rule and governance of the world. The gospel, that is, must be seen as including the law; in fact, it is itself a new law, the *lex Christi*, reaffirming and perfecting the old. No doubt the Jewish ceremonial law has been superseded as a merely temporary exigency, but the moral law was inscribed not only on the Mosaic tablets, but, from the beginning, in the very hearts of men. That we are justified by faith alone therefore does not remove the binding necessity of law after justification. Inasmuch as it is an expression of God's will for man it can never lose its authority or its obligation, being both a guide to the believer and a warning to the wrongdoer.[40] What the gospel does deny is legalism. Christian liberty is freedom from ecclesiastical ordinances and the impious and futile attempt to place confidence in the supposed merit of 'good works'.

37. Cf. H. Sasse, *This is My Body: Luther's Contention for the Real Presence in the Sacrament of the Altar*, (Minneapolis, 1959), 150.
38. Bromiley, 251f.
39. The *communicatio idiomatum*, or interchange of the properties appropriate to each nature, Zwingli explains as only a figure of speech, *alloiosis*, whereby one thing is stated but another meant.
40. *H.*, XI, 345, IX, 127–9.

## A disciplined church

It was on such issues, in fact, that the Zurich reform started, namely the legitimacy of practices instituted and imposed only by the church, and especially fasting, clerical celibacy and the cult of the saints. The requirement of fasting was challenged quite suddenly during Lent in 1522, when a group of men that included three priests, of whom Zwingli was one, broke the traditional fast at the house of the printer Frohschauer by eating a meal of sausages. Zwingli himself did not partake, but he subsequently defended his friends' action in a sermon on what he saw as the proper use of meats. News of the offence spread and became a public scandal, the immediate outcome of which was the upholding of the ancient practice by the city council until the matter could be authoritatively settled.

On the question of celibacy Zwingli was only too well aware of the existing situation in which many priests, though nominally celibate, were to all intents married men, and in July of the same year he was, as we have said, among the signatories of a petition to his diocesan. The latter's response being negative, the abandonment of celibacy thereafter proceeded apace, more or less with the authorities' tacit sanction. As for the invocation of the saints, it had been the subject of a disputation as early as the summer of 1521, the outcome of which was that François Lambert (1486–1530), a visiting friar from Avignon, was won over to reformist ideas, and by the autumn of 1522 the destruction of images in the churches had begun. Eventually the council followed the popular move by expressly forbidding the saint cult, a decision which, along with the formal abolition of the mass, placed Zurich outside the jurisdiction of the Catholic church, which in Zwingli's opinion had ceased through its corruptions to be a part of the *communio sanctorum*. As he himself did not scruple to pronounce: *Ecclesia pontificum est ecclesia inimici hominis hoc est diaboli*, 'the church of the pontiffs is the church of the devil, the enemy of man'.[41]

Zwingli's own view of the church coincided basically with Luther's as the communion of all true believers, who in the nature of the case can be known only to God, their faith being the mark of that election in which their redemption stands. Every man of faith, that is, may justly see in his faith assurance that he himself is of the elect, though without possessing any such assurance concerning the apparent faith of others. Thus, since the divine election is secret, the true church must be invisible. Moreover it is to the latter alone that the 'notes' of unity, holiness, catholicity and apostolicity rightly apply. Externally, however, the church is, as with Luther, identifiable with the preaching of the Word and the due administration of the sacraments; but Zwingli adds a third condition, discipline, of which Calvin after him was to make so much. For the Zurich leader frankly admits that within the visible church, which he sees, more definitely than does Luther, as a covenanted society, there are some who are 'called Christians falsely, seeing that they have no inward faith'. Accordingly, although certainty is perhaps impossible, there must be, he thought, some means of publicly removing unrepentant sinners or unbelievers from the fellowship of the visible community, and he himself had no doubt that

41. Cf. E. Egli, ed., *Actensammlung zur Geschichte der Zürcher Reformation in der Jahren 1519–33* (Zurich, 1879), nos. 460 and 446. See Potter, *Zwingli* (*Documents*), 27f.

there was the clearest scriptural authority for this. Hitherto the pope or the diocesan bishop had exercised it, but his own substitute was somewhat more subtle and less authoritarian. No single individual could so use the power of the keys as to deprive another of his membership of the church; this was a responsibility which the community of the faithful as a whole must assume. First, an offender was to be warned privately by his local pastor; if on the evidence of reliable witnesses he failed to mend his ways he could then be named by the congregation.[42] If again no repentance or amendment was forthcoming the sinner was to be placed under the ban. In such action, necessary for the peace and good name of the church, no breach of Christian charity could be urged.

It was not long before Zwingli was faced with the practical necessity of putting his discipline to the test, and in the case of Christian reformers yet more radical than himself. The Swiss Brethren were at no time self-declared followers of his, having existed as a clandestine group long before he arrived in Zurich and whose antecedents can be traced back to the medieval Waldenses. But as evangelicals they welcomed the Zurich reform movement even though they continued to entertain their own notions of what a genuine reformation ought to effect. Thus at the public disputation of October 1523, when their spokesmen were Konrad Grebel, whom Zwingli himself described as 'a noble and learned young man', and an ex-Franciscan, Simon Stumpf, they took the opportunity to press their views on the city council, without, however, receiving a very sympathetic hearing. The visible church as they conceived it consisted of true believers only, whereas Zwingli recognized that on earth the Christian community, disciplined though it must always endeavour to be, will inevitably comprise both believers and unbelievers, wheat and tares, and that to eliminate all false Christians is not finally possible. The Brethren, on the other hand, had insisted that the Christian community must be an *actual* 'communion of saints' and that sinners should be excluded from its fellowship by an unsparing use of the ban. The standard of Christian living invoked rested on a biblical literalism stricter even than Zwingli's, which to some extent was tempered by his humanist scholarship. But scholarship and a reasoned exegesis the Brethren scouted as a threat to faith. In addition they rejected not only state control of the church but even state support, and in accordance with this opinion proposed that tithes should be secularized, a suggestion to which the council by no means warmed.

Furthermore, the question of the propriety of infant baptism was becoming a public issue. Certain people were refusing on conscientious grounds to have their children baptized, and Zwingli's young friend Balthasar Hubmaier voiced their objections with spirit. Matters came to a head at the beginning of 1525, when the 'anabaptists' or re-baptizers, as they were called, were summoned to defend their principles at another public disputation, those present on this occasion (17 January) including Grebel and Felix Manz. Zwingli, who disliked sectarianism, opposed them in person, urging that baptism, as the Christian counterpart of Old Testament circumcision, ought to be retained.[43] The council was persuaded by this reasoning

---

42. *S.W.*, II, 281.
43. See T. George, 'The Presuppositions of Zwingli's Baptismal Theology', in *Prophet, Pastor, Protestant: the Work of Huldrych Zwingli after Four Hundred Years* eds E. J. Furcher and H. Wayne Pipkin (Allison Park, Penn., 1984), 71–87.

and formally enacted that no breach of the rule of child baptism be permitted. Among those who preached defiance of the new law was Manz, who for his obduracy suffered the penalty of death by drowning.

The Swiss Brethren, like other such radical groups whose beliefs will be considered in detail in chapter 9, sought to dissociate themselves from public affairs and as far as possible withdraw from the organized life of society. Zwingli, however, by temperament as by experience a man of action and a firm upholder of the republican traditions of his city, by no means stood aloof from politics, seeing his mission rather as spanning both the ecclesiastical and the temporal. In other words, religious reform was to be promoted by political power, to the reshaping of society as a whole. Thus every stage of his movement had to be endorsed by the civic authorities. Nor did his concern stop there; for years he busied himself with schemes as much political as religious, discussing with Pirkheimer, as early as 1524, the possibility of a league between Zurich and Nuremberg, and in 1527 actually bringing about an evangelical front within the Swiss confederacy in the form of the Christian Civic Union (*Christliche Burgrecht*), which subsequently included Zurich, Bern, Basel, St Gall, Biel, Strassburg, Mülhausen and Schaffhausen. Its purpose was to provide collective security in the event of any one of the allies being attacked because of its religious faith. Actually he went even further, for his secret conversations with Philip of Hesse, had they borne fruit, might well have threatened the break-up of the Empire itself. Melanchthon was made aware of this danger and warned Luther, whose loyalty not only to the imperial idea but to the person of the emperor himself never wavered.[44]

Such grandiose political designs would have been quite impossible had the Swiss Reformation, like the German, not maintained the territorial principle, which anabaptist convictions altogether disallowed. Hence the importance to Zwingli of keeping infant baptism as a mark not only of entry into the church but also of the Christian commonwealth itself. In his sacramental teaching baptism was not *per se* a means of grace – its ritual administration was not in fact a necessity – but simply a covenant sign or symbol pledging faith and discipleship, certainly no more: that is, it was in no way a pledge of a life of achieved perfection, as the anabaptists contended, which Zwingli thought could eventuate only in intolerable legalism. Essentially he saw it as a mark of initiation, representing but not effecting an inward change in those who receive it, an interpretation he based on Matthew 3 and Romans 6. It might even be no more than an act of public testimony.[45] The anabaptists he emphatically held to be in error in so far as they associated such inward change with the actual administration of baptism. Their criticisms of the sacrament as traditionally understood he viewed sympathetically, but any

---

44. G. W. Locker, 'Zwinglis Politik: Grund und Ziel', *Theologische Zeitschrift*, 36 (1980), 84–102.
45. 'It is given and received for the sake of fellow-believers, not for a supposed effect upon those who receive it.' See Bromiley, 136f. Zwingli used the term *Pflichtszeichen*, 'a demonstration of allegiance'. His view of the sacraments generally was that of an outward sign of the believer's disposition and intent, more particularly a pledge of obedience and loyalty. Thus sacraments, of their very nature, must be subordinate to the word of God, whence they derive their meaning. See W. P. Stephens, *The Theology of Huldrych Zwingli* (Oxford, 1986), 180–93.

suggestion of rebaptism, or 'catabaptism', he objected to vigorously. The universal practice of infant baptism could be defended not only on historical grounds – Zwingli thought it probable that it went back to the apostles themselves – but on theological as well, as admitting, like circumcision under the Old Covenant, to membership of the Israel of God, although he definitely refused to connect it with the supposed guilt of original sin.

### The eucharistic controversy

Zwingli's clash with Luther occurred on the issue of eucharistic doctrine.[46] Their concluding and most personal exchanges on this vexed subject took place at Marburg, whither representative German and Swiss divines had been invited by Philip, the Landgrave of Hesse, who was convinced that the unification of the reform movements had become an overriding political need. This famous colloquy, known as the Colloquy of Marburg, was held during the first three days of October 1529, with Luther and Melanchthon heading the Saxon delegation, and Zwingli, Oecolampadius and Bucer the Swiss. On fourteen of the fifteen articles which Luther had drawn up at the Landgrave's request agreement was reached, but on the fifteenth, that concerning the Lord's Supper, it was found to be impossible, and some harsh words were uttered, especially on the Lutheran side.[47] According to Zwingli Luther thought Oecolampadius another Eck, while Zwingli himself found Melanchthon 'uncommonly slippery'; Luther he described, with embittered candour, as 'foolish and obstinate', wrong on both biblical and philosophical grounds. Yet despite the remark at the end of the meeting, always attributed to the latter, though in fact it was made by Bucer, 'you are of a different spirit from us', Zwingli could still comment, perhaps double-edgedly, that enough agreement had been reached 'on the rest of the doctrines of the Christian religion' to 'prevent the papal party from hoping any longer that Luther will be on their side'.[48]

To comprehend their differences it is necessary to look a little more closely at Luther's teaching on the eucharist. That the sacrament is effective *ex opere operato* he denied as far back as 1518: it is not, he said, the sacrament but the faith of the sacrament that justifies. What he was really stating, both then and later, was not that the sacrament of the altar has no objective efficacy, but that its efficacy depends on its being received in faith. By 1520 he had rejected the doctrine that the mass is in itself a sacrifice, maintaining that such spiritual sacrifices as we ourselves purport to offer in it are really offered by Christ on our behalf.[49] In his *Babylonian*

---

46. For a full account of the controversy see W. E. Köhler, *Zwingli und Luther: ihr Streit um das Abendmahl*, 2 vols (Leipzig/Gütersloh, 1924–53). The second volume was edited by E. Kohlmeyer and H. Bornkamm.

47. Kidd, *Documents*, no. 110. Also Potter, *Zwingli (Documents)*, 89–109, and the same author's *Zwingli*, chapters 12 and 13. After the conference Luther revised the articles in the form of what came to be known as the *Schwabach Articles*, which in turn constituted the basis of the *Augsburg Confession*. An attempt to reconstruct the Marburg Colloquy was made by W. E. Köhler, *Das Marburger Religionsgespräch 1529: Versuch einer Rekonstruktion* (Leipzig, 1929); see also Sasse, *op. cit.*, 269ff.

48. *S.W.*, X, 316–18, and Potter, *Zwingli (Documents)*, 107f.

49. *P.E.*, I, 312ff.

*Captivity* he forthrightly declares the notion that the mass is a sacrifice to be 'the most wicked of all' and one that brought 'an endless host of others in its train'.[50] The reason of course was that the teaching prevalent at the time seemed to involve the repeated 'immolation' of Christ on the altar and thus to impair the uniqueness of the one sufficient sacrifice offered on Calvary, a view with which the Swiss reformers entirely concurred.[51] With the doctrine of the presence, on the other hand, Luther dealt much less drastically. Transubstantiation he did repudiate without hesitation as implying the priestly 'miracle of the mass', which ran counter to his basic idea of the priesthood of all believers. But he nonetheless continued to hold the doctrine that Christ is really present in the sacrament as an object of faith, if not of clear understanding; that is, that Christ is present 'in, with, and under' the species of bread and wine, whose own substances, along with their accidents, persist. Such is made plain in his tract *On the Adoration of the Sacrament*, dating from 1523, in which he explains the presence of Christ in terms of the 'ubiquity' of his glorified body. As he puts it: 'The Body which you receive, the Word which you hear, are the Word and Body of him who holds the whole world in his hand, and who indwells it from beginning to end.'[52]

This belief was connected with the German reformer's very 'Alexandrian' doctrine of Christ's Person, whereby the union of the divine and the human natures is represented as so intimate and inseparable that the glorified humanity necessarily shares in the omnipresence of the divinity. Hence to speak in a literal way, as did Zwingli, of Christ's being *seated at the right hand* of the Father is impermissible, for what the words properly mean is simply that Christ participates fully in the glory and power of the Godhead, which is and cannot but be ubiquitous. However, although omnipresence is an essential attribute of God it is not always or usually manifest; normally it is hidden (*absconditus*). Where his presence is manifest it is because he has expressly chosen to reveal himself under certain specific conditions: in his incarnate existence, in his Word, and in the Supper. Even so it is a revelation for faith rather than reason, since without the Word the eucharistic elements would be devoid of spiritual meaning.[53] He also points out that the term 'presence' may carry a variety of connotations, a number of which he lists, and this variety itself is, he thinks, sufficient to show that Zwingli's denial of the possibility of a 'bodily' or 'substantial' presence of the Lord in the eucharist cannot be sustained.

At the same time the idea of a substantial presence does call for further elucidation. Luther conceives of substance not as merely static but as dynamic, as 'being in action' (*ens in actu*), for Christ must be thought of as personally present, and personality naturally expresses itself in activity. That is why the term 'consubstantiation', commonly referred to Luther's doctrine, is misleading. Christ is present in the eucharist in a manner which requires the instrumentality of material elements, namely bread and wine. But the union of the spiritual and the material

50. *P.E.*, II, 186ff.
51. See B. J. Kidd, *The Later Mediaeval Doctrine of the Eucharistic Sacrifice* (London, 1898); but also F. Clarke, *The Eucharistic Sacrifice and the Reformation* (Oxford, 1960; 2nd edn, 1967).
52. *W.A.*, XI, 450.
53. *W.M.L.*, XL, 212f.

is sacramental, not just physical or substantial. As Luther concisely phrases it: *in usu, non in objecto, spiritus est*. The presence of Christ, that is, is in the eucharistic *act* rather than in the elements simply as such. Why it should continue to be appropriate to describe bread, albeit consecrated, as the body of Christ Luther sought to explain, not altogether convincingly perhaps, by resort to synecdoche, the figure of speech whereby when part of a thing is mentioned the whole that it belongs to is understood; thus, however, inviting Zwingli's rejoinder that he after all did not take the words of scripture, 'This is my body', in a literal way and that his objections to the Swiss teaching were therefore misdirected. But the truth is that Luther, ever concerned to stress the objectivity of God's promises and grace, could not forego the conviction that in a sacrament in which the celebrant repeats the very words of Christ, *Hic est corpus meum*, the Lord's body is actually there and that the subjectivist opinions of *Schwärmer* like Karlstadt, who argued that at the Last Supper Christ, in uttering the words, had in fact pointed to his own living body, deprived the sacrament of its essential reality and point. What the gospel said it said, and as Luther wrote in *Against the Heavenly Prophets in the Matter of Images and Sacraments* (1524–5), 'we are not to deviate from the words as they stand, nor from the order in which they stand'.[54] Recitation of Christ's words does not create the presence, nor do they merely indicate a symbol; Christ by virtue of the omnipresence of his glorified humanity is of necessity present, and to repeat his words at the eucharist is to give that presence sacramental meaning and efficacy. From this position, as the Marburg Colloquy was to show, he would not budge.

Zwingli's view was quite different. Neither of the sacraments imparts a grace which can alter the standing of the elect, whose salvation is already assured and testified to by their faith. The function of these rites – the very word 'sacrament', with its pagan origin, he disliked – is simply to serve as tokens or signs of allegiance or profession. Zwingli's thinking on the eucharist was at first influenced by Erasmus, who personally inclined to the opinion that the Supper is purely symbolical, although he considered it unwise publicly to question the received doctrine. When the Swiss reformer finally abandoned the traditional belief is not altogether clear, but it was not earlier than 1522, the date of his pamphlet, *Freedom of Choice in the Selection of Meats*. Even in June 1523 he wrote to his old teacher Wyttenbach that 'transubstantiation causes me as little difficulty as the changing of water into wine' in St John's gospel; but serious doubt was already latent in his mind and the direction of his subsequent thinking was indicated even now: 'Christ sits, properly speaking, either in heaven at the right hand of God, or on earth in the hearts of the believers. He is the food of the soul; and this should not be degraded into something taken in the hand.'[55]

That the mass is a sacrifice he had denied in the eighteenth of his *Schlussreden*. The following year he learned that the Dutch humanist Cornelisz Hoen (Honius) had argued that the word 'is' (*est*) in the statement 'This is my body' really means 'signifies' (*significat*).[56] He may also have been influenced by Karlstadt; Luther at least was ready enough to detect in the Swiss divine's ideas the flagrant errors of

54. *W.M.L.*, XL, 146.
55. *S.W.*, VIII, 85f., and Potter, *Zwingli* (*Documents*), 94–8.
56. See Köhler, *Zwingli und Luther*, I, 1, 4, 61.

his own former colleague. But it was Hoen's suggestion that took root in Zwingli's mind. He recurs to it in his *On the True and the False Religion*, denying, on the principle that 'the flesh profiteth nothing' (John 5:63f.), that the physical can ever itself communicate the spiritual:

> By faith we believe that the physical and perceptible body of Christ is here. Things are believed by faith that are completely alien from perception. All physical things, indeed, are perceptible; if they were not perceptible then they would not be physical. Believing and experiencing therefore are different.

Those 'on the other side' however have asserted

> . . . something that the senses cannot perceive – that the bread is flesh. Were it otherwise it would be the senses that decided and not faith. Faith does not arise from material objects which belong to the senses, and it is not concerned with them.[57]

If Christ is present in the Supper it is faith only that makes it possible.[58] The actual body of Christ is at the right hand of the Father and it is vain to seek it elsewhere. The eucharist is a rite of thanksgiving (*eucharistia*), an uplifting of the heart, a confession of belief. By it men proclaim themselves to be disciples of Christ and members of his body, the form of their testimony being that of a memorializing of his death.

Both reformers, not to mention their respective followers, had expended a great deal of time and trouble on this controversy. It had begun early in 1526 with Zwingli's *Brief Instruction concerning the Last Supper* as a general statement of his views.[59] But hearing that Luther was planning to attack him he issued in March of the following year his *Amica exegesis* ('Friendly Explanation'), which, as its title implies, was entirely irenic in intention.[60] He also published a reply to Luther's sermon *On the Sacrament of the Body and Blood of Christ against the Enthusiasts*,[61] both of which the Wittenberger in turn answered in his treatise of March 1526, *Dass diese Worte Christi: Das ist mein Leib, noch feststehen, wider die Schwarmgeister*.[62] Zwingli countered in June 1527 with *Dass diese Worte: Das ist mein Leib, ewiglich den alten Sinn haben werden* – 'That these words, This is my Body, shall for ever retain their old meaning'.[63] Finally, in March 1528, Luther brought out probably the most weighty of all his utterances on this subject, his *Grosses*

57. *S.W.*, III, 773–87.
58. *S.W.*, V, 553, 586: *dum fides adest homini, habet deum praesentem.*
59. *Ein klare underrichtung vom nachtmal Christi* (*S.W.*, IV, 773–862).
60. *Amica exegesis, id est expositio eucharistii negotii ad Martinum Lutherum* (*S.W.*, V, 548–75). A copy was sent to Luther personally on 1 April (*S.W.*, VIII, 78) but, as Köhler observes, this marked the start of the rift between the two leaders (*Zwingli und Luther*, I, 464–72).
61. *W.A.*, XIX, 482–523; *W.M.L.*, XXXVI, 331–61.
62. 'That the words of Christ, This is my Body, still stand firm against the fanatics' (*W.A.*, XXIII, 38–283; *W.M.L.*, XXXVII, 3, 150).
63. According to Zwingli, Luther was guilty of six errors, in teaching that (1) the body of Christ, like Christ's divine nature, is ubiquitous; (2) Christ shows himself to us in this sacrament so that we can know where we may find him; (3) Christ's body, bodily eaten, takes away sin; (4) Christ's body is an entirely spiritual body; (5) Christ's body bodily eaten preserves our body to the resurrection; and (6) Christ's body bodily eaten gives us increase of faith. See *S.W.*, V, 976f.

*Bekenntnis vom Abendmahl* ('Larger Confession of the Lord's Supper'),[64] which though containing nothing new called forth yet another reply, this time from Zwingli and Oecolampadius jointly and dedicated to John of Saxony and Philip of Hesse.[65]

Luther went to Marburg only with reluctance; this long and unhappy dispute had estranged him from the Swiss reform movement. Towards Zwingli his attitude, considering how much the two held in common, had become oddly prejudiced.

> For my own part [*he declared*], I insist that I cannot regard Zwingli and all his teaching as really Christian. He neither holds nor teaches any part of the Christian faith rightly, and he is seven times more dangerous than when he was a papist. . . . I publicly maintain before God and the whole world that I neither can be, nor ever will be connected with his doctrine.[66]

Perhaps also jealousy entered in; Luther's contempt for Zwingli – 'this insolent Swiss' – was mixed with personal bitterness.[67]

Before the Marburg meeting the ex-Dominican Martin Bucer had done his best to mediate, but at the conference itself nothing would shift Luther from the position he had always taken up. *Hoc est corpus meum* – he chalked the words on a table even before the discussion opened – meant what it said. The statement admittedly was a sheer mystery to the reason, but faith must simply accept it as such; obedience was all. That Luther's language was often intemperate and at times coarse did not help matters. Zwingli, a man not easily ruffled, was dismayed and discouraged, and when at the close Oecolampadius reminded the Saxon of what this unseemly division in the reformist ranks would mean, the latter brusquely retorted, 'Pray God that he will open your eyes!' The Swiss leader could only reciprocate the same pious wish.

If Zwingli and his friends might fairly charge Luther with a failure to produce any *argumenta rationis*,[68] or to distinguish in scripture between the literal and the figurative, their own doctrine was not above criticism from the evangelical point of view. Not only was Zwingli's exegesis in his writings on the subject long-winded, repetitious and occasionally forced, his explanation of the sacrament itself is hardly adequate; his approach is negative rather than positive, pinpointing error more readily than clarifying truth. The eucharistic rite appeared to him, one cannot help feeling, to be no more than a bare sign, lacking any real relationship between itself and the thing signified, a view therefore which goes to the opposite extreme to the Catholic one, in which the sign itself is to all intents abolished. In other words, as between symbol and grace, the external and the internal, no positive connection emerges – the very tendency which landed him in a dubious christology. As a result the whole area of Christian piety which has found the presence of Christ to be in some sense 'in' the sacrament is virtually ignored, despite the fact that Zwingli's opinions did, towards the end, undergo some modification, allowing that the sign

---

64. *W.A.*, XXVI, 241–509.
65. *S.W.*, VI, 1–248.
66. *W.A.*, XXXVI, 342.
67. See *W.A.*, XXIII, 283; XXVI, 342 and 371f.
68. 'Our opponents', wrote Bucer, 'call us rationalists because we follow our reason and the evidence of the Fathers' (*S.W.*, VIII, 649).

assuredly *points to* an objective reality. For what his teaching failed to do was to show why it is that Christians have always looked to the eucharist for a unique realization of the life of Christ in their midst.


### Oecolampadius and Bullinger

When Zwingli, armed with a helmet and sword that were not those only of salvation and the Spirit, met a premature death on the field of Cappel, his friend and follower Oecolampadius had himself but a few more weeks of life left to him. He died on 23 November 1531, leaving Heinrich Bullinger to carry on the leadership of the Swiss Reformation.[69]

Born in 1482 at Weinsberg in the Palatinate, Oecolampadius's real name was Hussgen, or possibly Haus-schein, 'house-light', whence the cumbersome pun. After attending the Latin school at Heilbronn he matriculated at Heidelberg in October 1499, and later entered the universities of both Tübingen and Basel, becoming a D.D. of the latter in 1518, immediately following his appointment as preacher at the cathedral there. This post was a fitting one for a scholar, since its occupant was required from time to time to give theological lectures at which he could count on the presence of a well-educated audience. Oecolampadius had already published a series of sermons *On the Passion of the Lord* some years before, and despite the criticism sometimes made that his discourses were over-long and his delivery poor he had acquired something of a name as an orator. From the first it was evident that he was a born scholar, mastering Hebrew as well as Greek. His closest friend, a man of like interests, was the scholar Wolfgang Capito, who spearheaded the reform at Strassburg and who for a while was professor of theology at Basel. He was also a member of Erasmus's circle and assisted the famous savant in producing his Greek New Testament. His interest in patristics was of long standing, but was undoubtedly stimulated by his contact with the Dutchman, whom he helped too with his nine-volume edition of St Jerome, although his own leanings were rather to the Greek Fathers, especially Chrysostom and the Cappadocians, than to the less mystical Latins. Numerous translations came from his pen, and even if his technical scholarship is occasionally less than perfect – and on this score he came in for a good deal of criticism from his Catholic opponents – as much could be said, and has been said, of Erasmus himself.

Oecolampadius's immediate sympathies thus were with scholars and scholarship, and a number of well-known humanists were among his associates, including Pirkheimer, Veit Bild and Christoph Scheurl of Nuremberg, and Konrad Peutinger and the Adelmanns, Bernhard and Konrad, of Augsburg. All were strongly reformist in outlook and partisans of Luther. The more surprising is it, then, that in April 1521 he should have entered the Briggitine house at Altomünster, although his chief reason for so doing was probably the belief that convent life would afford

---

69. The indispensable modern works on Oecolampadius are E. Staehelin, *Das theologische Lebenswerk Johannes Oeckolampads und die Reformation der Kirche zu Basel* (Leipzig, 1939), and the same author's *Briefe und Akten zum Leben Oekolampads* (2 vols, Leipzig, 1927–34). See also E. G. Rupp, *Patterns of Reformation* (London, 1969), 1–46.

him a retreat for the quieter pursuit of his studies. In this he soon found himself mistaken and he left the community towards the end of the following year. Thereafter he definitely threw in his lot with the reformers. In December 1522 he got in touch with Zwingli, and from the time of their first meeting, some months later, they became fast friends, the Basel scholar, though, being somewhat as wax to the imprint of the other man's stronger personality.

From 1523 onwards Oecolampadius led reformist opinion in the city on the Rhine, his sermons creating such a stir among the townsfolk that the bishop forbade their continuance. The favourite Swiss device of a public disputation was called for, and two were held in December 1524, one of which was conducted on the reforming side by the Frenchman, Guillaume Farel, a fervent Protestant who later, as events turned out, was to be Calvin's precursor at Geneva. In February 1525 Oecolampadius was made preacher at St Martin's church by the municipal council and given a free hand in bringing about whatever changes the word of God might in his judgement require. It soon became evident that Oecolampadius's views were more radical than those propagated from Wittenberg, and that on the doctrine of the eucharist he was in close accord with Zwingli. But while defending the Zurich divine's position on this emotive subject he sought also to emphasize its positive rather than its negative and polemical aspects. Thus he affirms the body of Christ to be present in the consecrated elements after the same manner as its presence in the word itself, 'through which the bread becomes a sacrament and a visible word'. On the other hand, to say that the bread is the 'substantive body' of Christ, or that the Lord's body can be 'in many places at once' is an 'unprofitable assertion' out of keeping with the true attitude of faith. Yet he castigates as 'unbelieving' those who say they receive the bread only as a sign, for here the sign is not to be separated from the thing signified, even though the word *corpus* is used only in a figurative sense. What Oecolampadius seems to be saying is that Christ is spiritually but not 'substantively' present in the sacrament, and that the notion of a veritable 'absence', as some extremists were teaching, is altogether inadmissible.[70]

In other doctrinal matters Oecolampadius followed Zwingli closely, except that on the issue of election he was rather more reserved. He was less inclined to speculate about the exercise of the divine sovereignty and preferred to construe the doctrine as a simple affirmation of the absolute priority and sufficiency of grace. He certainly thought that no conclusion could be drawn of a double predestination, to bliss or perdition, from such obscure passages of scripture as Romans 9:13 or Malachi 1:2.[71] If a man seeks to know what ultimately is the cause of his having saving faith he must be content to rest in the conviction that God has so willed it. His advice was to heed those things in which the divine purpose has been revealed and to leave the *arcana Dei* alone. For this reason, although predestination was not to be denied, he deplored the idle and divisive controversy between Luther and Erasmus.

---

70. See Staehelin, *Briefe und Akten*, II, no. 470. Oecolampadius's eucharistic teaching was known to Bishop Fisher of Rochester, who answered him in his treatise defending transubstantiation, *De veritate corporis et sanguinis Christi in eucharistia*, published at Cologne in 1527. This was translated into German by Cochlaeus. See Köhler, *Zwingli und Luther*, I, 241.

71. Staehelin, *Das theologische Lebenswerk Johannes Oekolampads*, 217f.

In respect too of the relations of church and civil society he assumed a more moderate stance than did Zwingli, for whom the establishment of a Christian state which unified the temporal and the spiritual was an end not only feasible but necessary. Oecolampadius felt, however, that ecclesiastical discipline, to which he attached high importance, should belong to the church's pastoral office and not be administered within the civil legal system, since by nature it was inward and educative rather than external and retributive. In other words, whereas the state's duty is to punish acts, the church's is to warn and inform consciences. With the eventual adoption of the Reformation at Basel in 1529 this difference of view caused a good deal of friction, the civic authorities fearing the replacement of Catholic clericalism by a new and Protestant one, in spite of Oecolampadius's assurances that such discipline would in fact be administered by laymen, 'elders' of wisdom and public standing; the pastors, he urged, should always remember that they are ministers of the church of Christ, with no authority apart from it.[72] Zwingli at first sympathized with his friend's standpoint but later changed his mind. Bucer, on the other hand, supported the Basel reformer, believing, like him, in the need to distinguish the two powers.

Johannes Heinrich Bullinger, who succeeded Zwingli in his charge at the minster of Zurich in December 1531, was some twenty years younger than he, having been born in 1504, the son of the parish priest of Bremgarten in the Aargau by a clerical 'marriage' that was not regularized until 1529. He studied at Emmerich-on-Rhine and at Cologne, where the prescribed theological textbooks, Peter Lombard's *Sentences* and Gratian's *Decretum*, induced him to carry his reading back to the early Fathers, chiefly Origen and Chrysostom among the Greeks and Ambrose and Augustine among the Latins, and from them to the New Testament itself, of which he and his fellow-students felt they knew all too little. About this time also he came across the early writings of Luther, and in 1521 turned eagerly to the newly published *Loci Communes* of Melanchthon.[73] By the following year he had embraced the reformed doctrine and took on a teaching post at the Cistercian monastery at Cappel, where the abbot, Wolfgang Joner, was known to favour the new tendencies. Here he stayed until 1529, in which year he married and also succeeded his father as pastor of Bremgarten.

In the meantime he had made the acquaintance of Zwingli and during 1527 their friendship speedily ripened. Next year he accompanied him to the Bern disputation, and after the latter's death the responsibility of continuing his work at Zurich devolved upon himself. He was however a man of a different temperament, more conciliatory and irenic and without that touch of pugnacity which was a feature of Zwingli's character. Moreover, as a result of Catholic pressure, attempts were made to prevent him raising political issues in the pulpit, but like Oecolampadius he was more ready than Zwingli to recognize a distinction between the spiritual and the temporal spheres. He believed firmly in the duties of the civil power under God, but the church's essential task was the unhindered preaching of the divine word, although admonition of the civic authorities in their Christian obligations

72. See Staehelin, *Briefe und Akten*, II, chaps 18–20 and 24.
73. F. Blanke, *Die junge Bullinger* (Zurich, 1942), 5ff. See also J. Staedtke, *Die Theologie des jungen Bullinger* (Zurich, 1960).

might also be necessary. In general however church and state should avoid interfering in each other's affairs, except that the administration of the church's temporalities was a civil concern; as too, it may be noted, was the execution of ecclesiastical punishments. For although Bullinger's attitude was at first somewhat tolerant towards heresy it later hardened. He strongly opposed the anabaptists, and if persuasion was always to be the first resort coercive measures were certainly not to be excluded, even to the capital sentence.

Bullinger joined in the eucharistic controversy as a defender of the Zwinglian position. Thus he replied both to Luther and to the Catholic polemist Johann Faber,[74] but he also associated himself with Bucer in an effort to reconcile the German and Swiss points of view, drawing up a provisional statement of belief which was circulated among the Swiss cities in 1534 and which most of them accepted. A subsequent, more formal document was the *First Helvetic Confession*, in which he was assisted by Myconius and Grynaeus,[75] although he criticized Bucer's *Wittenberg Concord* in spite of its having been approved by the cities of Upper Germany. A further attempt to appease Luther in November 1536 was without success; the Saxon reformer remained implacable and as late as 1544 he again bitterly attacked the Zwinglian teaching. Bullinger answered him in the *Zurich Confession* of 1545, but the division between the German Lutheran and the Swiss churches was fated to continue and deepen. Nevertheless a closer accord developed between the German-speaking and the French-speaking sections of the latter, something which the growing importance of Calvin's Geneva as a religious centre clearly necessitated. It was sealed by the *Consensus Tigurinus* of May 1549 between Calvin and Farel on the one side and Bullinger on the other.[76]

Bullinger was a prolific writer, but his works have never been collected, apart from the ten-volume edition which he himself prepared. He produced numerous Latin commentaries on the New Testament, covering all the books except the Apocalypse, and also delivered a great quantity of biblical sermons (there are no fewer than one hundred and ninety on Isaiah alone) as well as discourses on the Decalogue, the Apostles' Creed and the sacraments, published under the general title of *Sermonorum decades quinque*.[77] Among his theological writings especially

74. Faber, a native of Leutkirch in Württemberg, was a lifelong friend of Erasmus's and for a time was in considerable sympathy with the reform movements in Germany and Switzerland, but he would contemplate no basic split in doctrine and instead became a dedicated opponent of the new teachings. He was appointed bishop of Vienna in 1530. See the article by F. Zoepfl in *Dictionnaire de Spiritualité* (ed. M. Viller *et al.*), V (1964), coll. 16–21. Faber's *Malleus in haeresim Lutheranam* was published at Cologne in 1524 (modern edition by A. Nägele [*Corpus Catholicorum*, Münster, 1941–52]).

75. Oswald Myconius (1488–1552) was a native of Lucerne, but because of his Protestant opinions was forced to leave the city in 1522. An associate of Zwingli at Zurich, he stepped into Oecolampadius's shoes at Basel on the latter's death. Like Bullinger he was of a compromising disposition and endeavoured to mediate between the Swiss and the Lutherans on the eucharistic issue. He was the author of a 'Life' of Zwingli. See K. R. Hagenbach, *Johann Oekolampad und Oswald Myconius* (Basel, 1859), 30–462.

76. Its twenty-six articles dealt principally with eucharistic doctrine. For the text see H. A. Niemeyer, ed., *Collectio Confessionum*, 191–217; also Kidd, *Documents*, no. 319.

77. Zurich, 1557. An English translation, called *The Decades*, was made in 1577 and reprinted for the Parker Society (Cambridge, 1849–51).

noteworthy are *De providentia* (1553), *De gratia Dei justificante* and *De scripturae sanctae auctoritate et certitudine* (1538). But probably the work for which he is best remembered is his history of the Reformation down to 1532.[78]

On the subject of predestination Bullinger at first held that free will is incompatible with the divine foreknowledge, but he later came round to the Calvinist standpoint and his own position received final expression in the *Second Helvetic Confession*, which he drew up in collaboration with Peter Martyr Vermigli and issued in 1566 at the behest of the Elector-Palatine, Frederick III, who had been won over to Calvinism.[79] This statement, which is unusually lengthy for a document of its kind – it is little less than a theological treatise – was accepted by all the Swiss churches except that of Basel, and indeed by the reformed churches of France, Scotland and Hungary, as well as proving influential in Germany, Holland and England. In fact the extent of Bullinger's influence on the English Reformation, for he was a voluminous correspondent, is a subject of considerable interest in itself. He wrote to Henry VIII and Edward VI, and was in close personal touch with the leaders of the Edwardine reform: 'King Edward's reformation', he remarked, 'satisfieth the godly'; men like Hooper and Jewel not only prized his good opinion but regarded him as almost an oracle. Even Elizabeth I sought his advice in dealing with her more extreme Puritans and in framing her reply to the papal charges after her excommunication by Pius V in 1570.

---

78. There is an edition by J. J. Hottinger and H. H. Vogeli (Frauenfeld, 1838–40). The biography by C. Pestalozzi (Elderfeld, 1858) is still useful for reference purposes.
79. Latin text in Schaff, *Creeds of Christendom*, 233–306. There is an English translation in Cochrane, ed., *Reformed Confessions of the Sixteenth Century*, 220–301.

## Chapter 6

# MELANCHTHON AND THE DEVELOPMENT OF LUTHERANISM

*Loci Communes*

The theological thinking of Martin Luther was the product of creative religious genius, but as an academic theologian he lacked the capacity for systematizing, for the ordered and balanced articulation of ideas. Chance, or providence as some no doubt would prefer to say, furnished him with precisely the coadjutor to meet this need, when in the late summer of 1518 a fledgling humanist lately of Tübingen (he was only twenty-one years of age) was appointed to the newly founded chair of Greek in Luther's university of Wittenberg. His name was Philipp Schwarzerd, although by then he had already adopted its Greek equivalent, Melanchthon.[1] 'Magister Philipp', as Luther was wont to call him, possessed the very qualities that the older man wanted if his convictions were to receive the intellectual shape and formal structure which an age of religious dialectics regarded as not only appropriate but indispensable. Luther indeed was well aware of his personal deficiency in this respect; he himself, he said, was a fighter for the truth, ever ready for the conflict, or a pioneer accomplishing a task which while necessary was but roughhewn and unfinished. Master Philipp, on the other hand, proceeded quietly and with hands undirtied, 'building, planting, sowing and watering with pleasure according to the rich gifts with which God had endowed him'.

But his role, certainly in the light of subsequent events, was not the mere formulating of other men's notions. What came to be known as Lutheranism was, for better or worse, more than simply the transmission of Luther's own faith and teachings, and in the development of the Lutheran type of doctrine and piety his own contribution was in every way substantial: the classical formulary of the Lutheran religion, the *Confession of Augsburg*, came from his pen. But for whatever reason he long remained in relative obscurity, posing something of an enigma. This fact can in part be explained by his early involvement in controversies that frequently became bitter, for few can have suffered more than he, quiet and conciliatory as he always was himself, from the scourge of the *rabies theologorum*, and in the end he even prayed that death might deliver him from the torment of such trials. Yet Luther looked on him as among the greatest of theologians, if not the nonpareil itself, judging that his celebrated theological textbook, the *Loci communes*, deserved a place next to the Bible.

His trouble was that, in certain respects, like Erasmus himself, who held him in high esteem and always befriended him, he was not the man for a time of upheaval and partisan strife. His vocation was that of a scholar and thinker, his interest the

---

1. In Greek as in German the word means 'black earth'.

cultivation of the mind, while in temper he was peaceable to the point of diffidence. A reasoned opinion was a necessity to him, and even Luther was not above criticism. Moreover he discerned truth in diverse quarters, where zealots might see only error, and the division of Christendom grieved him. Thus he was accused alike of Romanism and of Calvinism, in any case of being a prevaricator. Ultimately, however, polemics gave way to neglect and the savant for whom the turbulence of his age was a source of profound distress was in after years set aside as more or less of a nonentity devoid of any real certitudes, or at best a mere shadow of Luther. Modern research, happily, has done much to correct this prejudiced and false view. We now can see him as, if not a forceful leader, at least as a man with a mind of his own, balanced, discerning and singularly free of the bigotry and fanaticism which marked so many of his contemporaries.[2]

Born at Bretten, a little town not far from Karlsruhe, in 1497, Philipp Schwarzerd was a child of the Renaissance: it was his great-uncle, the eminent Hebraist Reuchlin, who induced him while still a boy to change his name to Melanchthon. His formal education began under a private tutor, Johann Unger, until he reached the age of ten, when he was sent to the Latin school at Pforzheim. Here he worked at the classical languages and even, it is said, made a start on the philosophy of Aristotle. Two years later he entered the university of Heidelberg and quickly gained favour as a promising Greek scholar. But although he graduated in arts he was not much impressed by the available courses and preferred to read on his own account before moving on to Tübingen, where the academic prospects seemed brighter.[3] Here too his precocity soon became obvious; he assimilated knowledge with ease and wrote fluently. His studies continued to be mainly literary, but under Stadian, the professor of philosophy, he was drawn to the then fashionable nominalism, especially the works of Ockham, whom he afterwards, however, came to look on with distaste.[4] Taking his master's degree in 1516 – until then he had been considered too young to qualify – he devoted his time increasingly to theology, though the humanities remained his prime interest. That he should have succumbed to the influence of Erasmus goes without saying, and in all probability it was through him that he first learned to regard scholasticism as a perversion of true religion. In 1518 he published his *Rudiments of the Greek Language*[5] having already brought out an edition of Terence as well as contributing a preface to Reuchlin's

2. Melanchthon's collected works and correspondence, edited by K. G. Bretschneider and E. Bindseil, were published as vols I–XXVIII of the *Corpus Reformatorum* (Brunswick, 1824–60, referred to here as *C.R.*); this edition was by no means complete and a number of omissions were afterwards made good by a series of *Supplementa Melanchthoniana* (Leipzig, 1910ff). More recently a selected edition of his works, *Melanchthons Werke in Auswahl* (referred to here as *M.W.*), in eight volumes edited by R. Stupperich and others (Gütersloh, 1951ff), has given his more important writings greater accessibility, but a complete critical edition remains a desideratum. For a compendious survey of Melanchthon study during the last century see W. Hammer, *Die Melanchthonforschung im Wandel der Jahrhunderte* (2 vols, Gütersloh, 1967ff). For the results of such study in respect of Melanchthon's earlier life W. Maurer, *Der junge Melanchthon. Zwischen Humanismus und Reformation* (2 vols, Göttingen, 1967–9) should be consulted.
3. *C.R.*, X, 260; I, cxlvi.
4. *C.R.*, XX, 549.
5. See *C.R.*, I, 24; XVIII, 124; XX, 3.

*Epistolae clarorum virorum.* Accordingly, when he left for Wittenberg to teach Greek there he did so simply as a humanist and a scholar in no way committed to novel views on religious issues.

In his new sphere he immediately made a firm impact with his inaugural address, remarkable in view of his youth and inexperience, on the reform of the curriculum as a means to moral improvement, and in spite of his shyness, his high-pitched voice and his stammer, before long he was lecturing to audiences to be numbered in hundreds. But the turning-point of his life was his contact with Luther. Although at first somewhat cool towards the newcomer the theologian was soon entirely won over by 'the little Greek', who henceforth became his righthand man, in a sense his *alter ego*. It was Luther who introduced him to the serious study of the Bible, in particular St Paul's epistles, and in a matter of weeks he was the older man's disciple. In the summer of 1519 he accompanied Luther to Leipzig for the much-publicized disputation with Eck, although he did so only as, in his own phrase, 'an idle spectator' and not at all as a participant. Even so his 'touchline' comments were numerous and pointed enough to provoke the Catholic champion to attack him as well, with contemptuous references to 'the Wittenberg languages teacher who behaves like a cobbler wanting to know more than his last'.[6] Melanchthon replied with a *Defence against John Eck* in which, declining, as he put it, 'to answer rant with rant', he clearly set out the principle of biblical authority. 'Sacred Scripture has a simplicity and unity which can be comprehended by anybody who will follow the text with care. For this reason we are told to search the Word. It is an anvil on which to test the doctrines and opinions of men.' The ancient Fathers were to be treated with respect, but were by no means infallible; as for the scholastics, they had simply turned the word of God into that of men. The divine canonical scriptures were 'alone inspired and true and pure in all things'.[7]

The young Greek scholar thus made it plain that henceforth he would identify himself with the reform and that his enthusiasm for Aristotle, whose works, in their original tongue, it had but lately been his ambitious plan to edit, was no more. 'Philosophers imagine that they can reach the highest level of virtue by exercise and habit; on the contrary, the sacred writings teach that all human performances are polluted by sin, and can be cleansed only by the Spirit which Christ procured for men.' His lecture subjects were now to be drawn from the New Testament as well as the Greek poets, as increasingly he felt theology to be his proper path, a conviction externally registered by his joining the university's theological faculty. Meanwhile his devotion to Luther intensified. 'I would rather die,' he exclaimed, 'than be separated from this man; nothing worse could happen than to have to live without Martin.'[8] He had in fact become the leader's closest colleague and adviser, not only defending him against his opponents but assisting him generously with his literary work, editing his lectures on the psalter and the 1519 course on Galatians, and contributing prefaces to both series.[9]

He was if anything even more rigid in his scripturalism than Luther himself. But

6. *C.R.*, I, 103.
7. *C.R.*, I, 113ff.
8. *C.R.*, I, 160 and 209.
9. *C.R.*, I, 121 and 170.

he was also becoming a theologian in his own right. His baccalaureate theses, which gained him the degree of B.D. (the only formal theological qualification he ever received) consisted of twenty-four summary statements on the doctrine of justification which he was prepared to uphold in public debate.[10] Particularly challenging, at the time, was his assertion that the church needed no articles of faith other than those furnished by scripture and that the authority of general councils is inferior to that of the Bible.[11] On this score he even maintained that the doctrine of transubstantiation, for which he could discover no scriptural grounds, constituted heresy. In regard to justification he argued that human righteousness is in truth no righteousness, being essentially self-centred and so vitiated at its heart, and that the only righteousness man can possess is that which is imputed to him by God through Christ. Salvation therefore is purely gratuitous, for God cannot be coerced by man even in the name of religion.[12] The outspokenness of the theses surprised Luther himself, who considered his young friend to excel 'all the doctors in the arts and in true philosophy'.[13] He regretted however that the 'faithfulness and diligence' of the man were so great that he allowed himself no leisure.

Further theses followed in July 1520, again on justification and pointing out that the love of God and man is the fruit of faith only and not a natural virtue. 'Faith and love are works of God, not of nature, and love necessarily follows faith. Inasmuch as the sum of our justification is faith, no work can be called meritorious. All human works are but sins.' He denied that the mass is an *opus* effective for the good of others and insisted that all believers are priests and that the Petrine see enjoys no primacy by divine right.[14]

The year 1520, that of Melanchthon's marriage to the daughter of the burgomaster of Wittenberg – 'She had qualities', he fondly averred, 'I could expect only from the immortal gods'[15] – saw also the publication of two notable discourses of his on St Paul: his academic address in honour of the apostle in January;[16] and a lecture on the study of Pauline doctrine, *De studio doctrinae Paulinae*, though these had been preceded by a 'Theological Introduction to the Epistle to the Romans' (*Theologica Institutio in epistulam Pauli ad Romanos*), written expressly at Luther's request.[17] St Paul had in fact come to signify for him, more exclusively even than for Luther, in whose thought there was an important Johannine component, the only true understanding of Christianity, beside which the teachings of most other theologians (Augustine being the great exception[18]) and of all philosophers – the purveyors merely of 'darkness and error' – stood in painful contrast. As its title indicates, it was an exposition of the argument of Romans as, so to speak, the

10. Luther described Melanchthon's academic defence of his work as 'miraculous': '*Ita respondit, ut omnibus nobis esset id quod est scilicet miraculum*' (*W.A., Briefe*, I, 514).
11. *C.R.*, I, 128.
12. *C.R.*, I, 87ff.
13. *C.R.*, X, 302.
14. *C.R.*, I, 125n., 126f.
15. *C.R.*, I, 212.
16. *M.W.*, I, 27–43.
17. *C.R.*, XXI, 49ff.
18. See W. Maurer, 'Der Einfluss Augustins auf Melanchthons theologische Entwicklung', in *Melanchthon-Studien* (Gütersloh, 1964), 67–102.

pattern of what Christian instruction should comprise; for what the apostle offered was not speculative theorizing like the Lombard's *Sentences* but a practical form of life *(forma vitae)*. Unfortunately an unauthorized 'boil down' of the contents of his lectures was brought out in printed form by some of his students as 'Basic Topics in Theological Matters' *(Rerum theologicarum capita seu loci)*. This caused him some annoyance, since it was both sketchy and premature. The only way to dispose of it effectively was to publish something which would serve the desired purpose more adequately. The upshot was the work called *Loci communes rerum theologicarum*, 'Theological Commonplaces' or 'Theological Topics', published at Wittenberg in December 1521.[19]

Melanchthon's design in composing this work needs to be understood. The *Loci communes* is usually referred to as the first Protestant treatise in dogmatic theology, but the description, especially when applied to the original edition, is hardly accurate. It was not in his mind to attempt anything approaching a detailed *summa theologica*. His aim was more modest and also different, namely to produce an outline of theological doctrine in accordance with the principles and priorities of Luther's teaching; more particularly, as he states in his dedicatory letter to a contemporary divine, Tilemann Plettener, to itemize such doctrinal matters, *loci communes*, as one ought properly to look for in holy scripture, in contrast with the perverted complexities of the scholastic theology; or as he himself phrases it, 'the theological hallucinations of those who have offered us the subtleties of Aristotle instead of the teaching of Christ'.[20] In other words, he was concerned with theological *method* as well as content. Again to quote his own statement: 'I am discussing everything sparingly and briefly because the book is to function more as an index than a commentary.' His treatise, in short, was to serve as a guide to the right understanding of the Bible. If he did not embark on a commentary it was partly at least because he was aware of the danger of commentaries, that they tend to become a substitute for what they purport to elucidate.

It is of interest to note that, powerful though Luther's influence upon him was at this time, Melanchthon had not at all shaken off the effects of his humanist training, especially the impact of Erasmus and Agricola, by whose aid he had come to appreciate the use and importance of both rhetoric and dialectics when rightly conceived and employed.[21] For what an author intends to communicate is to be determined in no small measure by his method of doing so. This point Erasmus had himself stressed in a book of 1513 on 'words and ideas' *(De duplici copia, verborum ac rerum, commentarii duo)*, as too in his study of the proper procedure in biblical exegesis *(Ratio seu methodus compendio perveniendi ad veram theologiam)*.

19. *C.R.*, XXI and XXII; *M.W.*, II, 1, ed. H. Engelland, (2nd edn, 1977). This volume and its successor (II, 2) contains also the final version of the work, the *Loci praecipui theologici* of 1559. There is an English trans. of the 1521 edition in W. Pauck, *Melanchthon and Bucer* (Library of Christian Classics) (Philadelphia/London, 1969) and that of 1555 by C. L. Manschreck, with an introduction by H. Engelland (London/New York, 1965). On the composition of the work see W. Maurer, 'Zur Composition der Loci Melanchthons von 1521', in *Luther-Jahrbuch*, xxv (1958), 146ff.
20. See Pauck, *op. cit.*, 19.
21. Cp. P. Joachimsen, 'Loci Communes. Eine Untersuchung zur Geistes geschichte des Humanismus und der Reformation', in *Luther-Jahrbuch*, viii (1926), 27–97.

In the latter he counsels the student to draw up lists, illustrated with specific examples, of *theologici loci*, or leading ideas, and suggested that the Bible will afford up to as many as three hundred such heads – 'little nests in which you place the fruits of your reading'. Such an exercise would not only be illuminating intellectually, but, according to humanist thinking, have beneficent moral consequences, an enhancement of *humanitas*. This concern for the moral improvement of individuals (*emendatio vitae*) Melanchthon never relinquished. He was by nature a teacher, not least of the young – renowned later as *praeceptor Germaniae*, he was one of the greatest educationists of his century – and like any good teacher wanted to see some practical result for his pains. Hence, no doubt, the theological significance which he came increasingly to attach to law and precept. In his last letter to Erasmus, with whom after 1524 his relations had cooled, he spoke of his intention, in a new and enlarged edition of the *Loci communes*, to include 'sound doctrine and useful morals as well as piety'.[22]

Nevertheless what above all motivated him to write his book was his total conviction of the truth of Luther's account of the Christian gospel. Not that he endorsed all Luther's views without question or demur; even at this period he had opinions of his own on certain matters which were indicative of the divergences later to become manifest and lead to tension between the two men, though never to the extent of an estrangement. (The acuteness of Melanchthon's differences with many of Luther's followers is of course another issue, to which we shall shortly have to refer.) On the other hand, he could not subscribe to Erasmus's moralism: man, he held – and here he stood firmly with Luther – has no resources of his own whereby to save himself, ethical self-sufficiency being as inadequate spiritually as the dogmatic intellectualism of the schoolmen. The moral law is not to be derived, that is, from the reason of man, as Cicero, for example, had maintained, but from divine revelation: 'For in general the judgement of human comprehension is fallacious because of our innate blindness, so that even if certain patterns of morals [*formae morum*] have been engraved on our minds, they can scarcely be apprehended.'[23] Rather what we do know of the 'laws of nature' has been directly implanted in us by God. Philosophical virtue cannot be based on corrupt human understanding, a condition of which the pundits of antiquity seemed unaware, supposing instead that moral excellence could be achieved by a spirit of emulative pride.

> Socrates was tolerant, but he was a lover of glory, or surely was self-satisfied about virtue. Cato was brave, but because of his love of praise . . . Cicero . . . thinks that all motivation for virtue lies in love of ourselves or love of praise. How much pride and haughtiness are to be found in Plato![24]

As for Aristotle, of whom the scholastics make so much, what was he but a mere 'wrangler'?

With the passing of the years Melanchthon was to modify his opinions considerably, as is shown by the changes introduced into the successive revised versions

22. Allen, ep. 3120.
23. Pauck, *op. cit.*, 50.
24. *Ibid.*, 34.

of the *Loci* and by the various doctrinal disputes in which he became embroiled. Thus the second edition, published in 1535, besides being larger, differs from the first in a number of points. It was after 1540, though, that the most substantial changes were introduced, with the result that the edition of 1555 is not only very nearly four times as bulky as the original but has undergone fundamental alterations. In his preface Melanchthon affirms his belief in the Apostles', Nicene and Athanasian creeds, and is careful to state his purpose of arranging the contents of his work according to the articles of these ancient and authoritative symbols, eschewing 'any peculiar opinions or fantasies' not consonant with the tradition of faith embodied in the *Augsburg Confession*. But in the 1521 version his plan was squarely based on the teaching of Romans and Galatians, so that the presiding themes, or *loci communes*, are sin and grace, law and gospel. The foundation doctrines of God and Christ are passed over, the whole procedure being selective and with the several parts not always interrelated. His concern, as he himself stated, was not with abstractions and mysteries but with the *beneficia Christi*, the spiritual benefits with which Christ actually endows us.[25]

The first main topic is that of sin. Preparatory to this, however, is a discussion of the difficult issue of free will. Here attention is paid to human psychology, with special stress on the role of the emotional urges, or inner disposition (*affectus*), by which the will (*voluntas*) is to a large extent controlled.[26] Melanchthon himself dislikes the question-begging terms 'reason' and 'free will', preferring to speak of the 'cognitive faculty' and a 'faculty subject to the affections' – love, hate, hope, fear and so on. Certain it is that the reason is incapable of dominating the emotions, and any one feeling can as a rule be subdued only by another and a stronger.[27] Reason may advise, but it cannot compel, and it in no way follows that because we know the good we can also pursue it. Sin strikes deeply into human nature and is not simply a matter of external acts. To say therefore that since a man is free to do good works he can merit divine grace is a profound error. At the root of his being is self-love, *amor sui*, the first and most powerful of the basic motives governing his nature. If 'for its sake he seeks and desires only that which seems to his nature good, pleasant, sweet and glorious' he cannot effectively *choose* either to love or to hate, least of all to love God. Abstract talk about the will's freedom is sophistical. 'The Christian acknowledges that nothing is less in his power than his heart.'[28]

---

25. The well-known sentence, 'Hoc est Christum cognoscere, beneficia eius cognoscere', occurs in the Preface to the 1521 *Loci*. Pauck, 21.
26. Perhaps the best way of rendering this word as used by Melanchthon is 'disposition' or 'state of mind'. He himself elsewhere (*Philosophiae moralis epitomes*, *M.W.*, III, 188) defines *affectus* as 'the movement whereby the senses or the will are carried away by the thing presented to them, or else recoil from it'. These *affectus* are intrinsic to human nature, having been implanted by God (*sunt res divinitus conditae in natura hominis*), but whereas some accord with right reason (love of one's children, for example), others are evil, and contrary to it (as to be envious of another's happiness). Nevertheless all are in some measure corrupted (*vitiosi*), some intrinsically, others accidentally. See H. Bornkamm, 'Melanchthons Menschenbild', in W. Elliger, ed., *Philipp Melanchthons Forschungsbeiträge zur vierhundertsten Wiederkehr seines Todestages* (Göttingen, 1961), 76–90.
27. Pauck, 27.
28. *Ibid.*, 30.

It is because of this persistent misrepresentation of the actual state of man's nature that the character and scope of sin have been misunderstood, its depth and all-pervasiveness minimized. The truth is that *original sin*, that 'native propensity and innate force and energy by which we are drawn to sinning' and which has been propagated from Adam to his entire posterity, has mankind in its grip. Scholastic distinctions between orders of sin are trifling. 'Scripture does not call one sin "original" and another "actual", for original sin is plainly a kind of actual, depraved desire.' All sin is 'vice' (*vitium*), 'a depraved affection, a depraved activity of the heart against the law of God'.[29] When in this connection one speaks of the 'flesh' the word designates not only the 'body', as the scholastics suppose, but the whole tendency and disposition of the natural man; no aspect of his being is excluded.

Thus inevitably one is led to consider the nature of *law*, the proper function of which is to reveal the meaning of sin by commanding what is good and forbidding what is evil.[30] Such a revelation is necessary if human self-sufficiency is to be broken down. For whereas reason sees law only as a 'corrector of crimes' or an 'instructor of living', scripture describes it in language far more minatory: the 'power of anger', the 'power of sin', the 'sceptre of the avenger'. 'The work of the law is to kill and to damn, to reveal the root of our sin, and to perplex us. . . . It mortifies not only avarice and desire, but the root of all evils, our love of self, the judgement of reason, and whatever good our nature seems to possess.'[31] Aware, then, of the bondage of his will and confronted by the awful authority of the God-given law, it is no more permissible for man to talk of a 'natural' knowledge of God than of a 'natural' capacity to do good. Man is quite unable to comprehend either creation or providence, as still less the ultimate mystery of God's existence, spiritual truths which simply cannot be known by the flesh.

By contrast the *gospel* comes as the promise of grace and righteousness, of which Christ is the pledge.[32] By grace, again, should be understood not the scholastic notion of *gratia infusa*, the infusion or impartation of certain qualities or a certain 'habit', but, as in the Bible, the divine favour, the goodwill of God towards us.[33] Primarily it means the forgiveness or remission of sins, and justification follows from the acceptance of the gospel in faith.

> We are justified [*he writes*] when, put to death by the law, we are made alive again by the word of grace promised in Christ; the gospel forgives our sins, and we cling to Christ in faith, not doubting in the least that the righteousness of Christ is our righteousness, that the satisfaction Christ wrought is our expiation, and that the resurrection of Christ is ours. In a word, we do not doubt at all that our sins have been forgiven and that God now favours us and wills our good.[34]

So the whole concept of works-righteousness is false: 'When justification is attributed to faith, it is attributed to the mercy of God; it is taken out of the realm of

29.  *Ibid.*, 31.
30.  *Ibid.*, 49.
31.  *Ibid.*, 79.
32.  *Ibid.*, 72.
33.  *Ibid.*, 87.
34.  *Ibid.*, 88f.

human efforts, works, and merits.'[35] The only righteousness we have is what is imputed to us on the strength of Christ's own, an idea which, with its forensic overtones, was to receive further emphasis in Melanchthon's later writings.[36] At the same time he recognizes that justification is not complete so long as sanctification remains unperfected: 'For our sanctification began as an act of the Spirit of God, and we are in the process of being sanctified until the flesh is utterly killed off.'[37] Thus although the forgiven sinner is, as Luther always insisted, *simul justus et peccator*, justification must be seen to include sanctification.[38] Faith, moreover, in the biblical meaning of the word, is not to be equated with mere intellectual assent, which in the scholastic vocabulary is denoted by the term *fides informis*, or 'incomplete faith', as distinct from *fides formata*, or 'faith completed' by *caritas*, that is works. Faith is not simply an opinion as to *credenda*, matters to be believed regarding doctrine or historical facts. Properly speaking it is 'nothing else than trust [*fiducia*] in the divine mercy promised in Christ'. Unless we believe *in this sense* 'there is no mercy of God in our hearts'.[39] But to trust in God is to respond to him in every vicissitude of life and death, for he who by faith has Christ 'has all things and can do all things'.[40]

In his predestinarianism the young Melanchthon would appear on the face of it to be as rigid as Calvin himself. 'All things that happen', he states, 'happen necessarily, according to the will of God.'[41] The human will, then, cannot be free. What he is discussing, however, is not man's final destiny but the determinism whereby he is obliged to act in the way he does. This too Melanchthon considers to be taught in scripture, since for the biblical authors all things occur as God disposes. Not that an element of contingency is ruled out, for obviously there is in human nature 'a certain freedom in outward works': one may or may not greet a man, put on one's coat, or take a meal, as one chooses. Likewise one is free to obey or disobey the law. But to govern one's internal disposition is not possible. Here only divine grace is effective.

Turning to the *means* of grace, or more correctly to the signs by which God's promises are 'sealed' for us, Melanchthon denies that the sacraments have justifying power in themselves and apart from the faith through which alone they acquire their significance. But as testimonies of the gospel they are of the highest value in consoling and strengthening the conscience. Baptism is the sign of our 'transition through death to life' and thus of that mortification of the flesh which brings salvation.[42] Participation in the Lord's Supper involves the eating and drinking of the body and blood of Christ and as such is a 'certain sign of grace'. But nothing is said about the nature of Christ's presence, and all masses are godless 'except

---

35. *Ibid.*, 106.
36. It had already in fact been stated quite succinctly by Melanchthon in one of his baccalaureate theses: '*Omnia justitia nostra est gratuita Dei imputatio*', 'Our own righteousness is by the gracious imputation of God'.
37. Pauck, 130.
38. *Ibid.*, 123.
39. *Ibid.*, 92.
40. *Ibid.*, 103.
41. *Ibid.*, 24.
42. *Ibid.*, 137.

those by which consciences are encouraged for the strengthening of faith'. The Supper is not a sacrifice: 'A sacrifice is what we offer to God, but we do not offer Christ to God. He himself offered up himself once for all.'[43] There are two sacraments only; for penance no special sacramental ordinance is necessary.

Melanchthon concludes with a section on 'Magistrates'.[44] The civil authorities must be obeyed, he affirms, unless they command what is contrary to divine law, by which he means presumably what is explicitly laid down in scripture. On the other hand he concedes that there are certain laws we call 'natural', although he is dissatisfied with the account of them given by either theologians or lawyers. A law of nature may be said to be 'a common judgement to which all men give the same assent' and which is 'suitable for the shaping of morals', even though in general 'the judgement of human comprehension is fallacious because of our innate blindness'. Broadly speaking, the natural law tells us that God must be worshipped, that because men are social beings none should be harmed, and that human society demands that its members make common use of all things. Even so, Melanchthon veers between 'reason' and biblical precept, and the reader is left with the impression that the very idea of a 'law of reason' independent of scripture is one that the author of at least the first version of the *Loci communes*, with his pronounced biblicism, cannot easily assimilate.

## The *Augsburg confession*

Melanchthon had proved himself to be a convinced and loyal adherent of Luther, but his own mind was by no means decisively made up on all issues. While he was writing his book Luther had published his own important work *Against Latomus*, which raised questions that the younger man felt he too had to deal with. This both delayed publication and left him, nevertheless, dissatisfied with the result, although the *Loci* turned out to be an immense success, being reprinted no fewer than eighteen times in four years. But Luther's absence from Wittenberg from 1521 to 1522 meant that his colleague had to face alone the situation created in the university town by the *Schwärmer*, the 'fanatics' – men like Karlstadt and Zwilling – as well as the arrival there of the Zwickau 'prophets' and of that particularly disturbing character, Thomas Müntzer. In his practical handling of it his personal deficiencies as a leader became evident, but the 'spiritualist' presentation of Christianity was repugnant to him, as too was the anabaptism increasingly associated with it, and in his various memoranda he repeatedly attacked them both for perverting or bypassing the words of scripture and propagating, in effect, a new form of justification by works. Further, the argument on free will between Erasmus and Luther in 1524 and 1525 led him to reassess the role of the will in conversion, since his own sympathies with Erasmus's position were difficult to suppress. His doubts as to the implications of predestinarianism found expression in his commentary on Colossians in 1527, the doctrine seeming to him too obscure and too much of a mystery to be of help to simple souls, and in any case his strong

43. *Ibid.*, 146.
44. *Ibid.*, 148ff.

pedagogical bent meant that he had to leave room for freedom at least in respect of 'civil righteousness'. The facts of the religious life and the requirements of civil obedience ought not, he maintained, to be confused, as the 'fanatics of course did persistently confuse them'. Thus he insisted that because man has the responsibility he must also have the freedom to do good and avoid evil.

To many Lutherans this looked suspiciously like a reinstatement of the obligations of the Law, and they were offended by his *Instructions to the Visitors* of 1528,[45] which dealt with the unhappy state of the church in Electoral Saxony, although Luther himself, who with his friend Johann Bugenhagen, a highly competent theologian, had carefully perused the first draft, had described it as satisfactory in almost all points and most suitable for its object.[46] In the following year Melanchthon accompanied the Elector of Saxony to the Diet of Speyer to represent the Protestant cause, only to be disappointed and even shocked at the actual outcome.[47] He was also drawn into the eucharistic controversy and, after Luther, was the most important member on the Wittenberg side at the Colloquy of Marburg, firmly endorsing his leader's opposition to Zwingli's 'impious dogma'.

By the beginning of 1530 the emperor, now at last, through the Peace of Barcelona (29 June 1959), in accord with Pope Clement VII, and having also, by the Treaty of Cambrai – the so-called *Paix des Dames* – reached a settlement with Francis I of France, was in a position to give his full attention, after the lapse of ten years, to the religious situation in Germany. Under pressure as he was from the Turks (the Ottoman Suleiman II was already at the gates of Vienna), he realized his need of the united support of the German princes and hence of coming to some kind of terms with the Lutherans. With this end in view he summoned a diet of all the estates of the empire to meet at Augsburg on 8 April. No coercion was either threatened or hinted at, in spite of the adjurations of the nuncio Cardinal Campeggio and other papal representatives to eradicate heresy by fire and sword. Although Charles had absolutely no personal sympathy with the evangelical cause, what he wanted was peace, and his methods would be diplomatic and as far as possible conciliatory. As his rescript declared, it was his intent 'to give a charitable hearing to every man's opinion, thoughts and notions, to understand them, to weigh them, to bring and reconcile them to a unity in Christian truth, . . . to see to it that we all live in one common church and in unity.'[48] His task might have seemed the less difficult in that it was well known that the reform movement was sharply divided within itself and that even the Protestant princes were at odds with one another. Luther and Melanchthon, the latter in particular, were totally opposed to any resort to arms against the emperor and in no way ready to see the gospel defended by force. But these scruples were by no means shared by all.

The responsibility for drawing up a statement of evangelical doctrine and of evangelical requirements in matters of practical reform, asked for by the emperor

45. *Unterricht der Visitatoren an die Pfarherrn im Kurfürstenthumb zu Sachssen.* H. Lietzmann edited a reprint of the original edition (Bonn, 1912).
46. Melanchthon's Latin *Visitation Articles*, published a year earlier, are very characteristic of his mode of procedure, polemical though they are.
47. Smith, *Luther's Correspondence*, II, 272f., 470f.
48. *Ibid.*, 465n.

himself, devolved on Melanchthon, although the foundation of his work had already been laid in the Marburg-Schwabach and Torgau Articles.[49] Furthermore, the necessity of answering a new and formidable polemic from the tirelessly belligerent Eck of Ingolstadt in the shape of *Four Hundred and Four Theses* 'extracted from the writing of those who are causing schism in the Church'[50] – culled, that is, indiscriminately from the utterances of Karlstadt and Zwingli as well as those of Luther and Melanchthon – not to mention the effort of devising forms of words to satisfy the theologians among Luther's own followers, proved highly taxing and caused him great stress of mind. But eventually the document was ready, its author having done his best to present the reformers' case in as persuasive a manner as possible. He forwarded it for approval to Luther (himself prevented by the imperial ban from attending the diet in person), who on 15 May expressed his satisfaction, although he had to confess for his part that he could not 'move so softly and lightly'.[51] But even this draft was not final. Melanchthon discussed matters at length with one of the imperial secretaries, Alfonso Valdès, in an attempt to show how seriously Catholic controversialists had misrepresented the Protestant teaching. Indeed the Wittenberg professor – to Luther's own alarm, it should be said – seemed prepared to go almost any distance to meet Catholic objections, and at one moment it even appeared that the resolution of their differences was actually in sight, the points at issue having been reduced to certain specific abuses which the Lutherans had consistently pressed to have removed.[52] Unlike the irenic Melanchthon, however, the Lutheran party as a whole, and especially the princes, displayed little of the spirit of conciliation, to the emperor's evident displeasure; nor, it may be remarked, did many of the papists either, who continued to refer to the Protestants in highly opprobrious language. Charles moreover was becoming impatient at the delay and on 22 June gave peremptory notice to the Lutherans to have their statement ready within two days at the latest. So on the following day Melanchthon went once more through the entire text, and even then Philip of Hesse insisted on some last-minute changes.

On 25 June the diet met in the hall of the episcopal palace, and the *Confessio Augustana* (thereafter known as the *Augsburg Confession*), signed by seven princes and the representatives of the cities of Nuremberg and Reutlingen, was read out in the German tongue and in ringing tones by the Saxon chancellor, Christian Beyer. The emperor's behaviour at the time has been variously reported, some saying he listened attentively, others, with bored indifference or with closed eyes. As a *compte rendu* of Protestant 'opinion and grievances' it obviously was not to be taken as a comprehensive statement of doctrine, but it had the great merit of

49. The *Schwabach Articles* comprised a series of seventeen theological propositions presented at a conference held at Schwabach in October 1529, in the hope, despite the Marburg fiasco, of securing an agreement between at any rate the German representatives of the Lutheran and Zwinglian viewpoints respectively. They were largely of Luther's own drafting and contained a summary of his eucharistic doctrine in an uncompromising form. Little wonder, no agreement was reached. For the text see *C.R.*, XXVI, 129–60.
50. Kidd, *Documents*, no. 105.
51. *C.R.*, I, 1093f.
52. *C.R.*, II, 114f.

being concise and readily intelligible. Luther, who complained at not having been consulted about the final revisions, told Melanchthon bluntly that he thought too much had been given away, but the latter always looked on it – considering the toil and anguish it had cost him – as his own intellectual property, and did not hesitate to alter it as he thought fit, both before its appearance in print in the spring of 1531 and subsequently.[53]

After receiving it the emperor passed it on to a committee of Catholic theologians which included such bitter anti-Lutherans as Eck, Johann Faber and Cochlaeus. This body replied with a *Confutatio pontificia* which was read out at the diet on 3 August and which in turn elicited from Melanchthon a firmly worded *Apology for the Confession*, though the latter Charles declined to accept.[54]

From the outset the *Confessio Augustana* acquired the status of an authoritative formulary, although later editions were to vary somewhat both from the original and from one another. Melanchthon issued an extensively revised version in 1540 known as the 'Variata', but in 1580, when the compilation entitled *The Book of Concord (Konkordienbuch)* was published at Dresden, an attempt was made to revert to the text of 1530, and this form, which became known as the 'Invariata', although in fact it contains a large number of minor differences from the original document, remains to this day the classical confession of the Lutheran churches.[55]

The first part of the *Augsburg Confession*, consisting of twenty-one articles, provides a statement of the main doctrinal position adhered to by the Lutherans.[56] Article I, 'Of God', simply reaffirms the Nicene dogma, but the second goes straight to the doctrine of original sin, declaring that after the fall of Adam all men begotten by the natural process of procreation are born in sin [*cum peccato*] – 'that is, they are born without fear of God, without confidence towards God [*fiducia erga Deum*], and with concupiscence [*concupiscentia*]' or inordinate desire – and stating that 'this original disease or flaw is truly a sin, bringing condemnation and eternal death to those who are not reborn through baptism and the Holy Spirit'. The Pelagian heresy is expressly repudiated, especially the view that 'man can be justified in God's sight by his own strength of reason'. Article III, 'Of the Son of God', while in general terms affirming the Apostles' Creed, adds a clause on the atonement with the words '. . . that he [Christ] might reconcile the Father to us, and be an offering not only for original sin but also for all actual sins [*pro omnibus hominum peccatis*]'. The fourth article deals with the controverted issue of justification. 'Men',

53. For a critical edition of the text see H. Bornkamm, *Die Bekenntnisschriften der evangelisch-lutherischen Kirche* (1930; 2nd edn, Gottingen, 1952), 19–137. Latin text also in Kidd, *Documents*, no. 116. For an English translation see T. G. Tappert, ed., *The Book of Concord* (Philadelphia, 1959), 23–96; see also W. Maurer, *A Historical Commentary on the Ausburg Confession* (Philadelphia, 1976).
54. For Melanchthon's *Apology* see Bornkamm, *op. cit.*, 139–404 (English trans. in Tappert, *op. cit.*, 97–285). On the *Confutatio* see J. Ficker, *Die Konfutation des Augsburgischen Bekenntnisses* (Leipzig, 1891).
55. A critical edition of the *Konkordienbuch* by Lietzmann and others is to be found in *Die Bekenntnisse*. See note 53 above. See further E. W. Gritsch and R. W. Jenson, *Lutheranism: the Theological Movement and its Confessional Writings* (Philadelphia, 1976).
56. The preface and epilogue, like the articles themselves under revision up to the final moment, were the work of Bruck and Jonas Justus.

it says, 'cannot be justified before God by their own powers, merits or works, but are justified freely [*gratis*] on account of Christ through faith [*propter Christum per fidem*], when they believe that they are received into grace and their sins forgiven for his sake'; which faith God imputes for righteousness in his own sight. Article V, 'Of the Church's Ministry', teaches that the ministry of the Word and sacraments was instituted in order that the foregoing doctrines might be held and followed, the same Word and sacraments being the 'instruments' by which the Holy Spirit is given. Accordingly, the anabaptist idea that the Spirit can be conferred without either is repudiated. By the terms of Article VI, 'Of the New Obedience', faith should bring forth 'good fruits', the keeping of God's commandments being a consequence of his good will, not ours. Article VII, 'Of the Church', teaches that the church is 'a congregation of saints, in which the Gospel is rightly taught, and the sacraments duly administered', and that it will remain for ever; adding also that for the true unity of the church it is sufficient to have unity of belief concerning the teaching of the gospel and the administration of the sacraments, and that uniformity in matters of detail is unnecessary. The article following, VIII, 'Of the Nature of the Church', gives assurance that the imperfection of the ministers does not invalidate the sacraments which they administer, the contrary view, as held by the Donatists in antiquity, being condemned.

Articles IX to XIII are concerned with the sacraments as such. The first of them lays down that baptism is necessary to salvation and that by it children are 'offered to God' in order that they may be received into his favour, a matter on which the contrary anabaptist tenet is emphatically condemned. The article 'Of the Lord's Supper' states that 'the body and blood of Christ are truly present [*vere adsint*] and are distributed to those who partake therein'. Article XI recommends the retention of private absolution, 'so long as it is understood that it is not necessary to enumerate all sins in confession', which would not be possible. The twelfth notes that true penitence is always open to sinners, to whom therefore the church should dispense absolution, the two aspects of penitence being contrition – genuine sorrow for sin – and faith, whereby Christ's forgiveness is accepted. Anabaptist notions of the possibility of a perfection such as renders sin impossible, as well as the third-century Novationist rigorism which refused to receive even penitent sinners back into the church, are repudiated. Article XIII, 'Of the Use of the Sacraments', declares that they were 'ordained not only to be the marks of profession among men, but rather that they should be signs and testimonies of the will of God towards us, set forth unto us to stir up and confirm faith in such as use them'. However, the Catholic doctrine that the sacraments justify *ex opere operato* and apart from faith is rejected. Articles XIV and XV deal with the church's 'Orders' and 'Rites' respectively. Nobody may officiate in the church except he be duly called (*rite vocatus*), while such rites may be kept as can be 'observed without sin' and which promote peace and good order – holy days, fasts, and so forth. On the other hand, no man's conscience should be burdened by such things. Vows, fasts and the observance of days are not effective for salvation.

The sixteenth article, 'Of Civil Affairs', asserts the legitimacy under God of civil government and the lawfulness of punishment for wrongdoing, and of military service, contracts, property, oaths ('at the bidding of the magistrate') and marriage.

Anabaptist ideas about the non-engagement of Christians in political and social life are accordingly censured: all Christians have a duty to assume the obligations of citizenship.

The remaining articles are confined to more strictly theological matters. The seventeenth, 'Of Christ's Return to Judgement', again condemns anabaptism for its alleged belief in a final universal salvation, including even the 'impenitent and blasphemers [*impios ac diabolos*]', and affirms that it is the elect alone who are destined for eternal bliss. The 'Jewish notion [*Judaica opinio*]' of a post-resurrection rule of the godly in this world, along with a similarly temporal punishment of the wicked, is again scouted. Article XVIII, 'Of Free Will', affirms a certain liberty in ordinary human affairs and matters 'subject to reason', but insists that without the Holy Spirit the will has no power to effect the righteousness of God. Pelagian views are once more repudiated. Article XIX attributes the cause of sin to an evil will, 'a will which turns away from God of itself, not one which is turned away from God [*quae, non adiuvante Deo, avertit se in Deo*]'. The long article which follows, 'On Good Works', rebuts the charge that Lutherans prohibit these by pointing out that the emphasis in their preaching is not on religious observances as such but on faith, as to which in the past there has been only 'the profoundest silence [*altissimum silentium*]'. It is asserted yet again that works do not reconcile men to God and that faith alone can bring peace of conscience, in the knowledge that it is through Christ only that their reconciliation stands (*habent placatum Dei*), a truth that they who have not had the experience of faith cannot comprehend. Ascetic practices, however arduous, fail to inculcate it, for what is meant by faith is not bare mental assent but effective belief, which is itself, through the power of the Holy Spirit, the sole source of good works. Finally, Article XXI states that the memory of the saints should be kept in mind 'in order that we may follow their faith and good works according to our own calling'. On the other hand, scripture does not teach that we may invoke them for their aid. The summary concluding this part of the *Confession* claims the Protestant doctrine to be biblical and orthodox, being consonant with the teachings of the Catholic Fathers, and that in the liturgy ancient usages are retained where free from the abuses which have caused such scandal.

The rest of the *Confession*, or *Apology*, as Melanchthon preferred to call it, consisting of seven articles based on those of Torgau (March– April, 1530), deal with topics of practical reform (communion in both kinds, clerical marriage, etc.) and need not detain us, except to note that the third of them, 'Of the Mass', denies that the rite has been abolished but instead 'is retained among us, and celebrated with the utmost reverence'.

The whole tenor of the document was explanatory, moderate and conciliatory, avoiding as far as possible a polemical stance, its aim being to placate Charles V, for whom Melanchthon himself had the deepest respect, and to assure him that Protestant teaching was by no means the parcel of heresies which Rome declared it to be. Alas, it failed in its object. For the reformers of upper Germany it was too conciliatory, not laying sufficient stress on the differences separating the Protestants from the Romanists, especially in its somewhat terse and guarded statements on the eucharistic presence, and its omission of any reference to the papacy (to Protestant consciences an intensely emotive issue) or to that cardinal tenet of Luther's, the priesthood of all believers. So the four cities of Strassburg, Constance, Lindau and Memmingen presented on 9 July 1530 a statement of their own, the *Confessio Tetrapolitana*, which, although largely resting on the *Augsburg Confession*, contained notable modifications in a Zwinglian direction.[57] Zwingli himself of course stood altogether apart from the Lutheran formulary, having submitted his own *Fidei Ratio* on 3 July.[58] But above all the emperor, though he would have preferred to act in the role of adjudicator – something which Rome would not have contemplated – was swayed by the papal legate and the Catholic majority and would not accept the *Confession*, which, as we have seen, had already been assailed by Eck and others with their *Confutation*. On 22 September 1530 an imperial recess was announced which declared the Protestant statement to have been refuted and allowed the Protestant leaders until 15 April 1530 to conform, meanwhile forbidding further innovations and committing the enforcement of its terms to the *Reichskammersgericht*, the imperial supreme court. This recess the Protestants at once rejected, denying that their *Confession* had been refuted and offering in proof thereof Melanchthon's extended *Apology (Apologia Confessionis)* or defence of it which was published, along with the *editio princeps* of the *Confession*, in the spring of 1531. Charles V, however, remained obdurate.

The situation in Germany now looked ominous: fourteen imperial cities joined the princes in opposing the recess, and war seemed imminent. In face of it the Protestant Schmalkaldic League was formed, led by Electoral Saxony and Hesse. By April 1532 the defence of the Protestant cause by force of arms had become entirely feasible and in the following July a truce was arrived at known as the Peace of Nuremberg, which ensured their position until such time as a general council should be convened by the pope.

### Melanchthon's *Apology*: 'synergism'

Melanchthon's *Apology*, which engrossed his attention for some months, reveals nothing of the undue pliancy with which its author had been charged during the Augsburg negotiations. There was now much less call for diplomacy, less need to underline what the opposing sides had in common, and with heavier concentration on justifying the differences that separated them: original sin, justification *sola fide*, good works, the church, the eucharist, clerical marriage and ecclesiastical ceremonies. As the author remarked in a letter to Bucer: 'In it I have treated the articles on justification, repentance and some others in such a manner that our opponents will comprehend that the burden of proof is placed upon them.'[59] In his introduction he accused the papists of seeking neither truth nor concord, but only 'to drain our

57. Niemeyer, *Collectio Confessionum*, 740–70. English trans. in Cochrane, *Reformed Confessions*, 51–88.
58. The Protestant delegates had never been given a copy of the *Confutatio* and Melanchthon in answering it had to rely on information obtained through friends at Nuremberg (*C.R.*, XXVII, 227ff). His finished work was several times as long as the brief and hardly adequate document presented at the diet, and offers a considered account of Lutheran doctrine as a whole.
59. *C.R.*, II, 498.

blood'. In spite of what the 'blockhead of Rome' might say 'we cannot abandon truth that is manifest and necessary to the Church'. Responsibility for schism was therefore to be totally discounted. The book was immediately acclaimed by Lutherans everywhere and quickly won for itself a special place among the recognized statements of Reformation doctrine, side by side with the *Augustana* itself.

The pivot on which Melanchthon's exposition rests is justifying faith; abstract questions are set aside in favour of the concrete *beneficia Christi*. It is, he insists, faith in Christ, and that alone, which justifies the sinner in the sight of God. As Article IV of the *Augsburg Confession* puts it, 'men are not justified by their own strength, merits or works', but freely 'on account of Christ through faith', or as he says in the *Apology*, 'to be justified means to make [*effici*] unrighteous men righteous, or to regenerate them', in the sense of imputing to them a righteousness which is not their own (*aliena justitia*).[60] Faith moreover is not intellectual assent, but a complete trust and confidence in God's mercy and forgiveness in Christ. In affirming this – and Melanchthon is evidently speaking out of his own experience – he stands squarely with Luther himself. But after 1531 his theological views underwent a change, and the question arises whether in his later writings he actually separates sanctification (*regeneratio*) from justification in fact as well as in principle, thus making the former a second and distinct stage in the process of salvation, with justification proper a matter purely of an *imputed* righteousness. It is a subject on which much has been written.[61] However, although Melanchthon repeatedly uses language suggestive of bare imputation, we should note that even in the later editions of the *Loci* he says that Christ came 'in order to forgive us our sins and to begin in us new righteousness and eternal life through the Holy Spirit'.[62] Thus in the 1555 edition he declares: 'If we believe on the Son of God, we have forgiveness of sins; and Christ's righteousness is imputed to us, so that we are justified and pleasing to God for the sake of Christ', but adding also: 'We are reborn through the Lord Jesus Christ; he speaks comfort to our hearts, imparts to us his Holy Spirit; and we are heirs of eternal salvation'.[63] Passage after passage indeed may be cited to show that he does not disconnect the imputation of Christ's righteousness from 'the new and eternal life actually beginning in us, which is a new light and obedience towards God'.[64] 'Justification', he says, 'always brings new life and obedience with it', and 'the beginning of renewal always occurs at the same time as justification.'[65]

Nevertheless Melanchthon does not consider the human will, in this process,

60. It should be observed also that although Melanchthon employs the expression *justum efficere*, which in Roman usage meant to 'effect' a righteousness that is itself justifying, what he signifies by it is rather the 'forensic' view, as it is often called, of simply *accounting* righteous. See C. Stange, 'Zur Rechtfertigungslehre in der Apologie', in *Studien zur Theologie* (Gütersloh, 1928), 435ff.

61. Cf., e.g., K. Holl, *Die Rechtfertigungslehre im Lichte der Geschichte des Protestantismus* (Tübingen, 1923).

62. *C.R.*, XXI, 854.

63. C. L. Manschreck, ed. and trans., *Melanchthon on Christian Doctrine: Loci Communes 1555* (New York, 1965), 155f.

64. *C.R.*, XIII, 1342.

65. *C.R.*, XXI, 442; XXVIII, 401.

to be entirely passive. In other words, whereas forgiveness of sin, in which *justificatio* essentially consists, is the utterly gratuitous act of God and in no respect dependent on any supposed merit in man, it is at the same time inseparable from that gift of the Spirit, and therewith actual newness of life, which constitutes *sanctificatio*. Such was not Melanchthon's previous view. In the *Loci* of 1521 he states categorically: 'We can do nothing but sin. . . . Since all things that happen happen necessarily according to divine predestination, there is no freedom of the will [*voluntas*]'. But predestination itself he deliberately avoids discussing, as a mystery defying human curiosity. In his 1527 commentary on Colossians, though, doubts about the doctrine, stimulated perhaps by Erasmus's controversy with Luther, are already apparent, and in the *Augustana* it receives no mention at all, as being likely, he thought, only to cause confusion.[66] Further, what had more and more come to impress him was the universal nature of God's promises. As he wrote in the *Apology*, with men law and obligation are fundamental, but with God it is mercy that has the priority. 'The Gospel is itself the command that bids us believe that God pardons and saves on account of Christ', so that he who believes in Christ is not condemned. Yet why is it that, if mercy is open to all and God is no respecter of persons, some do not receive mercy, unless, that is, man himself has the responsibility and therefore the freedom to accept it? Even so Melanchthon is still unsure, at this stage, of the effectiveness of man's rational volition.[67] A little later, in a new commentary on Romans, written in 1532, and subsequently in the 1535 edition of the *Loci*, he has gained confidence, arguing now that the divine election is determined by 'something in us [*aliqua causa electionis in nobis*]', to the extent at least that man has the capability within him either to receive or to reject grace (*facultas applicandi se ad gratiam*).[68] 'God draws him who is willing.'[69] Years later (1553), in his treatise *De anima*, he clearly teaches that the human will is not inactive in the moral struggle: 'The will is the power to seek the highest things [*suprema*], and to act freely when, by the intellect, the object has been shown to it.'[70]

This doctrine, known as synergism (Gk, *sunergein*, to cooperate), appeared to many Protestants little short of Pelagian, and to clear the way for a return to Romanist notions of merit, although Luther himself, touchy enough on doctrinal points about which he had personal feelings, showed no signs of displeasure, in spite of the fact that his friend and spokesman was becoming increasingly hesitant even to include the word *sola* in the expression *justificatio fide*, noting that all ancient authors, Augustine alone excepted, 'place some cause of election in us'.

The conviction was in fact growing on Melanchthon that an out-and-out doctrine of predestination was contrary to Christian experience and subversive of morality. He himself was by nature a moralist to whom antinomianism in any guise was repugnant, and he was not unaware of the value of moral sensitivity in leading to conversion. 'The will hears the promise and tries to concur [*causa concurrens*] and

66. *C.R.*, II, 546.
67. *C.R.*, XV, 678ff.
68. *C.R.*, II, 658f.
69. *C.R.*, XXI, 330. 'Saul', says Melanchthon, 'is cast away and David accepted.'
70. *M.W.*, III, 344.

to end its deliberate sinning against conscience.'[71] On the other hand he admitted that the degree to which the will is active in conversion depends on 'how far God has healed it [*quatenus sanari divinitus coepit*]'.[72] For the measure of the will's non-resistance is a consequence of the Spirit's influence upon it.[73] Such qualifications notwithstanding, it was all but inevitable that Melanchthon's opinions on this important matter should provoke criticism and controversy. Particularly strong opposition came from Niklaus von Amsdorf (1483–1565) and Matthias Vlacich of Illyria (1520–75), usually known as Flacius Illyricus, both Lutheran divines of the most intransigent school. The former held that 'good works', so far from being good, were actually harmful, while according to the latter, who maintained that he was correctly interpreting Luther himself, sin constitutes the very substance of the natural man, who is bound to deny the will of God and to resist all the promptings of the Holy Spirit. Both contended that in regeneration the sinner is wholly passive, but Flacius even went so far as to teach that not only is the image of God in fallen man obliterated, he is transformed into the image of Satan. Johann Pfeffinger of the university of Leipzig, which in this dispute, with Wittenberg behind it, adopted Melanchthon's position, replied to Amsdorf, the newly founded university of Jena, where Flacius had his chair, taking up an opposing stance.[74]

Thus controversy raged, synergism *versus* strict predestinarianism, with the latter committed to the dogma that God does not will all men to be saved, and with the Wittenberg theologian Georg Major (1502–74), a pupil of Melanchthon's, maintaining that 'good works' are necessary to salvation inasmuch as faith must express itself in them, until in 1559 an attempt was made, in the *Book of Confutation and Condemnation*, issued on the orders of Johann Friedrich II of Saxony, forcibly to silence the synergists as heretics.[75] Melanchthon, whose disposition was far from combative, was much upset by this prolonged verbal strife but stuck to his opinion that it is idle to talk of conversion apart from the consent of the will, that man is not a stone, and that if freedom means anything then rejection of God's grace is a possibility. In the midst of the dispute death overtook him on 19 April 1560, but a partisan and former pupil of his, a certain Victorinus Strigel (of Jena, as it happened, though he had suffered imprisonment there) argued that man's spiritual capacity was not destroyed by the fall but only impaired, albeit grievously; he is sick, but not dead. In other words, it is not that he *cannot* will the good, but only that, from his sinful condition, he has no desire to do so. This position Strigel upheld at a public disputation with Flacius at Jena in the summer of 1560; his statements were not always clear, but what he seemed to be saying was that human volition is free but disoriented, and only the

71. *C.R.*, XXI, 658f.
72. *C.R.*, XXIV, 316.
73. *C.R.*, XV, 680.
74. Pfeffinger was the author of two works on the freedom of the will, *De libertate voluntatis humanae* and *De libero arbitrio*, both published in 1555. He spoke of 'the Holy Spirit moving, through the Word of God, the mind in the act of thinking, the will not resisting but complying whenever moved by the Holy Ghost'.
75. On the Majorist controversy see O. Ritschl, *Dogmengeschichte des Protestantismus*, II (Leipzig, 1912), esp. 371–98, and Seeberg, *Lehrbuch*, IV. 485ff. The controversy was renewed during the years 1558 and 1563 by Agricola and Musculus.

sustained operation of the Holy Spirit, extended perhaps over a lifetime, can restore its true direction.[76]

The synergist controversy was not brought to an end until the publication in 1577 of the last of the classical Lutheran formularies, the 'Formula of Concord', included in the *Book of Concord*. In this the Melanchthonist (or Philippist) views were rejected along with the Romanist; but disallowed also, with the Calvinism which it seemed to reflect, was the extreme language used by Flacius and the so-called Gnesio-Lutherans (Gk, *gnesios*, genuine). Article II of the Formula, *Of Free Will*, declares that in spiritual matters man's reason and understanding are totally blind and his unregenerate will is averse from and hostile to God. In the work of conversion the sole human agency is in the preaching of the word. On the other hand determinism is repudiated as Manichaean and the will after conversion, though only then, is said to be liberated. In the ordinary affairs of life reason can of course judge and free choice is possible. Article IV, *Of Good Works*, referring to the issues raised in the Majorist controversy, disapproves the use of the word 'necessary' in the statement that good works are necessary to salvation, and insists that the only necessity involved is that of their spontaneously following the condition of being saved. In themselves they contribute nothing to salvation.

## Melanchthon's later theology

But to return to the development of Melanchthon's own theological thought: we have already noted how his assessment of the nature of faith, as expressed in the original *Loci Communes*, was essentially that of Luther himself, an attitude of complete personal trust and confidence in God's promises and redeeming grace; the scholastic rationalism was decisively rejected. Later this 'existential' approach was modified or supplemented by an 'intellectualist' element not hitherto present, or at least, in the flush of Melanchthon's early enthusiasm for the *sola fide*, kept in the background. Thus in the 1543 version of the *Loci* we read that a 'true definition' of faith equates it with 'assent to the whole Word of God set before us, and therefore also to the promise of reconciliation freely given on account of Christ, the Mediator'. The existential factor is certainly not discounted: the 1555 edition expressly emphasizes, as against scholastic objections, that 'the faith of which St Paul speaks . . . is not only knowledge and thought but something in the will and heart, a burning reliance on the Son of God, an earnest, ardent desire and will to accept the precious treasure, forgiveness of sins and grace'.[77] Faith therefore is something very different from the abstract or notional knowledge possessed by the

---

76. Strigel, in a *Declaratio* of 3 March 1562, distinguished between the power (*efficacia*), lost in the fall, to do what is pleasing to God, and that inherent capacity (*capacitas, aptitudo*) for the divine vocation by which man as a rational being is marked off from other creatures. It is because of this rational capacity, and only so, that men, through the Holy Spirit, can assent to the Word. Against this idea Flacius urged that conversion must always be attributed to God alone; in so far as the will does cooperate it is only *after* the actual moment of conversion.

77. Manschreck, *op. cit.*, 164.

devils and by godless men. But there is now also a growing insistence on the place in faith of *belief* in the ordinary sense of the word. In the *Liber de anima* faith is defined as:

> the idea [*notitia*] by which we give our adherence unreservedly to an affirmation, convinced, that is, by witnesses or by authority. So, in accordance with the converging testimony of historians, we believe that Octavius Augustus succeeded Julius Caesar in the government of the Roman empire.[78]

Such belief plainly is assurance (*certitudo*), not conjecture. However in the things pertaining to God more than this is involved.

> In the words of the prophets and the apostles faith designates not only the assent given to historical narratives, but also that given to the divine promises. . . . Faith is the awaiting of what should be hoped for; that is, the confidence which is placed in the promise.[79]

Trust remains the controlling element, but a conviction amounting to the force of knowledge – that certain things are, or will come to pass – must accompany it. *Fiducia* and *assensio* are conjoined, and sound doctrine becomes one of the 'notes' of the church, whose membership indeed is constituted by those 'who hold pure doctrine and agree in it'.[80] This intellectual aspect of faith is especially shown in the way Melanchthon admits the possibility of a purely rational assurance of God's existence. The arguments are founded on several evident facts, as in addition to the principles of causation, efficient and final, there is the order manifested in nature, which, he contends, could be neither accidental nor the result of properties inherent in matter itself but requires a mind or spirit of order to explain it. Other considerations include the rational nature of man himself, which points to reason as its source of origin, his capacity also to make moral judgements, that native sense of the divine which all men seem to possess, and the emergence of ordered forms of society.

Clearly, then, God's being, Melanchthon thinks, is a truth of natural reason and does not, as such, rest on revelation. Rather, touching the knowledge of spiritual things, scripture reinforces and supplements what, in principle at any rate, is apprehended without its aid. Even divine providence is basically a matter for the rational understanding, although in fact, the human condition being what it is, this is not always evident and men need as well the particular instruction (*patefactio divina*), 'the plain and indubitable testimony', which the Bible alone can give.[81] Thus reason is confronted with its own limits and so recognizes a realm of knowledge not accessible by way of the common experience and understanding. It is a conclusion which, in effect, restores the scholastic concept of a balance between reason and revelation, with its corollary, to which later Lutheranism was to accord full weight, that faith includes *credenda* – what the church confesses, teaches and requires to be believed. As Melanchthon himself says: 'In our confession we profess

78. *M.W.*, III, 359.
79. *Ibid.*
80. *C.R.*, XV, 273. Melanchthon's *Declamatio de philosophia* is of special interest on this subject.
81. *C.R.*, XIII, 150f.

that we embrace the whole teaching of the Word of God, to which the Church gives testimony, and indeed in that sense which the symbols [*i.e. the creeds*] show;'[82] while elsewhere he states: 'In the true faith I include the whole doctrine handed down in the books of the prophets and apostles, and comprehended in the Apostles', Nicene and Athanasian creeds.' He firmly denies moreover that he and his fellow-reformers had introduced new dogma into the church. On the contrary, 'we renew and illustrate the doctrine of the Catholic Church'.[83]

The idea of reason and revelation as complementary determines Melanchthon's view of the relation of theology to philosophy, and so to all other sciences.[84] That natural knowledge of the divine which philosophy itself is able to afford is extended and enhanced by theology using the data of a revelation mediated through history.[85] But theology, the content of which is supernaturally disclosed, and philosophy, which draws on experience and applies rational principles that are universal, evidently differ in their respective methods, and on that account are not to be confused.[86] This is not to say that theology itself is unscientific, since revelation, if it is really to appear as knowledge, needs to be properly ordered and categorized, for which purpose dialectics is clearly necessary.[87] In short, philosophy is the proper aid to theology if the latter is to be both adequately systematized and related to the other spheres of human knowledge, for instance, psychology.[88] It might even be described as a propaedeutic introductory to the gospel itself,[89] for as Melanchthon saw it all human understanding is a pyramid, a hierarchical structure, whose apex or summit is the knowledge of God. Behind it of course was the Aristotelian principle that man's reason is the instrument for the comprehension of all things, earthly or heavenly. The Stagirite, of whose works the schoolmen had made such assiduous use, had been the young humanist's first love, only to be pushed aside in the earlier phase of his Lutheran zeal; yet the estrangement was to prove no more than temporary. Melanchthon later wrote in the shadow of an Aristotle he had once again come to admire, with, now, his eyes on the *Metaphysics* no less than on the *Organon*.

In the light of this revived Aristotelianism it is interesting to observe Melanchthon's new attitude to law, and particularly the natural law as covering the field of social ethics. Little space is accorded to this topic in the first *Loci Communes*, but in the later editions it assumes considerable prominence. Consonant with his estimate of reason Melanchthon sees knowledge of the divine law as something inherent in man's nature. This law is embodied in 'the orders [*Stande*] and works [*Werke*] which serve to keep the human race, and are ordained by God,

---

82.   *C.R.*, XXIV, 398.
83.   *M.W.*, III, 122.
84.   *C.R.*, XII, 689.
85.   *C.R.*, XXI, 605f.
86.   *C.R.*, XI, 282.
87.   *C.R.*, XI, 280; VII, 577; XI, 654. Hence the high importance Melanchthon attached to the education and training of the clergy. At Wittenberg the course comprised dialectic, rhetoric, poetics and science, notably Aristotle's *Physics*, a work for which Luther himself had no use at all (*C.R.*, XI, 501. Cf. *W.A.*, V, 457f.).
88.   *C.R.*, XI, 282.
89.   *C.R.*, XXIV, 689f.

with certain limits and means.'[90] Of these marriage is obviously primary as providing in an orderly way for the continuation of human life, although for the protection
and maintenance of society authority, justice, the penal law, just warfare, the
division of property and so forth are likewise necessary. Hence the *societas politica*,
the state, which on earth is the law's guardian. Civil government itself must
therefore be seen to exist by the will of God, and through its proper functions, as
Luther himself had taught, it is the temporal counterpart of and complement to
the ministry of the church, for in addition to preserving peace and security its duty
is also to promote true religion and piety and to suppress false doctrine and
idolatrous practice. This whole conception of the role of the state was opposed on
the one hand to the high papalism of medieval theory and on the other to the
anti-political notions of many of the sectaries, not to mention the revolutionary
excesses of the Peasants' War. For this purpose the *Politics* of Aristotle was an
invaluable guide, and Melanchthon's use of it was to leave a perdurable mark on
all subsequent Lutheran thinking in this realm.

Melanchthon's life as a theologian had seldom been easy and even in his last
years he was not to be spared the vexation of further controversy, often embittered.
One of these theological *fracas* involved the Nuremberg divine Andreas Osiander
(1498–1552),[91] who, following the exile enforced on him by the *Augsburg Interim*,[92]
took up a professorship at Königsberg. Here he had achieved notoriety as the
exponent of a mystical doctrine of justification according to which salvation,
though wholly through the free grace of Christ as apprehended by faith, rests not
simply on the *imputation* of Christ's righteousness but on a substantial *impartation*
or transference of that righteousness to the believer. He emphasized, that is, the
'Christ-in-us', as the principle of an actual righteousness, at the expense (or so his
critics alleged) of the 'Christ-for-us', which the strict Lutherans insisted was Luther's
own doctrine, and in this way he judged he was in closer accord with the original
Pauline teaching. Osiander in no respect questioned Luther's theory of the atonement: Christ's death was truly substitutionary even as his life was in all its aspects
a perfect fulfilment of the Law on our behalf, although Osiander himself tended
to minimize the part of Christ's human nature in the work of redemption and
perhaps to obscure the once-for-all effectiveness of the cross. Nevertheless the idea
that in justification we are 'made righteous' rather than simply 'declared righteous'
aroused an angry response among Osiander's fellow-Lutherans as savouring of
Romanism and 'works righteousness', while his claim to have Luther on his side

90. Manschreck, *op. cit.*, 323.
91. On Osiander see E. Hirsch, *Die Theologie des Andreas Osiander und ihre geschichtlichen
    Voraussetzungen* (Göttingen, 1919) and G. Seebass, *Das reformatorische Werk des
    Andreas Osiander* (Nuremberg, 1967).
92. The *Augsburg Interim* was the doctrinal formula drawn up in 1548 as a provisional
    basis for a settlement of the religious differences between Catholic and Protestant. It
    resulted from the defeat in 1547 of the Schmalkaldic League of Protestant states by
    Charles V, who then hoped to restore the church's unity. Accepted by the Diet of
    Augsburg in July 1548, its terms were set out in twenty-six articles, in which the main
    points conceded to the Protestants were clerical marriage and communion on both
    kinds. See Kidd, *Documents*, no. 148. A modification of it known as the *Leipzig Interim*
    took a direction a little more favourable to the Protestant position and was adopted
    for Saxony in December, 1548.

was rejected as an impudence. The debate was conducted with an extraordinary degree of animosity even for those days, and eventually led to an open breach, not excepting excommunication, between him and his 'orthodox' antagonists.

The repercussions of this dispute were felt throughout Protestant Germany and especially at Nuremberg. Osiander was not without his supporters, but for the most part his condemnation was considered fully justified. Melanchthon, as the leading Lutheran theologian of the age, was the immediate object of his attack, though in fact it was the Wittenberg teacher's over-zealous pupils who were most clamant in denouncing the Königsberg doctrines, which were too readily misunderstood and misrepresented. For Osiander genuinely believed that his own interpretation of Luther's very nuanced doctrine was the correct one. Indeed so obdurate was he in holding to his convictions that he in turn treated Melanchthon in a way that caused the latter lasting grief. The unhappy wrangle was terminated by Osiander's sudden death in 1552, although Melanchthon was further embroiled in argument with an Italian ex-monk, Francesco Stancari, who taught that Christ was our justification according to his human nature only. The issues held to be at stake in these controversies form the subject of Article III of the *Formula of Concord*.

Melanchthon's life was dedicated to constructive theological and educational work, and he found the sort of theological politics and polemics in which he seemed to be continuously involved distasteful and distressing, consuming of time and energy. This was not only a personal matter; his fear also was for the effect it would have on the unity of Christian fellowship. Schism he utterly deplored, believing that the way of conciliation must always be tried as far as possible. The 1521 *Loci Communes* does not treat specifically of the church, but it is evident from his writings of that period that the existence of the 'Church Universal' whose head was Christ himself was an integral part of his faith. Article VII of the *Augsburg Confession* affirms that the one Holy Church 'will remain for ever' and that essentially it is 'a congregation of saints in which the Gospel is rightly taught and the sacraments duly administered', 'notes' underlined in the *Apology* (Arts VII and VIII) and clearly enunciated in the later *Loci*, the final version of which states that 'the really true Church, the people of God, which we have called the visible Church, has the external marks of a pure doctrine and right use of the sacraments'.[93] In its visible character as the *coetus vocatorum*, 'the assembly of the called', it is inevitably of course a mixed society not all of whose members are truly regenerate, but the hierarchical conception is rejected, neither the papacy nor the episcopal succession being necessary for its constitution or its continuance. However, the ministry as such is divinely willed, and Melanchthon attaches particular importance to its teaching role: in fact, he divides the church's members into two categories, the *docentes* and the *audientes*, those whose responsibility it is to instruct and those whose duty is to listen. Hence no doubt the impression he sometimes conveys of stressing overmuch the externals of Christian profession. 'I believe', he once wrote, 'in the Creed; I make use of the sacraments, I am baptized, and obey the ministry; therefore I am a Christian.'[94]

This statement taken literally and in isolation would be altogether misleading,

93. Manschreck, *op. cit.*, 272.
94. *C.R.*, XXIV, 402.

since he never discounted the necessity of fiducial faith. Yet if 'pure doctrine' is really of prime importance then sound theological instruction is indispensable, and in time orthodoxy becomes an end in itself.

A sacrament Melanchthon defined in the final edition of the *Loci Communes* as 'a religious ceremony instituted in the Gospel as a witness to the promise which is contained in the Gospel, that is to say, the promise of reconciliation and grace'.[95] In common with the other leading reformers he recognized the two 'gospel' sacraments only. As against the anabaptists he urged the legitimacy and complete propriety of infant baptism, but on the eucharist his ideas came gradually to differ from Luther's, whose position he had so staunchly defended at Marburg against the 'word-spinning' Zwinglians. Thanks also in large part to Bucer's attempts to mediate between Zurich and Wittenberg, the Swiss themselves shifted from a purely symbolical interpretation and, as the *First Helvetic Confession* shows, approximated to Bucer's own view. The latter in discussions with Luther at Wittenberg managed to bring about the agreement known as the *Wittenberg Concord*, a doctrinal statement drawn up by Melanchthon which, although basically Lutheran, did not insist on the doctrine of the ubiquity of the Lord's glorified body.[96] Unfortunately for the unity of the Reformation movement, the Swiss refused to ratify the Concord, although the Protestants of south Germany, despite their strong Zwinglian attachment, were eventually brought into the Lutheran church.

However, Melanchthon's own opinions were now themselves veering in a Zwinglian direction. For Luther's theory of ubiquity he found no support at all in the early Fathers, whose eucharistic teaching in any case was not uniform, while on the other hand, as against all those, including Bucer and Calvin, who asserted that the body of Christ is located only in heaven he maintained that Christ can choose – *arcano modo* – to be present in more than one place at a time. In a word, the real presence is essentially a presence of *will*, hence the cumbersome term sometimes used of Melanchthon's view, a presence *multivolens*. In the Latin text of his 1540 revised version of the *Augsburg Confession* he significantly rewrote Article X (*Of the Lord's Supper*) thus: 'They [*the Lutheran churches*] teach that with [*cum*] the bread and wine the very body and blood of Christ are truly offered ['*exhibeantur*' in place of the earlier '*distribuantur*'] to those who eat in the Lord's Supper,' the words 'truly and substantially present' being now omitted. Clearly therefore, though he believed in a 'spiritual' presence, Melanchthon was no longer prepared to take his stand on the principle that in the Supper Christ's body and blood, albeit 'given with' the bread and wine, are not given (as distinct from received) without *faith*, an idea which Luther simply could not admit.[97] On this subject the great German reformer considered himself to be nearer to the pope than to the impious Swiss, although he never broke with his revered Philipp.

In certain respects Melanchthon, as has frequently been remarked, is an

---

95.  *M.W.*, II (2), 497.
96.  For the text see Kidd, *Documents*, no. 127; an English trans. is given in Tappert, *op. cit.*
97.  On Melanchthon's eucharistic theology see R. W. Quere, *Melanchthon's 'Christum cognoscere': Christ's Efficacious Presence in the Eucharistic Theology of Melanchthon* (Leiden, 1977).

enigmatic figure. He was at once an evangelical and a humanist, and tension between these two sides of his mind resulted in an ambivalence, not to say a duplicity, of attitude that disconcerted and even alienated many who otherwise would have deferred to him as Luther's unquestionable successor in the leadership of German Protestantism. Moreover his very genuine desire to conciliate and promote harmony, where this might prove at all feasible, was often taken for mere pusillanimity, and his apparent readiness to change his opinions as a mark of inconstancy and vacillation; sometimes he could even seem a crypto-Romanist. And if his contemporaries were suspicious or hostile posterity, for its part, was long content to neglect him, for not until well into the nineteenth century did interest in his career and achievements revive. Modern research, happily, has now at last brought both the man and his work into much clearer perspective, while his caution and moderation, combined with his ecumenical spirit, are qualities which today count strongly in his favour.[98] His natural inclination for philosophy, which Luther judged to be the root cause of his difficulties, no doubt did much to set Lutheran theology on the path of an intellectualism which later became arid. But what has to be recognized in estimating his contribution to the religious changes of his time was his deep sense of tradition and of the importance of continuity in the Christian church. The past he respected for its wisdom and experience, and especially the voice of antiquity in the surviving writings of the Fathers – a regard plainly reflected in his ideas on liturgical worship and ecclesiastical polity generally, in which he assigned high value to custom and usage, wherever these could properly be retained, and, in all points, to good order. With the anarchism of the 'enthusiasts' and free spirits of his age he could have had no kind of sympathy. As the years went by he increasingly came to esteem the worth both of constitutional principle and a soundly formulated theology. Excepting only Luther himself no man did so much to determine the historic identity of Lutheran Christianity, in its spirit as well as in its forms.

98. On recent Melanchthon research see P. Fraenkel and M. Greschat, *Zwanzig Jahre Melanchthonstudien, Sechs Literaturberichte (1945–65)* (Geneva, 1967).

# Chapter 7

# CALVIN AND REFORMED CHRISTIANITY:
# I. STRASSBURG AND GENEVA

## Martin Bucer at Strassburg

If Wittenberg was from the first the principal centre of the Reformation in Germany it was not long before Strassburg, the imperial free city on the upper Rhine, became an important tributary source, starting with the pioneer work of Jakob Sturm, a local magistrate, and Matthäus Zell (1477–1548), a priest at the cathedral, who in 1521 began preaching evangelical doctrine in a side chapel there, followed by the appearance some two years later (May 1523) of Wolfgang Fabricius Capito, formerly chancellor to the archbishop of Mainz and a professor in the university of Basel, versed in law, medicine and theology as well as a noted Hebraist and friend and collaborator of Erasmus,[1] and then, a month later, of a man at the time but little known, Martin Bucer (1491–1551), previously a Dominican friar at Heidelberg but now a warm admirer of Luther. A little later these were joined by Kaspar Hedio (1494–1552), a scholar and theologian from Mainz, and by François Lambert, subsequently leader of the reform in Hesse, whither he was called by the Landgrave Philip. Of this group of adherents of the 'new learning' Bucer was to become easily the most prominent and influential, a man whose concern for the unity of the church was certainly no less than Melanchthon's, and whose mediatorial activities in this respect we have already had occasion to mention. Indeed after the death of Zwingli Bucer's personal abilities marked him out as the most effective leader of the reformed churches of Switzerland and south Germany, tireless in his efforts to secure not only Protestant cohesion but, as the successive conferences at Hagenau (1540), Worms (1540) and Ratisbon (1541) prove, to bring about accord between Protestants of both Lutheran and Zwinglian complexion and the best representatives of the old religion. To promote religious peace he showed himself ready to enter into discussion with anybody, whatever his views or his learning or his status. In fact he was a genuine ecumenist, for whom the cause of truth was never well served by the spirit of mere dissidence. Towards the end of his life he was to play a not insignificant part in the English Reformation during the reign of the young king Edward VI, particularly with his interesting treatise *De regno Christi*; but of this more will be said in the appropriate place.[2] At present

---

1. Capito, whose real name was Köpfel, was an associate of Erasmus's, keenly interested in reform on Erasmian lines. For a time Luther was his idol, but, being of a tolerant disposition, he always believed in introducing change *suaviter*. On Capito's mature theological opinions see O. E. Strasser, *La Pensée théologique de Wolfgang Capito dans les dernières années de sa vie* (*Mémoires de l'université de Neuchâtel*, XI, 1938). On his life and work generally, J. M. Kittleson, *Wolfgang Capito: from humanist to reformer* (Leiden, 1975).
2. See below, p. 245.

we shall confine ourselves to the earlier phases of his work as a reformer, having especially in view his humanist aptitude and his influence upon Calvin, to whose extraordinary career Bucer's own provides a suitable introduction.[3]

As a Dominican Martin Bucer (or Butzer) developed a humanist enthusiasm, and it was in a humanistic rather than a dogmatic spirit that he turned to the study of the Bible.[4] At first it was Erasmus whom he heroized, but the turning-point of his life was hearing Luther speak at the Heidelberg conference in April 1518. A correspondence between the two ensued, and soon the younger man had become a devotee. In 1522 he married, thus being one of the first of the reformers personally to repudiate the vow of celibacy. He began his evangelical preaching at Wissenberg in Alsace, but for much the greater part of his career he held pastorates in Strassburg, where in 1530 he was elected president of the church council, by then the supreme ecclesiastical authority. The traditional mass was not abolished until early in 1529, although a complete reorganization of the church system was already well in progress, Bucer's own *Ordnung und Inhalt deutscher Messe* of 1524 setting out the new form of worship. In 1539 he instituted a service of confirmation. But besides his liturgical interests he was convinced of the need for good catechetical instruction, and in fact for a sound educational system generally, himself founding a gymnasium in 1538, and in 1544 a seminary for the training of pastors. His reforming activity, moreover, was not confined to Strassburg: not only did he cooperate, if unsuccessfully, with Hermann von Wied, the evangelically-minded archbishop of Cologne, but his advice was sought in the Low Countries, in France and even in Italy. Like the other principal reformers, however, he would have nothing to do with the radical innovators, whose ideas he strongly opposed. His open disapproval of the *Augsburg Interim* obliged him to quit Strassburg, which if with reluctance had accepted the emperor's terms, and in the following year he betook himself to England at the invitation of the archbishop of Canterbury, Thomas Cranmer. He was honourably received by Edward VI, but his appointment in 1549 as regius professor of divinity at Cambridge was of short duration; for health reasons he did not assume his duties until 1550 and he died there in the February of the next year, his remains being buried in Great St Mary's church.[5] Even so he made an impact on the English reform movement which was to have lasting effect.[6]

3. There is a collected edition of Bucer's Latin and German works edited by F. Wendel, *et al.* (Gütersloh, 1954ff), including an admirable critical edition of the Latin text of the *De regno Christi* by Wendel (Paris, 1955); an English translation of the latter work forms the second part of W. Pauck's Library of Christian Classics volume, *Melanchthon and Bucer*. On Bucer generally see A. Lang, *Der Evangelienkommentar Martin Butzers und die Grundzüge seiner Theologie* (Leipzig, 1990); G. Anrich, *Martin Bucer* (Strassburg, 1914); and H. Eells, *Martin Bucer* (New Haven, Conn., 1931; repr. 1971). Also M. Greschat, 'Der Ansatz der Theologie Martin Bucers', *Theologische Literaturzeitung* 103 (1978). 81–96.

4. See M. Greschat, 'Die Anfänge der reformatorischen Theologie Martin Bucers', in *Reformation und Humanismus: Robert Stupperich zum 65. Geburtstag*, ed. M. Greschat and J. F. G. Goeters (Witten, 1969), 124–140. On the influence of Erasmus see F. Krüger, *Bucer und Erasmus: eine Untersuchung zum Einfluss des Erasmus auf die Theologie Martin Bucers* (Wiesbaden, 1975).

5. During the reign of Queen Mary his body was exhumed and then burned in the town's market square.

6. See C. Hopf, *Martin Bucer and the English Reformation* (Oxford, 1946).

Thanks to the interest of Sturm, Bucer, along with Capito, started lecturing on the Bible shortly after his arrival at Strassburg, his discourses being delivered in Latin to clerical hearers but in German for more popular audiences. Capito concentrated on Jeremiah, Bucer himself on the gospels, the pastoral epistles and the psalter, while Lambert lectured on Romans, I and II Corinthians and Ezekiel. The lecturers' approach, so free of scholastic formalism, proved immensely popular and the successive courses soon began to appear in print as full-scale commentaries: Lambert on Hosea in 1525, and on Daniel and the Apocalypse in 1526, Capito on Habbakuk in the same year, Bucer on St Matthew and Ephesians in 1529 and a second edition of the St Matthew volume in 1530. The dedicatees were often highly placed personages like the Dauphin of France, Bishop Foxe of Hereford and Archbishop Cranmer. The overall aim of this studious effort at biblical interpretation was evident: to present in the clearest possible fashion the primary sources of all genuine Christian doctrine and ethics. Bucer's commentaries in particular, whatever one may think of them nowadays – and their long-winded discursiveness makes them scarcely readable – were greatly esteemed by his contemporaries, not least by Calvin, who used them in the preparation of his *Institutes*, and in the preface to his own commentary on Romans, probably the most important of all his exegetical works, he generously acknowledged his debt to the Strassburg divine, whom, despite certain reservations (Calvin was never wholly unqualified in his praise), he thought one of the best biblical scholars of the age – an impressive tribute as coming from the greatest of all sixteenth-century exegetes.[7]

Bucer fully appreciated the value of a sound text as the necessary basis for a good translation. But although for his commentary on the Psalms, for example, he went direct to the Hebrew, using not only the best grammars available but consulting Jewish commentators as well, neither philology nor textual criticism was his primary interest. For him the only point of studying scripture so closely was to discover its exact sense, in order to be able to draw out its full religious significance. This is emphasized in his prefaces. It is not enough, he says, merely to pick out passages here and there to suit some immediate purpose of the theologian's, a procedure more often than not both unintelligent in its arbitrary selectiveness and prone to overlook the truths contained elsewhere.[8] The gospels in particular should be read as wholes, if an authentic portrait of Christ is to emerge. Allegorical exegesis ought therefore to be avoided; it could 'prove' too much, whilst diverting attention from what scripture really had to offer.

The critical spirit of humanism is apparent in all Bucer's exegetical work. Each biblical author was to be studied for his own special and characteristic witness, particularly as faith is always a deeply personal matter: *sua fide justus vivat, non aliena*, the righteous lives by his own faith, not by somebody else's. For this reason, he thought, one should be tolerant of another man's sincerely held convictions, an attitude which made Bucer so good a mediator. For his part he confessed himself ready at all times to submit his own views to the judgement of other believers, who were free to accept or reject them as they saw fit.

Bucer was not a systematic theologian like Melanchthon or Calvin, and his

7. Cf. Lang, *op. cit.*, 36.
8. *Ibid.*, 377ff.

opinions on doctrinal matters have chiefly to be sought in the pages of his commentaries. St Matthew's gospel he judged of supreme value as a source for the Christian's knowledge of the work and teaching of Jesus, and after it the other synoptics, St Mark and St Luke, his studies of all three providing the centrepiece of his entire exegetical output. Next to the synoptics came the Pauline epistles, since no one had comprehended the meaning of Christ so well as the great apostle, nor had furnished the Christian with such excellent instruction in his duties. But the reader, he maintained, should not start with Romans or Galatians, books more often talked about than understood. Better was it to make a beginning with the Pastorals, I and II Timothy and Titus, and then work through the rest, leaving Romans, the most difficult of all, to the last.[9] As for the Old Testament, the most profitable study lay in the psalms, Bucer's commentary on which went through no fewer than five editions, Calvin again esteeming it so highly as to feel any exposition of his own to be unnecessary. Bucer also anticipated Calvin in holding that it is not enough to read the scriptures with intellectual concentration only; the enlightenment of the Holy Spirit is all-important. But he differed from the French divine in attaching more weight to the authority of the early church Fathers, the opinion, as he thought, of those who lived so much nearer to the age of canonicity giving them special qualification as interpreters of divine revelation.

Furthermore, Bucer, like other humanists, was persuaded that this had had its *praeparatio*, or at least its foreshadowing, not only among the Jews but in paganism itself, and did not doubt that St Paul himself had believed the same. The morally educative value of the pagan classics he considered obvious; outside the Bible there was no better preceptor than Cicero. But he also held that the Greek philosophers had been able to attain to such a genuine if limited knowledge of God and of the true righteousness as was bound to have promoted acceptance of the gospel in the pagan world. And he adds that in view of the fact that it was God's intention, following his self-revelation in Christ, to transfer the Kingdom from the Jews to the Gentiles, it is a fair presumption (*verisimile est*) that before the Lord's coming many among the latter would already have been set to discover the way to true righteousness. This must have been providential, for as the Jews had been given the Law, so Gentiles had enjoyed the God-implanted *lumen naturale* (*gentes sola luce quam naturae vocant, praeditos*), by which they became possessed of no small measure of the truth. Thus they knew much of the content of the divine law without having formally received it as such. That the philosophers, fallible men, for even Plato (not to mention Aristotle) at times goes wrong, were not always in agreement on men's actual moral duties is not surprising; understanding demands time and effort, and Christian theologians themselves are often notoriously at odds with one another. But the evident fact is that philosophy is on many matters demonstrably in accord with holy scripture. Both teach that all things were created by God and are subject to his guiding wisdom, and that man, although made in the divine image, has so fallen from his original state that he is now incapable of recovering his integrity without divine aid. Also, for those without the Law to live in

9. Bucer's *Metaphrases et enarrationes perpetuae epistolarum D. Pauli apostoli* was published at Strassburg in 1536. It has been described as the first modern commentary (Strohl, *La pensée de la Réforme*, 13, 20).

accordance with nature (that is, in obedience to God's will) is to recover to some extent this lost image. And the basic law which all men can obey is to do good and harm no man. The one great difference between Christian and pagan righteousness lies, as the apostle insists, in the forgiveness of sins through Christ. Apart from the knowledge of this supreme truth the pursuit of virtue too easily becomes the pride of moral self-sufficiency. Yet it is noteworthy that Bucer describes the fault as a defect of, so to say, pedagogical method (*ratio tractandi*) rather than as an error of substance.

This humanist strain in Bucer, which was to persist throughout his life, is evident in his interpretation of justification by faith. There can of course be no question of the deep impression first made on him by Luther's teaching, but in a letter addressed by him in 1518 to the humanist Beatus Rhenanus what he seems especially to be stressing is that a justified sinner is essentially a *new creation*.[10] The Law, he writes, can instruct the mind, but in itself it is not enough to move the heart. Only God's grace, the power of the Holy Spirit, can do this, for the Spirit at once illuminates, purifies, creates the impulse to do good and supplies the strength to accomplish it. Indeed in justification man does not so much act as he is acted on (*non tam agunt quam aguntur*). The Spirit is a kind of divine entelechy which descends on the soul to take possession of it and activate it in such a way that it is able to see and do what is right. But we have to remember that when God intends to give life he also first mortifies; before enriching he makes the sinner realize his own utter poverty. The wonder is however that the divine love which finds nothing in fallen man that is intrinsically lovable yet deigns to recreate him. Thus while the emphasis must necessarily fall on the love and condescension manifested in Christ it is always to show how God wills to create a new humanity. What Bucer is especially concerned to bring out is the teaching of Luther's tract *On the Freedom of a Christian Man* and the sermon *On Good Works*. For as he sees it it was God's purpose that men should cooperate with and help one another.[11] But sin, the essence of which is selfishness, prevented this. As a result all human relationships have been disrupted, causing a distortion that in some strange way has affected even external nature itself, which man now exploits simply for his own profit. God's plan, though, is to restore to mankind in Christ both the will and the capacity to love his neighbour as himself. Hence the need, in Bucer's mind, to show how not only the church but civil society itself ought to be ordered if such an end is to be realized. In a word, redemption takes account of man's material requirements as well as his spiritual, of the fact that he has a body as well as a soul, so that the alleviation of human need at the physical level must be seen as itself a constituent element of a proper spiritual relationship. It is a striking feature of Bucer's outlook which, present from the beginning, was to be given detailed expression in the *De regno Christi*.

To bring this new world order about the saving gospel of Christ must be

10. *Briefwechsel*, ed. A. Horwitz and K. Hartfelder (Leipzig, 1886), 108ff. Cf. *W.A.*, IX, 161–9. Beatus Rhenanus was, like Bucer, a native of Schlettstadt.
11. See his tract *Das ym selbs niemant sonder anderen leben soll* (1523) reprinted in a French translation (with introduction) in *Revue d'histoire et de philosophie religieuses* (Strasbourg, 1947), 141–213.

preached, heard and believed, for when men comprehend that God truly is their Father in heaven they will learn also to see each other as brethren. The sermons that date from the time of Bucer's pastorate at Wissenburg, before he settled at Strassburg, follow Luther closely.[12] Faith, he declares, is absolute trust in God, who bestows his grace on us freely, delivers us from all evil and forgives us our sins; it is a conviction (*persuasio*), amounting to a fixed and indubitable (*certa et indubitanda*) assurance, of God's purpose to redeem and restore fallen humanity, and is elicited by the teaching of Jesus Christ in the gospels.[13] But faith involves obedience, issuing in a righteousness which, claiming no inherent merit, is a grateful thank-offering to God. Again, its essential content is service of one's neighbour; nevertheless it also requires of us a self-discipline without which such service is not possible. Life itself tests us by providing abundantly the opportunities and the means of this discipline.

All these points find summary statement in the *Confessio Tetrapolitana*. Saving faith, it says, is the work of God through his Word and the Holy Spirit (Article III), but (Article IV) it must lead on to actual newness of life. For to love God is to become like him, fashioned after the image of his Son. To know God (Article V) is to learn to trust him utterly and to believe in his goodness towards us, such alone being the source of the 'good works' Christ himself bids us to perform. The roots here of much later evangelical pietism are apparent.[14] They were in fact extended by Bucer himself in his own homiletic practice, with the importance he attaches to the sermon's primary aim of edification.[15] The preacher's aim, he always believed, should be to guide his hearers towards a deeper understanding of the moral implications of faith; the exposition of doctrine (and the tendency even then was for this to become more and more abstruse) is subordinate. Moreover, in the preface to his commentary on Romans he makes it quite clear that, since the apostle himself teaches that faith manifests itself in love, justification and sanctification are to be seen as two simultaneous 'movements' in, or complementary aspects of, a single process of spiritual regeneration.


A mediating theology. Bucer and Calvin


What, then, was Bucer's view on predestination, an issue on which no reforming theologian could remain uncommitted? That it came to assume a growing importance

12. See A. Erickson, *Die Predigt Bucers zu Weissenburg* (Strassburg, 1891).
13. The actual nature of faith was of concern to Bucer, and he appended a treatise on it (*Disputatio de fide*) to his 1529 commentary on the psalter. But this view of it as a conviction, with understanding, of the mercy and beneficence of God is apparent throughout his commentary on the gospels (where the idea of faith as *assent* seems to receive special stress, modified somewhat in the 1536 edition), in the commentary on Romans, and in the *Tetrapolitana*. For while Bucer does not in any way seek to obscure the objective aspect of faith as a gift of the Spirit, he seems to have a particular interest in considering it subjectively in its psychological effects.
14. Cf. A. Lang, *Puritanismus und Pietismus. Studien zu ihre Entwickelung von M. Butzer bis zum Methodismus* (Neukirchen, 1941), 13–71.
15. And precept also. See P. Scherding and F. Wendel, 'Un traité d'exégèse pratique de Bucer', in *Revue d'histoire et de philosophie religieuses* (Strasbourg, 1946), 32–75.

in his mind is not to be doubted, but it is questionable whether it posed itself to him in the first place as a matter of basic principle.[16] It would appear rather to have been in the nature of a practical inference from his pastoral experience, which forced the question on him, as on any thoughtful parish minister, why it is that whereas some heed the gospel when preached to them others do not. From a knowledge of Bucer's general outlook one would have supposed it easier for him to attribute the difference to human causes: moral indifference, or sheer hardness of heart. That he should instead have referred it back to the divine purpose itself, though never, it would seem, to the point of actually denying the freedom of the human will, can perhaps best be explained by the influence of Zwingli, whom he held in the highest regard.[17] Further, the whole concept of the church itself was inseparable in much current thinking from the doctrine of election and reprobation, since the divine society, it was held, cannot but depend on what ultimately is an eternal and unchanging decree of God himself.[18] This, however, could well be offset by the practical conviction that in the teachings of the gospel the church has an indefeasible responsibility for its lost sheep. Plainly there were two truths here that had somehow to be balanced one against the other if the church were properly to fulfil its mission to the world. The whole problem was one to which Calvin was later to address himself much more systematically than the Strassburg theologian whose friend, and to some extent disciple, he became.

It is fair to say that none of the reformers – only Calvin, again, excepted – disclosed so great an interest in the nature and constitution of the church as did Bucer. His thinking on this subject was no doubt influenced by Luther, Zwingli and Oecolampadius, but here too the root of his convictions lay in his active pastoral concern, at once stimulated and moulded by his experience at Strassburg, where, given the ready encouragement of the city council, whose eyes were on the example of Zurich, he very soon found himself carrying the full burden of responsibility for the leadership and organization of church life, the effective power of the Catholic bishop of Geneva having already virtually collapsed. As by 1524 the parishes had been reorganized under evangelical preachers and new disciplinary measures introduced, it fell largely to Bucer to explain the new order to the townspeople, many of whom had succumbed to an individualistic illuminism or a sectarian radicalism with which he himself, unlike Capito, had very little sympathy. The *ius reformandi* he at first accepted as lying with the magistrates who had so warmly supported him, but he later yielded to Oecolampadius's argument that the church should be free to exercise its own autonomous discipline. The appointment in 1531 by the civic authorities of *Kirchenpfleger*, or 'churchwardens', was for a time a source of difficulty for him, since they found it in fact more agreeable 'to criticize the vicar' than to contribute much in the way of active pastoral help. Notwithstanding, he felt able to concede that as 'lay elders' they fulfilled a genuinely spiritual function, as well as embodying the principle of the priesthood of all believers, to which he had himself always attached a fundamental importance. At

16. Lang, *op. cit.*, 158–64 thinks otherwise.
17. Bucer discusses the question at some length in his Romans commentary (358ff).
18. Cf. J. Courvoisier, *La notion de l'Eglise chez Bucer dans son développement historique* (Paris, 1933), 65ff.

any rate their growing willingness to cooperate with their pastors was a welcome development. Meantime Bucer had warmed to the idea of forming *Gemeinschaften*, voluntary groups or fraternities within each parish consisting of dedicated Christians who would operate as a kind of spiritual leaven enhancing the quality of Christian living throughout the city.

The biblical grounds for his ecclesiology Bucer endeavoured to make clearer in the 1536 edition of his commentary on St Matthew and in the new work on Romans. But a greater stress is also evident on the institutional character of the church as not only a communion of regenerated believers living a life of mutual aid and care but as the sphere in which the true word of God is preached, the witness of the faith maintained and the sacraments duly dispensed as Christ had commanded. Both word and sacraments, that is, were to be understood as objective means of grace, not in any exclusive sense but as the recognized and assured vehicles of God's promised gifts to his people. Besides which it followed from the significance attached to preaching and the administration of the sacraments that the role of the minister himself should appear strengthened. In Bucer's view, though, the idea of the universal priesthood meant that the pastor did not stand alone but was to be assisted by other ministrations in accordance with, as he supposed, the testimony of scripture itself: namely, elders, teachers and deacons, the first of these being responsible, along with the ministers, for the discharge of that function of discipline which he was coming more and more to regard as an essential mark of a truly reformed church.[19]

Bucer's considered views on the nature, rights and mission of the church were expounded two years later and mainly for the benefit of the civic authorities in his treatise *Von der wahren Seelsorge und dem rechten Hirtendienst* ('Of True Pastoral Care'), perhaps the most carefully conceived of all his writings.[20] In it he asserts the church's inherent independence by virtue of its divine mission to continue Christ's work and to promote his Kingdom on earth, he alone being its Head and Lord, albeit invisible (*unbefindlich*). The church indeed is the 'Body of Christ', or visibly (*befindlich*), a 'body in Christ'. It is also the 'Kingdom' of God or of Christ, and all true believers are its citizens. Using another scriptural expression, it can be described as the 'bride of Christ', while in its warfare against sin and the devil it is an 'army', with Christ as its 'captain'. All these designations are valid and instructive, although none – and notably, perhaps, the phrase 'Body of Christ' (Pauline though it is) with its questionable suggestion of the church as an 'extension' of the incarnation – should be pressed to the exclusion of the others. Furthermore, it is the church's duty to educate, it may be even to re-educate, its own members, as it likewise is its right to excommunicate those whose presence within it is a shame and a scandal.

All through the work Bucer is at pains to document his statements from the Bible, listing what he judges to be the appropriate references at the head of each chapter. The church itself he defines at the outset as 'a community [*Gemeinschaft*] in which the word and the sacraments, love and discipline [*Zucht*] prevail'. Its

19. Courvoisier, *op. cit.*, 88.
20. For a detailed account see Courvoisier, *ibid.*, 97–115, to which the resumé in the text is indebted.

members, drawn from the world at large, are constituted a single body in Christ, their Lord, by the power of his agent, the Holy Spirit, and the proclamation of the word. Their vocation is to serve him in a brotherhood of mutual love, bearing one another's burdens, since 'none lives for himself alone', and striving to advance his Kingdom among men. Even so, Christ and his church, although in a significant sense one, are not to be confused. As the Head he is distinct from the body, even if the latter, to have life, must be animated by his Spirit. Hence the Lord's work requires the visible instrumentality (*befindliche Werkzeuge*) of recognized ministers charged with the exercise of special functions (*Ämter*) within the community of the faithful and on its behalf. Luther indeed admitted the need, which unless met would of course render any sort of organized communal life impossible, but Bucer takes a much more positive view, holding that the actual forms of ministry are themselves of scriptural origin and must therefore be said to be divinely provided. Pastors and teachers, elders and deacons, who all have their New Testament prototypes, are to be chosen from the Christian community by reason of their particular gifts and qualifications. The church's mission includes both pastoral care and evangelism, together with the exercise of paternal discipline in the name of Christ; a discipline, it may be added, conceived to be of benefit not only to the church but to society as a whole. For whereas justice and the enforcement of law are concerned with outward acts (with the conscience itself they cannot deal directly) the church's business is with souls, with men's inner selves. In this realm the ministry of elders is equipped to function. But the church always has the ultimate right to excommunicate.

These ideas Bucer presents not as a mere theoretical excursus but as a practically effective scheme of church organization, independent in important respects of the civic authorities but at the same time claiming public responsibility for the administration of charity and for education, in which the church already had a controlling interest. They met however with opposition in Strassburg itself, and in particular Bucer's plan of forming *christliche Gemeinschaften* in the parishes, on lines similar to those of Spener's *collegia pietatis* more than a century later, did not prove a lasting success. In Hesse, on the other hand, thanks to the support of the Landgrave, with whom he was on close terms, Bucer's objectives attained a considerable measure of concrete embodiment. Subsequently, as much elaborated and somewhat idealized in the *De regno Christi*, they were laid before the English government, although ineffectually as events turned out. The Strassburg reformer's vision did not, in fact, become practically feasible until the advent of Calvin at Geneva.

Bucer's intervention in the eucharistic controversy has already been mentioned. According to the *Tetrapolitana* the sacraments are 'sacred symbols' and 'visible signs of an invisible grace'; but the statements on the eucharist are ambiguous, the result plainly enough of the attempt to placate the susceptibilities of both the Lutherans and the Swiss. Luther's doctrine of what appeared to its critics to be an inadmissible 'localization' of Christ's presence in the elements did not satisfy Bucer, although the Wittenberg leader often said that he could never really think of God except as 'God made flesh' and that Christ was no less present in the act of preaching. Bucer's view was that while it is the bread and wine only that are outwardly received in the sacrament it is Christ's body and blood that are received inwardly by faith.[21] What he would not allow was that in the elements there is any *manducatio oralis* of the Lord's body and blood. Yet in the *Wittenberg Concord* of 1536 sufficient agreement was reached to admit the affirmation that 'with' the bread and wine – Luther did not now insist on the words 'in' and 'under' as well – the Lord's body and blood are truly and substantially present, offered and received, the relationship between the elements and the presence being described as a 'sacramental union'. Moreover, the validity of the sacrament was declared to be independent of the worthiness of either the ministrant or the recipient, although not to the extent of admitting it in the hypothetical case of a 'eucharist' celebrated by or for Jews or Turks.[22]

Bucer's endeavours to discover a way of stating the doctrine in a formulary which both Lutherans and Zwinglians could accept were untiring and ingenious – Heinrich Bullinger, during the 1544 controversy between the Lutherans and the Swiss, actually coined the word *bucerisare* to express the sort of thing he meant – but they made for him many enemies and sometimes left even his friends nonplused. Like Melanchthon he too suffered much from the *rabies theologorum*. Yet if his achievements were apt also to be failures for him personally they were destined to have a positive and durable outcome in those of Calvin. For Bucer more than any other reformer was the direct forbear of Calvinism.[23]

Indeed the close affinity between the theological outlook of Calvin and that of the Strassburg divine who was seventeen years his senior has repeatedly been noted and cannot seriously be disputed. Whether the subject is predestination, the sacraments, the church or ecclesiastical discipline there is so patent a resemblance between the teachings of the two men that the question at once presents itself: did Calvin derive certain of his basic tenets, more or less in the form in which he characteristically expounds them, straight from Martin Bucer? It has even been maintained that the older divine was actually Calvin's superior in 'theological originality'.[24] It is pretty certain that Calvin became acquainted with Bucer's writings while still a student in France, most probably through Volmar, his professor at Bourges, although he may already have heard of Bucer from his cousin Pierre Robert, or Olivétan, as he was usually called, who himself would appear to have studied at Strassburg.[25] Of any personal contact on Calvin's part with Bucer there is no sure evidence previous to a letter of 4 September 1534, sent by the former from his birthplace, Noyon, the wording of which suggests that some correspondence between them might already have taken place.[26] The earliest known letter of Bucer's to Calvin, who by that time was living at Geneva, is of 1 November 1536, seeking to arrange a meeting between them at the latter's convenience and regretting that they had not met when Calvin visited Strassburg, probably a few

21. Whence the remark of a modern commentator that 'we may look to Bucer for the origin of the custom of theologians to speak of a Real Presence when a Real Presence is not actually meant' (Sasse, *This is My Body*, 306).
22. See Jacob, ed., *The Book of Concord*, II, 287ff. ('Bucer's exhortation to his colleagues').
23. Anrich, *Martin Bucer*, 144.
24. O. Ritschl, *Dogmengeschichte des Protestantismus*, III, 125.
25. See J. Pannier, *Calvin à Strassburg* (Paris, 1925), 11, 12.
26. A. L. Herminjard, *Correspondance des Réformateurs dans les pays de langue française*, (9 vols, Geneva, 1866–1897), III, 202f.

weeks before.[27] The chances are, however, that the two reformers did not become personally acquainted until they met at Bern in the following year. In a letter of 12 January 1538 Calvin alludes to this meeting and discusses a number of matters, not omitting to criticize the Strassburg leader for not speaking out forcefully enough in dealing with opponents. He himself did not mince words. 'If you want a Christ', he says, 'who is acceptable to all, you must not fabricate a gospel for that purpose.'[28] But when, shortly afterwards, the young Frenchman was forced to leave Geneva and had settled at Strassburg as minister to the French congregation there, he came fully under Bucer's influence. Not that his correspondence indicates submission on all matters to the older man's viewpoint – Calvin's was not a submissive temperament – and he does not hesitate to register differences, but he now obviously finds himself in marked sympathy with him and is prompt to defend him against his critics. Further, through close personal contact with Bucer, his own theological opinions, especially on predestination and the Lord's Supper, attain a new clarity and precision.[29] He could in fact be fairly described at this time as a disciple of Bucer. Again, it was the Strassburg divine who made him properly aware of the Reformation as a European movement, putting him in touch with German Protestantism, notably in the person of Philipp Melanchthon, inviting him to conferences such as those at Hagenau and Ratisbon, and in general awakening in him that keen sense of the need for evangelical unity which persisted throughout his life.

The details of Bucer's relations with Calvin after the latter's return to Geneva are obscure because of the paucity of the surviving correspondence between them, although we do know that Bucer was very reluctant for him to leave Strassburg, and such letters as are extant plainly reveal the warmth of their mutual esteem.[30] For the years after 1547 we are much better informed. These were the dark days of the *Interim* and Bucer was deeply apprehensive for the future of the reformed churches. He kept up his personal courage, but was disquieted and depressed by the current course of events. At any rate it was becoming increasingly clear that he would have to leave Strassburg, and in the autumn of 1548 he wrote to Calvin expressing the hope that he might shortly be able to visit Geneva.[31] This was not to be fulfilled, far-off London being his destination instead. Yet even at that date he thought it might be possible for him to see his friend once more before departing. The tone of his letters, signed *Tuus totus Bucerus*, evidences the admiration and strength of regard he still felt for the man who had given such impressive articulation to the principles of the evangelical faith and was well on the way to

27. *Ibid.*, IV, 117ff., although the editor gives the date incorrectly as 1 December. See H. Eells, 'Martin Bucer and the conversion of John Calvin', in *Princeton Theological Review* (1924), 412ff.
28. *Johannis Calvini opera quae supersunt omnia*, ed. G. Baum, E. Cunitz, E. Reuss *et al.* (*Corpus Reformatorum*) (Brunswick and Berlin, 1863–1900, 59 vols), X, 142. Referred to hereafter as *Opera*. There is an English trans. of the 1536 *Institutes* by F. L. Battles (Atlanta, Mich., 1975). Very many of Calvin's works were published at Edinburgh by the Calvin Translation Society between 1843 and 1859.
29. See Pannier, *op. cit.*; also E. Doumergue, *La Vie de Calvin* (Lausanne and Neuilly-sur-Seine, 7 vols, 1899–1927), II, 203f, and Eells, *Martin Bucer*, 229ff.
30. Herminjard, III, 150f.
31. *Opera*, XIII, 56.

promoting in Geneva those ideals of a true Christian commonwealth which he himself had just failed to do at Strassburg.[32]

## Geneva

But although Calvin's name is for ever associated with the chief city of French-speaking Switzerland he was not the pioneer of its religious reform. Something had already been achieved, before he set foot there in the summer of 1536, by French refugees, the first among whom was Guillaume Farel (1489–1565).[33] A native of Gap in Dauphiné and a pupil of Lefèvre d'Etaples, who had fled from France in 1524 when suspected of 'Lutheranism', Farel had been conspicuous at the disputations of Basel and Bern – he was red-bearded, fiery-tempered and gifted with a certain ranting eloquence – in his role of itinerant preacher under commission from the Bernese civil authorities. Ejected from Basel, possibly at the instigation of Erasmus, who considered him an ill-bred nuisance, he arrived first at Lausanne and then at Neuchâtel, where his reformist agitation led to church-wrecking and iconoclasm. Nevertheless he succeeded in getting the mass abolished and thereafter went on to prosecute his campaign elsewhere. In May 1531 he was joined by Pierre Viret (1511–71) of Orbe, a man, happily, possessed of a quieter and more persuasive manner.[34] The two arrived in Geneva at the beginning of October 1532 bearing credentials from the Bernese government, but were obliged to flee as a result of strong local Catholic opposition backed up by the canton of Fribourg. Farel returned there, however, in the winter of 1533–4 under the protection of Bern and with Viret and another French refugee, Antoine Froment (1510–84), as his assistants, along with Calvin's cousin Olivétan (c. 1506–38), who in 1535 brought out – if with considerable aid from Calvin himself – a French translation of the Bible.

On 29 January 1534 a disputation was held to decide the issue of whether the city should now fully embrace the reform or not, the prince-bishop, Pierre de la Paume, having left six months previously. Farel and Viret successfully debated with

32. *Ibid.*, 199, 350, 358, 374. The dominant spirit at Strassburg after Bucer's departure was Johann Marbach (1521–81). A friend and one-time pupil of Luther's at Wittenberg, his life's work had the Rhineland city for its main scene: from 1545 to 1558 he was pastor of St Nicholas's church, and from 1552 presided over the convocation as well as being its representative at the Council of Trent. Marbach was always closely associated with Bucer, but later he took up a more rigidly Lutheran position than had previously won sympathy among his fellow-citizens, strongly of the Swiss and Calvinist stand points. That he had followers is evident from the *Kirchenordnungen* adopted in 1598, which for the most part was of his devising. Tirelessly energetic and polemical in the cause of what he saw as the truth, he engaged in repeated controversy, chiefly on eucharistic doctrine, but also on perseverance and predestination. That Strassburg eventually accepted the *Formula of Concord* is largely attributable to his efforts.

33. As much information on Farel as may be required is contained in *Guillaume Farel, 1489–1565*, edited by the Comité Farel (Neuchâtel and Paris, 1930) and A. Stuck, *Guillaume Farel* (St Gallen, 1942).

34. His correspondence is given in Herminjard. Viret's principal work was his *Instruction chrestienne en la doctrine de la Loy et l'Evangile*, published at Geneva in 1564; see also R. D. Linder, *The Political Ideas of Pierre Viret* (Geneva, 1964).

the Dominican Furbiti, as the Catholic champion, the relative authority of the church and the scriptures and the practice of fasting, but matters were still not quite settled. The Franciscan church was occupied by the reforming party in March, and when in April the Bernese were able to exert pressure without hindrance from Fribourg other changes were rapidly brought about, starting with the closure of the convents. A second disputation took place in June, a new form of celebrating the Lord's Supper was introduced by Viret and an attempt made by the bishop to gain control failed. In August the cathedral of St Pierre and the two principal churches, the Madeleine and St Gervais, were seized by the reformers, and after harangues by Farel many of their contents were destroyed or cast out. Finally the Council of Two Hundred – the Deux Cents, an administrative assembly which met monthly to deal with important legislation – agreed to abolish the old church system altogether. The bishop's jurisdiction was formally repudiated and the mass discontinued. Later an order was issued requiring public worship to be observed in a manner consistent with scripture. By the end of May 1536, three months before the arrival of Calvin, when an oath was imposed on all citizens to abide by the gospel, the reformation in Geneva was nominally complete.

Even so conditions in the city, socially and morally, were far from satisfactory, and Farel, accomplished though he was as an agitator, was devoid of administrative ability. If what the city needed was a man who could at any rate make good this defect then Calvin's appearance there was indeed an act of providence. His actual coming was an accident of circumstance, but it changed his whole life. His decision to remain at Geneva is best recounted in his own often quoted words, in the preface to his *Commentary on the Psalms*:

> As the most direct road to Strassburg, to which I then intended to retire, was closed by the wars, I had resolved to pass quickly by Geneva, without staying longer than a single night in that city. A little before this popery had been driven from it by the exertions of the excellent man whom I have named [*Farel*] and Pierre Viret; but matters were not yet brought to a settled state, and the city was divided into ungodly and dangerous factions. Then a person, who has now returned to the papists [*his friend Louis du Tillet, a canon of Angoulême*], discovered me and made me known to others. Upon this, Farel, who burned with an extraordinary zeal to advance the gospel, immediately strained every nerve to detain me. And after learning that my heart was set upon devoting myself to private studies, for which I wished to keep myself free from other pursuits, and finding that he gained nothing by entreaties, he proceeded to utter the imprecation that God would curse my retirement and the tranquility of the studies which I sought, if I should withdraw and refuse to help, when the necessity was so urgent.[35]

At the time Calvin was twenty-seven years of age, trained in the law but the author of a theological compendium, remarkable for its conciseness and clarity, *Christianae Religionis Institutio* – 'The Institutes of the Christian Religion', published only a few months earlier (March 1536) by the Basel printers Thomas Platter and Balthasar Lasius, and destined, through its successive editions, to be the most celebrated and influential work of its kind that the Protestant Reformation was

35. *Opera*, XXX, 23–6.

ever to produce. But before embarking on any discussion of this something must be said by way of introducing its comparatively youthful author and his achievement, such as it was, to that date.

## Calvin, humanist and reformer

Jean Chauvin (the original form of his name) was born 10 July 1509 at Noyon in Picardy, where his father Gérard was notary to the cathedral chapter and registrar to the bishop of the diocese. As a schoolboy he incurred notice for his quick intelligence and excellent memory, and when only twelve years old was assigned part of the stipend of a cathedral chaplaincy to meet the cost of his education for the priesthood, the career which his father, not unnaturally, at first had in mind for him. As a boy he was also, on account of his father's position, very friendly with members of the socially well-placed local family of Montmors, although his own ancestry was humble enough, and intercourse with them gave him early opportunity to acquire the self-confident ease and polished manners which were to be a mark of the man. In 1523 probably, although a date some two years previously has been plausibly suggested,[36] he was sent to Paris to attend the Collège de la Marche, one of the teaching establishments of the university, where for a time he was instructed in Latin by a distinguished pedagogue of the day, Mathurin Cordier, with whom he began a friendship that was to last into later life.[37] From this institution he went on to the Collège de Montaigu, a stronghold of theological orthodoxy, where Rabelais and Erasmus had likewise been students and who both, it must be said, spoke ill of the place, though Calvin himself seems not to have complained. Its rector, Tempête, would appear to have been aptly so named: in Rabelais's words, '*Horrida tempestas montem turbavit acutum*, Tempête was a great whipper of schoolboys'. Here the young Calvin began the study of philosophy, one of his teachers being Jean Mair (or Major), a capable theologian of the nominalist school. The *Sentences* of the Lombard were of course a staple part of the intellectual diet, but Aristotle would have been read in a Latin translation, and a good deal of attention was evidently given to logic and epistemology, from a firmly Occamist angle. It must have been here too that Calvin first became aware of the Lutheran heresy.

Then suddenly the boy's education was switched from theology to law. His father's decision was a matter of prudence: more money was to be made out of law than religion, although his own current difficulties with the ecclesiastical authorities at Noyon may also have induced him to change his son's course. Thus Jean found himself a law student at the university of Orléans, and enjoying a good deal more personal freedom than formerly. The effect of Calvin's legal training (and the faculty of law at Orléans was greatly esteemed) was to foster in him qualities of mind – clarity, precision and caution – which were never lost, although before long the budding lawyer was to turn from the *Digest* to the mysteries, once again, of sacred science. His circle of friends, moreover, was liberal-minded, and

36. By his recent English biographer, T. H. L. Parker, in *John Calvin* (London, 1975), 187f.
37. Doumergue, *op. cit.*, I, 60.

some of them were open to the new ideas in religion – one, Melchior Wolmar, was in fact a crypto-Lutheran – although there is no definite evidence that Calvin himself had reformist leanings.

The best teacher at Orléans was Pierre Taisan de l'Estoile, a sound lawyer of firmly orthodox religious views and a good man whom Calvin greatly respected, but in 1529 the young student moved to Bourges, drawn thither by the reputation of a newly arrived professor, the noted Italian jurist and humanist Andrea Alciati. Here Calvin stayed until 1530 or 1531, devoting some of his time, however, to other subjects, especially Greek, in which he took lessons from Wolmar, who was now lecturing at Bourges.[38] The sudden death of his father required his presence back home at Noyon for a time, but instead of resuming his studies at Bourges he returned to Orléans to sit for his licentiate in laws. Thereupon his legal career ended, and his movements afterwards are not very clear; certain family matters had to be attended to, but he also was at work on his first book, a commentary on Seneca's *De clementia*, published in Paris at his own expense in April, 1532. The title-page bore the name by which he has ever since been known, *Calvinus*.[39] His reasons for selecting this subject no doubt included the fact that Erasmus had twice brought out editions of the works of Seneca, in the second of which, issued in 1529, he had stated that he was not wholly satisfied with his editing and suggested, perhaps not altogether sincerely, that someone 'more learned, more felicitous, and with more time at his disposal' might improve upon it.[40] Nonetheless one may fairly look for a deeper motive, and a measure of apologetic interest need not be entirely ruled out. The ancient Roman statesman-philosopher had hoped to persuade the emperor Nero to adopt a more clement attitude towards his people; could not the hint therefore be dropped to the king of France, a patron of enlightened learning, to show a similar spirit towards his loyal Protestant subjects? Yet nothing that Calvin actually says indicates that any such thought was in his mind. A more plausible idea may be that, as a young man proud of his wide reading, he wished to demonstrate his own sympathy with a classical author then much in vogue among the intellectual *avant-garde*.[41] Stoicism, with its emphasis on the dignity and brotherhood of man, made a strong appeal to humanists. Some also were conscious of an affinity between the Stoic ethic and Christianity, and in all probability Calvin, with his intense moral seriousness, was struck by it too. Seneca, besides, was a favourite author of Zwingli's, as the latter's *De providentia* reveals: '*Ille* [Seneca] *unicum de gentibus animarum agricola.*' Certainly Calvin misses no opportunity to point out resemblances between this form of ancient paganism and the religion of Christ, particularly the doctrine of an overruling providence, one of Stoicism's central tenets.[42] 'Such also', he notes, 'is the teaching of our

38. *Opera*, XII, 364f.
39. *Opera* V. See F. L. Battles and A. M. Hughes (ed.), *Calvin's Commentary on Seneca's 'De Clementia'* (Leiden, 1969).
40. See Allen, ep. 2091.
41. Cf. L. Zanta, *La Renaissance du stoicisme au xvi siècle* (Paris, 1914). Also F. L. Battles, 'The sources of Calvin's Seneca commentary', in F. L. Battles *et al., John Calvin (Courtenay Studies in Reformation Theology)* (Abingdon, 1966), 38–62.
42. *Opera*, V, 18.

religion, that there is no power but of God, and that everything was ordained by him, according to Romans, chapter 13.'[43]

The concept of the *ius naturale*, the natural law, likewise interested him. But his humanism is chiefly evidenced by his critical method. The whole apparatus of book-learning is present. No fewer than seventy-four Latin and twenty-two Greek authors are either quoted or alluded to; nor are the Christian Fathers ignored: St Augustine's *City of God* indeed is mentioned fifteen times. Yet from the Bible there are no more than three quotations. The young savant had of course read the moderns, whom he lauds with becoming deference, although he is not afraid to state a difference of opinion: *tamen errat Erasmus*.[44] His general procedure however is not novel, having already been adopted by Erasmus in the *Paraphrases* and Budé in his *Annotations*: linguistic analysis, citation of parallels in the same or in other writers, and so forth. Yet in spite of the imitativeness natural to a tyro in authorship Calvin manages to leave on his work the imprint of a distinctive personality. For although he was never an originator of ideas, when he drew on those of others it was always to fuse them into a unity from which they gained fresh vitality and adaptiveness. What is remarkable about this particular work, considering that the *Institutes* was to follow in little more than a year's time, is the paucity of the allusions to Christianity itself. As has been said: 'It would be embarrassing to have to prove, from this *Commentary*, that the author had any special interest in religious problems',[45] though he is not uncritical of philosophy generally for being inconclusive on even the most important matters as well as having little practical value for ordinary men, and of Stoicism in particular for the frequently inhuman rigidity of its moral outlook. 'Pity', he says, 'is a virtue as well as fortitude',[46] and one has no right to affect indifference to the feelings and opinions of others.[47]

But Calvin's humanism was not simply a phase in his intellectual development which maturity and a deepening religious conviction would soon transcend.[48] On the contrary, he retained much of the humanist attitude throughout his life,[49] and never ceased to admire the wisdom of classical antiquity or the beauty of its literary expression. In the 1539 edition of the *Institutes*, prepared when he was at Strassburg and in close contact with Bucer, he allows that the fall did not destroy man's natural intelligence and that ancient paganism had to its credit literary works which 'by the wonderful light of the truth' they emit 'compel our admiration' and furnish us with clear proof that 'the nature of man, however he may have lost his former

43. *Ibid.*
44. *Ibid.*, 32.
45. W. Walker, *John Calvin, the Organizer of Reformed Protestantism* (London, 1906), 69.
46. *Opera*, V, 154.
47. *Ibid.*, 112.
48. Q. Breen speaks of Calvin's carrying over 'a precipitate of humanism into his theology' (*John Calvin: a study in French humanism*, Grand Rapids, Mich., 1931, 146), while F. Wendel considers that 'everything, even including the limitations of his knowledge, betrays the previous humanist in Calvin' (*Calvin: the Origins and Development of his Religious Thought*. English trans. by P. Mairet, London, 1963, 36).
49. 'In all his works he remains respectful to well-conducted reasoning, to chaste style and good taste. . . . In refinement of taste he comes very near to Erasmus' (Wendel, *op. cit.*, 35). Breen says: 'A certain elegance lies upon all that he wrote, the light of classical clearness' (*op. cit.*, 148).

integrity . . . nevertheless was not deprived of many gifts of God'.[50] He does not question that the classics contain 'many well phrased utterances concerning God', indicating that to some at least he had given 'an inkling of the truth of his deity'; all the same, such illumination as was afforded by these 'sparks' was insufficient to bring a single soul really 'to know God, his paternal will, or that favour in which lieth our salvation'. Furthermore, these 'little grains of truth' scattered throughout the books of the philosophers are repeatedly 'obscured by horrible lies'.[51] Thus a Demosthenes or a Cicero, a Plato or an Aristotle can 'wonderfully attract, delight and move us, even ravish our minds', but when we turn from these authors to the holy scriptures we at once realize the sheer inadequacy of mere rhetoricians and philosophers.

Doubtless as Calvin grew older his regard for the pagan writers, like Augustine's, lessened. Yet he never questioned their basic cultural value, even though bound to deplore the human pride and vanity all too often manifested in them. In his criticisms of the ancient wisdom he may indeed appear more negative than either Bucer or Zwingli, but in clarity of argument and elegance of style he profited immensely from his study of them, and none among the Protestant reformers seriously rivalled him in either respect. As a Latinist he was among the best of his century, and when it came to the use of his native tongue he commanded a lucidity, conciseness and grace which place him along with Montaigne, Descartes and Pascal as one of the founders of modern French prose.[52] Obviously, to such a mind, in some ways so like Erasmus's, the tortuosities of scholastic reasoning, and the jargon in which this was cast, could not but be repulsive. As a scholar his natural interests were philological, historical and philosophical, and without them, whatever the force of his religious convictions, he would not have been the man he was. 'The mental formation and the religion, the culture and the morality, went hand in hand.'[53]

However, although the learned young author would have had much less of his fair share of human vanity had he not expected to make something of a name for himself in the world of letters with this perhaps too self-conscious literary debut, he was in fact to be disappointed. The book caused no stir and seems to have been little considered, unless to be criticized for its arrogance. The modern historian should judge it in the light of other products of its kind and age, but even so its faults are patent.[54]

The date of Calvin's conversion to Protestantism is among the disputed topics

---

50. Bk II, ch.IV, 13–19 (in J. Pannier's edition of the French version of 1541 (Paris, 1936), I, 115–22).
51. Pannier, *op. cit.*, 120f.
52. 'Elle représente une étape essentielle de l'histoire de notre langue. Pour la première fois le français se ploie à traiter les plus hauts sujets de philosophie et de morale. Calvin contribue ainsi à forger l'outil qu'utiliseront après lui Pascal et Bossuet' R. Peter and J. Rott, 'Exposition Jean Calvin', in *Revue d'histoire et de philosophie religieuses* (1965), 129.
53. Seeberg, *Lehrbuch der Dogmengeschichte*, IV, 558.
54. On Calvin's humanism generally see J. Bohatec, *Budé und Calvin. Studien zur Gedankwelt des französischer Frühumanismus* (Graz, 1950). Also J. Boisset, *Sagesse et sainteté dans la pensée de Jean Calvin* (Paris, 1959) and Breen, *op. cit.*

of modern Reformation scholarship. When did it occur, and for what reasons and in what circumstances? These however are questions primarily for the biographer and there is no call to devote much space to them here.[55] Unfortunately for the problem of dating the evidence is sparse, consisting mainly of a passage from the Psalms commentary, published a quarter of a century later in 1557, and one of the few biographical references to be found in Calvin's writings. Here he relates how God drew him from 'obscure and lowly beginnings' to confer on him 'that most honourable office of herald and minister of the Gospel', but that at first he was 'so obstinately addicted to the superstitions of the Papacy' that nothing less than a 'sudden [or 'unexpected': *the word is 'subita'*] conversion' could have 'subdued to docility a mind too stubborn for its years'. And he goes on:

> Thus having received some foretaste of true godliness I at once burned with so great a zeal to progress that although I did not give up my other studies I yet pursued them more slackly, nor had a year gone by when all who were desirous of a purer doctrine turned to me, novice and beginner that I was, in order to learn it.[56]

Of interest also, in this connection, is the reference in Calvin's *Epistle to Cardinal Sadoleto*, where he puts into the mouth of an imaginary reformer words which it is difficult to suppose do not allude to his own experience:

> The more earnestly I contemplated myself [*it reads*] the more my conscience was pricked with sharp goadings; so much so that no other relief or comfort was left to me except to deceive myself by oblivion. But, as nothing better offered itself, I continued in the same way that I had begun. Then however there arose quite another form of teaching: not to turn away from the profession of Christianity but to reduce it to its own source, and to restore it, so to speak, cleansed from all filthiness to its proper purity. Nevertheless, being offended by this novelty, I could scarcely listen to it willingly, and must confess that at first I valiantly and bravely resisted it. For as men are by nature stubborn and opinionated in supporting institutions which they have once received, it irked me greatly to admit that all my life I had been fed on ignorance and error. One thing especially prevented me from believing in those people, and that was reverence for the Church. But after I had listened for some time with open ears and had suffered myself to be taught, I saw very well that such a fear, that the majesty of the Church might be lessened, was unnecessary and vain.[57]

Considerations of chronology, and what we know of Calvin's movements at the time, would suggest that this profound change of mind happened a year or more before his departure for Basel, that is, late in 1533 or early in 1534. It is the date which has on the whole been preferred by Calvin scholars. It was in May 1534 that he resigned his ecclesiastical benefices.[58]

55. On Calvin's conversion see Doumergue, *op. cit.*, I, 327ff., J. Pannier, *Recherches sur l'évolution religieuse de Calvin* (Strasbourg, 1924), P. Sprenger, *Das Rätsel um die Bekehrung Calvins* (Neukirchen, 1960), A. Ganoczy, *Le jeune Calvin: Génèse et évolution de sa vocation reformative* (Wiesbaden, 1966), Wendel, *op. cit.*, 37–45, Parker, *op. cit.*, 192–6, A. E. McGrath, *A Life of John Calvin* (Oxford, 1990) 69–78.
56. *Opera*, XXXI, 22.
57. *Opera*, V, 412.
58. Such is Wendel's view, as too J. T. McNeill's (*The History and Character of Calvinism*, 1954; repr. New York, 1967, 107–18). Dr Parker again argues, less plausibly, for an earlier date, towards the end of 1529 or early in 1530 (*op. cit.*, 195).

It is reasonable to suppose that Calvin's initial interest in reformist and even expressly 'Lutheran' ideas goes back, as we have already remarked, to his student days at Orléans. In spite of their attractiveness he still, seemingly, found it difficult to renounce his allegiance to the church in which he had been brought up, or indeed his respect for the papacy itself; so keen an intelligence must have realized from the outset that acceptance of reform in any radical shape would mean a breach with both. Only the bursting on him of a sudden conviction, a *subita conversio*, would be sufficient to force him out of this indeterminate state of mind. But all that we know of Calvin in 1533 indicates that he had not then decisively broken with Roman Catholicism. For example, the actual content of the sensational rectorial address which his friend Nicolas Cop delivered before the Sorbonne on All Saints' Day 1533 and which has been thought to have reflected Calvin's own views at that time, although it upset the hidebound traditionalists of that ancient institution, scarcely amounts to Protestantism, despite its *verbatim*, if unacknowledged, borrowing from Luther. After its delivery Calvin, as one of Cop's known associates, had for a while to go into hiding, and it could well have been then, or a little later, that the moment of positive decision presented itself to him. The moderate reformism of men like the aged Lefèvre d'Etaples would have been seen by him to fall short and that the axe had indeed to be laid at the root of the tree. So, *Deus subegit* . . .: his conversion was construed by him as an act of divine providence. Yet the experience, to judge from Calvin's own terse and guarded statement, does not appear to have involved any great emotional crisis; in essence it was an intellectual conversion. But it would be a mistake to think of Calvin, as has often been the case, as a man of cold disposition, without feeling: on the contrary, there is much on record to suggest that he was subject at times to intense emotion. His iron will, though, rarely failed to control it.

## *Christianae Religionis Institutio*, 1536

When, at Geneva in the late summer of 1536, Guillaume Farel sought out Calvin during what the latter intended to be only the briefest stay, it was because the young traveller, a fellow-countryman twenty years his junior, was already known to him as the author of a striking published statement of the principles of the reformed divinity. In Farel's eyes he was just such a man as the Swiss city needed if it were to be delivered from its troubles. Accordingly he urged him not only to remain there but to assume a responsibility which to a man of Calvin's retiring, scholarly nature could not but seem appalling. As Calvin himself describes the occasion, again in the *Commentary on the Psalms*, Farel

> strained every nerve to detain me. And after having learned that my heart was set upon devoting myself to private studies . . . he proceeded to utter an imprecation that God would curse my retirement, and the tranquility of the studies which I sought, if I should withdraw and refuse to give assistance when the necessity was so urgent.

And he continues: 'I felt as if . . . God from heaven had laid his mighty hand upon me to arrest me. To so imperious a call he could not but submit: so stricken with terror was I that I desisted from the journey which I had undertaken.'

The book which not only moved Farel but in time established its author's fame as the Protestant Reformation's greatest systematic theologian, was first conceived simply as an instruction in the catechism.[59] Yet it was also meant to serve a political and apologetic end as well, being prefaced by a dedicatory epistle to the king of France advising him that in this book he might learn truly 'what is that doctrine against which the furious so rage' who disturb the realm 'with fire and sword'.[60] It has, Calvin urges, been outrageously traduced by those who strive to portray it as a threat to law and order, peace and good government. 'Not without reason', therefore, does he request the king 'to assume the full cognizance of this cause.'

> Be not [*he says*] deterred out of contempt for our lowliness. Though we be but the offscouring of the earth, yet our doctrine is sublime above all the glory of the world and must stand, because it is not ours but the doctrine of the living God and his Christ. This teaching is calumniated as new, unconfirmed by miracles and refuted by its fruits which are sects, seditions, and sins. Opponents, however, call it novel only because Christ and the Gospel are new to them, which is why they think it uncertain.

He goes on:

> Most glorious King, although now your mind may be averse, alienated and even inflamed against us, we hope to regain your favour, if your Majesty will but once read this our confession with composure. If, on the contrary, your ears are lent to the malevolent and no defence is permitted to the accused, if we then continue to be persecuted, with connivance on your part . . . we shall in patience possess our souls and await the mighty hand of the Lord, who will undoubtedly come in due time to deliver the poor from their affliction and to castigate those who swagger in their security.

Although Francis I was known to profess an interest in reform and earlier in 1535 had actually invited Bucer and Melanchthon to Paris to discuss matters with him, these were bold words for a young and unknown scholar, the adherent of a suspect and even persecuted cause, to address to Europe's 'most Christian' monarch. But Calvin, timid though he may have been physically, was never lacking in moral courage. His inexpugnable conviction of his mission to expound the truth of God's Word gave him a fortitude which, though often tried, was never overcome.

The title *Institutio* is used in the then familiar sense of 'instruction' or 'education',[61] and was intended to denote the customary elementary teaching in the faith – now of course 'reformed' – based on the Decalogue, the Apostles' creed,

59. When exactly Calvin began work on the *Institutio* we do not know, but the book was more or less ready for press by August 1535, the date of the Epistle Dedicatory to Francis I. On its literary history see J.-D. Benoit, 'The history and development of the *Institutio*. How Calvin worked', in Battles *et al.*, *op. cit.*, 102–17. There is an admirable critical edition of the 1560 French version by J.-D. Benoit (*Institution de la religion Chrestienne*) in five volumes (Paris, 1957–63). An English translation, in two volumes, of the 1559 Latin edition by J. T. McNeill and F. L. Battles is published in the Library of Christian Classics (Philadelphia and London, 1961).
60. Calvin's friend Etienne de la Forge had been put to death in February 1535.
61. As in Erasmus's *Institutio principis christiani* (1516) or Budé's *L'Institution du prince* (written in 1516 but not printed until 1547). Cf. Breen, *op. cit.*, 119ff. Although the word is usually translated by the plural, 'institutes', the latter (*institutiones* in Latin) did not occur until 1564, when it was adopted in the Elzevir edition.

the Lord's prayer and the sacraments, to which topics the first four chapters are respectively devoted. The two remaining chapters (at this stage the book comprised only six in all) are more polemical in character and deal in turn with the so-called sacraments, five in number, which, added to the gospel rites, the two true sacraments of baptism and the Lord's Supper, made up the traditional 'Seven Sacraments' of medieval Catholic piety, and with the subject of 'Christian liberty', covering the powers of the church and of the civil magistracy. This concluding chapter is especially notable in that Calvin's views on the relations of the church to the civil authority never afterwards underwent any real change; on these matters his mind was made up early on and stayed so until the end. The *Institutio* was thus to all appearance a modest enough volume.[62]

Composed in Latin, this primal edition seems to have had no French counterpart. In the autumn of 1536 Calvin was at work on a French version of a quite brief text originally in Latin – he refers to it as a mere *libellus* – which was to be called *Instruction et confession de foy*, and was for use in the church at Geneva. This was published there early in 1537, but it is considerably shorter than even the first *Institutio*. The first French version of the *Institutes*, that of 1541, was made from the 1539 edition, and thereafter each fresh Latin edition was soon followed by its French equivalent.

The second (1539) edition of the *Institutio* was printed at Strassburg, whither Calvin had repaired after his expulsion from Geneva, and it contained a sizeable amount of new material, running now to seventeen chapters. As a result of his dispute during 1537 with a certain Pierre Caroli, a Romanist who had formerly been of Bishop Briçonnet's 'reformist' circle at Meaux and who had charged Calvin (as also Farel) with Arianism, an exposition of trinitarian doctrine was given prominent place, Calvin having all along protested his orthodoxy. Another chapter was included on the agreement between the Old and New Testaments, an echo of his conflicts with the anabaptists. New, too, are the chapters on repentance and justification by faith, neither of which subjects had received any special attention in 1536; a further chapter dealt with the mysteries of providence and predestination, which again had been only very cursorily treated in the earlier edition. Predestination, be it noted, was never the starting-point of Calvin's theological thinking.

In 1541 the first French edition greatly enhanced the work's appeal, with its readership no longer confined to the learned but open now to the *gens mécaniques* as well. It differs from the Latin in being more explanatory and frequently much more forthright in its turn of phrase, the style generally becoming more mobile and relaxed, more idiomatic and racy. Further editions of the Latin text followed in 1543 and 1545, the latter containing a section on the doctrine of angels, a theme not hitherto trenched on, as well as more copious allusions to the early Fathers, Calvin's reading of whom steadily enlarged. The years 1550 to 1557 saw yet further editions, seven in all, in either Latin or French. Here and there new topics are introduced: the authority of the Bible, it may be, or the meaning of the *imago Dei* in man, and still more patristic references.

62. But it was a marked success, the publisher's stock of copies being exhausted within twelve months, and a new edition was called for. Moreover, although the volume had appeared anonymously, Calvin's authorship did not for long rest a secret.

The final editions are those of 1559 and 1560, the one in Latin, the other in French. Both are far from being mere reprints; the entire work was reshaped and considerably enlarged; in fact so extensively revised was it as to have become virtually a new undertaking, the whole, now comprised in four lengthy 'Books', requiring some eighty chapters. Further, the old catechism plan had been dropped in preference for one based on the Apostles' Creed, with the doctrines of God, Christ and the Holy Spirit being treated each in order and with a new expansiveness, and with the church and sacraments completing the scheme. All now is more complex, more detailed, more exhaustive. Rearrangement is considerable, the doctrines of providence and predestination, for example, hitherto taken together, are now dealt with separately, providence under 'God' in Book I, predestination, as the ground of salvation, in Book III, while the chapter on the Christian life, in all former editions the conclusion of the whole, is also brought back to Book III by being related to the work of the Holy Spirit. The entire enterprise, once a handy compendium for more or less elementary instruction, has thus become a massive volume, heavy with biblical and patristic erudition and harking back again and again to the various controversies, whether with anabaptists and Socinians, with an Osiander or a Servetus, in which he had been embroiled over many years, and always, needless to add, with an eye on the corrosive errors of the 'Papists'. His overall purpose has been, he points out in his 'Address to the Reader', to expound a comprehensive biblical theology; or in his own phrases,

> to prepare and instruct candidates in sacred theology for the reading of the divine Word, in order that they may be able both to have easy access to it and to advance in it without stumbling. For I believe I have so embraced the sum of religion in all its parts, and have arranged it in such an order, that if anyone rightly grasps it, it will not be difficult for him to determine what he ought especially to seek in scripture, and to what end he ought to relate its contents.

What he offers therefore could well be described as an interpretative appendix to his massive work as a biblical exegete. It was to be the crown of his life's achievement as a scholar and a theologian.

## A holy commonwealth

But to return to Calvin's earlier days at Geneva: the task to which he was committed was a thorny one. Although their state was in decline economically, the citizens were still comparatively well-to-do, but they seem to have been pleasure-loving to excess, relaxed in morals, public and private alike, and with a reputation for turbulence. Whether they were more licentious than the inhabitants of many another late medieval city would not be easy to prove: Savonarola's Florence, for instance, was far from being a model of either civic or private virtue. Calvin and Farel thus not only had to consolidate and organize the religious reformation but, still more dauntingly, to bring about an effective moral reform. As its now recognized preachers they had from the outset taken a stand against what they saw as manifest evils, and as early even as September 1536 complaints were voiced about the severity of their reproofs. Thereafter a prolonged contest took place with the civic authorities about the rights of the church, in particular its claim to impose a *discipline ecclésiastique* that would include excommunication.

In January 1537 Calvin prepared a draft list of the reforms he wished introduced. Presented to the city's Small Council (of twenty-five members), it provides what virtually was the basis of Calvin's entire programme of ecclesiastical renovation at Geneva. It is concerned with four matters only: the Lord's Supper (*la Saincte Cène de Nostre Seigneur*), singing in public worship, the religious instruction of children, and the regulation of marriage. Special stress was laid on the first. Ideally the Supper should be celebrated every Lord's Day, or at any rate once in a month in each of the city's three churches. Unworthy persons are warned not to approach the Holy Table, and to prevent their doing so the right to excommunicate may be invoked. This memorandum, which came to be known as *Articuli de regimine ecclesiae*, or 'Articles on Church Government', was approved by both the Small Council and the Council of Two Hundred, who qualified it only with the specific regulation that the Supper be observed not less than four times a year.[63] The articles were further ordered to be read every Sunday from the pulpits in order to prepare the people for their adoption, and from the end of July all citizens were to be sworn individually to uphold the new polity. Failure to comply after 12 November would result in banishment.

Nevertheless things did not go well between the preachers and the civic authorities, who, while ready for a measure of reform, were not willing to go to Calvin's lengths in enforcing a clerically devised disciplinary system. The situation was aggravated by encouragement of French immigrants: Calvin himself did not become a legal citizen of Geneva until 1556. His opponents, whom he later stigmatized as the 'Libertines', were successful in their campaign against him, and on the question of the adoption by the city's governing bodies of the ecclesiastical usages of Bern, which regarded itself as having some kind of suzerainty over Geneva – it had defended Geneva in its resistance to the duke of Savoy and the prince-bishop – matters came to a head. Calvin and Farel did not necessarily object to these usages in themselves (stone fonts, unleavened bread at the Supper, and the observance of certain church festivals), but they were insistent that they be received by the Genevan church on its own account and not on the orders of the secular power; for with Calvin ecclesiastical autonomy was, and was to remain, a fundamental principle. So on 23 April, Easter Tuesday, the two men were banished from the city on the Rhone.

In time, however, Geneva discovered that it could not after all do without *ille Gallus*, 'that Frenchman'. When Cardinal Sadoleto urged the citizens to return to the Roman obedience it was Calvin whom the Bern municipality, to which the cardinal's letter had been passed on, requested to reply to it; this he did in magisterial fashion, his answer being among his most striking utterances.[64] More and more did the Genevan government come to regret the loss of the presence among them of so able a man, however prickly he may have been in his dealings with them, and on 20 October 1540 the city formally invited him to return. At first

---

63. *Opera*, Xa, 5–14.
64. See *Johannis Calvini opera selecta*, ed. P. Barth and W. Niesel (5 vols, Munich, 1926–36), I, 250.

he was very unwilling – as he wrote to Viret, 'There is no place under heaven I am more afraid of'[65] – but after some months of hesitant refusal he yielded once again to the entreaties of Farel and other friends and well-wishers, and on 13 September 1541 he re-entered the city, never to leave it again. The burden of responsibility facing him was terrifying, but he did not shirk it, beginning instead the work of building up in Geneva what he envisaged as a truly Christian commonwealth, some adumbration of which he had already witnessed at Strassburg under the admirable Bucer. (It was at Strassburg too, we may recall, that Calvin married in August 1540, Idelette de Bure, the widow of an anabaptist whom he had won over to the paedobaptist position. She died nine years later, but he did not marry again.)

Although Calvin was both by intellectual interest and personal temperament a typical scholar, not really happy unless in his study and at his books, he possessed in fact an astonishing practical gift, yoked to a power of will no less remarkable. What he saw to be necessary he set about unflinchingly to devise, whatever inward strain and distress it might cause him. The *Articuli* were soon superseded by new and more comprehensive regulations. On the very day of his arrival back in Geneva six laymen were at his request appointed by the Small Council to assist him and the other ministers in drawing up laws of church polity. Their report was ratified by the Two Hundred within a couple of months and finally adopted by all the Councils and the general assembly of citizens by the beginning of 1542. Thus the *Ordonnances ecclésiastiques de l'Eglise de Genève* came into being, embodying what their author claimed was a 'polity ecclesiastic . . . taken from the Gospel of Jesus Christ'.[66] For as he himself said: 'Immediately after I had offered my services to the Senate, I declared that a church could not hold together unless a settled government should be agreed on, such as is presented to us in the Word of God, and such as was in use in the ancient church.'[67] A church properly ordered and disciplined seemed to him absolutely indispensable to the preaching of the Word; indeed, in a sense, to be part of it. Organization was not, that is, a matter to be settled according to circumstances; the true principles of church order had been laid down in scripture.

The *Ordonnances*, which directly relate to the ecclesiology elaborated in the *Institutes*, are concerned with three main topics, the first being that of the ministers and other persons responsible for the organized life of the church, namely pastors, doctors, elders and deacons. Here, as we have already noted, he had found a valued mentor in Martin Bucer. The elders (*anciens*) were to be twelve in number, chosen from the three Councils and having the duty to cooperate with the pastors or ministers in the discharge of discipline. The function of the doctors would be to teach, and more specifically to interpret the scriptures; that of the deacons would be the care of the poor. Next to be arranged were the various practical matters

---

65. *Opera*, XI, 167.
66. *Opera*, Xa, 15–30; Kidd, *Documents*, no. 302; for a translation see J. K. S. Reid, *Calvin: Theological Treatises* (Library of Christian Classics, XXII) (Philadelphia/London, 1954), 58–71. The *Ordonnances* did not assume their final form until 1561.
67. *The Letters of John Calvin* (comp. by J. Bonnet, English trans. by D. Constable), ed. 1885, 260.

integral to the life of a reformed church: forms of worship and the ministration of the sacraments, marriage regulations, the visitation of the sick and of prisoners, the religious education of the young and the burial of the dead. Thirdly, there was the Consistory, the church's controlling body made up of six pastors and the twelve elders under the presidency of one of the city's syndics (himself of course an elder). Conceived as a court of discipline, it was to be invested with wide-ranging powers, touching in fact all aspects of the personal lives of Geneva's citizens. But the *Ordonnances* expressly stated that it had no civil jurisdiction, and to begin with its powers did not extend beyond verbal admonition. Much of Calvin's subsequent career, however, was taken up with his unrelenting struggle, in opposition to the Libertines, the freedom-loving party, to acquire for the church the full right of excommunication, with all that this would involve in practice. He did not in fact get his way until 1555.

It is not to our purpose here to attempt to summarize the course of events at Geneva during the years of Calvin's ascendancy, incomplete as this was during the earlier phase and not, perhaps, absolutely complete over the final nine years (he died on 27 May, 1564) covering the disputes with Castellio on the canon of scripture, with the anabaptists, whom he bitterly attacked in his *Brief Instruction* (1545), with Jérôme Bolsec, who denounced his doctrine of predestination as a 'false and godless notion', and, most painfully remembered of all, with Michael Servetus, on account of theological views, admittedly eccentric, for which Calvin hounded him to his death, objecting only, if we give him credit for sincerity, to the form of this last – burning alive. And always there was the contest with the Libertines, honourably led, on the one hand, by Ami Perrin, zealous for civic independence and personal liberty, and restive before the growing preponderance of foreign refugees, though including, on the other hand, the so-called Spirituals, 'secte fanatique et furieuse' – among whom Mesdames Perrin and Ameux were prominent – with their pantheistic and antinomian tendencies.

On the functions of the state itself Calvin had clearcut and characteristic opinions; indeed his political thinking is more developed than that of any other reformer apart from Bucer, whose influence on him in this respect also is very evident. In essence Calvin's doctrine was already fully present in the 1536 *Institutes*. He distinguishes in the usual way between the two jurisdictions, the civil and the ecclesiastical, assigning to each its own sphere of rights and responsibilities, the church to preach true doctrine and administer the sacraments, and the state to maintain law and order in a sinful world. But whereas both Luther and Zwingli, in their differing ways, yielded the church virtually to the state's control, Calvin insists on its independence. In his view church and state are autonomous powers, each of which, after its own fashion, expresses the divine will and witnesses to the authority of the divine law. It is incorrect therefore to speak of Calvin's Geneva as a theocracy, since theoretically at least church and state, although complementary, were certainly not to be identified with one another. Inasmuch, though, as the state is composed of Christian men it has the duty of aiding the church, whose members are its own citizens, in the discharge of its mission, just as it is the church's duty to instruct and advise the state, whose citizens are its own members, in all matters of spiritual and moral concern. But in the spiritual sphere Calvin would bate nothing of the church's right, strongly resisting any claim on the part of the magistracy to interfere with what was not its proper responsibility. In proclaiming its faith and determining its order and liturgy the church has no worldly master, the state's role being simply to ratify and confirm; although once the church's forms and activities have been confirmed and ratified it is the civil authority's duty to uphold and protect them. In fact the church has the unequivocal right to demand the state's cooperation in carrying out its decisions and requirements and in securing obedience and submission to them. In particular, when the church desires the imposition of disciplinary measures in the interest of the moral well-being of the whole community it is the state's obligation to comply, civil punishment giving sanction to ecclesiastical law. As Calvin puts it in the 1559 edition of the *Institutes*:

> Civil government has its appointed end, so long as we live among men, to cherish and protect the outward worship of God, to defend sound doctrine and the condition of the church. . . . It also prevents idolatry, sacrilege against God's name, blasphemies against his truth, and other public offences against religion from arising and spreading among the people. . . . In short, it provides that a public manifestation of religion may exist among Christians, and that humanity be maintained among men.[68]

The 'fanatics', that is the anabaptists, who regard it as 'a thing unworthy of us and set far beneath our excellence to be occupied with those vile and worldly cares which have to do with business foreign to a Christian man' are roundly condemned.[69]

It cannot be claimed that the church–state relationship at Geneva was ever established during Calvin's lifetime in a manner that satisfied him. From 1536 until he quitted the place in 1538 he found the city authorities antagonistic on many issues that appeared to him weighty, and even after his return things seldom went smoothly. Thus the ideal, as he conceived it, had to be sullied with compromise, the Councils maintaining an effective control over the Consistory in a way that came near to erasing that distinction between the spiritual and the temporal which to him was vital. Certainly the Genevan city-state was not prepared to submit without demur to the direction of the church; instead it chose to regard the latter as a province within its own sphere. After Calvin's death, in the period of his successor Beza (Théodore de Bèze, 1519–1605),[70] the balance was tilted even more sharply in favour of the magistracy. In the conditions prevailing at Geneva in the middle decades of the sixteenth century it was inevitable, however, that the two powers should become so intimately involved with one another as to convey the impression of a virtual identity.

68. *Institutes*, IV, xx, 2f. On Calvin's ideas generally concerning civil government and its relation to the ecclesiastical see H. Höpfl, *The Christian Polity of John Calvin* (Cambridge, 1982); as also G. Lewis, 'Calvinism in Geneva in the time of Calvin and Beza', in *International Calvinism 1541–1715*, ed. M. Prestwick (Oxford, 1985), 39–70.
69. *Ibid.*
70. The fullest exposition of Beza's theological views is his *Tractationes theologicae* (1570–82). He was a rigid predestinarian, holding that the fall and its consequences in human sinfulness were part of the eternal divine plan. He wrote a life of Calvin (*Vita Calvini*) in 1564. See E. Choisy, *L'Etat Calviniste chrétien à Genève au temps de Théodore de Bèze* (Geneva, 1903).

To the modern liberal intelligence the 'holy commonwealth', in embodiment as in principle a Christian totalitarianism, can scarcely be other than repugnant. Like Marxism, Calvin's theology was an all-comprehending theory, the vindication of which lay in a *praxis*. Its author was convinced beyond all shadow of doubt that in the scriptures men have been vouchsafed a unique and compellingly authoritative revelation of the will and purpose of God, to which the entire life not only of the individual but of society itself must conform, as by it they will surely be judged. So rigorous a standard, for a man of conscience, could not but lead to censoriousness, legalism, intolerance and persecution, especially when conjoined with a temperament, like Calvin's, inherently wilful and exacting. It is no wonder that even those closest to him were awed by him, while hostile legend has traduced him as a sanctimonious tyrant. Yet he had, as his modern apologists are eager to point out, his 'human' side. Although he was harsh in controversy, and not without a vindictive streak in his nature, he was neither gloomy nor cruel, nor even a killjoy, at least not to the extent of many who in after years professed to follow his religious and ethical tenets. (It is important always to recognize that historical Calvinism and the theological teaching of Calvin himself are not by any means simply to be equated.) Moreover, like any other of his contemporaries, he is to be judged by criteria relevant to the intellectual and moral conditions of his age. All the same, apology can easily become mere excuse and if his modern evangelical defenders may justly complain of the manner in which, for too long, he has been misinterpreted and misrepresented, their own account of him is sometimes apt to leave the reader at a loss to understand how distortions allegedly so gross could have arisen.

In the criticisms that have been made of Calvin's régime there is unquestionably much exaggeration, whether intentional or from ignorance; but there is also much that cannot fairly be rebutted. Those who stayed or settled in Calvinian Geneva were for the most part such as endorsed the religio-political experiment introduced there; those who did not usually found it more convenient to depart. But on any showing it was an audacious venture in the ideological ordering of a society; for this reason it is futile to judge it apart from the theological principles on which it ostensibly rested. If society is indeed to be reconstituted on the basis of a consistent theory, as has been widely believed in the present century, then Calvin's work still calls for appreciation on its own merits, however one assesses the truth claim of the theory itself. An undogmatic Christianity on the Erasmian model, and the kind of 'open' society which that would have implied, Calvin despised utterly; dubiety was never permitted to blur his vision of his objectives, which through his own century and later have made a profound appeal to the Christian conscience. It was with no trace of irony that John Knox could describe the Geneva he knew as 'the most perfect school of Christ that ever was on earth since the days of the Apostles.'

Chapter 8

# CALVIN AND REFORMED CHRISTIANITY:
# II. A PATTERN OF SOUND DOCTRINE

*Sola Scriptura*: Calvin as biblical exegete

We have stated that Calvin's aim in the *Institutes*, one which became increasingly overt with each successive edition, was to provide a compendium of biblical theology for the guidance of the student as he endeavours to thread his way through the sacred scriptures. The fact is that Calvin saw himself principally as a biblical scholar and exegete, with his work as a dogmatic theologian strictly ancillary to that of biblical exposition. As with Luther, scripture was for him the unique external and objective basis of authority in religion, the unfailing source of a knowledge whereby truth is established and error identified and refuted. It called therefore for the most diligent investigation, the reason adduced by Calvin for his personal determination 'to give the rest of my life, however much may still remain to me, chiefly to the study of it, if I can find the leisure and the freedom for it'.[1] These words were penned in 1551, in the writer's mid-career, but his exegetical work had begun more than a decade previously with the publication at Strassburg in the spring of 1540 – four years after Bucer's – of a *Commentary on St Paul's Epistle to the Romans*: 'the first', it has been remarked, 'and one of the most welcome of a long and brilliant series of exegetical works'.[2] It was based in all probability on his Genevan lectures of 1536–7; indeed the relation between this and other proposed Bible commentaries is indicated in the preface, in which Calvin states:

> If I shall hereafter publish any commentaries on scripture, I shall always condense them, for I have no need to undertake lengthy doctrinal discussions and digress into *loci communes*. Thus will the godly reader be spared great trouble and tedium, provided he approach them [*the commentaries*] fore-armed with a knowledge of the present work as a necessary instrument.

And he assures his reader that this study of Romans will itself furnish practical illustration of what he means.[3] In short, it was the *Institutio* which would deal with doctrines as such, leaving the author at liberty to elucidate his texts unhindered by the need for extended dogmatic discussions *en route*.

The series of commentaries which followed appeared in both Latin and French, although in certain instances in the latter only. In 1542 and 1543 Jude and I and II Peter were dealt with; from 1546 to 1548 I and II Corinthians, with Galatians and the Pastorals soon after (1548–9), although the same year saw also the commentary on Hebrews (a writing incidentally which Calvin did not himself regard

---

1. *Opera (Corpus reformatorum)*, XIV, 37.
2. Wendel, *Calvin: the Origins and Development of his Religious Thought*, 61.
3. P. Barth *et al.*, eds, *Johanni Calvini opera selecta*, III, 6.

as Pauline). I and II Thessalonians came next, along with a French version of the Romans book. The first of the Old Testament commentaries, that on Isaiah, appeared in 1551. A study of The Acts was published in two parts, the first in 1552 and the second two years later, the commentary on St John's gospel in 1553, a 'Harmony' of the synoptic gospels in 1555, and in 1556 a collected and revised edition of all the New Testament epistles with the exception of II and III John, which, along with the Revelation, Calvin did not treat (or if he did his work is not extant). The Old Testament series continued with Genesis (Latin and French) in 1554, Hosea in 1557, a second edition of the Isaiah commentary in 1559, all the minor prophets in 1560, Daniel in 1562, Jeremiah and Lamentations, and indeed the entire Pentateuch, in 1563. The final commentaries, on Joshua and Ezekiel, appeared posthumously in 1564 and 1565 respectively. It was a monumental achievement, on the strength of which, as to both quantity and quality, Calvin must be ranked as the greatest biblical exegete of his century.[4]

Certain of the New Testament and most of the Old Testament commentaries originated as lectures delivered before often large audiences at the Collège de Genève. When lecturing Calvin did not read from a script but spoke extempore; he did so slowly and in a way that made it fairly easy for his actual words to be taken down by his students, and he himself went over their work to correct any errors before sending it to press. His procedure in his Old Testament lectures was first to read the selected passage in the original tongue and then to translate it into Latin, preferring usually, despite his familiarity with the Vulgate, to make his own version. His knowledge of Hebrew has sometimes been questioned, but it would seem from the evidence of the commentaries themselves that he was proficient in the language, with a sound knowledge of its grammar and an appreciative under-standing of its style. In dealing with the New Testament, his comments on which were in the main dictated privately to secretaries,[5] he used the Latin versions of Erasmus as well as the Vulgate, though here again he would adopt his own rendering whenever it suited him. The Greek text itself was Erasmus's, which, as we have seen, the reformers generally found an indispensable tool; but he was of course a fine enough scholar in his own right not to be confined to it. After the text and translation he went on to explain the passage as a whole before going into details, but he always kept close to the text, discussing phrases and words with characteristic precision and orderliness. Finally, to make sure that the meaning had been clearly conveyed, he went over the passage once more, paraphrasing where necessary so as to underline the sense, and patiently elucidating any lingering points

4. The commentaries and biblical sermons make up the major part of Calvin's collected works – volumes XXIII to LV in the edition in the *Corpus reformatorum*. On his exegetical work generally see J. Baumgartner, *Calvin hébraïsant et interprète de l'Ancien Testament* (Strassburg, 1881), J. Haroutinian and L. P. Smith, eds, *Calvin: Commentaries* (Library of Christian Classics) (Philadelphia/London, 1958); T. H. L. Parker, *The Oracles of God: an introduction to the preaching of John Calvin* (London, 1947), and *Calvin's New Testament Commentaries* (London, 1971). A translation of the New Testament commentaries, ed. by D. W. and T. F. Torrance, began publication at Edinburgh in 1959.

5. Cf. Doumergue, *op. cit.*, III, 592f. Among those who assisted him were Jean Budé, son of the famous humanist Guillaume, and Charles de Jonvillers, his brother-in-law.

of difficulty, even at the cost of repetitiveness, not infrequently evident in the published text. But he was never afraid to be polemical, and his wit could be mordant.

Calvin's thorough acquaintance with humanist methods stood him in excellent stead as a biblical commentator. He had learned to respect a text as a text, and realized the need for a philological approach and the importance of comparing manuscripts and authorities. His equipment was enhanced also by the extraordinary width and depth of his classical and patristic reading, his knowledge of the Fathers especially being unrivalled, perhaps, in his day. His primary aim was to ascertain the plain or literal meaning of the text on which he was working, since in his view this was the only genuine one, in contrast with the allegorism which had been so grossly overworked by early and medieval commentators alike, though he himself resorted to typology, which can become hardly less fanciful. The proper course was to endeavour to penetrate the mind of the biblical author, to fathom his intention and purpose, whereas the allegorizing of a passage might easily invest it with a sense wholly removed from the original and so resulting in uncurbed abuse.[6] On this score Calvin could and did criticize even the revered Augustine himself. Nevertheless the goal which he set himself was not merely that of a historical investigator; questions of authorship, historical circumstances and so forth were clearly relevant to serious study, but what mattered, indeed validated the entire exegetical proceeding, was its spiritual significance. The Bible is the Word of God to man, written down and preserved through the ages for the building up of the church: 'The Church of God can be established only where the Word of God rules, where God shows by his voice the way of salvation. Therefore until true doctrine shed its light, men cannot be gathered in one place to constitute the true body of the Church.'[7] Thus inevitably the question is raised of the inspiration and authority of scripture.

Calvin was well aware that the biblical authors wrote in the first place for their own times and situations. The prophets – a Hosea, an Isaiah, a Jeremiah – delivered the 'oracles of God' for the instruction and warning of the people of God, to whom they believed themselves sent. But their message was not confined to a single age or set of conditions; it envisaged a distant future, anticipating and foretelling Christ and his church. Accordingly the two Testaments are providentially linked, the Old looking forward to the New, the New harking back to and applying the prophecies of the Old. For Calvin, like Luther, believed that the Bible preaches Christ throughout, the one part in a 'shadowy' (*umbratile*) manner, the other openly and plainly.[8] In

6. In Genesis 1:1, for instance, the Hebrew word *elohim*, although plural, should not be referred, as had commonly been done, to the persons of the Trinity, an interpretation which seemed to Calvin 'to have little validity', and rather to be in the nature of a 'violent gloss'. In exegesis he himself preferred what he termed a 'perspicuous brevity'. He thought it 'sacrilegious audacity rashly to turn Scripture this way and that (as we please), and to fool with it as though it were a game'. See his *Epistle* to Simon Grynaeus (1493–1541), prefacing his *Commentary on Romans* (Haroutinian and Smith, *Calvin: Commentaries*, 73–7).

7. Haroutinian and Smith, *op. cit.*, 79.

8. 'The Scriptures are to be read with the purpose of finding Christ there' (*Opera*, XLVIII, 125: comment on John 5:39).

fact, it was only in the light of the New Testament that the meaning of the Old became fully apparent. When, for example, St Matthew (17:35) alludes to the psalmist's words: 'They divide my garments among them, and for my raiment they cast lots' (Psalm 22:18), or recalls (21:42) the saying, 'The stone which the builders rejected has become the chief cornerstone' (118:22), he and his readers well know how much more truly applicable is the utterance to Christ than to David. In other words, what the Old Covenant promised the New fulfilled, the essential difference between them being chronological only, not substantial; for the New Testament restores rather than abrogates the Old: 'All men adopted by God into the company of His people since the beginning of the world were covenanted to him by the same law and by the same bond of the same doctrine as obtains among us.'[9]

Does this mean, as has often been objected, that Calvin deliberately obscures the differences between the two Testaments, thus minimizing the distinction, so manifest to Luther, between Law and Gospel? His reply, in effect, is that if both Testaments preach Christ they must cohere; in the nature of the case there can be no disparity between them. But this is in no way to compromise the truth that the Christ who was known to the Jews only by anticipation, under the form of the Law, was not fully revealed until his coming in the flesh and with the proclamation of the Gospel. It is our privilege that we can contemplate God's glory in the face of his Son. Even so, however, opposition between law and gospel ought not to be exaggerated: 'The Gospel did not so supplant the entire Law as to bring forward a different way of salvation. Rather, it confirmed and satisfied whatever the Law had promised, and gave substance to the shadows.'[10] The same point had been made by Bucer.[11] In any event it had been urged long before by St Augustine in his anti-Manichaean writings. The differences between the two Testaments really pertain, in Calvin's own phraseology, 'to the manner of dispensation rather than substance'.

The Bible, Calvin insists, has its authority from God, not from the church, which itself is grounded in the Bible, otherwise it would not be the church. For although the canon is the church's possession the scriptures themselves are self-authenticating:

> [*They*] obtain among believers only when men regard them as having sprung from heaven, as if there the living words of God were heard. . . . But a most pernicious error widely prevails that Scripture has only so much weight as is conceded to it by the consent of the church. As if the eternal and inviolable truth of God depended upon the decision of men!

On the contrary:

9. *Institutes* (1559), II, x,1 (English trans. by J. T. McNeill and F. L. Battles).
10. II, ix,4, Cf. II, vii, 16 and viii, 28f.
11. *Enarrationes in evangelia* (1536), 120, and *Metaphrases epistolorum Pauli* (1536), 25, 159, 187 (quoted Wendel, *Calvin*, 210f.)
12. I, vii, 1f. 'It is utterly vain to pretend that the power of judging Scripture so lies with the church that its certainty depends upon churchly assent. Thus, while the church receives and gives its seal of approval to the Scriptures, it does not thereby render authentic what is otherwise doubtful or controversial' (I, vii, 2). What Calvin however does not say is how we can be certain that in the compilation of the canon nothing was included which was not divinely inspired and nothing excluded which was. So, is the Apocrypha 'inspired' or not?

Scripture exhibits fully as clear evidence of its own truth as white and black things do of their colour, or sweet and bitter things do of their taste.[12]

This is not to say that the Bible does not contain discrepancies – compare, for example, Acts 7:16 with Genesis 1:13 and Joshua 24:32, on the burial-place of the patriarchs – and these may be attributed possibly to human error, though sometimes more probably to the specific purpose which the author concerned may have had in mind. Calvin at any rate recognizes the likelihood of the need to correct the received text at one point or another, as, for instance, with Matthew 23:24. Such difficulties however do not worry him unduly and he sees no reason to assert their importance. The humanist in Calvin was fully alive to the fact that ancient texts transmitted over many centuries present problems of their own which in no way detract from the value of what their authors have to say. What matters is that the biblical writers were the 'mouthpieces of God' and as such their utterances are infallible, although human nonetheless and thus capable of being mistaken as to factual details (compare, say, I Corinthians 10:8 with Numbers 25:30). Moreover if scripture as the Word of God for the edification of the church – something of immensely more significance than any human wisdom, however excellent in its kind – contains the gospel of salvation, then it is and must be divinely *inspired*. This implies that essentially it is the work not of men but of the Holy Spirit, that it was in all truth 'dictated' by the Spirit, so that we rightly and necessarily speak of God as its author.[13] Hence, 'when that which is set forth is acknowledged to be the Word of God, there is no one so deplorably insolent – unless devoid also of both common sense and humanity itself – as to dare to impugn the credibility of Him who speaks'.[14] 'The highest proof of Scripture derives in general from the fact that God in person speaks in it.'[15] Repeatedly Calvin uses such phrases as 'God speaking', 'God teaching', 'God preaching', when referring to the testimony of scripture, which can itself correctly be called *os Dei*, 'the mouth of God'.[16] Accordingly we owe to the Bible the same reverence which we owe to God, inasmuch as it has proceeded from him alone and has nothing merely human mixed with it. Its authority therefore is beyond all dispute or question.

Did Calvin then teach a doctrine of literal or verbal inspiration? On this point modern opinion has differed, though in the main favouring the view that he did, even if he did not actually invent it.[17] He certainly speaks of the apostles as 'the sworn and authentic amanuenses of the Holy Spirit',[18] and uses the words 'dictating' and 'dictation'. He also holds that inspiration covers the entire content of scripture, so that in this respect all its books are on the same level, thus plainly differing from Luther, who made no bones about distinguishing varying degrees of inspiration in the Bible. His dispute with Castellio, who had questioned the inspiration of the Song of Songs, focused on this precise issue. He further believed that although the language employed was perforce that of men what they set down was

---

13. Cf. St Thomas Aquinas, *Summa theologica*, I, i, 10.
14. I, vii, 1.
15. I, vii, 4.
16. I, vii, 5.
17. So, e.g., Seeberg, *Lehrbuch der Dogmengeschichte*, IV, 2, 567.
18. IV, viii, 9.

God's own utterance.[19] For this reason the authors of scripture can be relied on to have performed their task with complete faithfulness. Whether, notwithstanding, their witness did err, or failed at times to communicate the divine message accurately, Calvin does not expressly consider. But it is hardly plausible to suppose that, in anticipation of modern historical criticism, he drew any clear distinction between the divine *doctrina* and the human channels through which it has been conveyed. An amanuensis may make a slip – as still more those who successively copied the manuscripts – but that serious misunderstanding or error could have occurred in the original is excluded by everything Calvin says. Where he encounters a difficulty he is able as a rule to explain it, as we already have noted, and he rarely in his commentaries suggests emendations of his own. Naturally the Bible does not teach what is not its concern to teach – and the first chapter of Genesis, he recognizes, should be interpreted on that principle – but in what it is concerned to teach he undoubtedly accepts it as inerrant and containing no statement that is false. Hence, he maintains, we are bound to say that we owe to scripture the same reverence which we owe to God, inasmuch as it has proceeded from him alone.

What Calvin does not do is to state, or imply, that a doctrine of the inerrancy of scripture is first to be accepted as a *guarantee* that what the Bible teaches is divine; and to this extent he assuredly does not encourage the 'fundamentalist' biblicism of later times. Rather is the inspiration to be inferred from the content itself, as the Word of God; its value, that is, is intrinsic. But this content and this value are not sufficiently established by the light of reason only, any more than by the bare authority of the church. Were it otherwise scripture's credibility would ultimately remain in doubt. It is here that it differs essentially from the ancient classics.

> Read Demosthenes or Cicero; read Plato, Aristotle and others of that following. They will, I admit, allure you, delight you, move you, enrapture you in wonderful measure. But betake yourself from them to this sacred reading. Then, in spite of yourself, so deeply will it affect you, so penetrate your heart, so fix itself in the very depths of your being, that, compared with its profound impression, such vigour as the philosophers and rhetoricians have will but disappear.[20]

But why is this so? The answer is that, as the scriptures were composed not from the resources of mere human wisdom but by inspiration of the Holy Spirit, so it is to the witness of this same Spirit within the heart of the reader that they finally impress themselves on him as divine and life-giving.

> The prophets and apostles do not boast either of their keenness or of anything that wins credit for them as they speak; nor do they dwell upon rational proofs. . . . If we desire to provide in the best way for our consciences – that they may not be perpetually beset by the instability of doubt or vacillation. . . we ought to seek our conviction at

19.  The apostles, says Calvin, 'were to expound the ancient Scripture and to show that what was taught there has been fulfilled in Christ. Yet they were not to do this except from the Lord, that is, with Christ's Spirit as precursor in a certain measure dictating the words' (IV, viii, 8). The last phrase however, in Latin *verba quodammodo Christi Spiritu*, is noteworthy as introducing some possible qualification.
20.  I, viii, 1.

a higher level than that of human reasoning, judgements or conjectures – that is, in *the inward testimony of the Spirit.*[21]

Apart from this primal witness the Word will gain no credence in the minds of men. For unless the Spirit who spoke by the mouth of the prophets enter into our own hearts and touch them to the quick, says Calvin, we shall not really perceive or understand that their writings do indeed faithfully set forth what was given to them from on high. Moreover, this *testimonium internum Spiritus Sancti* relates to scripture alone; nothing else is to be judged by it.

On the other hand, once we have gained from this unique testimony an assurance far superior to that of any human judgement, then the various and probably more obvious reasons which present themselves for submitting to scripture's rule and guidance will acquire an added relevance and force. Here Calvin can remind his readers how, for instance, the Bible has survived all attacks, which it could scarcely have done had it only human strength to rely upon. 'The whole power of earth has armed itself to destroy it, yet all these efforts have gone up in smoke.'[22] And he points out how its authority has been further sealed by the blood of the martyrs: 'Having once received it, they did not hesitate courageously and intrepidly, and even with great eagerness, to suffer death for it.' They died to render testimony to their faith 'not with fanatic excess but with a firm and constant, yet sober, zeal toward God'.[23]

Calvin follows Zwingli, and diverges from Luther, in his conception of scripture less as a means of grace than as a revelation of the divine will; and, as we have seen, that will, being one and immutable, is revealed as certainly in the Old Testament as in the New. Necessarily, then, the two dispensations will cohere if both alike are the Word of God. Inevitably, however, the result is a tendency towards legalism markedly at variance with the attitudes of Luther, although again distinctly reminiscent of Zwingli. For Calvin, that is, the Old Testament must be approached as an authority in its own right, with a power to guide and to inspire not essentially different from that of the New. The teaching of the prophets stands alongside that of the apostles, to which it is in no way subservient and by which it is by no means rendered otiose.[24] This acceptance of the Old Testament as a 'law' for Christian living, the force of which the New Testament only makes all the plainer, pervades Calvin's thought and was to become even more explicit in his followers. Its effect was to imbue Calvinism with a practicality and clarity of aim which Lutheranism has sometimes seemed to lack and which stood it in good stead in the course of its historic struggles. Paradoxically, it has also conferred on Calvinism an undeniable affinity with Catholicism. At least Catholic and Calvinist, however acutely they might differ in both doctrine and polity, have always been in a position to comprehend one another's standpoint. It is no wonder that Calvinism was to prove Catholicism's most formidable opponent.

21. *Ibid.*
22. I, viii, 12.
23. I, viii, 13.
24. See, *e.g.*, the *Commentary on Romans* (*Opera*, XLIX, 271).

## The knowledge of God

The Bible, then, as the utterance of God himself, is the source of our knowledge of him. 'No one', says Calvin, 'can get even the slightest taste of right and sound doctrine unless he be a pupil of scripture.'[25] What we need to know of him, and what alone we can know of him, is contained there. But does this mean that apart from scripture there is absolutely no knowledge or even intimation of God, and that both the religious experience of the heathen and the speculations of the philosophers are vain? Calvin's reply is simply that they are and that the mysteries of God have meaning only for those to whom it is given. Rational proof is neither necessary nor possible,[26] since the testimony of the Spirit alone brings certainty. Natural theology on the scholastic pattern is therefore as inadmissible for Calvin as it was for Luther. 'Whatever we ourselves think concerning God is foolishness, and whatever we say, without sense.'[27] For the great truth is that his essence is incomprehensible and that his divinity eludes all human perception.[28] Only God knows himself in his inner being (*quid sit apud se*). 'For how can the human mind measure off the measureless essence of God according to its own little measure? . . . Indeed how can the mind by its own leading come to search out God's essence when it cannot even reach its own? Let us then willingly leave to God the knowledge of himself.'[29] And Calvin quotes Hilary of Poitiers, that God is the sole fit witness to himself, and except through himself is unknown.

Yet this is not to say that man is totally without some 'natural' apprehension or consciousness of God, and Calvin is careful to point out in the first Book of the *Institutes* what is to be understood by it. His words are worth quoting at some length:

> There is within the human mind and indeed by natural instinct, an awareness of divinity [*divinitatis sensum*]. This we assume to be beyond controversy. To prevent anyone from taking refuge in the pretence of ignorance. God himself has implanted in all men a certain understanding of his divine majesty, ever renewing its memory by distilling it, as it were, drop by drop. Since, therefore, men one and all discern that there is a God and that he is their Maker they are condemned by their own testimony because they have failed to honour him. If ignorance of God is to be looked for anywhere, surely one is most likely to find it among the more backward peoples and those more remote from civilization. Yet as the eminent pagan [*'ethnicus', i.e. Cicero*] says, there is no nation so barbarous, no people so savage, that they have not a deep-seated conviction that there is a God. And they who in other aspects of life seem the least to differ from brutes still continue to retain some seed of religion.[30]

This native awareness of God within man has a threefold root: in the manifestations of the divine in the natural world and in the nature of man himself,

25. I, vi, 2.
26. II, vii, 5.
27. I, xii, 3.
28. I, v, 1.
29. I, xiii, 21.
30. I, iii, 1. The work of Cicero's to which Calvin alludes is the *De natura deorum* (and notably I, xvii, 43).

especially the distinction between good and evil imprinted on his conscience; in the whole natural course and development of things, and in human history. Religion accordingly is no arbitrary invention, and even idolatry, in its perverted way, witnesses to the truth of the one God. Nevertheless, although such knowledge is in itself authentic enough, it is at most incomplete and imperfect. As Calvin observes, although experience teaches that the 'seed of religion' has been implanted in all men, yet 'barely one in a hundred can be found who in his own heart nurtures what he has conceived, and not even one in whom it comes to maturity, much less bears fruit in its season'.[31] Some are befogged by their own superstitions, while others, through evil intent, deliberately turn aside from God, with the result that 'no real piety remains in the world'. Thus even the knowledge which men do have serves in the end only to their own condemnation, in that in place of the one true God they fashion idols of their own devising.

It might appear that in affirming so much Calvin is in fact undermining his former emphatic assertion that there is no knowledge of God apart from the Bible. He himself says that whereas a merely speculative curiosity about the being and majesty of God is inordinate and to be discouraged, it is right for us 'to contemplate him in his works, by means of which he renders himself near and familiar to us, and in some manner communicates himself'.[32] Indeed he expressly speaks of a 'double knowledge': the historic scriptural revelation which culminates in Christ and that 'primal and simple knowledge to which the very order of nature would have led us if Adam had remained upright'.[33]

*If Adam had remained upright*: but there, unhappily, lies the rub. Man is not what he was when first created. God still is manifested in his creation, but man himself is now so conditioned by sin, his vision so darkened by pride and presumption, that he can no longer read the book of nature aright. Consequently we can know God only as he chooses to reveal himself to us, that is, only in his dealings with us (*qualis erga nos*). This knowledge, so far from being absolute and abstract, is essentially a relative and practical, or 'saving', knowledge, directed simply to the human situation as it is.

> The knowledge of God, as I understand it, is that by which we not only conceive that there is a God, but also grasp what befits us and is proper to his glory: in short, what is to our advantage to know of him. For rightly speaking, we cannot say he is known where there is no religion or piety ['*pietas*', *a word which combines the ideas of both love and fear*]. . . . For what good would it be to profess with Epicurus that there is a God of a sort who has cast aside the care of governing the world only to amuse himself in idleness? What help would it be to 'know' a God with whom we have nothing to do? Rather should our knowledge serve, first to teach us fear and reverence, and then to instruct and guide us to look to him for every good thing, and having received it, to credit it to his account.[34]

Hence,

31. I, iv, 1.
32. I, v, 9.
33. I, ii, 1.
34. I, ii, 1 and 2.

Because we have fallen from life into death, the knowledge purely of God as the Creator would be useless unless faith also followed, setting forth for us God as our Father in Christ. The nature order was that the fabric of the universe [*mundi fabrica*] should be the school in which we were to learn piety, the means which were to lead us to eternal life and perfect felicity. But since man's rebellion, our eyes, wheresoever they turn, encounter God's curse.[35]

Also, while the 'seed of divinity' planted within us is still there it is so corrupted 'that by itself it produces only the worst fruits'.[36] So, 'after the ruin of Adam no knowledge of God had power unto salvation apart from a mediator'.[37] With Zwingli's humanistic idea that even the sages of pagan antiquity possessed a genuine knowledge of God through moral enlightenment Calvin had no sympathy at all.[38]

What this teaching very clearly implies is the utter transcendence of God, which prevents us from speaking of him virtually at all except in the terms which he himself has made available to us. Beyond all else, therefore, what impresses us is his sovereign and awesome majesty. Calvin's whole system of doctrine is built on this foundation, which more than any other aspect of it constitutes his distinctive contribution to the theology of the Protestant Reformation. Rightly has it been said of Calvinism – most certainly so at least of Calvin's own thinking – that it is a 'passionate theocentrism'.[39] Calvin's views on the atonement, on the sacraments, on the church and on the Christian life are all more or less directly shaped by it and have to be seen in relation to it. Of recent years the tendency has been to stress, rather, the central importance for Calvin of Christ himself, his person and his work – to urge, in fact, that the Calvinism of Calvin, whatever may have been true of his followers, is Christocentric, tireless in declaring that Christ is our sole mediator, that the benefits of redemption come to us through him alone, that all scripture points to him, and that the task of the church is ever to proclaim and witness to the salvation which he brought. There is unquestionable truth in this; any suggestion that in Calvin's personal faith Christ was in some way of peripheral significance only would be to disregard what the great Reformer himself says over and over again. Nevertheless the belief that dominated his mind was his profound conviction that God, from whom all things come, by whom all things are sustained and ordered, and in whom all things have their end, should receive from them, and from man in particular, who was expressly created in the divine image, the glory which is his supreme due. The idea of God, omnipotent and omniscient, was ever present to Calvin and pervades everything he wrote, in a manner to which the history of Christian thought and spirituality offers few if any exact parallels.

First, then, the Almighty is Creator, as the scriptures teach at the outset, although Calvin is prompt to insist on the role of Christ the divine Word as the agent in creation. And the purpose of the created world, however glorious in itself the latter may be, is, Calvin does not hesitate to affirm, mankind.

35. II, vi, 1.
36. I, iv, 1.
37. II, vi, 1.
38. Cf. II, ii, 18.
39. Basil Hall, *John Calvin* (London, 1956), 20.

God himself has shown by the order of creation that he created all things for man's sake. For it is not without significance that he divided the making of the universe into six days, even though it would have been no more difficult for him to have completed in one moment the whole work together in all its details than to arrive at its completion gradually by a progression of this sort. But he willed to commend his providence and fatherly solicitude towards us in that, before he fashioned man, he prepared everything he foresaw would be useful and salutary for him.[40]

It can thus be said that if God brought the world into being for his own greater glory, man himself, as its culminating point, has in this regard a unique vocation. For although God lacks nothing, his principal aim in creating man was that his name might be glorified in him.[41]

But if God is Creator he also must be thought of as a sustaining Providence.

To make God a momentary Creator, who finished his work once for all, would be a cold and barren thing; and we must differ from the profane especially in this, that we see the presence of the divine power shining as much in the continuance of the world as in its inception.[42]

On this subject Calvin dwells at length. In the 1539 version of the *Institutes* providence is dealt with after predestination (itself scarcely noticed in the original edition), but in the final version it comes immediately after his already extended discussion of creation. What marks Calvin's thinking is his overriding sense of the absoluteness of the divine will, though there would seem little reason to doubt that in this he was influenced, as we have seen, by his contact with Bucer; for Calvin, like the Strassburg reformer, sees God not only as originating all things but as determining and controlling them at every moment, so that no place whatever is left for mere chance.

Suppose [*he says*] a man falls among thieves, or wild beasts; is shipwrecked at sea by a sudden gale; is killed by a falling house or tree. Suppose another man wandering through the desert finds help in his straits; having been tossed by the waves, reaches harbour; miraculously escapes death by a finger's breadth. Carnal reason ascribes all such happenings, whether favourable or adverse, to fortune. But anyone who has been taught by Christ's lips that all the hairs of his head are numbered will look farther afield for a cause, and will deem that all events are governed by God's secret counsels.[43]

Everything, in a word, is what it is because God has sovereignly willed it so; it derives solely from his determinate decree and thus can brook no questioning. Indeed to ask why God should have decided one thing rather than another is not only idle but impious, for what God wills he wills, and there is no higher authority to which he can be conceived of as answerable.

For Zwingli too, it will be recalled, God is omnipotent in the sense of being eternally active: not merely is he the first cause, he is the only cause; yet the Zurich theologian takes a basically more metaphysical view of the divine activity, seeing it as immutable law or an all-pervading energy rather than a continuously

40. I, xiv, 22.
41. *Opera*, VIII, 293f.
42. I, xvi, 1.
43. I, xvi, 2.

deliberate volition. By Calvin, however, God's power and rule are thought of through and through as personal. Further, his particular control obtains no less of the inorganic world than of the human or the sentient, since although each phenomenon 'has by nature been endowed with its own property, it yet does not exercise its own power except as it is directed by God's ever-present hand'. Inanimate objects are thus 'nothing but instruments to which God continually imparts as much effectiveness as he wills, and according to his own purposes bends and turns them to either one action or another'.[44] Calvin's meaning could hardly have been rendered more explicitly. God himself is limited by no law, whether physical or moral, and it is man's first duty simply to recognize God's absolutely unconstrained sovereignty.

It has been argued that the source of this conception in Calvin's thinking was the Scotism and Occamism which have usually been interpreted as identifying the divine will with arbitrary, not to say capricious, power.[45] But in the third Book of the *Institutes* Calvin at one point expressly repudiates what he calls 'the dream of papist theologians touching the absolute power of God',[46] holding that God's will, so far from being arbitrary, is a manifestation of his nature, which in turn means that he can do nothing self-contradictory. Yet the resemblance between Calvin's view and Ockham's is striking. According to the latter nothing is of itself good or evil, the free will of God being the sovereign arbiter of what is so. Likewise Calvin states that 'the will of God is so much the supreme and sovereign rule of justice that whatever he wills must be held to be just in so far as he wills it. So that when one asks, Why did God do this? we must reply, Because he willed it. If one goes farther and says, Why did he will this? that is to ask for something greater and higher than the will of God, which cannot be done.'[47] God, in truth, is his own law and above that which he prescribes for mankind, so that what he commands is right because, and only because, he commands it. Whether in propounding this doctrine Calvin took his cue from the later scholastics is of little relevance. The character of his own belief is surely perfectly clear.

But Calvin also distinguishes his idea of providence from the generalized fatalism of the Stoics, seeing the divine action as always particular.[48] Moreover providence especially relates to human events. Indeed what separates the God of the philosophers from the God of biblical faith is that for philosophy he is an absentee deity unconcerned with the world he has created, whereas in biblical teaching he is ever present, watchful and effectively operative. 'Let my readers grasp that providence means not that by which God idly observes from heaven what takes place on earth, but that by which, as keeper of the keys, he governs all events. Hence it pertains

44. *Ibid.* God, says Calvin, could as well have made man an ass or a dog.
45. Albrecht Ritschl was one of the first to maintain this, and he has been followed by many others since: e.g., W. Walker (*John Calvin, the Organizer of Reformed Protestantism*), R. Seeberg and H. Bois (*La philosophie de Calvin*, Paris, 1919), although the last-named writer later retracted his statements.
46. III, xxiii, 2.
47. *Ibid.*
48. Calvin rejects the opinion which 'concedes to God some kind of blind and ambiguous motion, while taking from him the chief thing: that he directs all things by his incomprehensible wisdom and disposes it to his own end' (I, xvi, 4).

no less to his hands than to his eyes.'[49] God cannot have knowledge of which his purpose and therefore his action are not the expression. In saying which, given his principles, Calvin is of course entirely logical.

## Predestination

So, then, we are brought to the doctrine of predestination, with which, rightly or wrongly, Calvin's name is invariably associated. Certainly in the final edition of the *Institutes* it assumes a prominent place, but in the various summaries of Christian doctrine which from time to time he drew up, as well as in the successive editions of the *opus magnum*, it receives very varying degrees of emphasis. In 1536 he did not treat it as a separate doctrine at all, and it is mentioned at two points only. However, in the French catechism composed at Geneva in the following year the question of predestination is definitely put as a matter of observation: Why is it that the seed of the Word comes to fruition in some but not in others, unless the former have by God's eternal decree been predestined to be his children and heirs of the Kingdom, whereas the rest, for whom the preaching of the gospel offers nothing but the smell of death, are also by the same divine counsel before the creation of the world non-elect and therefore reprobate?[50] Nonetheless are the faithful warned that the whole issue is a profound mystery into which it is dangerous to pry too closely. In the catechism of 1541, on the other hand, it is given no explicit statement at all. The 1539 edition of the *Institutes* does advert to the subject, linking it with the doctrines of both the church and providence, and by 1559 the author deals with providence and predestination together as aspects of one and the same fundamental truth, namely the eternal decree of God's will before the world and time. Calvin's views, as often with theologians, were sharpened by controversy, if not in substance then certainly in statement. Jérôme Bolsec, an ex-monk and one-time Paris theologian, engaged in argument with him on the subject of double predestination – predestination, that is, to both life and death, denying election and reprobation as eternal decrees and insisting that they are dependent on faith. To hold otherwise, he contended, would be to represent God as an unprincipled tyrant. This highly incensed Calvin, who attacked his opponent in savage terms, denouncing him as a villain who knew no more of the Bible than the filthiest pig, and eventually secured his banishment. The fact is that the significance of the doctrine came to loom ever larger in Calvin's mind, believing as he did that the honour of God and the salvation of the world rested on it. He was convinced that it had to be maintained and taught as a basic article of faith, though not pressed too hard unless it were deliberately assailed, in which case it would have to be defended with the utmost vigour. He himself admitted that it related to what can only be called an 'awful decree' (*quidem decretum horribile*),[51] but God's transcendent will is inscrutable and never to be questioned.

The idea of predestination, and even of double predestination, was not by any

49.  *Ibid.*
50.  *Opera*, XXIV, 46.
51.  III, xvi, 8.

means an innovation in Western theology, its origin taking us back into Christian antiquity. At any rate on this as on other topics the Augustinian tradition was a powerful component of medieval thought. In the ninth century the somewhat heterodox Saxon monk Gottschalk, an extreme Augustinian, had anticipated Calvin's views almost to the letter. Gottschalk's teaching proved highly controversial, no doubt, and three successive synods, at Mainz (848), Quiercy (849) and Lyons (854), pronounced differing verdicts upon it. During the course of the dispute the various arguments for and against predestinarianism, as they have been rehearsed again and again down to modern times, were fully deployed, the main point at issue being whether Christ died for all men or for the elect alone. So far in fact was the question from being settled that it cropped up periodically throughout the Middle Ages,[52] the debate however turning chiefly on the requisite degree of emphasis, not on the principle itself; it could, as with Wycliffe and Hus, for example, receive greater stress than usual, but the doctrine that those who inherit eternal life are elected thereto was part of the accepted pattern of belief. St Thomas Aquinas pays long and close attention to it, making it a special part of the general doctrine of providence and defining it as 'the type [*ratio*] of the direction of a rational creature towards the end of eternal life'.[53] He also holds that the number of the elect is determined.[54]

The sixteenth-century reformers, apart from certain of the radicals, all endorsed the idea, finding solid scriptural warrant for it, particularly in St Paul, and the clearest and most forthright exposition of it in St Augustine. With Luther it was a basic theological tenet, although he deplored a too anxious prying into the secrets of the divine will. Melanchthon at first adhered to it without question, but later found any attempt at precise formulation of the doctrine less and less to his liking, holding that it could only result in the confusing of simple souls. The belief that salvation depends on faith issuing in righteousness he deemed more edifying because more easily understood. Bucer, on the other hand, taught it unequivocally, and Calvin readily followed him, though he would not have been the man he was had he not also brought the matter to the bar of his own searching judgement. In any case he drew deeper inspiration from Augustine, considering indeed that he was himself doing no more than to reproduce 'that holy man's own plain and uncompromising teachings'. He quotes him repeatedly and even says that he would be content to present Augustine *verbatim* as an expression of his personal views.[55]

52. As with the revived Augustinianism of the *schola Augustiniana moderna*, of whom Gregory of Rimini (Ariminensis) (died 1358) was a signal representative. See P. Vignaux, *Justification et prédestination au xiv^e siècle. Duns Scot, Pierre d'Auriole et Gregoire de Rimini* (Paris, 1934).
53. *Summa theologica*, I, xxiii, 1.
54. *Summa theologica*, I, xxiii, 7.
55. Cf. III, xxii, 8: 'If I wanted to compile a whole volume from Augustine, I would readily show my readers that I need no other language than his.' Calvin's admiration for Augustine is very evident in the section of the *Institutes* (II, xxi–xiv) dealing with predestination, as also in his treatise *On the Eternal Predestination of God*, part of which is devoted to a point by point exposition of the saint's teaching.
   The main sources for St Augustine's teaching on predestination and grace, which in turn rests largely on his understanding of St Paul, are the retrospective analyses of its development given in *Contra duas epistulas Pelagii* (A.D. 421), *the Retractationes* (427),

The presupposition of Calvin's doctrine, as that of Augustine or Aquinas or his fellow-reformers, is the sinful condition of man consequent on Adam's fall. Created at first in God's own image, man's present state is one of complete moral corruption, to the extent that the divine image is virtually effaced; or as Calvin is careful to phrase it: 'Even though we grant that God's image was not totally annihilated and destroyed in man, yet was it so corrupted that whatever remains is a horrible deformity.'[56] Calvin is not of course denying that men are capable of any good at all at the human level – obviously some are more moral than others – or that, as society judges, individuals even among the heathen – a Socrates or a Zeno springs to mind – have not achieved a high level of virtue. But attainments of the kind, admirable as in themselves they may be, are in God's sight no more than 'splendid vices', to use Augustine's telling expression. Before him who is absolute Righteousness their defect is manifest: that residual element of selfishness and pride which mars all human actions, however seemingly well-intentioned. As Calvin himself pungently says, men 'are constrained from evil-doing not by genuine zeal for good, but either by mere ambition or by self-love, or some other perverse motive'.[57] They do good deeds, or avoid evil ones, for a variety of reasons, but for none that can be pronounced immune from the taint of sin which affects our entire nature. For that same nature is 'not only destitute and empty of good, but so fertile and fruitful of every evil that it cannot be idle', sin being ever active, ever self-reproducing.[58] This condition of original sinfulness – 'original' inasmuch as it is our inheritance from Adam in the beginning – is aptly called, in Augustine's word, *concupiscentia*, 'concupiscence', or the 'law of sin in our flesh'. 'Man, from the understanding to the will, from the soul even to the flesh, has been defiled and crammed with this concupiscence.'[59] For when Adam 'deserted the fountain of righteousness' not only did a lower appetite seduce him, 'but unspeakable impiety occupied the very citadel of his mind and pride penetrated to the depths of his heart'.[60] So man is, in another of Augustine's expressions, *massa perditionis*, deserving wholly of condemnation.

This hereditary depravity and corruption of human nature is not therefore simply a condition like a disease, which, though rendering a man helpless, is not, or at least may not be, his own fault. On the contrary, it is profoundly culpable. Even

---

55. *continued De praedestinatione natione sanctorum* (428–9), *De dono perseverantiae* (428–9) and the unfinished *Contra secundam Juliani responsionem* (429–30). In the last-named it is emphatically stated: 'All things work together for good to those who were chosen before the foundation of the world by him who calleth those things which be not as though they; to the elect according to the election of grace, who were chosen before the foundation of the world freely, and not on account of any good works foreseen. Within that number of the elect and the predestinated, even those who have led the worst lives are by the goodness of God led to repentance' (c.5). J. B. Mozley's *The Augustinian Doctrine of Predestination*, published in 1878, remains an authoritative treatment of its subject. L. Smits, *Saint Augustin dans l'oeuvre de Jean Calvin* (2 vols, Assen, 1957f.) is exhaustive.

56. I, xv, 4.

57. III, xiv, 3.

58. II, i, 8.

59. *Ibid.* Cf. II, iii, 5: 'So depraved in his nature that he can be moved or impelled only to evil.'

60. II, i, 9.

infants, says Calvin, are guilty, not of another's sin but their own.[61] The descendants of Adam are judged, that is, not for his defection as such but for the evil disposition and propensity which they all inherit from him. Thus is it that the entire human race is 'hostile and hateful to God', and worthy only of perdition. Nevertheless God in his mercy chose to elect *some* to life eternal. In no way, however, and by no foreknowledge of their actual worthiness, do they merit such a choice. (It is not indeed a question of any divine *fore*-knowing, in that, properly speaking, God does not foreknow, as if he were conditioned by the sequence of time: as the eternal all things are ever present to his mind.) Quite certainly election does not depend on faith, 'as if scripture taught that we are merely given the ability to believe, and not, rather, faith itself'.[62] The grace of God does not find, but makes, those who are elected fit for salvation. St Paul is quoted as authority for the principle that God bestows his favour on the elect simply because he so wills: 'He is moved to mercy for no other reason but that he wills to be merciful.' Moreover, what applies to the saved applies no less to the reprobate. In Calvin's classic definition:

> We call predestination God's eternal decree, by which he determined with himself what he willed to become of each man. For all are not created in equal condition; rather, eternal life is foreordained for some, eternal damnation for others. Therefore, as any man has been created for one or the other of these ends, we speak of him as predestined to life or to death.[63]

This fateful decision is a secret counsel of the divine will; we can see no reason for it, nor have we any right to demand one of God. As in the apostle's words, 'God has mercy upon whomever he wills to have mercy, and hardens whomever he wills to harden'.[64] But the decision is of course self-justifying to the extent that the elect bring forth the fruits of grace and faith.

Calvin, convinced that he had biblical authority behind him, did not shrink from the implications of double predestination, although he may somewhat veil his language. To his logical mind they were inescapable conclusions. God is no less a God of justice than of mercy, and if his mercy redounds to his greater glory, so too does his justice. Sinful man, in any case, has no claim on him. That the doctrine had its difficulties Calvin was aware, but he could always forestall objectors by pleading man's constitutional ignorance of God's ways. Is the Almighty arbitrary or capricious? By no means, he insists. God has given mankind the law, and they have disobeyed it; how then should they suppose that his righteousness will overlook the transgression? Rather should we be astonished and thankful that in his mercy he has spared some at least the retribution which alone is their due. On the other hand, for God to have saved all would have implied a suspension of his justice and an obscuring of the greatness of his mercy, neither of which would have promoted his glory. To the question why men should have been created only for reprobation, the answer is that life in this world, even for a limited time, is a good

61. II, i, 8.
62. III, xiv, 3.
63. III, xxi, 5.
64. Romans 9:18; cf. Calvin's *Sermon on Ephesians I, 3f*: 'If we ask why God takes pity on some, and why he lets go of others and abandons them, there is no answer but that it pleased him so to do.'

thing, for which man's gratitude is fully warranted. But again, if the outcome of the divine choice is thus settled what need is there to preach the gospel, to the elect as to the non-elect? Because, says Calvin, God works not by mere *fiat* but through means or with instruments. His word is necessary to instruct, whether by the gospel or by the law; for thus the elect learn how their salvation comes about, and the reprobate why they are worthy of condemnation. 'Even now', he muses, 'they are striking and beating their consciences.'[65]

Such objections are, in a sense, only debating points. The real difficulty is much more fundamental. Is not God, on Calvin's showing, himself responsible for the world's sin and misery? Man, however, we are assured, sins by his own volition, as Adam himself did; for what he does he wills by virtue of his sinful nature. Men's wills now, evidently enough, are in bondage, yet Adam's was free before he transgressed.[66] Calvin states indeed quite categorically that 'Adam could have stood if he wished, seeing that he fell solely by his own will'.[67] Yet it is equally true that, on the arguments Calvin adduces, his fall resulted from no chance impulse, no 'Shall I, shan't I?' decision. God knew that Adam would fall *because* he had also decreed that he would do so. 'Scripture proclaims that all mortals were bound over to eternal death in the power of one man. Since this cannot be ascribed to nature, it is perfectly clear that it has come forth from the wonderful plan of God.'[68] To say that Adam sinned *willingly* therefore may be true, but his will already was deflected, 'bent', and his consequent action predetermined according to the deliberate purpose of his Maker. And this simply in order that God might enact the scenario of parading his 'glorious' attributes before the all but uncomprehending gaze of his puppet creatures! Calvin disliked the term 'free will' as derogating from God's sovereignty, whereas the idea of predestination, which he cherished whatever rational and moral problems it might raise, maintained it. Any objection that the price was too high for God so represented to retain his credibility could ever be met with the dialectically unanswerable rejoinder that 'we must always at last return to the sole decision of God's will, the cause of which is hidden in him'.[69] Thus

---

65. II, v, 5. What proportion, out of the entire race of mankind, should in Calvin's view be regarded as of the elect? He wisely never ventured to say, but it was not large. 'Some object that God would contradict himself if he should universally invite all men to him, but admit only a few as elect', an objection however which Calvin finds quite inadmissible (III, xxii, 10).

66. 'Man, as he was corrupted by the Fall, sinned willingly, not unwillingly or by constraint; by the most eager inclination of his heart, not by forced compulsion; by the promptings of his own lust, not by pressure from without' (II, iii, 5). That man is responsible for his acts, and feels himself to be so, Calvin regards as demonstrated by the promptings of conscience. The trouble with man is, not that he has no will, but that it is enslaved. 'Because of the bondage of sin by which the will is held bound, it cannot move toward God, much less apply itself thereto. . . . Nonetheless the will remains, with the most eager inclination disposed and hastening to sin. For man, when he gave himself over to this necessity, was deprived not of will, but of soundness thereof' (*ibid.*).

67. I, xv, 8. 'His choice of good and evil was free; and not that only, but the highest rectitude imbued his mind and will, and all the organic parts were rightly composed to obedience until in destroying himself he corrupted his own blessings' (*Ibid.*).

68. III, xxiii, 7. See the whole of section 4.

69. III, xxiii, 4.

might agnosticism, under the cloak of faith, conveniently silence both reason and conscience.

But does Calvin believe that free will is restored to the regenerate? Contrary to Augustine's opinion he holds that it is not. A *right* will, as he calls it, is one subject to the will of God and the good works which spring from it are in fact God's own gifts. Man's good will, that is, is not really his own at all, whereas his sinful will is. Hence while for the latter he is justly condemned, for the former he can claim no credit. To ask why man should be held responsible for the evil in him but not for the good is to receive from Calvin the reply which by now we must expect: it is not right to exact from God a reason for his actions; whatever he does is for his own glory.[70]

The debates concerning supralapsarianism and infralapsarianism were to consume the interest of Calvin's followers, and it can fairly be argued that the latter did not avoid distorting his perspectives or shifting his emphases. This perhaps was inevitable; the teachings of no really influential thinker are merely reproduced by his disciples, but the case against the Calvinists, as distinguished from the master himself, can be over stated. It is true that the scriptural base of the latter's doctrine sometimes tended to recede before speculative and formalistic, even Aristotelian, theologizing, but Calvin himself cannot be wholly exculpated. He may not have taught supralapsarianism in so many words (his language is sometimes tortuous) but the least that can be said is that those who interpreted him as having intended it are not to be blamed for wanton misrepresentation: the idea is implicit in one statement of his after another,[71] even though he deprecates, no doubt sincerely, an excess of dogmatic precision. Again, to maintain that he did not teach a limited atonement – in other words, that Christ's death was for the sake of the elect only – is surely to prevaricate. If he had not done so he would not have gone as far, in this regard, as Augustine, who explained that the idea of Christ's dying for all mankind was only a way of saying that no class or condition of men was as such excluded. The Calvinists, whatever their faults, are scarcely to be censured for making explicit what Calvin himself seemed well enough to mean despite ambiguousness of phrase or the silence of discretion.[72]

70. Among Calvin's leading contemporary critics on this subject were the Romanist theologian Albertus Pighius, who, strangely, had charged Calvin with ethical indifference and against whom the reformer published his *Defensio sanae et orthodoxae doctrinae de servitate et liberatione humani arbitrii* (1543; see *Opera*, XXXIV, 225ff). Another was the unfortunate Castellio. Calvin's pamphlet against his fellow-Genevan is marked by a degree of acrimony and venom which, even in an age given to vituperation, displays its author in a far from flattering light. But there were many among Calvin's adherents and associates – with no intention, therefore, of calumniating him – who nevertheless had misgivings about certain features of his teaching. His meaning, all too often, seemed elusive, even when his words appeared not deliberately evasive.

71. Cf., e.g., *Institutes* II, xv,8 and III, xxiii 8 ('The first man fell because the Lord had judged it to be expedient; why he so judged is hidden from us').

72. Calvin's teaching is not of course to be *equated* with that of his followers, as they developed it in the later 16th and early 17th centuries. That was an age in which systematization was prized for its own sake, something as true of Lutheranism as it was of the Reformed theology. And in both Aristotle was enlisted as an invaluable *aide*. Thus a Protestant scholasticism emerged which neither Luther nor Calvin would,

*Calvin II: A pattern of sound doctrine*

## Christ, his person and his work

The objection has been urged against Calvin's predestinarianism that, since election to blessedness lies in God's eternal decree, the atoning work of Christ is rendered otiose or unnecessary. But this is not at all how the reformer himself viewed the matter. It would be wholly unfair to him to suggest that his doctrine is so strictly *theo*centric as to imply that the significance of Christ in the scheme of salvation is no more than nominal, or at most peripheral.[73] Calvin's insistent teaching is that it is through Christ alone that man can know God, and that election takes place only in Christ. For God and man, mutually alienated by the latter's sin, can be reconciled only through a mediation whereby the satisfaction of God's righteousness and the demonstration of his mercy are united. Christ, then, is he through whom and in whom this is achieved, to mankind's inestimable benefit. 'From the beginning of the world he had consequently been set before all the elect that they should look unto him to put their trust in him.'[74] St Irenaeus was correct in saying that the Father, himself infinite, becomes finite in the incarnate Son, 'for he has accommodated himself to our little measure lest our minds be overwhelmed by the immensity of his glory'.[75] The work of redemption could not, that is, as the ancient Fathers clearly taught, have been accomplished unless the mediator were himself both God and man. The task he had to perform was 'no common thing', but so to restore us to divine grace:

> as to make of the children of men, children of God; of the heirs of Gehenna, heirs of the heavenly Kingdom. Who could have done this had not the self-same Son of God become the Son of man, and had not so taken what was ours as to impart what was his to us, and to make what was his by nature ours by grace?[76]

Thus Calvin readily adopts the Chalcedonian doctrine of the union of the two natures in Christ. On the one hand, there can be no question but that Christ was truly man, in soul as in body; upon that scripture is plain and emphatic, although such infirmities as Christ knew were voluntarily borne and he could have been exempt from them without detriment to his humanity. On the other, he was truly God; hence by his complete identification with us, sin only excepted, we have a sure trust of being ourselves made children of God.

The union of Godhead and manhood came about 'not by confusion of substance but by the unity of person'.[77] Following the course of patristic orthodoxy Calvin

72. *continued* we may surmise, have readily endorsed. Nevertheless those who initiate great movements of thought cannot be excluded from all responsibility, however unwitting, from the course which such movements eventually take. The connection between Marxism and Karl Marx can at no point be severed. On Calvinism in its further historical dimension see J. T. McNeill, *The History and Character of Calvinism* (London and New York, 1954) and, more recently, M. Prestwich (ed.), *op. cit.*; W. S. Reid, *John Calvin: his Influence in the Western World* (Grand Rapids, Mich., 1982) should also be consulted.
73. See note on Calvin's trinitarian doctrine (p. 192 below).
74. II, vi, 4.
75. Calvin cites *Adv. haeres.* IV, iv, 2.
76. XI, xii, 2.
77. II, xiv, 1.

stresses the oneness of the God-Man, reducing the Nestorianizing tendency which we noted in Zwingli, while at the same time rejecting any monophysite commingling of the two natures such as even Luther has been accused of: 'We affirm [Christ's] divinity so joined and united with his humanity that each retains its distinctive nature unimpaired, and yet the two natures constitute one Christ.'[78] The humanity is in no essential respect to be separated from the divinity, but the distinction must nonetheless be maintained between them if the Godhead is not to suffer change and diminution. Thus although Calvin allows the idea of the *communicatio idiomatum* in accordance with the evidence of scripture itself, he would not press it as far as does Luther, for whom the ubiquity of the divine nature is imparted to the human itself. Qualities which are utterly alien to man belong exclusively to Christ's divinity and cannot be transferred:[79] only so much was communicated to the human nature as was needful for our salvation, otherwise this divine power was kept as though hidden. Anything therefore that might tend to erase the distinction between the two natures was to be rejected. Christ's sinlessness, moreover, was not the result of his miraculous birth but rested on the sanctifying power of the Holy Spirit, who preserved his human generation as pure as it would have been before the fall.[80]

Christ's work, Calvin thinks, can be described in terms of his threefold office as prophet, priest and king.[81] All these functions are implied, he maintains, by the very name *Christ*, since under the law prophets, priests and kings were all anointed with holy oil. For this reason the 'illustrious name of "Messiah" was also bestowed upon the promised Mediator'.[82] As prophet Christ, beyond all others, is a herald and witness of the Father's grace. Indeed the perfection of his teaching has closed the line of prophecy: 'Outside Christ there is nothing worth knowing.' As king he rules over a spiritual kingdom, which as such is eternal. Under his protection the church's perpetuity is assured, while for the individual it proffers the hope of a blessed immortality.[83] Further, Christ's kingship endows his people with all the gifts of the Spirit,[84] while his heavenly session means that he is the Father's representative not only to govern and defend the church but to destroy his enemies.[85] Finally, in

78. *Ibid.*
79. *Opera*, XVV, 104.
80. Calvin's doctrine of the incarnation is epitomized in a couple of sentences in the 1559 *Institutes*: 'Even if the Word in his infinite essence united with the nature of man into one person, we do not imagine that he was confined therein. . . . The Son of God descended from heaven after such a manner that, without leaving heaven, he willed to be born in the virgin's womb, to go about the earth, and to hang upon the cross, yet he continuously filled the world even as he had done from the beginning' (II, xiii, 4). On Calvin's Christology as a whole see J. S. Witte, 'Die Christologie Calvins' in *Das Konzil von Chalkedon* (ed. A. Grillmeier and H. Bacht), (Frankfurt-am-Main, 1951–4) 487–529, and W. Niesel, *The Theology of Calvin* (English trans. by H. Knight) (London, 1956), 155ff.
81. This categorization is not mentioned in the original *Institutio*. It appears first in the 1539 version, receiving its final, extended treatment in that of 1559 (II, xv).
82. II, xv, 2.
83. II, xv, 3.
84. II, xv, 4.
85. II, xv, 5.

his priestly office he acts as 'a pure and spotless Mediator' to reconcile men to God. '[For] God in his capacity as judge is angry towards us. Hence, an expiation must intervene in order that Christ as priest may obtain God's favour for us and appease his wrath. To perform that office, therefore, Christ had to come forward with a sacrifice.' And for this only his own death as a pure and spotless victim would suffice. 'Neither we nor our prayers have access to God unless Christ, as our High Priest, having washed away our sins, sanctifies us and obtains for us that grace from which the uncleanness of our transgressions and vices debars us.'[86] It is to the death of Christ therefore that we must look in order that the efficacy and benefit of his heavenly priesthood may reach us.

Unlike Anselm, for whom the atonement is a meritorious satisfaction, Calvin sees it as penal, a substitutionary punishment whereby one suffered what the many deserved. In his own consciousness, says Calvin, Christ bore the weight of the divine anger, 'since he was "stricken and afflicted" by God's hand, and experienced all the signs of a wrathful and avenging God'.[87] If it cannot be urged that he bore the exact penalty due to us on account of sin – although Calvin believed that Christ endured the torment of the damned in descending into hell – he underwent in our stead what was virtually its equivalent. But, though he recognizes that God as retributive justice demanded the punishment, the motif which Calvin (along with Luther) consistently sounds is that of Christ's total and willing obedience. The ground of our forgiveness is in fact his entire life, 'the whole course of his obedience', not only his death. But that death was, in truth, crucial. Christ died a judicial death, although the judge, Pontius Pilate, who condemned him, himself testified to his innocence. Thus our guilt is seen to be transferred to Christ, so that he voluntarily became our substitute to appease the wrath which should have been visited upon us. The very cross itself is symbolic, accursed not only in the opinion of men but by enactment of the divine law, as stated in Deuteronomy 21:23.[88] Other benefits include deliverance from death and the devil, as St Paul teaches, and a beginning of the mortification of our own flesh.[89] It is through union with Christ, and only so, that the elect are assured of redemption; it follows therefore that redemption is logically dependent on election and that Christ's atoning work was not effective for the non-elect. Calvin himself, it is true, is not explicit on this point, but had he been confronted with it in the context of subsequent debate there can be no real doubt that he would have endorsed it.

What place, then, does Calvin assign to justification by faith? Referring to it as 'the principle article of our religion', he characterizes it simply as 'the acceptance with which God receives us into his favour as righteous men', and states that it 'consists in remission of sins and the imputation of Christ's righteousness'.[90] In no sense does he see it as involving an *infusion* of grace. Essentially it is the forgiveness of sins as a wholly gratuitous divine act: 'We are justified by God solely by the

---

86. II, xv, 6.
87. II, xvi, 11.
88. II, xvi, 6.
89. II, xvi, 7.
90. III, xi, 2.

intercession of Christ's righteousness', which we apprehend by faith.[91] Repentance, newness of life and free reconciliation ensue.[92] To the charge that justification thus understood obviates the need for good works Calvin's firm reply is, like Luther's, that although in no respect can good works become the ground of our holiness a living faith is never devoid of such works. Thus justification necessarily has its consequence in sanctification. And sanctification in turn means a change not only in external conduct, but inwardly, by a renewal of the heart, stimulated thereto by the fear of God, who will sit in judgement upon us.[93]

> If, when all the gifts God has bestowed upon us are called to mind, they are like rays of the divine countenance by which we are illumined to contemplate that supreme light of goodness; much more is this true of the grace of good works, which shows that the Spirit of adoption has been given to us.[94]

Nevertheless it has always to be clearly recognized that our salvation stands not on faith, let alone good works, but on election.[95]

Faith itself Calvin defines as 'a firm and certain knowledge of God's good will towards us, founded upon the truth of the freely given promise in Christ, both revealed to our minds and sealed upon our hearts through the Holy Spirit'.[96] This has a somewhat intellectualist ring, but Calvin wishes to press the fact of the cognitive element in faith as against anything resembling mere feeling.[97] Luther too admitted this element, but he was prone to dwell on the subjective aspect, on faith as receptivity, the soul's 'openness' to God. Calvin, temperamentally more of an 'intellectual' than the German leader, senses the danger of subjectivism and hence includes in his definition the object of faith itself. 'By this knowledge [*of the reconciliation effected by Christ*], I say, not by submission of feeling, do we obtain entry into the Kingdom of Heaven.'[98] It is not enough, he warns, for a man implicitly to believe what he does not understand or even investigate. Contrariwise, he is thoroughly alive to the perils of scholastic rationalism, and clearly states that assent should be of the heart rather the brain.[99] After all, 'of what sort is that faith which distinguishes the children of God from the unbelievers, by which we call upon God as Father, by which we cross over from death into life, and by which Christ, eternal salvation and life, dwells in us?'[100]

### The church and the sacraments

Calvin's conception of the church was as positive as was that of traditional Catholicism, and he vehemently rebutted the charge that the Reformation signified

91. III, xi, 23.
92. III, iii, 1.
93. III, iii, 6 and 7.
94. III, xiv, 18.
95. III, xxiv, 3.
96. III, ii, 7.
97. III, ii, 2.
98. *Ibid.*
99. III, ii, 8.
100. III, ii, 13.

a breach with the historic church, or that the reformers were indifferent to the institutional forms of Christianity. The Roman Church, however, he denounced as so corrupt – it was, he declared, like Israel under Jeroboam – as to have all but forfeited the true character of a church; although this was not to deny that many of its members, as individuals, were of the true church. But that there could be no Christianity without the church he was insistent; and in so maintaining he meant, also, the *visible* church. To quote his own words, with their echo of St Cyprian:

> There is no other way to enter into life unless this mother conceive us in her womb, give us birth, nourish us at her breast . . . and keep us under her care and guidance until, putting off mortal flesh, we become like the angels. . . . Away from her bosom one cannot hope for any forgiveness of sins or any salvation.

And it is of the same visible, institutional church that he proclaims:

> 'What God has joined together it is not lawful to put asunder', so that, for those to whom he is a Father, the church may also be Mother.[101]

The article of the creed affirming the one, holy, catholic church was in no way impugned because of the faults of the papal communion. The church still is nothing less than the pillar and ground of the truth, and wilfully to detach oneself from it is sin. With an eye on the contemporary anabaptists and spiritual 'fanatics' – the Karlstadts and the Müntzers as well as the Donatists and Cathari of old, he bitterly attacked those 'who, imbued with a false conviction of their own perfect sanctity, as if they had already become a sort of airy spirits, spurned association with all men in whom they discerned any remnant of human nature'.[102] Membership of the church is not a matter of individual choice and preference, and to separate from it amounts to a denial of God and Christ.

But the visible church must be seen in its wider setting. In principle it is the body of Christ, as St Paul teaches. To be 'in Christ' is thus to be within that body. The individual believer indeed is united with Christ only through membership of it. At the most fundamental level the church is constituted by the number of the elect from the beginning of the world (*universus numerus electorum*), and as such comprises many more than 'the saints presently living on earth'.[103] It is from this company, the membership of which is known to God alone, since to men it is invisible, that the visible church has to be distinguished.

The function of the latter is stated in the opening of Book IV of the *Institutes*. Man, being the creature that he is, both ignorant and slothful, has need of outward aids if faith is to be engendered and grow within him. Hence, obviously, the aim and purpose of *preaching*. And in order that the preaching of the gospel should continue and flourish Christ, he says, committed 'this treasure to the church'.

> He instituted pastors and teachers through whose lips he might teach his own; he furnished them with authority; as, finally, he omitted nothing that might make for the holy agreement of faith and good order. Above all he instituted the sacraments,

---

101. IV, i, 4; IV, i.1.
102. IV, i, 13.
103. IV, i, 7.

which we who have experienced them feel to be more than useful aids to foster and strengthen our faith.[104]

Thus the institutional church is necessary both to our vocation and to our sanctification. Faith is awakened by preaching and teaching, and is brought to fruition in holiness of living within the community of the faithful through the means of grace which Christ has provided. Like Luther Calvin sees the church as the milieu in which the word of God is proclaimed and heard in all its completeness and purity, and the sacraments are duly administered. To these he adds, with Bucer, the requirement of a vigilant discipline. Wherever these elements are present there, he holds, is the true church. It should be remarked, though, that as the essential and distinguishing *notae* or marks of the church Calvin – here departing from Bucer – lists only the first two.[105] For whatever faults a particular church may have – and he fully allows that, although 'gathered from all nations', the church on earth is 'divided and dispersed in separate places' – yet if, despite this, it retains these two constituent features, it must not be rejected. In that sense therefore discipline is not a note of the church, and in the *Institutes* Calvin nowhere presents it as such, even if in his reply to Cardinal Sadoleto he lays it down that 'there are three things on which the safety of the church is founded and supported: doctrine, discipline, and the sacraments'. And he actually adds a fourth, 'ceremonies by which to exercise people in the offices of piety'.[106]

Discipline for Calvin was of course a principle of major importance. The test of faith lay in a life of scrupulous moral obedience, and freedom in Christ could have nothing to do with antinomianism. If the church's preaching were not to be rendered vain and its ministration of the sacraments were to be effectual, the church must practise a constant self-examination. Naturally it could not exclude the non-elect *per se*, inasmuch as they are not certainly identifiable by men. But scandalous conduct had to be dealt with by the church itself, for since it is the body of Christ 'it cannot be corrupted by such foul and decaying members without some disgrace falling upon its Head'. From this sprang the duty to excommunicate as warranted by scripture and lawfully observed in the primitive church. Excommunication was designed at once to safeguard the honour of God, to preserve good church members from corruption through intercourse with evil, and to afford wrongdoers, of very shame at such public exposure, opportunity to repent.[107] But this positive sanction, the only one open to an ecclesiastical court – and it was not, emphatically to be extended to individual pastors – was a final resort, 'the church's last thunderbolt'. Yet it was necessary if the sacrament of the Lord's Supper, to which Calvin always attached the highest value, was to be kept from profanation.

That in actual use the discipline fell short of its ideal purpose is little wonder, and its record has not fared well at the hands of posterity. The Geneva consistory, which exercised it, pronounced judgements which the civil authorities were expected to implement, and thus it quickly became one with the penal measures applicable

104. IV, i, 1.
105. IV, i, 9.
106. See J. K. S. Reid, ed., *Calvin: Theological Treatises* (Philadelphia and London, 1954), 232.
107. IV, xii, 5.

to the community as a whole. All too frequently the cases brought before it were of a trivial and pettifogging kind (even laughing at Calvin in the pulpit was an indictable offence) and were the cause of widespread complaint. But, as we have seen, what occasioned the most sustained objection was the church's claim to an *exclusive* right to excommunicate, with all its civil consequences. On this point Calvin was adamant, and whatever the arguments at Bern or Zurich or Lausanne against it, at Geneva his tenacity paid off.

An integral part of Calvin's doctrine of the church was his theory of the ministry. Neither its function nor its form was, he considered, a matter of *ad hoc* arrangement but had been expressly determined by Christ. Lutheran teaching presented the ministerial office in the close context of the general priesthood of the faithful, but Calvin saw it rather as an order distinct from the congregation and 'the chief sinew by which believers are held together in one body': 'Through the ministers to whom he has entrusted this office and has confined the grace to carry it out, Christ dispenses and distributes his gifts to the church; and he shows himself as though present by manifesting the power of his Spirit in this his institution.'[108]

Consonant with this view he maintained that the power of the keys, not withstanding the fact of its abuse by the Roman hierarchy, is given to the ministry as such, whereas Luther had regarded it as the possession of the believing community as a whole, every member of which could as such act as an *alter Christus* to his neighbour. The church's ministers are at once Christ's instruments, his ambassadors to the world, interpreters of his sacred will and representatives of his person.[109] For laymen to perform ministerial functions Calvin deemed improper, even in the instance of emergency baptism.[110]

The forms of the ministry are explained at length in the 1543 edition of the *Institutes*, the influence of Bucer being everywhere evident, even to the letter.[111] Ephesians 4:4 is cited as the main scriptural authority, although Calvin points out that it is neither necessary nor feasible to adhere strictly to the example of the primitive church, in which certain types of ministration were appropriate only to the conditions then obtaining.[112] The permanent orders, as we saw in the previous chapter, were those of pastor, teacher, elder and deacon. In the New Testament the first of these was designated by a variety of terms: bishop, presbyter, pastor, minister.[113] The next, that of doctor or teacher, had responsibility for scriptural interpretation: 'to keep the doctrine whole and pure among believers'.[114] The elders (or presbyters) were concerned, in conjunction with the pastors, with moral discipline, often severe: in a city of some twenty thousand inhabitants, within the five years 1542–6, seventy-eight persons were exiled and fifty-eight sentenced to death. The deacons, lastly, served the church by ministering to the poor.

108. IV, iii, 2.
109. IV, iii, 1.
110. IV, xv, 20.
111. The first edition of the work to appear, that is, after the publication of the *Ordonnances ecclésiastiques*.
112. IV, iii, 5.
113. IV, iii, 8.
114. IV, iii, 4. In the *Ordonnances* provision was to be made for two theological lecturers, one each for the Old Testament and the New.

On the making of a minister Calvin is with Luther in stressing the prime necessity of the call.[115] But how and by whom should the pastor be appointed? On this Calvin felt that scripture offers no specific instruction. Ought he to be chosen by a single individual, by his fellow pastors and the elders, or by the church as a whole?[116] Calvin's own preference is for plural authority in this as in other matters, and in the *Institutes* he expresses the opinion that the actual rite of ordination should properly follow the apostolic practice of the laying-on of hands, it 'being useful for the dignity of the ministry to be commended to the people by this sort of sign', as well as being a warning to the ordinand that 'he is no longer a law unto himself' but is bound in servitude to God and the church.[117] In the *Ordonnances*, on the other hand, Calvin did not enjoin it, in view of the superstition associated with the Roman conception of the priesthood. It is however a mistake to suppose that Calvin insisted on the presbyterian system of church government as alone *de jure divino*. Dogmatic presbyterianism was a subsequent development, chiefly under Beza's influence. Calvin himself was by no means consistently opposed to episcopacy, so long as it did not degenerate into a secularized autocracy.

Like Luther Calvin relates the sacraments directly to the Word; they are 'an aid', he says, 'to faith similar to the preaching of the Gospel'. (He points out that faith can waver and fail unless supported by means that take account of human limitations.) Accordingly he defines a sacrament as 'an outward sign by which the Lord seals on our consciences the promises of his good will towards us in order to sustain the weakness of our faith; and we in turn attest our piety toward him in the presence of the Lord and of his angels and before men'. Or again, more briefly: 'A testimony of divine grace towards us, with mutual attestation of our piety towards him.'[118] The sacraments, nonetheless, are secondary to the word as deriving their significance from it alone, their function being to supplement it because of our human need of material assistance. A sacrament is thus, so to speak, a 'visible word', an image or token of that divine grace which the word itself presents more explicitly.[119] Yet the gospel in itself is independent of the sacraments and could dispense with them.

However, the parallelism between scripture and the sacraments must, Calvin stresses, never be lost sight of; indeed, a sacrament is constituted by both the Word and the external sign: 'Let Word be added to the elements and it will become a sacrament.'[120] Again, as the sacraments were expressly ordained by Christ they afford a means of union with him, a union involving both our souls and bodies and pointing forward to ultimate and complete union with him in heaven. Further, as the understanding of the Word is made possible only by the power of the Spirit so too is the right reception of the sacraments. 'If the Spirit be lacking the sacraments can accomplish nothing more in our minds than the splendour of the sun shining upon blind eyes, or a voice sounding in deaf ears.'[121]

115. IV, iii, 10.
116. IV, iii, 1.
117. IV, iii, 16.
118. IV, xiv, 1.
119. Cf. IV, xiv, 6.
120. IV, xiv, 3f.; IV, xvii, 4.
121. IV, xiv, 9.

Baptism Calvin understands as 'the sign of the initiation by which we are received into the society of the church, in order that, engrafted in Christ, we may be reckoned among God's children'.[122] It was given also both as a means of strengthening the believer's faith and of serving as a confession of that faith before men. But primarily it is the sign and seal of the remission of sins, and so is much more than a bare outward mark or badge of religious profession. On the other hand the water has no inherent spiritual power of its own, the whole point of the symbol being 'to fasten our minds on Christ alone'. In other words, while Calvin is certain of the objectivity of the sacrament he is at pains to avoid any suggestion of an *ex opere operato* efficacy, as Luther at times seemed to teach. He chooses his language with signal care. The baptismal rite exhibits, he says,

> the surest rule of the sacraments, that we should see spiritual things in physical, as if set before our eyes. For the Lord was pleased to represent them by such figures, not because such graces are bound and enclosed in the sacrament so as to be conferred upon us by its power, but only because the Lord, by this token, attests his will towards us.

He does not confront us with a mere appearance only, but 'leads us to the present reality and effectively performs what it symbolizes'.[123] Yet the necessity of baptism is conditional, not absolute, since salvation is ultimately determined by divine election: 'God adopts our babies before they are born.'[124] Against the anabaptists, however, Calvin was undeviatingly firm, defending infant baptism on biblical grounds by drawing a close parallel between the Christian rite and Jewish circumcision and by fastening on Christ's own example in receiving little children.[125]

Turning now to the doctrine of the Lord's Supper we observe a similar emphasis. What Calvin draws attention to is the promise of divine grace which the eucharistic action signifies and confirms. His teaching is compounded of elements to be found in the early church Fathers, particularly Augustine, as well as in Luther and Bucer, but the subtlety and skill with which he appropriates them amount to a degree of personal originality for which he can take full credit. What he sought to do, and as some would claim succeeded in doing, was to break the deadlock of the antagonistic Lutheran and Zwinglian views by restating the issue, by posing the question how it is that the body and blood of Christ become, in the Supper, ours, the faithful possessing the whole Christ crucified so that they enjoy all his benefits, rather than asking how, objectively, the bread and wine become the body and blood of Christ. This shift of viewpoint is indicated even in the 1536 edition of the *Institutes*, and subsequently, under Bucer's influence to no small extent, was further clarified.[126] As against Zwingli he conceived the Supper as much more than a mere

---

122. IV, xv, 1.
123. IV, xv, 14.
124. IV, xv, 20.
125. IV, xvi, 7.
126. In each new edition of the *Institutes* Calvin dealt with the theme of the Lord's Supper in increasing detail; but he also treated it more or less systematically in separate treatises, especially the brief *Confessio fidei de eucharistia* of 1537, the *Petit traité de la Sainte Scène* of 1541 and his defence of his views against the Lutheran polemist Joachim Westphal (1555–7), the *Petit traité* being particularly worthy of attention (see

commemoration of Christ's sacrifice; rather is it a true act of communion with the Lord himself made possible by the operation of the Holy Spirit. The words of institution are not to be taken literally, that is: Calvin, like Zwingli, denied the Lutheran doctrine of the ubiquity of Christ's glorified body – 'a monstrous notion', he called it[127] – but *sacramentally*. By this he meant, following biblical usage, the naming of the sign or symbol from the thing signified (or metonymy): for example, that 'circumcision is the covenant' (Genesis 17:13), or that 'the lamb is the Passover' (Exodus 12:11), or that 'the rock from which the water flowed in the desert was Christ' (I Corinthians 10:4). 'Those things [*he says*] ordained by God borrow the names of those things of which they always bear a definite and not misleading signification, and have the reality joined with them.'[128] The body of Christ is thus called bread, in that it is the symbol or sign by which 'the Lord offers the true eating of his body'.[129] But that body is not corporeally present, and there is no manducation in the receiving of it. Christ is 'with' the bread but not 'in' it, since it is 'not lawful to drag him down from heaven'.[130] Accordingly the Lutheran as well as the Roman doctrine has to be rejected. Calvin sums up his view in the simple and moving statement that Christ 'bids me take, eat and drink his body and blood under the symbols of bread and wine. I do not doubt that he himself truly presents them, and that I receive them'.[131] But of course reception always depended on faith.

On the central place of the eucharistic rite in the Christian life Calvin never wavered, and to the end of his life he strove, if unsuccessfully, for its weekly celebration.

What Calvin did for the Protestant Reformation within the span of a by no means extended career (he died in 1564 at the age of fifty-five) can hardly be overestimated. His achievement was quite extraordinary, even if its immediate

---

126. *continued Johanni Calvini opera selecta*, I, 503–30). Calvin uses the term 'substance' (*substantia*), but conceives it as 'power' rather than 'essence'. Hence his view of the nature of Christ's presence in the Supper can best be described as dynamic rather than static, the latter notion, as he thought, having been responsible for most of the difficulties which the various attempts to define the doctrine had encountered. As he saw it the 'power' of Christ's body and blood is made ours through the action of the Holy Spirit.

127. IV, xvii, 30. Calvin's dismissal of Luther's theory of ubiquity is perhaps to be explained by his own somewhat materialistic idea of the Lord's glorified and ascended body. Cf. *Institutes*, IV, xvii, 29f. Luther's more mystical belief he could not appreciate or even, possibly, understand. He quotes with approval Peter Lombard's principle (*Sentences*, III, xxii, 3) that 'although the whole Christ is everywhere, still the whole of that which is in him is not everywhere' (IV, xvii, 21).

128. IV, xvii, 21.

129. 'In this Sacrament we have such full witness of all things that we must certainly consider them as if Christ here present were himself set before our eyes and touched by our hands' (IV, xvii, 3).

130. IV, xvii, 31.

131. IV, xvii, 32. 'Calvin believed that the simpler the view taken of the sacrament, consistent with the significance attributed to it by Christ and his Apostles, the greater would be the potency, the more would it be a real means of grace; also, the more likelihood would there be of general agreement', A. M. Hunter, *The Teaching of Calvin* (London, 1950), 167.

setting was a community numbering no more than the population of what today would be considered only a small country town. The type of Christianity that soon came to be associated with his name outstripped that of Luther and his followers in energy alike of thought and of action, as too in its capacity not only to develop internally, if sometimes in ways that its author himself might not have favoured, but also in its power to attract adherents of diverse national and cultural traditions. As a theologian Calvin has had few peers, though less for any notable originality of view or insight than for his capacity to integrate, correlate and clarify; his talent, appropriate to a reformer of the second, consolidating generation was essentially architectonic.[132] So too, of course, was Aquinas's, but what distinguishes Calvin is that he was not simply a thinker, however perspicuous and resourceful, but a religious leader of such astonishing practical ability as to place him among the most influential of the world's men of action. His mind could leap with apparent ease from the highest reaches of theological abstraction to the smallest particulars of day-to-day administration, the reason being, no doubt, that he could always see, with a perceptiveness far sharper than is normal, the interconnection between governing principles and detailed policies. In his untiring self-application to the tasks he undertook he aroused the wonder, if not invariably the sympathy, of all who came in contact with him. In short, he was a dedicated doctrinaire. Thus he was never slipshod and never indifferent, and although the opposition or thoughtlessness or inertia of others forced him into compromises, he at no time lost sight of the goals he had set himself. From the outset of his work as a religious reformer his beliefs were clear-edged and consistently marshalled, and subsequent thought in no way caused him to change or seriously modify them, even when diplomacy required him to express himself with perhaps more than his customary reserve. The inherent rightness of his judgement on any matter he seems never to have questioned. That these signal qualities had their corresponding defects was to have been expected, and historical memory has since tended to dwell upon the latter to the cost of the former. When the system that traditionally has borne his name entered its decline, as with the emerging of the European mind from its long theological trauma it was bound to do, his fame, if not actually eclipsed, was also (to say the least) not much cherished.

Even before Calvin's death Geneva, adorned with its new university founded in the summer of 1559 with Beza as its rector, had become the intellectual centre of Protestantism, which, apart from the variegated fringe movements we shall have to consider in the next chapter, had firmly divided itself into two camps, the Lutheran or 'evangelical' and the Calvinist or 'reformed', alien to each other even when not in open antagonism. In Switzerland the single Helvetic church, set up after the *Consensus Tigurinus* (or 'Zurich Agreement') of 1549 had united the Zwinglian and Calvinist followings, acquired in 1566 a formal confession of its own, known as the *Second Helvetic Confession* to distinguish it from the *First*,

---

132. This judgement is only slightly qualified by Wendel's opinion (*op. cit.*, 358) that 'Calvin's is not a closed system elaborated around a central idea, but. . . . draws together one after another, a whole series of Biblical ideas, some of which can only with difficulty be logically reconciled'.

dating from 1536.[133] Comprising thirty-six articles, its teaching was closely akin to that of Calvin himself, if not at all points in full accord with it. Outside Germany and Scandinavia Calvin's doctrine now supplied the real inspiration and impetus of religious reform, not only Calvinist ideas but also the characteristically Calvinist type of piety and church polity soon making their appearance in France, the Rhineland, Holland, England and Scotland, while in eastern Europe they spread to Bohemia, Hungary and Poland. Confessions of faith, all of a Calvinist hue, proliferated, the most important being the *Scottish Confession of Faith* (1560), the German *Heidelberg Catechism* (1563), the *Canons* of the Synod of Dort (1619), the *Westminster Confession* (1647) and the *Helvetic Consensus Formula* (1675), although no single Calvinist formulary gained an authority comparable to that of the *Augsburg Confession* among Lutherans.

## Note on Calvin's trinitarian doctrine

On the evidence, as he judged it, of the original edition of the *Institutes*, Pierre Caroli, a former member of the Briçonnet circle at Meaux, accused Calvin of Arianism. The latter, ever prompt to attack others but immediately resentful of attacks on himself, indignantly affirmed his loyalty to the traditional doctrine of Christ's person, but declined to make a public subscription to the three ancient creeds, the Apostles', the Nicene and the Athanasian, as Caroli had demanded. Not unnaturally his refusal aroused suspicion of his orthodoxy, though in the upshot he was vindicated. Subsequent editions of the *Institutio* made it clear beyond question that Calvin embraced the trinitarian dogma without demur. Although he points out that in scripture Almighty God, 'to keep us sober, speaks sparingly of his essence', yet 'he so proclaims himself to be God as to offer himself to be contemplated clearly in three persons'. 'Unless we grasp these only the bare and empty name of God flits about our brains, to the exclusion of the true God' (I, xiii, 2). He admits that there are those who dislike the term 'person', and that any theory which divides God's simple essence goes far to justify these objections, but Christ's divinity must be safeguarded, even by the use of language which is not itself scriptural. It is incompatible with the unity of God that each of the three persons could have 'a portion of the divine essence', so that 'in all three that essence must be absolutely one and unbegotten'; that is, there is no 'sharing' of or participation in an essence which could be regarded as a sort of fourth entity in the Godhead. 'We do not separate the persons from the essence, but distinguish among them while they remain within it' (I, xiii, 25). Thus it is the one true God who was incarnate in Jesus Christ.

> The God who manifested himself in Isaiah was the true and only God, the God whom nevertheless John affirms to have been in Christ. He who also through the mouth of Isaiah testified that he would be a stone of stumbling for the Jews was the only God, whom Paul declared to have been in Christ (I, xiii, 23).

133. For Latin text see Schaft, *The Creeds of Christendom*, III, 233–306; an English trans. is included in Cochrane, ed., *Reformed Confessions*, 220–301.

But although Calvin, following the Western theological tradition,[134] upholds the unity of the divine essence so strongly he tries not to do so at the expense of the distinction of the persons. 'The words "Father", "Son" and "Spirit" imply a real distinction – let no one think that these titles, whereby God is variously designated from his works, are empty – but a distinction, not a division' (I, xiii, 17). For although the entire Godhead is present in each person, a diversity of 'functions' or attributes can be assigned to each individually. 'To the Father is attributed the beginning of activity, and the fountain and wellspring of all things; to the Son, wisdom, counsel, and the ordered disposition of all things; but to the Spirit is assigned the power and efficacy of that activity' (I, xiii, 18).

134. Calvin closely follows St Augustine, *De Trinitate*, but he also quotes Cyril of Alexandria's treatise of the same title.

# Chapter 9

# THE RADICAL REFORMATION

*'Be ye separate'*

Luther and Zwingli, Melanchthon and Calvin were the great leaders of Reformation thought in what may be called its classical forms, but the movements initiated or shaped by them were by no means the only expression of the contemporary urge to recall historic Christianity to what was conceived to be its properly evangelical state. Many others there were, for the most part relatively obscure as individuals, who went farther and sought not merely a reformation or cleansing of religion of its abuses but rather a restitution, or literal restoration, of its primitive condition as portrayed in the New Testament and by writers of early post-apostolic times. For these reform would necessarily have to be effected in a much more drastic and reductive way than anything envisaged by Luther or even Zwingli. The one pattern to be followed was that of the days when the church was composed not of Christian citizens going about their normal pursuits and willingly submitting to if not actually exercising civic authority, but of committed believers eschewing all power other than spiritual and prepared for the sake of their principles to endure suffering and persecution like their Christian forbears in the church's heroic age when the Spirit-filled community was a people apart and the way of faith, in all likelihood, that of martyrdom as well.

For these enthusiasts the test of discipleship was to be reviled and rejected, as their divine Master had himself been. Subtle doctrines and dogmas, an elaborate ecclesiastical organization, above all subservience to or alliance with the political order were for them no part of the genuine Christian vocation and life. Regarding the world's future they were frankly pessimistic, but its ultimate fate was, they recognized, not their concern. Assuredly no man of whom the world spoke well could be held to have maintained an unsullied witness. Lutherans and Zwinglians may have purged church teaching of many grievous errors, but the bodies they themselves were establishing were no less implicated in the interests and pursuits of a still far from regenerate society than was the old and corrupt system they strove to displace. The actual quality of Christian living had changed too little. What the 'radicals' preached and exemplified was a simple, dedicated faith express-ing itself in a strictly observed morality. To the purity of their living, indeed – apart, that is, from the extraordinary aberration at Münster in 1534 – even their most obdurate opponents readily testified.

This type of uncomplicated evangelical belief had its roots in some of the popular piety characteristic of the later Middle Ages, especially in Germany, where its adherents were usually if vaguely referred to as the 'Brethren'. In those days also simplicity of creed, love of one's neighbour, devotion to scripture and a dislike of all clericalism, were the readily perceptible marks of their common attitude; but whereas the earlier evangelicals had perforce to follow their way of life as unobtrusively as possible, those who made their appearance after the revolts of Luther in Saxony and Zwingli in Switzerland were bolder, more outspoken and demonstrative, with the unhappy consequence – inevitable, given the then existing climate of opinion – that they had soon to endure the harshest persecution, at the hands of Protestants as well as of Catholics. Nevertheless they can now be identified, in their collective aspect and irrespective of the sometimes bewildering variety in their views and expectations (in certain instances blatantly heretical) as unquestionably a major articulation of the religious movement of the sixteenth century. Together they constituted, with the Lutheran, Calvinist and, as we shall later observe, Anglican reforms, a fourth 'Reformation' the influence of which has continued and spread far beyond the lands of its origin down to our own time.[1]

Important as has been the modern revival of scholarly interest in the leaders of classical Protestantism, it does not surpass that of parallel study of the history of the radicals, or the anabaptists as they used as a whole, but not very accurately, to be called; for what has signalized research in this field is the great amount of newly discovered and edited source materials as well as the not at all easy task of general reassessment.

Even now, as one of the principal contributors to this work, the American scholar G. H. Williams, has stated, it would be premature to attempt a definitive account of the 'radical' Reformation. For our very limited purpose here, however, the emerging picture is clear enough to enable us to present certain summary impressions. At the very least one is not likely to question Professor Williams's judgement that 'for good or ill, the Radicals were to shape the contours of the world that was to come after them far more than they or their Catholic and Protestant opponents realized'.[2]

It is nowadays usual to classify the diverse and in certain instances widely disparate radical or 'left-wing' elements of the Reformation movement into three groups, the anabaptists proper, the spirituals, and the rationalists,[3] though an excessive rigidity of classification should not be attempted, since overlapping is frequent and at times it is difficult to say precisely to what type a given individual belongs. Thus if anabaptists like Balthasar Hubmaier or Menno Simons are fitly described as evangelical, it would nonetheless be misleading to deny the epithet to the rationalists, while the so-called spirituals are for their part so variegated in appearance that no sharp dividing line can be drawn between them and the other two groups. Again, it would be a mistake to represent Reformation radicalism as a self-consistent movement. The radicals were indeed fervent for reform, root and

---

1. G. H. Williams and A. M. Mergal, eds, *Spiritual and Anabaptist Writers* (Library of Christian Classics) (Philadelphia/London, 1957), 19. See also H. Fast, ed., 'Der Linke Flügel der Reformation: Glaubenzeugnisse der Täufer, Spiritualisten, Schwärmer und Antitrinitarien' (*Klassiker der Protestantismus*, IV, Bremen, 1962).
2. G. H. Williams, *The Radical Reformation* (Philadelphia/London, 1962), xix.
3. The term 'left-wing' is used by, among others, R. H. Bainton, as in his article 'The left wing of the Reformation', in *The Journal of Religion*, xxi (1941), 127; see also R. Friedmann in *Church History*, xxiv (1955). 132–51. The expression may pass, but because of its modern political connotation it is not really an appropriate one. Certainly the radicals' aim was not the reconstruction of contemporary society.

branch, but they definitely cannot be said to have organized reformist campaigns after the manner of the Lutherans, the Zwinglians and the Calvinists. At no time did they produce a great spiritual leader, nor did they have any common body of doctrine – the *Schleitheim Articles* alone come nearest to a formal epitome of their views – and of institutions of any sort they were deeply suspicious, even though they did create three distinctive communities which have survived down to the present day, namely the Mennonites, the Amish and the Hutterites.

Where beyond doubt they shared a like attitude was in their common determination to avoid involvement with governments and even to shun the ordinary paths of social intercourse. For them separation of their own conventicles from the national or territorial state was a fundamental principle and one which the revolutionary activities of a Thomas Müntzer or the apocalyptic fantasies of the New Jerusalem at Münster did nothing to qualify. As the fourth of the *Schleitheim Articles*, the *Brüderliche Vereinigung* or 'Brotherly Union', puts it: 'For truly all creatures are in but two classes, good and bad, believing and unbelieving, darkness and light, the world and those who are out of the world, God's temple and idols, Christ and Belial; and none can have part with the other.'[4] To traffic with the world was to compound with evil. Warfare was denounced utterly, and the radicals would themselves carry no weapons, believing in the force only of personal persuasion, missionary preaching, philanthropy and martyrdom. In modern eyes the intense sincerity of their idealism evokes admiration, but their rejection of the secular order, along with their total pacifism, looked to their contemporaries, Protestant and Catholic alike, to be a direct threat to the integrity of the state and civil society. Repression therefore was inevitable, and if suffering for conscience's sake be itself a sign of divine favour then their expectations of heavenly bliss were well founded. But let us consider the various types of radical reformism in order.

## The anabaptists

For the beginnings of evangelical anabaptism we may look to Zurich soon after the Reformation was introduced there in the early 1520s. As compared with those of Luther, Zwingli's ideas were themselves distinctly radical and thus likely to make an immediate appeal to men who by disposition were potentially still more revolutionary. So at the second public disputation at Zurich in October 1523 Balthasar Hubmaier (*c.* 1485–1528), parish priest at Wildshut and formerly a student of Eck's at Ingolstadt, who had become a follower of Zwingli, expressed strong sacramentarian views, denouncing the sacrifice of the mass and describing the Supper as simply 'a publishing of Christ's testament, in which is celebrated the memorial of his death'.[5] Closely associated with him were Konrad Grebel, a young man of patrician family, Ludwig Hätzer and Felix Manz, all of them sacramentarians and fervent iconoclasts. Hätzer had already published a book entitled *The Judgement of God*

4. See J. C. Wenger, 'The Schleitheim confession of faith', in *The Mennonite Quarterly Review*, xix (1945), 249, as quoted by Williams, *op. cit.*, 183.
5. H. C. Vedder, *Balthasar Hubmaier: the leader of the Anabaptists* (New York and London, 1905), 63f.

*our Spouse as to how one should hold oneself toward all Idols and Images*, in which he plainly drew on the sentiments of Luther's turbulent colleague at Wittenberg, Karlstadt, although on the other hand both Grebel and Manz were of a scholarly bent, having received humanist training and possessing a knowledge of Hebrew as well as the classical languages. All four men, however, left the three-day disputation far from satisfied with the opinions of one who up till then they had regarded as their leader. 'Zwingli, the herald of the Word', wrote Grebel, 'has cast down the Word, has trodden it underfoot, and has brought it into captivity.'[6] He and Mantz tried indeed to persuade Zwingli to adopt their views and to set up a new church 'according to evangelical truth and the Word of God', that is, on the supposedly New Testament pattern, in which tithes would be renounced, the ministers instead relying on the freewill offerings of the faithful, and in which all things would be held in common, as in the primitive church at Jerusalem. But their plea fell on deaf ears; Zwingli's concept of a 'civic' Christianity had little in common with his erstwhile friends' belief in a 'gathered' church and their absolute rejection of the magistrate's role in the ordering of the Christian life. For them therefore the way forward was now to be through a 'second reformation' brought about by persons whose commitment would be wholehearted and uncompromising. Henceforward they looked for inspiration not to Zwingli but to men like Karlstadt and Thomas Müntzer, spirits more akin to their own.

At this time, although they saw the Lord's Supper as no more than a commemoration, adult baptism evidently had not become a principle with them. Further, complete non-violence and a readiness to submit to persecution were a constituent element in what they regarded as the true imitation of Christ. Thus was it that the so-called Swiss Brethren came into being as a sect deliberately dissociating itself not only from Roman Christendom but from any sort of church reformed in cooperation with the magistracy. It looked on itself as a fellowship of believers apart from the world, the breach therewith now being marked, very significantly, by a repudiation of its members' original baptism in infancy and acceptance in its stead of a new rite that implied the virtual nullity of their former Christian profession. Its inauguration may be exactly dated, namely 21 January 1525, when a small group of dissenters met at the home of Felix Manz to consider their next step. Among those present, besides Manz himself, were Grebel and Georg Blaurock ('Blue Coat') (*c.* 1492–1529), a married ex-priest who had arrived in Zurich from Church the previous year. After prayer together Blaurock called on Grebel to baptize him, which the latter, a layman, at once did. 'Each confirmed the other in the service of the Gospel, and they began to teach and keep the faith. Therewith began the separation from the world and its evil works.'[7] Blaurock himself then baptized a number of other persons.[8]

This baptism, the first adult baptism on record from Reformation times, was by

6. In a letter of 18 December 1523 to Vadianus. See E. Arbenz, *Die Vadianische Briefsammlung der Stadtbibliothek St Gallen* (7 vols, St Gallen, 1890–1913), III, 50.
7. See A. Zieglschmid, *Die älteste Chronik der Hutterischen Brüder* (Philadelphia, 1943). The words quoted are cited by Williams, 122f.
8. See H. S. Bender, *Conrad Grebel, c. 1498–1526: the Founder of the Swiss Brethren sometimes called Anabaptists* (Goschen, Ind., 1950).

aspersion, not total immersion. A day or so later Grebel was present at a similar gathering at the house of one Jakob Hottinger at Zollikon, a few miles from Zurich. A simple form of service was then held, consisting of a reading from the New Testament, with a preachment on the Lord's Supper and a baptism, followed by the distribution of the bread and wine, again by laymen, to the assembled company. This kind of observance was repeated again and again, the act of communion betokening not only fellowship but community of goods as well. Such 'believer's baptism' was seen by them as the only entry to the new life, although no sacramental meaning was attached to it and emphasis was less on the positive attestation of faith, or even on the capacity to believe, than on repentance and a transcending of the past, prompted by an anguished consciousness of sin and of the need for forgiveness.[9] Religion as living experience became the focus of attention.

The baptist movement spread, to the alarm of the city authorities. Within a few weeks numbers of people were baptized in neighbouring villages and townships and an anabaptist congregation was established at Zollikon. On 18 January 1525 the order was given that all unbaptized children must be brought to baptism within the ensuing eight days, expulsion from Zurich being the penalty for failing to do so. On 1 February the order was repeated. Some who did not comply were arrested, and Mantz, Blaurock and a few others were taken into custody. Zwingli tried to reason with them, but without avail. Subsequent discussions, on 16 March and again on 20 March, ranged over several matters keenly at issue – the possibility of a 'pure' church, the use of the ban for wayward members, community of goods, tithes, civil government, the working of the Spirit – but no progress was made. The authorities felt therefore that they had no alternative but to take stern action against the dissidents. Not only were Grebel, Mantz and Blaurock imprisoned but Hubmaier was subjected to torture before being banished. In March 1526 it was enacted that anabaptists (or 'catabaptists') were to be executed by drowning, and in January of the following year this sentence was carried out on the luckless Felix Mantz, as it also would have been upon Grebel but for his death from the plague. Blaurock, not being a citizen of Zurich, was first flogged through the streets and then expelled. In July 1527 Zwingli attacked the Brethren's teaching in a 'Refutation of the Teachings of the Catabaptists' (*Elenchus in Catabaptistarum strophas*), mainly as these had been set out in Grebel's book and the *Schleitheim Articles*.[10]

This last, the 'Brotherly Union' previously mentioned, had been composed at Schleitheim in the canton of Schaffhausen in February 1527 at a synod of the Swiss Brethren under the leadership of Michael Sattler.[11] Addressed to 'the children of light . . . scattered everywhere', it was aimed principally at 'false brethren' guilty, in their newfound freedom in the Spirit, of antinomian excesses.[12] 'They think faith

---

9. F. Blanke, *Brüder in Christo; die Geschichte der ältesten Täufergemeinde* (Zurich, 1955), 35ff.
10. Zwingli had just completed his *Täuferbüchlein*, or *Little Book on Baptism*, see Bender, *op. cit.*, 294ff.
11. On this see B. Jenny, 'Das Schleitheimer Täuferbekenntnis, 1527', in *Schaffhauser Beiträge zur vaterländischen Geschichte*, xxviii (1951), 5–81.
12. Wenger, *op. cit.*, 247ff.

and love may do and permit everything and that nothing will harm them or condemn them, since they are believers.' But the seven articles, although in no sense a confession of faith, cover the typical anabaptist positions: the right of the brethren to choose their own pastors and to exclude sinners, after due warning, from their 'purified' churches (i.e. the pre-communion ban), the refusal of oaths and of civil and military service, and the principle of non-violence. On the question of the ban it was stated that: 'Whoever has not been called by the one God to one faith, to one baptism and to one Spirit, to one body, with all the children of God's church, cannot be made one bread with them, as indeed must be done if a man is truly to break bread according to the command of Christ.' In congregational worship Bible-reading and instruction were assigned the most prominent place, and although the pastor, discharging a settled ministry, might lead in prayer, other members of the gathering inspired to do so could follow suit. It was also recognized that the congregation had the right to discipline their minister. The refusal of the civic oath was of course taken by their opponents as clear proof of their subversive social attitudes.[13]

Zwingli had denounced anabaptist views on previous occasions, twice in 1525 and again in 1526,[14] but the *Elenchus*, written in Latin, was his hardest blow.[15] In it he assailed the dissidents for what he saw as their pig-headedness, their malice and their hypocrisy. Arguments from scripture simply did not move them, inasmuch as they openly disparaged the Old Testament, while their pretension to a special sanctity was no more than spiritual pride. They were, he contended, a sect outside the church, novelty-seeking and superstitious, attaching more importance to works than to faith, and by their teaching and practice alike dishonouring the sacrament of baptism. Further, they were Pelagian in their doctrine of the will, laying too much stress on the earthly example of Christ and too little on his resurrection and ascension to the right hand of God. He also ridiculed them as killjoys, while darkly hinting at sexual irregularity at their surreptitious gatherings in woods and forests. Most dangerous of all, however, was their attitude to duly constituted government authority, a disposition the only result of which would be to destroy the sacred ties of the Christian commonwealth.

But if anabaptists were eradicated from Switzerland their numbers multiplied elsewhere, chiefly though not exclusively among the peasantry and the poorer class of townsfolk in the Netherlands and north Germany, Austria and even as far afield as Poland and Lithuania. Thus a sizable anabaptist congregation established itself in Moravia under the protection of the Count of Lichtenstein and having a connecting link with the Swiss Brethren in the person of Balthasar Hubmaier, who became their leader at Nikolsburg, whither he had gone after leaving Zurich. Here he wrote several doctrinal works, in particular on baptism and on the freedom of

13. The full title of the *Schleitheim Articles* was 'The Brotherly Union of a Number of Children of God concerning Seven Articles'. The German text is given by B. Jenny (see note 11 above). A good English translation is that of J. C. Wenger; see also Williams, 182–5.
14. *Von der Taufe, von der Wiedertaufe und von der Kindertaufe (Sämmtliche Werke*, IV, 188–337), and his answer to Hubmaier's *Taufbüchlein (ibid.*, 577–642).
15. *S.W.*, VI, I, 1–196.

the will, in which he developed an anabaptist theology differing sharply in certain respects from the ideas of other evangelical anabaptists.[16] His concept of man was trichotomous, that is, distinguishing between spirit, soul and body, in a way more Platonist than biblical, although for biblical authority he cites I Thessalonians, 5:25. After the fall, he maintained, the spirit preserved its original integrity, a notion he supported by appeal to St Paul's words in I Corinthians, 2:15: 'But he that is spiritual judgeth all things, yet he himself is judged of no man', an idea which brings him closely into line with the spirituals. Each component of man's tripartite being has, he held, its own will, but if the spirit-will is still intact, that of the soul, symbolized by Adam, succumbed to the temptations of the flesh, represented by Eve, so losing its capacity to identify good from evil. The body-will Hubmaier sees as given over to universal corruption, 'good for nothing', and enmeshing the uncomprehending soul in its own sensual impulses. Salvation is achieved by the restoration to the soul of its power to know good from evil and to fight on the side of good, its understanding of which is furnished by the gospel of Christ, though through the gospel man attains to a state of grace higher than that of his prelapsarian condition, thus qualifying him for membership of the community of the truly regenerate.

> So now, the soul, after restoration, is whole, through the sent Word, and is truly made free. Now it can choose and do good, as much as is required of it, since it can command the flesh, tame it, dominate it, to such an extent that it must make it go against its own nature even into the fire [*of martyrdom*] with the spirit and the soul, for the sake of the name of Christ.[17]

In his doctrine of God Hubmaier distinguishes between the divine will or power as absolute (*potestas absoluta*), and the same as revealed (*potestas ordinata*), the former inscrutable, but the latter forming the basis for a scheme of salvation in which the role of Christ is of course central. But in it man's will retains its essential freedom.

> Now as soon as God turns to us, calls us and warns us to follow him, and we abandon wife and child, ship and cargo, everything that hinders our journey toward him – our help has already come to us, namely, his attracting, drawing will. By it, he wills and draws all men unto salvation. Yet choice is still left to man, since God wants him without pressure, unconstrained, under no compulsion. Such as do not receive him, hear him, or follow him, God turns and averts himself from them, and lets them be as they wish to be. . . . Even as God is holy with the holy, so is he withdrawn from those who withdraw. The first will may be called in Scripture *voluntas conversiva*, from *convertendo*; the second, *voluntas aversiva*, from *avertendo*. Not that there are two wills in God, as said above. There is only one will in God, but we have to speak of God humanly and with human words, as if, for example, he had eyes, ears, a face and a back.[18]

16. Hubmaier's *Schriften* were edited by G. Westin and T. Pergsten (*Quellen und Forschungen zur Reformationsgeschichte*, XXIX, 1962). There is a 'Life' by Bergsten (*Acta Universitatis Upsaliensia*, III, Casel, 1961); see too J. H. Yoder, 'Balthasar Hubmaier and the beginnings of Swiss anabaptism', in *The Mennonite Quarterly Review*, XXXIII (1959), 5–17.
17. *Von der Freyheit des Willens* (1527), Part ii, section 3; see Williams and Mergal, *op. cit.*, 126.
18. *Ibid.*, 135.

Baptism, Hubmaier insists, can be believer's baptism only. Acceptance of it ensures forgiveness and affords admission to the church, to whose discipline the baptized then submits himself. Breach of the discipline will incur the ban, for

> whomever the church binds and casts out of her assembly on earth he is bound before God in heaven and excluded from the Catholic church on earth (out of which there is no salvation), since Christ himself, while he was yet on earth, hung both keys at her side, giving them to her alone, his spouse and beloved bride.[19]

As for the Lord's Supper, Hubmaier maintains that its significance lies simply in the mutual pledge of believer to believer: 'In baptism one pledges oneself to God, in the Supper to his neighbour, to offer body and blood in his stead, as Christ for us.'[20] He thus went far beyond Zwingli in voiding the sacrament of all idea of a distinctive presence of Christ therein.

A scholarly man and a serious thinker, Hubmaier unfortunately did not enjoy his immunity at Nikolsburg for long. Arrested there by the agents of the imperial government, he and his wife were taken to Vienna, where he was burnt at the stake on 10 March 1528, she, loyal to him to the end, being drowned in the Danube a few days later. With Hubmaier's removal the Nikolsburg congregation dispersed.

A marked characteristic of evangelical anabaptism was its community spirit. Those, for example, who settled near Austerlitz, some miles to the north of Nikolsburg, developed a strong communitarianism under the able leadership of Jakob Hutter (d. 1536), who brought with him a fair number of his Tyrolese adherents. Indeed in the space of only a few years he established over eighty anabaptist settlements in Moravia, although at times he had great difficulty in reconciling the many quarrelling factions among them. Under his direction, however – and from August 1533 until the late spring of 1535 he was to all intents their 'bishop' – they turned themselves into disciplined and hard-working communities.[21]

Hutter's followers wished for separation from the world, but they were not ascetics. Adopting a strict morality, along with spiritual *Gelassenheit* or 'yielding to God', they nevertheless saw work as a virtue and in time became expert agriculturists and stock-raisers, while their skill in manufacture brought them European fame. Hymn-singing played a large part in their simple worship, but doctrinal matters had little interest for them and their few publications have not in the main survived, although a sufficient idea of what specially concerned them may be gained from Ulrich Stadler's *Cherished Instructions on Sin, Excommunication, and the Community of Goods*.[22] In this the author writes movingly of the 'communion [*Gmain*] of the faithful in Christ and of the one community [*Gmainschaft*] of the holy churches called of God'. United in heart and mind, he says, they

19. Vedder, *op. cit.*, 135.
20. *Ibid.*, 108.
21. On Hutter see *Jakob Hutter: Leben, Frömmigkeit, Briefe (Mennonite Historical Series, no. 4, Newton, Kansas, 1956)*.
22. An English translation of part of it is given in Williams and Mergal, 274–84.

must move about in this world, poor, miserable, small, and rejected of the world, of whom, however, the world is not worth. . . . In this community everything must proceed equally, all things must be one and communal. . . . *One, common* builds the Lord's house and is pure; but *mine, thine, his, own* divides the Lord's house and is impure. . . . Where there is ownership and one has it . . . he is outside of Christ and his communion and thus has no Father in heaven.

In brief, a brother should serve, live, and work for the other, none for himself; indeed, one house for another, one community [*Versammlung*] for another in some other settlement in the land.[23]

Hutter himself died at the stake at Innsbruck in February 1536 by order of Ferdinand of Austria, but his work was continued by Johann Amon (d. 1542), a Bavarian cloth-weaver, and later and more effectually by the Silesian Peter Riedemann (1506–56), the community's leading thinker, whose 'Account of our Beliefs' (*Rechenschaft unserer Glaubens*) of 1540 is probably the fullest statement of the Hutterite tenets that has come down to us.[24] Written for the information of Philip of Hesse, who at the time held the author in custody, it falls into two parts, the first and longer, based on the Apostles' Creed, dealing with the twelve essential articles of faith, and the second taking the form of meditations on special themes. Little attention is given to original sin, and justification by faith is passed over in silence, emphasis falling rather on the regenerative work of the Holy Spirit. The church also is seen as having an active role, namely to leaven the world, 'to be a lantern of righteousness, in which the light of grace is borne and held before the whole world . . . that they may also see and know the way of life'.[25] Unselfishness, brotherly love and service, and community of goods are again repeatedly stressed. 'All those who have fellowship [*with Christ*] likewise have nothing for themselves, but have all things with their Master and with all those who have fellowship with them, that they may be one in the Son as the Son is in the Father.'[26]

But by no means all the anabaptists were quiet, peaceable and industrious, seeking in their religious life only recovery of the simple idealism of New Testament times. From the early 1520s an apocalyptic and revolutionary strain manifested itself which was to culminate, a decade or so later, in the Münster catastrophe. During Luther's stay at the Wartburg from 1520 to 1521 conditions at Wittenberg, lacking his control, became chaotic, and with the arrival there of the Zwickau 'prophets', Niklaus Storch and Thomas Stübner, a fanatical revivalism set in, a feature of which, already, was the denunciation of infant baptism. 'He who *believes*', they proclaimed, quoting Mark 16:16, 'and is baptized will be saved.' Powerfully influenced by these *Schwärmer*, as Luther contemptuously dubbed them, was a certain Thomas Müntzer, himself at first one of Luther's followers.[27] Born at

23. Williams and Mergal, 277f., 284.
24. *Account of our Religion, Doctrine and Faith given by Peter Riedemann of the Brothers whom Men call Hutterians* (English trans. by K. Hasenberg, London, 1950).
25. *Op. cit.*, 39.
26. *Ibid.*, 43.
27. See P. Wappler, *Thomas Müntzer in Zwickau und die Propheten Zwickau* (Leipzig, 1908). On Müntzer's ideas and activities see O. H. Brandt, *Thomas Müntzer: sein Leben und seine Schriften* (Jena, 1933), H. J. Goertz, *Innere und aussere Ordnung in der Theologie Thomas Müntzers* (Leiden, 1967) and E. G. Rupp, *Patterns of Reformation* (London, 1969), 157–353.

Stolberg in the Harz Mountains in 1488 or 1489, he had been a priest and was a well-educated man, having studied at Leipzig, Frankfurt and Mainz. He had also deeply imbibed the ideas of Joachim of Fiore and the mystical Tauler. The Lutheran spell, however, did not hold him for long – Luther himself he dismissed as a mere *Schriftsgelehrter*, a 'scribbler' – and the spiritualism to which his mind was prone displayed itself in ways increasingly fervid and even violent. From Germany he went on to Prague, where he tried, in vain as it happened, to incite the Hussite Brethren to an uprising. Returning to Saxony, he settled for a time at Alstedt, where he laced his preaching of radical religious change with heady rant about a social revolution that would eventuate in the setting up of the New Jerusalem and the dispossession of the ungodly by force. In 1524 he became involved in the Peasants' Revolt, and when this collapsed at Frankenhausen in May of the following year he was captured, tortured and executed.

Müntzer's beliefs were compounded of diverse elements. On the one hand he embraced a kind of natural theology, drawing on the *Theologia Naturalis* of the early fifteenth-century Spanish Franciscan Raimund de Sebunde. Simple people, he judged, could learn the essentials of the gospel of Christ from the book of nature itself, man's relation to the animals presenting a clear analogy with that of God to men. On the other hand, as is to be seen from the manifesto he issued while in Prague, he speaks of the bestowal of the sevenfold gift of the Spirit as the final aim of redemption. With this Spirit endowment instruction would be conveyed by way of visions, dreams and ecstatic utterances, although the elect alone could expect to receive revelations of this sort, and even then they would have to undergo the harrowing of fear if they were to attain to true godliness. Christ's own suffering on the cross was to be taken as the image and type of that which the elect themselves must gladly endure, for affliction is the bitter draught that has to be drunk if perfection is to be reached.

Thomas Müntzer was a hot-headed fanatic and is only marginally to be classed among the anabaptists. More characteristic of at any rate one side of the movement was Melchior Hofmann (c. 1495–c. 1543). A native of Swabia, and by trade a leather-dresser and furrier, he was attracted first by Zwingli and then by Luther, under whose influence he became an itinerant preacher, visiting Livonia in 1523 and Stockholm three years later. In 1529 he engaged in a disputation with Luther's friend Johann Bugenhagen, in which he attacked Lutheran doctrine at certain points and spoke slightingly of Luther himself as no more than the precursor of true reform. Expelled from Denmark he went to Strassburg, where he joined the anabaptists, who were numerically strong there, and submitted to rebaptism. Between 1530 and 1533 he carried out a successful evangelistic tour of Holland and East Friesland, returning in the latter year to Strassburg, which he now hailed as the scene of the coming New Jerusalem. Unhappily for him and his fellow-sacramentarians, when the city authorities accepted the *Confession of Augsburg* the religious climate quickly changed. Melchior Hofmann was arrested and spent the last ten years of his life in prison there.

Hofmann was a zealot whose wild ideas were fostered by his own lack of formal education and open contempt for learning.[28] Among the more curious of his notions

28.   See F. O. zur Linden, *Melchior Hofmann: ein Prophet der Wiedertaufe* (Haarlem, 1885).

was the belief that Christ's flesh was not taken from Mary, but that as the divine Logos he transformed himself into flesh for man's salvation.[29] Nevertheless his truculent millenarianism gained him many followers, and there can be little doubt that it was largely his preaching which moved the Netherlanders who in 1533 and 1534 migrated *en masse* to the episcopal city of Münster in Westphalia on hearing the news that the brethren there were proving themselves strong enough not only to defy the Catholic bishop but even to counter the Lutheran element. The leadership of these strange enthusiasts was assumed by the young Haarlem baker, Jan Matthijs, who rapidly drew to his cause converts from towns all over Holland, declaring himself to be the true Enoch to the exclusion of all other aspirants for the role. He appointed twelve apostles, among them the Leyden tailor Jan Beuckels, soon himself to play a bizarre but fateful part in Münster's destiny. Within the city itself, moreover, the tide of anabaptist conviction was flowing fast under the ex-Lutheran Bernhard Rothmann and his dedicated follower, the rich cloth merchant Bernhard Knipperdolling. Events moved swiftly and by January 1534 the radicals, with mob support, gained control of the city. Matthijs, though admittedly only when Münster came under siege from both Catholic and Lutheran forces, insisted on universal baptism and ruled the common possession of all property.

When Matthijs was killed in a sortie outside the city walls his place as leader was assumed by Beuckels, John of Leyden, as he had come to be called, a young man of some eloquence and much force of personality who was fast turning into a ruthless egomaniac out of touch with reality. He proclaimed himself king with all the trappings of royalty – splendid robes, a court, armed guards and so forth. Matthijs's rule had been violent enough, but Beuckels was the prey both to his own vagrant fantasies and a strongly sensual nature. He set up twelve 'Elders' or 'Judges of Israel' for the control of every aspect of life, private as well as public, and a long catalogue of sins was published that were declared punishable by death. Further, the great numerical preponderance of women over men at Münster, their numbers having been swollen by an influx of refugees as well as enthusiasts, was the ready excuse for the introduction of polygamy: Beuckels himself took several wives.

Meantime the city's siege was maintained unremittingly, and attempts by other anabaptist groups to relieve it were easily foiled. In June 1535 it fell at last, but even then only as the result of treachery from within. Thus the shortlived apocalyptic kingdom was brought to an appropriately tumultuous end. Rothmann died in the fighting, but Knipperdolling was tortured to death and the corpses of both were placed in cages and hung from the tower of St Lambert's church, where they remained indeed until 1881. After this brutal reprisal the old religion was restored and vigorous action against anabaptists everywhere in Europe became the order of the day.

But although these luckless evangelicals were harried unmercifully they were by no means exterminated. In particular the Netherlanders, in spite of their disastrous participation in the New Jerusalem experiment, proved themselves, under the able leadership of Menno Simons (1496–1561), a former priest of Witmarsum in Dutch

29. C. H. Schoeps, *Vom himmlischen Fleisch Christi* (Tübingen, 1951) and zur Linden, *op. cit.*, 39.

Friesland who had undergone believer's baptism in 1536, capable of rallying the more moderate elements, banding themselves together into a coherent sect which came in time to acquire the name of Mennonite. Simons, described as 'a man of integrity, mild, accommodating, patient of injuries, and so ardent in his piety as to exemplify in his own life the precepts he gave to others',[30] had already adopted sacramentarian views while still discharging his Catholic ministry. 'It occurred to me [*he afterwards wrote*] as often as I handled the bread and wine in the Mass that they were not the flesh and blood of the Lord.'[31] But what really shook his earlier convictions was his reflection on the question of baptism. He noted St Cyprian's approval of adult baptism, but other statements also of the Fathers sowed doubt in his mind. 'They taught me that children are by baptism cleansed from original sin. I compared this idea with the Scriptures and found that it did violence to the blood of Christ.'[32] For Christ's death on Calvary, he was now convinced, had freed the whole world from sin, whether or not this truth was actually recognized, and because of it baptism is to be seen as a liberation of the individual believer from his personal sins. Hence 'faith does not follow from baptism but baptism follows from faith'.[33] Menno Simons stood, though, with Luther in holding that faith is not a 'work' of man but a gift of God and that man's righteousness is not his own but solely the imputation to him of the righteousness of Christ.[34] 'All our righteousness is as filthy rags.'[35] Of himself man is only a miserable sinner; it is through Christ alone that he is 'justified and pleasing unto God and adopted by him in eternal grace', though faith, if genuine, necessarily works through love.[36]

Although Menno Simons spent years as an itinerant evangelist and pastor, visiting the scattered brethren, catechizing, baptizing and doing whatever he could in extremely difficult circumstances to build up the churches, he yet found time for a considerable amount of writing, the best-known of his tracts including *The Spiritual Resurrection* (*c.* 1536), *The New Birth* (*c.* 1537), *Christian Baptism* (1539) and *The Foundation of Christian Doctrine* (1540). Of these the last-named, composed originally in Dutch and commonly called *The Foundation Book*, is the most interesting, providing as it does a conspectus of its author's religious opinions and something in the nature of a confession of Mennonite tenets for his spiritual descendants. But it may be noted that his doctrine of the incarnation, though he claimed to uphold the Nicene faith,[37] was certainly not orthodox by Chalcedonian standards. Like Melchior Hofmann's, it was a form of mono-physitism, since the dogma of the two natures seemed to him to divide the one Christ, whereas we ought to 'confess him entirely to be the true Son of the true

30. T. M. Lindsay, *A History of the Reformation* (Edinburgh, 1907), II, 469.
31. J. C. Wenger, ed., *Menno Simons: the Complete Writings*, English trans. by L. Verduin (Scottdale, Pa., 1956), 668.
32. *Ibid.*, 669.
33. *Ibid.*, 120.
34. *Ibid.*, 116, 342, 1053.
35. *Ibid.*, 95.
36. *Ibid.*, 116.
37. For Menno's trinitarianism see his tract, 'A Solemn Confession of the Triune, Eternal and True God, Father, Son and Holy Ghost' (1550), in *Works*, 488ff.

and living God'.[38] Accordingly his flesh must itself be thought of as heavenly, for had he been really born of Mary 'he would have sprung from the sinful flesh of Adam', so that man's salvation would then have come through his own sin-tainted flesh, an idea totally unacceptable.[39] Christ therefore must have been born not 'of' Mary but rather 'by' or 'through' her.[40] This notion was indeed integral to Simon's views as to both rebirth and the church as a 'pure' community: 'For all who are in Christ are new creatures, flesh of his heavenly flesh, bone of his bone, and members of his body' – understood, that is, in an exclusively spiritual sense.[41] Menno even seems to say that, as Christ was the eternal Logos made flesh, he was generated by the Holy Spirit, although nourished by Mary,[42] an idea deriving from the belief, still current in the sixteenth century, that it is the male parent who originates the child, the female being no more than the soil, 'the prepared field', in which the seed is planted. This unsullied purity of the Lord's human nature was demanded, in fact, by Menno's insistence that the church, as the body of which Christ is the head, must itself be without spot or blemish.

Menno's view of the Christian life was thus radically different from Luther's. Luther too, no doubt, saw the church as a *communio sanctorum*, in a spiritual sense, but for Menno it had to be a 'communion of saints' quite visibly, its holiness being not only a principle or *nota* but an empirical reality, something actually attained here and now. A man's regeneration, in other words, was to be assessed in terms of his day-to-day moral conduct. The church would then be understood as 'an assembly of the pious' in a positive and manifest way.[43] It is not and must never be allowed to become a 'mixed' society, with tares in it as well as wheat, for in that case it would have become the church not of Christ but of anti-Christ.[44] In this respect the 'territorial' churches of Luther and Zwingli were no better than that of the pope.

Menno was no 'illuminist' and took his stand firmly on the Bible, maintaining that 'the Word of the Lord is the only doctrine by which our souls can live for ever'.[45] He also scouted the millenarian illusions which had brought such disaster on the disciples of Melchior Hofmann, and any personal visions of his own he utterly eschewed. Scripture was the sufficient source of truth without supplementation by further revelations supposedly given to Spirit-filled individuals. A favourite text of his was I Corinthians 3:11, 'For other foundation can no man lay than that is laid, which is Jesus Christ.' Like Luther he understands scripture as everywhere preaching Christ, in whose gospel both Testaments have their unity. But because of his strong Christocentrism he cannot concede an actual equality of the two; the New Testament must for Christians always be the primary witness;

39. *Ibid.*, 800. 'For Christ Jesus, as to his origin, is no earthly man, that is, a fruit of the flesh and blood of Adam. He is a heavenly spirit in man. For his beginning or origin is of the Father like unto the first Adam, sin excepted. (*Works*, 437).
39. *Ibid.*, 797.
40. *Ibid.*, 768.
41. *Ibid.*, 402.
42. *Ibid.*, 436.
43. *Ibid.*, 734.
44. *Ibid.*, 743.
45. *Ibid.*, 165.

plainly so in, for example, the instance of the *lex talionis*, where the Old Testament law is superseded. Yet Menno agrees with Calvin in identifying scripture effectively with the word of revelation and his exegesis tends to be both literalist and legalist. Thus his objection to infant baptism, although reinforced by the argument that the presence of original sin in infants would seem to entail their damnation, is mainly founded on the absence of any explicit reference in the New Testament. Curiously, however, he does not put the lack of saving faith in infants at the head of his case, although he denies that it is legitimately administered to those who are not instructed in the faith because of their natural inability to receive it; indeed, to confer it upon those who at birth have less sense than 'irrational creatures' is as idolatrous as it is futile.[46] Yet he also contends that infants stand in no need of ceremonies in order to be saved, since if they die before reaching years of discretion they die under the promises of God.[47]

Menno Simons's teaching on the Lord's Supper was, as one would expect, baldly sacramentarian; any doctrine of a real presence he derides as 'contrary to nature, reason, and Scripture; an open blasphemy of the Son of God; an abomination and idolatry'.[48] The Holy Spirit, he holds, needs no mediation, his operation on the believer's soul being direct, bringing to it the unique benefits of Christ's atoning death. Yet although he sees the rite as no more than a memorial of the Lord's self-sacrificing love he esteems it highly and speaks of it as 'Christian marriage', commanded and ordained of the Lord himself.

It was through the work and example of Menno Simons that what was best in the anabaptist religious tradition was perpetuated into the seventeenth century, ultimately to become influential much beyond the limits of the sect that bore his name. From East Friesland its adherents spread throughout the Low Countries and north Germany, where it absorbed what remained of the other anabaptist conventicles. Separation from the world continued a basic principle, along with a puritan mode of life that included extreme simplicity in dress, food and household furnishings. The ban, moreover, continued to be a distinctive feature of the sect's practice, although the Dutch Mennonites produced a more liberal wing known as Waterlanders, who preferred to adopt a less exclusive attitude towards the society in which they lived, modifying the old rigidity and encouraging a generally more tolerant outlook, even to the extent of allowing their members to hold office under government, so long as this in no way implicated them in the use of force or the shedding of blood. Nevertheless Mennonitism did disclose a certain tendency to anti-trinitarianism, as in the instance of the one-time priest Adam Pastor, who left the sect in 1547 to found a unitarian group of his own in the Cologne–Münster region. Another dissident was Henrik Niclaes (*c.* 1502–80), who believed himself to be the prophet of a new age of Christianity and established a following calling themselves the Family of Love. Niclaes based his activities on Emden, but he travelled widely. Thus he visited England, where he gained a number of devotees, although his teachings, with their pantheistic and antinomian leanings, created scandal. Even so, his writings were reprinted during the Commonwealth period.

46. *Ibid.*, 240, 238.
47. *Ibid.*, 120, 130.
48. *Ibid.*, 48.

## The spirituals

The second group of religious enthusiasts who in the past were usually included under the anabaptist label are those who nowadays are more aptly described as 'spirituals', and who are distinguishable by their mystical bent and their concern for the inwardness of true religion through the enlightenment and guidance of the Spirit. They differed from the great majority of the reformers, of whatever shade of doctrine, in maintaining that scripture, the written word, does not define and interpret the Spirit, but that it is the Spirit which defines and interprets the word. Only he who has the Spirit's direct illumination can, they held, perceive the inner truth of revelation and can know Christ according to the Spirit and not merely from the letter. The use of scripture was therefore primarily to mirror or articulate a personal religious experience rather than to create one. The exteriorization of religion in formularies and social institutions, however simple and supposedly restitutive of primitive conditions, did not much interest them. In fact they hark back rather to the mystical tendencies evident in the later Middle Ages, to Joachim of Fiore, to the Spiritual Franciscans and to the Beghards and Brethren of the Free Spirit.

In both, we may note, apocalyptic and millenarian expectations were also present, even where counterbalanced by an element of contemplative rationalism as well. Spiritualism, as it may be termed, is most signally represented by Hans Denck, Sebastian Franck and Caspar Schwenckfeld, though they differ in a number of respects from one another, and each in turn merits consideration in some detail.

First, however, we may mention David Joris, a curious personage not easy to categorize. A Dutchman born about 1501, he too inclined to mysticism and possessed some talent as a painter and poet, but his religious views were to become increasingly eccentric. He joined the Melchiorites on receiving baptism from Obe Philips, a leading figure in the sect, in 1534 and later befriended Castellio, as he also wrote in defence of the heretic Servetus. Insisting that water-baptism is in itself of no account, but that Christian baptism is essentially a baptism of the Spirit, he similarly maintained that scripture, again purely of itself, is of no avail to the believer without the inner light of the Spirit to guide him. Hailed as a prophet by a pious woman named Anneken Jansdochter, he came to regard himself as the Third David – third, that is, in succession to the biblical king of that name and his descendant Christ, above whom indeed Joris was disposed to exalt himself. He taught a doctrine of the intrinsic virtue of suffering in preparation for the coming New Age.

> All the godly must drink
> From the chalice of bitterness, 'pure red wine'.
> But the dregs shall God give to the godless to drain.
> They shall spew and belch and fall into death without end.[49]

Known as Davidians or Davidists, Joris's followers, whose perfervid spirit is well caught in the writings of Anneken,[50] won no sympathy from Menno Simons, who

49. R. H. Bainton, *The Travail of Religious Liberty: nine biographical studies* (Philadelphia, 1951), 127. The lines quoted are cited by Williams, *The Radical Reformation*, 382.

firmly dissociated himself from them. To escape the persecution in 1543 Joris fled to Basel, where he concealed himself under the alias of Jan van Brugge, supposedly a simple refugee for the gospel's sake. His true identity was not in fact discovered until three years after his death in 1556; he was then proclaimed a heretic and his remains exhumed and burnt.

Hans Denck (or Denk) was a man of indubitable intellectual ability and spiritual insight. A Bavarian from Heybach (or Hubach) to the south-west of Munich, his birth may be dated about 1495; he studied at Ingolstadt university (1517–19), where he developed a warm humanist interest and a proficiency in Latin, Greek and Hebrew. He began his career by teaching languages at Regensburg, but soon moved on to Basel, attracted thither by the fame of Erasmus and Oecolampadius. The latter obtained for him the rectorship of the St Sebaldus school at Nuremberg, where his circle of friends included men like Pirkheimer, Osiander and the painter Albrecht Dürer. From this post, however, he was dismissed two years later on a charge of heresy, for he had in the meantime come under the influence of Karlstadt and Müntzer. Thereafter he had no fixed abode: Mülhausen, Augsburg and Strassburg were places only of temporary sojourn. He also had by now adopted anabaptist views, and it was he who baptized Hans Huth. But the extremism of his opinions alienated the moderates of Strassburg, a city which the brethren were accustomed to look on as a 'refuge of righteousness'; he was denounced by Bucer as the 'anabaptist pope' and eventually expelled. He then moved on to Worms, where in 1527 he composed his best-known tract, 'Of True Love' (*Von der wahren Liebe*), in which his deeply devotional spirituality finds beautiful utterance.[51] In the summer of 1527 Denck was again at Augsburg in the company of Huth and others for a synod at which, it seems, a second Pentecost was expected. Later Huth was arrested and put to death, Denck himself escaping only to die shortly afterwards of the plague.[52]

Even his severest critics allowed Denck to be a man of the highest probity and of good scholarship. And he was not a fanatic; on the contrary, he combined a sober and modest disposition with the capacity for reasoned judgement. Recognizing, for example, the disparities within scripture itself, he believed that these could be reconciled only inwardly, by such a spiritual enlightenment as enables one to grasp the truth as a whole. Luther's teachings failed to satisfy him, as being dogmatically too restrictive, leaving little room for the progressive self-revelation of God in the individual soul. Thus his case against the Lutheran doctrine on predestination and the bondage of the will is presented in carefully chosen terms in his dialogue *Whether God is the Cause of Evil*, published at Augsburg in 1526.[53] In this he urges the freedom of the will and the possibility of a responsible decision for Christ in the life of any adult person. He argues that salvation is *in* us but not

---

50. See T. van Braght, *The Bloody Theater, or Martyr's Mirror* (English trans. by J. F. Sohm) (Scottdale, Pa., 1951), 453f.
51. Denck's writings have been published in a modern two-volume edition by G. Baring and W. Fellmann (*Hans Denck Schriften*, Gütersloh, 1955f.).
52. On Denck see A. Coutts, *Hans Denck, 1495–1527: humanist and heretic* (Edinburgh, 1927).
53. See Williams and Mergal, 86–111, for an abridged translation.

*of* us, its essence being the soul's self-surrender to God.[54] 'Scripture speaks of a tranquillity [*Gelassenheit*] which is the means of coming to God, that is, Christ himself, not to be regarded physically, but rather spiritually.'[55] In fact there is no other 'way of blessedness' than simply to lose one's self-will. On the other hand, the believer must be active; of Luther's passivity he will have nothing. 'It is a fabrication when false Christians say that they can do nothing but what God works in them.'[56] And to the question why God does not take away the 'creaturely' and make us 'as he himself would have us', Denck's reply is that 'if he already takes away the creaturely, as often happens for many, then he gives man absolute freedom of choice, as he gave it at the beginning, in such a way that a man might embrace either the good or the bad'. God does not wish to compel, but only that his mercy should be recognized and accepted.[57] Denck's view of evil itself has a Neo-Platonist slant: it is negative, not positive, and sin is non-being: 'How sin [really] is nothing may be perceived by whoever gives himself over to God and becomes nothing, while at the same time he is created something by God.' Each man, he says, will understand this according to the degree of his self-resignation.

A similarly free spirit was Sebastian Franck, born at Donauwörth, in the vicinity of Augsburg, in 1499. He was a personal friend of Denck's, but of more consequence as a scholar and of deeper learning as a humanist – he had studied under Agricola and Urbanus Rhegius – as he also was more prolific as a writer.[58] He entered the university of Ingolstadt in 1515, but later moved to Heidelberg, where in April 1518 he met Bucer, who was attending the famous disputation there at which Luther explained and defended his then still novel views. Ordained a priest in the Augsburg diocese, he acknowledged himself a Lutheran in 1526 and took up a clerical appointment at Gustenfelder, near Nuremberg. He also married, one Ottilie Behaim, the sister of two painter brothers, actually pupils of Dürer, who were known anabaptist sympathizers, although during his Lutheran phase he was hostile to both Zwinglian and anabaptist positions. But by 1530, when he published his 'Chronicle of Turkey', (*Türkenchronik*), a German translation of an anonymous Latin original which favourably contrasted the life and worship of the Muslims with the divisions and scandals of Christendom – his own 'off-beat' radicalism had become quite evident. Thus in discussing the dozen sects into which, as he thinks, the Christians were already divided he is obliged to add three more, namely the Lutheran, the Zwinglian and the Anabaptist. These diverse bodies, he allows, possess the truth in varying measure, but he now sees also a fourth type emerging, an invisible because purely spiritual community subject only to the Word of God internally received and without any of the traditional exterior forms such as ordained ministry and preaching, sacraments and ceremonies.

Meanwhile he had given up his Nuremberg pastorate and gone to Strassburg,

54. *Ibid.*, 93.
55. *Ibid.*, 97.
56. *Ibid.*, 92.
57. *Ibid.*, 97.
58. On Franck's work and ideas see A. Hegler, *Geist und Schrift bei Sebastian Franck* (Freiburg-im-Breisgau, 1892). Also W. E. Peuckert, *Sebastian Franck: ein deutscher Sucher* (Munich, 1943).

to start on his career as a popular religious writer pursuing a path of his own. Here he came into contact with Caspar Schwenkfeld, with whose opinions he at once realized he had much in common. In the autumn of 1531 he published his grandiose *Chronica, Zeitbuch und Geschichtsbibel* (a panoramic history of Christianity) in which all the Christian churches come in for sharp attack. He denounces both Romanism and the imperial system, but is little less unsympathetic towards popular movements likely to challenge established authority by violence. His survey of heresies and heretics – among whom, incidentally, he included Erasmus, much to the latter's annoyance – is especially interesting. Although his account of Luther's achievement is positive, this audacious broadside of his led nevertheless to his imprisonment as a dangerously subversive character and the book itself was suppressed. On his release the city fathers of Strassburg, who were no longer willing to tolerate his presence in the place, expelled him. He next settled at Ulm where he set up a printing press and began to publish his own works. Once again, however, he found himself at odds alike with the theologians and the magistracy. He insisted on his principle that true religion is inward and spiritual and that not only were there saints before Christ but that conscientious Mohammedans and pagans may have possessed it through the Spirit, even though they knew nothing of Christ's gospel.

> The unitary Spirit alone baptizes with fire and the Spirit all the faithful and all who are obedient to the inner Word in whatever part of the world they be. For God is no respecter of persons, but instead is the same to the Greek as to the Barbarian and the Turk, to the lord as to the servant, so long as they retain the light which has shone upon them and the joy in their heart.[59]

'My heart', Franck declared, 'is alien to none.'

Further expositions of these unconventional teachings followed in the *Paradoxa* of 1534 and 'The Seven Sealed Book' (*Das . . . mit sieben Siegeln verschlossene Buch*), written some five years later. The former is mystical in feeling and was plainly inspired by the *Theologia Germanica*. A paradox, in Franck's view, is a statement apparently incredible but nonetheless true when considered from a certain standpoint; indeed we have to say that, whatever is affirmed of God, its contrary is likewise the truth. His dislike of scriptural literalism is plain: it is a misuse of the Bible, the 'sword of Antichrist' which in fact kills the true Christ and is the breeding-ground of heresies and sects. In 'The Seven Sealed Book' he again denounces the narrow-minded sectarianism that is incapable of seeing Jew and Samaritan in a brotherly light, and he claims that Plato and Plotinus 'spoke to him more clearly than did Moses'. While deprecating overcharged emotionalism and ecstatic outpourings he continued to stress the presence in the soul of a divine element, described variously as the 'Word of God', the 'Inner Light' or the 'True Light', which is the ground and starting-point of all spiritual advance – a view of man that naturally implies the will's freedom and hence a capacity for active cooperation with the divine Spirit.

The medieval antecedents of Franck's thought are evident enough, yet he is one of the most modern in outlook of all the religious thinkers of his time. For

59. Williams and Mergal, 150.

ecclesiastical institutionalism he had no use and the current attempts at a repristi-
nation of the church he held to be wholly illusory. Indeed the mature mind had
no need of external props of any kind. Even the Bible is a dubious guide, containing
as it does so many contradictions and paradoxes, and if the reader is to profit from
its doctrine it must be interpreted at the deepest level.[60] Jesus as he lived and taught
is certainly disclosed to us in the gospels, but the figure there depicted is only the
symbol of the eternal Word which has communicated with man down the ages and
in diverse places.

Franck left Ulm at the beginning of 1539 for Basel, where he married again
shortly after his first wife's death and also resumed his trade as a printer, bringing
out, among other things, a Latin-Greek edition of the New Testament in 1541. He
died in the autumn of the following year.

But of all the spiritualist writers probably the most remarkable, as certainly the
weightiest intellectually, is the Silesian nobleman and lay theologian Caspar
Schwenckfeld.[61] A landowner and a knight of the Teutonic Order, Schwenckfeld
was won over to Lutheranism as early as 1518 and became the leader of the reform
movement in Silesia. He adhered firmly to the Lutheran teaching for some years
and was well known to Luther personally. Eventually, however, he was repudiated
by the Saxon reformer because of his deviant ideas on the eucharist. Disillusioned,
Schwenckfeld turned to radicalism, but to a form of it that owed nothing to
Karlstadt or Müntzer, revolutionary action being completely out of accord with
his convictions. By 1526 he had rejected any outward expression of the Lord's
Supper, maintaining that Christ's flesh is purely spiritual and that to 'feed' on
Christ is simply to receive him inwardly, in the depths of the soul. Yet at this stage
in his career Schwenckfeld sought only what he called a middle or 'royal' road in
religion.

> We are prone [*he wrote in 1524*] to swerve from the right hand to the left, contrary
> to the Lord's command: 'Turn not to the right hand nor to the left. We must walk
> on the royal road and seek to find the mean between the former hypocritical life. [*i.e.*
> *Romanism*] and the present liberty [*i.e. Lutheranism*]. Otherwise all will be futile'.[62]

60. Franck vigorously opposed any appeal to the Old Testament as an authority on a par
    with the New. Speaking of the early Christian Fathers – 'of whom', he declares, 'not
    even one knew the Lord . . . nor was sent by God to teach' – he says that 'they mix
    the New Testament with the Old, as also today their descendants do. And when they
    have nothing with which to defend their purposes they run at once to the empty quiver,
    that is, to the Old Testament and from it prove the legitimacy of war, oath, government,
    power of magistracy, titles, priesthood; and praise everything and ascribe this all forcibly
    to Christ without his will. And just as the popes have desired all this from it, so also
    many of those who would have themselves be called Evangelicals hold that they have
    nobly escaped the snare of the pope and the devil and have nevertheless achieved, with
    great effort and sweat, nothing more than that they have exchanged and confounded
    the falsehood of the pope with the Mosaic kingdom!' (from a letter to John Campanus,
    1531; Williams and Mergal, 151).
61. See S. G. Schulz, *Caspar Schwenckfeld von Ossig (1487–1561): spiritual interpreter of
    Christianity, apostle of the middle way, pioneer in modern religious thought* (Norristown,
    Pa., 1946). Schwenckfeld's numerous writings are contained in the successive volumes
    of the *Corpus Schwenckfeldianorum* (Leipzig, 1907–61).
62. *Corpus Schwenck.*, II, 62.

Neither a religion of works nor one of resting on a purely forensic doctrine of imputed righteousness would suffice. But the royal road was likely to be one few would find.

Yet Schwenckfeld's own way was later to be changed, lying this time between 'territorial' Protestantism, typified by Lutheranism (or Calvinism), and the outright radicalism of the anabaptist sects. In fact, Schwenckfeld was to veer towards a more errant course than that even of the latter, much to the disgust of Luther, who described him as 'a stupid fool, possessed by the devil, understanding nothing', and who especially objected to being 'pestered with the pamphlets the devil spews out of him'. But Schwenckfeld had now passed well beyond any position with which Luther could have sympathized to one that implied a quite different view of what Christianity is. Like Franck, he had come to believe, contrary to all 'classical' Protestantism, in the freedom of the human will, although at the same time not bypassing the essential Protestant doctrine of solafideism, for that principle he never rejected. What he was concerned for were the real grounds of the moral life and the ability to achieve by self-discipline a progressive and manifest sanctification. This, he maintained, 'derives from the knowledge (*Erkenntnis*) of Christ through faith',[63] a knowledge which must come from within, nurtured by that interior feeding upon Christ which a true because wholly spiritual participation in the Supper renders possible. Incorporation into the second Adam through membership of the invisible company of the truly faithful delivers the soul from the bondage of sin and gives it freedom at last. Although Schwenckfeld thought it impossible for the old and corrupt man to keep the commandments of God, this was possible for the new and regenerated man, loving God with his whole heart and his neighbour as himself.[64] Such could not but be so in view of the transforming power of Christ in the soul. But if a real sanctification is possible – in effect a 'deification', in Schwenckfeld's term, of fallen humanity – then the Lutheran notion of *simul justus et peccator* is inadmissible, depending as it does on a mistaken conception of the Christian life. The believer in Christ can learn to master his sensual appetites, can in fact be visibly transfigured by the security of that interior 'castle of peace' in which he now dwells. The test of true religion thus lies in experience, in an inward transformation expressing itself in complete renewal of life. Yet Schwenckfeld was well aware of the danger of spiritual pride, and he always insisted that Christian living is a continuous progress rather than an actual attainment.

> We, who are as yet poor souls, inexperienced in divine things, poor and weak in the spirit and faith, hope that God the Lord will in time help us and others further, as it may please him. Meanwhile we are zealous in the pure wholesome doctrine about the Lord Jesus Christ and endeavour through him to live piously in his grace.

The church too, therefore, must be an entirely new, dedicated and select body.

> We hope that the Lord, through this pure wholesome doctrine of his saving knowledge, because it came out of his divine revelation in the Holy Spirit, will build his chosen

63. *Corpus Schwenck.*, X, 707.
64. *Corpus Schwenck.*, XII, 901.

church and through it will gather the children of God which are scattered over the whole earth.[65]

Schwenckfeld's last years were spent at Ulm, where he died in 1561. Theological controversy, chiefly about eucharistic and Christological doctrine, engrossed much of his time. His own standpoint was now far from the Lutheran positions formulated at Augsburg, which he rejected as inimical to true freedom in the Spirit. That the sacraments could not in themselves be means of grace seemed to him obvious. Infant baptism he of course did not approve, but neither had he any belief in the efficacy of adult baptism. As for the Supper, he dismissed all idea of a veritable presence, even to the extent of arguing that the words of institution as reported in the gospels were a misrepresentation of what Christ himself had really said on the eve of his death. Behind this conclusion lay what for him was an initial principle, that all creatures are 'external to God' as likewise is God to all creatures, so that creatureliness can never be the vehicle of divinity. Thus the eucharistic rite has no more than a symbolic significance and its observance is not a necessity. Still more fundamentally, the same axiom determined Schwenckfeld's Christology.[66] Christ's flesh was no ordinary human flesh but came direct from God by (or through) the Virgin Mary, an opinion which he defended on the grounds that Christ being one with God, since he was 'begotten' not 'created', his human nature must itself be unique. Thus although Schwenckfeld professed to maintain the distinction between the divine and the human natures, what he seems actually to have taught was a kind of mutual absorption of the two, in a way that really amounts to the old Eutychian heresy.[67]

As regards the atonement Schwenckfeld held that salvation was the work of the historic Christ redeeming mankind from the power of the devil, but that it is dispensed by the glorified Christ in the purifying of human nature, so bringing about regeneration and adoption into sonship, an idea which explains his requirement of an actual moral and spiritual change, inasmuch as 'God looks on none as righteous in whom his own intrinsic righteousness is not present'.

For all Schwenckfeld's individualism and dislike of sectarian conventicles, his followers became a sect known as Confessors of the Glory of Christ, or, after 1539, simply as Schwenckfeldians, mainly congregated in Silesia and Swabia, although subsequently in Prussia too. In time they were augmented by a number of anabaptists and by disciples of Jakob Boehme. The sect survives yet in Pennsylvania.

Idiosyncratic though they appear, the spirituals were by no means mere eccentric dreamers, and their teachings came as an inspiration to many. Within the limits of

---

65. *Corpus Schwenck.*, XVI, 280f.
66. Schwenckfeld's chief theological treatises are *Von der göttlichen Kindschaft und Herrlichkeit des Gantzen Sones Gottes* (1538) and *Konfession und Erklärung vom Erkenntnis Christi und seine göttlichen Herrlichkeit* (1540). He was opposed by Martin Frecht at Ulm and condemned by a Lutheran synod presided over by Melanchthon in 1540.
67. Eutyches was condemned at the Council of Chalcedon in 451 for confounding the natures in a way that amounted to monophysitism; see J. N. D. Kelly, *Early Christian Doctrines* (5th edn, London, 1977), 330–4. In Schwenckfeld's eyes even Luther was to be suspected of Nestorianism.

the present chapter space has been found for the consideration only of three or four of the principal figures among them. But others, such as Johann Bünderlin (*c.* 1499–1533) of Linz, who worked at Strassburg and later in Silesia, and Christian Entfelder (his dates are unknown) a follower of Denck and a friend of Hubmaier's,[68] who had formerly, it seems, ministered to congregations of the Swiss and Austrian Brethren, are worthy at least of mention. The latter firmly rejected the current biblicism – nothing, he declared, could be drawn from the Bible unless the seeker had first discovered within himself what to look for – while the church of his ideal would be 'a chosen, saved, purified, sanctified group in whom God dwells, upon whom the Holy Spirit has poured out his gifts, and with whom Christ the Lord shares his offices and his mission'.[69] Another for whom an affinity with the spiritualist standpoint might well be claimed was the Swiss physician and neo-Platonist thinker Theophrastus Paracelsus (Philip von Hohenheim) (1493–1541), who, although neither anabaptist nor anti-trinitarian, wrote extensively on a variety of theological topics, the sacraments especially, besides producing biblical commentaries of some interest.

In all these personages what above all else is to be observed is a deep religious conviction stemming directly from a fifteenth-century Christian piety in which elements of Platonism and Kabbalistic nature-mysticism intermingle. In this they in turn foreshadow the type of piety which in the seventeenth century assumed a number of differing forms and evokes in particular the names of Jakob Boehme, George Fox and John Smith, the Cambridge Platonist. Although not by disposition or interest the founders of churches or sects their influence was nonetheless pervasive, continuing when their own were all but forgotten.

## The rationalists

The last group of radicals to be considered is that comprising what have not inaptly been designated the evangelical rationalists.[70] Like the anabaptists and the spirituals they were only in part the outcome of the Protestant Reformation, having other and in certain regards older origins, among which humanism was predominant, especially in the case of the Sozzinis. Reference to the latter is a reminder also of the fact that many of them were Italians thoroughly imbued with the spirit of the Renaissance and essentially intellectual and critical in their approach to theology, which, in its traditional shape, demanded in their view reconstruction from its foundations. Alienated from Rome by its manifest corruption, men like Camillo Renato, Giovanni Gentile, Matteo Gribaldi, Bernardino Ochino and Giorgio Eindrata nevertheless lacked the strong impulsion of a common animating religious conviction, directing their attention instead to the quest for a rationally intelligible doctrine. Of cultured minds, they were all of them pronounced individualists for whom rejection of the ecclesiastical system in which they had been nurtured left them with little if any sense of a possible alternative other than the solitary road

68. R. M. Jones, *Spiritual Reformers* (London, 1914), 39–143.
69. *Ibid.*
70. Williams, xxix.

of private thought and speculation, although Ochino (1487–1547), one-time vicar-general of the Capuchins, became a Protestant and was welcomed at Geneva by Calvin, under whom he was given the pastorate of the Italian refugees. The creation of a communion or sect on the basis of a shared belief was not for most of them an option, though their ideas did have some effect on reformed churches in eastern Europe, whence the Transylvanian Unitarians, the Lithuanian Brethren and the Socinians in Poland, even if the last-named included elements of an anabaptist and spiritualist tendency in addition to the theological rationalism which so marked the opinions of Fausto Sozzini. 'A loose band of ethical theists',[71] their tenets covered pacifism, psychopannychism (the sleep in death of the souls of the elect until they awaken to share in the rule of Christ at his second advent)[72], a minimizing of all the external appurtenances of traditional Christianity, and, last but by no means least in importance, a distinctive anti-trinitarian bias stressing the humanity of Christ to the near elimination of his divinity, unless possibly in an adoptionist sense.

All these features emerge clearly in the teaching of Sozzini, or Socinus, to use the Latinized form under which he is usually known. However, one of the earliest and, because of the fatal encounter with Calvin in 1553, best remembered of these anti-trinitarians was, not an Italian but a Spaniard, Miguel Servede, or more familiarly Servetus.[73] Born in 1511 at Tudela in Aragon of a long line of jurists, he too was destined for the law, but his preference was for humanist studies. In 1530 he corresponded with Oecolampadius, meeting him later at Basel, but it is evident from his letters that he had already adopted very unorthodox opinions. The following spring saw him at Strassburg, where he intended to get his book 'On the Errors of the Trinity' (*De Trinitatis erroribus libri septem*) published, as also to discuss the problem of the authority of the Bible with Capito and Bucer, the latter's commentary on the synoptic gospels having particularly attracted him. The theological treatise, which finally made its debut at Hagenau in June, 1531, falls into seven parts, the first of which contains an exposition of the author's characteristic modalism comprising the view that Christ is Son of God not eternally but by generation of the Holy Spirit, the Spirit in turn being conceived less as a distinct 'person' than a divine potency. The remaining six parts either develop these ideas further or else engage in acrimonious polemic against

71. *Ibid.*, 856.
72. Psychopannychism, much canvassed in the early sixteenth century in Italy, was a theory concerning the after-life of the soul. Briefly, it turned on the idea that after the death of the body the soul succumbed to a profound sleep, as against the accepted view of purgatory, reaffirmed at the Council of Florence in 1439, that the souls of the dead are fully conscious and therefore capable of both satisfaction and suffering. Servetus adhered to it, as did many of the anabaptists and some of the spirituals, as also the Socinians later. Calvin took the notion seriously enough to publish a weighty treatise (*Psychopannychia*) against it in 1542 (modern edn by W. Zimmerli, *Quellenschriften zur Geschichte des Pietismus*, XIII, Leipzig, 1932).
73. See R. H. Bainton, *Hunted Heretic: the life and death of Michael Servetus* (Boston, 1953). Anti-trinitarian ideas were found also in the circle of another Spanish humanist, Juan de Valdés (*c.* 1498–1541), on whom J. Heep, *Juan de Valdés: seine Religion, sein Werden, seine Bedeutung* (Leipzig, 1909) and J. C. Nieto, *Juan de Valdés and the Origins of the Spanish and Italian Reformation* (Geneva, 1978) may be consulted.

Lutheran doctrine.[74] Some readers were impressed by the work's boldness and evident learning, but on the whole reception of it was unfavourable. Bucer attacked its teaching in a series of lectures, while Oecolampadius in Basel anathematized it as blasphemous. The upshot was that Servetus was expelled from Strassburg, although, somewhat surprisingly he at once returned to Basel, presumably still hoping for a sympathetic hearing there. The Swiss city, however, was no more friendly, despite his effort to present his curious heresy in a more conciliatory fashion in a shorter work entitled 'Dialogues on the Trinity' (*Dialogorum de Trinitate libri duo*, Hagenau, 1532).[75] In this he made some attempt to use traditional theological language and to explain more clearly what he had meant by Christ's divine Sonship.

From 1541 to 1553 Servetus was personal physician to the archbishop of Vienne, during which time he entered into correspondence with Calvin, to whom in 1546 he sent a draft copy of his *Restitutio Christianismi*. Their exchanges were prolonged, Calvin becoming increasingly wearied and irritated by them; in any case he found Servetus's anti-trinitarian ideas totally unacceptable. Eventually the Inquisition at Lyons intervened, and although Servetus escaped from his detention in April 1553 and went into hiding, he appeared at Geneva in the August of that year, was recognized and was arrested by the authorities. Tried for heresy and condemned, he was executed at the stake on 27 October. His *Restitutio*, the most important of his writings, which had been published at the beginning of the year, provides a comprehensive statement of his mature opinions. It is clear that by now he had gone a good way beyond the position taken up in his two earlier disquisitions on the Trinity, and that he objected to the doctrine as an intellectual abstraction without warrant of scripture, even though he seemed loath, oddly enough, to dispense with the traditional terminology, such as speaking of the Son's *generatio* rather than *prolatio* as previously. His views nonetheless remained speculative to the point of the bizarre. Yet he manages to retain a kind of 'economic' or 'revelational' Trinity whereby the Logos and the Spirit, signifying primal light and primal power respectively, are understood as a progressive disclosure of the unitary personality of the one God, who alone is eternal. The Logos again, as the archetype of all created things, was figured in Adam and the Old Testament theophanies, but finally became incarnate in Christ. The role of faith, in Servetus's view, and here he anticipated Socinus, is the intellectual recognition of this divinity. To Calvin all such notions were abhorrent, not to mention their author's quirky and abusive attitude; but in its way Servetus's system was unquestionably Christocentric – his personal devotion to Christ seems to have been genuine – and he himself claimed that it was more truly biblical than any of the other reformed 'orthodoxies'.[76]

Although frequently classed among the evangelical rationalists, Fausto Sozzini, nephew of the scarcely less free-thinking Lelio Sozzini (1525–62) and a member of a prominent Sienese family of lawyers, takes us to the margin of the radical

74. There is a translation (*Two Treatises on the Trinity*) by E. M. Wilbur, in *Harvard Theological Studies*, XVI (1932).
75. Wilbur, *op. cit.*, 85–264.
76. Of Servetus's theological doctrines the fullest account is that of H. Tollin, *Das Lehrsystem Michael Servets, genetisch dargestellt* (3 vols, Gütersloh, 1876–9).

movement in the audacious flight of his ideas.[77] A man both of marked intellectual ability and of qualities of leadership, he was born at Siena in 1539. He received little formal education, yet at the age of twenty-three he published a treatise on St John's gospel in which he denied the essential divinity of Christ and also cast doubt on the natural immortality of man. From 1565 to 1575 he was employed in the service of Mabella de' Medici, daughter of the Grand Duke of Tuscany, and during these years he at least conformed outwardly with the beliefs and practices of the church. Later he made his home at Basel where he applied himself to theological studies, publishing in 1578 his *De Jesu Christo servatore*, in which he now made clear his opposition not only to Catholicism but to the teachings of the Protestant reformers as well. In the same year he visited Klauserberg in Transylvania, apparently expecting to gain the sympathetic ear of its ruler Johann Sigismund, who himself was known to hold anti-trinitarian opinions. As matters turned out Socinus found himself called upon instead to resist the still more extreme views of the local bishop Franciscus Davidis (1510–79).

In the following year he moved on to Poland, the country in which he was to spend the rest of his life and to achieve the work which gave him his lasting influence. Thanks to the feudal conditions still persisting there fugitive anabaptists had been able to settle on the estates of tolerant Polish magnates, and one of the sects which Socinus encountered was a 'unitarian' body known as the Minor Reformed Church of Poland. Its main congregations were located at Vilna in Lithuania, and at Rakow in the domain of a nobleman, Jan Sieninski, the latter place in particular having become a centre of attraction to radical dissidents throughout Poland, Moravia and even Germany. Indeed Rakow had acquired fame as a kind of New Jerusalem organized on what were thought to be strict New Testament lines, where social reforms were carried out, a puritan mode of life established and unitarian doctrines disseminated. In 1602 a unitarian college was founded there by Sieninski's son, Jakob. Opinions among these sectaries differed considerably, but Socinus did much to bring about some sort of unity by his moderating approach. All the same, his popularity at Rakow declined and he left the place in 1598, his closing years being passed at Ludowice, where he died in 1604. The classical Socinian confession, the *Racovian Catechism*, was brought out shortly after his death, he himself, with the help of Petrus Statovius (Stoiński), having been largely responsible for the revision of the original statement. This catechism was first printed in Polish in 1605, but an enlarged edition in German was published in 1608, while a Latin edition dedicated to King James I of England appeared in 1609.[78] But for a proper understanding of early Socinianism recourse must be had to the writings of Socinus himself and of other Socinian divines down to the mid-seventeenth century. All are contained in the *Bibliotheca Fratrum Polonorum*, published at Amsterdam in 1656.

77. See G. Pioli, *Fausto Socino: Vita, opere, fortuna* (Modena, 1952) and M. Martini, *Fausto Socino et la pensée socinienne* (Paris, 1967). There is an informative article on the two Sozzinis by L. Cristiani in the *Dictionnaire de théologie catholique*, XIV (part 2, 1941), cols 2326–34.
78. An English translation by Thomas Rees, made from a revised and enlarged Latin edition of 1680, was published in London in 1818.

The whole cast of Socinus's mind was rationalist and critical, and for him reformation, last and first, meant a reconstruction of doctrine. In purely religious feeling he seems to have been deficient.[79] It is therefore incorrect to describe Socinianism, as has sometimes been done, as the logical development of 'orthodox' Protestantism. It drew its inspiration very largely from the Renaissance humanist spirit and the individualism which this fostered, although behind these lay also medieval scholasticism in its Scotist-Pelagian form. In any case basic to Socinian teaching was the conviction of man's inherent moral capacity. Its conception of the nature of Christianity was through and through ethical, anticipating both the Deists and Kant in its principle that what in the traditional Christian doctrine was not morally serviceable should be jettisoned. But clearly, if the essence of religion is morality it must be assumed that man has the intrinsic moral ability to fulfil its demands. Thus Luther's insistence on the bondage of the will struck them as completely misconceived, for if there is no morality without responsibility, equally there can be no responsibility without freedom, and no fault can be attached to sin. As to this the *Racovian Catechism* offers the plainest statements. However, the will needs to be instructed and the instruction effective, for salvation man himself cannot provide. Hence the necessity of divine revelation, since of any merely 'natural' religion Socinus and his followers had no notion. As the *Catechism* puts the matter in its very opening words: 'The Christian religion is the way of attaining eternal life which God has pointed out by Jesus Christ; or, in other words, it is the method of serving God, who will reward the obedient with eternal life, and punish the disobedient with death.'

This emphasis on man's permanent need of teaching in turn determined the Socinians' idea of faith itself, which they understood as neither more nor less than a saving knowledge or doctrine apprehensible by 'right reason' (*recta ratio*). So to the question of the use of right reason, 'if it be of any, in those matters which relate to salvation', the answer given is: 'It is indeed of great service, since without it we could neither perceive with certainty the authority of the sacred writings, understand their contents, discriminate one thing from another, nor apply them to any practical purpose.'[80]

Rejecting as they did all ecclesiastical authority and interpreting the Bible firmly in accordance with what they held to be the axioms of natural reason, their attitude to questions of faith and doctrine could scarcely be other than intellectual. To religious experience – the pangs of conscience or the inward sense of forgiveness – they made no appeal whatever; for them the evidences of Christianity were wholly external, especially Christ's virgin birth, his miracles, and his death and resurrection. These it was which authenticated his prophetic office as a divine teacher on whose precepts and their observance a godly life, and so final salvation, must depend. The Socinian rationalism thus differed in an important way from that of a later age, in that it remained strongly impregnated with supernaturalism, itself the result of a naïve scriptural literalism, necessary, it was held, if the Bible is to preserve its authority. At the same time, and rather oddly, they set little store by the Old

79. C. A. Harnack: 'The religious motive in the deepest sense is absent in these Italians' (*History of Dogma*, VII (English trans. by W. M'Gilchrist), 163).
80. Section I, ch. ii.

Testament, the greater part of which the Socinians saw as having historical value only. Nor indeed did they insist on the inerrancy of scripture: even the apostles could err. The one sole purpose of the biblical revelation was to furnish the patterns of a rationally ordered way of life. Ultimately, therefore, salvation depended on good works, and certainly not on 'faith' as a subjective disposition.

It followed that Socinianism could allow no room for the doctrine of predestination, which was judged to have sprung from a grave misreading of scripture. Again, the *Racovian Catechism* is uncompromising in its teaching: 'This notion of predestination is altogether false – and principally for two reasons, whereof one is that it would necessarily destroy all religion, and the other that it would ascribe to God many things incompatible with his nature.' But along with this rejection went that also of original sin, whether in its Catholic or its Protestant form. Adam's fall, it was declared – as the Pelagians of antiquity had maintained – affected himself alone, and mankind as a whole lost neither life nor freedom thereby.[81] Human nature therefore is not essentially corrupted and calls for no essential transformation. Also no atonement is needed to reconcile God to men, for God can forgive sins of his sovereign will, which is in no respect constrained by principles as it were external to himself.[82] Accordingly no 'substitute' or 'satisfaction' was required to meet the demand of the divine righteousness. This latter point, in fact, is vital to the whole Socinian system because rendering entirely otiose the dogma of Christ's divinity, at any rate in the sense of a divine pre-existence and subsequent incarnation. Jesus Christ was indeed unique as a man, born as he was of virgin, with infinite wisdom conferred on him by God, as likewise raised at the last from the dead and elevated miraculously into heaven as a pledge and earnest of the eventual salvation of all the just, for to the unheeding and godless there could be only final annihilation. But in himself Christ was not divine, divinity belonging to the one God alone: actually he was by nature passible and mortal; such divinity as was bestowed on him 'adoptively', at his ascension into heaven, was simply of a kind to render him a fitting object of worship. Plainly then, in Socinian theology, trinitarianism had completely collapsed, though anti-trinitarianism was more in the nature of an inference than a basic principle, and relatively little attention is paid to it in the *Racovian Catechism*. Moreover, from so drastic a revision of the fundamentals of Christian teaching it comes as no surprise that the Socinian account of the church and the sacraments was reductive in the extreme, the church being thought of as no more than a community of the like-minded and the sacraments as purely symbolic: baptism was a sign of conversion and the Supper a bare memorial of the Lord's death.

Only a few groups among the radical reformers became stabilized into sects capable of sustaining a historic existence; the Socinians were one, the Mennonites another. But because of their diversity and not infrequent eccentricity it would nevertheless be a serious mistake to suppose that together they did not constitute, taking a general view of them, an aspect of the sixteenth-century religious Reform

81. See too Socinus's *De statu primi hominis ante lapsum* (*Bibliotheca Fratrum Polonorum*, II, 253ff.).
82. *Racovian Catechism*, section V, ch. viii; cf. Socinus, *De Jesu Christ servatore* (*Bibliotheca*, II, 121ff.).

movement in Europe no less significant, both in its outlook and attitudes and in its long-term influence, than others which, until latterly at least, have figured much more prominently in historiographical perspective, a perspective set in fact by the radicals' very first historian, Heinrich Bullinger in 'The Rise of Anabaptism' (*Der Widertaufer Ursprung*) of 1560. As has fairly been said, 'the Radical Reformation contained impulses which were at once more primitive and more modern than the driving forces of classical Protestantism'.[83] Indeed it would be true to say that modern sectarian Protestantism owes far more to the spirit and characteristic beliefs of these people than it does to the great historic systems of Luther and Calvin, which in retrospect, as we on the hither side of the Enlightenment now see, appear for the most part archaic, with their cardinal doctrines of predestination and justification *sola fide* as pieces in an ideological museum rather than as deep-seated convictions having the power to move hearts and stir wills. Not of course that the tenets of anabaptists and spirituals were always of a sort to make any wide extension of their hold probable: their intense assurance of, for example, the imminent end of the world and the apocalyptic state of mind it induced are alien to our modern standpoint, and the actual beliefs in which these were articulated are to the vast majority of Christians today merely naïve when not absurd. But the doctrine that baptism should follow a personally held faith and not simply anticipate it, or the principle that church and state must be entirely separate, are by no means now the reprehensible and dangerous things which the radicals' contemporary opponents judged them to be, while the idea that the spirit of religion transcends any or all of its institutional embodiments is in no way remote from modern thinking, but rather speaks to it. In any case the immense fortitude with which the sectaries faced not only universal obloquy but at times bitter and bloody harassment on the part of their fellow-Christians, Protestant no less than Catholic, abides perhaps as the most impressive phenomenon of all the troubled religious history of their era.

83.  Williams, *op. cit.*, 848.

# Chapter 10

# THE REFORMATION IN BRITAIN:
# I. CRISIS

## 'Henrician' catholicism

It has often been said that the Reformation in England was essentially an act of state, a 'parliamentary transaction'.[1] There is truth in the assertion, obviously. Every stage of the movement, as likewise the sharp reaction against it under Mary Tudor, was effected by political action and in accordance with state policy. Apart from this fact it surely would be extremely difficult to surmise how, or even whether, Protestantism would have made any real headway in a country which, for the most part, was conservative in its religious outlook and certainly not eager for the introduction of doctrinal and liturgical novelties. Yet to regard the English Reformation as purely an act of state carried through despite the indifference of, or even in opposition to, public opinion at large would be to misread the situation. The state reformation was one thing, but the change of religious orientation which occurred during the course of the century, a change that affected all ranks of society, is another, and not less substantial. For the truth is, to quote a distinguished modern authority, that 'while English religion was predominantly Catholic in 1520, it had become predominantly Protestant well before 1600'.[2] Moreover the process which led to this outcome did not await state action to make a beginning, and it subsequently gathered momentum in the face of government opposition carried to the point of rigorous persecution.

Years before Henry VIII summoned his reform parliament in 1529, heresy, feared and keenly resisted by a man of such personal integrity as Thomas More, was sometimes decidedly louder than a whisper, even if heretical opinions were not widespread, while anticlericalism, prompted by abundant causes of dissatisfaction, was rife. What is not clear is how dissatisfaction and potential dissidence would have been rallied and organized had it not been for the government initiative, for in religious leaders of high ability and dedication England was signally lacking. No one remotely comparable to a Luther or a Calvin ever emerged, and of original theological thinking, even on a much lower plane, nothing can be cited. Doctrinally, the English Reformation was the debtor to the continentals. Only when what was long after to acquire the designation Anglicanism began to shape itself towards the end of the century, out of the turmoil, political and religious, of the earlier and revolutionary decades, did a recognizably new type of reformed Christianity make its appearance.

The England of the last years of the fifteenth and the opening decades of the

1. Cf. F. M. Powicke, *The Reformation in England* (London, 1941), 34.
2. A. G. Dickens, in *The Reformation Crisis*, ed. J. Hurstfield (London, 1965), 44.

sixteenth centuries by no means presented the spectacle of a land in which religion was neglected or in decline. On the contrary, the standard of outward observance, as attested by foreign visitors, was high. The churches were well attended, and on the whole well furnished and cared for – the fifteenth century had been an age conspicuous for parish church building and rebuilding – and popular devotionalism, superstitious though much of it may have been, was spontaneous. Further, the religiosity of the English people is fairly testified by the number of religious books published. The statistics show that from a third to one half of the literature that came from the press was of a pious character: it has been ascertained that of the 349 books printed between 1468 and 1530 no fewer than 176 were of this nature.[3] And of course many more titles were imported from the continent. On the other hand the Bible seems to have been relegated to the background, though this can be attributed more or less to the prohibition in 1408 of any vernacular version not sanctioned by the bishops. The truth nevertheless is that in this period no English version at all was made available, whereas in Germany twenty complete translations were brought out between the years 1466 and 1522, while in France a printed translation appeared in 1477 and ten years later an old one, dating from 1291, found a publisher, and by 1521 even this had been reprinted seven times. England unfortunately was obliged to wait for its vernacular scriptures until William Tyndale produced his Protestant New Testament in 1526.

But a dissident evangelicalism was not missing. Wycliffe's teachings in the fourteenth century had given rise to Lollardy, and this had persisted, although driven underground by persecution, down to Tudor times: indeed in the early sixteenth century, as may be inferred from diocesan records and other sources, it was quite evidently recrudescent. In York, for example, more than seventy cases were brought against heretics during the reigns of Henry VIII and Mary, a large proportion of them involving Lollards.[4] The incidence of Lollardy was thus, clearly, frequent, even if the actual numbers of its adherents are difficult to compute and probably in the aggregate were not great. Congregations were to be found in London, Essex, Kent, Buckinghamshire and the Midlands and North, the members of which were for the most part artisans and peasants, although merchants of some standing were occasionally among them. Their beliefs were generally based on scripture-reading – Purvey's English Version was much used – and old Wycliffite tracts, but could hardly be said to amount to a coherent body of doctrine. Lollardy was anticlerical in bias and sharply critical of the worldliness and pomp of the church, as in truth of any priestly intervention at all between the believer and his Saviour. It also minimized the importance of the sacraments as compared with preaching, objected to clerical celibacy, auricular confession and prayers for the dead, and derided the superstition of pilgrimages, the cult of the saints and images. In all this Lollardy reveals a close affinity with the clandestine evangelicalism of the various groups of 'brethren' on the European continent. What it was wanting in, however, was a coordinating theological principle.

Yet it did provide a fertile soil for the reception of Lutheran ideas, which began

---

3. P. Janelle, *L'Angleterre catholique à la veille du schisme*, 13ff.
4. See A. G. Dickens, *Lollards and Protestants in the Diocese of York, 1509–1558* (Oxford, 1959).

to percolate through at an early date, Lutheran literature, from 1520 if not before, finding its way into the country by the eastern ports from the Netherlands and north Germany. In fact the two evangelical influences, the home product and the imported, were to continue for a good many years side by side, although to speak of the Lollard 'leaven' as having 'permeated the English people' is to exaggerate.[5] But it is indubitable that the leading English reformers were acquainted with Wycliffe's own writings, as they themselves testify, Cranmer declaring that Wycliffe had set forth the truth of the gospel, while Hooper and Ridley commended him for having resisted 'the popish doctrine of the Mass' and denied transubstantiation.[6] Dickens's conclusion, that 'Lollardy survived and contributed in some significant degree toward the Protestant Reformation' is a fact based on 'massive and incontrovertible evidence', must be held to stand.[7]

Lutheranism also soon made an impression at the universities, or at least at Cambridge, where scholars like Robert Barnes, the Augustinian friar, and Thomas Bilney were wont to meet at the White Horse Tavern expressly to discuss the new theology – whence the name it acquired of 'Little Germany' – even if there is nothing to show that Thomas Cranmer, then a fellow of Jesus College, was ever of their company. The circulation of Lutheran literature in England was considerable enough to worry the authorities and intelligence of it even reached the ears of Pope Leo X, who wrote to the king and to Cardinal Wolsey urging them to bring it to a halt. On 12 May 1521 Wolsey went in state to St Paul's cathedral to hear a sermon against Lutheran errors preached by Bishop Fisher of Rochester before a distinguished congregation, and on the same occasion a large quantity of Lutheran books was burnt in the adjoining churchyard.[8] Even the king himself entered the controversy with his treatise *Assertio septem sacramentum*, attacking the Lutheran sacramental doctrine. It is thus clear that England was not at all unprepared, for its part, to reflect the religious changes that were affecting her continental neighbours. When Henry VIII summoned his 1529 parliament he could count at all events upon a not unsympathetic reception for any measures he might deem it necessary to take against papal authority, which was not popular, in his own realm.

The political Reformation began with Henry's breach with Rome as a result of his failure to secure papal sanction for the divorce of his wife, Queen Katharine, desired by him partly for personal reasons but partly also from his genuine anxiety for a male heir in order to secure the continuity of his dynasty. With the series of Acts of parliament passed between 1532 and 1534 whereby the ancient *Ecclesia Anglicana* was severed from the papacy we are not here concerned, so they need not be examined in detail. Their effect was first to ensure the submission of the clergy and then to cut one by one the ties which from time immemorial had bound the church in England to Rome. Annates, 'Peter's Pence' and appeals to the Roman courts were abolished, the pope was denied any voice in ecclesiastical appointments, and the power of granting licences and dispensations was transferred from him to

5. T. M. Lindsay, *A History of the Reformation* (Edinburgh, 1907) II, 318.
6. A. F. Pollard, *Thomas Cranmer and the English Reformation* (London, 1904), 9.
7. A. G. Dickens, *The English Reformation* (London, 1964), 37.
8. *Letters and State Papers*, III, i, 485.

the archbishop of Canterbury. The monarch himself was declared to be 'Supreme Head' of the church with no qualifying clause and authority was likewise given him to impose an oath on any subject requiring his acceptance of the new regime, refusal to take it being judged high treason, as in the cases of More and Fisher. Thus within three years a complete constitutional revolution was carried through almost entirely on the king's own initiative, not to say his whim, although he had had enough sagacity to make certain at every stage of the acquiescence of parliament in what he sought to do.[9]

But apart from the subsequent suppression of the monastic houses and the destruction of certain shrines like that of St Thomas at Canterbury, nothing was done to change the church's familiar aspect in the eyes of laymen attending its services. To all appearance England remained as Catholic as she had been, except that the papal jurisdiction (and antipapal feeling had further increased) had now been totally abolished. For although it was the king's will to unite the ecclesiastical with the civil power under his own supreme authority it certainly was not his intention to patronize heresy, and those accused of it met their judicial deaths along with dissentients from his anti-Roman policy. He was content, in short, to preserve the old religion but under strict state control, his minister, the astute and somewhat impassive lawyer, Thomas Cromwell, being appointed vicegerent of the church.[10] In this Henry was supported by Bishop Stephen Gardiner (*c*.1490–1553), who argued in his *De vera obedientia* (1535) that the pope had no legitimate power over national churches, and by Cuthbert Tunstall and Edmund Bonner, bishops of Durham and Hereford (later London) respectively, none of whom was in any mind to entertain Lutheran doctrine and practices.[11] The archbishop of Canterbury, Thomas Cranmer, on the other hand, was a known sympathizer with the so-termed 'new learning', and tension between the two factions, the conservative and the reformist, grew. In July 1536 convocation, under Cromwell's presidency, adopted certain articles, ten in number, in the compiling of which the king himself had had a part, their express purpose being 'to stablish Christian quietness and unity among us, and to avoid contentious opinions'. Cromwell himself would have preferred a more distinctively Protestant formulary, whereas on the whole the articles take up a traditionalist position regarding the sacraments of baptism, the eucharist and penance, and are moderate and compromising on the use of ceremonies, images, the invocation of saints and prayers for the dead. But no mention is made of the remaining four sacramental rites, confirmation, holy order, matrimony and

9. Besides Dickens's *The English Reformation*, which is indispensable reading for the student, there is an admirable account of the course of events in G. R. Elton, *Reform and Reformation: England 1509–1558* (London, 1977).
10. It is G. R. Elton's opinion that 'so far as one can give a label to (Cromwell's) political philosophy it could be called Aristotelian' (*op. cit.*, 171). He was certainly familiar with the ideas of Marsiglio of Padua, a decided Aristotelian. But he had also read Machiavelli. He had too his fair share of anti-clerical feeling. As Elton remarks of Cromwell's vicegerency: 'High-sounding phrases notwithstanding, the Henrician Reformation signalled the triumph of the laity in the realm of religion' (199).
11. On Gardiner see J. A. Muller, *Stephen Gardiner and the Tudor Reaction* (London, 1926), and for a summary of the argument of *De vera obedientia*, P. E. Hughes, *The Reformation in England*, I (London, 1953), 337–41.

extreme unction, while in the definition of justification Lutheran phraseology is discernible.[12]

A further instance of the compromising spirit was provided a year later with the publication of a treatise entitled *The Institution of a Christian Man*, commonly known as the *Bishops' Book* in having in the main been the work of Cranmer and Bishop Foxe of Hereford, with the concurrence of the entire episcopate, although Hugh Latimer, a man of markedly Protestant outlook, had strong reservations. The book, which bore no explicit commendation from the king, refers to the sacraments as numbering seven, but at the same time justification is attributed exclusively to the merits of Christ, by whose passion and death 'all my sins and the sins also of them that do believe in him and follow him, be mortified and dead', though the obligation to perform good works thereafter is made plain. The Roman doctrine of purgatory is affirmed, but abuses of it are denounced, as too the notion 'that through the bishop of Rome's pardons souls might be clearly delivered out of purgatory and the pain of it'. Prayers for the dead are declared to be laudable.[13]

A significant move in the reformist direction was the order in the Royal Injunctions of 30 December 1538 for a copy of the Bible in English to be placed in every church so that it might be read by the parishioners. This move may be attributed in part to Cranmer, but also to Cromwell, who had long had a personal interest in the translation of the scriptures. The version adopted, the 'Great Bible', was basically William Tyndale's, formerly forbidden, as revised and completed by Miles Coverdale, who in Edward VI's reign became bishop of Exeter.[14] Cranmer's preface to the edition of April 1540 commended it to 'all manner of persons, of what state or condition soever they be', as 'the most precious jewel and most holy relic that remaineth on earth'. Nevertheless the bishops generally were critical of it, wanting it to be brought more closely into line with the Latin version. Moreover, a sharp turn back to the old religious position came with the passage through parliament in 1539 of the notorious Act of the Six Articles – 'the whip with six cords', as some said – which insisted rigidly on transubstantiation, communion in one kind only as necessary, clerical celibacy, the inviolability of vows of chastity, private masses and compulsory auricular confession. Savage penalties were attached – denial of transubstantiation, as heresy, meant death by burning – but it proved

12.  The text of the *Ten Articles* is to be found in C. Hardwick, *A History of the Articles of Religion* (Cambridge, 1851), 231–48 (39–59 contain introductory matter).

13.  The text is reprinted in C. Lloyd ed., *Formularies of Faith as set forth by Authority during the Reign of Henry VIII* (1825), 21–212.

14.  William Tyndale's translation of the New Testament was begun at Cologne in 1525, but before it was finished he had to flee to Worms, where it was printed in the following year. Subsequent editions were printed in Holland and copies soon reached England. His rendering of the Pentateuch was published at Antwerp in 1529–30. Afterwards he worked on the remainder of the Old Testament as well as revising the New. He also supplied prefaces and marginal notes bearing a strong Lutheran colour. For the production of his version he used Erasmus's Latin New Testament, the Vulgate and Luther's German version. He was burned as a heretic at Vilvorde in Holland in 1536. See C. Gray, *William Tyndale and the English Bible* (London, 1938) and S. L. Greenslade (ed.), *The Cambridge History of the Bible: The West from the Reformation to the Present Day* (Cambridge, 1963), 141–47. For a 'life' see D. Daniell, *William Tyndale, a Biography* (New Haven and London), 1994.

less severe in its operation. Cranmer, who on account of the chastity clause was obliged to conceal his wife, opposed the Bill with vigour in the Lords, yielding however when the king appeared in the House in person and pressed for its immediate adoption. This capitulation, though doubtless irreconcilable with the archbishop's true conscience, was not, it is to be feared, untypical of the man.

Conservative forces gained further ground with the publication in May 1543 of another extended doctrinal statement intended for lay instruction, *The Necessary Doctrine and Erudition of a Christian Man*, popularly known as the *King's Book* because of its express authorization by the monarch, who indeed was personally involved in its composition, besides furnishing it with a preface. Its obvious purpose was to put a stop to the spread of Protestant ideas, fully endorsing the provisions of the Six Articles statute. The actual drafting of the book – its style is felicitous – owed a good deal to the archbishop, but its standpoint was far removed from his own and represented a defeat for his policy.[15] The Lutheran touches in the *Bishop's Book*, the statements on the church for example, are mitigated, and all seven sacraments are expounded in the traditional way. The article on justification was entirely rewritten, with supplementary sections on faith, free will and good works. The part of man's freedom is recognized: 'Man hath free will also now after the fall of our first father Adam', a view pronounced to be scriptural. To say that 'we be justified by faith' is not to be taken as meaning that faith is 'separated from hope and charity, fear of God and repentance'. But a distinction is drawn between faith as intellectual assent and 'as it hath hope and charity, annexed and joined unto it'. The office of a priest is stated to consist

In true preaching and teaching the Word of God unto the people, in dispensing and ministering the sacraments of Christ, in consecrating and offering the blessed body and blood of Christ in the sacrament of the altar, in loosing and assoiling from sin such persons as be sorry and truly penitent for the same, and excommunicating such as be guilty in manifest crimes, and will not be reformed otherwise.

But the nomination of bishops is the king's right, while national churches are to be understood as having 'distinct and divers heads on earth', even though they compose nonetheless 'one holy catholic church'. Their unity 'standeth not by acknowledgement of one on earth over all churches', and no one church 'may or ought to challenge over another . . . any superiority or pre-eminence'. Rome's claims are declared flatly to be a 'usurpation'. All told, the book stood for 'Henrician', or a non-papal 'national' Catholicism, a religion, that is, which the plain man, for whom the book was intended, would at once recognize as Catholic even if some of its theological phraseology might not satisfy Roman orthodoxy.

The *King's Book*, then, evidently registers Henry's religious principles during the final years of his reign. Yet these were not wholly a time of reaction. Protestant beliefs made headway, not least among the upper ranks of society, and an influential party at court led by the Earl of Hertford (the Protector Somerset to be) made no secret of their interest in the new opinions. Much Protestant literature continued

15. A reprint of the *King's Book*, edited by T. A. Lacey, was published for the Church Historical Society in 1932 (London). For a careful discussion of it see Hughes, *op. cit.*, 46–57.

to be smuggled into the country from abroad, the English Bible was still available to be read, and the king's young son Edward was placed under tutors with known Protestant inclinations, while the archbishop was by now, in heart and mind, himself a Protestant. Certainly by 1546 he had come to accept justification by faith alone and had rejected transubstantiation. Plots to destroy him were uniformly unsuccessful, and the king, with a degree of indulgence he extended to no one else, retained confidence in him to the end. When Henry died on 28 January, 1547 Cranmer was at his bedside to afford him both spiritual and personal comfort.

## Thomas Cranmer

With the new reign, and power in the hands of the regency council under the new king's uncle, Edward Seymour, now Duke of Somerset, Thomas Cranmer came into his own. It was plain from the start that religious change could be delayed no longer. Men like Latimer, a divine of definitely Protestant outlook, as still more Hooper, the forerunner of puritanism, acquired prominence, while an influx of foreign reformers – such as Ochino, Vermigli, Bucer, Laski – fleeing either from the Roman Inquisition or the Augsburg Interim, brought with them both practical experience and clearcut views. Straight away Cranmer turned the liturgical studies which had long engaged him – even during Henry's latter years he had composed an English litany (1544) – to specific use, first (1548) in a Lutheran-influenced form of prayer to be introduced into the mass, and then (1549) a complete English prayer book. But before detailing these innovations and the trend of thinking they embody, we must take a rapid glance at Cranmer's earlier career and the shaping of his religious convictions.

Born in 1489 at Aslacton in Nottinghamshire, the second son of the local squire, he went to Cambridge in 1503, and seven or eight years later was elected to a fellowship at Jesus College. Ordination directed his thoughts to a more serious concern with theology and in time he became deeply learned in the subject (even as archbishop he devoted as many hours a day as he could to his books) although he was never to display any personal originality of mind as a thinker. But in 1529 a very unexpected change occurred in the fortunes of this rather retiring don when he was introduced to the king as a man with relevant opinions on the momentous issue of the royal divorce. Henry was so far impressed by this meeting as to engage him forthwith in his service, appointing him one of his chaplains, along with the archdeaconry of Taunton to sustain him. He also secured the patronage of the influential Boleyn family.

Further studious leisure was interrupted by the diplomatic missions on which the monarch despatched him, including one in 1532 to the Emperor Charles V, with instructions to make contact while in Germany with the Lutheran princes. It was on this embassy that he met and wedded, in spite of the celibacy to which as a priest he was committed, the niece of the Nuremberg reformer Andreas Osiander. Then suddenly in the same year undreamt of preferment was thrust on him by his nomination, on the death of Archbishop Warham, to the archbishopric of Canterbury and the primacy of all England, a promotion advancing him above the prelate who appeared, and assuredly considered himself to be, the most eligible for the great office, Stephen Gardiner of Winchester. Cranmer, however, was a man wholly without ambition of a political kind, and he accepted the distinction, and the heavy responsibilities accompanying it, with an uneasy heart. Long afterwards, at his trial, he declared that 'there was never a man come more unwillingly to a bishoprick than I did to that'. But consecrated he was on 30 March 1533, the king having seen to it that the necessary papal bulls were sent, although Cranmer circumvented the difficulty of the papal oath by making an express reservation to do nothing contrary to the law of God, the king's prerogative or the laws of the realm, and by swearing the oath before and not after that to the king. One of the first tasks to fall to him was that of pronouncing the annulment of the king's marriage to Katharine (as, subsequently, of two others of his numerous matrimonial ties). Henry's breach with Rome he of course endorsed entirely, ascribing to the monarch an authority superior to anything the pope could rightly claim. 'All Christian princes', he believed, though the actual words were penned in 1540, 'have committed to them immediately of God the whole cure of all their subjects, as well concerning the ministration of God's Word for the cure of souls as concerning the ministration of things political and of civil government.' The preamble to the Act in Restraint of Appeals and the Oath of Supremacy thus gave his conscience no trouble. His erastianism, although in fact no more extreme than that of Gardiner, was as thoroughgoing as that of the author of the *Defensor Pacis*, whose doctrine he echoes at point after point, even if we may doubt whether he ever supposed the monarch's *potestas jurisdictionis* could be extended at need to become a *potestas ordinis*.[16]

Cranmer's reformist interest may be traced back as far as the time of the publication of Erasmus's Greek Testament and Luther's Wittenberg *Theses*. The earliest principle to establish itself in his mind, in all likelihood under humanist influences, was that of the absolute primacy of scripture in the determination of Christian belief and doctrine. He had been educated in the old scholastic tradition, but it was the current return to the Fathers, and beyond them to the New Testament itself, which now stirred him. According to his first biographer he for three years 'applied his whole study to the scriptures', using the original Greek and Hebrew and seeking the plain or literal meaning in preference to that supplied by patristic and scholastic commentators.[17] Thus as an examiner in the divinity school he demanded from candidates a firsthand knowledge of the biblical texts. It was, too, by this same biblical criterion that he subsequently judged the matter of the royal divorce, holding that the original papal dispensation had contravened the unambiguous law of Leviticus, which he evidently took to be a moral and not merely a ceremonial prescription. But the scriptural principle carried him farther still, for how, he had to ask himself, did the claims of the papacy stand when seen in the light of the New Testament witness? The answer, he concluded, was manifest: the Bible did not confer supreme authority on the Roman pope; whereas, as he himself

16. An English translation of Marsiglio's book by William Marshall was issued under the patronage of Thomas Cromwell in 1535.
17. J. G. Nichols, *Narratives of the Days of the Reformation* (Camden Society, London, first series, LXXVII, 1859), 218–33.

judged, not only the Old Testament but the New as well pointed to the headship in spiritual affairs of the 'godly prince', the monarch – a conviction which settled in his conscience and to which to the end he strove to adhere, even if, under the papist sovereign Mary, to his ultimate confusion and undoing.

Cranmer was not a systematic theologian, and his output of purely theological writing, much of it, even then, in polemical form, is small;[18] consequently we have no consistent statement of his view of scripture and its inspiration or of the principles for its exegesis. What he does, rather, is to bring particular issues as they arise to the scriptural test. Of confirmation, for example, he says that 'there is no place in Scripture that declareth this sacrament to be instituted of Christ';[19] or, in regard to private celebration of the mass, he thinks it 'more agreeable to Scripture and the primitive Church that the first usage should be restored again, that the people should receive the sacrament with the priest'.[20] His insistence on the letter of scripture led him, besides, to discount the supposed authority attaching to 'unwritten traditions'. The treatise which bears the title *Confutation of Unwritten Verities* underwent considerable rearrangement by an anonymous editor, but that it is substantially Cranmer's in content and phrasing is plain enough.[21] The Bible he deems to be basically self-authenticating, yet he is ready to admit a degree of authority to patristic interpretations of it, and he himself quotes extensively from the Greek and Latin Fathers, as even at times from medieval writers. But this is because the Fathers themselves can be seen to acknowledge scripture as final. He affirms the role of the Spirit in guiding the church 'into all truth', but only in respect of the teaching which Christ himself had already imparted and for which the New Testament provides the objective witness. Had the apostles given instruction not mentioned therein then this could refer only to 'variable traditions, observations, and ceremonies, and outward rites and bodily exercises, which must certainly be kept, but which the church has power to alter, replace, or suppress'.[22] Always for what is essential to faith the Old and New Testaments are the sufficient authority.

On the other hand, for what is not essential express biblical authority is not requisite, so long as what is done – and the field envisaged here is that of church order and ceremonies – is not contrary to scripture; rather, what is permissible or impermissible has to be determined in accordance with circumstance. By the same token also not all things which were observed in the primitive church, even on the attestation of scripture, should be regarded as of obligation under the altered conditions of a later age. Precisely on what grounds Cranmer would allow this liberty of deciding is never made clear, and in reaching a practical decision on any given matter inconsistency may at least appear to arise. Notwithstanding, the

18. *The Remains of Thomas Cranmer*, edited by H. Jenkyns in 4 vols, were published at Oxford in 1833; *Writings and Disputations . . . relative to the Sacrament of the Lord's Supper and Miscellaneous Writings and Letters* were edited by J. E. Cox and published by the Parker Society, Cambridge, 1844–6 (referred to below as *Works*). An edition by C. H. H. Wright of Cranmer's *Defence of the True Doctrine of the Last Supper* was published in 1907 (London).
19. *Works*, II, 80.
20. II, 151.
21. II, 1–67.
22. II, 55.

distinction was one by which the reformed Church of England was to set much store. It was integral to the Elizabethan Settlement and to the long-sustained argument of Hooker's *Ecclesiastical Polity*. On it Cranmer himself, and Anglicanism as it eventually developed, stood and stands with Luther as against Calvin.

Again, with this readiness to concede that in things inessential a church has power and authority to establish its own rule and law – a principle, clearly, which recognizes the part of reason in the ordering of religion – goes Cranmer's respect for the secondary authority of the Fathers. Where they afford a unanimous or near unanimous testimony regard must be paid to them, even if not unconditionally. For the early church was in a sense a 'golden age', alike in faith and in piety. The ground for this respect for the past was that in Cranmer's eyes reformation did not mean innovation. The authentic Catholic doctrine and practice can and should be seen to have had the support of antiquity as well as, ultimately, scripture. He certainly could not admit to be heresy what had been taught and believed from the first age of the Catholic church.

But a profound concern for the scriptural basis of Christian doctrine did not in itself mean that Cranmer, who somewhere about 1520 had obtained a licence to read Lutheran writings, already being surreptitiously circulated in Cambridge,[23] was himself in any mind as yet to embrace Lutheran tenets, and we have no evidence that he was personally in touch with men like Barnes and Bilney. Where he did encounter Lutheran ideas at first hand and, it seems, imbibed them, was, suitably enough, in Germany. Even back in England rumour now had it that the king's emissary was himself a heretic, though during his first three years as archbishop he gave no definite indications of any declension from orthodoxy apart from his rejection of the pope. In a sermon at St Paul's Cross on 6 February 1536 he even went so far as to stigmatize the pope as Antichrist. In 1538, when a Lutheran delegation arrived from Germany with the object of reaching an agreement on a formulary of faith preparatory to that alliance with the Lutheran princes which Cromwell so desired, it was apparent that in Cranmer and most other bishops on the English side the Germans had a sympathetic audience. A consensus on the doctrine of justification was arrived at, even if with the slight modification that while men could be justified only by grace through faith, such faith itself demanded the performance of good works. The other outstanding issue, the dogma of transubstantiation, was sidestepped by a simple assertion of the real presence.

There is nothing to suggest that Cranmer was at all easily won over to the Lutheran teaching on justification *sola fide*. By nature cautious, he had all the scholar's scrupulosity in refraining from hasty conclusions and in doctrinal matters his thinking was always slow.

Yet the issue was one on which, given his biblicism, he would have felt bound to make up his mind. His extant 'Notes on Justification' provide ample evidence of the care with which he studied the question.[24] At what date he compiled these is by no means certain; that the manuscript is in his own hand, not that of his secretary, would seem to point to a relatively early date, although the actual positions stated imply definite conviction rather than tentative consideration. The

23.  J. Ridley, *Thomas Cranmer* (Oxford, 1962), 21.
24.  *Works*, II, 203–11.

notes themselves are brief, but they are supported by copious citations from the Bible, the Fathers and even the schoolmen. Cranmer is emphatic that justification is in no sense the work of man but of God only.[25] Human effort would never have sufficed to merit the remission of sin; Christ alone brought this about: he 'who was offered upon the cross for our sins, and rose again for our justification'.[26] And by works must be understood not merely external observances – 'ceremonials and judicials' – but also 'all manner of works of the law'.[27] Solely by faith do we 'know God's mercy and grace promised by his word (and that freely for Christ's death and passion's sake) and believe the same, and being truly penitent, we by faith receive the same'.[28] This teaching reappears in the *Ten Articles*, the *Bishops' Book* and the *Forty-Two Articles* of 1553. But the fullest exposition is that furnished by the 'Homily of Salvation' in the *Book of Homilies* issued in 1547, and is as fine a statement of this classic Reformation doctrine as may be found anywhere:[29] it has fittingly been described as 'one of the cardinal documents of the Reformation as England knew it'.[30] In it Cranmer is at pains to stress the one and only ground of justification as God's mercy and the merits of Christ's redeeming work.

> Our justification doth come freely, by the mere mercy of God, and of so great and free mercy that, whereas all the world was not able of their selves to pay any part toward their ransom, it pleased our heavenly Father, of his infinite mercy, without our desert or deserving, to prepare for us the most precious jewel of Christ's body and blood, whereby our ransom might be fully paid, the law fulfilled, and his justice fully satisfied.[31]

This great truth is embraced by faith, but not so that faith itself becomes a 'good work', 'for that were to count ourselves to be justified by some act or virtue that is within ourselves', whereas 'we must renounce all our said virtues of faith, hope, and charity, and all other virtues and good deeds, which we either have done, or shall do, or can do'.[32] But if faith alone is necessary it is as 'an earnest trust and confidence in God', 'a true, lively, and Christian faith', not a mere 'dead belief'.[33] It is this alone which brings forth good works, such indeed being necessary fruit of faith.

On the doctrine of the church Cranmer has little direct to say. Like all the

25. II, 203, 206.
26. II, 209.
27. II, 207.
28. II, 210.
29. These homilies, twelve in number, were ordered 'to be declared and read by all parsons, vicars, and curates, every Sunday in their churches where they have the cure'. About half of them are devoted to moral exhortation, but the first five at least are a forthright expression of the 'new learning'. An earlier book of the sort had been prepared by Cranmer in 1542, but not printed. The 1547 book was reprinted at Oxford in 1859. The 'Homily of Salvation' is included in T. H. L. Parker, *The English Reformers* (Library of Christian Classics, XXVI) (Philadelphia and London, 1966), 262–82.
30. Hughes, *op. cit.*, II, 96.
31. Parker, *The English Reformers*, 264.
32. *Ibid.*, 267.
33. *Ibid.*, 270 ('Even the devils knew and believed that Christ was born of a virgin', *etc.*) The words, 'an earnest trust and confidence in God' are from the homily 'Of a True, Lively, and Christian Faith'.

reformers he is driven to distinguish between the church as it had become in his time – the Roman institution, so obviously corrupt and false in its claims – and the 'true' church as 'the holy, elected people of God'.[34] But where is the latter to be found? Cranmer was no anabaptist sectarian and could not therefore look on it as confined to a mere band of the visibly regenerate. On the other hand, it was no real answer to say that the true church is invisible. In an ultimate sense, no doubt, invisible it is: those who truly are in Christ can be known to God alone. But in the article of 1553 that dealt with the church it is spoken of as visible, 'a congregation of faithful men, in which the pure Word of God is preached, and the Sacraments be duly administered according to Christ's ordinance', phraseology unmistakably Lutheran in tone.[35] The visible church however can err and has done so; yet 'truth it is indeed', Cranmer would assure us, 'that the church doth never wholly err; for ever in most darkness God shineth unto his elect, and in the midst of iniquity he governeth them so with his holy word and Spirit, that the gates of hell prevail not against them'.[36] One nevertheless may ask where precisely, and how, is this final inerrancy maintained. To reply, as Cranmer does, that 'God hath preserved a good number, secret to himself, in his true religion', is an assertion of faith but an evasion of the difficulty. How the 'truth' of the church is recognized is, once more, by reference to the word of God. Such a church 'containeth itself within God's Word, not that deviseth new articles contrary to God's Word'.[37] The church, that is to say, is identifiable only in relation to the gospel. But behind this, to a more positive, as indeed more essentially scriptural, conception Cranmer does not go.

In regard to the church's ministry Cranmer had given up, long before he composed the ordinal of 1550, the belief that holy orders constituted a sacrament – at any rate in the strict and exclusive sense of medieval teaching – considering that there was no more specific promise of grace 'in the committing of the ecclesiastical office, than in the committing of the civil office'.[38] But the ordinal leaves the historic threefold ministry intact, claiming indeed that

it is evident unto all men, diligently reading holy Scripture, and ancient authors, that from the Apostles' time there hath been these orders of Ministers in Christ's Church: Bishops, Priests, and Deacons: which offices were evermore had in reverent estimation, that no man by his own private authority might presume to execute any of them, except he be first called, tried, examined, and known to have such qualities as were requisite to the same: And also by public prayer, with imposition of hand, approved and admitted thereunto . . .

adding that 'these orders should be continued, and reverently used, and esteemed, in this Church of England'.[39] This fact was of the utmost importance for the

34. *Works*, I, 376.
35. Article 20 of the *Thirty-Nine Articles*. Cf. E. J. Bicknell, *A Theological Introduction to the Thirty-Nine Articles* (3rd edn revised by H. J. Carpenter, London, 1955), 229ff.
36. *Works*, I, 377.
37. I, 378.
38. II, 116.
39. *The First and Second Prayer Books of Edward VI* (with introduction by E. C. S. Gibson; rev., with additional introduction by E. C. Ratcliff, Everyman Library, London, 1949), 438.

development of a distinctively English, or Anglican, type of reformed Christianity, episcopacy having been abandoned by both the German and the Swiss churches. Although certainly influenced by the *De ordinatione legitima* of Martin Bucer, who had settled in England at Cranmer's own invitation, it was a moderate and even conservative document, modelled on the Sarum pontifical but greatly simplified and with the medieval ceremonial drastically curtailed.[40] In the first ordinal the delivery of the 'instruments', that is the paten and chalice to priests and the pastoral staff to bishops, was retained, but in the second the Bible only is given, to bishops and priests alike. (In both ordinals the New Testament is the instrument of the deacons.) This change is significant as pointing Cranmer's concern for a biblical theory of the ministry as against the older exaltation of the *sacerdotium*.

The fact of Cranmer's erastianism, already alluded to, requires some further discussion. To modern liberal ways of thinking it was extreme, elevating the civil authority – then an absolute and wilful monarch – to the point where it assumes almost a spiritual potency.[41] In consequence the ecclesiastical office is not merely subjugated to the temporal, it appears to become dependent on it for the very exercise of its functions. This has often been urged against Cranmer as yet another proof of his craven subservience to his royal master, or, even worse, to those who, in Edward VI's reign, wielded power in his name. R. W. Dixon, not a deliberately hostile critic, speaks of him as 'needful to the men of violence and craft who now held in their hands the destinies of the country and the Church'. 'He became', he says, 'their scribe, their tool, their voice.'[42] 'He acquiesced', says a more recent biographer, 'in every change of religious doctrine during the twenty years in which he, almost alone among the leading statesmen, survived every turn of official policy.'[43]

That Cranmer was indecisive and pliable cannot be denied, but he was not merely a time-server, and assuredly not a coward. The temporal supremacy was for him, however mistakenly, a fundamental principle, of hardly less weight than his belief in the primacy of scripture. We now may wonder why and how he could have held so tenaciously to this conviction, for his personal sincerity is not – though sometimes in spite of appearances – to be doubted. He was unreservedly anti-papal, and wholly a patriot. But without the pope what alternative of an external authority was there, especially if the image of the 'godly prince' were itself, as he was

---

40. On Bucer's liturgical influence see F. E. Brightman, *The English Rite* (2 vols, London, 1915), II, 932–1017. In Bucer's estimation there were only two kinds of ministry, 'according to the institution of the Holy Spirit', namely that which related to the ministry of the word, sacraments and discipline and which belonged properly to bishops and priests, and that which pertained to the care of the poor and was committed to deacons. Cf. C. H. Smyth, *Thomas Cranmer and the Reformation under Edward VI* (Cambridge, 1926), 229ff.

41. *Works*, II, 117.

42. *A History of the Church of England from the Abolition of the Roman Jurisdiction* (2nd, rev. edn, London, 1893), I, 155f.

43. Ridley, *op. cit.*, 66. Or as A. G. Dickens puts it: 'He saw in the strong hand of monarchy the nation's hope of vanquishing false doctrine, aristocratic faction, popular rebellion and foreign invasion. With his eyes wide open he accepted for the English Church a new bondage in place of the old bondage of Rome' (*The English Reformation*, 168f.)

persuaded, so plainly scriptural? 'To blame Cranmer for being an erastian', it has been remarked, 'is as reasonable as to blame him for living in the first half of the sixteenth century.' [44] At the end the archbishop found himself in a fatal dilemma, caught between the same two principles he hitherto had judged coincident, but which now were starkly antagonistic. The tragedy of his martyrdom was thus inevitable, since of the two he chose that which, in his inmost conscience, he could not deny without abjuring the very truth for which the Protestant Reformation itself stood.

### 'The True and Catholic Doctrine of the Sacrament'

Cranmer's eucharistic doctrine has been the subject of prolonged debate, and especially his view of the 'true', 'spiritual' or 'sacramental' presence of Christ in the Supper. Thus even at his formal examination in St Mary's, Oxford, before James Brooke, bishop of Gloucester, in September 1555, it was observed by his interrogator, Dr Martin:

> Ye say you have God's word with you, yea, and all the doctors. I would here ask but one question of you, whether God's mercy be contrary to itself, and whether the doctors teach doctrine contrary to themselves, or no? For you, Master Cranmer, have taught in this high sacrament of the altar three contrary doctrines, and yet you pretended in every one *verbum Domini*.

To which the former archbishop made reply: 'Nay, I taught but two contrary doctrines in the same',[45] an answer which, so far from clearing up confusion, has rather added to it ever since. So again and again the questions have been raised: When did Cranmer give up transubstantiation? Was he at any time a Lutheran? Did he finally embrace teaching usually attributed to Zwingli, and is it this which is presupposed in at any rate his second Prayer Book? Or was his real position consistently neither the one nor the other, but something closely akin to the 'mediating' stance of Martin Bucer? Although, as we have said, Cranmer was not a great or an original theological thinker, he nonetheless had a good theological mind fed by wide reading, patristic, medieval and contemporary, and to arrive at an understanding of his doctrine a variety of sources must be drawn upon, namely the two liturgies issued during the reign of Edward VI, his printed controversial writings, in particular *A Defence of the True and Catholic Doctrine of the Sacrament of the Body and Blood of Our Saviour Christ* of 1550, with his *Answer* to Bishop Gardiner's rejoinder, and certain manuscript writings in the British Library and the library of Corpus Christi College, Cambridge.[46]

44. Smyth, *op. cit.*, 30.
45. *Works*, II, 217f.
46. MSS Royal, 7 B XI and XII; *Collectiones ex S. Script. et Patris* MS 102, foll. 151–93, and 113, foll. 345–89. Gardiner's tract was entitled *An Explication and Assertion of the True Catholic Faith touching the most blessed Sacrament of the Altar with confutation of a book Written against the same*, published soon after Cranmer's *Defence*. The archbishop countered this with *An Answer unto a crafty and sophistical Cavillation by Stephen Gardiner . . . against the true and godly doctrine of the most holy Sacrament* (1551), to which Gardiner in turn replied (1552). Cranmer's final response to Gardiner was never finished.

The main difficulties are that Cranmer's eucharistic theology was of slow development, that the expression of his thinking is often tentative and guarded, and that at times he appears to be actually contradicting what he has said elsewhere. Unfortunately discussion of his views has been too eager to affix to them labels that can be easily comprehended, without always giving careful enough consideration to what really it was that he was seeking to articulate. He himself once said, 'I have come to the conclusion that the writings of every man must be read with discrimination',[47] and of his own literary work this is eminently true.

Moreover, before attempting to unravel the meaning of Cranmer's frequently veiled and even evasive statements, it is important to see them in their broader theological context. If his understanding of the eucharistic presence took years to mature, his basic concepts of the nature of salvation, justification, grace and remission of sins were reached much sooner. Redemption, he was convinced, was wrought solely by the 'oblation and sacrifice' of Calvary. In his own eloquent phrases:

> Our heavenly Father can by no means be pleased with [us] again, but by the sacrifice and death of his only-begotten Son, whereby God had made a perpetual amity and peace with us, doth pardon the sins of them that believe in him, maketh them his children, and giveth them to his first-begotten Son Christ, to be incorporate into him, to be saved by him, and to be made heirs of heaven with him.[48]

Accordingly the late medieval teaching on the sacrifice of the mass impaired for him as for all others of the reformers the uniqueness of that 'one oblation of himself once offered' as a 'full, perfect, and sufficient sacrifice, oblation, and satisfaction, for the sins of the whole world'. The eucharist was not and could not be in any sense a repetition of that sacrifice. On the contrary, as he wrote in 1547, the oblation and sacrifice of Christ in the mass, 'is not so called, because Christ indeed is there offered and sacrificed by the priest and the people, . . . but . . . because it is *a memory and representation* of that very true sacrifice and immolation which was before made upon the cross'.[49] Hence his preference for a table instead of an altar:

> For the use of an altar is to make a sacrifice upon it: the use of a table is to serve for men to eat upon. Now when we come to the Lord's board, what do we come for? To sacrifice Christ again, and to crucify him again; or to feed upon him that was once only crucified and offered up for us?[50]

Hence too the all-important change of emphasis from the mass as a sacrificial rite to the communion service as a feeding on Christ's flesh and a drinking of his blood spiritually.[51] On this interpretation of it the service clearly sets forth the truth that justification is by faith alone and by no work whatsoever of man.

But, it might be asked, is the eucharist's sacrificial aspect sufficiently portrayed by describing it only as a 'memory and representation'? That it is a memorial is obviously not open to question in view of the gospel words of institution, 'Do this

47. *Zurich Letters* (ed. H. Robinson) (Parker Society, Cambridge, 1845), III, 14.
48. *Defence* (ed. Wright), 27.
49. *Works*, II, 150.
50. II, 524f.
51. Cf. *Defence*, 244.

in remembrance of me', yet Cranmer hardly seems to see more in it than a *figurative* representation of the Lord's death, a symbol appealing to the imagination.

> The priest should declare the death and passion of Christ, and all the people should look upon the cross in the mount of Calvary, and see Christ hanging, and the blood flowing out of his side into their wounds to heal all their sores; and the priest and people all together should laud and thank instantly the chirurgeon and physician of their souls.[52]

He fails, apparently, to grasp the idea of it as an objective representation of the sacrificial death itself through the operation of the Holy Spirit, preoccupied as he is with the subjective or human aspect, with what the remembrance of Christ's can and should stimulate us to do. So, we are told, 'the humble confession of all penitent hearts, their acknowledging of Christ's benefits, their thanksgiving for the same, their faith and consolation in Christ, their humble submission and obedience to God's will and commandments, is a sacrifice of laud and praise'.[53] It would, however, be fair to urge that, even granting this subjective emphasis in Cranmer's thinking, the 'sacrifice of praise and thanksgiving' and the 'oblation of ourselves, our souls and bodies' would have been understood by him to depend absolutely on Christ's original self-offering for us, apart from which our own self-oblation would be worthless. It is therefore, we should say, the unique, 'objective', self-offering of Christ which the sacrament of the Supper recalls and represents, even though Cranmer himself is content to describe it simply as a 'representation'. For what, rather, he is impelled to stress is the 'eating and drinking' whereby the believer is nourished spiritually by Christ's body and blood, a nourishment not only for the individual but for Christians corporately. For in this sacrament, he points out, 'all faithful Christians [be] spiritually turned into the body and blood of Christ, and so be joined to Christ, as St Paul saith: "We be one bread and one body, as many as be partakers of one bread and one cup".'[54]

At this point of course the question arises of the *manner* in which the presence is to be conceived; it is also where we come up against the real difficulty in interpreting Cranmer's thought, since to determine how, precisely, it came to shape itself on this subject has not proved possible. By the summer of 1538 he was disposed to doubt transubstantiation,[55] although adhering the while to a doctrine of the real presence, thus suggesting that his ideas on the matter had by then taken a Lutheran direction, in which in fact he would seem to have persisted until 1546 or later. Yet to speak confidently of Cranmer as a Lutheran during this period in his sacramental doctrine would be misleading; certainly so if by that designation it is to be inferred that the archbishop actually embraced the theory of consubstantiation, a scholastic concept which even Luther himself never explicitly adopted.[56]. What

---

52. *Works*, I, 359.
53. I, 352.
54. I, 42.
55. II, 375.
56. Cf. Smyth, *op. cit*, 50–9. Among those who have maintained that Cranmer was at first a Lutheran are (besides his opponent Gardiner and John Foxe the martyrologist): Gilbert Burnet (*A History of the Reformation in England* [1679–1714]), John Strype (*Memorials of Thomas Cranmer*, 1694), Henry Jenkyns, A. F. Pollard (*Thomas Cranmer and the English Reformation, 1489–1556*, London, 1904), and Darwell Stone (*A History of the Doctrine of the Eucharist*, 2 vols, London, 1909, II, 125–9, 177–84).

Cranmer held in this, the earlier phase of his disillusionment with the traditional dogma, was a doctrine of the real or substantial presence, a view which he afterwards spoke of disdainfully as an 'error' like that of transubstantiation or of 'the sacrifice propitiatory of the priests in the mass'.[57] In any case a rational explanation of how the 'real' presence subsisted there he made no attempt to supply. To him it was a mystery of faith, to be accepted simply as such. His change of mind seems to have come about under the guidance of the bishop of London, Nicholas Ridley, who himself had been much affected by study of the ninth-century monk Ratramnus's *De corpore et sanguine Domini*, which in turn caused him 'to search more diligently and exactly both the Scriptures and the writings of the old ecclesiastical fathers in this matter'.[58] Discussions on the subject with Ridley may have dated in the first instance from 1546, or at all events before the end of 1548, when the archbishop spoke in the House of Lords debate on the Sacrament (14–18 December). Cranmer by then had definitely committed himself to a theory of the presence as 'spiritual' only, since in the *Order of Communion* published in 1548 he stated that 'God doth vouchsafe in a sacrament and mystery to give us his said body and blood spiritually: to feed and drink upon'.[59] The question is whether from this time onwards Cranmer was not in truth moving still farther to the theological 'left' and into Zwinglianism, as a number of modern scholars have firmly maintained.[60]

Those who uphold this opinion are disposed to attribute the change to the influence of the Polish reformer Jan Laski, or à Lasco, who stayed with the archbishop at Lambeth in the autumn of 1548, and without doubt statements of Cranmer's can easily be cited which on the face of it have a Zwinglian aspect: 'The Spirit and the body are contrary', 'Christ is in the world in his divinity, but not in his humanity', 'The change is inward, not in the bread, but in the Receiver'.[61] Yet in view of his well-known concern to find a doctrinal platform on which Protestants could unite, a standpoint on a matter of the highest theological import so objectionable to the Lutherans would seem very unlikely to have been urged by him. Hence the argument that his mature position, at which he arrived after rejecting the idea of a 'real' or 'substantial' presence, was essentially a mediating one, approximating closely to Bucer's.[62]

But, let us repeat, it is better to read Cranmer himself – a scholar of independent judgement – with an open mind than to attempt to 'place' him according to some predefined classification. In a written *Explicatio* as to whether Christ is really present in the sacrament, prepared for the Oxford disputation of 1555, he states

---

57. *Works*, I, 374.
58. *The Works of Nicholas Ridley*, ed. H. Christmas (Parker Society, Cambridge, 1843), 206.
59. *The Liturgies of Edward VI*, ed. J. Ketley (Parker Society, Cambridge 1844), 3.
60. Notably Gregory Dix, *The Shape of the Liturgy* (London, 1945) and in the *Church Quarterly Review*, cxlv (1947–8), 145–76, and cxlvi (1948), 44–60 (in reply to G. B. Timms), *Dixit Cranmer et Non Timuit* (London, 1946); see also C. C. Richardson, *Zwingli and Cranmer on the Eucharist* (Evanston, Illinois, 1949).
61. Cf. Richardson, *op. cit.*, 20ff.
62. So C. H. Smyth – although he designates Cranmer's position by the absurd name of 'Suvermerianism' (*op. cit*, 23f.) – and Timms (*op. cit.*).

categorically that 'If ye understand by this word "really", *re ipsa*, "in very deed and effectually", so Christ, by grace and efficacy of his passion, is indeed and truly present to all his true and holy members,'[63] present, that is, not only in his deity but in his risen and glorified humanity. For as Cranmer averred later, at his examination: 'I believe, that whoso eateth and drinketh that sacrament, Christ is within them, whole Christ, his nativity, passion, resurrection and ascension.'[64] But this presence, he insists, is a 'true' presence through being a 'spiritual' one, not a substantial, corporal or natural presence, inasmuch as substantially, corporally and naturally Christ in his human nature is with his Father in heaven. In that sense indeed Christ is *absent* from the Supper. So in his *Answer* to Gardiner Cranmer explains the twofold nature of the rite thus:

> In the sacrament or true ministration thereof be two parts, the earthly and the heavenly: the earthly is the bread and wine, the other is Christ himself: the earthly is without us, the heavenly is within us: the earthly is eaten with our mouths, and carnally feedeth our bodies; the heavenly is eaten without inward man, and spiritually feedeth the same: the earthly feedeth us but for a time, the heavenly feedeth us for ever.[65]

For the effect, he continues, of 'godly eating',

> is the communication of Christ's body, and the wine the communication of his blood, but to the faithful receiver, and not to the dumb creatures of bread and wine, under whose forms the catholic faith teacheth that the body and blood of Christ invisibly is hidden.[66]

It is in those only who worthily receive 'the outward sacrament'. As the bread and wine are consumed outwardly, so the body of Christ is received inwardly by faith.

The doubt left in the reader's mind is whether this view does not in fact throw all the emphasis on the subjective attitude of the communicant, thus amounting to pure receptionism: that is, that the presence is 'real' only in the mind of the faithful recipient at the moment of his reception of the sacrament. Such an assessment of Cranmer's teaching is possible, inasmuch as the case for an objective presence – in the sacrament as given, that is, as well as received – he seems not to consider, being satisfied that 'evil men do not eat the very body and drink the very blood of Christ'.[67] What he fails to make clear is whether the communicant is to know that in the bread broken and the wine outpoured Christ truly is offered by the Spirit, even though, where faith is lacking, he is not received. Cranmer may have believed this himself, but his words somehow always fall short of actually saying so, as certain of his own contemporaries were quick to perceive: for example, during the Lords' debate in December 1548 Bishop Holbeach of Lincoln pinpointed the matter when he asked 'whether the body is in the sacrament or in the receiver?'

On the whole, though, despite much prosiness and prolixity in Cranmer's eucharistic writings, the doctrine conveyed is not obscure. Where ambiguity does lie is in its liturgical expression, especially in the first prayer book; although there,

63. *Works*, I, 395.
64. II, 213.
65. I, 337. For further discussion see P. Brooks, *Thomas Cranmer's Doctrine of the Eucharist* (London, 1965).
66. I, 36.
67. I, 13.

understandably, it could serve, and was indeed intended to serve, the practical end of a reasonable comprehension of diverse opinions. The second prayer book is more explicit and leaves little room for any other interpretation of the eucharistic presence than what Cranmer had stated at length in the *Defence* and the *Answer*.

## The beginnings of Anglicanism

If Thomas Cranmer was not, in all accuracy, the architect of Anglicanism, it was he, surely, who laid its foundations, the foundation-stone itself, one could say, being the Book of Common Prayer, a publication which, the Authorized Version of the Bible alone apart, has done more than anything else to determine the historic character and ethos of Anglican faith and piety. Yet in claiming that Cranmer set out the basis of Anglicanism one has to remind oneself that the full portent of his work was by him largely unforeseen. He desired, most earnestly, a reformed Christianity in England, and strove for much of his life to bring it about, but it cannot be said that he began with any clear plan or principle of procedure, let alone an overall conception of what precisely he would wish to see result. For that, probably, the times were too turbulent, the oscillation of government policy too sudden and extreme. Nor was he a born leader, whether in thought or in action. By no means without deep convictions, he yet tended ever to await events, to accommodate and to compromise. His peculiar talent, however, was as a liturgist. His sense of the nature, and in particular the requisite 'tone', of public worship was all but unerring, his one weakness perhaps being an excessively homiletic or didactic propensity. But the felicity of his language has gained and merited the highest praise; so mellifluous indeed is it that one is apt to overlook what is vague, ambiguous or questionable behind it. Yet, as a twentieth-century Roman Catholic writer, Hilaire Belloc, has put it: 'Cranmer constructs with a success only paralleled by the sonnets of Shakespeare.'

The archbishop's practical interest in liturgy was of long standing, going back, it would appear, at least to the days of his visit to Germany and his personal contacts with Lutherans. It was spurred also by the editions of ancient liturgies then coming from the presses – the Greek liturgies of St John Chrysostom, of St Basil and of the Presanctified were published at Rome in 1520, while Latin versions of that of St Chrysostom, one of them from the hand of Erasmus, were also soon made available. With the medieval uses, and especially that of Sarum he was of course thoroughly familiar, while from Lutheran sources came numerous *Kirchenordnungen*, or 'Church Orders', printed between 1527 and 1545, one of which, 'A Simple and Religious Consultation' (*Simplex et pia deliberatio*), was published in Latin in 1545, with two English editions following in 1547 and 1548.[68]

68. The 'Consultation of Hermann of Cologne', on the basis of which a Lutheran reformation was to be introduced in the diocese of Cologne on the initiative of Archbishop Hermann von Wied himself, was the joint work of Melanchthon and Bucer, and brought about a reconciliation between Wittenburg and Strassburg, despite certain reservations on the part of Luther himself. It was from the 'Consultation' that Cranmer derived his *Order of Communion* of 1548.

Its pattern is Lutheran, even though its eucharistic theology is to all intents Bucerian. Moreover, from Roman sources came the *Breviarium Romanum nuper reformatum* of the Spanish cardinal Quiñones in 1535, with the start of a further revision in the following year.[69]

Cranmer's early experiments in liturgical reform comprise two Latin schemes, one Lutheran in type, and dating from 1538, the other on the lines of Quiñones' revision and composed sometime between 1543 and 1546.[70] But the first complete liturgical scheme in English was the compilation which bore the title *The Booke of Common Prayer and Administration of the Sacramentes, and other Rites and Ceremonies of the Churche after the use of the Churche of England*, and which was ordered to be used throughout the land from Whitsunday 1549.[71] A single volume containing all the church services was a novelty, but its skill in combining the old with the new is remarkable. Cranmer's aims were partly doctrinal, to increase the scriptural component and to eliminate everything suggestive of medieval superstition; partly practical, to provide a simplified, vernacular and genuinely congregational form of public worship. The medieval daily offices were reduced to two, a morning service created by a fusion of the old services of mattins and lauds, and an evening service similarly compounded of vespers and compline. Traditional practices such as 'kneeling, crossing, holding up of hands, knocking upon the breast, and other gestures' were left optional, as also was auricular confession, concerning which a paragraph was inserted at the end of one of the exhortations at communion: such, it said, as were satisfied with a general confession were not to be offended at those who preferred auricular and private confession to a priest, and *vice versa*. On the other hand, the petition in the litany seeking divine deliverance form 'the tyranny of the Bishop of Rome and all his detestable enormities' was retained, while the traditional practice of elevating the host, reserving of the sacrament for purposes of adoration, veneration of images and so forth were excluded. The communion service was still referred to as the mass, its framework being, more or less, that of the old service, though with Lutheran modifications in the shape of exhortations, communion devotions and an unvarying post-communion collect. Thanksgiving is rendered for 'the wonderful grace and virtue' of the saints, including 'the glorious and most blessed Virgin Mary', and in the prayer of consecration a clause was added for the sanctification of the elements by the Holy Spirit and the words 'that they may be unto us the body and blood of Thy most dearly beloved Son Jesus Christ'. The words used at the administration of the sacrament are: 'The body (or blood) of our Lord Jesus Christ which was shed for thee preserve thy body and soul unto everlasting life.' It is directed that wine be mixed with water at the offertory, and that the *Benedictus* and *Agnus Dei* be sung. The traditional mass vestments are also ordered to be used.

69. An edition of Quiñones' breviary by J. Wickham Legg was printed at Cambridge in 1888. See too the same editor's *The Second Recension of the Quignon Breviary* (Henry Bradshaw Society, XXXV [1908] and XLII [1912]).

70. See J. Wickham Legg, ed., *Cranmer's Liturgical Projects* (Henry Bradshaw Society, I; 1915).

71. Printed in *The Liturgies of Edward VI* (see note 59 above).

The influence of Lutheran forms in the baptismal office is fairly obvious, but the familiar aspect of the service, with anointing and the sign of the cross and the use of the chrisom, or white baptismal veil, remained. The whole book was clearly intended as a means of comprehending both the Catholic reformists and those who desired more far-reaching change.

To what extent could its success in this regard be expected? Stephen Gardiner, by declaring his belief that the new communion service involved no denial of transubstantiation, did nothing to allay the misgivings of Protestants like Hooper, who in a letter to Bullinger criticized the book as 'inadequate and ambiguous, even in some parts manifestly impious'. For them the reforms did not go nearly far enough. The papists for their part also disliked it for what they sensed to be its implicit Protestantism, and in the south-west of England it was the occasion of a serious uprising. That a further and more thoroughgoing revision would have to be undertaken was plain, repugnant though this was to Cranmer's own feelings. Pressure for 'the more perfecting of the said order', in other words, for its quite overt Protestantizing, became too strong to be resisted, especially now that the hand of the Protestant 'left' had been considerably strengthened by the accession to power of the rapacious John Dudley, newly created Duke of Northumberland, in place of Somerset, who had been imprisoned. Cranmer, although not eager for fresh changes, had no stomach for open resistance. Furthermore he had himself submitted the book for detailed examination and comment to Martin Bucer, now installed at Cambridge, and the latter's characteristically long-winded *Censura*, or report, was completed early in January 1551. He found himself, he admitted, in the main satisfied with the book, but listed numerous reservations on particular points, notably the rubrics at the communion service, especially that on the wearing of the eucharistic vestments, the wording of the consecration prayer and the inclusion of a petition for the souls of the departed in the prayer for the church. The Italian immigrant, Peter Martyr Vermigli, who was likewise asked for his opinion, agreed with Bucer in general, but added his own objection to reservation for the sick.

The new prayer book, which was adopted by parliament in 1552 (there is no evidence it was ever brought before convocation), clearly reveals the effect of these criticisms. Zwinglian ideas, championed among the bishops by Hooper, who now occupied the see of Gloucester, were in the ascendant. The earlier book was declared by parliament to be indeed 'agreeable to the word of God and the primitive church', but doubts, it was alleged, had arisen through 'curiosity' and the compilation should therefore be explained and improved. The process of 'more perfecting' turned out to be drastic. The canon of the 1549 communion service, based as it was on the medieval form, was broken into three separate parts, the prayers for the church being brought forward to a place immediately after the offertory sentences, the prayer of consecration significantly reworded, and the prayer of oblation (with the phrase implying the mediation of angels dropped) shortened and inserted after the administration. The 1549 words of administration were deleted and replaced by 'Take and eat this, in remembrance that Christ died for thee, and feed on him in thy heart, by faith with thanksgiving', and 'Drink this in remembrance that Christ's blood was shed for thee, and be thankful', expressions which apparently indicate

Zwinglian doctrine. The word 'altar', along with 'mass', was struck out and the eucharistic vestments prohibited. No provision was made for the anointing of the sick or for reservation.

How far the book embodied Cranmer's personal views and wishes has been a good deal discussed, positive evidence one way or the other being lacking, but Hooper's voice was influential with the Privy Council, as too was John Knox's, who in a sermon protested before the king against the rubric directing the people to kneel to receive communion. His objection indeed was so far heeded by the Council that it inserted, purely on its own authority, a further rubric – the so-called 'Black Rubric' – denying that any adoration 'is done, or ought to be done, either unto the sacramental bread and wine there bodily received, or unto any real and essential presence there being of Christ's natural flesh and blood', words manifestly aimed at excluding the doctrine of the real presence. Although Cranmer himself had refused to modify the original rubric on kneeling, his official responsibility for the revised prayer book as a whole is unquestionable. Important amendments were to be made a few years later, after the accession of Elizabeth I, but the 1552 liturgy is in substance that which the Church of England has used until the revisions and innovations of modern times.

The worship of the reformed *Ecclesia Anglicana*, which thus may fairly be described as Cranmer's achievement, needed however a doctrinal platform more specific than the ancient creeds and stating its beliefs as they related to current issues of controversy. This likewise the archbishop sought to provide in the *Forty-two Articles* which received the royal signature on 12 June 1553. Their express aim, according to their official title (in Grafton's imprint) was 'for avoiding of controversy in opinions, and the establishment of a godly concord, in certain matters of religion'. The further statement, that they had been 'agreed on by the Bishops and other learned men in the Synod of London' was entirely false, since convocation had not passed them and they were without formal ecclesiastical authority, the body responsible for reviewing and recommending the articles being in all probability the commission of thirty-two divines and laymen appointed for the purpose of revising the canon law which produced the *Reformatio Legum Ecclesiasticarum*. Behind them lay the series of *Thirteen Articles*, based on the *Augsburg Confession*, drawn up by Cranmer at the time of the conference with Lutheran divines in 1538 but never published. It is apparent from the list of their contents that they were not advanced as a systematic formulary of belief (only *certain* matters of religion' were touched on), and in seeking to avoid 'controversy in opinions' their use was evidently practical and provisional only. Thus although the first of the articles gives a summary statement on the Trinity, there is no exposition of the doctrine of Christ's divinity, and no article on the Holy Spirit. The fifth article declares the sufficiency of scripture but makes no allusion to the canon and provides no list of accepted books. In general the articles were mediating, and meant to be as comprehensive as possible in the circumstances.

Extremists at either end of the scale are excluded: both the medievalists, papists and scholastic theologians, and the anabaptist radicals. Articles 12, 13, 23, 26, 29 and 30 expressly condemn the doctrines of the 'School authors' concerning merit, works of supererogation, purgatory and pardons, grace *ex opere operato*, transubstantiation and the 'sacrifice of Masses'. Article 36 rejects the claims of the pope, while Articles 20 and 22 deny the infallibility both of the Church of Rome and of general councils. On the other side the anabaptists come in for sweeping censure. It is true that they are referred to by name only twice, but their alleged errors regarding the doctrines of the Trinity and the Person of Christ (Articles 1–4 and 7), free will (8–10), antinomianism (14 and 15), the authority of scripture (5), infant baptism, ecclesiastical discipline (20 and 32), the nature of the resurrection and the future life (39 and 40), the millennium (41), the salvation of all men (43) and the authority of the state (36–38) are all condemned. Yet if the tone of the articles is rasping and polemical they showed, as Dixon said, a surprisingly comprehensive and moderate spirit: 'the broad, soft touch of Cranmer lay upon them'. Although both anti-Roman and anti-radical, their aim was concord, and they eschew the precise definitions, even in such a matter as justification, which in the circumstances of the time could only have provoked division. But their sacramental teaching is meagre, the consequence no doubt of the current eucharistic disputes, disputes that may very well also have been the cause of the delay in publishing them, for on this issue the battle between the Saxon and the Swiss was now being fought out in this country.

Nevertheless, with an English Bible, a reformed and vernacular liturgy, and a doctrinal platform which, although far from systematic, at least indicated the church's position in relation to controverted points of doctrine, Anglicanism may be said to have come to birth. Its exact identity, however, was as yet by no means clear, showing its mind more in what it repudiated than in what it affirmed. Over the whole English church, furthermore, lay the menacing shadow of the temporal government justifying its repeated acts of spoliation in terms of a harsh and domineering erastianism.

But the Protestant revolution was suddenly halted in its tracks by the death of the sixteen-year-old Edward VI and the accession of his half-sister Mary, daughter of Katharine of Aragon and a woman whose devotion to Catholicism and the papacy verged on the fanatical. The political side of the religious changes in sixteenth-century England was once again to be forcefully asserted. The settlement of religion was a primary concern of the state, and not even a policy of reaction was possible unless with the parliamentary sanction. The new sovereign was crowned in Westminster Abbey on 1 October, and her first parliament not only restored immediately the legality of her mother's marriage but rescinded the entire legislation of the previous reign, thus abolishing both the new liturgy, which in any case had been in use for only a few months, and the ordinal. Imprisoned bishops were released and reinstated in their sees, and Stephen Gardiner was made chancellor of the realm. Foreign refugees were ordered to leave the country within twenty-four days, and the medieval services were restored. Nor was all this carried out in the teeth of popular opinion. Mary, a devout and courageous woman, personally well thought of, was regarded everywhere as the rightful queen.

At first nothing was said about the reconciliation of England with the papacy, and had she done no more than return to the condition of things obtaining at the close of her father's reign, so consolidating a national Catholicism, all might have been well. But she had made up her mind to do more than this, and embarked upon a policy of restoring papalism by force – a policy underlined by her decidedly unpopular marriage with Philip II of Spain. The outcome of it, within the space of but five years, was calamitous. Her kinsman Cardinal Reginald Pole, arrived in England as papal legate and was appointed to the primacy in succession to the now deposed and imprisoned Cranmer. He formally absolved sovereign and parliament for their alleged sin of schism, as also possibly convocation, although the English church as such had at no time incurred the pope's condemnation. Pole himself was a reformist of Counter-Reformation stamp, and although scholarly and high-principled had, after a long absence from his native country, little personal knowledge of either England or Englishmen, and he found the compromises necessary in his new sphere painful. When he died – as it happened on the very same day as the queen herself (17 November 1558) – he was under recall to Rome on a charge of heresy.

The persecution of Protestants during the reign included the execution of five reforming bishops – Hooper of Gloucester, Ferrar of St David's, Ridley, Latimer and finally Cranmer himself. Hooper notoriously held views of an extreme Protestant type, but Ridley's and Latimer's opinions were less distinctive. The accusation against them was of denying the presence in the sacrament of the 'natural' body of Christ – an expression itself of dubious meaning and perhaps less than orthodox – of affirming that the substance of bread and wine remains after consecration, and of repudiating the doctrine that the mass is a propitiatory sacrifice. Cranmer at the last made repeated and rather abject recantations, but his final act reversed them as 'things written with my hand contrary to the truth which I thought in my heart, and written for fear of death, and to save my life, if it might be'. He then added: 'Forasmuch as my hand offended, writing contrary to my heart, my hand shall first be punished therefore; for, may I come to the fire, it shall first be burned. And as for the pope, I refuse him as Christ's enemy and antichrist, with all his false doctrine.' On his continued adherence to the eucharistic doctrine set out in his *Answer* to Gardiner he was adamant. 'And as for the sacrament, I believe as I have taught in my book against the bishop of Winchester' containing 'so true a doctrine of the sacrament, that it shall stand at the last day before the judgement of God, where the papistical doctrine contrary thereto shall be ashamed to show her face.' An old and sorely tried man, he met his death with conspicuous bravery.

Cranmer's martyrdom, along with that of many other sufferers less eminent, contributed in no small measure to the survival of the Anglicanism which he had inaugurated by his work. Hatred and cruelty had made the name of Catholic ominous, if not odious, and of the restored papalism Englishmen had had enough. On Mary's decease an unhappy reign was brought to a finish. Her heir was her half-sister Elizabeth, a Protestant.


Note on Bucer's *De regno Christi*


Martin Bucer's treatise *De regno Christi* ('On the Kingdom of Christ'), was the last and most permanently interesting of his works, embodying as it does the fruits of his thinking and experience as a reformer over three decades. Certainly it is the work by which, as theologian and administrator, he is best judged. It was written in 1550 within the space of three months (it was completed by 21 October of that year) with a view to instructing the young king Edward VI in the principles and procedures requisite for the ordering of the national life in accordance with true because reformed religion. On the strength of it the university of Cambridge awarded him the degree of doctor of divinity. Not that it is free of its author's characteristic faults of repetitiveness and verbosity, and the long section on marriage and divorce comprising more than a quarter of the whole book (it would appear to have been composed earlier as a separate treatise) is out of proportion; but it is well thought out and remarkable for the scope and variety of its contents. It is notable, moreover, for the width of its understanding of English life and institutions, since Bucer had never previously visited England, had by then been in the country but a short time, and could neither speak nor read English. His achievement must therefore be attributed to the quickness of his observation and intelligent and experienced grasp of the human situation whatever the circumstances. Also during his sojourn at Cambridge, cut short though it was by his premature death, he was in close contact with men like Walter Haddon, Master of Trinity and vice-chancellor, Matthew Parker, Master of Corpus Christi, Edmund Grindal – each of the two last a future archbishop of Canterbury – and Roger Ascham the humanist, from whom he would have learned much.

The *De regno Christi* envisages a 'Christian commonwealth', *respublica Christiana*, within which no detail of the common life, spiritual or temporal, would remain unregulated. Much of what Bucer has to say no doubt matured in his mind during his Strassburg years, but its relevance to England is pressed with conviction. In any case his concept of the Kingdom of Christ is no disembodied ideal but is always related to the practical necessities of church and state alike, just as, in its turn, the 'idea of a Christian Society' (to use a modern expression) is itself related to the fundamental tenets of the Christian faith as revealed in scripture. Thus he stresses the immediate responsibility of temporal rulers for the spiritual and moral welfare of their subjects, for which indeed 'the kings of this world ought also to be ready to undergo any dangers, exile and even death'. This will be effected primarily through the church, with an appropriate discipline duly imposed. On this last Bucer is very explicit. But the church is no mere inward-looking company of the pious. 'It is not enough for the churches of Christ to care for the mere life of their people, they must also make provision so that they live to the Lord by being useful to one another and to the whole commonwealth and the Church.' For the church, it could be said, is the state in respect of its members, as the state likewise is the church. Both exist to serve Christ and promote his kingdom; but whereas the state may finally resort to force the church is bound to use persuasion, their respective roles being in this way complementary. More, there is a kind of mutual subordination: the church to the state inasmuch as the magistrates are responsible for the life of the community as a whole, and the state to the church inasmuch as those who exercise temporal authority do so with the instruction and guidance of the church's ministers, who, as such, are charged with making known Christ's will. The aim of both the spiritual and the temporal orders is thus the establishment of Christ's rule in the community, which as a body of faithful Christians, will always be motivated by love and mutual service. Such is the goal which even the most detailed prescriptions concerning the common life are designed to attain.

It cannot be claimed that Bucer's hopes were fulfilled. His book was not printed in England but at Strassburg several years after his death. That it found readers in England is very doubtful; it was not translated into English, though it did appear subsequently in German and in French. King Edward – 'a second Josiah', in Cranmer's flattering description – did read it, and himself composed a tract entitled *Discourse on the Reformation of Abuses* in which Bucer's ideas may have been of influence. But the Marian interlude ousted Protestant notions for a quinquennium, and when Elizabeth succeeded the continental divine who for a brief while had been honourably received among Englishmen passed out of mind. In any case his own thinking was taken up and to some extent transcended in Calvinism, the ideological force which in the new reign was to become pervasive. (There is a critical edition of the *De regno Christi* by F. Wendel in *Martini Buceri Opera Latina* [XV, Paris, 1955]; for an abridged English translation see W. Pauck, ed., *Melanchthon and Bucer*, 153–394. On Bucer's connection with the English Reformation see C. Hopf, *Martin Bucer and the English Reformation* [Oxford, 1946].)

# Chapter 11

# THE REFORMATION IN BRITAIN:
# II. CONSOLIDATION

## The Elizabethan Settlement

As a Protestant Elizabeth could adopt no other course than to overthrow the papist religious settlement of her Catholic predecessor. But her position was far from easy. The need of the hour was for national unity. The foreign situation demanded careful handling: England was still at war with France and dependent on the Spanish alliance, since militarily and financially the country was weak. However, the Catholic opposition amounted to much less than might have been expected; the bishops stood by Mary's policy but otherwise gave little effective leadership. Public opinion moreover, after such frequent and sudden changes of religious direction imposed from above, was remarkably apathetic. The queen's own views too were not entirely clear. Mass was still said in the royal chapel according to the Sarum rite, but the host was not elevated, although she herself was reputed to hold the doctrine of the real presence. Epistle, gospel and litany were read in English. She likewise approved of vestments and would even, it seems, have preferred the continuance of clerical celibacy. Her coronation on 15 January 1559 was according to the Latin rite. Probably her own standpoint was Lutheran, but with more than a tinge of the humanist temper added, for she was without religious fervour. Soon after her accession a document entitled 'A Device for the Alteration of Religion' was put out anonymously, although not, as it would appear, from any governmental source, even if it turned out in fact to be a rehearsal of the programme which the queen and her council were actually to adopt.

Elizabeth's first parliament met in January 1559, and proceeded to pass two Bills of the highest importance, the Acts of Supremacy and of Uniformity. The former, besides restoring Henry VIII's anti-Roman legislation and an Act of Edward VI requiring holy communion to be administered to the laity in both kinds, imposed an oath on all officials, both clerical and lay, acknowledging Elizabeth not indeed as 'Supreme Head' – a designation obnoxious to many on theological grounds – but as 'Supreme Governor' of the church as well as the state, the meaning of the title being explained further as implying that the monarch claimed no more than the authority 'which is and was of ancient time due to the imperial crown of this realm, that is, under God, to have the sovereignty and rule over all manner of persons within these her realms'.[1] The Bill met with little opposition, and had parliament done no more the situation would have been in almost all respects a reversion to that of 1547. But a vigorous Protestant group soon made its influence felt, and parliament was induced to pass the second of the two Bills, the Act of

---

1. Gee and Hardy, *Documents Illustrative of English Church History*, 442–58.

Uniformity, the effect of which was to reintroduce, not the first Edwardine prayer book, which Elizabeth herself would most likely have wished, but the second, a more overtly Protestant compilation, provision being made that it should come into use on 24 June 1559.[2] Nevertheless a few changes were made which were of no inconsiderable doctrinal significance. The 'Black Rubric', or more accurately, the 'Declaration on Kneeling', at the end of the communion service, was deleted, and at the administration the words used in the 1549 book, 'The Body of our Lord Jesus Christ, which was given for thee, preserve thy body and soul unto everlasting life', were now directed to be repeated before those prescribed by the second book, namely, 'Take and eat this, in remembrance that Christ died for thee, and feed on him in thy heart with faith and thanksgiving'. Thus although phraseology indicating commemoration was retained it was preceded by words that could readily and naturally be taken as implying belief in the real presence. In addition, the eucharistic vestments enjoined by the first book but disallowed by the second were again to be permitted under the terms of the so-called 'Ornaments Rubric', placed among the general rubrics before the orders for morning and evening prayer.

The task of revision had been assigned to Matthew Parker (shortly to be replaced by Edmund Guest), Edmund Grindal, Richard Cox and some others, assisted by a lawyer, Sir Thomas Smith, and directed by the queen's secretary, Sir William Cecil.

The new book was therefore essentially a compromise between the wishes of the queen and her government on the one hand, and the more advanced reformers in the Commons, backed by returned emigrés, Zurich-orientated, on the other. Both sides thus had to make concessions that were distasteful to them, and the process of finding a consensus of opinion was slow enough to irritate the more militant spirits. As John Jewel, later bishop of Salisbury, wrote to Peter Martyr:

> Our adversaries [*i.e. the Romanists under Mary*] acted always with precipitancy, without precedent, without authority, without law; while we manage everything with so much deliberation, and prudence, and wariness, and circumspection, as if God himself could scarce maintain his authority without ordinances and precautions. . . . This dilatoriness has grievously dampened the spirits of our brethren, while it has wonderfully encouraged the rage and fury of our opponents.[3]

But this concern for compromise was the pivot of the Elizabethan Settlement, and in spite of all subsequent attempts to overthrow it, it proved durable, the forms of public worship then adopted largely determining the whole character of Anglicanism over the ensuing generations.[4]

2. *Ibid.*, 458–67.
3. *Zurich Letters*, I, ed. H. Robinson (Parker Society, Cambridge, 1842), 17.
4. For the 1559 prayer book see W. K. Clay, *Liturgies and Occasional Forms of Prayer set forth in the Reign of Queen Elizabeth* (Parker Society, Cambridge, 1847). A Latin version of the Book of Common Prayer (*Liber Precum Publicarum*) was authorized by the queen in April 1560 differing in certain respects from the English original. These all appear to indicate the monarch's personal preference for the 1549 liturgy and include provision for the reservation of the sacrament for the sick and prayers for a requiem celebration of holy communion. In 1561 a new and fuller calendar was published. See F. Streatfeild, *Latin Versions of the Book of Common Prayer* (Alcuin Club Pamphlets, XIX, London, 1964).

On 9 December 1559 a new primate of All England was consecrated in the chapel of Lambeth Palace, in the person of Matthew Parker, the see of Canterbury having been vacant for over a year; the rite used followed the form set out in the 1552 prayer book. The consecrating bishops were William Barlow, formerly of Bath and Wells, John Scory, formerly of Chichester, Miles Coverdale, formerly of Exeter, and John Hodgkins, suffragan bishop of Bedford. The theological and canonical validity of this act has been the source of much Anglican-Roman controversy and need not be further discussed here. An account of the proceedings, however, was compiled on the orders of Parker himself which leaves no doubt that every care was taken to secure regularity, since the episcopal succession within the reformed Church of England depended on it. The new archbishop, who assumed the heavy burden of his responsibilities only with the greatest reluctance, was primarily a scholar, a man of a retiring and contemplative disposition not by nature cast as an administrator. But his innate conservatism, respect for constituted authority and deep sense of tradition meant that at all events his primacy would be likely to exert a restraining and steadying influence, though the extremists on either side despised such moderation. Educated at Corpus Christi College, Cambridge, he became interested in reformist ideas while in his mid twenties, Thomas Bilney and Hugh Latimer having been two of his close friends; but his prolonged studies in the early Fathers acted as a counterweight to the Lutheran principles which otherwise attracted him. After various preferments, including that of chaplain to Anne Boleyn when queen, he was appointed dean of Lincoln in 1552, although under Mary he was deprived and obliged to live in strict retirement. A firm upholder of the royal supremacy, his aim was to maintain the 1559 settlement and preserve continuity with the past. The doctrine and polity of the national church he envisaged indeed as constituting a *via media* between Romanism and Calvinist puritanism. Among his principal achievements as a scholar was his editing of a collection of Anglo-Saxon sermons to which he gave the characteristic title *The Testimony of Antiquity, shewing the ancient faith in the Church of England touching the Sacrament of the Body and Blood of the Lord*, and which contained a declaration signed by the two archbishops and thirteen bishops affirming, with regard to Aelfric's Easter sermon, *Of the Paschal Lamb*, that

> The whole discourse of the Sermon is about the understanding of the sacramental bread and wine, how it is the body and blood of Christ our Saviour: by which is revealed and made known what hath been the common taught doctrine of the Church of England on this behalf many hundred years ago, contrary to the unadvised writing of some nowadays.[5]

The great work of the convocation which met on 13 January 1563 was the drawing up of the *Thirty-nine Articles*, on the basis of the earlier *Forty-two*. Permission to revise the latter was granted by the queen to Parker, who then sought the aid of some other bishops – Grindal of London, Cox of Ely and Guest of Rochester – in carrying out the task, he himself, however, remaining in control. When the draft was completed it was submitted to the upper house of convocation on 19 January 1563, and to the lower house ten days later. In this first draft the

5.  Quoted Dixon, *Hist. of the Church of England*, V, 354f.

revised articles still numbered forty-two, four old ones, concerned with anabaptist errors, having been removed and four others added. But three were struck out after debate in convocation, thus reducing them to thirty-nine. A clause was inserted in Article 20 ('Of the Authority of the Church') derived from the 1552 Lutheran *Confession of Württemberg*, stating that 'the Church hath power to decree rites or ceremonies and authority in controversies of faith', words clearly directed at the more extreme reformers who denied to the church any power or authority to enforce a rite or ceremony not explicitly warranted by scripture. The twenty-ninth article, which referred to 'the wicked which do not eat the body of Christ, in the use of the Lord's Supper', was dropped, it has been said, at the wish of the queen herself, and was not replaced until the final revision of 1571, when the papal bull *Regnans in Excelsis* rendered it no longer necessary to conciliate Romanist feeling.[6]

The main differences between the new set of articles and those of 1553 thus comprise the inclusion of certain new ones and the enlargement of others, as, for example, the reference in Article 2 to the eternal generation and consubstantiality of the Son, and the whole of Article 5 ('Of the Holy Ghost') – additions taken almost word for word from the *Württemberg Confession* – or the changes in the eleventh article, 'On Justification' which was expanded and given a more distinctively Lutheran emphasis: 'We are accounted righteous before God, only for the merit of our Lord and Saviour Jesus Christ by faith, and not for our works or deservings.' The twelfth article, 'Of Good Works', was likewise based on the *Württemberg Confession*, declaring that good works, 'which are the fruits of faith and follow after justification, cannot put away our sins and endure the severity of God's judgement', but yet are 'pleasing to God in Christ, and do spring out necessarily of a true and lively faith'. Lutheran overtones are detectable too in Article 19, on the Church, which is still defined (as in 1553) as 'a congregation of faithful men, in which the pure word of God is preached and the sacraments duly administered according to Christ's ordinance in all those things that of necessity are requisite to the same.'[7]

On the other hand echoes of the Swiss Reformation as well are plainly audible, thanks to the influence both of the returned Marian exiles and of Heinrich Bullinger

---

6. In the early years of her reign Elizabeth and her advisers still entertained the possibility of comprehending the Romanists, or at any rate the majority of them, in the national church. The action of Pope Pius V in 1570 in declaring Elizabeth a heretic and purporting to deprive her of her 'pretended right' to her realm and absolving her subjects of their allegiance to her frustrated this hope. On the article in question see Bicknell, *The Thirty-Nine Articles*, 399–407.

7. The influence of the Lutheran *Confession of Augsburg* on the *Forty-Two Articles* is clearly detectable, by way of Cranmer's *Thirteen Articles* of 1536. The *Thirty-Nine Articles*, however, disclose a fresh Lutheran influence through the *Confession of Württemberg*, a formulary consisting of thirty-five articles compiled by Johannes Brenz (Brentius) (1499–1570) and presented to the Council of Trent in 1552 by envoys of the state of Württemberg. For the text see H. Hoppe (ed.), *Die Bekenthissschrift der altprotestantische Kirche Deutschlands* (Cassell, 1855). See also P. Schaff, *History of the Creeds of Christendom* (Grand Rapids, 1896), I, 343f., 627ff. Several of Archbishop Parker's additions to the 1553 Articles were drawn from this source. Cf. B. M. G. Reardon, 'The Thirty-Nine Articles and the Augsburg Confession', in *Lutheran Quarterly*, III (1989), 91–106.

in Zurich, who was kept in close touch with the situation in England. Thus the lengthy Article 17, on predestination and election, looks Calvinist-inspired, especially in its opening sentence; yet essentially it would not have been unacceptable to Lutherans also, since it says nothing about irresistible grace, or a limited atonement, or double predestination. Of 'curious and carnal persons' lacking the spirit of Christ it avers merely, if somewhat rhetorically, that 'to have continually before their eyes the sentence of God's Predestination is a most dangerous downfall, whereby the devil doth thrust them either into desperation or into wretchlessness of most unclean living no less perilous than desperation'.

The Church of England's position as against Rome is of course succinctly indicated; at that time it could not be other than unequivocally on the Protestant side of the great divide. Thus, contrary to the findings of the Council of Trent, which in 1546 had issued a decree affirming both scripture and tradition equally to be sources of doctrine, Article 6 lays it down that scripture itself contains all things necessary to salvation, 'so that whatsoever is not read therein, nor may be proved thereby, is not to be regarded of any man to be believed as an article of faith, or deemed needful for salvation'. The same article lists the canonical books of the Old Testament and those of the Apocrypha, stating of the latter that they are not to be used for the determination of doctrine but only as an 'example of life and instruction of manners'. Article 25 denies the teaching that the 'Seven Sacraments' were all of Christ's institution, saying that the five 'commonly called Sacraments' – confirmation, penance, holy orders, matrimony and extreme unction – are not 'sacraments of the Gospel' but have grown up partly of 'the corrupt following of the Apostles' and are partly 'states of life allowed in the scriptures'. The preceding article condemns the use in public worship of 'a tongue not understanded of the people', and Article 30 disallows communion in one kind only. Article 32 is emphatic in asserting the lawfulness of clerical marriage, 37 asserts the validity of orders as conferred by the Edwardine rite (so anticipating subsequent Roman objections), and insists on the authority of 'every particular or national church' to ordain, change or abolish such ecclesiastical rites or ceremonies as have 'only a human authority'. Other articles condemn medieval teachings or practices judged to be contrary to scripture, namely, works of supererogation (14), and the 'Romish' doctrine of purgatory, pardons, image worship and the invocation of saints (22). The thirteenth article, 'Of Works before Justification', censures the scholastic doctrine of congruous merit.[8]

Regarding the sacraments of baptism and the Lord's Supper the articles exclude anabaptist and the more extreme sacramentarian teachings. Thus of the sacraments generally it is stated (Article 25) that they are 'not only badges or tokens of Christian men's profession, but rather certain sure witnesses and effectual signs of grace and God's good will towards us, by the which He doth work invisibly in us, and doth not only quicken, but also strengthen and confirm, our faith in Him,' while the phrase *ex opere operato*, referred to and rejected in the corresponding article of 1553, is here omitted. Article 26, again, affirms that the minister's personal

---

8. That is the doctrine that further divine grace can be earned, as it were, by perseverance in good works. See Bicknell, *op. cit.,* 216f.

unworthiness is of itself no hindrance to the efficacy of the sacraments he administers. The following article, on baptism, declares that baptism is not only a 'sign of profession, and mark of difference' distinguishing Christians from the unchristened but one also of

> regeneration or new birth, whereby, as by an instrument, they that receive baptism rightly are grafted into the Church; the promises of forgiveness of sin, and of our adoption to be the sons of God by the Holy Ghost, are visibly signed and sealed; faith is confirmed, and grace increased by virtue of prayer unto God

is evidently aimed not only at the anabaptist (infant baptism is described as 'most agreeable with the institution of Christ') but also at the sacramentarian position, although the necessity of baptism for salvation, asserted in the 1549 prayer book, is not expressly claimed. Articles 28 to 31, dealing with the controversial issues of the Lord's Supper, seek to steer a middle course. The first of them, much changed from 1553, condemns transubstantiation as unscriptural, besides overthrowing in principle the nature of a sacrament, while the statement that 'the body of Christ is given, taken, and eaten in the Supper', albeit 'only after an heavenly and spiritual manner', would certainly appear intended to allow a doctrine of the real presence. But it is also pointed out that the means by which the body of Christ is received and eaten in the Supper is faith. The twenty-ninth article, already alluded to, is ambiguous, but the simplest interpretation is that although the 'inward part' of the sacrament, the body and blood of Christ spiritually present, is offered to the wicked, or those 'void of a lively faith', they are incapable of actually receiving it, the profanity of their approaching it indeed bringing down upon them a deserved condemnation. Article 30 asserts communion in both kinds to be the rule of the church, while 31, proclaiming the sufficiency of Christ's atonement – the offering of the crucified Christ 'once made being the perfect redemption, propitiation, and satisfaction for all the sins of the whole world, both original and actual' – goes on to exclude all idea of 'the sacrifice of masses', according to which it was commonly believed that the priest 'did offer Christ for the quick and dead to have remission of pain or guilt'. Seemingly its purpose was to reject later medieval conceptions of the eucharistic sacrifice that could be said to imply the insufficiency of the cross and the need for its repetition or supplementation in the mass itself.[9]

Various subjects covered by the remaining articles require no more than selective mention. Article 21 maintains that general councils may not be called 'without the commandment and will of princes' and are themselves not inerrant; 23 lays down that no one may minister in the congregation unless lawfully called by 'men who have public authority in the congregation'; 24, 'Of the Traditions of the Church', contends with all Reformation thinking, that ceremonies need not be the same in all places, and that, where man-made, may be altered anywhere and at any time, although what is scriptural is of course unalterable. The thirty-seventh article, which contains the well-known statement that 'the Bishop of Rome hath no jurisdiction in this realm of England', asserts the royal supremacy, but with the somewhat guarded admission that 'the Queen's majesty hath . . . chief government of all

---

9. See B. J. Kidd, *The Later Mediaeval Doctrine of the Eucharistic Sacrifice* (London, 1898); but cf. also F. Clark, *Eucharistic Sacrifice and the Reformation* (London, 1960).

estates of this realm, whether they be ecclesiastical or civil'. It adds, once more against the anabaptists, that Christians are not exempt from the death penalty and that at the bidding of the secular authority they may serve in war.

Such, then, is the broad content of the articles. Although on the whole a decided improvement on the 1553 set, they do not offer a digest of Christian doctrine. The very order in which they appear, if not haphazard, scarcely lays out a consistent dogmatic scheme. In short, they do not aim at, to quote Bishop Pearson's words, 'a complete body of divinity, or a comprehension and explanation of all Christian doctrine necessary to be taught: but an enumeration of some truths, which upon and since the Reformation have been denied by some persons'.[10] They are, that is, for the most part concerned with matters of doctrine, as also of practice, which were then the subject of vigorous and often embittered debate, even among Protestants, during the period in which they were drawn up, seeking to indicate the Church of England's mind thereon. Unlike many of the continental confessions – argumentative, wordy and diffuse – they are terse to the point of obscurity, sometimes stopping laconically short when the reader could well have done with a more explicit statement or greater detail. Their tone, in line with the controversial style of the age, is not free from asperity, but they are not abusive, nor are they sweeping in their condemnations. For their purpose was not to explain, within their self-imposed limits, the full doctrinal position of the reformed *Ecclesia Anglicana*, the liturgy of which had preceded them, but to commend themselves as a basis of agreement among men whose religious convictions were nevertheless by no means harmonious even when more or less in unison on fundamentals. Hence they refrain as far as possible from antagonizing by excess of precision. As Dixon justly observes: 'Regarded whether as a symbol or a code, the English Articles . . . can scarcely fail to move admiration, in comparison with similar performances of the age.'[11]

All the same, it has frequently been stated that their basis is Calvinist. This is only a part truth, since it could as well, and perhaps better, be said that their teaching is Lutheran. In the main, they articulate the teachings on which evangelicals, whether Lutheran or Calvinist, could and did come very near to reaching a common mind. Even so there is an Englishness about them – the practicality of their concern and approach, and avoidance of theological hair-splitting – which singles them out among the comparable formularies of the time. English divines moreover, then as since, were respectful of the testimony of the early Fathers, and were suspicious of a dogmatism too rigid in its interpretation of what it claimed as the one exclusive meaning of scripture. Yet this very moderation and traditionalism were, in the eyes of their critics, their cardinal fault. One notes, for instance, how in Article 9 the condition of fallen man is not stated to be one of total depravity but only to be 'very far gone from original righteousness'. Unsurprisingly, the

---

10.  Quoted Hardwick, *A History of the Thirty-Nine Articles*, 158.
11.  Dixon, *op. cit.,* V, 395. In the words of an eminent Scottish divine of the last century, 'there is present everywhere a touch of moderation, the softening influence of a conciliatory doctrinism which is true to the positive aspects of Augustinianism and the evangelical import of the great question raised by the Reformation' (J. Tulloch, *Rational Theology in England in the Seventeenth Century*, 2nd edn., Edinburgh, 1874, I, 65).

puritans in after years made repeated attempts to get them amended or supplemented. Had they been satisfied that their content was the pure doctrine of Geneva such manoeuvres would have been unnecessary.[12] Even their anti-Romanism may be more apparent than real, as the efforts of Christopher Davenport (better know to history as Franciscus a Sancta Clara) in the seventeenth century and John Henry Newman in the nineteenth to de-Protestantize them might seem to prove.

The thirty-fifth article refers to a second *Book of Homilies* and lists their titles – in number twenty-one at the revision of 1571 – the aim of which was the starkly practical one of doing something to make good the dearth of satisfactory preachers among the clergy, owing either to incompetence or to excessive partisanship of a kind not favoured by the government. Their purpose was thus to put a collection of sermons, as in the case of the first book issued in 1547 composed by members of the episcopate, in the hands of the parish clergy, wherewith to provide their congregations with weekly edification. The queen herself was not enthusiastic for the project, but the royal authorization was granted after convocation's approval in 1563. The contents cover a wide variety of matters, some of the homilies dealing with seasonal themes (Christmas, Good Friday, Easter, Whit Sunday and Rogationtide, discourses which might not inappropriately be used at other times as well) while others treated of fasting, alms-giving, prayer and the right reception of holy communion – the last of these (no. 15) being marked by unmistakably Calvinistic language. Others again dealt with certain difficulties of scripture (10), with matrimony (no. 18) and with forms of moral delinquency (5, 6, and 20). The homily for Whit Sunday gives the essential notes of the church, in Calvinistic fashion, as three: true doctrine, the sacraments and discipline; it also attacks the Roman church in scurrilously abusive terms. To the student the collection is relevant for an understanding of the feeling and direction of Elizabethan churchmanship, but it cannot be cited as in any manner recording the official voice of Anglicanism.[13]

12. The 'Declaration of Doctrine' prepared for the queen by a group of Marian exiles approved itself to Jewel as wholly conformable with the 'doctrine of Zurich'. The bishops, however, compiled an earlier series of eleven articles which they authorized at a meeting at Lambeth on 12 April 1561 (see Hardwick, *op. cit.* 357ff). It was evidently understood that these, which were certainly concise, were not only intended to secure the consent of the clergy but to serve 'the instruction of the people'. But this formulary never acquired any other authority than what the bishops themselves conferred on it. For the instruction of schoolchildren a Latin catechism (*Catechismus puerorum*) was composed by Alexander Nowell, prolocutor of the lower House of Convocation, but this likewise never gained synodical authority. Its source was plainly Calvin, and more especially the *Geneva Catechism* (see G. E. Corrie's edition, Parker Society, Cambridge, 1853).

13. It was completed in all probability by the beginning of 1563, being mostly the work of Bishop Jewel, though it was not published in its final form until 1571. The titles of the various homilies are listed in Articles 35 of the Thirty-Nine Articles. For both this and the earlier collection see *The Two Books of Homilies appointed to be read in Churches*, ed. J. Griffiths (Oxford, 1859).

## A twofold apologetic

The earlier years of Elizabeth I's reign were not a period of any distinction in English theology, but it is necessary to note, at this point in our survey, that the one outstanding theological treatise of the day took the form of, in Mandell Creighton's words, 'the first methodical statement of the position of the Church of England against the Church of Rome, and the groundwork of all subsequent controversy'.[14] This was John Jewel's *An Apology of the Church of England (Apologia Ecclesiae Anglicanae)*, published in 1562.[15] Commissioned by the government and appearing originally in Latin with no indication of authorship, the book from the first enjoyed a status above that of a private and personal utterance, being to all intents an official explanation and vindication of the English religious settlement against the Romanists. More than a generation after its first publication the then archbishop of Canterbury, Richard Bancroft, still saw fit to give order that all parish churches should possess a copy of its author's works, by that time available in a single volume. It is true that some doubt has been raised as to whether it was solely Jewel's composition, but that his was the principal hand is beyond question.[16] Written in the main for a foreign readership, and in particular with a view to the findings of the Council of Trent, to which the Church of England had declined to send a representative, it won the warm commendation of Peter Martyr, Bullinger and other Zurich divines, although at home Nicholas Bacon, the Lord Keeper, was disposed to criticize it for not having defended, as against the Calvinists, the preservation of many features of the old Catholic heritage. But generally it was welcomed in the country as an admirably succinct account of what the national church stood for, as well as a riposte to the rumours circulating abroad that ecclesiastical affairs in England were in a state of chaos, and that libertinism was rampant.[17]

A Devon man by birth, Jewel (1522–71) was educated at Merton and Corpus Christi Colleges, Oxford, and was elected to a fellowship at the latter in 1542. While at the university his Protestant convictions were deepened by a systematic study of the Bible, as later by personal contact with Peter Martyr, who in 1547 assumed the regius professorship of divinity. After ordination he was appointed to a benefice near Oxford, but with Mary's accession he lost his fellowship and subsequently fled the country, going first to Frankfurt, thence to Strassburg, where his acquaintance

---

14. *Dictionary of National Biography*, X (1908), art. 'Jewel', 817.
15. Jewel's works, edited by J. Ayre, were issued by the Parker Society, Cambridge, 1845–50. A modern edition of the *Apology*, in the translation by Lady Bacon, wife of the Lord Keeper Nicholas Bacon, has been edited with an introduction by J. E. Booty (New York, 1963).
16. See J. E. Booty, *John Jewel as Apologist of the Church of England* (London, 1963), 57 ff.
17. Mr Booty quotes a manuscript at Corpus Christi College, Cambridge, alluding to a report that the papists charge 'that our doctrine is detestable heresies, that we are fallen from the doctrine of Christ's catholic church, that we are subtle sectaries, that we dissent among ourselves, and that every man nourisheth and maintaineth his peculiar opinion, and that we are teachers of carnal liberty' (*An Apology of the Church of England*, Introduction, xxv).

with Peter Martyr began, and finally to Zurich. On receiving news of the queen's death he returned to England in March 1559, and in January of the following year was made bishop of Salisbury. That he was influenced by his foreign travels and contacts is to have been expected, but he was no extremist, and like so many Anglican theologians he attached special weight to the 'consent' of the early Fathers.[18] But Jewel's presiding concern throughout the Apology is with the reasons for the English church's rejection of Rome, and he is far from emphasizing the differences dividing the Reformers themselves. His most capable opponent on the Roman side was an old Oxford contemporary of his, the recusant Thomas Harding (1516–72), then at Louvain university, whose *Confutation* of Jewel's book came out in 1564, thus provoking Jewel's final blow in his massive *Defence of the Apologie of the Church of England* three years later.

The essence of the Anglican divine's case is that it was not the Church of England which should be charged with departing from the Catholic church but rather Rome herself, for whereas she had departed 'from God's word, from Christ's commandments, from the apostles' ordinances, from the primitive church's examples, from the old fathers' and councils' orders', England, by contrast, has returned to the faith of apostolic and patriotic times.

> For the people of God are otherwise instructed now than they were in times past, when all the bishop of Rome's sayings were allowed for gospel, and when all religion did depend only upon their authority. Now-a-days the holy scripture is abroad, the writings of the apostles and prophets are in print, whereby all truths and catholic doctrine may be proved, and all heresy may be disproved and confuted.[19]

If Rome insists she is right let her show it from the scriptures. In the second part Jewel proceeds to itemize the doctrines of the historic Catholic faith held in the Church of England – each paragraph begins with the words 'We believe' – including her belief in the 'Church catholic and universal', and her commitment to maintain the threefold order of ministers, bishops, priests and deacons, while rejecting the claim of the pope to universal supremacy: 'We say that there neither is, nor can be, any one man, which may have the whole superiority.' Further, the English church holds that ministers, who must be duly called to their office, have the power to bind and loose. Of the eucharist Jewel says: 'We affirm that bread and wine are holy and heavenly mysteries of the body and blood of Christ, and that by this Christ himself, being the true bread of eternal life, is so presently given to us, as that by faith we verily receive his body and blood.'[20] Transubstantiation, however, must be repudiated as something which neither expresses the meaning of scripture nor is endorsed by the doctrine of the Fathers. Part III rebuts the charge of heresy and dissociates the English church from the sectarian growths lately sprung up abroad. 'The world seeth now right well . . . that we neither have bred,

---

18. See C. W. M. Southgate, *John Jewel and the Problem of Doctrinal Authority* (Cambridge, Mass., 1962). There is no need to dispute Booty's opinion that 'all of the authorities which Jewel recognized, the primitive Church, the Fathers, the Councils, he subordinated to the primary authority of the Scriptures' (*John Jewel as Apologist*, 137). The most moderate of the Reformers insisted on that.
19. Jewel, *Works*, III, 57.
20. *Ibid.*, 63

nor taught, nor kept up these monstrosities.'[21] Part IV resumes the assault on the Roman church, and this is continued in Part V, which judges contemporary Rome in the light of patristic teachings and finds it wanting.

> Wherefore, though our departing were a trouble to them [*the Romanists*], yet ought they to consider withal how just cause we had of our departure. . . . Let them compare our churches and theirs together, and they shall see, that themselves have most shamefully gone from the Apostles, and we most justly have gone from them.[22]

The final part deals with questions concerning supremacy and authority in the church, whether the papacy, councils, or the crown, concluding that: 'We see by histories and by the examples of the best times, that good princes ever took the administration of ecclesiastical matters to pertain to them only.'[23]

But the most pressing opposition to the state religious settlement came not from Roman Catholic controversialists but from the sustained puritan effort to subvert it from within. At first it concerned merely peripheral matters like clerical vesture – although even to such points the dissidents attached high importance of principle – but later the attack opened on a wider front, with an attempt to undermine the whole Anglican polity by gradually presbyterianizing it. The leader of this opposition was the Lady Margaret's professor of divinity at Cambridge, the redoubtable Thomas Cartwright (1535–1603), a man whose impressive learning did nothing to temper his vitriolic polemicism and who at least claimed to have no scruples about wanting the death penalty for all who could be identified as 'false teachers'. 'If this', he declared, 'be bloody and extreme, I am content to be counted with the Holy Ghost.'[24] Although he was deprived of his academic seat in 1570 he continued to fight elsewhere, and it was probably his mind behind the anonymously issued puritan manifesto of two years later, *The First Admonition to Parliament*, a violent critique of the ecclesiastical usages to which the party objected, but above all advocating, if the work of reform were to be complete, the abolition of episcopacy altogether.[25] A second such *Admonition* was the work of Cartwright himself and composed in a style thoroughly characteristic of its author; bishops, for instance, were 'a remnant of Antichrist's brood'.[26] Its vituperation apart, though, Cartwright's purpose in writing it was plain enough: to destroy the episcopal system and replace it with a presbyterian consistory. In addition the remaining vestiges of medievalism in public worship were to be eradicated and nothing permitted for which the express warrant of scripture could not be adduced.[27] Besides Cartwright the puritans also had Walter Travers (*c.* 1548–1643), again a man of ability, who

21. *Ibid.*, 67.
22. *Ibid.*, 91f.
23. *Ibid.*, 98
24. See A. F. S. Pearson, *Cartwright and Elizabethan Puritanism, 1535–1603* (Cambridge, 1925).
25. The actual authors were the London printers John Field and Thomas Wilcox.
26. On the two *Admonitions* see W. H. Frere and C. E. Douglas, *Puritan Manifestoes: a study in the origin of the Puritan revolt* (London, 1907).
27. According to M. M. Knappe it was in 1557, among the congregation of the English emigrés at Frankfurt that 'the cry of "No Prelacy" was raised for the first time in English controversy' (*Tudor Puritanism*, Chicago, 1939, 157).

after serving a ministry in Antwerp for some years, became, in 1581, lecturer (or reader) of the Temple Church in London. Already in 1574 he had published, in both Latin and English, a *Full and Plain Declaration of Ecclesiastical Discipline*,[28] covering much the same ground as the *Admonitions* and in a manner to emulate that of Cartwright himself. Once more, it is the presbyterian system that is called for, even if the actual name of bishop is retained.

But the puritan offensive was not confined to manifestoes and controversial treatises; it was a highly organized and active conspiracy. About five hundred beneficed ministers made known their assent to a presbyterian book entitled *Disciplina Ecclesiae Sacra*, the aim of which was to demonstrate how the entire scheme of Calvinistic doctrine and ecclesiastical order might be set up within the Church of England. 'Prophesyings', as they were termed – theoretically they were meetings of local clergymen for Bible study, discussion and instruction, but in practice occasions for much fiery puritan exhortation and denunciation – became more and more widespread and in some instances were actively encouraged by the bishops. The failure of Archbishop Grindal, who succeeded Parker at Canterbury in 1575 and who himself had strong puritan leanings, to stop this indiscipline, along with his tactlessness in dealing with the queen personally, led to his suspension from all administrative duties, though he kept his primatial dignity until his death in 1583. John Whitgift (*c.*1530–1604), who succeeded him, although a Calvinist in theology – witness the *Lambeth Articles* of 1595[29] – adopted a more stringent attitude in compelling the assent of the clergy generally to both the Book of

28. The place of printing was not stated, but another edition appeared in 1580 giving it as 'at Geneva'.
29. During the seventies and eighties Calvinism was the ascendant theology in England, and was strongly represented among the bishops themselves. The *Thirty-Nine Articles*, as finally revised in 1571, by no means satisfied the more advanced puritans on a number of doctrinal points. 'Indeed', according to the *Second Admonition to Parliament*, 'the Book of the Articles of the Christian religion speaketh very dangerously of falling from grace', and there was no mention of reprobation at all. At the universities, and especially at Cambridge, Calvin's theology had become entrenched and the *Institutes* was assiduously studied. But the voice of protest was not altogether silent. Thus on 29 April 1595 a fellow of Caius College, William Barrett, preached in St Mary's, the university church, against the doctrines of the indefectibility of grace, of assurance and of reprobation, only to find himself forthwith denounced by the authorities, led by Dr Whitaker, the master of St John's and regius professor of divinity. Both he and they then appealed to the archbishop of Canterbury, himself a moderate Calvinist, who discussed the matter at considerable length with a deputation from Cambridge. The upshot was the calling of a conference at Lambeth in November 1595 which resulted in the drawing up of nine propositions that were plainly Calvinist in substance. However, that such discussions had even taken place displeased the queen, who informed the archbishop that she 'misliked much that any allowance had been given by his grace and the rest of any such points to be disputed'. No attempt therefore was made to impose them as interpretative of the *Thirty-Nine Articles*, and Whitgift let it be known that they were to be taken only as the 'private judgements' of the compilers. An effort some years later (1604) to gain official sanction for them failed.

A highly influential writer on the puritan side was William Perkins (1558–1602), the first folio edition of whose collected works appeared in 1600. Educated at Christ's College, Cambridge, he held a fellowship there from 1584 to 1594. A Calvinist in theology, he nevertheless was a man of liberal views, to the extent at least of recognising

Common Prayer and the *Thirty-Nine Articles*. The puritans' rejoinder, however, was renewed opposition, instanced by the 'Martin Marprelate' tracts, scurrilous and even libellous in content, and in the government's view treasonable in implication. But here they overreached themselves. Parliament in 1593 passed an Act prohibiting attendance at schismatic conventicles, under which the law could take the sternest measures against actual separatists, three of whom, Barrow, Greenwood and Penry, were hanged. Yet if the puritan objections were to be countered more was wanted than physical repression. It was to meet this need that Richard Hooker embarked on his great work of Anglican defence, *The Laws of Ecclesiastical Polity*, a most fitting and impressive sequel to Jewel's own *Apology*, but this time with Protestant extremism as its target.

## Richard Hooker

In 1585 Hooker was appointed master of the Temple Church, where Travers was already installed as reader and fostering hopes of the mastership himself. The nomination was the queen's, but in this case it was Whitgift's advice that prevailed, despite strong puritan influence on Travers's behalf. Hooker, born at Heavitree, near Exeter, in 1553 or 1554, was a protégé of his fellow-Devonian Bishop Jewel, whose assistance enabled him to enter Corpus Christi College, Oxford, in 1571. After holding a fellowship at the college he came to London from the country living of Drayton Beauchamp in Buckinghamshire. At the time he was not well known, and was of an unusually shy and retiring disposition, but he was a dedicated scholar who even then, at the age of thirty-one, had acquired a massive learning, classical, biblical, patristic and medieval. His sermon on *Justification*, preached soon after his entry upon his new benefice, did nothing to placate puritan susceptibilities. 'Christ', he declared, 'hath merited righteousness for as many as are found in him', and allowed that even a papist, 'yea, a cardinal or pope', will not be rejected by a merciful God ready to make 'the best of that little which we hold well'.[30]

Controversy between men of views so divergent as those of master and reader was inevitable, and as the seventeenth-century church historian Thomas Fuller puts

29. *continued* that on any controverted issue opposing beliefs can be held with sincerity by both parties. This is shown in his *Reformed Catholike* (1597), a book which gained considerable attention and which sought to demonstrate how much was in fact held in common by theological opponents and to reduce the dividing differences between them. On the Catholic side it was answered in detail by William Bishop (under the initials D. B. P.), titular bishop of Chalcedon (two parts, dated 1604 and 1607). This provoked further controversy, with two Anglican replies and a rejoinder by Bishop (1608). Perkins also wrote on moral theology and on the art of preaching, as well as an *Exposition* of the Apostles' creed (1595). See W. F. Mitchell, *English Pulpit Oratory* (1932) and the discussion of Perkins in W. E. Houghton, *The Formation of Thomas Fuller's Holy and Profane States* (Harvard, 1938). For a modern edition of Perkins see *The Works of William Perkins* (ed. I. Breward) in the *Courtenay Library of Reformed Classics* (Sutton Courtenay, Berks, 1970).

30. *Of the Laws of Ecclesiastical Polity*, ed. C. Morris (London, Everyman Library, 1969), 21.

it, 'the pulpit spake pure Canterbury in the morning and Geneva in the afternoon'. In fact these Sunday disputations became a matter of so much comment, although they were conducted with a seemliness of expression rare in those days, that Travers was inhibited by the archbishop from further preaching. But it was no doubt from them (for they were delivered before a congregation of learned lawyers who enjoyed the verbal sword-play) that Hooker got the idea, as probably the title too, of a 'treatise in which', as he wrote to Whitgift, 'I intend a justification of the Law of our Ecclesiastical Polity'.[31] The task he set himself was an onerous one which occupied him for the remaining fifteen years of his life. Part of the work would seem to have been composed in London, while Hooker was residing at the house of his father-in-law, John Churchman.[32] The first four Books were published in 1593, and the long and important fifth in 1597. The last three were drafted but never completed for the press before Hooker died, at the early age of forty-six. At the time of his death he was vicar of Bishopsbourne in Kent. The manuscript of Books VI to VIII did not see print till long afterwards.[33]

Hooker's aim in *The Laws of Ecclesiastical Polity* was to defend the Anglican settlement of 1559, although as C. S. Lewis pertinently observes, he himself never heard of a religion called Anglicanism.[34] In this he followed his patron Jewel, but the scope of his endeavour is far wider. The work may take the form of an apology but it has more of the range and system of a *summa theologiae* steering a middle course between the poles of Rome and Geneva. It would probably be an exaggeration to say that this 'treatise did for the Church of England what Calvin's *Institutes* had done for the Genevan Church' – certainly it has never exercised the kind of hypnotic authority over Anglicans which the latter did over Calvin's followers – but it can fairly be claimed that it gave to Anglicanism 'a voice and a character' which hitherto had not properly been heard or revealed.[35] Its merits were from the

31. The letter is given in Isaac Walton's 'Life of Hooker'. See J. Keble's edition of the *Polity*, (Oxford, 1836; 1850 ed.), I, 85f.
32. There is no evidence that Hooker ever lived at the master's official residence. In his literary work he had advisers and assistants, especially Dr John Spenser, of his own college at Oxford, and two former pupils, George Cranmer, greatnephew of Archbishop Cranmer, and Edwin Sandys, son of the archbishop of York. Whitgift also was well aware of the project and deeply interested. Much new light was shed on Hooker's life by the researches of J. C. Sisson, in his *Judicious Marriage of Mr Hooker* (Cambridge, 1940), who disposed of certain of the yarns about Hooker, in particular that of his very 'injudicious' marriage to Joan Churchman, daughter of his friend, served up in Walton's entertaining but gossipy and unreliable biography. Nevertheless, one need not wholly discredit the impression of Sandys and Cranmer that the great but temperamentally rather timid scholar was henpecked.
33. They were made over to the safekeeping of Dr Spenser, but Edwin Sandys may have tampered with Book VI on doctrinal grounds, and so came into conflict with Bishop Lancelot Andrewes, who was anxious about the unpublished Books 'lest they be embezzled and so suppressed, or come into great hands who will mutilate them for their own purpose'. However, Sisson's view in regard to Books VII and VIII is that 'there is no reason for doubting their authenticity, even allowing for the chequered history of these manuscripts from 1600 onwards' (*op. cit.*, 106). The complete edition of *The Laws of Ecclesiastical Polity* did not appear until 1661.
34. *English Literature in the Sixteenth Century* (Oxford, 1954), 454.
35. R. Bayne, 'Hooker', in Hastings's *Encyclopaedia of Religion and Ethics*, VI, 774.

outset recognized far beyond purely Anglican circles, while its magisterial sweep and tone, if they did not silence the puritan opposition, were such that no serious attempt was made to meet Hooker's arguments with a like thoroughness. His close reasoning, his moderation and balance, have coupled with his name, most appositely, the epithet 'judicious'. Invective and partisanship are absent, but not irony which, especially in the later Books, can often be penetrating. ('An opinion', he remarks, 'hath spread itself very far, as if the way to be ripe in faith were to be raw in wit and judgement.'[36]) His determination to avoid the *rabies* and *odium* that so commonly marred contemporary religious debate cannot better be described than in his own words:

> It is no part of my secret meaning to draw you hereby into hatred, or to set upon the face of this cause any fairer glass than the naked truth doth afford; but my whole endeavour is to resolve the conscience and to show as near as I can what in this controversy the heart is to think, if it will follow the light of sound and sincere judgement, without either cloud of prejudice, or mist of passionate affection.[37]

Not least, for the lover of the English tongue, *The Laws of Ecclesiastical Polity* is a landmark in the history of the nation's literature. In the words of Saintsbury, it is 'a book in which matter and manner are wedded as in few other books of the same kind'.[38]

Hooker sets out to refute the puritan contention that in religion holy scripture affords the sole and absolute authority and rule. But he can achieve his end only by showing that this principle is altogether too narrow, and that it disregards that larger context of the divine law in creation within which even the scriptural revelation must be placed if we are to understand its proper scope and purpose. What first is wanted therefore is an examination of the essential nature of law itself and of the various kinds or categories into which it falls, a task on which Hooker embarks in what is probably the most masterly part of the whole treatise, Book I. For here is the root, so to say, from which the entire scheme of the *Ecclesiastical Polity* stems. In its most general sense law is defined as 'that which doth assign unto each thing the kind, that which doth moderate the force and power, that which doth appoint the form and measure'.[39] Although law is thus to be conceived as a rule or canon 'whereby actions are framed', Hooker does not hesitate to apply the notion to God himself, on the principle that ultimately law and law-giver are one. 'The very being of God', [*he states,*] 'is a kind of law to his working: for that perfection which God is, giveth perfection to that which God doth.'[40] God is therefore both a law to himself and to all else besides.[41] So from this one source several types of law descend in hierarchical order. And primarily there is that which Hooker terms, with reference to such 'operations as have their beginning and being by a voluntary purpose, wherewith God hath eternally decreed when and how they

36. *Eccles. Pol.*, VIII, 4.
37. Preface, vii.
38. *A History of Elizabethan Literature*, (London 1887; 9th edn., 1907), 46.
39. *Eccles. Pol.*, I, ii, 1.
40. I. ii, 2.
41. I, ii, 3.

should be', the 'first law eternal'.[42] By this he means nothing less than the basic reason for the existence of things and of the ends they serve. The 'second law eternal' is, accordingly, that order which, under the divine will, all creatures keep.[43] Recognizing these fundamentals, then, reason can proceed to determine the different categories of law, whether of natural agents, or of heavenly beings, or of men. With regard to the last of these three types of law are distinguishable: the law of reason, 'which binds all creatures reasonable in this world'; the divine law, known to us only by 'special revelation from God'; and human law – the laws which, by the light either of reason or of revelation, men themselves enact. In framing these categories Hooker is clearly drawing on the tradition of the 'natural law' (*ius naturale*) which stretches back through medieval scholasticism to the Stoic philosophy of antiquity.[44]

The function of law in the life of man is to guide him to choose the good. His actual choice lies between will and appetite: 'The object of Appetite is whatsoever sensible good may be wished for, the object of Will is that good which Reason doth lead us to seek.'[45] Hence law of its very nature presupposes the possibility and responsibility of rational volition. In Hooker's philosophy this is of cardinal importance, however dubious it may have appeared to his Calvinistically-minded readers. Thus the way is cleared to deal with the question of scripture: whether the latter is, in truth, 'the only rule of all things which in this life may be done by men', as the puritans insisted. Actually the biblicist position has already been out-flanked by what was said in Book I; what has now to be appreciated is the real grounds on which the scriptures demand our assent. It cannot simply be claimed that the Bible is self-authenticating: 'It is not the word of God which doth or possibly can assure us that we do well to think it his word.'[46] In the last resort we have nothing else to guide us but reason and conscience, as many passages in the scriptures themselves imply. That the Bible contains the word of God is therefore a subject for reasoned argument. So Hooker arrives at the essentially humanist conclusion that 'the authority of man is, if we mark it, the key which opens the door of entrance into the knowledge of the Scripture', for 'Scripture could not teach us the things that are of God, unless we did credit men who have taught us that the words of Scripture do signify these things', a statement which also raises the question of the place of tradition.[47] The Bible has great authority – the Roman idea that it is insufficient of itself and needs supplementation by extra-scriptural tradition is an error; but it is no less erroneous, and even dangerous because conducive to scepticism, to claim that it offers more than it does.

The third Book concerns itself with the church, especially the assertion that 'in Scripture there must be of necessity contained a form of Church polity' the laws of which are unalterable. Hooker's purpose here is to meet the puritan contention

42. I, ii, 2.
43. I, iii, 1.
44. On Hooker's debt to St Thomas see P. Munz, *The Place of Hooker in the History of Thought* (London, 1952), 175ff. Cf. G. Hillerdal, *Reason and Revelation in Richard Hooker* (Lund, 1962), 40f.
45. *Eccles. Pol.*, I, vii, 3.
46. II, iv, 2.
47. II, vii, 3.

that by reference to the scriptural standard the Church of England was inadequately reformed. In other words, how could that church rightly maintain that reform may be taken so far but no further without seeming to compromise with the grave defects of Rome? Hooker's answer is that whereas in matters of saving faith the criterion of scripture is indeed sufficient and immutable, in matters of church polity or order, which do not pertain to the faith itself, there need be no limitation to a single form or usage only. In this field human judgement is free to decide what is or is not to be desired. 'Much of that which the Scripture teacheth is not always needful; and much the Church of God shall always need which the Scripture teacheth not.'[48] And: 'Because discretion may teach the Church what is convenient, we hold not the Church further tied to Scripture, than that against Scripture nothing be admitted in the Church, lest that path which ought always to be kept even, do hereby come to be overgrown with brambles and thorns.'[49]

It is in the light of this principle that questions of ecclesiastical polity must be approached, and especially, in view of the puritan objections to it, the episcopal form of church government. The puritan claim was that presbyterianism is the sole order of church government to have biblical authorization, but Hooker refrains from making a like claim on behalf of episcopacy.

> If [*he sagely observes*] we did seek to maintain that which most advantageth our cause, the very best way for us and the strongest against them were to hold even as they do, that in Scripture there must needs be found some particular form of church polity which God hath instituted, and which for that very cause belongeth to all churches, to all times. But with any such partial eye to respect ourselves, and of cunning to make those things seem the truest which are the fittest to serve our purpose, is a thing which we neither like nor mean to follow.[50]

It is enough that the Church of England should adhere to government by bishops as 'that which agreeth best with Scripture'.[51] The rightness of a ministerial hierarchy and the due subordination it entails can, Hooker believes, as against puritan insistence on the parity of ministers, be shown to be scriptural. We may note that in the seventh Book of the *Polity*, published in 1662, he states quite plainly:

> This we boldly therefore set down as a most infallible truth, 'That the Church of Christ is at this day lawfully, and so hath been sithence the first beginning, governed by Bishops, having permanent superiority, and ruling power, over other ministers of the word and sacraments'.[52]

Indeed, on the evidence of both scripture and history we are to conclude that 'if anything in the Church's government, surely the first institution of Bishops was from heaven, was even of God, the Holy Ghost was the author of it'.[53] Even so exceptions, Hooker allows, may occur, should circumstances warrant it. Episcopacy,

48. III, xii, 20.
49. III, iii, 3.
50. III, x, 8.
51. III, ix, 4.
52. VII, iii, 1.
53. III, v, 10.

therefore, is not invariably necessary, and Hooker will not unchurch bodies that lack it.

The last of the Books published in 1593, the fourth, treats of the rites and ceremonies of the church and rebuts the charge that they are 'popish'. The English church, continuous with that of the Middle Ages and antiquity, may use such traditional forms as she may deem appropriate, and the mere fact that Rome likewise does so is no reason for disowning them.

Thus we arrive at last at the great fifth Book, considerably more bulky than all four of its predecessors put together, for it is here that the author reaches the heart of his enterprise – to present a positive account and a vindication of the church's position upon the various particular matters as to which, in puritan eyes, it was defective.[54] Hence the book's detail. But the dominant motif is that whereas 'all things cannot be of ancient continuance, which are expedient and needful for the ordering of spiritual affairs', the church 'being a body which dieth not hath always power, as occasion requireth, no less to ordain that which never was, than to ratify what hath been before'.[55] A formal liturgy, including the simple reading of scripture without homiletic comment, is entirely defensible on the score of ancient and traditional usage, 'although not in all things everywhere the same', and Hooker stresses the value of liturgical order – 'a prescriptive for common prayer' – in comparison with not only extempore prayers but also preaching, which to the puritans was central for the whole act of worship: 'Sermons are not the only preaching which doth save souls', since 'preaching is a general end whereunto writing and speaking do both serve'. (As he himself however was a rather ineffective orator, Hooker probably goes too far in depreciating pulpit exhortations.)

In his sacramental teaching – and in chapters 1–lxvii, which are among his best, Hooker returns to theological fundamentals – he bases his position on the doctrine of the incarnation.

> Sacraments [*he reminds his readers*] are the powerful instrument of God to eternal life. For as our natural life consisteth in the union of the body with the soul, so our life supernatural is the union of the soul with God. And forasmuch as there is no union of God with man without that mean between both which is both, it seemeth requisite that we first consider how God is in Christ, then how Christ is in us, and how the sacraments do serve to make us partakers of Christ.[56]

On the question of the eucharistic presence he is somewhat elusive, although his general position would seem to be that of the prayer book rather than the *Thirty-Nine Articles*. 'There holy mysteries', he writes, 'received in due manner do instrumentally impart unto us ever in true and real though mystical manner the very Person of our Lord Himself, whole, perfect, and entire.'[57] But he also states that 'the real presence of Christ's most blessed body and blood is not to be sought for in the sacrament'.[58] On the face of it this is pure receptionism, but the passage

54. Francis Paget's *Introduction to the Fifth Book* (2nd edn., Oxford, 1907) remains useful.
55. V, viii, 1.
56. V, i, 3.
57. V, lxvii, 8.
58. V, lxvii, 6.

needs to be read in context, which seems to call for stress on the words 'sought for': the important thing is the presence of Christ in the heart of the communicant, and the spiritual participation in him which this implies.[59] 'What these elements are in themselves it skilleth not, it is enough that to me which take them they are the Body and Blood of Christ'.[60] He does not deny the sacramental presence of Christ in the elements, that is to say, but he does not think that inquiry as to how precisely that presence subsists there is of any great relevance. It is recognition of the effect which matters, not exact determination of the cause.

The rest of the *Polity* – the last part of Book V and Books VI to VIII – admit here of no more than cursory reference. Their central theme is the relation of church and state, and the ideal which Hooker presents is that of a national church, an order in which church and commonwealth are seen as one, each showing a complementary aspect of the same society: 'There is not any man of the Church of England but the same is a member of the Commonwealth, nor any member of the Commonwealth which is not also of the Church of England.'[61] Sectarianism is thus firmly rejected. Thus too the civil ruler is necessarily 'supreme governor of the Church'. Hooker maintains that it is a 'gross error' to suppose that the royal power serves only the nation's material interests, or 'men's temporal peace' and not their 'eternal safety', as if God had ordained things for no other end and purpose 'but to fat up men like hogs and to see that they have their mast'. In principle therefore sovereign and parliament are as representative of the English church as they are of the state itself; their joint duty and responsibility are to safeguard religion. Apparently Hooker's standpoint is thoroughly erastian, yet it does not in his mind amount to absolutism. The sovereign's headship of the church is, as he points out, *intra ecclesiam non supra ecclesiam*. 'Kings have dominion to exercise in ecclesiastical causes, but according to the laws of the Church.'[62] Sovereignty is itself subject, as on the Bractonian principle, to God and the law.

Hooker's immediate aim was to defend the English church establishment against the attacks of its puritan critics; his final achievement was to furnish it with a rationale which, while covering even the details of ritual practice, had its foundations in the broadest philosophical maxims. Accordingly his appeal is always beyond special authorities and precepts to the dictates of 'right reason'. So too he is confident that a natural theology is both possible and necessary if revelation itself is to be open, as it rightly should be, to the grasp of the rational understanding. Reason, that is, can of itself attain to the knowledge that God exists, as 'mere natural men' have known,[63] that all things therefore depend on him, and that he is the proper object of worship and obedience. Moreover, it is by reason that the axioms of morality are discoverable: to love one's neighbour is itself a rational decision. Such elementary obligations are apprehensible by us 'without the help of Revelation supernatural and divine'.

59. C. Darwell Stone, *A History of the Doctrine of the Holy Eucharist* (2 vols, London, 1909), II, 125–9, 177–84.
60. *Eccles. Pol.*, V, lxvii, 2.
61. VIII, i, 2. On Hooker's theory of civil government see below, 275f.
62. VIII, ii, 17.
63. I, viii, 7.

As a Christian theologian Hooker cannot of course discount the fall and its outcome, and simply to be aware of the laws of reason is not the same thing as to follow them: rather, in his depraved nature 'man is little better than a wild beast', 'obsolete, rebellious, and averse from all obedience unto the sacred laws of his nature'. But the essence of his humanity was not destroyed by sin, since the law of reason is still valid and in a measure effective even in his existing condition. Man's sense of perfection has not wholly left him, although it needs the light of revelation to enlarge it. But 'the complete sufficiency of . . . Scripture must . . . be understood with this caution, that the benefit of a divine light be not thought excluded as unnecessary, because the necessity of a divine light is magnified'.[64] The danger of the appeal to scripture alone has been, Hooker thinks, to introduce personal and private judgement as though it were the deliverance of the Holy Spirit. He admired Calvin greatly as a theologian, yet in an age when Calvinism was seemingly triumphant he himself stood aside from the great Genevan's following.

But Hooker tempered his insistence on the ultimate authority of reason by appeal to the gathered experience of the ages. Not only was it true that 'the ancienter the better ceremonies of religion are', but it must be judged, 'in all right and equity', that 'that which the Church hath received and held so long good, that which public approbation hath ratified, must carry the benefit of presumption with it to be accounted meet or convenient'.[65] And this in turn presupposes the wider principle that 'that which all men's experience teacheth them may not in any wise be denied'.[66] Indeed it may be said that the general and perpetual voice of men is as the sentence of God himself. 'For that which all men have at all times learned, nature herself must needs have taught.' In this trust in reason, experience and custom, as against all forms of *a priori* radicalism, Hooker goes far towards expressing, by anticipation, the genius of historic Anglicanism, for which the doctrinaire logic of Geneva has been no more to its liking than has the authoritarian institutionalism of Rome.

### The origins of English separatism

Hooker's ideal of an equivalence of church and nation was beyond realization even in his own day. The determined adherents of the old faith, now spiritually reinvigorated by the work of the Counter-Reformation, would not accept the national religious settlement in any respect and became henceforth an entrenched opposition, although their personal loyalty as citizens was for much the most part not seriously to be doubted. On the other side, the puritans, 'morose and obstreperous', as Bishop Cox of Ely called them, exerted substantial political influence and were as yet by no means convinced that the struggle to gain control of the national church and remould it in accordance with their own wishes might have to be abandoned. Nevertheless there were some among them who felt in all conscience that they could not go on conforming, and who began to devise a church system of their own

64. I, xiv, 4.
65. Preface, iv, 4.
66. III, viii, 14.

independent of the state. Of these irreconcilables the most prominent was Robert Browne (*c.* 1550–1633), a born dissident and mentally, perhaps, not altogether stable. He it is who is usually regarded as the pioneer of independency or congregationalism and who actually founded an independent conventicle at Norwich, an act for which he was imprisoned. On his release he and members of his flock migrated to Middleburg in Holland, where in 1582 he published his two principal literary works. The first of these, his *Treatise of Reformation without Tarying for Anie*, purported to explain what its author considered the true relationship of church and state, to refute the sort of charges made against himself and his followers – in essence, disloyalty to the queen as head of the Church of England – and to castigate preachers who sought to evade responsibility for not pursuing reform more consistently and energetically by pleading dependence on the secular authority.

Browne's main contention was that neither parliament nor the sovereign herself had any legitimate jurisdiction over the church, which he saw, after the manner of the continental anabaptists, as a separate spiritual realm, or community of saints, constituted by wholly voluntary covenant and in no way subservient to temporal rulers, Christ alone being its head. In fact Browne could not even concede that the church has a mission to the world if the end in view be the transformation of the worldly into something approximating to the Kingdom of God. The civil authorities have their proper functions to fulfil, though these do not include religious and ecclesiastical responsibilities, and in truth the church has throughout history best flourished when opposed. Hence the form or polity of a church is solely a matter for its own committed membership, which should not tarry in shaping it according to its convictions, for those who belong to a church live the life of grace in community of worship and edification, as far as possible in separation from the world.

To the Brownists internal discipline was of special importance, with excommunication imposed not simply for immorality or manifest irreligion but for almost any form of backsliding or evident tepidness of faith. Further, they demanded complete independence and autonomy for every congregation, so that wherever a group of truly regenerate believers constitutes itself as a worshipping community there the true church must be said to exist. And each such congregation was, on Browne's insistence, to be democratically organized, its officers being neither self-appointed nor supplied from without, but chosen by the congregation itself, to which they were responsible and by which they might be deposed.

The point on which Browne differed from the familiar anabaptist position was in his retention of infant baptism. As he wrote in his other treatise, *The Book which showeth the Life and Manner of all True Christians*, 'we must likewise offer and give up our children and others being under age, if they be of our household and we have full power over them'.[67] But the Lord's Supper is defined in typically anabaptist terms simply as 'a Sacrament or mark of the apparent Church sealing unto us by breaking and eating of bread and drinking the Cup in an holy communion'.[68]

67. A. Peel and L. H. Carlson, eds, *The Writings of Robert Harrison and Robert Browne* (London, 1953), 256.
68. *Ibid.*, 279.

Unfortunately Browne's personal fractiousness led to dissensions within his Dutch congregation and he moved on first to Scotland, where however he found himself little welcome, and then back to England, only to suffer there a further term of incarceration. In the end, curiously enough, he made his submission to the established church, accepting ordination and spending many years as incumbent of a Northamptonshire parish, although, it would seem, not without making some further difficulties for himself.

An exact contemporary of Browne's was Henry Barrow (*c.* 1550–93), a man converted at the age of thirty to a strict puritanism from, it is said, a dissolute life as a courtier. His views were very similar to those of Browne, but he eventually fell foul of Archbishop Whitgift, on whose orders he passed most of the remainder of his days in custody. Barrow was a dedicated separatist, at odds even with Browne himself, holding that a church organization of any sort must inevitably be corrupt. His writings, which include *A True Description of the Visible Congregation of the Saints* (1589) and *A Brief Discovery of the False Church* (1590), were printed in Holland by the efforts of his friends.[69] Charged in 1590 with circulating seditious books, he was executed by hanging three years later.

Barrow, like Browne, insisted that the church visible is the only church, whether in the New Testament or in living experience, and it exists exclusively in its particular and localized embodiments.[70] In *A True Description out of the Word of God, of the Visible Church*, printed, probably at Dort, in 1589, he writes:

> This Church as it is universally understood containeth in it all the elect of God that have been, are, or shall be. But being considered more particularly, as it is seen in the present world, it consisteth of a company and fellowship of faithful and holy people gathered together in the name of Christ Jesus, their only king, priest, and prophet, worshipping him aright, being peaceably and quietly governed by their officers and laws, keeping the unity of faith in the bond of peace and love unfeigned.[71]

But Barrow's main work, much longer and more polemical, was the *Brief Discovery*, written when its author was detained in the Fleet prison. The whole book is a sustained attack on the religious settlement of 1559. The English church is denounced as unscriptural, Calvinistic perhaps in its professed tenets but really untrue even to Calvin. On every count – state establishment, undiscriminating membership, neglect of discipline, 'popish' hierarchical ministry and a horde of ecclesiastical officials, formalized liturgy ('a quenching of God's spirit'), 'Jewish and popish' feasts and fasts – the church is violently castigated. Archbishop Whitgift, whom Barrow reviled as 'a monster . . . neither ecclesiastical nor civil, even that second beast spoken of in the Revelation', showed in fact remarkable patience and no sign of resentment in dealing with him and other separatists.

A collaborator of Barrow's was his friend John Greenwood, like him a Cambridge man, who received ordination in the Church of England but who in

---

69. C. F. J. Powicke, *Henry Barrow, Separatist, and the Exiled Church in Amsterdam* (London, 1900).
70. See L. H. Carlson, ed., *The Writings of Henry Barrow 1587–1591* (2 vols, London, 1962) and *id., The Writings of John Greenwood and Henry Barrow 1591–1593* (2 vols, London, 1970).
71. Carlson, *The Writings of Henry Barrow 1587–1591*, 214.

1586 was arrested and imprisoned for setting up a dissenting conventicle in London. Despite this he organized in 1592 the first separatist body in the capital, becoming, as he described himself, its 'teacher'. His writings include a short pamphlet, *The True and the False Church* (1588), in which he too excoriates the established church as a counterfeit: 'These churches consist not of a company of faithful people, but of a multitude of profane people. They worship not God truly, but after a false and idolatrous manner, as witnesseth their popish liturgy, their stinted book of their common prayer.'[72] By contrast, the 'true planted and rightly established Church of Christ' is defined as 'a company of faithful people; separated from the unbelievers and heathen of the land; gathered in the name of Christ, whom they truly worship, and readily obey as their only king, priest, and prophet; joined together as members of one body; ordered and governed by such officers and laws as Christ in his last will and testament hath thereunto ordained'.[73]

In 1592 Greenwood was rearrested, tried and condemned, along with Barrow, for uttering seditious publications, the two men being hanged at Tyburn early in April the following year. A few weeks later Henry Penry (1559–93), a Welshman from Brecknock and an Oxford graduate, was likewise executed on a charge, dubiously substantiated, of exciting rebellion, although he may well have been directly involved in the production of the Marprelate tracts. The deaths of these honest and sincere men are a deplorable fact in the history of Anglicanism, but with their extremist opinions they seemed to their contemporaries, even indeed to men like Cartwright, only subversive and revolutionary. Their uncompromising aim was the total abolition of the established church, and although as much as possible was done to dissuade them from their convictions by reasoned discussion they remained obdurate, attacking Archbishop Whitgift personally, as well as the religious system which he represented, in the most opprobrious language.

## Calvinist presbyterianism in Scotland

In Scotland as in England Protestant doctrines were at least anticipated by Lollardy – Scottish Lollardy was known to the Hussites as early as 1433 – and to some extent also by humanism. But during the reign of James V Lutheran ideas were reaching the populace by way of tracts smuggled into the country through the east coast ports; to such an extent in fact that in 1525 the Scottish parliament, the Estates, forbad the importation of Lutheran literature, in which they included Tyndale's New Testament, on pain of imprisonment and confiscation of goods and ships. Three years later the terms of the Act were extended to cover all who in any way assisted the spread of heretical views. The first well-known teacher of the new doctrines was Patrick Hamilton, who, although a scion of a noble and powerful family, was burned at St Andrews in 1528. Other executions followed until the king's death in 1542, when the regent favoured Protestantism and parliament authorized the use of the Bible in English or Scottish. Prominent among the

---

72. Carlson, *The Writings of John Greenwood 1587–1590*, 97–102.
73. *Ibid.*, 98.

reformist leaders was George Wishart, who had travelled in Germany and Switzerland and had imbibed Zwinglian opinions while at Zurich and Basel. Returning to England in 1542 he studied for a time at Cambridge and then betook himself to Scotland, where he began preaching at Montrose and Dundee, quickly gaining a following. He too went to the stake (1546), but not without having secured a perfervid and dedicated disciple in the young John Knox, destined to become the most famous of all the Scottish reformers and a man whose achievements, if not his personality, compel admiration.

Knox was born at Haddington, probably in 1514, but little is known of his early life, although it seems certain that by 1540 he was in priest's orders, serving not in a parish but as tutor in the households of the lairds of Longniddry and Ormiston. In 1545 he publicly confessed Protestantism, but two years later was captured by the French at St Andrews and sentenced to the galleys: for nineteen months he was chained to an oar. On his release early in 1549 his real work as a Protestant activist began. After some five years ministering to congregations at Berwick, at Newcastle and in London he was offered in 1552 the bishopric of Rochester by Edward VI, as well as a London living, but he declined both. Later he found his way to Geneva, getting to know Calvin there, and from thence to Zurich, where he stayed with Bullinger. Apart from a brief visit to Scotland in 1555 the years 1554 to 1558 were spent by him on the continent, for a time at Frankfurt, where disagreements arose with the English refugees which caused him to leave; but also, and more happily, at Geneva, that 'very school of Christ', as he called it. These were years in which he acquired considerable practical experience and a wide personal acquaintance with reformers in France and Switzerland.

Meanwhile the Scottish Protestants were continuing to organize themselves through a covenant. The Lords of the Congregation – the designation by which the leaders were generally known – swore before

> the majesty of God and His congregation that we (by His grace), shall with all diligence continually apply our whole power, substance, and very lives, to maintain, set forward, and establish the most blessed Word of God and His Congregation; and shall labour at our possibility to have faithful Ministers purely and truly to minister Christ's Evangel and Sacraments to his people.[74]

Knox, then at Geneva, was besought by the Lords to return to his native land, which he at last succeeded in doing in the early summer of 1559. Events thereafter moved quickly; the ancient Catholic system was obviously crumbling, despite efforts by the French queen-regent, mother of the young Queen Mary, to prop it up. The reformist party, with strong popular support, and exhorted powerfully by Knox, moved from triumph to triumph. Finally, in August 1560, parliament decreed the abolition of the papal authority and jurisdiction in the realm, annulled all the Acts of previous parliaments deemed contrary to the reformed doctrine, and prohibited the saying of or attendance at mass. Scotland thus opted for sweeping religious changes of a kind inspired and guided by the example of Calvin's Geneva.

The classical documents of the Scottish Reformation are the *Scots Confession*, the *Book of Discipline* and the *Book of Common Order*, the first of which provides

---

74. See D. Laing, ed., *The Works of John Knox* (Edinburgh, 1845–55), I, 273.

a fundamental doctrinal statement, drafted in 1560 by Knox and five collaborators within the space of four days.[75] The preface, boldly worded, invites correction if need be on the basis of scripture and disclaims any idea that the ensuing articles are inerrant. Of these, twenty-five in all, the first fifteen treat in order of the doctrine of God and the Trinity, the creation and fall of man and the prophetic promises of redemption, the incarnation (affirming the duality of the two natures in the unity of the one Person), the passion, resurrection and ascension of Christ, and sanctification through the Holy Spirit. In each the teaching, although Calvinistic in tone, is that of Catholic orthodoxy, and calls for no special mention, except to note that the doctrine of election (Article VIII) is stated in rather less than explicit terms, observing simply, and in a subordinate clause, that God 'of mere mercy' elected us 'in Christ Jesus, His Son, before the foundation of the world', while of predestination, a teaching which Knox himself embraced with fervour, nothing at all is said. Even justification by faith, although clearly assumed, is not defined. A decidedly Protestant note, however, is sounded in the articles on good works (XIII and XIV), which firmly reject all idea of merit or supererogatory virtue, among evil works those being included that 'in matters of religion and worshipping of God, have no assurance but the invention and opinion of man, which God from the beginning has ever rejected' – an oblique thrust at Rome; indeed throughout the whole confession the anti-Roman animus is intense. Article XVI, 'Of the Kirk', declares the church to be indefeasible and to consist of

> a multitude of men chosen of God, who rightly worship and embrace Him by true faith in Christ Jesus who is the only Head of the Church, which is also the body and spouse of Christ Jesus; which Church is Catholic, that is, universal because it contains the elect of all ages, of all realms, nations, and tongues . . . who have communion and society with God the Father and with His Son, Christ Jesus, through the sanctification of the Holy Spirit, . . . out of which there is neither life nor eternal felicity.

The notes of the church (Article XVIII) are said to be 'neither antiquity, title usurped, lineal descent, place appointed, nor multitude of men approving an error', but the true preaching of God's Word and the right administration of Christ's sacraments, together with ecclesiastical discipline uprightly administered, 'as God's Word prescribes', stress being placed, in typical Calvinist fashion, on particular 'kirks', 'such as were in Corinth, Galatia, Ephesus, and other places in which the ministry was planted by Paul, and were of himself named the Kirks of God'. The absolute authority of scripture is forcefully asserted in Article XIX: it is of God, depending neither on men nor on angels. The notion that the Bible has no other authority but that which the church itself invests it with is denounced as blasphemous 'and injurious to the true Kirk, which always heareth and obeyeth the voice of her own spouse and pastor, but taketh not upon her to be mistress over the

75. To these three documents should be added Knox's own chronicle of and commentary upon the course of events, the famous *History of the Reformation in Scotland* – utterly partisan but indispensable as a source of information. It was not printed in its author's lifetime and the first edition did not appear until 1586, and then was immediately suppressed for political reasons. The earliest complete and correct text came out in 1722. A modern edition of it is by W. C. Dickinson (London, 1949).

same'. It should be observed, too, that (though the statement actually occurs in the previous article) the interpretation of scripture does not depend either on private judgement or on the decisions of public persons, 'but appertaineth to the Spirit of God, by which also the Scripture was written'; this in turn being explained to mean, not so much the *testimonium internum* of the Spirit as the perspicacity of scripture itself, by which the less clear is explicated by what is more so.

With the articles (XXI to XXIIII) on the sacraments the language of the confession becomes sharper and more polemical. The position adopted is clearly Calvinist as distinct from Lutheran, but underlines as against Zwinglian teachings the objectivity of the spiritual gift conveyed by them: 'We utterly condemn the vanity of those that affirm sacraments to be nothing else but naked and bare signs.' By baptism, which is very properly administered to infants, 'we are' says the confession, 'ingrafted in Christ Jesus to be partakers of his justice [righteousness], by which our sins are covered and remitted'; while in the Supper, 'rightly used, Christ Jesus is so joined with us, that He becomes that very nourishment and food of our souls'. Although the transubstantiation dogma is condemned as pernicious, it is declared that 'believers do at the Lord's table so eat His body and drink His blood that He remaineth in them and they in Him', the union of Christ and communicant being 'wrought by operation of the Holy Ghost', who by faith lifts us above all earthly things, asking us 'to feed upon the body and blood of Christ Jesus, which was once broken and shed for us, which now is in that heaven, and appeareth in the presence of the Father for us' – phraseology pretty well identical with Calvin's own. But since the efficacy of the sacraments is inseparable from true faith both minister and communicant must properly understand their meaning and purpose, for if the opinion of the recipient is changed, the right use (so it is averred) ceases – a questionable view in that it approaches, on the one side, the Roman doctrine of 'intention', and on the other the Wycliffite notion that the value of the sacrament depends on the moral character of the ministrant. The ministers of the 'papistical Kirk' are abjured as 'no ministers of Christ Jesus'.

Article XXIV, 'Of the Civil Magistrate', is strongly anti-anabaptist. It states that the magistrate's office is ordained of God 'for the singular profit and commodity of mankind', and that civil rulers are 'to be loved, honoured, feared, and held in reverent estimation', for not only are they 'appointed for civil policy, but also the maintenance of the true religion, and for suppressing idolatry and superstition' – once again a typically Calvinist standpoint.

The *Scots Confession*, although approved by parliament, was not adopted as a constitutional document in the sense of a doctrinal test for ministers and others, and was not included in the *Book of Common Order*. In 1648 it was replaced by a theologically much more systematic and elaborate formulary, the *Westminster Confession*, even if the older statement be preferred on account of its directness of feeling and utterance and as a spontaneous expression of the circumstances which produced it.[76]

While the *Confession* set out the basic theology of the Scottish Reformation a

76. The most recent edition of the *Scots Confession* is that by G. D. Henderson (Edinburgh, 1960).

comprehensive scheme of practical reform was supplied by its accompanying *Book of Discipline*, again drawn up by Knox and his five colleagues. The whole spirit and ethos of this document too are distinctly Calvinist. It is a strikingly original composition, not precisely to be matched by anything else which the age produced, even if it has to be criticized as 'uneven and ill-proportioned', defects attributable no doubt to the haste with which the work on it was done.[77] Various influences are to be traced in it – Calvin's *Institutes* and *Ordonnances* are fairly obvious – but these touch matters of detail rather than of general content and scope, which were to indicate how a total 'Reformation of religion in the whole realm' was to be effected. It is set out under nine different heads, covering doctrine, the sacraments and the abolition of 'idolatry', the education and provision of ministers, the election of elders, the administration of ecclesiastical discipline, and what is termed the 'policy' of the church: 'an exercise of the Church in such things as may bring the rude and ignorant to knowledge, inspire the learned to greater fervency, or retain the Church in good order' – broadly and in a word, its mission.

The orderly calling of ministers was insisted on, but their admission was to be marked by no ceremony involving imposition of hands, the public approbation of the people and the declaration of the appointment by the chief minister being deemed sufficient. 'Papistical priests' are stated to have neither power nor authority to administer the sacraments. Thus the system adopted was in principle presbyterian, although the developed order of later times was of only gradual growth and may be said not to have attained its final shape until 1689. In 1572 an attempt was made to reintroduce a form of episcopacy, but the new bishops, contemptuously referred to as 'tulchans', or dummies, were held in low esteem, and when Knox's successor as leader of the Scottish religious settlement, Andrew Melville (1545–1622), returned to Scotland in 1574, he pressed the view that episcopacy was unscriptural and not to be further tolerated. So by 1580 the bishops, so-called, had disappeared. Two years previously a second *Book of Discipline* was compiled and endorsed by the General Assembly in 1581.

The work of Reformation would have been incomplete without appropriate liturgical forms to supersede the old Catholic worship. Knox had a qualified admiration for the 1552 English prayer book and even recommended its use to his Berwick congregation. But later, while ministering to the English exiles at Frankfurt, he decided in favour of a simpler worship, although on this his ideas did not please his flock and he moved on to Geneva. There it was that, with Calvin's personal approbation, he completed his *Book of Geneva*, which he brought back with him to Scotland in 1559. It was published at Edinburgh in 1562 and adopted by the General Assembly forthwith. An enlarged edition, with a metrical version of the psalter added, came out two years afterwards, and this, the *Book of Common Order*, remained the public liturgy of the Scottish church until its replacement in 1645 by the *Westminster Directory*. Curiously, the doctrinal confession included in the book was not the *Scots Confession* but that of the Church of Geneva. In addition to the regular public services there were forms for the election of superintendents, ministers, elders and deacons, as well as for the occasional offices and

77. G. Donaldson, *The Scottish Reformation* (Cambridge, 1960), 62.

for ecclesiastical discipline. The Lord's Prayer and Apostles' Creed were to be recited at every service, and the expectation was expressed that the Lord's Supper would be celebrated monthly, 'or so oft as the Congregation shall think expedient'. Baptism was directed to be administered before the sermon at Sunday worship. All these forms had a certain rough-hewn dignity, but the felicity of the English prayer book is noticeably absent. In fact, what has been said specifically of the *Book of Discipline* is essentially true of all three of these documents, namely, that their real significance and permanent importance lay in their concentration and definition of the ideas by which the Scottish reformers were guided, and in the tone which they imparted to the religion and character of the nation.[78]

## Note on Hooker's Theory of Civil Government

The theory of the civil government adumbrated in *The Laws of Ecclesiastical Polity* attempts to reconcile Thomist natural law philosophy with the practical exigencies of social reality. As such it is very characteristic of its author, a man always insistent on relating particular issues to basic principles while ever mindful of the contingent circumstances to which they have to be adapted. 'First, it is manifest', he declares, 'that obedience of creatures unto the law of nature is the stay of the whole world' (I, iii, 2). Natural law binds men absolutely as men, 'although they never have any settled fellowship, nor any engagement among themselves what to do or not to do' (XI, x, 1). But they have a natural desire for fellowship as well as need of the benefits which co-operative association will bring them. Thus the idea of the Social Contract is introduced, although not by that name. 'All public regiment of what kind soever seemeth evidently to have risen from deliberate advice, consultation, and composition between men, judging it convenient and behoveful: there being no impossibility in nature considered by itself, but that men might have lived without any public regiment' (I, x, 4). This, clearly, pertains to man's essential nature as a rational being. However, this essential rationality is marred by the actual and all too evident defects of man's nature as we see it. Selfishness and sensuality are men's undoing, as also the lethargy which deters them from doing the good they should do. Hence government to control men's actions is requisite; for while, on the one hand, it is an expression of their true nature, it is, on the other, an accommodation to the facts of men's lives as actually lived. So positive law has to be devised and imposed, which will make use of the constraining efficacy of rewards and punishments.

Positive law is founded on the natural law, but whereas the latter binds universally the former does not, for natural law enunciates what is right *per se*, positive law what is right because enjoined. But Hooker adds: 'Most requisite therefore it is that to devise laws which all men shall be forced to obey none but wise men be admitted' (I, x, 7). But the form of government may vary: 'The kinds thereof being many, nature tieth not to any one, but leaveth the choice as a thing arbitrary' (I, x, 5). Hooker holds the medieval and ultimately Aristotelian view of society as a

---

78. A. R. MacEwen, *A History of the Church in Scotland* (2 vols, London, 1918), II, 168.

community or commonwealth. 'Power belongs not to any one individual but to the community under the law.' Tyranny is illegitimate. 'By the natural law, whereunto [God] hath made all subject, the lawful power of making laws to command whole politic societies of men belongeth so properly unto the same entire societies, that for any prince or potentate of what kind soever on earth to exercise the same of himself, and not allow by express commission immediately and personally received from God, or else by authority derived at first from their consent upon whose persons they impose laws, it is no better than mere tyranny' (I, x, 8). 'Laws they are not therefore which public approbation hath not made so.' Such approbation does not have to be direct; it can rightly be given through representatives.

Hooker thus clearly asserts the sovereignty of the commonwealth through parliament, and in so doing takes his place – a forward one – in the history of English political constitutionalism. Principles are fundamental, but the theorist must have his eye on the situation confronting him. The *Ecclesiastical Polity* looks out, if a little complacently, over a happy contemporary settlement in both church and state.

# Chapter 12

# COUNTER-REFORMATION: THE COUNCIL OF TRENT

## Catholic reform and revival; the Jesuit theologians

A major consequence of the Protestant Reformation which in the sixteenth century tore western Christendom asunder was that the old church of the papal obedience, besides losing vast territories north of the Alps, itself underwent profound internal changes, partly in the reform of administrative abuses long recognized and widely deplored, but partly also, and more importantly, through a spiritual and moral revival from which it was able not only to recover self-confidence but to mount a vigorous and in many respects highly successful counter-offensive against its antagonists. This process, at once of reaction and rejuvenation, constituted what is usually designated the Counter- or Catholic Reformation, either term being appropriate if not taken as exclusive of the other. From it modern as distinct from medieval Catholicism finally emerged. For the Roman Catholic church of today is hardly less an outcome of the Reformation crisis than are the communions which, no doubt with varying eagerness and emphasis, recall the sixteenth century as the age of their nativity.

Not all aspects of this remarkable movement need demand our attention here. As a spiritual revival it gave new impetus to the religious life in the professional sense, at first in the Roman Oratory of the Divine Love, then in new religious orders or congregations, among them Theatines, Somaschi, Barnabites and Capuchins (a resuscitation of St Francis's medieval ideal), though most significantly of all the Jesuits.[1] The type of spirituality which these, the last especially, represented may be characterized as 'activism in grace': divine grace, that is, as unconditionally necessary for the soul's health, but expressing itself, through a subdued and disciplined will, in works of charity and social service. Such activism, of which a popular devotional book, *The Spiritual Combat*, attributed to the Theatine Lorenzo Scopuli, is a characteristic example, may in some measure at least be seen as a reply to Lutheran solafideism. Moral effort, fortified by a spiritual *askesis*, was the keynote, while the source of grace itself was judged to lie less in inward conviction of salvation than in the sacraments, notably the eucharist and penance more frequently and consistently used, and in assiduous prayer.

This stress upon a rigidly controlled but morally reinvigorated will nowhere found more striking utterance than in the famous *Spiritual Exercizes* of the Jesuits' founder, St Ignatius of Loyola (1491–1556), a work more readily comparable with

---

1. On the founding of the Society of Jesus see J. Brodrick, *The Origin of the Jesuits* (London, 1940). For the other orders mentioned see L. Cristiani, *L'Eglise à l'époque du Concile de Trente* (Fliche et Martin, *Histoire de l'Eglise*, XVII) (Paris, 1948), 245–95.

a military manual than a devotional writing of the usual sort.[2] 'Love', says the author, 'should consist in works far more than in words.' 'Laying aside', he goes on to say, 'all private judgement, we ought to hold our minds prepared and prompt to obey in all things the true spouse of Christ our Lord, which is our Holy Mother, the hierarchical Church.' Concomitant with discipline, that is, is obedience, and obedience to the church, or more exactly to the supreme pontiff himself, was paramount for all who sought enrolment in the Society of Jesus. Ultimately, however, the thing that mattered most was 'to honour and serve God, and save one's soul'. Well has it been said that 'this simple, slight, unassuming book was to make its weight felt to the ends of the world'.[3] From 1540, when the Society received incorporation by the bull *Regimini Militantis Ecclesiae* of Pope Pius III, onwards through the century, those in whose training it provided an essential stage became what probably was the most potent single influence in a Catholicism now reformed, renewed, propagandist and vehemently anti-Protestant.

This influence quickly showed itself in Counter-Reformation theology, particularly in the work of two of Loyola's original band of six associates who first took vows at Paris on 15 August 1534 and who thus formed the Society's nucleus, namely Diego Lainez (1512–65) and Alfonso Salmerón (1515–85). Lainez, a man of acute intellect, was from the start a personal force, an energetic preacher and teacher who, before succeeding Ignatius as general in 1558, was professor of theology at the Sapienza in Rome. At the Council of Trent, where he enjoyed the status of a papal theologian and later one of its fathers, his views on justification, the eucharist and penance carried considerable weight. On the theory of 'double justification', as to which agreement had been reached at the Conference of Ratisbon (Regensburg) in 1541,[4] he vigorously opposed the ideas put forward by

2. For a critical edition with introduction, notes and bibliography see *Monumenta Historica Societatis Jesu: Munementa Ignatiana*, Series 2, i (Madrid, 1919; 2nd rev. edn, Rome, 1969). There is an English trans. of *The Spiritual Exercises of St Ignatius* by T. Corbishley (London, 1963).

3. P. Janelle, *The Catholic Reformation* (Milwaukee, 1949; repr. 1963), 108.

4. The Conference of Ratisbon (Regensburg) met from 27 April to 22 May 1541, at the behest of Charles V, to discuss the possibility of a Catholic–Protestant understanding, other negotiations of the kind having already taken place somewhat earlier, first at Hagenau and then at Worms. Each side was represented by three leading theologians, the Catholics by that hardy controversialist Eck of Ingolstadt, by Julius von Pflug (1499–1564), bishop of Naumburg, a man of humanist sympathies, and Johann Gropper (1503–59) of Cologne, whose *Enchiridion* (1536; it later was placed on the Index) was thought by some Catholics capable of providing an acceptable basis for a reconciliation. On the Protestant side were Melanchthon, Bucer and Johannes Pistorius (1513–83). The pope was represented by the 'liberal' Cardinal Gasparo Contarini (1483–1542), who did his best to foster agreement wherever he could. The first four topics on the agenda – the condition of man before the fall, free will, the cause of sin, and original sin – created little difficulty, but the issue of justification gave rise to sharp contention. Even on this, though, accord was at last reached, thanks largely to Contarini's efforts, his *Epistola de justificatione* (25 May 1541) providing a formula on which minds not mutually antithetic could meet. Even Eck did not dissent, although he subsequently expressed regret for his action in acquiescing. Unfortunately the agreement was repudiated at Rome, while Luther himself was dissatisfied with it. Regarding the other matters discussed – the doctrinal authority of the church, the hierarchy, discipline and the

Girolamo Seripando (1493–1553), general of Luther's own order of Augustinian Eremites, who drew what seemed to him a necessary distinction between imputed and inherent righteousness, maintaining that the latter depended entirely on the former, an argument by which the council was much moved until Lainez's intervention. The Jesuit did not reject the distinction and even, in principle, allowed the sole efficacy of imputed righteousness. But he insisted, not implausibly, that no such differentiation is possible in life and that there is no imputed righteousness which at the same time is not realized in act. His pressure undoubtedly swayed the council and left its mark on the decree as finally drafted.[5] Lainez wrote no extended or systematic doctrinal treatise. Earlier on Ignatius Loyola had urged him to produce a new *summa theologica*, but this the manifold concerns of an active life prevented him from ever attempting.

With Lainez's name is always joined that of Salméron, who like his colleague was an effective presence at Trent. He was the Society's most forceful preacher, though as a writer he is less memorable, being as diffuse as he was prolific: his chief literary work was an immense homiletic commentary on the whole of the New Testament, though it did not appear until some years after his death.[6]

But the Jesuit theologian about whose teaching controversy within the Roman church was to become keenest was another Spaniard, Luis de Molina (1535–1600). Molina entered the Society in 1553 and held academic appointments successively at Coimbra, Evora and Cuenca before settling first at Lisbon and then at Cuenca again to a life of study. It was at Lisbon that he published his 'Harmony of Free Will with the Gifts of Grace' (*Concordia liberi arbitrii cum gratiae donis*) in 1588, devised originally as a commentary on certain passages in St Thomas Aquinas. His characteristic views, which in theological history still bear the label of his name (Molinism), envisage the divine gift of grace as effectual not simply in and of itself (*ab intrinseco*) but as depending on God's foreknowledge of a man's actual use of that gift. Molina saw this as a mediating doctrine (*scientia media*) capable of reconciling the principles of grace and free will. By distinguishing, that is, between prescience and predestination human freedom might be seen to coexist along with divine providence and prevenience. For when the sinner reacts positively to the option of faith, repentance and justification the requisite grace is afforded him by God, although on the ground only of Christ's merits, not his own. In this respect Molina believed that he had succeeded in harmonizing the Augustinian strain in St Thomas with the semi-Pelagianism associated with the Franciscans, and claimed that had such a theory as this prevailed before Lutheranism would have been forestalled. His opinions, however, met with resistance, especially from those

4. *continued* sacraments – there was no accord at all. Thus the conference ended in failure. For the Acts see Kidd, *Documents*, 136–40. Cf. also L. von Pastor, *Die kirchliche Reunionsbestrebungen während der Regierung Karls V* (Freiburg-im-Breisgau, 1879), 218–78. On Contarini's part see P. Matheson, *Cardinal Contarini at Regensburg* (Oxford, 1972).

5. See his *Disputationes Tridentinae*, ed. H. Grisar (2 vols, Innsbruck, 1886). Also F. Cereceda, *Diego Lainez en la Europa religiosa de su tiempo, 1512–1565* (2 vols, Madrid, 1945f.) and J. Brodrick, *The Progress of the Jesuits* (London, 1946), 66–111.

6. At Madrid, 1598–1601. It was based on his sermons, in which scripture is firmly harnessed to Roman dogma. See G. Boero, *Vita del servio di Dio, padre Alfonso Salmerón* (Florence, 1880).

traditional custodians of Thomism, the Dominicans. A special congregation, *Congregatio de Auxiliis*, was set up in Rome by Pope Clement VIII to adjudicate on the matter, but although it deliberated from 1598 until 1607 no final decision was pronounced, even when its feeling was against Molinism. Hence the latter doctrine continued to be taught.[7]

Nevertheless Augustinianism did not remain merely on the defensive. In the writings of the Louvain theologian Michel de Bay (or Baius) (1514–89) it was energetically reasserted in a form which can now be seen as a signal anticipation of the Jansenism of the following century. About 1550 Baius, who was principal of the Standonck College at Louvain, found himself, along with a colleague of his, Jan Hessels, in trouble with both the university authorities and the archbishop of Malines regarding his teachings on sin and grace, the orthodoxy of which was suspect. But the affair did not prevent him and Hessels from attending the reopening of the Council of Trent in 1551 as the university's representatives. Ten years later a series of propositions attributed to him were censured by the Sorbonne, ever sensitive to the whiff of heresy. Baius was by no means a contumacious man and he intimated his readiness to accept the ruling whether of Rome or of the council, which by then had resumed its sittings. For a time dispute again died down but flared up with the publication in 1563–4 of certain dogmatic treatises of his, among them those on free will (*De libero arbitrio*), righteousness (*De justitia*) and justification (*De justificatione*). In 1567 Pius V, in the bull *Ex Omnibus Afflictionibus*, condemned seventy-nine propositions extracted from Baius's works (though the author is not named personally) as false, heretical and scandalous. The ambiguous phraseology of the papal document may have rendered exact interpretation of it somewhat problematic, but final censure was conveyed in a brief of 1569 and Baius dutifully submitted. Thereafter he took no further part in theological controversy.

Baianism rested on the fundamental Augustinian doctrines of man's total depravity and moral incapacity consequent upon the fall. Thus he was led to oppose the scholastic teaching, sustained at Trent, that man's prelapsarian state was one of 'pure nature' (*pura natura*), to which an additional gift of grace (*donum superadditum*) was brought, so raising man to a preternatural condition of innocence. In Baius's view such innocence was rather an attribute or complement of human nature itself, so that the fall was to be explained not simply as a privation of special grace but as an essential corruption of man's being, making any true freedom of will impossible (*liberum arbitrium hominis non valet ad opposita*). The work of redemption restored man's original innocence; original sin indeed persists as a condition of his actual nature, but charity, through grace, overcomes concupiscence as a motive for action. Even so, justifying righteousness, according to Baius, lies more surely, given the practical impossibility of achieving

---

7. See F. Stegmüller, ed., *Geschichte des Molinismus, I: Neue Molinaschriften* (*Beiträge zur Geschichte der Philosophie des Mittelalters*, xxxii, 1935); also J. Rabeneck, 'De vita et scriptoris Ludovici Molina', in *Archivum Historicum Societatis Jesu*, xix (1950–1), 75–145; and E. Vansteenberghe, 'Molinisme', in *Dictionnaire de Théologie catholique*, x (1928), coll. 2094–2187.

spiritual and moral perfection in this life, in the forgiveness of sins.[8]

The condemnation of Baius and the maintenance of semi-Pelagianism were symptomatic of the consistent Jesuit influence in Counter-Reformation theology, or at least of that insistence on the freedom of the will and the need for perseverance in good works characteristic of the activism with which the Society has always been associated.

One more notable representative of the order should be mentioned here, as probably the most able of its controversialists. Robert Bellarmine (Roberto Bellarmino, 1542–1621) was an Italian from Tuscany who became a Jesuit in 1560 and held a professorship in theology at Louvain from 1570 until 1576, when he took up an appointment in Rome at the Society's then newly founded college. Created a cardinal in 1599, he was from 1602 to 1605 archbishop of Capua, although preferment to high ecclesiastical office was rarely accepted by members of the order. By inclination wholly a scholar, much of his time and energy were given over to controversial exchanges with Protestants – one of these was with James I of England – and he was not only well versed in Protestant doctrine but invariably treated it with fairness and understanding. His main work, *Disputatio de controversiis Christianae fidei adversus huius temporis haereticos*, published at Ingolstadt between 1586 and 1593, in which the Tridentine platform was clearly and forcefully defended, is noteworthy for its carefully presented case for papal supremacy and infallibility.[9]

## The summoning of the Council

Strange as it may seem, the medieval Catholic church, deeply concerned though its teachers and savants were with the niceties of theological doctrine, had little in the way of precise dogma on which to rest its theological structures beyond the fundamentals bequeathed to it from antiquity. The result had been a crop of theological variations, embodied in rival school traditions between which there was often keen dispute. Doctrine tended, in fact, to be regarded as a technical matter on which the vast majority of believers, not being professionally equipped to deal with it, could not be expected to hold an opinion. It was sufficient to accept what the church was presumed to teach by an act of implicit faith, and in the fifteenth century, certainly, attention was directed more to personal and practical religion than to its dogmatic framework. With the coming of the Reformation, however, and with it the propagation of doctrines not only novel but in most instances contradictory of the beliefs of the Roman church, a reassessment of Catholic

8. See F. X. Jansens, *Baius et le baianisme* (Museum Lessianum, section théologique, XVIII, 1927). Also H. de Lubac, 'Deux augustiniens fourvoyés, Baius et Jansenius: i, Baius', in *Recherches des sciences religieuses*, xxi, (1931), 422–43, and E. van Eijl, 'L'interprétation de la bulle de Pie V portant la condemnation de Baius', in *Revue d'Histoire ecclésiastique*, i (1955), 499–542.
9. See J. Brodrick, *The Life and Works of Blessed Robert Cardinal Bellarmine* (2 vols, London, 1928). Bellarmine's collected works were reprinted at Paris 1870–4. His canonization took place in 1930.

teaching regarding disputed issues and leading, it might be, to exact and authoritative statements thereon became urgent. Whatever else the Council of Trent may have achieved this it did accomplish, expending on its task a truly remarkable degree of care and deliberation. Without the challenge of Protestantism, indeed, this work of definition might never have been undertaken. For in the words of Adolf Harnack, 'the decrees of the Council of Trent are the shadows of the Reformation. That it was given to Catholicism to understand itself, to give expression to its distinctive character and to rescue itself from the uncertainties of the Middle Ages, was a debt it owed to the Reformation.'[10] It was at Trent that Roman Catholicism transformed what to a large extent had been speculative theology into a scheme of rigid if not always entirely unambiguous dogma, with, in the main, Thomism as its informing spirit.

The summoning of a general council, pressed on the papacy by the Emperor Charles V, had been consistently shirked by Rome from fear of a resurgence of conciliarism, which in the greatly changed conditions of the sixteenth century might well have reduced the papal power to, at best, that of a constitutional monarchy. Catholic princes, on the other hand, deplored ecclesiastical abuses and saw in a council the only hope of their eradication. For years the popes, one after another, stalled: Alexander's advice to Clement VII was taken to heart. 'Never', said the legate, 'offer a council, never refuse it directly; on the contrary, show a readiness to comply with the request but at the same time stress the difficulties that stand in the way; by this means you will be able to ward it off.'[11] But, confronted by the rapid spread of Protestantism and the ecclesiastical disintegration it brought with it, a council sooner or later was unavoidable. Rome was determined that it would not be summoned by a temporal ruler or convened in any locality where papal influence could not be directly exerted. Eventually the bull *Laetare Hierusalem* fixed the meeting-place of the assembly at Trent (Lat. *Tridentum*), a free city of the empire in northern Italy with a mixed German and Italian population; easy of access therefore from Italy, but within the imperial jurisdiction. The papal legates arrived there in March 1545, but the delegates themselves were slow in following them and months passed before the council was ready to open.

The formal opening took place on 13 December, but the members present even then comprised no more than fifty bishops and fewer than fifty theologians and canonists. At no time, in fact, were the numbers of the former large and the Italian element was always far more numerous than the rest: of the 255 prelates who signed the final acts of the council 189 were Italians, though even so it would be a mistake to think that all of them dutifully supported the papal interest. Paul III's legates were, besides, themselves men of mark: Gian Maria Cardinal del Monte (later Pope

10. *A History of Dogma*, VII, 36.
11. J. J. I. Döllinger, *Beiträge zur politischer, kirchlicher und Kulturgeschichte der sechs letzten Jahrhunderte* (3 vols, Munich, 1862–82), III, 254 (quoted H. Jedin, *History of the Council of Trent*), I (English trans. by E. Graf, London, 1957), 224. Contarini complained of Clement VII that though the pope 'desires the suppression of abuses in holy church he never carries his desires into effect and takes no steps to that end' (Jedin, *op. cit.*, 222). But Clement had every reason to dread a council.

Julius III), Marcello Cervini (as Marcellus II he was to have one of the briefest pontificates in history), and the Englishman Reginald Pole. Of these the first was an unbending conservative; the second, although keen enough on disciplinary reform, was in no way in favour of concessions in the dogmatic field; and the third may be said to have belonged to the 'liberal' reformist group led by men like Contarini, Giberti of Verona and Fregoso of Salerno. Charles V, even at that late date, saw the council in an oecumenical light and hoped that it would be able to win over at any rate the Lutherans, thus overcoming the schism in Germany and restoring ecclesiastical unity within the empire. But to less sanguine minds it was evident that any such reconciliation was of only the remotest possibility. The real work of the council – from which, as an obviously papal gathering, the Lutherans from the very first stood aloof – would be at once that of internal reform, which could now no longer be delayed, and of the codification of Catholic doctrine in a manner that would clarify it for the benefit of the faithful and declare beyond all doubt wherein it differed, and had to differ, from the heresies of Protestantism. The task of formulation devolved on the bishops and heads of religious orders (*diffinitores*) exclusively, but they were to be assisted by panels of theological and legal experts (*consultores*) among whom Jesuits and Dominicans carried great weight.

Difficulties arose at the outset as to the order of procedure. Cervini, expressing Paul III's own view, was anxious that the doctrinal issues should first be dealt with, leaving curial reform to the pope himself, and with this order of priorities Protestant opinion would have been in agreement: as the reformers saw matters it was Rome's false teachings that were the real source of corruption. Not a few of the delegates, however, led by Madruzzo the prince-bishop of Trent, thought otherwise, believing that the root cause of Luther's revolt had been the church's institutional disorder and holding that the practical end of moral and administrative reform was the more pressing; and in this of course they reflected the firmly held view of Charles V. The upshot was a compromise whereby the two sides of the council's work would receive simultaneous discussion in separate commissions whose reports would be laid before the council fathers alternately. This decision did not please the pope, but his attempt, through his legates, to have it rescinded were unavailing. The mode of procedure was thus settled: the synod would divide itself into two, each commission having separate agenda the several items of which would be considered first by a committee of experts and then debated, with the latter's recommendations before it, by the commission itself. If the recommendations were approved they would be brought before a general congregation of the whole synod. Finally, if adopted there, they would be promulgated by the council in solemn session. Doctrinal decisions would take the form both of decrees (*decreta*) containing positive statements of the church's teaching and canons (*canones*) anathematizing the contrary Protestant teachings. The decrees are, it must be allowed, altogether notable for the skill with which they are phrased. Protestant views, on the other hand, are treated without sympathy and at times without real understanding, and in any case tend to be presented only in an extreme or one-sided manner.

In general the doctrinal positions reached at Trent represent a thorough reassessment of the received teachings and are certainly not a mere reiteration and endorsement of medieval theologizing, much of which was eliminated, especially in the Scotist-nominalist line. The Jesuit influence, as we have said, was marked, but the council's work signified in the main a reaffirmation of Thomism and hence in its way a resuscitation of Augustinianism. So in reaching their conclusions the council fathers were not seldom subject to tensions which the records of the preceding debates render quite evident. All the same, over the whole long process of rethinking Catholic doctrine fell the shadow of Protestantism and the formulations arrived at must be seen primarily as Rome's defiant riposte to the challenge which the Protestant reformers had thrown down. Proof of the council's concern is apparent in the selection and order of the theological topics discussed. For Trent, although modern Roman Catholicism has in large part been built upon it, has to be placed in the context of the time and circumstances in which the post-medieval church found itself. Where in all probability it most signally failed – apart, that is, from its inability to appreciate what lay at the heart of the Protestant revolt – was in giving expression to the humanist spirit and so of conceding the importance of biblical and historical theology, the study of which humanism had pioneered. It is of significance that in 1558 the works of Erasmus, for long suspect in orthodox eyes, were condemned *in toto* by Pope Pius IV.[12]

The council's meetings, which all told extended over a period of eighteen years, for four and a half of which it was actually sitting, cover three periods: 1545–7 (sessions i–ix), under Pope Paul III; 1551–2 (sessions x–xvi), under Julius III; and 1562–3 (sessions xvii–xxv), under Pius IV. Trent was the scene of all except sessions ix and x, which from 21 April till 2 June 1547 were held at Bologna, within papal territory. Despite the long intervals when the synod was not meeting and the changes of personnel which these entailed, the council's record is one of continuity; it was a single assembly, not a succession of three. And at the end of it the papacy itself, *mirabile dictu* now reformed, was triumphant. The Catholic church had become indeed papal in a more stringent sense, as also more evidently Latin, than ever before in its history.

### Sessions iii–vi: basic issues

The substantive business of the council started with the third session, as the first two were taken up with procedural matters.[13] To begin with, the rule of faith itself

---

12. Trent modified this absolute censure, but it was afterwards reimposed by Sixtus V (1590).
13. The initial question to be settled was the title of the assembly itself, the legates proposing *Sacrosancta Tridentina Synodus, in Spirito Sancto legitime congregata, in ea presidentibus tribus apostolicae sedis legatis*. The more 'progressive' party wanted to add the words *'Ecclesiae universalis repraesentans'*, but the proposal was rejected, probably as too reminiscent of the conciliarist demands at Constance and Basel. Full accounts of the council's deliberations are provided in the Görres-Gesellschaft's *Concilium Tridentinum: diariorum, actorum, epistolarum, tractatuum nova collectio* (13 vols, Freiburg-im-Breisgau, 1901ff., referred to here as *C.T.*). The definitive history of the council is Hubert Jedin, *Geschichte des Konzils von Trient* (Freiburg-im-Breisgau, 1949ff., English trans. in 2 vols, London, 1957–61).

was considered, and as at earlier councils the Nicene (Niceno-Constantinopolitan) creed was affirmed (4 February 1546) as the *Symbolum fidei quo sancta Romana ecclesia utitur.*[14] Then, at the fourth session, the council fathers embarked on the question, all-important in view of the Protestant insistence on the sole sufficiency of scripture, of the sources and documents to which appeal in matters of doctrine was properly to be made. Thus the issue of what the canon of scripture actually comprises was introduced in the general congregation on 12 February. This, however, occasioned little discussion, and three days later it was decided to follow the decree of the Council of Florence of 4 February 1441, which, in accordance with tradition, identified as books of the Old Testament those of the Greek canon, which included the apocryphal books as well, so imposing on Catholics the acceptance of all of them as *de fide*, a decision ratified by the First Vatican Council in 1870.[15] The Augustinian general, Seripando, had sought to distinguish between the protocanonical books (those of the Hebrew canon), 'canonical and authentic' and so constituting a *canon fidei*, from the deuterocanonical ones, 'canonical and ecclesiastical', which should be regarded rather as a *canon morum* (a standard for morals).[16] But the council was not impressed by the argument. In the list of the New Testament books the *Epistle to the Hebrews* appeared as the fourteenth of St Paul's epistles.[17]

Ecclesiastical tradition, on the other hand, was a subject not so easily disposed of. What exactly such tradition included and what was its relation to scripture were inescapable problems inasmuch as the Lutherans repudiated all tradition which did not conform to the scriptures. If the Protestant case was to be heeded would it then follow that ecclesiastical tradition had no authority of its own? As to its content, traditions certainly existed in regard to worship and discipline which were not to be found in scripture; but what of doctrine? Questions like these did not admit of an immediate answer and the *consultores* themselves were none too successful in clarifying matters. The Jesuit theologian Claude Lejay, however, was of influence in securing a distinction between dogmatic traditions (*quae ad fidem pertinent*) and all others, ceremonies and the like. Even so, what was it that the former could be shown to have taught? The council was tempted actually to compile a list of traditions, and one such was submitted by a lay theologian, Count Lodovico Nogarola in a dissertation, *Institutiones apostolicae*, itemizing no fewer than thirty-four apostolic traditions.[18]

Then the whole concept of tradition as an authority independent of scripture was suddenly challenged by an Italian bishop, Giacomo Nacchianti of Chioggia. Were not all doctrines necessary for salvation, he asked, already contained in Holy

14. *C.T.*, IV, 579–88.
15. Hitherto no council claiming oecumenical status had listed the canonical books in a decree, though such a list was made at a Roman council held probably in 382 under Pope Damasus. This and the Tridentine list are identical.
16. See his tractate 'De libris S. Scriptorum', in *C.T.*, XII, 483–96.
17. On Trent and the canon of scripture generally see K. D. Schmidt, *Studien zur Geschichte des Konzil von Trient* (Tübingen, 1925), 125–209, and A. Maichle, *Der Kanon des biblischen Bücher und das Konzil von Trient* (Freiburg-im-Breisgau, 1929).
18. H. Jedin, 'Un laico al Concilio di Trento: el Conte Lodovico Nogarola', in *II Concilio di Trento: Rivista commemorativa de IV Centenario*, ed. P. Paschini, I (1942–3), 25–33.

Writ? 'To put scripture and tradition on a parity', he said, 'is ungodly (*impium*).' How could one 'accept the practice of praying eastward with the same reverence as St John's Gospel?' In the circumstances it was a bold utterance. 'One almost imagines Luther speaking', observes Jedin, 'as one listens to this Italian bishop's earnest warning against putting the traditions . . . by the side of scripture.'[19] Yet surprisingly his interjection did not antagonize the council fathers as much as might have been expected. Further, his view was shared by Agostino Bonuccio, the general of the Servites, who objected that scripture contained the entire gospel and not a part of it only. Rightly understood tradition was not a complement of the scriptural revelation but its interpretation. Thus between the two there could be no parity.

In spite of objections like these from a minority of its members what the council quite certainly had in mind in approving the decree was that tradition brought to scripture not simply an exegesis but a material supplementation. As finally accepted (8 April 1546) the document stated that:

> In order that errors may be removed and the purity of the Gospel be preserved in the Church, which was promised through the prophets in the Holy Scriptures and which our Lord Jesus Christ the Son of God first published by his own mouth and then commanded to be preached through his Apostles to every creature as a source of all saving truth and of discipline of conduct; and perceiving that this truth and this discipline are contained in written books and unwritten traditions, which were received by the Apostles from the lips of Christ himself, or, by the same Apostles at the dictation of the Holy Spirit, and were handed on and have come down to us; following the example of the orthodox Fathers, this Synod receives and venerates, with equal affection and reverence [*pari pietatis affectu ac reverentia suscipit et veneratur*], since one God is the author of both, together with the said traditions, as well those pertaining to faith as those pertaining to morals [*tum ad fidem, tum ad mores pertinentes*].[20]

As for the biblical text itself, after a discussion of what language or languages – the original tongues, as the humanists had urged, or an officially recognized version (Latin) – it was to be used in, it was decided that the Vulgate (*vetus et vulgata editio*) should be accepted, even though in the course of the debate it was acknowledged that the text ought to be corrected in the light of the Septuagint and other ancient witnesses.[21] As to vernacular versions, inconvenience and even danger

19. Jedin, *History of the Council of Trent*, II, 64.
20. *C.T.*, V, 91f. But see further J. R. Geiselmann, *Die Heilige Schriften und die Tradition* (Freiburg-im-Breisgau, 1962); also, by the same writer, 'Das Missverständnis über das Verhältnis von Schrift und Tradition in der katholischer Theologie', in *Una Sancta*, xi (1956), 131–50. According to Geiselmann Trent rejected a form of words which stated that the 'truth' (of salvation) and 'rule' (of conduct) are contained 'partly' (*partim*) in written books, partly in unwritten traditions, so that in fact the Council – contrary to a common interpretation of its decree, by both Catholics and Protestants– did *not* affirm that some revealed truth is contained in tradition but not in scripture. See likewise Y. M.-J. Congar, *La Tradition et les traditions* (Paris, 1960–63) (Engl. trans. by M. Naseby and T. Rainborough, London, 1966). Congar holds that what Trent should be taken to teach is that all saving truth is contained, at least implicitly, in scripture, tradition being no more – if no less – than its true interpretation in the life of the church.
21. For Cervini's defence of the Vulgate see *C.T.*, X, 468.

to the faith were, it was felt, likely to attend their circulation. On the interpretation of scripture arbitrariness and idiosyncrasy were to be avoided: the church alone could expound it authoritatively. No books of scripture were to be printed or published without the name of the editor and the permission of the ordinary, in accordance with the bull *Inter Sollicitudines* of the Fifth Lateran Council.

In its next session (v) the synod turned to the doctrine of original sin, on which again there were fundamental differences from Protestantism. The subject was first referred to the theologians (24 May 1546), the particular topics which they were asked to examine being, first, the testimony of scripture and apostolic tradition appealed to by the early Fathers, the councils and the Apostolic See against those who denied original sin; secondly, the nature of original sin, by reference to its effects; and thirdly, the means by which man is delivered from original sin, and especially whether redemption effects its complete removal or whether certain traces (*vestigia*) remain, and if so, what their consequences might be. What exactly the *consultores* had to report on these matters is not known, except for the views of a Spanish secular priest, Juan Morilla, in whose thinking there was evidently a pronounced Augustinian strain instanced by what he says on the effects of baptism, which, he points out, expunges the guilt of original sin and its eternal damnation (*reatum peccati et damnationis aeternae*), but does not destroy concupiscence, which so persists as always to demand moral effort (*ad agonem*). Thus although concupiscence is not itself, strictly speaking, sinful, it is, as it were, a weight dragging even the regenerate downwards into sin. It is because of concupiscence, in other words, that our righteousness is never more than imperfect.[22] Here, plainly, was material for controversy. Luther had maintained that concupiscence is a condition actually sinful. Indeed St Augustine and St Thomas had themselves described it as 'sin', though this might be taken to mean only that, by presenting an obstacle to the attainment of good, it necessarily 'inclines' to evil – an interpretation which Seripando rejected: to him, as an Augustinian, it was of the essence (or 'act', *actus*) of original sin; for this it is, he argued, which, along with the guilt (*reatus culpae*), is the cause of inherited guilt in the unbaptized; if after baptism it is not sin in a positive or active sense, yet 'in some sense' (*aliqua ratione*) it still is so, at least as being the root and cause of actual sin. Seripando sought nevertheless to distinguish his position from Luther's on the ground that although concupiscence is displeasing to God it does not of itself render the baptized liable to eternal damnation, since guilt is washed away in baptism. But he did press the point that the effectiveness of the baptismal rite is inseparable from faith, whether that of the catechumen himself or, in the case of infants, that of the sponsors.[23]

The first draft of the original sin decree succeeded in avoiding scholastic technicalities almost completely, confining itself to biblical and patristic language, but it gave rise to searching discussion.[24] For example, was Adam's original righteousness a supernatural *sanctitas*, 'holiness', or was it, as the Spanish prelate, Cardinal Pedro Pacheco, bishop of Jaen, thought, better described as *rectitudo* or *innocentia*? Again,

22. For Morilla's tractate on sin see *C.T.*, XII, 553–65.
23. For his statement on original sin see *C.T.*, XII, 549–53. Also H. Jedin, *Girolamo Seripando* (Würzburg, 1937), I, 354–8.
24. *C.T.*, V, 196f.

the decree's final clause, which had an Augustinian bias, declared that the Thomist teaching, according to which the *formal* element in sin is removed by baptism, whereas the *material* element is not, was stated to be not unacceptable (*non improbat*). Incidentally, Pacheco had also posed the question of the immaculate conception of the Virgin Mary, a belief that had been a good deal disputed in the schools, Scotists who favoured the doctrine opposing Thomists who did not, and a lengthy wrangle over it seemed inevitable, especially when Pacheco found that by the terms of the draft decree the dire consequences of the fall which had been transmitted to the whole human race 'in accordance with a universal law' seemed to preclude it altogether. A revised draft therefore was brought before the general congregation (14 June), in which the points made by Seripando and the Augustinians were ignored,[25] while an added fifth canon anathematized the doctrine that in baptism the guilt of original sin is not removed but merely 'covered up' (*radi*) or not imputed. But on the subject of the immaculate conception the council declined to make a statement and the decree in its final form was approved on 17 June.[26] Not only Pelagian but also, it would appear, semi-Pelagian ideas were rejected, although certain turns of phrase are somewhat less than clear: for example, what precisely is the meaning of 'that holiness and righteousness in which [Adam] had been constituted [*in qua constitutus fuerat*]'? The loss only of Adam's supernatural endowment? Or what really is to be understood by the assertion that free will is *minime extinctum*? Or that by the fall Adam was 'changed for the worse [*in deterius commutatus*]'?[27]

With the council's sixth session there began the long debate on the central issue of justification, one of palmary significance for Protestants but which, with the exception of men like Cajetan (in his *De fide et operibus* of 1532) and Gasparo Contarini, had received little enough serious attention from Catholic theologians. On 21 June Cervini addressed the general congregation on it, stressing for his audience the great importance of the subject and reminding them that it had not been adequately dealt with by any previous council.[28] Also he impressed on them that if they would discover the source of the Lutheran errors on other doctrinal matters they should seek it there. He was well supported by Cardinal Pole, who, however, put it to the council to consider the question with an open mind and not forthwith to condemn a teaching simply because it happened also to be Luther's. On the following day the subject was passed to the *consultores*, who were asked to treat it under six heads: its meaning; its causes, including the respective parts of God and of man in the process; the role of faith; the place and value of works, both before and after justification; the process itself; and the basic proofs, biblical, patristic and conciliar by which the Catholic position was upheld.[29] The theologians' discussion lasted from 22 to 28 June, except for the 24th, a holy day, and such

25. *C.T.*, V, 118f.
26. *C.T.*, V, 238ff.
27. *Tametsi in eis liberum arbitrium minime extinctum esset, viribus licet attenuatum et inclinatum.* For a careful discussion of the decree see W. Koch, 'Das Trienter Konzilsdekret *De peccato originali*', in *Tübinger Theologische Quartalschrift*, xcv (1913), 430–50 and 532–64; xcvi (1914), 101–23.
28. *C.T.*, X, 531ff.
29. *C.T.*, V, 262–5.

differences as arose were between Scotists and Thomists; nominalism was not represented. Although information on these six days is regrettably meagre, it is clear that the Augustinian–Lutheran viewpoint was by no means without a voice, a group of theologians, it seems, maintaining the passivity of the human will in justification; indeed a Greek prelate, the bishop of Melapotamos and Chironissa, squarely denounced the two Augustinian Eremites on the commission as Lutherans pure and simple.

On 30 June the bishops themselves took up the subject.[30] A Thomist, Pietro Bertano, bishop of Fano, who was in close touch with the legates, stated the Catholic argument with clarity and force.[31] There is, he said, a threefold righteousness (*justitia*): that of God himself, as shown by his sending of his Son into the world for the redemption of man; that of Christ, whose merits are appropriated by us to become our own (*justitia inhaerens*); and the righteousness of good works, by which we exemplify our own righteousness. We are, certainly, justified by faith, but by an active faith (*per fidem*), not a passive one (*ex fide*), for faith, in order to be effective, must, as St Paul teaches, be united with hope and love. Only by such meritorious faith is man united with Christ; otherwise, as St James says, it is dead faith. The Lutheran formula, *sola fide*, Bertano rejects as too limited, since it seemed to exclude hope and love; while good works are not merely the sign or expression of justification but a necessary and integral part of it.

Seripando's views, always of interest to the student of Trent, are best ascertained from his tractate on justification especially drawn up for the council.[32] The decree ought not, he thought, to be cast in technical language but in words the layman could understand, and should relate to the facts of experience, especially as exemplified in the classic instances of the conversions of St Paul and St Augustine. Four factors, he maintained, are in this regard to be borne in mind: the absolute prevenience of divine grace (*gratia praeveniens*), by which we are called to repentance; our own act in repenting, with grace aiding us (*adiutorium gratiae*); the righteousness of God embodied in the redeeming work of Christ (*justitia Dei*); and the faith and trust whereby we receive the divine forgiveness and are made one with Christ. Thus reconciled to God we receive the gifts of the Spirit, and in particular that charity which enables us to fulfil God's commands (*justitia operans*).

What Seripando appears here to be saying is that the remission of sins is in respect of fiducial faith, and that charity, or the capacity for good works, is bestowed on the pardoned sinner as a consequence. But would not this have been taken by many as to all intents and purposes solafidianism? To forestall such criticism Seripando tried to make it clear that the distinction he drew between justification proper, as the remission of sins, and sanctification as the performance of good works, was a logical one, not a chronological, and that in the subject himself they are in fact simultaneous. Also, he saw justification–sanctification as a continuing process requiring sustained moral effort, and grave sin could nullify it,

---

30. *C.T.*, V, 282–5.
31. *C.T.*, V, 309f.
32. *C.T.*, XII, 613–36. See also Jedin, *Girolamo Seripando*, I, 326–35. Cf. P. Pas, 'La doctrine de la double justice au Concile de Trente', in *Ephemerides Theologicae Louvanienses*, xxx (1954), 5–53.

although resort to the sacrament of penance would provide a fresh start. In any case, justification was not complete until a man's final entry into eternal life, which is possible for him partly as a reward – union with Christ – and partly as a grace, for no perseverance in well-doing can ever meet the strict demands of the divine righteousness. In this way he succeeded, he believed, in combining the ideas both of free grace and of merit, emphasizing at once the objectivity of God's act and the disposition of the repentant sinner.

These opinions, as stated by the Augustinian general, seemed to have caused little or no offence. Other speakers, however, and notably the bishop of La Cava, Tommaso Sanfelice, took up positions which to some council fathers were indistinguishable from Lutheranism. Sanfelice indeed declared roundly that it is by faith alone that the ungodly man is reunited with God (*ex impio factus pius*), although like Seripando he would make no chronological difference between justification and sanctification.[33] Another bishop whose ideas looked Lutheran was the Englishman, Richard Pate, bishop of Worcester. It was also at this general congregation of 17 July, after Sanfelice had spoken, that the bishop of Melapotamos and Chironissa called the bishop of La Cava, to his face, 'either a fool or a knave', an insult for which the Greek had his beard so violently tugged that hairs were pulled out! For this behaviour Sanfelice was disciplined by a temporary excommunication.

The first draft of the justification decree was prepared towards the end of July. The authorship is not definitely known, but not improbably it was the bishop of Bitonto's. After stating in a rather floridly homiletic style that justification is offered freely on account of Christ's sacrifice, it proceeds, in eighteen canons, to condemn numerous errors that had come to be associated with the doctrine, and chiefly the idea that it consists exclusively in the imputation of Christ's merits (*sola imputatio Christi*) and does not involve any actual gift of righteousness (*donatio justitiae*) in the form of an inherent sanctifying grace *(gratia gratum faciens nobis inhaerens)*. But the draft was sharply criticized by the bishops for its verbosity and prolixity as well as for its failure to deal with certain other themes, as, for example, the certitude, or assurance, of grace and salvation. The Servite Bonuccio even found it 'unacceptable in all its parts [*in omnibus displicet*]'. Further discussion, however, was for a time interrupted by external events.

The subject was resumed in the autumn when in the general congregation of 23 September the legates put before it an entirely new draft, this time from the hand (although anonymous) of Seripando, but considerably worked over by a number of other persons to whom it had been submitted, probably at the end of August.[34] Among these was the learned Spanish Dominican, Domingo Soto of the university of Salamanca, and the effect of the alterations was undoubtedly to dilute Seripando's Augustinianism.[35] The discussions following its presentation in the assembly were prolonged and the document's every sentence was minutely examined.[36] When at last the archbishop of Palermo praised the 'exquisite skill' and the

33. *C.T.*, V, 384–91.
34. For Seripando's preliminary draft see *C.T.*, V, 821–33.
35. Jedin, *History of the Council of Trent*, II, 240–4.
36. See *C.T.*, V, 442–97 for the views of the council fathers in the general congregation, 1–11 October.

'masterly and scholarly' order with which the decree had been prepared he was but voicing the prevailing impression of the council's members. The bishop of Verona's coadjutor, Luigi Lippomani, reported to Rome (9 October) that 'if all the universities of the world and the Lutherans as well were here, the subject could not have been more thoroughly discussed than has been done'.[37] Even so, the question of the certitude of grace was still unsettled, and indeed was to remain so.[38] But the great issue was that of imputed or inherent righteousness. Seripando's 'double justification' found few defenders, the theologians, influenced by Lainez, having rejected it at the end of their sitting (15–26 October) by thirty-two votes to five.

On 13 January 1547 the synod's decree was promulgated, fifty-nine prelates being present.[39] It was, in the words of Jedin, 'the Church's authoritative answer to the teaching of Luther and the *Confessio Augustana* on grace and justification'.[40] The doctrine that man can be justified before God by his own works and apart from divine grace through Jesus Christ is anathematized, as also is the opinion that justifying grace can be merited without the prevenient inspiration of the Holy Spirit. But so too is the view that 'the free will of man, moved and aroused by God (*a Deo motum et excitatum*), in no way cooperates by responding to God's awakening call (*nihil cooperari assentiendo Deo excitanti et vocanti*) so as to dispose and prepare itself for the acquisition of the grace of justification, nor can it, if it so will, refuse that grace, but that, like some inanimate thing, it does nothing at all and is completely passive (*sed velut inanime quoddam nihil omnino agere mereque passive se habere*)'.

That human free will has been 'wholly lost and destroyed' (*amissum et extinctum*) by Adam's fall is likewise negated. Other teachings explicitly condemned are: that all works done before justification are actually sinful and deserve God's hatred only; that 'the more vigorously a man strives to dispose himself to receive grace, the more grievously he sins'; that the godly is justified by faith alone (if, that is, what is meant by *sola fide* be 'that nothing else is required by way of cooperation in acquiring the grace of justification and that it is not at all necessary for a man to be prepared and disposed by the motion of his own will'); and that 'a man reborn and justified is bound by faith to believe that he is assuredly of the number of the predestinate'. The further notions that a man once justified can no more sin or lose grace and that justification once received is not preserved or even increased in God's sight by good works, the latter being but 'fruits and signs of justification, not causes of its increase', are also anathematized.

Positively, the decree upholds the view that justification includes not only remission of sins but also sanctification and inward renewal through the willing reception of divine grace. Cooperation with grace in other words, is both possible and necessary. Sins, it declares, are really remitted and not merely not imputed, although concupiscence, as a *fomes peccati*, or liability to sin, persists after baptism. Faith certainly is indispensable, but it is not the sole condition of justification, even

---

37. Jedin, *op. cit.*, II, 246.
38. On this see G. Schreiber, ed., *Das Weltkonzil von Trient* (2 vols, Freiburg-im-Breisgau, 1951), I, 117–43, 145–67; cf. Jedin, II, 247–53.
39. *C.T.*, V, 790–820, cf. A. Michel, *Histoire des Conciles* (Hefele), X, 1 (Paris, 1938), 65–165.
40. Jedin, II, 307.

if it is 'its beginning, foundation and root', since hope and love are likewise requisite. And by keeping God's commandments justifying grace is increased, although it can be lost by mortal sin, with however the possibility of regaining it through the sacrament of penance.

Unquestionably the decree is a very careful compilation, and its sixteen chapters and thirty-three canons should be studied in their entirety if the Tridentine stand-point is to be appreciated. It is clear, and it is precise; and it is not simply an evasive compromise aimed at obscuring scholastic differences. Nor did Seripando's arguments go for nothing, even if too much allowance for them might have looked dangerously like a sell-out to Lutheranism. Rejection of the ideas of assurance and final perseverance prove likewise that the fathers yielded nothing to Calvinism. Ludwig von Pastor calls it 'a masterpiece of theology'.[41] Harnack indeed finds it 'a product of artifice', but concedes that it is remarkably well constructed.[42] He even thinks that 'it may be doubted whether the Reformation would have developed itself if this decree had been issued at the Lateran Council at the beginning of the fifteenth century', although he adds, fairly enough, that the fact that the Roman church should have expressed itself on the issue of justification in the way the decree does 'was itself a consequence of the Reformation'.[43]

### Sessions vii–xxv: the sacraments and other topics

With the seventh session the whole subject of the sacraments was broached. At the general congregation of 17 January 1547 thirty-five alleged errors on sacramental teaching, culled from Protestant writings mainly by Luther and Melanchthon, were read out.[44] Examined first by the theologians and divided into three groups – the sacraments in general, baptism and confirmation – they were again referred to the council fathers on 7 February, who discussed them until 21 February. After the long and difficult debate on justification, however, this new assignment presented far fewer problems, for here the prelates felt themselves to be on much firmer ground. Sacramental doctrine had long been in the forefront of the church's concern and the scholastics had given the whole field minute attention; though even so divergences between the theological schools were by no means lacking.[45] What was now to be decided was which of the cited propositions were heretical and which merely erroneous; whether any of them had in fact been condemned by earlier councils or by the Fathers; and whether the list was exhaustive. The legates also warned that points on which differences of opinion were recognized should be set aside. In the course of debate fifty-one theses were submitted to the council, and

41. *The History of the Popes from the Close of the Middle Ages*, English trans. ed. by R. F. Kerr, XII (London, 1950), 344.
42. *History of Dogma*, VII, 56–71.
43. *Ibid.*, 57.
44. *C.T.*, V, 835–9.
45. See in particular A. M. Landgraf, *Dogmengeschichte der Fruhscholastik*, iii (Ratisbon, 1954) and F. Cavallera, 'Le décret du Concile de Trente sur les sacrements en général', in *Bulletin de Littérature ecclésiastique*, vi (1914), 361–77, 401–25; vii (1915), 17–33, 66–88; ix (1918), 161–81.

these again were reduced to thirty canons, as to which the fathers easily made up their minds.[46]

The decree opens with a short preface containing an emphatic declaration of the vital importance of the sacramental principle, stating that it is by means of the sacraments that 'all true righteousness either begins, or, having begun, is increased, or, having been lost, is restored [*per sacramental omnis vera justitia vel incipit vel coepta augetur vel amisse reparatur*]'. How it is that the sacraments possess this power is not indicated, nothing being said to meet the Protestant insistence on their inseparable relation to the word. Nor is the place of faith mentioned. There is only the bare statement that what follows rests on the holy scriptures, the apostolic tradition, conciliar decisions and the common witness of the Fathers. The language used harks back to the school terminology, although on the other hand no technical exposition of the sacramental theory is offered; even the long-established distinction of form, matter and ministrant is not referred to. In the very first canon it is affirmed, without qualification, that all the sacraments were instituted by Christ, while the fourth canon asserts that they are necessary to salvation, although not all of course are necessary for every man. The purpose of the sacraments (canon 5) is not simply to nourish faith (*propter solam fidem nutriendum*), nor are they mere external signs of a righteousness received through faith (canon 6). On the contrary, they themselves contain the grace they signify, *ex opere operato*. Those who deny this are anathematized (canon 8).

Three of the sacraments – baptism, confirmation and holy orders – are said to convey an indelible 'character' and so may not be repeated, though what precisely is to be understood by such a *character in anima* it is chary of saying. Normally the ministrant of the sacraments is a priest (canon 10), who in administering them must have the intention of doing what the church does (canon 11); the idea of the priesthood of all believers is thus scouted. The effectiveness of the sacraments, moreover, does not depend on the ministrant himself being in a state of grace. Finally (canon 13) it is declared that:

> if anyone shall say that the received and approved customs of the Catholic Church, which are usually applied in the solemn administration of the Sacraments, may either be despised or omitted by ministers as they please without sin, or changed into other new ones by any pastor of the Church, let him be anathema.

As to baptism, the Christian rite is stated to be more than that of John the Baptist and must be of water and in the threefold name of Father, Son and Holy Spirit, and that it is necessary to salvation. The third canon declares that the Roman church, 'the mother and mistress of all churches', has the true doctrine of the sacrament of baptism and condemns all who deny it. Regarding confirmation it is maintained that it is no 'idle ceremony' nor a mere occasion for adolescents to testify their belief, and that its ordinary minister is the bishop. Clearly little if anything in all this could be read as a concession to Protestantism.

Meanwhile the increasing tension between the pope and the emperor, who was not satisfied with the council's progress in the reform of abuses – to him a most pressing concern – and who was also at odds with Paul III over the ambitions of

46. *C.T.*, V, 984ff.

the latter's son, Pier Luigi Farnese, as duke of Parma and Piacenza, caused the Roman pontiff to seek the removal of the council from imperial territory altogether. An outbreak of the plague at Trent gave him a convenient pretext for instructing his legates to persuade the assembly to vote its own translation to Bologna; which, accordingly, its members did, by a majority of thirty-eight votes to fourteen, and in face of Charles's strong displeasure, expressed in his order to his own prelates to stay where they were. However, on 10 November 1549 Paul III died, and del Monte was elected to succeed him as Pope Julius III. The new pontiff, having no desire to quarrel with the emperor, was content that the assembly should be reconvened at Trent. Accordingly its second meeting, covering six sessions, opened on 1 May 1551, with Cardinal Marcello Crescenzio as sole legate, but with the archbishop of Siponto and the bishop of Verona assisting him as nuncios.

In the doctrinal field – although now the council was to address itself chiefly to matters of practical reform – it continued its work on the sacraments, with the promulgation of decrees on the eucharist, penance and extreme unction. The first of these subjects, one obviously of very wide scope as well as high importance, commanded the assembly's attention in its thirteenth session. Questions of eucharistic doctrine had indeed already been submitted to the council at the end of January 1547 in the shape of ten articles drawn from the writings of alleged heretics, and had been discussed by it from time to time down to the end of the first week in March of that year. These same articles were taken up again by the synod at the beginning of September 1551, and for the ensuing weeks were under more or less continuous review. The first speakers on 8 September were the Jesuits Lainez and Salmerón, who now had the status of papal theologians. Another Spaniard, Melchior Cano (1509–60), a Dominican and professor of theology at Salamanca, also played a notable part in the preparation of the decree (especially articles 3, 8 and 10); but it was again agreed that differences known to exist between the theological schools were to be avoided. What needed to be discussed were straight issues between Catholic teaching and Protestant heresy.

The commission charged with the task of drafting the decree consisted of the archbishops of Mainz and Sassari, and the bishops of Agram, Bitonto, Badajoz, Guadix, Astorga and Modena, under the presidency of the legate himself and his assistants. The work was finished by 2 October, but in view of the subject's importance it was decided (6 October) that, as in the case of justification, the canons condemning Protestant errors should be preceded by a positive exposition of the Catholic doctrine, so that a new draft became necessary. This was prepared under Luigi Lippomani's direction and was adopted by the general congregation on 10 October. On the following day, at the council's thirteenth session, it was solemnly promulgated in the presence of two cardinals, five archbishops and thirty-one bishops, besides abbots and generals of religious orders and numerous distinguished laymen. The document consisted of eight chapters and eleven canons.[47] The matters dealt with were the real presence, transubstantiation and the conditions and fruits of holy communion. The language, however, is not always as exact as might have been expected, owing to the council's determination not to trench on points of current debate within the church itself.

47. *C.T.*, VII, 1, 200–4.

First, it is stated that the 'whole Christ' – flesh, blood, soul and divinity – is present in the sacrament 'truly, really, and substantially under the forms of things sensible' (*vere, realiter, et substantialiter sub specie rerum sensibilium in hoc sacramentum*). The presence, that is, is not symbolic or figurative only; and this is said always to have been the teaching of the Fathers. The uniqueness of the eucharist among the sacraments is also stressed:

> It is common indeed to the most holy Eucharist with the other Sacraments that it is symbol of a sacred thing, and the visible form of invisible grace; but there is this point of pre-eminence and distinctiveness found in it, that the other Sacraments have power to sanctify only when actually used, while in the Eucharist the Sacrament is itself the author of sanctification previous to use [*ut in eucharistia ipse sanctitatis auctor ante usum est*].

Further, each species or element, as likewise every separate part of each species, contains the 'whole Christ' (*totus Christus in qualibet specie*). The presence itself is defined more precisely in terms of the dogma of transubstantiation: 'Through consecration of the bread and wine there comes about a conversion of the whole substance of the bread into the substance of the body of Christ our Lord, and of the whole substance of the wine into the substance of his blood.' It is right therefore that full worship (*latriae cultum*), such as is due to God, be rendered to the sacrament of the altar. The self-communication of priests is described as an 'apostolic tradition'. The idea that the forgiveness of sins is the principle fruit of the eucharist is condemned, as too is the teaching that faith alone is sufficient preparation for the reception of the sacrament. In short, all characteristically Protestant teachings on the eucharist, Lutheran and Calvinist as well as Zwinglian and anabaptist, were anathematized. The mind of the council could not have been expressed in a more uncompromising way.

At its fourteenth session the council turned to the sacrament of penance, its discussions eventuating in a formal statement on 25 November 1551. But before considering these it is appropriate to remark how the Tridentine divines settled the other outstanding matter in eucharistic doctrine, namely the sacrifice. The debate on this subject and on holy orders had actually begun on 2 January 1552, but it could not continue because of the dangerous political situation which had developed from the alliance of the German princes with France against Charles V. War broke out in the spring, with the result that, following the emperor's defeat at the hands of the turncoat Elector Maurice of Saxony and the latter's march into the Tyrol, the council on 28 April had to suspend its sittings. With its work on both doctrine and reform still far from complete it was not to assemble again for an entire decade.

Cardinal Caraffa, who was elected as Paul IV in May 1555, was a man who had always been heartily opposed to a council and his sentiments, as a Neapolitan, were almost obsessively anti-Hispanic. When at last the council was reconvened in the middle of January 1562 it was under a new pope, Pius IV, more amiable and politic than his irascible and headstrong predecessor. Nevertheless a sharp contest had arisen over whether this assembly was really a continuation of the earlier ones, or whether in fact it did not constitute a new council altogether. The king of Spain,

Philip II, was so firmly of the opinion that it was not a new synod that he refused his assent to its assembling until assured by Pius that it was indeed a continuation and not a fresh start. The legates, however, concerned to please the French and the emperor Ferdinand I, took the line of diplomacy and avoided any express declaration on the point, although it was generally understood that despite the time lapse the new assembly was continuous with the past ones at least to the extent that decisions already reached would on no account be reconsidered.

Thus the council fathers, who now numbered 113, agreed straight away to resume discussion of the agenda broken off in 1552, on which the chief item was the sacrifice of the mass, one of the most divisive issues between Catholics and Protestants. The latter, of whatever shade of opinion, rejected it utterly, whereas to the former it was the heart of the eucharistic rite and hence of vital significance for the church's whole religious life and outlook. At the same time the theology of it, endlessly discussed as it had been by the schoolmen, was complex and ill-defined, especially as touching the relation of the sacrifice both to Calvary and to the Last Supper. The first general congregation opened on 15 January, the legates including Seripando, now a cardinal and archbishop of Salerno, and a learned and able Pole, Stanislaus Hosius, bishop of Ermland. Certain other pressing matters had to be examined, including the *Index Liborum Prohibitorum* and the question of restoring the chalice to the laity, but by 19 July the synod was ready to consider thirteen articles which had been referred to it raising fundamental questions such as whether the mass is only a commemoration of Christ's sacrifice or whether it was itself sacrificial; and whether in the words *Hoc facit in meam commemorationem* Christ conferred on the apostles the power to offer his body and blood in the mass. A lively debate ensued, but at the end of it agreement was unanimous; where doubt had chiefly occurred was on whether Christ's sacrificial self-offering took place at the last supper or only on the cross. The Jesuit Salmerón, who spoke first, argued for the former, relying on the words of the canon of the mass and on the gospel injunction 'Do this in remembrance of me'. The Dominican De Soto, with the support of many of the council fathers, took the contrary position. Lainez, however, urged that Christ's whole life and work as well as his death were sacrificial, even though it was the latter that focused the truth of the self-giving divine love most vividly. The upshot was the adoption of a mediating view; at the Last Supper Christ had in fact offered himself sacrificially, but only on the cross did this self-oblation become propitiatory. Thus the first chapter of the decree says gradually that

> ... our God and Lord, although he was about to offer himself once on the altar of the cross unto God the Father by means of his death, nevertheless in the last supper, in order that he might leave to his Church a visible sacrifice, whereby the sacrifice of the cross might be represented, and the memory of it remain and its saving virtue applied, he offered up to God the Father his own body and blood under the species of bread and wine,

and by the words *Hoc facit in meam commemorationem* 'he commanded both his apostles and their successors in the priesthood to offer them, as the Catholic Church has always understood and taught'.

On the question whether the sacrifice of the mass is itself truly propitiatory the decree is explicit.

> For God, propitiated by the oblation of this sacrifice, granting us grace and the gift of penitence, remits our faults and even our most heinous sins. For there is one and the same victim, now offering through the ministry of the priesthood, who then offered himself on the cross; the only difference is in the method of the offering. The fruits of this (the bloody) oblation are perceived most fully through the bloodless oblation; so far is it from taking any honour from the former. Wherefore it is rightly offered, in accordance with the tradition of the Apostles, not only for the sins, penances, satisfactions and other necessities of the faithful living, but also for the dead in Christ, whose purification is not yet accomplished.[48]

The decree went on to state that the mass may be celebrated in honour of the saints, and that a mass without communicants is legitimate. All teachings contrary to these doctrines are anathematized.[49]

Throughout the debate on the sacrifice it was maintained that, since it is the same body and blood as were offered on the cross which are likewise offered in the eucharist, the sacrifice of the mass and that of Calvary are one and the same. Accordingly the mass is in no sense an addition to the cross but rather is an application of its benefits. Little attention was paid to the idea, both patristic and Greek Orthodox, of Christ's continuing self-offering in heaven.

One important matter in this connection that some were pressing to be resolved was the granting of the chalice to the laity, and on what conditions. The denial of the cup, so far from being an ancient practice, was of late western origin and was recognized to be a question of expediency, not of principle. Charles V was anxious to meet the Lutherans on this point and actually made it the major concession in his *Interim* of 1548. The French also were in favour of changing the existing custom. At Trent the subject had been mooted at the thirteenth session in October 1551; now, at their twentieth session, the fathers turned to it again when on 6 June five articles were put before them for consideration, the first of which contained the straight question whether it is obligatory on every Christian, by God's ordinance, to receive the sacrament in *both* kinds. Any suggestion of change, however, was bitterly opposed by the Spaniards, led by the archbishop of Granada, Pedro Guerrero, and the legates found it convenient to be evasive.[50] The council's eventual decision was registered at its twenty-first session on 16 July, in a statement of four chapters and four canons affirming that communion under both kinds is not of divine obligation, and that the 'whole' Christ is present under either species.[51]

It now only remains for us to glance briefly at the synod's findings on the sacraments of penance, extreme unction and holy orders, and on the doctrines of purgatory and the invocation of saints. Discussions on the first of these (*de poenitentia*) took place at Bologna in March 1547, when fourteen impugned articles were presented to the council, but it was not until the fourteenth session, on 25

48. *C.T.*, VIII, 699f.
49. *C.T.*, VIII, 959–62.
50. *C.T.*, VIII, 899–909, cf. E. Jamoulle, 'Le sacrifice eucharistique au Concile de Trente', in *Nouvelle Revue Théologique*, lxvii (1945), 513–31.
51. *C.T.*, VIII, 698–700.

November 1551, that the decree was agreed on and accepted. This states that the sacrament of penance was instituted by Christ himself, according to John 20:21, and that it is a rite essentially different from baptism (also for the remission of sins), with a different form and matter. Penance is said to consist of three parts or acts, namely contrition, confession and satisfaction (*satisfactio*). It is noteworthy that the view which held attrition (*attritio*, shame and the fear of punishment) to be sufficient for the effective reception of the sacrament was not accepted, although the utility of such a state of mind as an 'imperfect contrition' was deemed to be a salutary preparation (*ad Dei gratiam impetrandam disponit*). Where, doubtless, the influence of the reformers' teachings carried weight was in the emphasis now placed on inward sorrow and detestation of the sin itself and the resolution to offend no more. Satisfaction, or the penalties for sin imposed on the sinner, is rendered effective only through the sacrifice of Christ, although it is affirmed that the reconciliation which the sacrament is designed to bring about is not to be ascribed to contrition alone 'and without a vow to receive the sacrament'. Nothing, more-over, is said about faith, a distinction being drawn simply between *contritio* and *contritio caritate perfecta*.[52] The decree also states categorically that

> the whole Church has always understood that full confession of sins is by divine law necessary for all who have fallen after baptism, because Christ, at the moment of his ascension from earth into heaven left behind him priests [*sacerdotes*] representative of himself, as overseers and judges [*praesides et judices*] to whom all mortal offences are to be made known.

The priest in confession thus has a judicial role. Protestant objections to the idea that sacramental confession was neither instituted by divine authority nor is necessary to salvation, or that the method of private confession to a priest alone, 'a method always observed from the first down to this day by the Catholic church', is 'alien to the institution and command of Christ and a mere human invention' are condemned.

The definition on the sacrament of extreme unction follows that on penitence. Extreme unction is said to be of dominical institution, its matter oil, and its effect the forgiveness of sins.[53]

The sacrament of orders (*de ordine*) came up for discussion in the twenty-third session, when seven heretical propositions were submitted, the first and chief of which was that orders is not a sacrament at all. On 3 November 1563 they were resubmitted with amendments. An important point here was the status of bishops, the curialist party maintaining that bishops as such possess no intrinsic superiority to priests and that the authority they exercise is conferred on them by the pope. Against this Guerrero urged that bishops were instituted by divine right and that their intrinsic superiority to priests derived from that fact.[54] In this respect the pope is not essentially different from other bishops, each of whom is no less a 'Vicar of Christ' than he is. Guerrero's arguments gained him strong support, especially from

---

52. Harnack's tart comment was that 'what the 4th chapter of the Decree really does is to throw dust in the eyes of Protestants' (*op. cit.*, 52).
53. *C.T.*, VII, 1. 343–59.
54. *C.T.*, IX, 48–51.

his fellow-Spaniards, the bishop of Segovia, for instance, reminding the synod that while in the primitive church there were undoubtedly bishops, there was, with equal certainty, no papal supremacy; from which it is obvious they drew their power from Christ himself, not from the pope. Similarly the bishop of Oronse recalled that the keys were given to the other apostles as well as to St Peter. Lainez, however, as a Jesuit, took up the papal case with warmth. He distinguished between order and jurisdiction. The bishops in general, he conceded, had jurisdictional power by divine right, but the question was of the exercise of such power by individual bishops. The latter, he insisted, derived from the pope by virtue of his universal jurisdiction.[55] This speech hardly commended itself to the assembly and the debate became so acrimonious that the sitting had to be suspended. It was not until July 1563 that agreement on the terms of the decree was definitely reached.[56] It opens with the emphatic declaration that 'the sacrifice and priesthood are so conjoined by the appointment of God that both exist in very law [*sacrificium et sacerdotium ita Dei ordinatione conjuncta sunt ut utrumque in omni lege exstiterit*]'. In other words, because the church itself is sacrificial it necessarily has a sacrificing priest-hood. The seven orders of ministry – bishops, priests, deacons, subdeacons, porters, exorcists and acolytes – are stated to have been in existence from 'the very beginning of the Church', as also that holy orders is truly one of the seven sacraments. The question of the relation of bishops to priests is however left open, no more being said than that bishops are superior to priests as having taken the place of the apostles. Denials of these truths are anathematized.

The doctrines of purgatory and the saints were dealt with in session xxv, on 3 and 4 December, as the council, the members of which were now growing weary, drew towards its close. The decree on purgatory speaks of a 'sound doctrine' of the intermediate state which should be believed and taught everywhere, thus implying that some of the prevalent teaching was not sound; and it goes on to say that 'among the unlettered folk the more difficult and subtle questions, which do not tend to edification and from which no increase of piety is wont to arise' should be excluded from public preaching. So too 'things which pander to curiosity and superstition, or which savour of base lucre', are to be prohibited as 'scandals and sources of offence to the faithful'. The invocation of saints is recognized, the negative Protestant view being dubbed 'impious'. Likewise honour is due to relics, and images may be lawfully used.[57] That all these matters have been abused is admitted, but the tone of reproof is mild: 'If any abuses, however, have crept into (*irrepserint*) these holy and salutary observances the holy Synod has the intensest desire (*vehementer cupit*) that they be forthwith abolished.' Finally, in regard to indulgences, which after all provided the original spark of the whole religious conflagration, it is declared that the power of conferring them has been granted to the church by Christ and that she has made use of this divine privilege even from the earliest times. Their continuance, therefore, which is affirmed to be of great benefit for Christian people, is required, even though fear is expressed lest ecclesiastical

55.  *C.T.*, IX, 94–101.
56.  *C.T.*, IX, 620–2.
57.  *C.T.*, IX, 1077–9.

discipline be weakened by too great facility in granting them (*ne nimia facilitate ecclesiastica disciplina enervetur*).[58]

On 26 January 1564 Pope Pius IV solemnly confirmed the council's work, and on 2 August he appointed a congregation of cardinals to supervise the implementation of its enactments, so manifesting, by implication, his own plenary authority over the synod and its findings, both dogmatic and practical. On 13 November, by the bull *Injunctum Nobis*, he gave summary form to the faith of the Catholic church, as Trent had clarified and defined it, in the statement which has come to be known as the Creed of Pius IV.[59] It was to be recited publicly by all bishops and beneficed clergy, while for converts to the faith it was to be adopted as the formal, *ex animo* expression of the beliefs they now embraced. Scripture, 'according to that sense which Holy Mother Church has held and holds' is acknowledged, any other interpretation than that of 'the unanimous consent of the Fathers' being repudiated. The decrees of Trent on original sin and justification are explicitly professed, along with the definition of the seven sacraments. So too are the propitiatory sacrifice of the mass and transubstantiation, purgatory (the souls detained there being helped by the intercession of the faithful), the invocation of saints and the veneration of images. The 'Holy Catholic, Apostolic and Roman Church' is again declared to be 'the mother and mistress of all churches', and the Roman pontiff, to whom obedience is sworn, the successor of Peter and representative (*vicarius*) of Jesus Christ. In fine, the believer accepts and professes 'without doubting' all 'the traditions, definitions and declarations of the sacred Canons and Oecumenical Councils, and especially those of the holy Council of Trent'; while everything contrary thereto, and indeed all things 'condemned, rejected and anathematized by the Church', he likewise rejects and anathematizes.

'In spite', says Pastor, 'of all the disturbances, both from within and from without, in spite of all the delays and obstructions, as well as the many human weaknesses which had come to light during the course of its proceedings, the Council had accomplished a mighty work, and one of decisive importance'.[60] It was a major, probably indeed the most significant, step in the revival of Catholicism after its late medieval decline and the onslaught of Protestantism. But the overall object on which some hopes at least had been fixed, the restoration of Christian unity in the west, was not achieved, for by 1545 the breach was already too great, and by the close of the century Europe had to reconcile itself to the permanent coexistence of two wholly diverse and antagonistic forms of the Christian religion. But Catholicism itself, now more obviously Latin, in character as in the sphere of its actual obedience, had taken a close look at itself and had established its own identity the more certainly as well in its own eyes as in the sight of those who

58. *C.T.*, IX, 1105f.
59. *Forma professionis fidei catholicae Tridentinae.* See H. Denzinger, *Enchiridion symbolorum, definitionum et declarationum de rebus fidei et morum* (33rd edn by A. Schönmetzer, Freiburg-im-Breisgau, 1965); English translation in H. Bettenson, *Documents of the Christian Church* (Oxford, 1933), 372ff.
60. *The History of The Popes*, XV, 366. Also, as A. G. Dickens very aptly remarks, 'the canons and decrees [of Trent] remain one of the greatest monuments of committee-thinking in the whole history of religion' (*The Counter Reformation* [London, 1968], 133).

repudiated it. A great body of dogma had been formulated and countless abuses and defects recognized, and in intention, at all events, reformed. The Roman church was cleansed, but with definition and discipline went also a new hardness, if not of heart yet of mind, for with the disruptive forces of the Protestant world there was to be no compromise. Harnack's statement, though, that Trent's decrees 'had the effect of binding the Catholic Church to the soil of the Middle Ages and of Scholasticism' needs qualification. Assuredly the enquiring spirit of Renaissance humanism was largely banished, but as the same author himself concedes, 'the formulations adopted were ambiguous in all the questions to which the Church itself cannot give an unmistakable answer', so that 'the necessary freedom of development was preserved in spite of the huge burden of dogmatic material'.[61]

That Roman theology since Trent has not been a mere embalming of the doctrines defined there is certainly the case. But the most curious *lacuna* in the dogmatic field was the council's failure – inevitable though it may have been in the circumstances of the time – to present a considered ecclesiology, a doctrine of the nature of the church as such, and with it a balanced view of the position of the pope. Three or even four centuries were to elapse before these matters came before another oecumenical synod of Catholic bishops. But at any rate the practical consequence of Trent was, if somewhat paradoxically, to make it plain to the world that any council representative exclusively of the Roman church would be a council subordinate to the Roman pontiff, whose supremacy was now beyond challenge. For the Vatican assembly of 1870 did no more than articulate what had long since ceased to be an open question.

### Trent and Protestantism

During the early phase of the Reformation movement the demand for a council had been insistent, especially in Germany. The emperor saw it as the only feasible means of preserving, or restoring, the unity of western Christendom, being convinced in his own mind that on the true fundamentals of the faith, as these are listed in the ancient creeds, Catholics and Protestants were in agreement and that the doctrinal issues on which they differed could be resolved, given good will on both sides, by negotiation in conference. The reform of abuses in the Catholic church, a matter granted to be of pressing necessity, would, he sincerely believed, meet the reformers' most solid objections and so, sooner no doubt rather than later, lead to a healing of the calamitous breach. With the characteristic Protestant teachings he himself had no sympathy, but he was prepared to make concessions in practical matters such as the administration of the chalice to the laity and even the marriage of the clergy.

To Luther, however, the question of a council presented itself in a quite different light. At the start indeed he not only desired a council but demanded it, so long at all events as it might be a German council for the reform of the church in German lands. Later his attitude changed. No council, he was convinced, which

61. Harnack, *op. cit.*, VII, 71.

was not general, free and representative of Christian aspiration as a whole would be worth convening. An assembly under the tutelage of the pope, who to Luther increasingly assumed the aspect of Antichrist, would be none of these things. Furthermore, even a council must be subject to the word of God, and unless the word were recognized by it as the one source and standard of Christian truth its deliberations would be worse than useless. This he made clear to the Elector Johann Freidrich when in 1533 the papal legate Rangone conveyed an invitation to the Saxon prince to attend a council.[62] Two years later Paul III sent Pietro Paulo Vergerio (who himself was later to become a Protestant) to Germany to find out how the princes might regard the prospect of such a gathering.[63] The nuncio met Luther at Wittenberg, only to be told that he and his followers saw no need of a council so far as concerned themselves, inasmuch as they already possessed the evangelical faith, although it might be a good thing for Christendom as a whole if through it the papacy learned at last to distinguish truth from error.

In 1536 it was proposed to hold a council at Mantua in the following year, which the Protestants also were invited to attend, and the Schmalkaldic League was to meet in the February of 1537 to consider this. At the request of the elector, who at the time rather favoured the idea of a council, Luther drew up his *Schmalkaldic Articles* in order to make quite plain what the basic Protestant position was, one therefore from which any retreat was impossible.[64] The actual meeting Luther, for health reasons, did not attend, but the *Augustana* was reaffirmed at it, and a statement of Melanchthon's on the power and primacy of the pope was adopted. In the event, however, this Mantua proposal was called off, for the good reason, so Luther suspected, that the prospect of a genuinely free council Rome simply would not contemplate.[65] His own comments on the report (1537) of Paul III's commission, under Contarini's chairmanship, of cardinals and other prelates on ecclesiastical reform, a copy of which he had managed to get hold of, were typically scathing.[66] He had come, in fact, to look on the whole notion of a papal general council as a fraud and in his treatise *Von den Consiliis und Kirchen* ('On the Councils and the Churches') he set out his considered view of the subject, namely, that the ancient councils, which truly were authoritative and normative, had been summoned not by popes but by the Roman emperors; that the decisions even of these had always been subject to the truth of scripture; and that papally controlled councils would only reflect the arbitrary and erroneous opinions of the popes themselves.[67] Even so, this was still not Luther's final word on the matter. Within a year of his death (for in this respect time had in no way mellowed him) his hatred of the papacy again flared up in the shape of yet another denunciation of an

62. *C.T.*, IV, lxxxixff.
63. *C.T.*, IV, cxiff.
64. Luther's *Works*, Weimar edn (*W.A.*) L, 192–253.
65. Jedin, *op. cit.*, I, 313–30.
66. *W.A.*, L, 288–308. For the *Consilium de emendanda ecclesia* see *C.T.*, XII, 131–45; cf. Jedin, *op. cit.*, I, 424ff; also S. Ehses, 'Kirchliche Reformarbeiter unter Paul III vor dem Trienter Konzil' in *Römische Quartalschrift*, xv (1901), 153–74, 397–411.
67. Published in 1539 (*W.A.*, L, 509–653). There is an English trans. by C. M. Jacobs and E. W. Gritsch in (*Works*, ed. Pelikan and Lehmann), XLI, 3–178.

institution which he declared 'was founded on the devil'.[68] His answer was the same as ever: there could be no truck at all with Rome. Thus when, in 1551, the Protestants were asked to send a delegation to Trent they declined to do so unless the topics already discussed and agreed upon by the council were reopened *ab initio*; which, not unreasonably, the synod refused to do.[69]

So when Trent settled to its work in the new year of 1546 any chance of dialogue with the Lutherans was effectively past. All that the Roman church could now do was to apply itself to the task of internal reform and, on doctrinal issues, to proclaim its mind to the world. Yet the amount of contemporary non-Roman comment on the Tridentine definitions was very small, the most significant being Calvin's animadversions on Paul III's angry brief regarding the emperor's offer to the German Protestants, made without reference to the pope, to convene a German council. Calvin bitterly attacked Paul, not only for his personal life but also, and chiefly, for his presumptuous claim that the papal authority was superior to that of a council, a pretension supported neither by scripture nor by the practice of the early church, while to condemn Protestants as heretics merely on his own judgement was unwarranted and unfair.[70] Calvin also accused Paul of dissimulation in appearing to favour a council while at the same time having not the slightest intention of actually summoning one.

When the council at last did meet and had formulated some of the most important of its decrees Calvin published his own commentary on them in a broadside entitled *The Canons of the Council of Trent, with the Antidote*.[71] After laying down the basic evangelical principle once more that the Bible is the sole standard of doctrine he admits the prestige which throughout the ages general councils have enjoyed in Christendom, and concedes that a genuinely representative assembly even at this late date might accomplish some good. But no council under papal domination would be representative, any more than it would be free. Trent certainly was not so; it was poorly attended, and mostly by Italians at that, while the theologians and canonists advising the prelates were less than competent and in any case too subservient to legatine pressure; in addition, the council fathers themselves too easily assented to the draft decrees submitted to them. The objections were in fact by no means fully justified, but they were preliminary only: the substance of Calvin's tract is reached when he goes on to cite the canons in turn and to supply detailed criticisms of them. His arguments are of course what one would expect and serve only to show how irreconcilable the Roman and Protestant dogmatic positions essentially were.

In truth the only relationship between Protestant and Roman was that of open enmity, issuing, where persecution by the latter was not possible, at least in verbal warfare. Each side had its own doctrinal palladium and defended it hotly. In the

---

68. *W.A.*, LIV, 206–99.
69. With a view to Protestant representation at the council Melanchthon drafted a 'Repetition of the Augsburg Confession' (*Confession Saxonica*) (*Corpus Reform.*, XXVIII, 380–468).
70. *Calvini opera*, VII, 258–87; English trans. by H. Beveridge in *Tracts Relating to the Reformation by John Calvin* (Edinburgh, 1844), I, 237–86.
71. *Acta synodi Tridentini cum Antidoto* (*Opera*, VII, 371–506).

Lutheran camp the leading polemist was Martin Chemnitz (1522–86), a pupil of Melanchthon's and one of the most perceptive as well as learned theologians of his day. Born at Treuenbrietze, some fifteen miles from Wittenberg, he was educated at Magdeburg and at the university of Wittenberg. From there he moved on to Königsberg, where as librarian to Duke Albrecht of Prussia he was able to pursue his theological studies more intensively. In time he attained prominence as a churchman with a reputation also as a gifted preacher. Although in later life he probably did more than anyone else to secure acceptance of the *Formula of Concord* his fame rests mainly on his anti-Catholic controversial writings. These were initially prompted by the publication in 1560 by the Cologne Jesuits of a critical review of a current Lutheran catechism, to which Chemnitz replied in a tract entitled *Theologiae Jesuitarum praecipua capita*. This itself was countered by a Portuguese Jesuit, Payva d'Andrada – another of the Society's contingent at Trent – in two separate works, one of which expressly appealed to the council's decrees.[72] The outcome was the publication, over several years (1565–73), of Chemnitz's 'Examination of the Council of Trent' (*Examen concilii Tridentini*), in four parts, in which the synod's decrees and canons are subjected to a detailed analysis comparing Roman doctrine with the teachings of the New Testament and the early Fathers. It is a work at once of great erudition, discernment and moderation, singularly free as it is from the invective which almost always mars the utterances of sixteenth-century controversialists. It quickly established itself as an authoritative exposition not only of the Protestant case against Rome but of Lutheran divinity generally.[73]

So, then, the great divide in western Christendom stood. Neither Protestantism in any of its forms, nor Roman Catholicism, was in the mood to learn from its opponent. The Roman sacramental-sacerdotalist conception of the church was wholly rejected by the former, while the principles of justification by faith alone and the priesthood of all believers found no acceptance with the latter. Rome had in effect enshrined the still living medieval tradition in a dogmatic system regarded now as fixed and final, thus absolutizing and virtually dehistoricizing it. It says much therefore for the revitalizing power of the Catholic reformation that in spite of its backward-looking and reactionary stance the Roman church was able, during the following century, to draw on so great a reserve of inner inspiration, such that not only was the immense labour of practical reform carried through but a truly remarkable spiritual awakening made possible. Thus a new catechism, partly modelled on that of the Jesuit Peter Canisius, was drawn up and translated into several languages, the missal and breviary were revised – the latter drastically so, with the old hagiology thoroughly pruned – a corrected edition of the Vulgate was brought out and the standards of public worship in general greatly improved. Most important of all, however, was the gradual appearance of a better educated, disciplined and dedicated secular clergy, the weakest element in the medieval church

72. *Orthodoxarum explicationum de controversiis religionis capitibus libri X.*
73. English trans. by F. Kramer, *Examination of the Council of Trent, Part I* (St Louis, 1971). On Chemnitz see H. Hachfeld, *Martin Chemnitz* (Leipzig, 1867) and R. Mumm, *Die Polemik des M. Chemnitz gegen das Konzil von Trient* (Leipzig, 1905). On the reformers' attitude to Trent generally see R. Stupperich, 'Die Reformation und das Tridentinum', in *Archiv für Reformationsgeschichte*, xlvii (1956), 20–63.

structure. In Rome itself during the last quarter of the century colleges were established for the training of priests of various foreign nationalities – German, Hungarian, English, Greek, Armenian – as well as one for converts from Judaism and Islam. Jesuit influence, radiating from its college in Rome (later the Gregorian university), was increasingly potent and persuasive.

The fruits of the Counter-Reformation were first gathered in Spain and Italy, but with the advent of the seventeenth century it was to yield some of its finest in France, to which the names of Pierre de Bérulle, Charles de Condren, François de Sales and Jean Eudes bear eloquent testimony Nor, of course, may the extraordinary outburst of Catholic Augustinianism in the work of Cornelius Jansen, bishop of Ypres, be disregarded, and in association therewith the singular genius of Blaise Pascal. But these splendid recollections take us beyond the era of the Reformation and Counter-Reformation, in the chronologically more restricted sense, and properly introduce the history of modern Catholicism with its astonishing blend of rigidity and resilience, its missionary energy and its centralist cohesion – its capacity, in short, not only to survive but to revive, to live and to grow.

Protestantism, after the trauma of its early struggle for existence and the spiritual vision, freedom and reinvigoration which were then infused by it into the Christian inheritance, tended subsequently, although its institutions continued to flourish and spread, not merely to rest on its achievements but to identify itself with a motley sectarianism, always resolutely anti-Roman yet inwardly divided and fractious. The impulse which had moved it from the beginning – that religion must be founded in personal conviction and that its concrete articulations derive meaning and effectiveness only from a Bible-inspired individual faith – persisted. Nevertheless the momentum of renewal flagged with time. The deaths of Luther and Calvin removed from the European scene leaders in whom, whatever their personal faults, vivid spiritual insight and indefatigable zeal for truth and righteousness were of epoch-making consequence. Thereafter the two religious systems to which, by common usage, their respective names became attached experienced a decline in spiritual creativity, marked by a hardening of dogmatic attitudes, an increasing intellectualism, and with this, irresistibly, an obsessive concern for orthodoxy seemingly for its own sake, and an insistence on denominational distinctiveness and self-sufficiency. Calvinism in particular, at first the most vigorous and expansive of all the manifestations of Protestant belief and life, entered on, in the years following the Synod of Dort (1618–19) – an assembly so large and widely representative as almost to amount to a general council of the Reformed churches – the long decline from which it was never to recover. And indeed Protestantism in all its guises was to suffer acutely, on account it may be of its lack of any clearcut principle of authority, from the corrosive rationalism of the age of the Enlightenment; more so, it must be said, than did Rome, whose defences, erected primarily against the Reformation, served also, in some measure at least, against attack from this other and even more dangerous quarter.

# BIBLIOGRAPHY

## General

Bainton, R. H., *The Reformation of the Sixteenth Century* (Boston, 1952)

Bossy, J., *Christianity in the West 1400–1700* (Oxford, 1985)

Cameron, E., *The European Reformation* (Oxford, 1991)

Chadwick, O., *The Reformation*, Pelican History of the Church (vol. 3, London, 1972)

Daniel-Rops, H., *The Catholic Reformation*, English trans. by J. Warrington (London, 1962)

Delumeau, J., *Catholicism between Luther and Voltaire: a New View of the Counter-Reformation*, English trans., with Introduction, by J. Bossy (London and Philadelphia, 1977)

Dorner, J. A., *History of Protestant Theology, especially in Germany*, English trans. by G. Robson and S. Taylor (I, Edinburgh, 1871; repr. New York, 1970)

Elton, G. R. (ed.), *The Reformation*, New Cambridge Modern History (2nd ed., Cambridge, 1990)

George, T., *The Theology of the Reformers* (Nashville, Tenn., 1988)

Grimm, H. J., *The Reformation Era 1500–1650* (2nd ed., New York and London, 1973)

Hillerbrand, H. J., *The Protestant Reformation* (New York, 1968)

Hillerbrand, H. J., *The World of the Reformation* (London, 1975)

Kidd, B. J., *Documents Illustrative of the Continental Reformation* (Oxford, 1911)

Léonard, E. J., *Histoire générale du Protestantisme* (I, Paris, 1961)

Lortz, J., *The Reformation in Germany*, English trans. by J. Walls (2 vols, London and New York, 1968)

McGrath, A. E., *Reformation Thought: an Introduction* (2nd ed., Oxford, 1993)

Noll, M. A., *Confessions and Catechisms of the Reformation* (Grand Rapids, Mich., 1991)

Ozment, S. E., *The Age of Reform 1250–1550* (New Haven, Conn., and London, 1973)

Pauck, W., *The Heritage of the Reformation* (Oxford, 1961)

Pelikan, J., *The Christian Tradition, IV: Reformation of Church and Dogma* (Chicago and London, 1984)

Rupp, G., *Patterns of Reformation* (London, 1969)

Spitz, L. W., *The Protestant Reformation 1517–1559* (New York, 1986)

Strohl, H., *La pensée de la Réforme* (Neuchâtel and Paris, 1951)

Todd, J. M., *Reformation* (London, 1972)

Whale, J. S., *The Protestant Tradition: an Essay in Interpretation* (Cambridge, 1955)

## Chapter 1 The eve of the Reformation

Allen, P. S., *The Age of Erasmus* (Oxford, 1914)

Black, A., *Council and Commune: the Conciliar Movement and its Fifteenth Century Heritage* (London, 1979)

Bolton, B., *The Mediaeval Reformation* (Baltimore and London, 1983)

Bradshaw, B., and Duffy, E., *Humanism, Reform and the Reformation* (Cambridge, 1989)

Burger, H. O., *Renaissance, Reformation, Humanismus* (Bad Homburg, 1969)

Cameron, E., *The Reformation of the Heretics: the Waldenses of the Alps 1480–1580* (Oxford, 1984)

Dowling, M., *Humanism in the Age of Henry VIII* (London, 1986)

Fox, A., *Thomas More: History and Providence* (Oxford, 1982)

Gilmore, M. P., *The World of Humanism* (New York, 1952)

Holborn, H., *Ulrich von Hutten and the German Reformation* (New Haven, Conn., 1937)

Huizinga, J., *The Waning of the Middle Ages* (London, 1924; repr. Pelican Books, 1955)

Hyma, A., *Renaissance to Reformation* (Grand Rapids, Mich., 1951)

Kaminsky, H., *History of the Hussite Revolution* (Berkeley, Los Angeles, 1967)

Kristeller, P. O., *Renaissance Thought and its Sources* (New York, 1979)

Leff, G., *Heresy in the Later Middle Ages* (Manchester, 1967)

McFarlane, K. B., *John Wycliffe and the Beginnings of English Nonconformity* (London, 1952)

McGrath, A. E., *The Intellectual Origins of the European Reformation* (Oxford, 1987)

Oberman, H. A., *Forerunners of the Reformation: the Shape of Late Mediaeval Thought Illustrated by Key Documents* (2nd ed., Philadelphia, 1981)

Overfeld, J. H., *Humanism and Scholasticism in Late Mediaeval Germany* (Princeton, N.J., 1984)

Ozment, S. E., *The Reformation in Mediaeval Perspective* (Chicago, 1971)

Reynolds, E. E., *The Field is Won: the Life and Death of St Thomas More* (London, 1968)

Sears, J., *John Colet and Marsiglio Ficino* (Oxford, 1963)

Spitz, L. W., *The Religious Renaissance of German Humanism* (Cambridge, Mass., 1963)

Strauss, G., *Manifestations of Discontent in Germany on the Eve of the Reformation* (Bloomington, Ind., 1971)

Trinkhaus, C., *The Scope of Renaissance Humanism* (Ann Arbor, Mich., 1983)

## Chapter 2 Desiderius Erasmus

Bainton, R., *Erasmus of Christendom* (New York, 1969)

Bouyer, L., *Autour d'Erasme* (Paris, 1955)

Dickens, A. G. and Whitney, R. D., *Erasmus: the Reformer* (London, 1994)

Dolan, J. P., *Erasmus: Handbook of the Militant Christian* (Notre Dame, Ind., 1962)

Halkin, L. E., *Erasmus: a Critical Biography*, trans. by J. Tonkin (Oxford, 1994)

Huizinga, J., *Erasmus* (London, 1952)

Hyma, A., *The Youth of Erasmus* (Ann Arbor, Mich., 1930)

Kohls, E. W., *Die Theologie des Erasmus* (2 vols, Basel, 1966)

McConica, J. K., *Erasmus* (Oxford, 1991)

Olin, J. C. (ed.), *Christian Humanism and the Reformation: Selected Writings of Erasmus with the Life of Erasmus by Beatus Rhenanus* (New York, 1975)

Payne, J. B., *Erasmus: his Theology of the Sacraments* (Richmond, Va., 1969)

Phillips, M. M., *Erasmus and the Northern Renaissance* (London, 1959)

Renaudet, A., *Erasme, sa pensée religieuse et son action d'après sa correspondance (1518–1521)* (Paris, 1926; repr. Geneva, 1970)

Schoeck, R. D., *Erasmus of Europe: the Making of a Humanist 1467–1500* (Edinburgh, 1990)

Stupperich, E., *Erasmus von Rotterdam und seine Welt* (Berlin, 1977)

## Chapters 3 and 4 Martin Luther

Althaus, P., *The Theology of Martin Luther*, English trans. by R. C. Schultz (Philadelphia, 1966)

Bainton, R. H., *Here I Stand: a Life of Martin Luther* (Nashville, Tenn., 1950)

Bizer, E., *Fides ex auditu: eine Untersuchung über die Entdeckung der Gerechtigkeit Gottes durch Martin Luther* (Neukirchen, 1958)

Bornkamm, H., *Luther's World of Thought*, English trans. by M. H. Bertram (St. Louis, 1958)

Brendler, G., *Martin Luther: Theology and Revolution* (New York, 1991)

Dickens, A. G., *Martin Luther and the Reformation* (London, 1967)

Dickens, A. G., *The German Nation and Martin Luther* (London, 1974)

Ebeling, G., *Luther: an Introduction to his Thought*, English trans. by R. A. Wilson (London, 1970)

Erikson, E. H., *Young Man Luther: a Study in Psychoanalysis and History* (New York, 1958)

Friedenthal, R., *Luther*, English trans. by G. J. Nowell (London, 1970)

Gogarten, F., *Luthers Theologie* (Tübingen, 1967)

Green, V. H. H., *Luther and the Reformation* (London, 1964)

Hendrix, S. H., *Luther and the Papacy* (Philadelphia, 1981)

Holl, K., *Gesammelte Aufsätze zur Kirchengeschichte: I, Luther* (Tübingen, 1927)

Loewenich, W. von, *Luther's Theology of the Cross*, English trans. by H. J. A. Bowman (London, 1976)

Lohse, B., *Martin Luther: an Introduction to his Life and Writings* (Philadelphia, 1986)

McDonough, T. M., *Law and the Gospel in Luther* (Oxford, 1963)

McGrath, A. E., *Luther's Theology of the Cross* (Oxford/New York, 1985)

Oberman, H. A., *Luther: Man between God and the Devil* (New Haven, Conn., 1989)

Pelikan, J., *Spirit versus Structure: Luther and the Institutions of the Church* (London, 1968)

Prenter, R., *Spiritus Creator: Studies in Luther's Theology*, English trans. by J. M. Jensen (Philadelphia, 1963)

Rupp, E. G., *Luther's Progress to the Diet of Worms* (London, 1951)

Rupp, E. G., *The Righteousness of God: Luther Studies* (London, 1952)

Sasse, H., *This is My Body: Luther's Contention for the Real Presence in the Sacrament of the Altar* (Minneapolis, 1959)

Steinmetz, D. C., *Luther in Context* (Bloomington, Ind., 1986)

Strohl, H., *Luther, sa vie et sa pensée* (Strasbourg, 1953)

Watson, P. S., *Let God be God: an Interpretation of the Theology of Martin Luther* (London, 1947)

## Chapter 5 Huldrych Zwingli

Bouvier, A., *Henri Bullinger, le successeur de Zwingli, d'après sa Correspondance avec les réformés et les humanistes de langue français* (Neuchâtel and Paris, 1940)

Bromiley, G. W. (ed.), *Zwingli and Bullinger* (Philadelphia and London, 1953)

Brüsser, F., *Huldrych Zwingli* (Göttingen, 1973)

Courvoisier, J., *Zwingli: a Reformed Theologian* (Richmond, Va., 1963)

Farner, O., *Huldrych Zwingli* (4 vols, Zurich, 1943–1960)

Farner, O., *Zwingli the Reformer: his Life and Work*, English trans. by D. G. Sear (New York, 1952, repr. 1968)

Gäbler, U., *Huldrych Zwingli: his Life and Work* (Philadelphia, 1986)

Gestrich, G., *Zwingli als Theologe: Glaube und Geist beim Zürcher Reformator* (Zurich and Stuttgart, 1967)

Köhler, W. E., *Huldrych Zwingli* (Leipzig, 1943; 2nd ed., Stuttgart, 1952)

Locher, G. W., *Huldrych Zwingli in neuer Sicht. Zehn Beiträge zur Theologie der Zürcher Reformation* (Zurich and Stuttgart, 1969)

Pollet, J. V., *Huldrych Zwingli et la réforme en Suisse* (Paris, 1963)

Potter, G. R., *Zwingli* (Cambridge, 1976)

Rupp, E. G., *Patterns of Reformation* (London, 1969)

Stephens, W. P., *The Theology of Huldrych Zwingli* (Oxford, 1986)

## Chapter 6 Melanchthon and the development of Lutheranism

Boisset, J., *Mélanchthon, éducateur de l'Allemagne* (Paris, 1967)

Bornkamm, H., *Philipp Melanchthon. Zur 450 Wiederkehr seines Geburtstages* (Nuremberg, 1947)

Burgess, J. A., *The Role of the Augsburg Confession* (Philadelphia, 1980)

Elliger, W. (ed.), *Philipp Melanchthon. Forschungsbeiträge zur 400 Wiederkehr seines Todestages* (Göttingen, 1961)

Flack, E. E. and Satre, L., *Melanchthon: selected writings* (Minneapolis, 1962)

Händler, K., *Wort und Glaube bei Melanchthon* (Gütersloh, 1968)

Herrlinger, A., *Die Theologie Melanchthons in ihrer geschichtlicher Entwicklung* (Gotha, 1879)

Hildebrandt, E., *Melanchthon: alien or ally?* (Cambridge, 1946)

Hill, C. L., *The Loci Communes of Philip Melanchthon* (Boston, 1944)

Holl, K., *The Cultural Significance of the Reformation*, English trans. by K. and B. Hertz and J. H. Lichtblau (New York, 1959)

Kisch, G., *Melanchthons Rechts- und Soziallehre* (Berlin, 1967)

Manschreck, C. L., *Melanchthon: On Christian Doctrine* (London, 1965)

Manschreck, C. L., *Melanchthon, the Quiet Reformer* (New York, 1958)

Maurer, W., *Der Junge Melanchthon. Zwischen Humanismus und Reformation* (2 vols, Göttingen, 1967–9)

Maurer, W., *Melanchthon-Studien* (Gütersloh, 1964)

Pauck, W., *Melanchthon and Bucer* (Philadelphia/London, 1969)

Pelikan, J., *From Luther to Kierkegaard* (St Louis, 1950)

Richard, J. W., *Philip Melanchthon, the Protestant Preceptor of Germany* (New York, 1898)

Schafer, R., *Christologie und Sittlichkeit in Melanchthons früher Loci* (Tübingen, 1961)

Sperl, A., *Melanchthon zwischen Humanismus und Reformation* (Munich, 1959)

Stupperich, R., *Melanchthon*, English trans. R. H. Fischer (London, 1966)

Tappert, G. T., *The Book of Concord* (Philadelphia, 1959)

Vajta, V. (ed.), *Luther and Melanchthon. Papers of the International Congress on Luther Research* (Münster, 1960; Philadelphia, 1961)

## Chapters 7 and 8 Calvin and reformed Christianity

### BUCER

Bornkamm, H., *Martin Bucers Bedeutung für die europäische Reformationsgeschichte* (Gutersloh, 1952)

Chrisman, M., *Strasbourg and the Reform* (New Haven, Conn., 1967)

Courvoisier, J., *La notion de l'Eglise chez Bucer dans son développement historique* (Paris, 1933)

Eells, H., *Martin Bucer* (New Haven, Conn., 1931, repr. 1971)

Hopf, C., *Martin Bucer and the English Reformation* (Oxford, 1946)

Müller, J., *Martin Bucers Hermeneutik* (Gütersloh, 1961)

Pauck, W. (ed.), *Melanchthon and Bucer* (Library of Christian Classics, XIX, Philadelphia and London, 1969)

Pollet, J. V., *Martin Bucer: études sur la correspondance* (2 vols, Paris, 1958–1962)

Stephens, W. P., *The Holy Spirit in the Theology of Martin Bucer* (Cambridge, 1970)

Strohl, H., *Bucer, humaniste chrétien* (Paris, 1969)

Thompson, B., 'Bucer Study since 1918' *Church History*, XXV (1956), 63–82

Wendel, F., *L'Eglise de Strasbourg, sa constitution et son organisation* (Paris, 1942)

Wright, D. F. (trans and ed.), *The Common Place Books of Martin Bucer* (Abingdon, Berks, 1972)

CALVIN

Battles, F. L. *et al.*, *John Calvin,* Courtenay Studies in Reformation Theology (Abingdon, Berks., 1966)

Boisset, J., *Sagesse et sainteté dans la pensée de Jean Calvin* (Paris, 1959)

Boisset, J., *Calvin* (Paris, 1964)

Bouwsma, W. J., *John Calvin: a Sixteenth Century Portrait* (Oxford, 1989)

Bratt, J. H., *The Heritage of Calvin* (Grand Rapids, Mich., 1973)

Breen, Q., *John Calvin: a Study in French Humanism* (2nd ed., Hamden, Conn., 1968)

Dakin, A., *Calvinism* (London, 1940; repr. New York, 1972)

Doumergue, E., *Jean Calvin: les hommes et les choses de son temps* (7 vols, Lausanne, 1899–1927; repr. in 4 vols, Geneva, 1969)

Dowey, E. A., *The Knowledge of God in Calvin's Theology* (New York, 1952)

Ganoczy, A., *Le jeune Calvin: génèse et évolution de sa vocation réformatrice* (Wiesbaden, 1966. English trans., Edinburgh, 1988)

George, T. (ed.), *John Calvin and the Church: a Prism of Reform* (Louisville, Ky., 1990)

Jansen, J. F., *Calvin's Doctrine of the Work of Christ* (London, 1956)

Leith, J. H., *Calvin's Doctrine of the Christian Life* (Atlanta, Ga., 1989)

McGrath, A. E., *A Life of John Calvin* (Oxford, 1990)

McNeill, J. T., *The History and Character of Calvinism* (London and New York, 1954)

McNeill, J. T. (ed.), *John Calvin on God and Political Duty* (2nd ed., New York, 1956)

Mouter, E. W., *Calvin's Geneva* (New York, 1967)

Niesel, W., *The Theology of Calvin,* English trans. by H. Knight (London, 1956)

Parker, T. H. L., *Calvin's Doctrine of the Knowledge of God* (Edinburgh, 1969)

Parker, T. H. L., *Calvin's New Testament Commentaries* (London, 1971)

Parker, T. H. L., *John Calvin* (London, 1975)

Reid, W. S., *John Calvin: his Influence in the Western World* (Grand Rapids, Mich., 1982)

Reist, B. A., *A Reading of Calvin's Institutes* (Louisville, Ky., 1991)

Schmidt, A. M., *Calvin and the Calvinistic Tradition* (London, 1960)

Selinger, S., *Calvin against Himself: an Inquiry in Intellectual History* (Hamden, Conn., 1984)

Torrance, T. F., *Calvin's Doctrine of Man* (London, 1949)

Wallace, R. S., *Calvin, Geneva and the Reformation* (Edinburgh, 1988)

Wendel, F., *Calvin: sources et évolution de sa pensée religieuse* (Paris, 1950)

Wendel, F., *Calvin: the Origins and Development of his Religious Thought,* English trans. of the above by P. Mairet (London, 1963)

Chapter 9 The radical Reformation

Bainton, R. H., *The Travail of Religious Liberty: nine biographical studies* (Philadelphia, 1951)

Bainton, R. H., *Hunted Heretic: the Life and Death of Michael Servetus* (Boston, 1953)

Blickle, P., *The Revolution of 1525* (Baltimore and London, 1981)

Cory, D. M., *Faustus Socinus* (Boston, 1932)

Estep, W. R., *The Anabaptist Story* (Nashville, Tenn., 1963)

Friedmann, R., *Hutterite Studies*, ed. H. S. Bender (Goschen, Ind., 1961)

Jones, R. M., *Spiritual Reformers* (London, 1914)

Keeney, E., *The Development of Dutch Anabaptist Thought and Practice from 1539–1564* (Nieuwkoop, 1968)

Kot, S., *Socinianism in Poland* (Boston, 1957)

Krahn, *Dutch Anabaptism: Origin, Spread, Life and Thought (1450–1600)* (The Hague, 1968)

Littel, H. F., *The Anabaptist View of the Church*, 2nd ed. (Boston, 1958)

Martini, M., *Fausto Socino et la pensée socinienne* (Paris, 1967)

Pioli, G., *Fausto Socino: vita, opere, fortuna* (Modena, 1952)

Smith, C. H., *The Story of the Mennonites*, 3rd ed., rev. C. Krahn (Newton, Kans., 1950)

Stayer, J. M., *Anabaptists and the Sword*, 2nd ed. (Lawrence, 1976)

(Symposium) *The Mennonite Quarterly Review*, XXIV (1950); special issue on Anabaptist theology

Wilbur, E. M., *A History of Unitarianism* (2 vols, Cambridge, Mass., 1945–52)

Williams, G. H., *The Radical Reformation* (Philadelphia and London, 1962)

Williams, G. H. and Mergal, A. M. (eds), *Spiritual and Anabaptist Writers* (Library of Christian Classics: Philadelphia and London, 1957)

## Chapter 10 The Reformation in Britain I. Crisis

Ayris, P. and Selwyn, D. (eds), *Thomas Cranmer: Churchman and Scholar* (Durham, 1993)

Bromiley, G. W., *Thomas Cranmer, Theologian* (London, 1956)

Brooks, P., *Thomas Cranmer's Doctrine of the Eucharist* (London, 1965)

✔ Chester, A. G., *Hugh Latimer: Apostle to the English* (Philadelphia, 1954)

Clebsch, W., *England's Earliest Protestants, 1520–1535* (New Haven, Conn., 1964)

Dickens, A. G., *Lollards and Protestants in the Diocese of York, 1509–1558* (Oxford, 1959)

✔ Dickens, A. G., *The English Reformation* (London, 1964; rev. ed., 1989)

Dugmore, C. W., *The Mass and the English Reformers* (London, 1958)

Elton, G. R., *Reform and Reformation: England 1509–1558* (London, 1977)

Gee, H. and Hardy, W. J., *Documents Illustrative of English Church History* (London, 1896)

Gray, C. M., *Hugh Latimer* (Cambridge, Mass., 1949)

✔ Haigh, C., *The English Reformation Revised* (London, 1987)

Hopf, C., *Martin Bucer and the English Reformation* (Oxford, 1946)

Hughes, P. E., *The Reformation in England* (2 vols, London, 1950–53)

Hughes, P. E., *The Theology of the English Reformers* (London, 1965)

✓O'Day, R., *The Debate on the English Refo*

Parker, T. H. L., *The English Reformers (I*
Philadelphia and London, 1966)

✓Pollard, A. F., *Wolsey* (London, 1929)

✓Powicke, F. M., *The Reformation in England (*

Ridley, J., *Nicholas Ridley* (London, 1957)

Ridley, J., *Thomas Cranmer* (Oxford, 1962)

✓Rupp, E. G., *Studies in the Making of the English*
1947)

Smith, R. W., *John Fisher and Thomas More* (Lo

Smyth, C. H., *Thomas Cranmer and the Reformatic*
1926)

## Chapter 11 The Reformation in Britain

Bicknell, E. J., *A Theological Introduction to the Thir*
H. J. Carpenter (London, 1957)

Booty, J. E., *John Jewel as Apologist of the Church of*

✓Brook, V. J. K., *Whitgift and the English Church* (Lon

Brook, V. J. K., *A Life of Archbishop Whitgift* (Oxford,

Burrage, C., *The Early English Dissenters in the Light o*
*1641)* (2 vols, New York, 1912; repr. 1967)

Dawley, P. M., *John Whitgift and the Reformation* (Lond

Donaldson, G., *The Scottish Reformation* (Cambridge, 19

Frere, W. H., *The English Church in the Reigns of Elizabeth*
1904; repr. New York, 1977)

Gee, H. and Hardy, W. J., *Documents Illustrative of Er*
✓(London, 1896)

George, C. H., and George, K., *The Protestant Mind of the*
(Princeton, N.J., 1961)

Haugaard, W. P., *Elizabeth and the English Reformation: the*
*Settlement of Religion* (Cambridge, 1968)

Hill, W. S., *Studies in Richard Hooker* (Cleveland and London,

Hillerdal, G., *Reason and Revelation in Richard Hooker* (Lund,

Hooker, R., *Of the Laws of Ecclesiastical Polity*, ed. C. Morris (Ev
✓ 2 vols, London, 1969)

Hughes, P., *The Reformation in England III* (London, 1954)

✓Knappen, M. M., *Tudor Puritanism* (Chicago, 1939)

Knox, S. J., *Walter Travers: Paragon of English Puritanism* (Londo

McAdoo, H. R., *The Spirit of Anglicanism* (London, 1965)

✓McGrath, P., *Papists and Puritans under Elizabeth I* (London, 1967)

Marshall, J. S., *Hooker and the Anglican Tradition: a Historical and*
*Study of Hooker's Ecclesiastical Polity* (London, 1963)

Meyer, C. S., *Elizabeth I and the Religious Settlement of 1559* (St Loui

Morgan, I., *The Godly Preachers of the Elizabethan Church* (London, 1

Munz, P., *Th*

New, J. F.
(London,

Paget, F., *A*
*Ecclesiast*

Ridley, J.,

Cristiani,
de L'Eg
Delumeau
and wi
Denzinger
im-Bre
✓ Dickens,
✓ Dudon,
Evenett,
✓ 1968)
Janelle,
Jedin, H
tran
Jedin,
by
Kidd,
Miche
(Pa
Mich
19
Park
C
Past
(
Ral

Ric

Sc

S

 *Place of Hooker in the History of Thought* (London, 1952)
H., *Anglican and Puritan: the Basis of the Opposition, 1558–1640*
1964)
 *Introduction to the Fifth Book of Hooker's Treatise of the Laws of
ical Polity* (Oxford, 1899; 2nd ed., 1907)
ohn Knox* (Oxford, 1968)

## Chapter 12 Counter-Reformation: the Council of Trent

.., *L'Eglise à l'époque du Concile de Trente*, Fliche et Martin, *Histoire
lise*, XVII (Paris, 1948)
 J., *Catholicism between Luther and Voltaire*, English trans. by J. Moiser
h introd. by J. Bossy (London and Philadelphia, 1977)
, H., *Enchiridion symbolorum* (33rd ed. by A. Schönmetzer) (Freiburg-
isgau, 1965), nos 1500–1870 (principal decrees and canons of Trent)
A. G., *The Counter Reformation* (London, 1968)
.., *St Ignatius of Loyola*, English trans. by W. J. Young (Milwaukee, 1949)
H. O., *The Spirit of the Counter-Reformation*, ed. J. Bossy (Cambridge,

P., *The Catholic Reformation* (Milwaukee, 1949)
.., *Geschichte des Konzils von Trient* (Freiburg-im-Breisgau, 1949ff.); English
. by E. Graf (London, 1957ff.)
H., *Papal Legate at the Council of Trent: Cardinal Seripando*, English trans.
. C. Eckhoff (St Louis and London, 1947)
B. J., *The Counter-Reformation 1550–1600* (London, 1933)
, A., *Les décrets du Concile de Trente*, Histoire des Conciles (Hefele), X, 1
ris, 1938)
l, A., 'Trente, Concile de', in *Dictionnaire de Théologie catholique*, XV (Paris,
46), coll. 1414–1508
er, T. M., 'The papacy, Catholic reform, and Christian missions', in New
ambridge Modern History, III, ed. T. M. Wernham (1968), 44–71
or, L. von, *The History of the Popes from the Close of the Middle Ages, XII–XV*
London and St Louis, 1950f.)
ner, K., *Ignatius von Loyola als Mensch und Theologe* (Freiburg-im-Breisgau,
964)
hard, R., *Les décrets du Concile de Trente*, Histoire des Conciles (Hefele), IX,
1 and 2 (Paris, 1930f.)
hreiber, G., ed., *Das Weltkonzil von Trient: sein Werden und Wirken* (2 vols,
Freiburg-im-Breisgau, 1951)
hroeder, H. J., *Canons and Decrees of the Council of Trent: Original Text with
English translation* (St Louis, 1941)

# INDEX

# RELIGIOUS THOUGHT IN THE REFORMATION